Hiking Michigan

SECOND EDITION

W9-AEB-868

Roger E. Storm
Susan M. Wedzel

Human Kinetics

Library of Congress Cataloging-in-Publication Data

Storm, Roger.
  Hiking Michigan / Roger E. Storm, Susan M. Wedzel. -- 2nd ed.
    p. cm.
  ISBN-13: 978-0-7360-7507-7 (soft cover)
  ISBN-10: 0-7360-7507-0 (soft cover)
  1. Hiking--Michigan--Guidebooks. 2. Parks--Michigan--Guidebooks. 3.
Wilderness areas--Michigan--Guidebooks. 4. Michigan--Guidebooks. I.
Wedzel, Susan M., 1953- II. Title.
  GV199.42.M5S86 2009
  917.7404'44--dc22
                                        2008043165
  ISBN-10: 0-7360-7507-0
  ISBN-13: 978-0-7360-7507-7

The Web addresses cited in this text were current as of September 2008, unless otherwise noted.

Acquisitions Editor: Justin Klug; **Developmental Editor:** Amanda Eastin-Allen; **Assistant Editor:** Laura Podeschi; **Copyeditor:** Bob Replinger; **Proofreader:** Anne Rogers; **Permission Manager:** Martha Gullo; **Graphic Designer:** Nancy Rasmus; **Graphic Artist:** Kim McFarland; **Cover Designer:** Keith Blomberg; **Photographers (cover and interior):** Roger E. Storm and Susan M. Wedzel; **Photo Production Manager:** Jason Allen; **Art Manager:** Kelly Hendren; **Associate Art Manager:** Alan L. Wilborn; **Illustrator:** Tim Shedelbower; **Printer:** Versa Press

The maps on the following pages were adapted from maps from the Michigan Department of Natural Resources: 8, 12, 26, 43, 50, 70, 77, 93, 106, 110, 122, 125, 129, 132, 136, 140, 144, 156, 160, 164, 172, 175, 179, 199, 206, 209, 216, 231, 242, 250, 254, 270, 288, 294, 298, and 306. Map on page 4 adapted by permission of Drummond Island Tourism Association; maps on pages 16, 20, and 148 adapted by permission of Mackinac Island State Park Commission; map on page 54 adapted by permission of City of Negaunee, Jim Thomas; map on page 58 adapted by permission of Michigan Nature Association; map on page 62 adapted by permission of Grant Township; map on page 66 adapted by permission of The Fumee Lake Commission; maps on pages 114, 118, 195, and 285 adapted from maps from the U.S. Forest Service, Huron-Manistee National Forests; map on page 152 adapted by permission of Emmet County; map on page 168 adapted by permission of Grass River Natural Area, Inc.; map on page 219 adapted by permission of Wayne County Parks and Recreation; map on page 223 adapted by permission of West Bloomfield Parks & Recreation; map on page 227 adapted by permission of Huron-Clinton Metropolitan Authority; map on page 235 adapted by permission of Genesee County Parks and Recreation Commission; map on page 239 adapted by permission of Washtenaw County Parks and Recreation Department; map on page 258 adapted from "Hidden Lake Gardens Trail Map" authored by Gregory J. Kowalewski, Copyright Board of Trustees, Michigan State University; map on page 262 adapted by permission of Chippewa Nature Center; map on page 266 adapted by permission from a map created by Maggie LaNoue; map on page 274 adapted by permission of Kalamazoo Nature Center; map on page 278 adapted by permission of the City of Grand Rapids, Michigan; map on page 282 adapted by permission of North Country Trail Association; map on page 302 adapted by permission of Sarett Nature Center.

Human Kinetics books are available at special discounts for bulk purchase. Special editions or book excerpts can also be created to specification. For details, contact the Special Sales Manager at Human Kinetics.

Printed in the United States of America   10 9 8 7 6 5 4 3 2 1

Human Kinetics
Web site: www.HumanKinetics.com

United States: Human Kinetics
P.O. Box 5076
Champaign, IL 61825-5076
800-747-4457
e-mail: humank@hkusa.com

Canada: Human Kinetics
475 Devonshire Road Unit 100
Windsor, ON N8Y 2L5
800-465-7301 (in Canada only)
e-mail: info@hkcanada.com

Europe: Human Kinetics
107 Bradford Road
Stanningley
Leeds LS28 6AT, United Kingdom
+44 (0) 113 255 5665
e-mail: hk@hkeurope.com

Australia: Human Kinetics
57A Price Avenue
Lower Mitcham, South Australia 5062
08 8372 0999
e-mail: info@hkaustralia.com

New Zealand: Human Kinetics
Division of Sports Distributors NZ Ltd.
P.O. Box 300 226 Albany
North Shore City
Auckland
0064 9 448 1207
e-mail: info@humankinetics.co.nz

Acknowledgments

This collection of Michigan day hikes came about by combining two of our passions—Michigan and hiking. Our thanks go to the many staff and volunteers whom we had the pleasure to meet at the various parks and nature centers across the state. By giving freely of their time in providing information, answering our questions, and pointing us in the right direction, they made our task easier, as well as more enjoyable.

Besides everyone who helped with the first edition, special thanks go to Mark Mandenberg, Annamarie Bauer, Jim Radabaugh, Paul Yauk, Dan Lord, Robin Pearson, Loretta Cwalinski, Ken Phillips, Ron Yesney, Brenda Curtis, Rob Corbett, Paul Johnson, Don Mankee, Steve Walker, Jason Perkins, Howard and Janet Chilson, Shelby and Christa Newhouse, Mary Lee Turner, Rochelle Cody, Jim from Grand Island Ferry & Tours, Carol Fulsher, Jim Thomas, Dave Johnson, Joan Schumaker Chadde, Charlie Eshbach, Clare Rosen, Sherri Laier, Dana Richter, Dick Powers, Sam Raymond, Sharon Eaton, Tom Paquin, Gregory J. Hokans, Ronald L. Crandell, Mary Clark, Chuck Bauer, Chuck Fales, Eric and Carrie Myers, Steve West, Bill Cashmen, Betsie Winters, Warren M. Mullen, Harvey Silver, Patty Marshalek, Bill Underwood, Becky Goche, Chuck Dennison, Steven Courtney, Rose Norwood, Len Baron, and Jenelle Tokarczyk. Thanks also to Deborah Mulcahey, Barbara Nelson-Jameson, and their spouses for the use of their homes.

Our deepest appreciation goes out to Colleen Carey for stepping in as a hiking partner, to Michelle Massey for her helpful tips on using our new digital photography software, and to Leinnine from Pawsitively Purrfect Pet Sitting LLC for taking care of the kids.

This fine-looking book you are holding did not happen by itself. It is the result of a lot of hard work done by the staff at Human Kinetics, including Pat Sammann, who held our hands through the preparation of the first edition; all of the editors, graphic artists, and marketing staff involved in the project; and Justin Klug, who asked us back. To all, we say thank you.

"Good boy, Stasha!"

Contents

How to Use This Book

Hiking is an antidote to the rigors of modern life. It gives the body some much-needed (and enjoyable) exercise, and it gives the mind both rest and stimulation. Hiking even lifts the spirit to connect again with this earth that we are a part of but seldom have time to think about. With this book, we hope to provide you with an incentive to start or continue hiking, for the pleasure and the challenge of it.

Preparation of this second edition of *Hiking Michigan* was a labor of love. Michigan is a beautiful state and, with over 7.5 million acres of public land, has much to offer in the way of day-hike opportunities. We expanded this new edition to include over 20 new parks and nearly 50 new trails. We also included hikes on nine islands in the Great Lakes. In total, we feature nearly 500 miles of trail for the day hiker.

The trails in this book range from short, easy hikes for occasional hikers and families with young children to longer, more rugged ones for the experienced trailblazer. None of the trails takes more than a day to hike, although some trails may be linked together to create a hike of several days.

The trails are divided into three areas—Upper Peninsula, northern Lower Peninsula, and southern Lower Peninsula. Within each area, trails are listed from east to west. Divider pages signal the beginning of each new area, and those pages include information on the local topography, major rivers and lakes, flora and fauna, weather, and the best features of the area.

The innovative format of the book is designed to make exploring new parks and trails easy. Information on each park begins with the name of the park and a small state map that shows its general location. Bulleted highlights then point out features of the park. A description of the history and terrain of the park comes next. Practical information follows about how to get to the park, park hours, available facilities, permits and rules, and the address and phone number of a contact who can give you more information. The section titled "Other Areas of Interest" briefly mentions nearby parks and recreational opportunities, and provides phone numbers or Web sites to obtain more information. After the general information, a selected list of trails in the park follows. The length and difficulty of hiking each is given, along with a brief description of its terrain. The difficulty rating, shown by icons, ranges from one (the easiest) to five (most difficult).

Following the introduction are descriptions of the best trails in the park, along with a trail map. (A few parks have only one hike, with just one map that primarily shows the trail.) Each hike begins with information on the length and difficulty of the trail and the estimated time to walk it, as well as cautions to help you avoid potential annoyances or problems. The description of the trail provides more than directions; it is a guided tour of what you will see as you hike along. The scenery, wildlife, and history of the trail are all brought to life. Points of interest along the trail are numbered in brackets within the text, and those numbers are shown on the trail map to guide you. The approximate distance from the trailhead to each point of interest is given.

If you are in a hurry to find a park or trail to explore, use the trail finder on pages vi to xvii. It gives essential information about each highlighted trail in the book, including its length, difficulty, special features, and the facilities in the park.

Please note that conditions are changeable. When we prepared the first edition, the year was exceptionally wet. In contrast, conditions were extremely dry as we researched this new edition. So, as you hike the trails contained herein, be prepared, expect the unexpected, know your limits, have a great time, and take the second tree.

We hope that this book inspires you to get out and enjoy a wide range of outdoor experiences. We have included interesting trails from all parts of the state. Some are unexpected treasures—places that you would never dream exist in the state. Some may be favorites that you have already hiked and recommended to friends. But whether you live in a city or in the country, are away vacationing or are at home, some of these trails will be near you. Find one that you like, lace up your hiking boots, and go!

Trail Finder

Park	Trails	Miles	Difficulty	Hills	Escarpment	Forest	Lake	Wetlands	Overlook	River/Stream	Page
UPPER PENINSULA											
1 Drummond Island	Island Heritage Trail	1.6	2 boots	X	X	X	X				5
	Unamed Loop on 17, 19a, and 24	5.5	3 boots	X	X	X		X	X		6
2 Lime Island	N. Beach (Yellow) Trail	1.4	2 boots	X		X	X				9
	S. Beach (Red) Trail to Little Lime Island	7.8	2 boots	X		X	X				10
3 Bois Blanc Island	Snake Island–Mud Lake Nature Study and Natural Area	1.2	1 boot					X	X		13
	Lighthouse Point	6	2 boots	X		X	X	X			14
4 Mackinac Island State Park	Natural and Historical Features Tour	3.2	3 boots	X	X	X	X		X		17
	Tranquil Bluff Trail	3.2	3 boots	X	X	X	X		X		18
5 Mackinac Bridge	Mackinac Bridge Walk –Michigan's Annual Labor Day Hike	5	1 boot						X	X	21
6 Hiawatha National Forest East Unit	Horseshoe Bay Trail	2.2	1 boot			X	X	X		X	24
7 Tahquamenon Falls State Park	Giant Pines Loop With Upper Falls Tour	4	3 boots	X	X	X		X	X	X	27
	Clark Lake Loop	5.2	3 boots	X		X	X	X	X		28

RV camping   tent camping   swimming   canoeing   fishing   boating   picnicking   biking

	Park	Trails	Miles	Difficulty	Landscape							
					Hills	Escarpment	Forest	Lake	Wetlands	Overlook	River/Stream	Page
UPPER PENINSULA												
8	Seney National Wildlife Refuge	Pine Ridge Nature Trail	1.4	👣			X	X	X			31
9	Pictured Rocks National Lakeshore	Chapel Basin Trail	9.2	👣👣	X	X	X	X	X	X	X	34
		Beaver Basin Loop	5.1	👣👣	X	X	X	X	X	X	X	35
		White Birch Trail	2.1	👣	X	X	X	X		X		36
		Au Sable Light Station	3	👣👣	X		X	X	X	X	X	37
10	Grand Island National Recreation Area	East Ridge Trail	10.8	👣👣	X	X	X	X	X	X	X	40
		West Ridge Trail	10	👣👣	X	X	X	X	X	X	X	41
11	Fayette Historic State Park	Townsite Trail	1.7	👣	X	X	X	X		X		44
		Overlook Trail and Loop 1	2.6	👣	X	X	X	X		X		45
12	Hiawatha National Forest West Unit	Au Train Songbird Trail	2	👣	X		X	X	X	X	X	48
13	Little Presque Isle Tract	Lake Superior–Little Presque Isle Point to Wetmore Landing	3.6	👣	X	X	X	X		X		51
		Hogback Mountain Loop	5	👣👣👣	X	X	X	X	X	X	X	52

» continued

RV camping   tent camping   swimming   canoeing   fishing   boating   picnicking   biking

	Park	Trails	Miles	Difficulty	Hills	Escarpment	Forest	Lake	Wetlands	Overlook	River/Stream	Page
							Landscape					
UPPER PENINSULA												
14	Old Town Negaunee	Miners Trail Mix North	2.4	🥾🥾	X	X	X		X	X		55
		Miners Trail Mix South	2.9	🥾🥾	X	X	X		X	X		56
15	Estivant Pines Nature Sanctuary	Cathedral Grove Loop Trail	1.5	🥾🥾	X		X		X		X	59
		Memorial Grove Loop Trail	1.5	🥾🥾🥾	X		X		X		X	60
16	Hunter's Point Park	North and South Beach Loop	1.3	🥾		X	X	X				63
		Trail to Marina	.8	🥾			X	X	X			64
17	Fumee Lake Natural Area	Little Fumee Lake Loop	1.8	🥾			X	X	X		X	67
		Big Fumee Lake Loop	6.2	🥾🥾	X	X	X	X	X		X	68
18	Van Riper State Park	Upper Loop–River Trail With Old Wagon Road Trail Loop	2.1	🥾🥾🥾	X	X	X		X	X	X	71
		Lower Loop–Old Wagon Road Trail, Main Trail, Miners Loop, River Trail Spur	2.7	🥾🥾	X		X		X	X	X	72
19	McCormick Wilderness	White Deer Lake	6.6	🥾🥾	X	X	X	X	X		X	75
20	Craig Lake State Park	Crooked Lake Trail	4	🥾🥾	X	X	X	X	X			78
		Craig Lake Trail	6	🥾🥾🥾	X	X	X	X	X	X	X	79
21	Isle Royale National Park	Stoll Memorial Trail to Scoville Point	4	🥾🥾🥾	X	X	X	X	X	X	X	82
		Rock Harbor, Suzy's Cave, Tobin Harbor	3.8	🥾🥾🥾	X	X	X	X		X		83

RV camping   tent camping   swimming   canoeing   fishing   boating   picnicking   biking

	Park	Trails	Miles	Difficulty	Hills	Escarpment	Forest	Lake	Wetlands	Overlook	River/Stream	Page
UPPER PENINSULA												
22	Sylvania Wilderness (tent camping, swimming, boating, picnicking)	Clark Lake Trail	8.1	👣👣	X		X	X	X	X	X	86
		Unnamed Trail– Loon Lake Access	5.4	👣👣	X		X	X	X	X		87
23	Ottawa National Forest (tent camping, swimming, canoeing, fishing, boating, picnicking, biking)	Beaver Lodge Nature Trail	1.3	👣👣	X		X	X	X	X		90
		Cascade Falls Hiking Trail	1.7	👣👣👣	X	X	X			X	X	91
24	Porcupine Mountains Wilderness State Park (RV camping, tent camping, canoeing, boating, picnicking)	Overlook Trail	3.4	👣👣👣	X		X		X	X	X	94
		Escarpment Trail	4.2	👣👣👣	X	X	X	X	X	X	X	95
		East and West River Trails	2.5	👣👣👣	X	X	X	X	X	X	X	96
		Summit Peak Trail and South Mirror Lake	4.8	👣👣👣	X	X	X	X	X	X	X	97
25	Black River Harbor National Forest Recreation Area (RV camping, tent camping, swimming, boating, picnicking)	North Country Trail to Sandstone, Gorge, Potawatomi, and Great Conglomerate Falls	3.6	👣👣👣	X	X	X		X	X	X	100
		North Country Trail to Rainbow Falls– West and East	3.2	👣👣👣	X	X	X	X	X	X	X	101
NORTHERN LOWER PENINSULA												
26	Negwegon State Park (swimming, fishing, picnicking)	Potawatomi Trail	3.3	👣			X	X	X			107
		Algonquin Trail	6.7	👣👣			X	X	X		X	108
27	Thompson's Harbor State Park (fishing)	Loops 1 and 2	2.9	👣			X	X				111
		Loop 3	2.9	👣			X	X				112

Landscape

» continued

RV camping   tent camping   swimming   canoeing   fishing   boating   picnicking   biking

» continued

Park	Trails	Miles	Difficulty	Landscape							Page
				Hills	Escarpment	Forest	Lake	Wetlands	Overlook	River/Stream	
NORTHERN LOWER PENINSULA											
28 Huron National Forest, Lumberman's Monument	Highbanks–Sid Town to Lumberman's Monument	2.7	👣	X		X		X	X	X	115
	Highbanks–Iargo Springs to Lumberman's Monument	3.6	👣	X		X		X	X	X	116
29 Hoist Lakes Foot Travel Area	Hoist Lakes Little East Loop	4.8	👣👣👣	X		X	X	X			119
	Hoist Lakes Little West Loop	6.4	👣👣👣	X		X	X	X			120
30 Ocqueoc Falls Bicentennial Pathway	Ocqueoc Falls Bicentennial Pathway–Medium Loop	4.6	👣👣	X		X		X	X	X	123
31 Sinkhole Area	Sinkholes Pathway–Short Loop	.9	👣👣👣	X		X	X		X		126
	Sinkholes Pathway–Long Loop	2.2	👣👣👣	X		X	X		X		127
32 Clear Lake State Park	Clear Lake Nature Trail	4.7	👣👣	X		X	X				130
33 Pigeon River Country	Shingle Mill Pathway–Upper Loop	6	👣👣	X		X	X	X	X	X	133
	Shingle Mill Pathway–Middle Loop	6.3	👣👣	X		X	X	X	X	X	134

RV camping   tent camping   swimming   canoeing   fishing   boating   picnicking   biking

Park	Trails	Miles	Difficulty	Hills	Escarpment	Forest	Lake	Wetlands	Overlook	River/Stream	Page
						Landscape					
NORTHERN LOWER PENINSULA											
34 George Mason River Retreat Area	Mason Tract Pathway–North	2.4	👣👣	X		X			X	X	137
	Mason Tract Pathway–South	6.4	👣👣	X		X		X	X	X	138
35 Wakeley Lake Semi-Primitive Non-Motorized Area	Wakeley Lake–Inner Loop	3.6	👣👣	X		X	X	X			141
	Beaver Pond Loop	1.7	👣			X		X			142
36 Hartwick Pines State Park	Old-Growth Trail	1.2	👣👣	X		X					145
	Au Sable River Foot Trail	3.9	👣👣	X		X		X	X	X	146
37 Historic Mill Creek Discovery Park	Evergreen, Beaver, and Sugar Shack Forest Trails	1.9	👣👣	X		X		X	X	X	149
	Beaver Pond Trail	1.8	👣👣	X		X		X	X	X	150
38 The Headlands	Trillium Trail	1.6	👣			X			X		153
	Voyager–Beach–McCormick Lake Trail Loop	3.4	👣👣	X		X	X		X		154
39 Wilderness State Park	East Ridge–Nebo–South Boundary–East Boundary Trails Loop	5.4	👣👣	X		X		X			157
	Big Stone–Pond-side–Red Pine–Hemlock Trails Loop	4.2	👣👣	X		X		X			158
40 Gaylord Forest Management Unit	Spring Brook Pathway–East Loop	1.6	👣			X		X		X	161
	Spring Brook Pathway–West Loop	4.8	👣👣	X		X		X	X	X	162

» continued

RV camping   tent camping   swimming   canoeing   fishing   boating   picnicking   biking

» continued

Park		Trails	Miles	Difficulty	Hills	Escarpment	Forest	Lake	Wetlands	Overlook	River/Stream	Page
							Landscape					
NORTHERN LOWER PENINSULA												
41	Jordan River Valley	Three Mile Pathway Loop–Deadman's Hill	3		X		X		X	X	X	165
		Warner Creek Pathway	3.7		X		X		X		X	166
42	Grass River Natural Area	Woodland/Wildfire Trail	1.3				X		X	X	X	169
		Cabin–Sedge Meadow–Tamarack–Fern Trails Loop	1.3				X		X	X	X	170
43	Wm. Mitchell State Park	Heritage Nature Trail	2.5				X		X	X	X	173
44	Leelanau State Park	Lake Michigan Trail	2.2		X		X	X		X		176
		Mud Lake Trail	3.2		X		X	X	X			177
45	Beaver Island	Miller's Marsh Nature Trail	1				X		X			180
		Buffalo's Camp, Doty's, and North Lake Trails	6.7				X		X		X	181
46	Sleeping Bear Dunes National Lakeshore	Dunes–Sleeping Bear Point Hiking Trail	2.5		X		X	X		X		184
		Pyramid Point Hiking Trail	2.7		X		X	X		X		185

RV camping tent camping swimming canoeing fishing boating picnicking biking

	Park	Trails	Miles	Difficulty	Hills	Escarpment	Forest	Lake	Wetlands	Overlook	River/Stream	Page
						Landscape						
NORTHERN LOWER PENINSULA												
47	North Manitou Island	Small Northeast Loop	6.4	🥾🥾	X		X	X				188
		Waiting for the Ferry	2.3	🥾			X	X				189
48	South Manitou Island	Lighthouse, Shipwreck, Cedars, Dunes	10.3	🥾🥾🥾	X		X	X		X		192
		Farm Loop	5.9	🥾			X	X				193
49	Nordhouse Dunes Wilderness	Four-Mile Loop	3.9	🥾🥾	X		X	X	X	X		196
		Six-Mile Loop	5.9	🥾🥾	X		X	X	X	X		197
50	Ludington State Park	Skyline–Sable River–Island Lake–Lost Lake Trails	3.5	🥾🥾	X		X	X		X	X	200
		Big Sable Point Lighthouse Loop	4.4	🥾🥾	X		X	X	X	X		201
SOUTHERN LOWER PENINSULA												
51	Sanilac Petroglyphs State Historic Park	Petroglyphs Park Nature Trail	1.4	🥾🥾	X		X		X		X	207
52	Port Crescent State Park	Camping Area Trail	1.8	🥾🥾	X		X	X		X	X	210
		Day-Use Area Trail	2.7	🥾🥾	X		X	X	X	X	X	211
53	Detroit International Riverfront	East RiverWalk	2.5	🥾							X	214

RV camping   tent camping   swimming   canoeing   fishing   boating   picnicking   biking

» continued

Park	Trails	Miles	Difficulty	Hills	Escarpment	Forest	Lake	Wetlands	Overlook	River/Stream	Page
SOUTHERN LOWER PENINSULA											
54 Wm. C. Sterling State Park	Sterling Marsh Trail	3.1	(1 boot)			X	X	X	X		217
55 William P. Holliday Forest and Wildlife Preserve	Tulip Leaf–Beech Trails	1.9	(1 boot)	X		X		X		X	220
	Ellsworth–Tonquish–Wildflower Trails	3.5	(3 boots)	X		X		X	X	X	221
56 West Bloomfield Woods Nature Preserve	West Bloomfield Woods Nature Preserve Trail	2.1	(2 boots)	X		X		X	X	X	224
	West Bloomfield Trail Network	4.3	(1 boot)			X	X	X	X		225
57 Indian Springs Metropark	Woodland Trail	3.5	(1 boot)			X	X	X	X	X	228
	Farmland Trail	1.6	(2 boots)	X		X		X			229
58 Maybury State Park	History Trail	1.2	(1 boot)	X		X					232
	Trail to Pond	3.1	(2 boots)	X		X	X	X			233
59 For-Mar Nature Preserve and Arboretum	Ground Water Pond and Hawthorn Trail	1.2	(1 boot)			X		X	X	X	236
	Ground Water Pond and Sugar Bush Trail	.7	(2 boots)	X		X		X	X	X	237
60 Parker Mill Park	Hoyt G. Post Trail	1.3	(1 boot)			X		X	X	X	240

RV camping   tent camping   swimming   canoeing   fishing   boating   picnicking   biking

	Park	Trails	Miles	Difficulty	Hills	Escarpment	Forest	Lake	Wetlands	Overlook	River/Stream	Page
SOUTHERN LOWER PENINSULA												
61	Bay City State Recreation Area	Frank N. Andersen Nature Trail	3.2	👢			X	X	X	X		243
		Tobico Marsh Loop	4.7	👢			X	X	X	X		244
62	Shiawassee National Wildlife Refuge/Green Point Environmental Learning Center	Ferguson Bayou Trail	5.2	👢			X	X	X	X	X	247
		Songbird–Duck Trails	1.4	👢			X		X	X	X	248
63	Pinckney Recreation Area	Crooked Lake Trail	5.1	👢👢👢	X		X	X	X	X	X	251
		Losee Lake Hiking Trail–Large Loop	3.3	👢👢👢	X		X	X	X	X		252
64	Waterloo Recreation Area	Waterloo-Pinckney Hiking Trail–Portage Lake to Sackrider Hill	5.8	👢👢👢	X		X	X	X	X	X	255
		Oak Woods–Waterloo-Pinckney Hiking Trail–Hickory Hills Nature Trail	4.7	👢👢👢	X		X	X	X	X		256
65	Hidden Lake Gardens	Pine-Tree Trail	1.3	👢👢	X		X	X				259
		Hikers' Trail	2.8	👢👢	X		X	X	X			260
66	Chippewa Nature Center	River Point Woodland Trail	1.5	👢			X		X		X	263
		River Trail	2.9	👢			X	X	X	X	X	264

» *continued*

RV camping | tent camping | swimming | canoeing | fishing | boating | picnicking | biking

» *continued*

Park	Trails	Miles	Difficulty	Hills	Escarpment	Forest	Lake	Wetlands	Overlook	River/Stream	Page
SOUTHERN LOWER PENINSULA											
67 Whitehouse Nature Center	River's Edge Trail	.9	👣			X		X		X	267
	Prairie Trail	1	👣			X		X		X	268
68 Yankee Springs Recreation Area	Hall Lake Trail	2.5	👣👣	X		X	X	X	X	X	271
	Long Lake Trail	5.2	👣👣	X		X		X	X	X	272
69 Kalamazoo Nature Center	Beech Maple–Riverwalk Trail	1.1	👣👣👣	X		X		X	X	X	275
	Fern Valley Trail	.6	👣👣	X		X		X	X		276
70 Aman Park	Yellow Trail	1.1	👣	X		X			X	X	279
	Red Trail	1.4	👣👣	X		X			X	X	280
71 North Country National Scenic Trail, Birch Grove Schoolhouse	Birch Grove Trail	9	👣👣	X		X	X	X			283
72 Manistee National Forest, Loda Lake Wildflower Sanctuary	Loda Lake Wildflower Sanctuary Trail	1.2	👣			X	X	X	X	X	286

RV camping   tent camping   swimming   canoeing   fishing   boating   picnicking   biking

	Park	Trails	Miles	Difficulty	Hills	Escarpment	Forest	Lake	Wetlands	Overlook	River/Stream	Page #
											Landscape	
SOUTHERN LOWER PENINSULA												
73	Saugatuck Dunes State Park	North Trail With Spur to Lake–Outer Loop	2		X		X	X				289
		Beach Trail	1.4		X		X	X				290
		Livingston Trail	2		X		X	X				291
		South Trail	4.6		X		X	X				292
74	P.J. Hoffmaster State Park	Loop of Homestead and Dune Climb Stairway	2.4		X		X	X		X		295
		Walk-a-Mile Trail	1.6		X		X	X				296
75	Muskegon State Park	Dune Ridge Trail Loop	1.7		X		X					299
		Lost Lake Trail	1.7				X	X	X		X	300
76	Sarett Nature Center	River–Gentian–Two-Board Trails Loop	.5		X		X		X	X	X	303
		Lowland–Upland Trails Loop	2.1		X		X		X	X	X	304
77	Warren Dunes State Park/ Warren Woods Natural Area	Nature–Blue Jay–Beach–Mt. Randal Trails Loop	4		X		X	X	X	X	X	307
		Warren Woods Natural Area Trail	1.1		X		X		X	X	X	308

RV camping   tent camping   swimming   canoeing   fishing   boating   picnicking   biking

Michigan

Upper Peninsula

Promoted as "Nature's Theme Park," Michigan's Upper Peninsula became part of the state as a consolation prize in a boundary dispute between Michigan and Ohio in the mid-1830s. Ohio got to keep Toledo. Michigan was granted statehood as well as the vast land and riches of the Upper Peninsula.

Topography

Known as the U.P., not northern Michigan, the peninsula contains one-third of Michigan's total land area. Long and narrow, the U.P. stretches over 380 miles from Ironwood on the west to the tip of Drummond Island on the east, and is surrounded by three of the Great Lakes—Superior, Michigan, and Huron.

The eastern end of the U.P. is low lying, often swampy, cut by small streams, and carpeted by marshland and woodland. Rolling limestone hills, part of the Niagara Escarpment, stretch across its south side. In the north, multicolored sandstone formations tower 50 to 200 feet above Lake Superior at the Pictured Rocks National Lakeshore.

The western U.P., with its rugged hills and escarpments (rock cliffs), is unlike any other part of the state. It contains outcroppings of some of the oldest known rocks on earth. West of Marquette, in the Huron Mountains you find the state's highest elevations. The western U.P. also has vast iron ore deposits. The discovery of a copper vein in the Keweenaw Peninsula enabled Michigan to be the number one copper-producing state for 40 years.

Major Rivers and Lakes

Lakes Superior, Michigan, and Huron define much of the U.P.'s shape and provide the peninsula with 1,700 miles of coastline. The shores are rocky and picturesque, varying from beach to dune to precipice.

Over 4,300 inland lakes speck the peninsula. Lake Gogebic is the largest. The Manistique Lakes, Indian Lake, and Lake Michigamme are some other large lakes.

The U.P. has 12,000 miles of rivers and streams that, while generally short, are wildly boisterous in their haste to reach the lakes. Some 250 waterfalls exist across the U.P., with most located in the western and central portions. The eastern U.P. has the mighty Tahquamenon Falls.

Common Plant Life

Forests of virgin white pine dominated much of the U.P. before the lumber era. Today, over 85 percent is forested by what is broadly called the north woods, a zone between the needleleaf, boreal forest of Canada and the broadleaf trees that stretch south.

Here in the north woods, the species of both forest communities flourish. Sugar maple, basswood, beech, and the red maple reach northward into the region typified by white spruce, balsam fir, tamarack, and quaking aspen. Also found in the zone are red pine, eastern hemlock, yellow birch, and eastern white pine.

Having been logged out, the U.P. has pockets of old-growth forest, but only three large tracts of old-growth forest remain. They are found in the Porcupine Mountains Wilderness, the Sylvania Wilderness, and on the private lands of the Huron Mountain Club.

In spring, a profusion of wildflowers blossoms across the U.P. While arbutus and violet scent the air, look for trillium, marsh marigold, blue carpets of forget-me-not, over 30 species of wild orchid, and one of the rarest plants in the world—the Michigan monkey-flower, found only in a couple of counties near the Straits of Mackinac. These are followed in early summer by daisies, hawkweed, fireweed, and sunflower, and then, in September, by goldenrod. The thimbleberry is a U.P. specialty. Blueberries are also plentiful in sandy soils and bog environments.

A bog is a unique wetland habitat that often occupies a glacial depression. Sphagnum moss grows in thick, floating mats on the surface of the water and is often mistaken for solid ground. The floating mats hold in the cold of winter and allow tundra shrubs like Labrador tea and leatherleaf to survive far south of their normal range. Carnivorous pitcher plants are also common in the bog environment.

Common Birds and Mammals

In Michigan, to view moose or catch a glimpse of a wolf in the wild, you once had to travel to the remote setting of Isle Royale. Set in Lake Superior about 50 miles northwest of the Keweenaw Peninsula, Isle Royale is a rugged island wilderness. It is 45 miles long and 9 miles wide, and contains more than 160 miles of some of the authors' favorite hiking trails. But in 1985, and again in 1987, moose were reintroduced to the U.P. from Canada and are thriving in their new home. Wolves also came back to the U.P. as they expanded their range from Minnesota during the 1980s.

As romantic as the notion of seeing moose or wolf is, you have a much better chance of seeing white-tailed deer or even black bear. Other mammals to look for include coyote, red fox, bobcat, beaver, porcupine, fisher, and snowshoe hare. At an old iron ore mine in Iron Mountain, up to one million big and little brown bats—one of the largest concentrations of bats in the world—gather to hibernate for the winter.

Birds are the most visible of wild animals, but unlike what occurs with a soaring eagle, a perched hawk, or circling vultures, you are more likely to hear the call of the loon, the honking of a Canada goose, or the caw of a raven long before you see it. In spring, thousands of birds congregate at Whitefish Point during the migration north. Over 230 bird species have been recorded there. The tip of the Keweenaw Peninsula is an important spring migration route for raptors. For a migration of a different type, monarch butterflies congregate at Peninsula Point in fall before they cross Green Bay into Wisconsin.

A note about insects: Be prepared. Late May to mid-July is the peak season for an assortment of critters such as the black fly, mosquito, no-see-um, deerfly, and stable fly. As a consolation, no poisonous snakes live in the U.P.

Climate

People say that the U.P. has two seasons, shoveling and swatting. In truth, the U.P.'s weather is highly influenced by the Great Lakes that surround it. Temperature extremes are moderated by the presence of the lakes, and in winter the lakes help generate the highest snowfalls in the Midwest. The average maximum January temperatures range between 20 and 25 degrees Fahrenheit, while the lows average between −1 and 11 degrees. In July the average maximum temperatures range from 75 to 79 degrees Fahrenheit, and the lows average between 50 and 58 degrees. Annual snowfall totals vary from 51 inches at Escanaba, to 150 inches at Ironwood, to nearly 200 inches in the snowbelt of the Keweenaw Peninsula.

Best Natural Features

- Lakes Superior, Michigan, and Huron
- Pictured Rocks' multicolored sandstone cliffs
- Grand Island
- Grand Sable Dunes
- Tahquamenon Falls
- Isle Royale, a U.S. Biosphere Reserve
- Porcupine Mountains Wilderness
- 4,300 inland lakes
- 12,000 miles of rivers and streams
- 250 waterfalls
- Keweenaw Peninsula, the U.P.'s upper peninsula
- Brockway Mountain

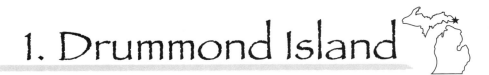

- View the rare alvar grassland prairies of the Maxton Plains.
- Catch far-reaching views from the Upper Peninsula's easternmost point.
- Explore a diverse environment.

Park Information

This 136-square-mile-island is one of the largest in the Great Lakes. About 150 miles of shoreline encircle 87,000 acres; two-thirds of the island is owned by the State of Michigan. A small community of 1,000 to 1,200 full-time residents occupies the island.

Rocky shores, sandy beaches, groves of hardwoods, prairie meadows, and miles of water speckled with numerous islands provide a diverse environment for a plethora of activities. Michigan's Department of Natural Resources (DNR) has 76 miles of designated off-road vehicle (ORV) trails, which are used by mountain bikers, hikers, motorcycles, ATVs, and ORVs. Bike the innumerable trails, kayak from island to island, or snowmobile on 100 miles of groomed trails.

The island is home to an ecological jewel—the Maxton Plains. This fragile area of rare alvar grassland prairie can be found in a handful of places around the world, the Great Lakes area being one of them. In this open landscape, grasses and sedges grow on flat limestone bedrock where a thin layer of soil precludes the growth of most trees.

Drummond Island Township Park provides 43 campsites and a sandy beach along Sturgeon Bay.
Directions: Pick up the ferry in De Tour. Take M-134 east from I-75 to De Tour Village.
Hours Open: Visit the Maxton Plains, Drummond Island Township Park, and state land year-round from dawn to dusk. The ferry runs year-round, but hours are reduced from January 2 through March 31.
Facilities: Hiking, biking, cross-country skiing, snowmobiling, ATV, ORV, swimming, canoeing, kayaking, hunting, fishing, camping (tent and backcountry), and golfing.
Permits and Rules: No charge is assessed for day use of the trails, although camping requires a fee. Those who camp must obtain a permit for backcountry camping from the Department of Natural Resources (DNR). Round-trip ferry service costs $12 per car and driver plus $2 for each additional adult. The Nature Conservancy manages most of the Maxton Plains. While there, keep ORVs and bicycles on the roadways; tread lightly on the grasslands; do not collect plants, animals, rocks, or other natural objects; and carry out your trash.

For Further Information: Call Drummond Island Ferry at 906-235-3170. To reach the Drummond Island Township Park, call 906-493-5245, or contact the Drummond Island Tourism Association (DITA) at 906-493-5245, 800-737-8666, or www.drummond islandchamber.com. For camping permit information, call the DNR in De Tour at 906-297-2581. Get in touch with the Nature Conservancy Michigan Field Office at 517-316-0300. Steve Walker at the Bear Track Inn—906-493-5090—has maps and is knowledgeable about the trails.

Other Points of Interest

Take a tour of the **De Tour Reef Lighthouse**, including a 6-mile round-trip boat ride to the lighthouse. Limited narrated tours are offered on weekends from June through August. For more information, contact the De Tour Reef Light Preservation Society (DRLPS) at 906-493-6609 or www.DRLPS.com.

Woods & Water Ecotours offer custom or packaged ecotours. Explore Drummond Island by foot, sea kayak, and mountain bike; explore the ecology on Lime Island; sea-kayak the Les Cheneaux Islands, the St. Mary's River areas, or Lime Island; or snowshoe, dogsled, or ski along the snow-covered dunes of Lake Superior. For more information, contact Woods & Water Ecotours, P.O. Box 114, 20 Pickford Avenue, Hessel, MI 49745; 906-484-4157; www.WoodsWater Ecotours.com.

Park Trails

The ORV trails on state land are numbered and marked, so you can use them in increments. Stop in the visitor center at the Four Corners blinking light for color-coded maps. The Drummond Island Resort and Conference Center allows the public to hike and bike 6 miles of trail. It is located at 33494 S. Maxton Road. For information, call 906-493-1000.
Rainbow Trail (🥾, 4.6 miles). Cross-country skiing and hiking trail. The mostly flat trail is off Maxton Cross Road. It is maintained by the Drummond Island Cross Country Club.
Marble Head View Point (🥾🥾🥾, 6 miles round-trip). The viewpoint is a headland 100 feet above Lake Huron on the easternmost point of the island. It provides far-reaching views of Lake Huron's North Channel.

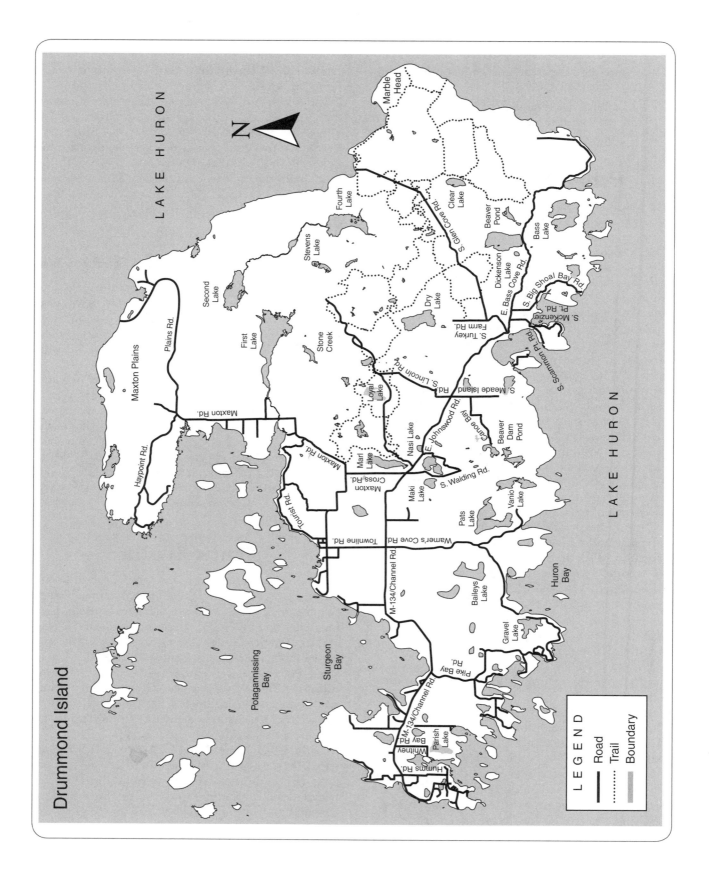

Drummond Island

LAKE HURON

LAKE HURON

Marble Head

Fourth Lake

Clear Lake

Beaver Pond

Bass Lake

Stevens Lake

S. Glen Cove Rd.

Dickenson Lake

E. Bass Cove Rd.

S. Big Shoal Bay Rd.

Second Lake

Dry Lake

S. McKenzie Pt. Rd.

S. Turkey Farm Rd.

First Lake

Stone Creek

S. Lincoln Rd.

Loyal Lake

S. Meade Island Rd.

S. Scammon Pt. Rd.

Maxton Plains

Plains Rd.

Maxton Rd.

Canoe Bay

Beaver Dam Pond

Haypoint Rd.

Maxton Rd.

Marl Lake

Nasi Lake

E. Johnswood Rd.

Vanio Lake

Maxton Cross Rd.

S. Walding Rd.

Tourist Rd.

Maki Lake

Pats Lake

Townline Rd.

Warner's Cove Rd.

Huron Bay

Potagannissing Bay

Sturgeon Bay

M-134/Channel Rd.

Baileys Lake

Gravel Lake

Pike Bay Rd.

M-134/Channel Rd.

Whitney Bay Rd.

Parish Lake

Humms Rd.

LEGEND
Road
Trail
Boundary

Island Heritage Trail

Distance One-Way: 1.6 miles
Estimated Hiking Time: 1 to 1.5 hours

Cautions: The trail has some moderately steep climbs and descents, so wear proper footgear. Roots and rocks may be slippery when wet. Some parts of the trail may be hard to follow, so watch for the pink and orange markings to keep you on track. Bears inhabit the island, so take care. Take along insect repellent.

Trail Directions: From the ferry, take M-134 east 5.7 mi. to Township Park Road. Turn left into the Drummond Island Township Park. Park about .3 mi. down on the left side of the road, where you start the trail **[1]**.

Don't let the first part of the trail fool you with its downed trees and less-than-spectacular entry; you won't be disappointed. This trail takes you through cedar-birch forest and down to the shores of Lake Huron. At the first junction (.1 mi.), turn left and gently climb to the next one, which soon follows **[2]**. Turn left here as well and climb the cushioned trail past the rock escarpment on your right. Make a hairpin turn right at the end of the escarpment and climb it (.3 mi.) **[3]**. Walk the ridge on the pine- and cedar-cushioned trail, looking down from where you came. Cedar perfumes this wet, dark environment where a moss-covered rock garden lies to your left.

Stay to the left when you reach a junction. The trail winds along more moss-covered ledges, rocks, and crevasses. You pass a junction to the lower level at .4 mi. **[4]**. Stay left to climb a higher escarpment and hairpin to a higher point. The trail switchbacks up the ridge.

Descend the ridge through more moss-covered rock (.6 mi.) **[5]** and pass a velvety green rock wall on your right. Stay to the right of the junction that heads down and make the hairpin turn to the left off and around the ridge where you came up **[3]**. Stroll past the junction that shortcuts up the ridge to the junction that leads back and turn right. The next junction, which leads to the lower trail, follows shortly afterward (.8 mi.) **[2]**. This closes the upper trail loop. Now follow the path to the lower loop, heading gently down.

There are fewer cedars on this loop than on the other. At 1 mi., you reach a trail at Lake Huron **[6]**. A sign directs you to the right for the campground and to the left to the upper trail. Follow to the left along the rocky shore and listen to the waves lapping on the shore as ducks, loons, gulls, and terns go about their business.

At the trail sign (1.1 mi.) **[7]**, stay to the left, gradually winding up. You soon start to notice a more moss-covered environment. The slope becomes more serious (1.3 mi.) as you pass fallen birch trees **[8]**. Shortly, swing left and walk along the base of a mossy ledge. You pass two spurs that lead up the escarpment before you arrive at the sign that splits the upper and lower loops (1.5 mi.) **[2]**. Stay to the left of both spurs and continue straight at the sign for the short stretch back to the parking area.

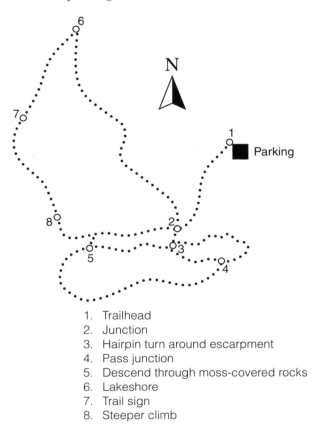

1. Trailhead
2. Junction
3. Hairpin turn around escarpment
4. Pass junction
5. Descend through moss-covered rocks
6. Lakeshore
7. Trail sign
8. Steeper climb

Unnamed Loop on 17, 19a, and 24

🐾🐾🐾 **Distance Round-Trip:** 5.5 miles
🐾🐾🐾 **Estimated Hiking Time:** 2.5 to 3 hours

Cautions: Hiking, bicycling, and ATV use are permitted on the trail. Be careful. The trail includes some steep climbs. Roots and rocks are often underfoot. Bears inhabit the island. Take care and take insect repellent.

Trail Directions: From the Four Corners to where you park is almost 13 mi. Head east 7 mi. along Johnswood Road (M-134) to Kreetan Road. Turn left and go up to Sheep Ranch Road (which may be unmarked) and go right to Corned Beef Junction. Turn right. The grassy parking area is about .3 mi. on the left. Given the abundance of wildlife that we saw on this trail, the bumpy drive is well worth it. Start your hike at the parking area **[1]**.

Follow the road to the right about .05 mi., where you turn left at the junction. You soon pass another junction, descend over rocks off a ledge, and enter a meadow briefly before swinging left and climbing through pines and ferns (.2 mi.) **[2]**. You pass through saplings and skirt yet another meadow. This weaving from meadow to woods identifies this trail. Likely because the woods offer cover and food (raspberry) grows in the open areas, we saw several deer and sandhill cranes along the way.

You cross the road you came in on at .6 mi. **[3]** and continue to the right to traverse another meadow. The trail swings left through a future forest that has remnant stumps of the past (.7 mi.) **[4]**. Ruts and grass encumber the trail for a stretch.

A pond lined with cattails is on your left (.9 mi.) **[5]**. A deer stomped away from us here, its tail bobbing. Raspberries line the trail.

You weave past wetlands and pass through meadows, at times edged with trees. Deer bounded off.

You reach a junction at 1.5 mi. **[6]**. Turn left and go about .2 mi. to the next junction. It is narrow and may not have a sign at the trail. Watch carefully for this. You want to turn right through grasses and wildflowers, and then climb through tamaracks toward a rocky ledge.

At 1.9 mi., you reach the 19a junction **[7]**. Turn left. In the summer, grasshoppers might explode up like popcorn. Now on the rocky ledge, you wind along the perimeter of a meadow. At 2.1 mi., you reach an overlook where we saw sandhill cranes **[8]**. The trail winds right and down along the ridgeline, only to climb steeply at 2.2 mi. **[9]**, where you soon reach an overlook. Wind down, pass a wet area, and reach a junction at 3 mi. **[10]**. Stay to the right and cross the road. The winding, rolling trail takes you through rock piles on either side. You make a sharp right at 3.3 mi. and then climb steeply up another ridge **[11]**. Look for pudding stones as you walk the top of the ridge. Look to the northwest for a glimpse of an interior lake.

You come off the ridge and through a meadow with popping grasshoppers to cross a two-track (3.7 mi.) **[12]** to arrive at the junction for 24 (3.8 mi.) **[13]**. Stay to the right to enter the woods. The pattern of meadow and woods reappears. We heard deer sneezing and snorting as we passed through more raspberries. You reach another junction at 4.6 mi. **[14]**. Stay straight. The trail narrows so much that it seems only a deer could use it. Snorting confirms this. Roll through the raspberries and along the rutty, muddy trail to arrive at a junction, where you turn left (5.3 mi.) **[15]**. This takes you up to the road where you left your vehicle (5.5 mi.) **[16]**. Turn left to walk back to it.

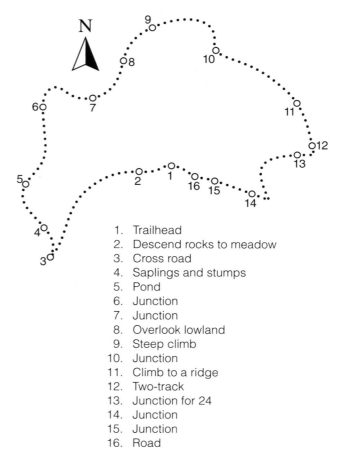

1. Trailhead
2. Descend rocks to meadow
3. Cross road
4. Saplings and stumps
5. Pond
6. Junction
7. Junction
8. Overlook lowland
9. Steep climb
10. Junction
11. Climb to a ridge
12. Two-track
13. Junction for 24
14. Junction
15. Junction
16. Road

- Watch and feel oceangoing freighters pass through St. Mary's River.
- Explore historic buildings, lime kilns, and ongoing archaeological excavations.
- Experience a nesting colony of common terns.

Park Information

This isolated 980-acre island located in the middle of St. Mary's River is a challenge to access, but the effort is not only worthwhile but fun. If you don't have a boat to travel the 3 miles from Raber in waters that you share with oceangoing ships, you will need to charter one.

The island has a long history as a base for lime supply, ship refueling, and recreation. A 30-room hotel catered to the likes of Diamond Jim Brady and Mae West. The hotel is gone, but seven cottages, an old schoolhouse, a superintendent's home (dragged across the ice to the island in 1912), an old fuel dock, warehouse, boiler building, and oil storage tanks remain. Six of the cottages, which sit high on a bluff overlooking the shipping channel, may be rented. They are solar powered and have knotty pine paneling, rustic wood furniture, and wood stoves. Ships pass near the dock, lit from bow to stern at night. The thrum of the propellers is so intense that vibrations can often be felt in the cottages.

Tent platforms are located 400 feet from the dock and on the southeast end of the island. Nonplatform camping is also available.

A 900-foot dock, a remnant of the island's history as a fuel stop, helps to harbor smaller boats and is home to some protected terns that nest there. The harbor offers 40 slips. In 1907 a wood-hulled steamer, the *Rome*, went down in the harbor. Its hull was filled with limestone, and today it serves as a breakwall at the entrance of the harbor.

Hike the several miles of trails, swim the sandy beaches, fish on- or offshore, or explore the archaeological excavations along a wood walkway.

Directions: Raber and De Tour are good locations from which to embark. Cross the Mackinac Bridge to the Upper Peninsula and take I-75 to M-134 and head east. Go north on M-48 to Raber or continue on M-134 to De Tour.

Hours Open: Cottages and camping sites are available from Memorial Day weekend through mid-September.

Facilities: Hiking, picnicking, camping, swimming, fishing, boating, kayaking, historic buildings, boat slips, cottages, and portable restrooms.

Permits and Rules: No fee is required to use the island, but there are fees for camping and for cottage rental. Reservations must be made for the cabins, and a two-day minimum stay is required. Pets are permitted, but they are not allowed in the buildings and must be on a 6-foot leash. Public use of motorized vehicles is not permitted.

For Further Information: Contact Sault Ste. Marie Management Unit, 2001 Ashmun, Box 798, Sault Ste. Marie, MI 49783; 906-635-5281, for information or for cabin reservations. To charter a boat, contact Sturgeon Bay Charter at 906-493-6087 or www.sturgeonbay charters.com; Les Cheneaux Islands Water Tours & Charter Service at 906-484-3776, 866-322-3776, or www.fishingwithnorm.com; or Michigan Charter Boat Association, 800-MCBA-971. No parking is available at the dock in Raber, but vehicles can be parked in De Tour.

Other Points of Interest

From De Tour, take a ferry to **Drummond Island** (see park #1). For information, contact the Drummond Island Tourism Association (DITA) at 906-493-5245, 800-737-8666, or www.drummondislandchamber .com.

Park Trails

A series of trails may be connected to form various trips that crisscross the island. Get a map from the information board near the dock or from the caretaker.

Kiln Trail (🥾, 5 miles round-trip). This trail takes you to the archeological sites, lime kilns, and the shore of St. Mary's River, where you can watch ships as they veer near the island.

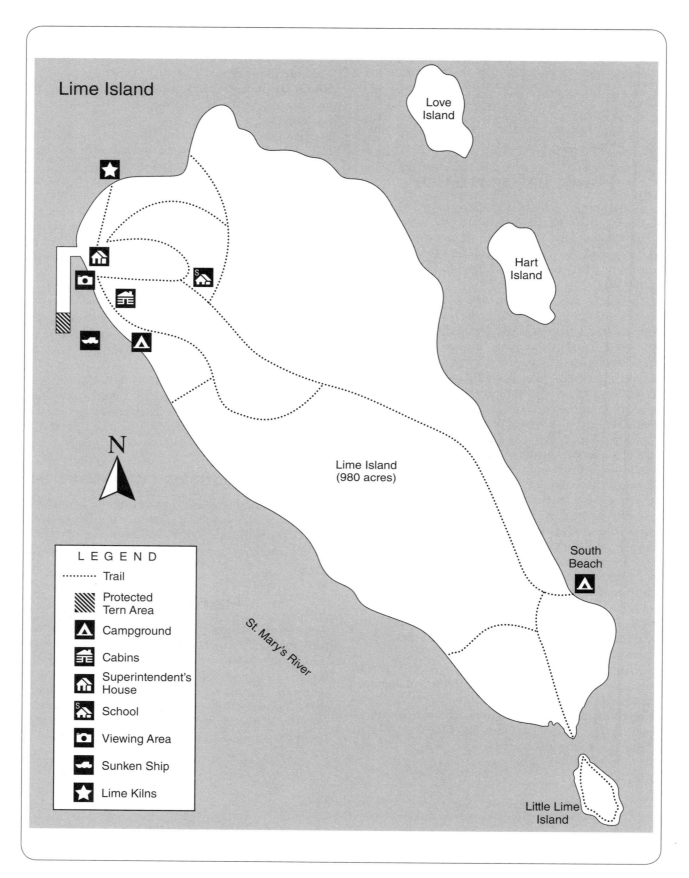

Lime Island

Love Island

Hart Island

Lime Island
(980 acres)

N

St. Mary's River

South Beach

Little Lime Island

LEGEND
········· Trail
Protected Tern Area
Campground
Cabins
Superintendent's House
S School
Viewing Area
Sunken Ship
Lime Kilns

N. Beach (Yellow) Trail

Distance One-Way: 1.4 miles
Estimated Hiking Time: 1 to 1.5 hours

Cautions: Roots and rocks at times litter the trail and may be slippery when wet. Bears inhabit the island, so take care. Watch out for poison ivy. Take along insect repellent.

Trail Directions: Start this pine-cushioned, cedar-scented trail off the service road, just north of the superintendent's house **[1]**. The trail ascends. Near the top the trail is thick with moss. Soon you walk high on a ridge. Moss and wildflowers are your trail.

Start to descend into the shadows of mixed hardwood trees, ducking under some low-lying branches (.3 mi.) **[2]**. You reach a junction at .4 mi. **[3]**. Turn left and descend past large boulders and evidence of beaver. The area is laced with ferns and moss cushions your steps. At .6 mi., you reach the beach **[4]**. You can see Round Island in the distance. Relax. Go uphill back to the junction (.8 mi.) **[3]**. Stay to the left on this trail marked with orange.

Step out of the woods and into an open meadow blanketed by grasses, ferns, and wildflowers (1 mi.) **[5]**. Soon an ethereal trail joins in; veer to the right along the grassy two-track. You find remnants of the past here—asparagus and apple trees—from when there was a small town on the island.

You reach a junction at 1.1 mi. **[6]**. Follow to the right on the two-track that leads back to the old townsite. Monarch butterflies flutter by enjoying the milkweed in the sun along this stretch. Evidence of the island's past industrial life shows up in the borrow pit that lies behind the school. When you reach the school, step inside to view a botanical lesson as the children of the old town would have (1.3 mi.) **[7]**. The service road is just in front of the school. Follow this road to the right back to your starting point.

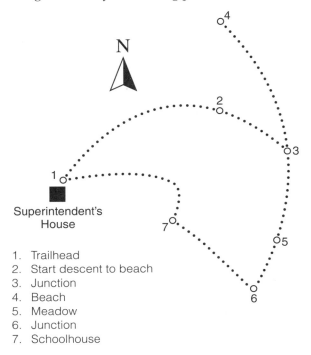

N

Superintendent's
House

1. Trailhead
2. Start descent to beach
3. Junction
4. Beach
5. Meadow
6. Junction
7. Schoolhouse

S. Beach (Red) Trail to Little Lime Island

Distance Round-Trip: 7.8 miles
Estimated Hiking Time: 3.5 to 4 hours

Cautions: Roots and rocks litter the trail and may be slippery when wet. Bears inhabit the island, so take care. Watch out for poison ivy. Take along insect repellent.

Trail Directions: Start off the service road, just north of the superintendent's house **[1]** and climb to a junction (.4 mi.) **[2]**. At the left is a spur to the shore. A number of such spurs appear on the route; veer right. Paper birch lie about like fallen soldiers in white uniforms. Boulders are scattered about.

Shasta daisies pepper the meadow—a bright relief from the darker woods that you've been in (.6 mi.) **[3]**. Veer right along a grassy two-track. You'll find remnants from past island life—asparagus and apple trees—before reaching a junction (.7 mi.) **[4]**.

Turn left, following the red arrow along this two-track. Keep to the left when the trail appears to split at .9 mi. **[5]**.

The woods become mixed, scattered with remnant large oaks and colorful fungus. You later find boulders strewn about the forest floor before arriving at the junction with the blue trail (1.3 mi.) **[6]**. Stroll past it; you will return to it on your way back.

The trail descends through more conifers, especially large cedars. The trail becomes rockier, and your descent becomes steeper (1.5 mi.) **[7]**. Moss-covered boulders are a prelude to the large one that you pass (1.6 mi.) **[8]**. Large cedars predominate as the trail rolls and winds until it descends steeply again into darkness where moss carpets the floor and the debris on it.

The canopy opens a bit, and you transition away from the cedar forest (2.2 mi.) **[9]** into hardwoods. At 2.4 mi., you reach the junction for the south camp beach

(red) **[10]**. Follow to the right and soon pass the junction for the brown trail. The area around the trail becomes wilder and then lush with sedges, wildflowers, and sensitive ferns. You soon reach the shore (2.9 mi.) **[11]**. Bear to the right for an opening to the beach. Daisy, iris, and yarrow line the trail. Little Lime Island comes into view. When water levels are low, it is no longer an island. Be prepared to explore it at 3.1 mi. **[12]**.

There is no trail here, just a beach crowded with wonderful rocks and boulders. Walk the perimeter to the right. If you brought a lunch, this is the spot to enjoy it.

When you loop back and face the larger island, look up in the tall, barren pine for a large nest with perhaps a bald eagle resting in the branches above it.

Follow the trail back the way you came. At the junction for the brown spur, turn left and wind down past large cedars to reach the beach (5.1 mi.) **[13]**. Listen for freighters passing before you return to the main trail and head left to reach the spur to the camp beach (5.5 mi.) **[10]**. It is less than .1 mi. to the beach, where you pass a tent platform. This spot would be a wonderful place to camp, offering solitude, waterfowl, and a beach with a view overlooking Canada. Now head back to the main trail and go north to the spur for the blue trail (6.7 mi.) **[6]**. Follow this lightly used trail to the left through darker, denser woods that have pockets of light and reach the spur to the beach (7.2 mi.) **[14]**. Turn left and descend into a sunny area past old ant mounds before you are swallowed by dark, dense forest growth. Arrive at the shore (7.3 mi.) **[15]** for yet another perspective of St. Mary's River.

Back on the main blue trail, head north through mostly young maples. The trail again becomes matted with moss and then weaves and rolls through cedar and pine. You pass through waist-high bracken ferns and notice that you come to a grassy opening with two fire pits behind the cottages. Here the trail ends. Note the large pile of coal on the left.

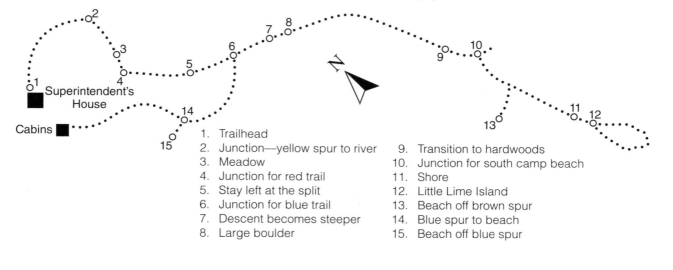

Superintendent's House

Cabins

1. Trailhead
2. Junction—yellow spur to river
3. Meadow
4. Junction for red trail
5. Stay left at the split
6. Junction for blue trail
7. Descent becomes steeper
8. Large boulder
9. Transition to hardwoods
10. Junction for south camp beach
11. Shore
12. Little Lime Island
13. Beach off brown spur
14. Blue spur to beach
15. Beach off blue spur

3. Bois Blanc Island

- Venture to a pristine and isolated island.
- Enjoy fiery sunsets that set sky and water ablaze.
- Mountain-bike the perimeter of the island.

Park Information

The island has no state parks. Camping is primitive—no restrooms, no grills, no electric, and no water hookups. The roads are dirt, and some unmanageable by car. So why visit Bois Blanc (known to the locals as Bob-lo) Island? All of the above.

This 22,000-acre island located southeast of Mackinac Island in the Straits of Mackinac provides rugged adventure. Permanent residents numbered 71 in 2000. The population explodes to roughly 1,200 in the summer, but a lot of open land remains available to explore. Besides the 39 miles of old roads, several unofficial primitive trails branch out from them. You need a good map for these trails and one that shows state versus private land. Portions of the island are designated natural areas, where dedicated trails cannot be developed. Some of the roads are used by cars, some by ORVs and ATVs, and some by mountain bikes.

Thirty miles of shoreline supply endless opportunities for fishing, swimming, and kayaking.

Roughly half of the island is managed by the Indian River Field Office of the Michigan Department of Natural Resources. Although there are no facilities to speak of, there are a couple of camping areas—one to the northwest off Bible Road and one east of Central Drive just south of Lake Thompson. Not all is rustic. Cottage and room rentals are available if you choose to stay overnight. Further luxuries include a general store with a gas pump and a tavern. And yes, there are latrines by the dock.

Directions: Although the island is part of the Upper Peninsula's Mackinac County, you pick up a ferry at 412 Water Street in Cheboygan. The ferry does transport vehicles. Contact Plaunt Transportation Co. at 231-627-2354, 888-PLAUNTS, or www.bbiferry.com. You can also fly over from Cheboygan or St. Ignace. Contact Great Lakes Air at 906-643-7165 or www.greatlakesair.net.

Hours Open: The ferry generally runs May through November and into December, weather permitting.

Facilities: Hiking, biking, swimming, fishing, hunting, snowmobiling, ATVs, and primitive camping.

Permits and Rules: There is no charge for visiting the island or for camping, but a permit is needed for campfires. Leave only footprints; take home only memories. The ferry costs $14.25 per adult, $47.50 per car or light truck, and $4.00 per bicycle.

For Further Information: Contact Indian River Field Office at 231-238-9314. You can obtain a campfire permit from Hawk's Landing Island Store, Bois Blanc Island, Pointe Aux Pins, MI 49775; 231-634-7375. For general information and lodging, contact the Cheboygan Area Chamber of Commerce, 124 North Main Street, Cheboygan, MI 49721; 800-968-3302 or 231-627-7183; www.cheboygan.com.

Other Points of Interest

While you are island hopping, Drummond, Lime, and Mackinac Islands are nearby. (See park #s 1, 2, and 4.)

Camping is available at **Cheboygan State Park**, located at 4490 Beach Road, Cheboygan, MI 49271, 3 miles east of town. Call 231-627-2811. You can also camp at **Aloha State Park**, located 5 miles south of Cheboygan via M-33. Contact Aloha State Park, 4347 Third Street, Cheboygan, MI 49721; 231-625-2522.

The **Insel Haus Bed and Breakfast** offers luxury accommodations on the island, and they provide a color map of the main trails to their guests. You can reach them at Insel Haus Bed and Breakfast, HCR 1, Box 157, Bois Blanc Island, MI 49775; 231-634-7393 or 888-634-7393; www.inselhausbandb.com.

The **Bois Blanc Island Landmark Trail**, developed by the B.B.I. Historical Society, is a driving tour that features 24 historic and natural sites around the island. Contact the Historical Society of Michigan, P.O. Box 933, Pointe Aux Pins, MI 49775; 231-634-7406; www.hsmichigan.org/pteauxpins.

Park Trails

The main trails are basically along roads or old roads. Those that skirt the backcountry are untamed, so you need a good map and compass.

About .1 mi. south of the Snake Island–Mud Lake Nature Study and Natural Area, the Nature Conservancy has marked and enhanced trails.

Bois Blanc Island

Lafayette Point

Walker Point

Snake Isle

Rosie Point

Nichol's Point

Packard Point

Bob-Lo Dr.

Lake Mary

Mud Lake

Lake Thompson

Lost Lake

Deer Lake

Base Line Rd.

Lighthouse Point

McRea Bay

Central Dr.

McRea Rd.

Twin Lake Cr.

Ferryboat Landing

Beaver Dam Rd.

Bob-Lo Dr.

Twin Lakes

Sucker Cr.

Hawk's Landing

Pointe Aux Pins

Bob-Lo Dr.

Point De Tachee

Sand Bay Rd.

Sand Bay

Zela Point

Bible Rd.

Point Catosh

Lime Kiln Point Rd.

Lime Kiln Point

Round Island

N

LEGEND

———	Good Dirt Road
= = =	Poor Dirt Road
· · · · ·	Trail
▲	Camping
🗼	Lighthouse
✕	Bois Blanc Landing Field

Snake Island–Mud Lake Nature Study and Natural Area

Distance Round-Trip: 1.2 miles
Estimated Hiking Time: 30 minutes to 1 hour

Cautions: Cobblestones are scattered along the trail. You will find loose footing with sand and stones. Walk with care and take along insect repellent.

Trail Directions: The nature area is about 4.5 mi. east of town on Bob-Lo Drive, where you park on the south side. There is no designated trail, but you'll find a distinct path to and along the shore. On this point-to-point trail you will be going out and turning around to come back. Start from right of the sign that identifies the area. From here you get a view of the bay **[1]**. You'll find yarrow, butterflies, and bergamot lacing the trail. To your right is the cobbled beach with grasses, sedges, and cattails. Follow the sandy path and pass a fence railing onto the peninsula and onto a cobblestone path. When water levels are high,

this peninsula becomes an island. The area is home to the dwarf lake iris, Michigan's state flower. The plant is found only in the Straits area and is bountiful in spring.

Young white cedar line up to greet you on your left. Notice the grazing line on them. Deer find them scrumptious. The trail veers right, and you reach the shore (.2 mi.) **[2]**. Walk the wide, cobbled path to the left. Tamarack, cedar, and other pines line the trail on your left. Water foams onto the shore on your right.

At .4 mi., you reach the base of the spit—the bar that you see extending out into the water **[3]**. If the water remains low, continue along the cobbled spit out to the tip (.6 mi.) **[4]**. You've just walked out across a small island to an area that, in higher waters, would be underwater.

Go back the way you came in, paying attention to the potentilla and other wildflowers that you may have missed as you were going in.

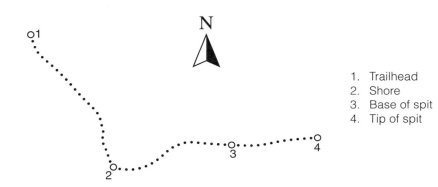

N

1. Trailhead
2. Shore
3. Base of spit
4. Tip of spit

Lighthouse Point

Distance Round-Trip: 6 miles
Estimated Hiking Time: 2.5 to 3.5 hours

Cautions: You'll find gravel, rocks, and roots along the trail. Watch your footing. Take along insect repellent.

Trail Directions: Take Bob-Lo Drive about 1 mi. east of town to Central Drive. Head north and follow it as it winds to the north end of the island and you again reach Bob-Lo Drive (although at the north end of the island it is a rough two-track). Park in the stones just north of Bob-Lo Drive. The trail starts there as Bob-Lo Drive heading east **[1]**. Sign post #17 here references a historical point that is part of the Bois Blanc Island Landmark Trail, which is a trail that you can drive. Your trail is a point-to-point trail through a designated wilderness area.

As you pass along this cedar-scented trail, you get glimpses of McCrea Bay through the trees. An area opens to the beach at .2 mi. **[2]**. After moving away from the beach, you arrive at another open area where you may reach the beach that houses a rusty reminder of the island's lumbering past. This was what #17 was referencing. Can you hear the loons in the distance?

The trail dips through a low, wet area, and then opens for another view (.7 mi.) **[3]**. Watch for kayakers in the bay.

You soon reach a muddy patch. Thereafter, a cover of cedars darkens your way. The trail rolls through a cedar swamp and then through red pine. A narrow path crosses, which you could take for a visit to the shore if you wish (1 mi.), or keep straight and soon pass another open view **[4]**. As you progress, trees become larger. Fallen trees litter the floor.

The trail splits at 1.5 mi. **[5]**. Take a brief visit to the small lake on the right. Tall pointed snags protrude from the other side. Watch for great blue herons or hawks. Raspberries line the path to the lake. Listen carefully for deer.

Pass large red and white pines to reach a junction (1.7 mi.) **[6]**. Follow to the left and enter the darkness of cedar and pine as the trail descends. You get a peek of the bay to your left through the trees (1.9 mi.) **[7]**. Cedar perfumes the air, and you pass a curb of white pine roots.

Cedars surround you. Downed trees and those leaning on one another creak as you pass through them. Cedar fragrance wafts past you.

At 2.2 mi., the trail is braided with roots **[8]**. You come closer to the bay as you continue north. At 2.7 mi., you see water on your right **[9]**. Soon you reach the gate of the lighthouse (3 mi.) **[10]**. That's as far as you can go. The lighthouse is private. Forge a path to the right and sit on the rocky dune. Have lunch and watch for freighters, shorebirds, and waterfowl before turning around and heading back.

1. Trailhead
2. Opens to beach
3. View of bay
4. Path crosses over to shore
5. Trail splits—quick visit to small lake
6. Junction
7. View of bay
8. Braided roots in trail
9. Water view to right
10. Gate at the lighthouse

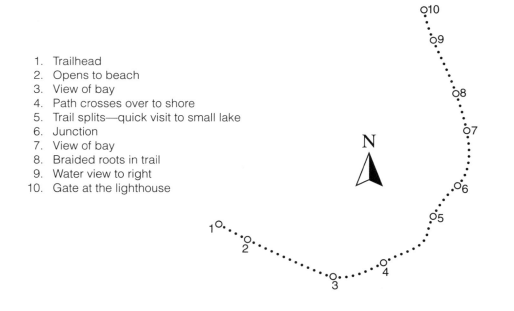

4. Mackinac Island State Park

- Step back in time to experience an era before the automobile.
- Enjoy historic reenactments at Fort Mackinac.
- Visit unique geologic formations.

Park Information

This state park makes up over 80 percent of the small island located in the Straits of Mackinac. The world-renowned retreat has more history than just the 18th-century fort within its bounds.

Before it became Michigan's first state park in 1895, it had been Mackinac National Park, the country's second national park, after Yellowstone. For history buffs, there's history on the bluffs. Fort Mackinac, perched on the bluff overlooking the straits, was built by the British in 1780. Cannon and musket firings and period reenactments offer visitors a taste of yesteryear.

Fort Mackinac, Fort Holmes, and a plethora of barracks, missions, and old cemeteries also take you back. Add to that palatial Victorian cottages, the stately Grand Hotel, the clip-clop of hooves, and creaking harness leather from horse-drawn carriages, and you live a bygone era.

Directions: Ferry transportation is available from St. Ignace and Mackinaw City. Three ferry lines serve the island. For information on schedules and rates, contact Arnold Transit at 800-542-8528, Shepler's at 800-828-6157, or Star Line at 800-638-9892.

Hours Open: The state park is open daily, but Fort Mackinac is open from 9:00 a.m. to 8:00 p.m. from June 20 to August 24, with reduced hours in spring and fall.

Facilities: Hiking, biking, cross-country skiing, snowmobiling, bridle paths, picnicking, interpretive trails.

Permits and Rules: No charge is required to visit Mackinac Island State Park, but admission to Fort Mackinac requires a fee of $10.00 for adults and $6.25 for children age 5 to 17. Combination packages, which allow seasonal access to Fort Mackinac, Colonial Michilimackinac, and Historic Mill Creek Discovery Park, are available at $59.00 for a family.

For Further Information: Mackinac State Historic Parks, 207 W. Sinclair Street, P.O. Box 873, Mackinaw City, MI 49701; 231-436-4100; www.mackinacparks.com.

Other Points of Interest

The Mackinac Island Chamber of Commerce can provide information on horse and buggy sightseeing tours, bicycle rentals, island hotels and guest houses, and horse-drawn taxi services. Contact Mackinac Island Tourism Bureau, P.O. Box 451, Mackinac Island, MI 49757; 877-847-0086; www.mackinacisland.org.

Other state parks are nearby: **Wilderness State Park** (see park #39), **Historic Mill Creek Discovery Park** (see park #37), and **Colonial Michilimackinac State Historic Park** are located in the Lower Peninsula. Only Wilderness State Park provides camping facilities. Colonial Michilimackinac provides an overview of British, French, and Indian life in the 18th century. For more information, contact Colonial Michilimackinac, c/o Mackinac State Historic Parks, P.O. Box 873, Mackinaw City, MI 49701; 231-436-4100.

Camping is also available in the Upper Peninsula's **Straits State Park**, which has an awesome view of the Mackinac Bridge. For more information, contact Straits State Park, 720 Church Street, St. Ignace, MI 49781; 906-643-8620.

Mackinaw City has parks, museums, walks, and points of interest. For information, contact the Mackinaw City Chamber of Commerce; 231-436-5574 or 888-455-8100; www.mackinawchamber.com; or the Mackinaw City Chamber of Tourism; 800-577-3113; www.mackinawcitychamber.com.

Park Trails

Although most people who arrive at the island scurry about Huron Street, weaving in and out of the clapboard buildings that house fudge and souvenir shops, relief from the crowds and mayhem of peak tourist visitation is nearby. With over 100 miles of non-motorized roads and trails, plenty of opportunities are available for bicycling, hiking, or horseback riding—set out and explore. Be sure to stop at the visitor center across from Marquette Park, near the docks, for more trail information.

Round the Shore (, 8.2 miles). A favorite hiking and bicycle route, this road hugs the shoreline as it circles the island on M-185, the only highway in Michigan on which automobiles are banned.

Upper Peninsula

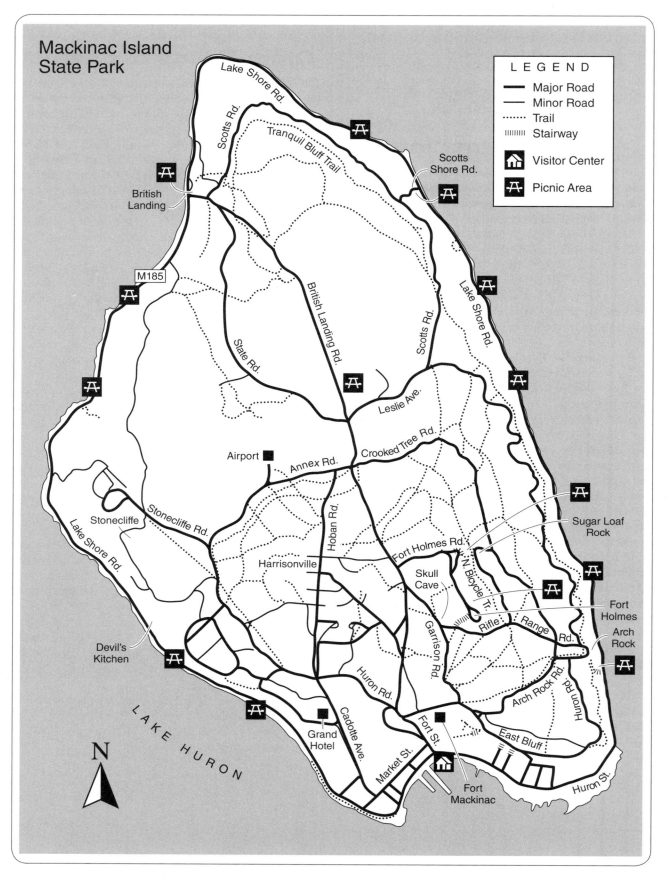

Mackinac Island
State Park

LEGEND
━━ Major Road
— Minor Road
···· Trail
⊪⊪⊪ Stairway
⌂ Visitor Center
🎪 Picnic Area

Lake Shore Rd.
Scotts Rd.
Tranquil Bluff Trail
Scotts Shore Rd.
Lake Shore Rd.
British Landing
M185
British Landing Rd.
State Rd.
Scotts Rd.
Leslie Ave.
Crooked Tree Rd.
Airport
Annex Rd.
Sugar Loaf Rock
Stonecliffe
Stonecliffe Rd.
Hoban Rd.
Fort Holmes Rd.
N. Bicycle Tr.
Fort Holmes
Harrisonville
Skull Cave
Rifle Range Rd.
Arch Rock
Lake Shore Rd.
Devil's Kitchen
Garrison Rd.
Arch Rock Rd.
Huron Rd.
Huron Rd.
Grand Hotel
Cadotte Ave.
Huron Rd.
Fort St.
East Bluff
Market St.
Fort Mackinac
Huron St.

LAKE HURON

N

Natural and Historical Features Tour

Distance Round-Trip: 3.2 miles
Estimated Hiking Time: 1.5 to 2 hours

Cautions: Both hiking and bicycling are permitted on the trails. Be careful. You cross roads that are shared with horses. Watch your step. Steps are slippery when wet. Take care and take insect repellent.

Trail Directions: Start at the visitor center at the southeast corner of Fort and Huron streets **[1]**. Cross Huron Street and head up the sidewalk along Fort Street. This climb up the hill takes you past Marquette Park, past a replica of a bark missionary chapel, and then past the entrance to Fort Mackinac. The governor's summer residence is at the top of the hill (.2 mi.) **[2]**. The house is open to the public from 9:30 a.m. to 11:30 a.m. on Wednesdays during the summer.

Turn right and stroll over to Fort Mackinac, where you are invited to "Step into History" (.3 mi.) **[3]**. Watch where you step as you continue walking to the junction with a directional board that directs you straight to the pedestrian and bicycle path (.4 mi.) **[4]**. Stroll through the wooded setting where white cedar is predominant. White pine and spruce help perfume the air.

The narrow Lime Kiln Trail cuts across your trail just before you curve left to parallel Arch Rock Road (.7 mi.) **[5]**. Listen for the shifting of bicycle gears and the clopping of horses as they pull touring carriages down the road. After passing a bench, you begin to descend. A sign warns, "Danger, Bicycles Slow" (.9 mi.) **[6]**. A sharp turn awaits you just before you reach the busy circle at Arch Rock Road.

Carriages line up as they wait for the tourists viewing Arch Rock (1 mi.) **[7]**. The arch-shaped rock rises 146 feet above the water. Nicolet Watch Tower adjoins the rock. Named after John Nicolet, the first white man to enter the Old Northwest, it offers a climb of almost 60 steps to a bluff overlooking Lake Huron.

Head back down to Arch Rock Bicycle Trail, which parallels Leslie Avenue, follow around the circle, and then continue north along Leslie Avenue. The trail winds through woods. Occasionally, you have views of the lake. Follow along the ridge. A rail fence protects you from getting too near the steep bluff at about 1.3 mi. **[8]**.

Take the left fork at the Y-junction (1.5 mi.) **[9]** and roll along the North Bicycle Trail through the shade of the woods. At 2 mi., you reach Sugar Loaf **[10]**. The towering stack of 75-foot-high rock was once a tiny island when water levels were higher.

Turn around and you'll notice steps. Take all 137 of them up the steep slope, past the sheer rock wall with cavelike holes, and onto the bluff for a different view of the Sugar Loaf formation.

Turn left on Fort Holmes Road (2.2 mi.) **[11]** and go on to Fort Holmes (2.3 mi.) **[12]**, which is situated on the island's highest point. In the War of 1812, the British moved to this high ground overlooking Fort Mackinac. The Americans, taken by surprise, surrendered. Surrender to the heights and take in the spectacular view—Bois Blanc Island (see park #3) amid a Lake Huron that is punctuated with boulders and a lighthouse.

Backtrack to the steps along the southwest side of the fort and take all 141 down to Rifle Range Road (2.4 mi.) **[13]**. Turn right. Just to the right, on Garrison Road, is Skull Cave, where, according to tradition, fur trader Alexander Henry hid during the Indian uprising of 1763. He claimed that the floor of the cave was covered with human bones (2.5 mi.) **[14]**.

Turn back and head south on what is Garrison Road as it descends back to the information board by the bicycle and pedestrian trail (2.8 mi.) **[4]**. From here, retrace your steps to the visitor center.

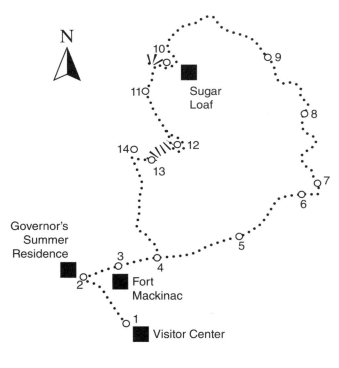

1. Trailhead
2. Governor's summer residence
3. Fort Mackinac
4. Directional board
5. Intersection with Lime Kiln Trail
6. Descent
7. Arch Rock
8. Rail fence
9. Y-junction
10. Sugar Loaf
11. Fort Holmes Road
12. Fort Holmes
13. Rifle Range Road
14. Skull Cave

Upper Peninsula

Tranquil Bluff Trail

Distance One-Way: 3.2 miles
Estimated Hiking Time: 1.5 to 2 hours

Cautions: This point-to-point trail starts at the southeast side of the island, near Arch Rock, and ends at the northwest side of the island, near the north end of British Landing Road. You may share this trail with mountain bicyclists. Getting to and from the trail will more than double your mileage. Plan your time accordingly.

The eastern portion of the trail includes a number of steep climbs and descents that are extremely slippery when wet. The trail has exposed rocks and roots, and portions of the trail flood when it rains. Wear appropriate footgear. This section of the trail is also along the edge of steep cliffs. Watch your step. Finally, take along insect repellent.

Trail Directions: Climb the steps to the Nicolet Watch Tower, which is next to the Arch Rock viewing area. The sign for the trail is to the left of the rock with the plaque that commemorates John Nicolet, the first white man to enter Michigan and the Old Northwest **[1]**.

The Tranquil Bluff Trail, the longest hiking trail on the island, provides an opportunity to walk the island in relative tranquility, although the first part of the trail, belying its name, contains some of the least tranquil hiking on Mackinac Island. The trail follows the edge of the cliffs along the east side of the island, rising and falling as it provides a number of scenic overlooks. This part of Mackinac Island is not what most tourists will see or remember. If the trail is more than you bargained for, Leslie Avenue is close by on the left. The trail does pop out onto this paved road briefly (.2 mi.) **[2]** and then veers right to climb to a cedar-scented overlook (.3 mi.) **[3]**.

The next mile is the roughest part of the trail as it rises and falls along the edge of the cliff. You are rewarded for your effort with numerous scenic views through the trees that cling to the rocky ledge. About 1 mi. into the hike, enjoy a series of spectacular views of Lake Huron from the bluff **[4]**.

When you reach the junction with the Murray Trail (1.3 mi.) **[5]**, the Tranquil Bluff Trail leaves the bluffs behind. The trail now becomes a peaceful walk through the woods. At 1.7 mi., cross Scotts Road **[6]**. This road is again accessible when it appears below on the right as you reach an opening in the trees (2.1 mi.) **[7]**.

You are near the northernmost point of the trail at 2.5 mi., and Big St. Martin Island is barely visible through the trees on the northern horizon **[8]**. The trail soon descends and swings wide to the left, and you find yourself heading south toward the junction with Porter Hank's Trail (3 mi.) **[9]** and the British Landing Nature Trail (3.1 mi.) **[10]**.

Continuing past the nature trail, the Tranquil Bluff Trail ends when you reach British Landing Road (3.2 mi.) **[11]**. The British used this road to reach the high ground above Fort Mackinac, an action that resulted in the fort's surrender during the War of 1812. From here you can take the shore route along the west side of the island or follow British Landing Road through the center of the island, back to the village.

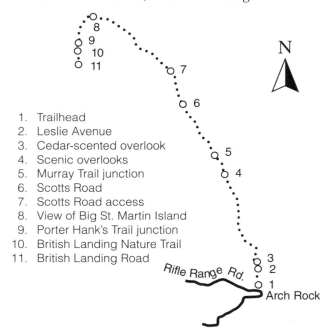

1. Trailhead
2. Leslie Avenue
3. Cedar-scented overlook
4. Scenic overlooks
5. Murray Trail junction
6. Scotts Road
7. Scotts Road access
8. View of Big St. Martin Island
9. Porter Hank's Trail junction
10. British Landing Nature Trail
11. British Landing Road

- Cross one of the longest suspension bridges in the Western Hemisphere.
- Visit two distinct peninsulas.
- Enjoy two tourist havens—St. Ignace and Mackinaw City.

Bridge Information

The Mackinac Bridge is located where Lake Michigan and Lake Huron meet, at the crossroads of the Great Lakes. Also known as the Mighty Mac or Big Mac, the Mackinac is a suspension bridge that spans the Straits of Mackinac and connects the Upper and Lower peninsulas of Michigan. The 2nd longest suspension bridge in the world (measured by length of main span) when it was built, after the Golden Gate Bridge, it now ranks as the 12th longest in the world. Ranked by total length of suspension, the Mackinac Bridge is the 6th longest in the world.

A bridge had been envisioned connecting the two peninsulas since the 1880s. They had originally been linked by ferry. The dream came to fruition when the bridge opened on November 1, 1957. It took 3.5 years to build and cost the lives of five men who worked on the bridge.

About 4 million vehicles cross annually between the two municipalities—Mackinaw City and St. Ignace. Every year since 1958, the bridge has been open to walkers on Labor Day for the Mackinac Bridge Walk. Between 50,000 and 70,000 people walk the bridge each year.

Directions: Mackinac Bridge is the I-75 connector between the Upper and Lower peninsulas.

Hours Open: All year, weather permitting.

Facilities: Sightseeing, bus ride, annual hike, and biannual Big Mac Shoreline bike tour.

Permits and Rules: New fees instituted in 2008 are $1.50 per axle for passenger vehicles and $3.50 per axle for all other vehicles. Maximum speed is 45 mph, no stopping is allowed on the bridge, and you should use four-way flashers and stay inside your vehicle if it becomes disabled. Other restrictions may be in effect because of weather conditions or construction projects.

For Further Information: Mackinac Bridge Authority, 906-643-7600. For information on the Upper Peninsula, visit www.uptravel.com. The St. Ignace Visitors Bureau and Chamber of Commerce share a Web site at www.stignace.com. The visitors bureau is at 6 Spring Street, Suite 100, St. Ignace, MI 49781; 800-338-6660. The chamber is located at 560 N. State Street, St. Ignace, MI 49781; 800-970-8717. The Mackinaw Area Visitors Center is located at 10800 W. US 23, Mackinaw City, MI 49701; 231-436-5644 or 800-666-0160; www.mackinawcity.com.

Other Points of Interest

A growing demand for fur led the French to build Fort Michilimackinac in 1715 at the site of present-day Mackinaw City. Trade flourished here because the site was conveniently located near three lakes, making it an easy rendezvous spot for the Indians. Now the **Colonial Michilimackinac State Historic Park**, which has its entrance under the bridge, it is part of the Mackinac State Historic Parks. Other historic sites in the Straits of Mackinac region include **Fort Mackinac** and **Mackinac Island State Park** (see park #4) on Mackinac Island and **Historic Mill Creek Discovery Park** (see park #37), east of Mackinaw City. For more information, contact Mackinac State Historic Parks, P.O. Box 873, Mackinaw City, MI 49701; 231-436-4100; www.mackinacparks.com.

Camping is available in the Upper Peninsula's **Straits State Park**, which has an awesome view of the Mackinac Bridge (the bridge is lit up at night). Across I-75 from this unit is the **Father Marquette National Memorial and Museum**, administered by Straits State Park and dedicated to Jesuit priest Father Jacques Marquette. For more information, call Straits State Park, 720 Church Street, St. Ignace, MI 49781; 906-643-8620.

About 11 miles west of Mackinaw City, **Wilderness State Park** (see park #39) offers 25 miles of Lake Michigan shoreline, modern campsites, a sandy beach, and about 12 miles of hiking trails. For more information, contact Wilderness State Park, 933 Wilderness Park Drive, Carp Lake, MI 49718; 231-436-5381.

Annual Bridge Walk

There are no trails. The walk is permitted only once each year—on Labor Day.

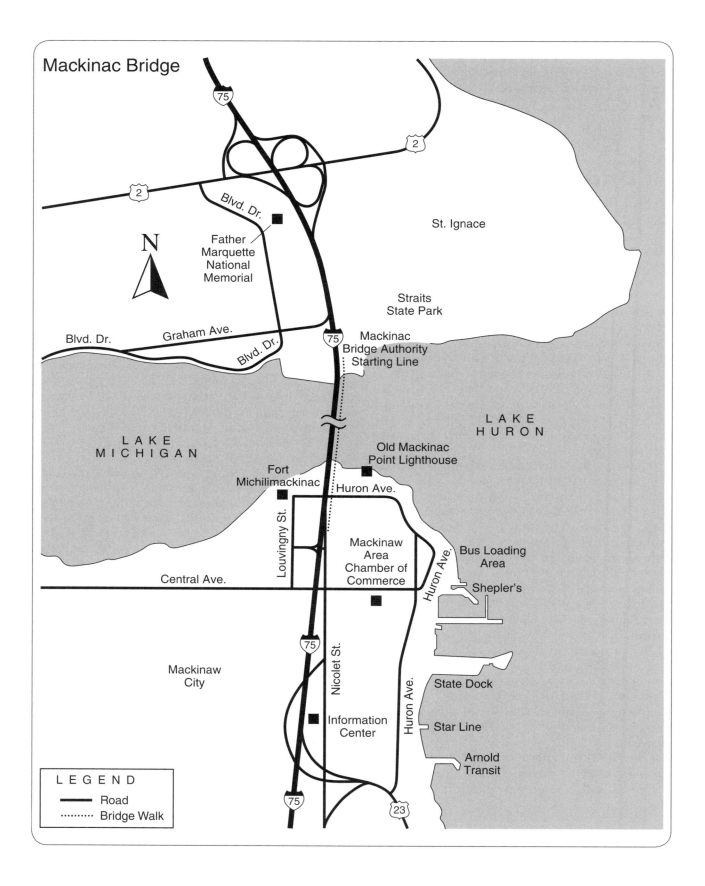

Mackinac Bridge

Mackinac Bridge Walk— Michigan's Annual Labor Day Hike

Distance One-Way: 5 miles
Estimated Hiking Time: 1.5 to 2 hours

Cautions: The bridge spans 26,372 feet, almost 5 mi. There are no restrooms on the bridge. Portable toilets are generally located at both ends of the bridge and at the bus loading areas. Maximum depth of water midspan is 295 feet. The drop from the roadway at midspan to the water is 199 feet, so stay away from the railings. Vehicular traffic is open on the west lanes. Stay away from the center mall that divides you from this traffic. Take along sunscreen, water, and insect spray.

Hike Directions: Michigan's annual hike begins on the north side of the bridge in the Upper Peninsula and ends on the south side in Mackinaw City **[1]**. You may park your vehicle in St. Ignace, walk the bridge, and then take a bus back, or you may park in Mackinaw City, take the bus over, and walk back. Limited parking space is located west of the Mackinac Bridge Authority plaza on the north end. Bus loading areas are at Conkling Park and the State Dock on South Huron Avenue in Mackinaw City. The walk is free, but there is a $2 fare for the bus. Buses start transporting in Mackinaw City at 5:30 a.m.

This event has been an annual occurrence since Governor G. Mennen Williams led about 60 hikers over the bridge on June 25, 1958. The next year it was moved to Labor Day, where it has been ever since. The current governor still leads the walk.

Hike along with 50,000 to 70,000 others, ranging in age from a few months (strapped to backs or in strollers) to about 90 years. As long as they are fit, people of all degrees of agility participate—runners (only those prequalified in the Governor's Council on Physical Fitness Jog) to walkers to those with walkers to those in wheelchairs. Peak attendance occurred in 1992 at over 82,000 when George H.W. Bush led the walk as he courted Michigan voters for his reelection. He lost, but you win as you watch the sun glistening on blue waters. See sailboats navigating in the distance. Listen to freighters rumbling beneath you. Catch a grand view of the Grand Hotel as it stands prominently on Mackinac Island.

The walk begins at 7:00 a.m. You can begin any time after the governor's party starts. No one may start after 11:00 a.m. The two east lanes of the bridge are used by walkers heading south up until 9:30 a.m. After this, only one east lane is available for walkers. Bus service from Mackinaw City to St. Ignace ends at 2:30 p.m. Start early if you parked in St. Ignace so that you can wind down into Mackinaw City and have plenty of time to enjoy the town (5 mi.) **[2]**.

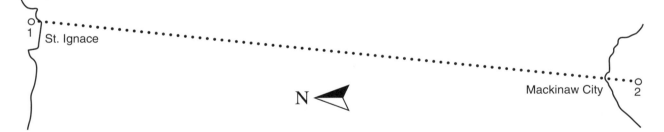

1. Beginning of walk
2. End of walk

- Have fun in the waters of three Great Lakes—Huron, Michigan, and Superior.
- Seek solitude in the four designated wilderness areas.
- Explore all or portions of the 83 miles of North Country Trail as it meanders through the heart of the forest.

Park Information

Named after Longfellow's celebrated poem "Song of Hiawatha," the Hiawatha National Forest includes water as a key element. Nearly 46 percent of the forest's 880,000 acres are wetland, featuring roughly 775 miles of rivers and streams, 413 lakes, and 100 miles of Great Lakes shoreline. Sandwiched between the Great Lakes, the Hiawatha's rolling hills are forested with northern hardwoods, white pine, and hemlock, and the flatter lands more typically are covered by red pine, jack pine, and aspen. The Hiawatha is separated into two large units. The East Unit extends north from St. Ignace, along Lakes Michigan and Huron, to the shore of Lake Superior west of Sault Ste. Marie. The West Unit (see park #12) stretches north from the towns of Rapid River and Manistique, along Lake Michigan, to Munising on Lake Superior. An abundance of recreational opportunities awaits fishermen, hunters, hikers, backpackers, canoeists, kayakers, snowmobilers, and cross-country skiers.

The East Unit features four wilderness areas (Delirium Wilderness, Horseshoe Bay Wilderness, Mackinac Wilderness, and Round Island Wilderness); a scenic drive (Whitefish Bay Scenic Byway); two designated national wild and scenic recreational rivers (Carp River and East Branch Tahquamenon); around 100 miles of hiking trails; over 20 miles of cross-country ski trails; and untold miles of snowmobile and ATV trails. Eight campgrounds and backcountry camping provide serene and scenic camping opportunities.

Directions: Facilities and points of interest are spread out over a large area. Contact the forest supervisor's office or the individual district offices of the Hiawatha National Forest for more information.

Hours Open: Most facilities are open year-round.

Facilities: Hiking, cross-country skiing, snowshoeing, snowmobiling, ATV, swimming, fishing, hunting, boat launch, canoeing, camping (tent and backcountry), picnicking, interpretive trails, and visitor center.

Permits and Rules: Generally, fees or permits are not required for hikers, canoeists, or other users. There is a $6 per vehicle per day fee for using the day-use areas at Lake Michigan and Brevoort Lake campgrounds. Camping fees vary by site. No fee is required for backcountry camping. Motorized and mechanized vehicles or equipment are not allowed in the wilderness areas. Leave no trace. Carry out what you carry in. Most of the lands within the Hiawatha boundaries are federally owned, but small parcels of privately owned lands exist. Obtain permission to enter such lands.

For Further Information: Hiawatha National Forest, Forest Supervisor's Office, 2727 N. Lincoln Road, Escanaba, MI 49829; 906-789-4062. Alternatively, you may contact the district offices of the Hiawatha National Forest East Unit: Sault Ste. Marie Ranger District, 4000 I-75 Business Spur, Sault Ste. Marie, MI 49783; 906-635-5311; or St. Ignace Ranger District, 1900 W. US 2, St. Ignace, MI 49781; 906-643-7900.

Other Points of Interest

The Hiawatha National Forest East Unit covers a huge territory. For more information about what is available in the area, contact Upper Peninsula Travel and Recreation Association, P.O. Box 400, Iron Mountain, MI 49801; 800-562-7134; www.uptravel.com; Sault Ste. Marie Chamber of Commerce, 2581 I-75 Business Spur, Sault Ste. Marie, MI 49783; 906-632-3301; www.sault stemarie.org; and St. Ignace Chamber of Commerce, 560 N. State Street, St. Ignace, MI 49781; 800-970-8717; www.stignace.com.

Park Trails

More than 100 miles of trails weave through the East Unit. Some are interpretive trails, such as the Ridge Interpretive Trail at the Brevoort Lake Campground. Some are scenic, such as the Monocle Lake Interpretive Trail at the Monocle Lake Recreation Area. Some are historic, like the Point Iroquois Boardwalk at the Point Iroquois Lighthouse. Others are for backpacking, like the 83 miles of the North Country Trail that passes through the forest. The potential in the wilderness is limitless.

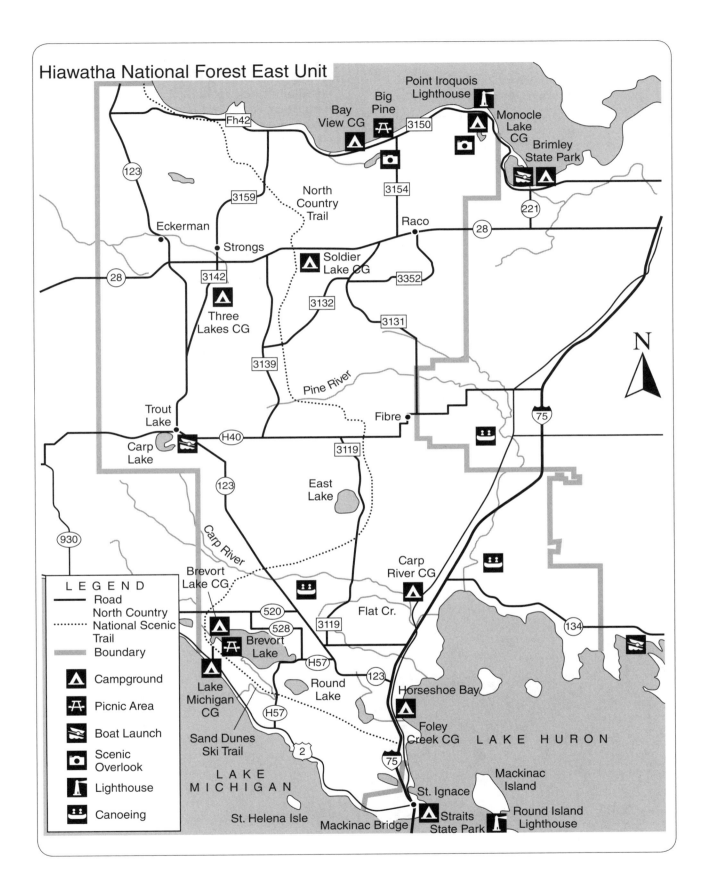

Hiawatha National Forest East Unit

Point Iroquois Lighthouse

Big Pine

Bay View CG

Monocle Lake CG

Brimley State Park

Fh42

3150

3154

123

3159

North Country Trail

Eckerman

Strongs

Raco

28

221

28

Soldier Lake CG

3352

3142

3132

3131

Three Lakes CG

3139

Pine River

Fibre

75

Trout Lake

H40

3119

Carp Lake

East Lake

123

930

Carp River

Carp River CG

Brevort Lake CG

520

528

3119

Flat Cr.

134

Lake Michigan CG

Brevort Lake

H57

123

Horseshoe Bay

N

LEGEND

Round Lake

Sand Dunes Ski Trail

H57

Foley Creek CG

LAKE HURON

— Road
North Country
⋯ National Scenic
Trail
Boundary

2

LAKE MICHIGAN

Mackinac Island

75

🏕 Campground

🏕 Picnic Area

🚣 Boat Launch

📷 Scenic Overlook

🗼 Lighthouse

🚣 Canoeing

St. Helena Isle

Mackinac Bridge

St. Ignace

Straits State Park

Round Island Lighthouse

Horseshoe Bay Trail

Distance Round-Trip: 2.2 miles
Estimated Hiking Time: 1 to 1.5 hours

Cautions: Roots and rocks are exposed along the trail, and some areas are wet. Wear proper footgear. Take along insect repellent in the warmer months. Portions of the trail are seasonally open for hunting, so take care.

Trail Directions: This trail through the Horseshoe Bay Wilderness starts at the Foley Creek Campground, which is on H-63 (Mackinac Trail), 2.5 miles north of I-75 business junction; or 2.3 miles south from Highway 123 junction. Parking is available on Mackinaw Trail, just north of the entrance to the campground. You can access the camp road from the lot and then walk north about .4 mi. to the trailhead [1]. A couple of parking spots may be available near the trailhead, so you may want to drive through the camp and check it out first during the mid-May to early October season. No user fee is required. Although your hike starts out with audible traffic floating over from nearby I-75, the trail sweeps to the right and away from the highway at .1 mi. [2].

Bracken ferns lace the pine-cushioned trail that passes through mixed conifers, many of which are hemlock. You then walk through seasonal wet areas and enter a cedar swamp (.2 mi.) [3]. This northern white cedar ecosystem is winter habitat for white-tailed deer when snow is deep.

You travel deeper into the dense, swampy woods after hiking over planks and a boardwalk (.4 mi.) [4]. Cedar and balsam perfume the air as trunks and branches of the dark, swampy forest creak and moan. The canopy opens a bit at .5 mi., but planks are still there to keep your feet dry [5]. The air is thick with the perfume of fir and cedar.

The woods become dense again (.6 mi.) [6]. Notice that you cannot hear the highway anymore. You cross more planks and pass a small stream on your left before the trail narrows so much that needles of firs brush you as you pass through.

Logs are grouped in the ground for your passage (.8 mi.) [7]. Bunchberries line the way. In the intermittent swampland, you cross more planks before arriving at what is now a sandy trail (1 mi.) [8]. This is your tipoff that you will soon cross through grasses and wildflowers that wave in the breeze off the bay (1.1 mi.) [9]. The turquoise, blue, and green bay is woven with ponds typical of coastal wetlands. The ponds are the preferred habitat for shorebirds, many species of ducks, and great blue herons. From the sandy shore you can see Mackinac Island to the southeast and St. Martin Island to the northwest. If you've packed a picnic lunch, you can enjoy the sun, shells, seagulls, and serenity that the white sandy bay has to offer before you turn around and head back.

1. Trailhead
2. Trail veers right
3. Cedar swamp
4. Boardwalk
5. Planks; canopy opens
6. Dense woods
7. Log planks
8. Trail becomes sandy
9. Horseshoe Bay

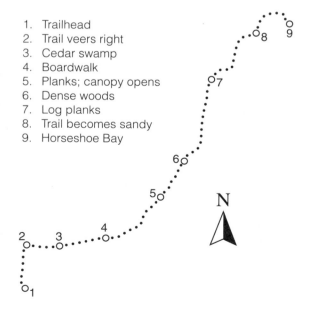

7. Tahquamenon Falls State Park

- Visit the land of Longfellow's Hiawatha.
- Watch root beer–colored water plunge over one of the largest waterfalls east of the Mississippi.
- Experience the moose capital of Michigan.

Park Information

With over 45,000 acres, Tahquamenon Falls State Park is the second-largest state park in Michigan. Much of the park is undeveloped and is managed as a wilderness area. The lifeblood of the park is the Tahquamenon River, which flows through the park and twice plunges into dramatic waterfalls.

The Upper Falls, sometimes called the Little Niagara, is one of the largest waterfalls east of the Mississippi River. It is over 200 feet across and has a vertical drop of nearly 50 feet. Hiking and cross-country ski trails start from the Upper Falls parking area. Gift and food concessions are located here, along with a picnic area and a privately owned restaurant and gift shop.

The Lower Falls are a series of smaller falls that cascade around an island. Although less dramatic than the Upper Falls, they are no less scenic. Rent a boat and row out to the island for a unique way to view the falls. Hiking trails, park concession, picnic area, and campgrounds are located at the Lower Falls.

Tannin leached from the spruce, cedar, and hemlock swamps that drain into the Tahquamenon River gives the water its amber, or root beer, color. The foam beneath the falls results from the soft waters being whipped as they tumble over the falls.

The park contains 13 inland lakes, 24 miles of river, 20,000 acres of natural area, and over 40 miles of hiking trails. The warmer months present camping, backpacking, fishing, canoeing, and nature study opportunities. Autumn brings color to the trees. Snowshoeing, cross-country skiing, and snowmobiling are available in winter.

Two modern campgrounds are located at the Lower Falls. Modern and rustic campgrounds are located at the Rivermouth site.

Directions: From Paradise, the Lower Falls entrance is 10 miles west on M-123. The Upper Falls are about 4 miles farther west. The Rivermouth unit is 4 miles south of Paradise on M-123.

Hours Open: Open year-round from 8:00 a.m. to 10:00 p.m.

Facilities: Hiking, cross-country skiing, snowshoeing, snowmobiling, swimming, fishing, hunting, picnicking, boat launch, boat rental, canoeing, camping (tent and RV), sanitation station, and interpretive trails.

Permits and Rules: A park fee is required for a motor vehicle ($6 daily, $24 annually for residents; $8 daily, $29 annually for nonresidents). Camping is permitted in established areas only.

For Further Information: Tahquamenon Falls State Park, 41382 W. M-123, Paradise, MI 49768; 906-492-3415.

Other Points of Interest

At **Whitefish Point**, visit the **Great Lakes Shipwreck Museum**. Experience the tales of ships and men who braved Lake Superior's cold, deep waters and violent storms, from the 1816 wreck of the *Invincible* to the wreck of the *Edmund Fitzgerald*. For more information, call 888-492-3747; www.ShipwreckMuseum.com. In spring, visit **Whitefish Point Bird Observatory** to watch the birds migrating at one of Michigan's premier bird-watching sites. For more information, call 906-492-3596.

Park Trails

Tahquamenon River Trail (, 4 miles). Follows the Tahquamenon River between the Upper and Lower Falls.

Overlook Campground Nature Trail Loop (, 2 miles). Starts near campsite #179 in the Overlook Campground and winds its way to the Lower Falls.

Wilderness Loop (, 7.4 miles). The park's most primitive trail, this path has few footbridges and no boardwalks. It traverses pine ridges, peat lands, and old-growth hemlock.

North Country National Scenic Trail (, 16 miles). Linking the Lewis and Clark National Historic Trail in North Dakota with New York's Crown Point Historic Site on Lake Champlain, this 4,600-mile-long trail includes 16 miles within Tahquamenon Falls State Park.

Emerson Foot Trail (, 2 miles round-trip). This trail passes through shrub swamp and black spruce, following a road that leads to the abandoned sawmill town of Emerson and then on to Lake Superior.

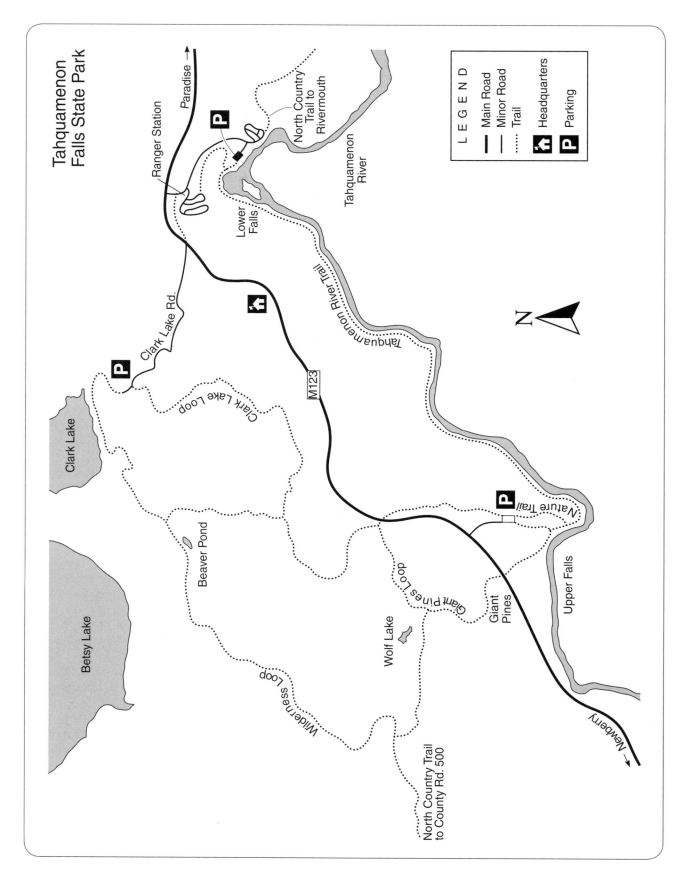

Tahquamenon Falls State Park

LEGEND
Main Road
Minor Road
Trail
Headquarters
P Parking

N

Paradise →

Ranger Station

North Country Trail to Rivermouth

Tahquamenon River

Lower Falls

Clark Lake Rd.

Tahquamenon River Trail

M123

Clark Lake Loop

Clark Lake

Betsy Lake

Beaver Pond

Wilderness Loop

Wolf Lake

Giant Pines Loop

Nature Trail

Giant Pines

Upper Falls

Newberry →

North Country Trail to County Rd. 500

Giant Pines Loop
With Upper Falls Tour

Distance Round-Trip: 4 miles
Estimated Hiking Time: 1.5 to 2 hours

Cautions: The trail may be intermittently wet. Wear hiking boots and be prepared to cross logs and rocks. Take insect repellent. You don't want mosquitoes and black flies to ruin your hike through one of Michigan's finest examples of primeval beech–sugar maple–hemlock forest. You're in bear country; act accordingly.

Trail Directions: Take the Old Growth Forest Nature Trail at the southwest corner of the Upper Falls parking lot [1]. This small portion of the trail rolls and winds through what had been old-growth woods before a fungus recently decimated it. The trees were cut to prevent further damage.

At .4 mi., turn left on the paved path that leads to viewing points along the Tahquamenon River [2]. This path leads you to a staircase that takes you down 117 steps to a boardwalk (.6 mi.) [3]; here you have several opportunities to view the root beer–colored water as it cascades over the edge, frothing as it plunges into the river below. Rest on one of the benches before climbing back up to the trail.

Follow the falls-viewing trail on its ridge above the river, stopping at the many viewing spots. From up here, the falls sound like wind whispering through the trees.

At 1 mi., another staircase takes you almost 100 steps down to a platform right at the falls [4] where the river rushes past you before it spills down below. Climb back up. You can rest here on a bench if you wish before continuing to the northwest to plunge onto the Giant Pines Trail.

Step into the northern hardwoods and revere the large beeches and sugar maples around you. Your boots may get muddy on this loop, but the experience is worth it. Hemlock mixes in with the other trees before you carefully climb out of the woods to cross M-123 (1.4 mi.) [5].

Dip back into the forest and arrive at one of the trees that gave the trail its name, a giant white pine (1.6 mi.) [6]. Stare up in silence at the 120-foot-high tree with its 4-foot, 8-inch diameter. Combined with its mate down the trail, these two trees contain enough board feet to build a five-room house. One can only imagine what the forest looked like before giants like these were depleted.

As it winds through the forest, the trail crosses firm ground and then a footbridge (1.7 mi.) [7]. At 2 mi., planks keep your boots dry [8]. Hemlocks line the way.

The trail descends and winds right. This next stretch is particularly intermittent with wet and dry patches. This pattern continues even after the North Country Trail leaves at 2.3 mi. [9].

After passing under overhead wires, you arrive at the junction for the Wilderness and Clark Lake loops (3.1 mi.) [10]. A picnic area is located here; to its right is M-123. Cross the highway, jog to the right to pick up the trail on the other side, and enter the dark cover of hemlock and beech.

At times lined with ferns, the trail is drier here. Maple saplings work hard for a comeback. The trail gently rolls, and at about 3.7 mi., you may have to maneuver around one more wet area [11] before winding down to the northeast end of the parking lot.

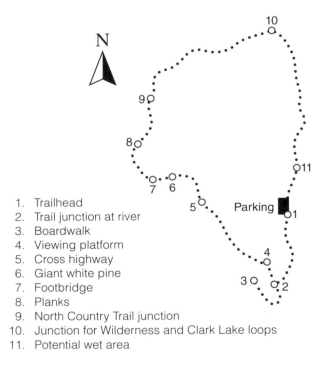

1. Trailhead
2. Trail junction at river
3. Boardwalk
4. Viewing platform
5. Cross highway
6. Giant white pine
7. Footbridge
8. Planks
9. North Country Trail junction
10. Junction for Wilderness and Clark Lake loops
11. Potential wet area

Clark Lake Loop

Distance Round-Trip: 5.2 miles
Estimated Hiking Time: 2 to 3 hours

Cautions: Be prepared for wet trail conditions and bog walking. Wear appropriate footgear. Take insect repellent. Mosquitoes, black flies, and deer flies are numerous, particularly from mid-May to mid-July. You're in bear and moose country; take care.

Trail Directions: From the Lower Falls, take M-123 west to Clark Lake Road. Follow Clark Lake Road, a single-lane, dirt road, to its terminus at a small parking area for the Tahquamenon Natural Area **[1]**.

Enjoy the wide, sandy trail as it rises from the southwest end of the parking area and skirts a bog. Look to your left for a narrow footpath, your gateway to a boardwalk excursion out onto a bog (.1 mi.) **[2]**. The Tahquamenon Falls State Park is home to the largest contiguous ecosystem of this type in the state. The Clark Lake Loop will let you experience a portion of this unique landscape firsthand.

Clark Lake first comes into view as the trail rises onto a ridge of red pine. The best views of the pristine lake come after a slight descent to trail marker post #5 (.4 mi.) **[3]**. Take pleasure in the solitude of the lake as the trail rolls along the uneven shore, on a ridge cushioned with sand and pine needles.

After crossing a boardwalk over root beer–colored water, look for the blazes on trees or the blue-tipped post that guides you away from the lake (.7 mi.) **[4]**. You are now entering landscapes dominated by ferns, patchworks of silver and green lichens, blueberries, ridges of red pine, jack pine uplands, and sphagnum moss–carpeted lowlands.

By the time you reach trail marker #4, (1.6 mi.) **[5]**, you will have walked on logs to cross several low-lying wet areas. Enjoy the spartan log crossings while you can, because you will soon be walking on less log and more bog.

Turn left at trail marker #4 and walk the perimeter of a beaver pond. The skeletons of dead trees still stand like a forest of ghosts. The trail shortly makes a sudden right, so be looking for blue paint on the trees. Arrive at the first of many bog crossings (1.7 mi.) **[6]**. In a wet season, this crossing will be a unique spongy experience.

By the time you reach trail marker #7 (2.6 mi.) **[7]**, the experience may no longer be so novel; the bogs become ubiquitous. Turn left at the post, proceed past a wet area, and descend through mixed pines into a forest of large hemlock trees (2.8 mi.) **[8]**.

As you approach a utility corridor, the trail swings left (3 mi.) **[9]**. Follow the blue blazes. Continue to cross a number of bogs in this section. The third crossing is a particularly long one (3.3 mi.) **[10]**. Look for the blue markers after crossing as the trail turns sharply left. After passing a number of stumps, you may notice that some carry the scars of an old forest fire (3.6 mi.) **[11]**.

Continuing past ridges of fern, lichen, and blueberries and over low-lying wet areas, the trail eventually enters a white cedar swamp on an old logging railroad corridor (4.6 mi.) **[12]**. Chugging in on the old corridor, you reach trail marker #6 at Clark Lake Road (5 mi.) **[13]**. Turn left to return to the parking area.

1. Trailhead
2. Boardwalk onto bog
3. Trail marker #5
4. Blue-tipped post
5. Trail marker #4
6. Bog
7. Trail marker #7
8. Hemlocks
9. Utility corridor
10. Long bog crossing
11. Fire-scarred stumps
12. Railroad corridor
13. Trail marker #6

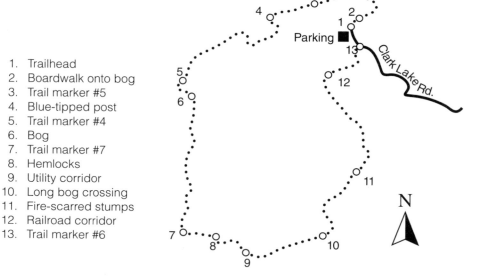

8. Seney National Wildlife Refuge

- Learn about nature from displays, multimedia shows, and a touch table at the visitor center.
- Hike or bike on roughly 70 miles of trails through woods, past rivers, or along pools.
- Discover an abundance of wildlife.

Park Information

Wisconsin, Minnesota, Alaska, Ontario—license plates from these places are often seen at the visitor center parking lot of the Seney National Wildlife Refuge. What makes this place such a desirable destination? The refuge encompasses only 95,212 acres of land intricately mottled with marsh, bog, swamp, and forest; 25,150 acres are wilderness. Drive, bike, or hike through the refuge and you'll learn that wetlands make up the bulk of the landscape. Pools—some green with algae, some blanketed with floating pads, some interrupted with small nesting islands or turtle-encrusted logs—envelop you. Two-thirds of the refuge is wetlands.

Lumbermen depleted many of the northern hardwoods and swamp conifers that covered the area about a century ago. Fires and drainage of the land for farming followed. But the soil was poor. As with much of the public land in Michigan, failure to pay taxes caused the land to revert to the state. The federal government was encouraged to take over the land, and in 1935 the refuge was created for the protection and production of migratory birds. The Civilian Conservation Corps stepped in, and the restoration began. Roads, dikes, and ditches were established to create an intricate water-control system. All of this maintains the refuge and its diverse habitat.

Visitors in vehicles are not the only migrants to pass through the refuge. The biological diversity within the refuge provides suitable habitat for over 200 species of birds. Viewing opportunities are plentiful for common loon, bald eagle, trumpeter swan, and sandhill crane, as well as white-tailed deer. The refuge also embraces black bear, river otter, beaver, and bobcat—even wolf, although a sighting would be a rare privilege.

The visitor center offers multimedia shows, displays, audio presentations, and a touch table with diverse animal furs and print molds for deciphering various animals' footprints.

About 70 miles of trails provide plenty of viewing or recreational ground for hikers or bikers. One of the trails is an interpretive nature trail. Canoeists can seek refuge along the Driggs and Manistique rivers. The refuge also has a 7-mile auto tour, the Marshland Wildlife Drive. A brochure assists visitors in understanding the refuge and its wildlife, and observation decks provide an opportunity for viewing wildlife in their habitat.

Winter gives rise to different opportunities—cross-country skiing and snowshoeing. Trails are groomed as needed.

Directions: The visitor center is located about 5 miles south of Seney on M-77 (or about 2 miles north of Germfask). The entrance is on the west side of the highway.

Hours Open: The refuge is open year-round from dawn until dusk, but the visitor center is open only from 9:00 a.m. to 5:00 p.m. from May 15 through October 15. The auto tour runs from May 15 through October 15.

Facilities: Hiking, biking, cross-country skiing, fishing, hunting, canoeing, interpretive trails, and interpretive center.

Permits and Rules: No fee is required. Off-road biking is not permitted. Keep your pets on a leash. Pick up your trash. Allow others room to pass you on the road. Leave all plants and animals as you found them. Roads or trails are periodically closed; respect this rule.

For Further Information: Seney National Wildlife Refuge, 1674 Refuge Entrance Road, Seney, MI 49883; 906-586-9851; www.fws.gov/midwest/seney.

Other Points of Interest

Canoes may be rented locally from Big Cedar Campground and Canoe Livery on M-77 in Germfask, 906-586-668, or from Northland Outfitters on M-77 in Germfask, 906-586-9801. Northland Outfitters also rents mountain bikes. The **Fox River Pathway** stretches 27.5 miles from north of Seney to the Kingston Lake campground in the Pictured Rocks National Lakeshore. For more information, contact the Shingleton Management Unit, 906-452-6227.

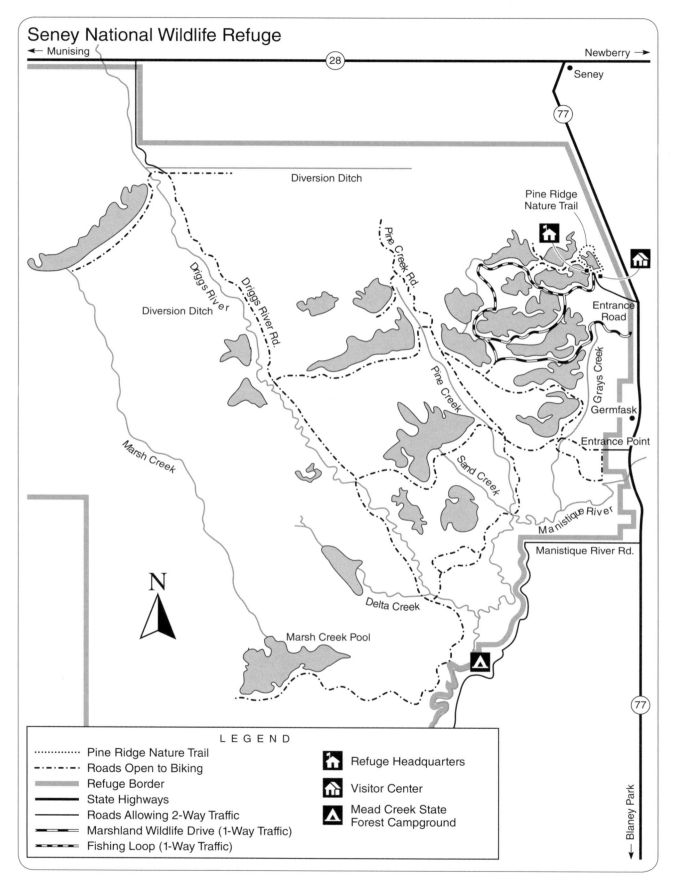

Seney National Wildlife Refuge

← Munising

→ Newberry

28

• Seney

77

Diversion Ditch

Pine Ridge Nature Trail

Pine Creek Rd.

Driggs River

Driggs River Rd.

Diversion Ditch

Entrance Road

Grays Creek

Germfask

Pine Creek

Marsh Creek

Entrance Point

Sand Creek

Manistique River

Manistique River Rd.

N

Delta Creek

Marsh Creek Pool

77

Blaney Park

L E G E N D

············· Pine Ridge Nature Trail	🏠 Refuge Headquarters
─·─·─·─ Roads Open to Biking	🏠 Visitor Center
▬▬▬ Refuge Border	△ Mead Creek State Forest Campground
▬▬▬ State Highways	
─── Roads Allowing 2-Way Traffic	
▬▬▬ Marshland Wildlife Drive (1-Way Traffic)	
▬▬▬ Fishing Loop (1-Way Traffic)	

Pine Ridge Nature Trail

Distance Round-Trip: 1.4 miles
Estimated Hiking Time: 1 hour

Cautions: The trail is in wet terrain, so the area is a magnet for mosquitoes. Certain portions of the trail are prone to flooding. Black flies, deer flies, and wood ticks may also be a problem. You're in bear country; act accordingly.

Trail Directions: The trail starts at the north end of the visitor center [1]. Head off through the grass between two pools; the one on your right has a green, textured cover of lily pads. Step onto a small bridge between the two pools and admire the handiwork of the Civilian Conservation Corps, which helped establish the elaborate water-control system within the refuge. Much of the trail is on dikes. Hence you are surrounded by water as you circle one of the pools.

At about .1 mi., the trail wraps around the pool to your left [2]. Along your right side, grasses, reeds, and cattails wave at you from the marsh.

Pass the ghost forest of drowned trees and gain a brief respite from the sun under a tunnel of brushy foliage before you emerge to a small, sandy reprieve with a bench (.3 mi.) [3]. This spot is an excellent place for watching whatever wildlife is in the pool during your visit.

The trail takes you past some paper birches and red pines standing at attention before it curves left (.5 mi.) [4]. A footbridge crosses over a pool of lily pads before it deposits you on an extensive boardwalk where you can hear the hollow clump of your passage for almost .25 mi. A sea of cattails fences you in along the way. Perhaps you will be rewarded with a viewing of a black bear, as we were.

Just before you step back onto terra firma on an island of pine needles the color of burnt sienna, the boardwalk bends left and you cross another footbridge (.7 mi.) [5]. The trail continues along this red carpet laid out for you through woods and over another bridge; then it passes an interpretive sign that lets you know about Seney's neotropical migrants. You can rest on a bench to view the wetlands that you are passing (.8 mi.) [6].

Cross one boardwalk and then another to view the large pool to your right. After a few steps more of the red-carpet treatment, a knob of land forms a point into the large pool. Here a bench in the pines awaits

you (.9 mi.) [7]. Use it while you view the many nesting islands in this pool. Listen for sandhill cranes or watch the bobbing buoys of geese and duck tails as the birds submerge their heads in the water searching for food.

Over the next stretch, you walk along a dike between two pools until you arrive at a service road (1.1 mi.) [8]. Turn left. Within 200 feet or so, watch for the sign that directs you back onto a path to the left. Depending on the season or weather, the trail could be wet and muddy just before you cross one footbridge and then another (1.2 mi.) [9].

A grassy path winds you back to the visitor center but first passes the refuge headquarters at the back of the fire tower (1.3 mi.) [10]. Having returned to the visitor center parking lot, look at the interpretive boards that shed light on a 1976 fire in the refuge and the reintroduction of Canada geese.

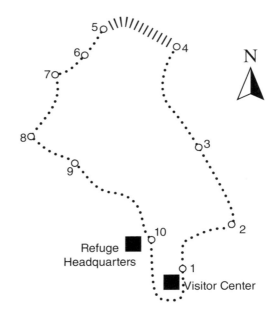

1. Trailhead
2. Trail wraps left around pool
3. Bench
4. Trail curves left
5. Footbridge
6. Interpretive sign
7. Bench
8. Service road
9. Footbridge
10. Refuge headquarters

9. Pictured Rocks National Lakeshore

- Explore colored cliffs, pebbled beaches, white sand dunes, and waterfalls.
- Discover the shipwrecks of the Alger Underwater Preserve.
- Cruise the waters along this unforgettable Lake Superior coastline.

Park Information

This 42-mile strip along Lake Superior's shoreline offers such splendor that in 1966 it was designated as the country's first national lakeshore. At the forefront are its cliffs, rising from Lake Superior to heights of 200 feet. Sculpted by water and weather, the arches and caves resemble castles and battleships. Water mixed with minerals seeps from the rocks, staining the cliffs with various hues. The earthy palette of colors changes as shadow and light continually alter the picture. But there's more than just the pictured rocks.

The mosaic of aqua-, blue-, and emerald-colored Lake Superior waters needs no introduction. Spray, exploding from cliffs, paints another scene. Waterfalls add a tint, and the massive Grand Sable Banks offer a soft contrast to the rigid cliffs of the colorful rocks. Weave in forests and inland lakes for a multilayered work of art—Pictured Rocks National Lakeshore.

Some park highlights include the Au Sable Light Station; a shoreline accentuated with shipwrecks; natural features like Sable Falls, Miners Castle, and Chapel Falls; the Munising Falls Interpretive Center; the Log Slide; and the white sand and pebbled Twelvemile Beach.

Three campgrounds can be reached by vehicle; there are also 8 group camps and 13 backcountry camps.

Directions: The Interagency Visitor Center is located on H-58, just east of M-28 in Munising. The Grand Sable Visitor Center is located on H-58 about 5 miles west of Grand Marais. The Munising Falls Interpretive Center is located on Sand Point Road, north of H-58, about 2 miles east of downtown Munising.

Hours Open: Open year-round. Some roads are subject to snow closures. The Interagency Visitor Center is open daily except Sundays and holidays from 9:00 a.m. to 4:30 p.m. Hours are extended from Memorial Day weekend through mid-September. Grand Sable Visitor Center and Munising Falls Interpretive Center are open from Memorial Day weekend through mid-September.

Facilities: Hiking, cross-country skiing, snowshoeing, snowmobiling, fishing, hunting, canoeing, kayaking, swimming, camping (tent and backcountry), picnicking, interpretive trails, and interpretive centers.

Permits and Rules: Camping requires a fee. Do not climb on cliffs. Bicycles are permitted only on roads where automobiles are permitted. Wheeled or motorized vehicles and pets are not allowed in the backcountry. Do not disturb shipwreck remains or remove plants.

For Further Information: Pictured Rocks National Lakeshore, P.O. Box 40, Munising, MI 49862-0040; 906-387-2607; www.nps.org/piro.

Other Points of Interest

Pictured Rocks Boat Cruises offers narrated tours, leaving Munising Bay every day from Friday before Memorial Day to the day after Labor Day. For more information, contact Pictured Rocks Cruises, Inc., P.O. Box 355, Munising, MI 49862; 906-387-2379 or 800-650-2379; www.picturedrocks.com.

Grand Island Shipwreck Tours offers tours for viewing the shipwrecks of the **Alger Underwater Preserve**. Tours run from June through September. For details, contact Shipwreck Tours, 1204 Commercial Street, Munising, MI 49862; 906-387-4477; www.shipwrecktours.com.

A publicly operated **shuttle bus** offers transportation for point-to-point hikers who need transportation back to their vehicles. For more information, contact ALTRAN, 530 E. Munising Avenue, P.O. Box 69, Munising, MI 49862; 906-387-4845; www.altranbus.com.

Park Trails

About 100 miles of trails traverse the park. Pick up a map at one of the visitor centers to plan other hikes.

Lakeshore–North Country Trail (, 42.8 miles). Follows the cliffs and shore of Lake Superior from Munising to Grand Marais and is the backbone of the trail system. Many day hikes incorporate portions of this trail.

Mosquito Falls Trail (, 3.8 miles round-trip). Starts at the Chapel Falls parking area and provides views of the Mosquito River, its series of waterfalls, and the Mosquito River canyon.

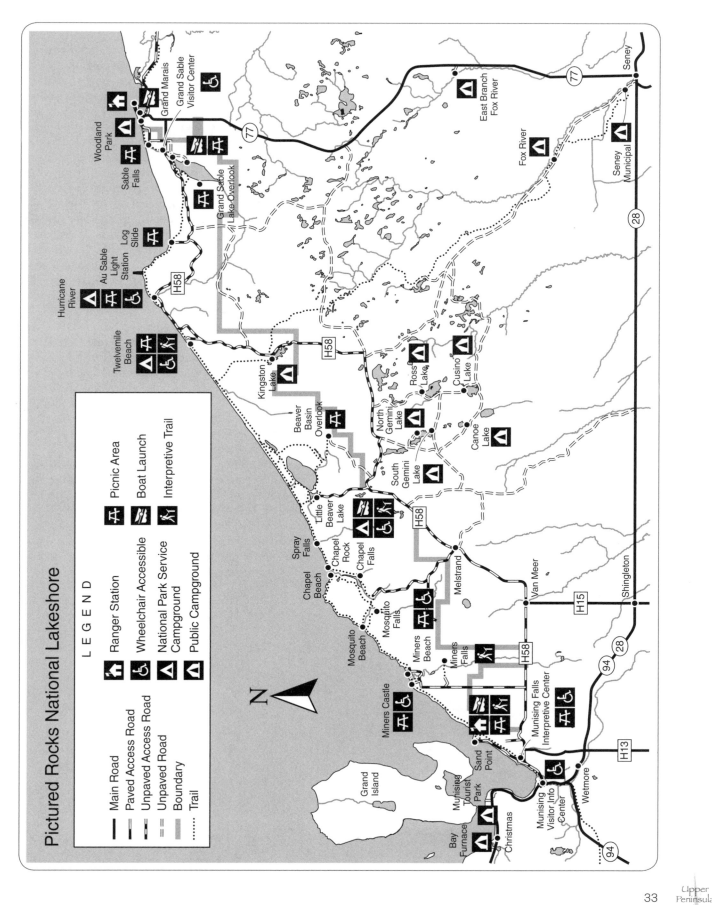

Pictured Rocks National Lakeshore

LEGEND

- Main Road
- Paved Access Road
- Unpaved Access Road
- Unpaved Road
- Boundary
- Trail

- Ranger Station
- Wheelchair Accessible
- National Park Service Campground
- Public Campground
- Picnic Area
- Boat Launch
- Interpretive Trail

N

Chapel Basin Trail

Distance Round-Trip: 9.2 miles
Estimated Hiking Time: 5.5 to 6.5 hours

Cautions: The trail winds along cliffs. Rocks and roots are sometimes exposed, and parts of the trail may be wet. Wear proper footgear. Take insect repellent and water. This is bear country.

Trail Directions: Start at the Chapel Falls parking area, just right of the information map [1], and head through dense hardwoods to arrive at the Chapel Lake overlook spur (.9 mi.) [2]. Follow this short path to a rocky perch for a view of Chapel Lake through the trees.

You hear the falls before you reach their overlook spur at 1.2 mi. [3]. Step down to a viewing platform that gives you a close-up of water free-falling over a 90-foot sandstone cliff.

Back on the main trail, cross the footbridge and take the root-laden path to the viewing platform on a bluff (1.4 mi.) [4], which opens up another view of the falls. Follow the trail to the right. Planks and foot and land bridges usually support your steps through wet areas. Waves on Lake Superior beckon as you descend to arrive at Chapel Rock (3.2 mi.) [5].

Walking the ridge above Lake Superior, you soon cross a bridge over Chapel River as it rushes into the turquoise waters of the lake (3.3 mi.) [6]. Step onto a carpet of pine needles and reach a clearing. Welcome the pine perfume and the rainbow-colored cliffs below.

Pass through the Chapel Beach camping area where steps lead down to Lake Superior (3.5 mi.) [7]. After the campground you'll find a junction. Stay right to Mosquito River. For the next 4 mi., walk the ridge overlooking Lake Superior. Near the end of Chapel Beach, the trail takes a short left where the cliffs jut out into the water. Watch for a close right, which takes you down what may or may not be a dried-up streambed (3.6 mi.) [8]. Go left and climb steeply out of this ravinelike trench and veer to the right, along the cliff.

The trail rolls through forest, occasionally weaving to clearings along the cliffs. One clearing reveals coves where the cliffs resemble battleships (3.7 mi.) [9]. After a few more steps you will see pottery-colored cliffs, etched with bowls and arches standing erect in mottled green and aqua water. A few steps farther on you come to another clearing that reveals another formation. Each time you move, the colors and shapes are different.

If you packed a lunch, enjoy it at Grand Portal Point (4.8 mi.) [10]. Here, you get a sweeping view of Lake Superior and its ragged shoreline of cliffs. Stay clear of the edge as you work your way back into the woods at the end of this sandy ledge (5 mi.) [11]. The trail soon cuts left and rolls through a carpet of bunchberries spilling down the steep slopes (5.2 mi.) [12] and shortly makes another turn to the left.

Cut across another sandy opening (5.5 mi.) [13]. Look back at the previous cliff that is carved like an Indian's head with a Mohawk haircut of foliage. At 6.1 mi., the trail cuts close to the edge [14]. From here you can see Grand Island. Ensuing overviews reveal cliffs etched with caves. Travel through more trees, pass another sandy stretch, and then arrive at Mosquito Camp. Pass by the camp and follow the NCT marker to the junction for the trail that leads back (7.5 mi.) [15].

Turn left and follow the north side of Mosquito River, through the camp and over a series of planks that cross over wet areas in the woods, until you arrive at the spur to Mosquito Falls (8.8 mi.) [16]. Stay straight unless you wish to hike the .2 mi. round-trip to the falls. You soon reach the trail that leads back to the parking area (9 mi.) [17]. Turn right and follow it down, over a bridge, and then up rocky steps to the parking area.

1. Trailhead
2. Chapel Lake overlook spur
3. Chapel Falls overlook
4. View of Chapel Falls
5. Chapel Rock
6. Chapel River
7. Steps to Lake Superior
8. Ravine
9. Overlook with view of coves
10. Grand Portal Point
11. Reenter woods
12. Bunchberries
13. Sandy opening
14. Cliff edge
15. Mosquito Beach trail junction
16. Mosquito Falls spur
17. Parking lot trail junction

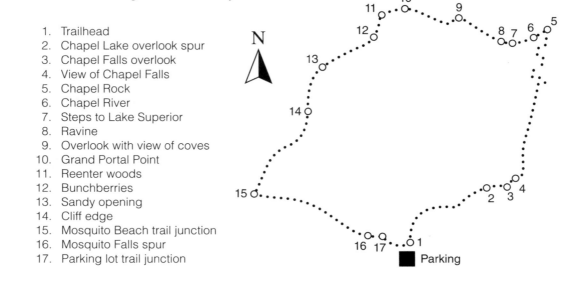

Beaver Basin Loop

Distance Round-Trip: 5.1 miles
Estimated Hiking Time: 2.5 to 3.5 hours

Cautions: Rocks and roots are sometimes exposed, and parts of the trail can be wet. Wear proper footgear. Take insect repellent and water. This is bear country.

Trail Directions: Start from the west end of the Lakeshore Trail parking area located just south of the Little Beaver Lake Campground. A mile-marker post indicates that the distance to the Lakeshore Trail and Lake Superior is 1.5 mi. and the distance to Beaver Lake is 1.4 mi. **[1]**.

Step into the dark, beech-maple forest and step down a series of ledges to a trail marker for the White Pine Trail (.1 mi.) **[2]**. Follow this numbered trail in reverse order. The trailhead for this interpretive loop actually begins at the Little Beaver Lake Campground, where a self-guiding brochure is available. Continue past the marker and descend to cross a boardwalk.

At .2 mi., the trail descends sharply, switching back and forth below a rocky ledge. On the hill are a number of white pines estimated to be around 300 years old **[3]**. At the bottom of the descent, a boardwalk carries you alongside a rushing stream. You soon cross this stream by a footbridge just past the trail junction to the Little Beaver Lake Campground (.3 mi.) **[4]**.

After a short climb, the trail levels out. Step across a lengthy boardwalk that leads you toward a sandstone outcrop. Swing around the outcrop, passing several sea caves cut into the rock some 500 to 600 million years ago (.4 mi.) **[5]**.

The trail descends to cross another boardwalk, leading you to a small footbridge over open water (.5 mi.) **[6]**. When climbing away from the boardwalk, the trail swings right, passes a number of fire-scarred stumps, and reaches a trail junction overlooking Little Beaver Lake (.6 mi.) **[7]**. Stay to the right and look for waterfowl as you follow along the north side of the lake. Look carefully and you might see evidence of the mammal from which the lake got its name—the beaver.

After walking the length of Little Beaver Lake, you soon reach a sandy beach (1.1 mi.) **[8]** along the shore of the much larger Beaver Lake. The trail gradually rises above the clear lake; from the higher elevation, you can see the sandy bottom. At 1.9 mi., you reach a trail marker near the creek that drains Beaver Lake **[9]**. Turn left toward Lake Superior. Before reaching it, you come to a trail junction (2.3 mi.) **[10]**. If you were to go left on the Lakeshore Trail, you would get to the Little Beaver Trail in 1.4 mi. Go right. When the trail turns right again, toward Beaver Creek, continue straight on a well-worn, but unmarked, path that provides a shortcut to Lake Superior. Soon, perched on a sand dune, you get an overview of the beach. Climb down the dune and turn left at the lake (2.4 mi.) **[11]**. The protruding point of land that you see off in the distance from here is Grand Portal Point.

Walking the Lake Superior beach amid driftwood, listening to the pounding surf, and hunting through the myriad rocks scattered about your feet make a pleasant diversion. Looking for the correct turnoff from the beach to the trail, on the other hand, is a lesson in futility. Before reaching the rocky point at the end of the beach, you'll notice a number of paths that lead away from the beach (3.5 mi.) **[12]**. Take your pick of paths and climb the steep, sandy bank to reach the Lakeshore Trail. Then turn left to arrive at the junction for Little Beaver Camp (3.7 mi.) **[13]**.

Hike inland .6 mi. to return to the trail junction that overlooks Little Beaver Lake (4.3 mi.) **[7]**. Turn right and retrace your steps to the parking area.

1. Trailhead
2. White Pine Trail junction
3. White pines
4. Little Beaver Lake Campground trail junction
5. Sea caves
6. Footbridge
7. Trail junction
8. Beach
9. Trail marker near Beaver Creek
10. Lakeshore Trail junction
11. Lake Superior
12. Number of paths
13. Trail junction

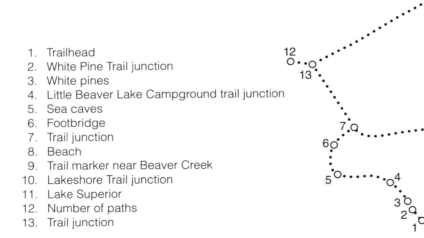

White Birch Trail

Distance Round-Trip: 2.1 miles
Estimated Hiking Time: 1 to 1.5 hours

Cautions: Rocks and roots are sometimes exposed, and parts of the trail can be wet or muddy. Wear proper footgear. Mosquitoes and black flies may be abundant, especially in the warmer months. Portions of the trail are extremely narrow and at the edge of a ridge; take great care. This is bear country, so take proper precautions.

Trail Directions: Take H-58 north to Twelvemile Beach. Park in the day area for Twelvemile Beach camp. Start at the map board on the northwest end of the parking lot and head out along the narrow path **[1]**. This path leads you to the camp road. Turn right along the road. At about .3 mi., steps lead down to Lake Superior **[2]**. Save those for when you finish your hike.

The trail actually starts on the left of the road next to camp #6 (.4 mi.) **[3]**. Brochures should be available there to guide you along this interpretive trail. You soon see that you are high and dry above the lake—the goatlike trail winds up the side of a ridge where you walk along with the moss-covered bluff at your side **[4]**.

You reach the top at .5 mi. for a sweeping view of Lake Superior **[5]**. Your walk high on the bluff is cush-ioned by pine needles. Sound carries well up here; you can hear the waves rushing onshore down below.

You pass a red pine plantation (.7 mi.), and the trail swings in away from the bluff edge **[6]**. Thereafter, the scruffy jack pine becomes more dominant. At 1 mi., the trail bends left **[7]**. After winding through lichen, stop #11 interprets the jack pine habitat and its need for regeneration by fire. As fire heats cones, they open and release seeds. At about 1.2 mi., look for old fire scars **[8]**.

The trail gently undulates. Notice the quiet. Few birds or animals build their homes here. You start to descend off the bluff at 1.6 mi. over roots **[9]**. Take care; they are slippery when wet. Post #16 (1.7 mi.) reminds you that you will ascend and that you have one more hill to climb before you reach the namesake of the trail, white birch **[10]**, which you do in about .1 mi.

The white birch lights up the forest. Birch often follows fires where soil quality is better. Lush ferns blanket the understory.

Continue walking the ridge along the Nipissing beach bluff (1.9 mi.) **[11]** before descending off it and arriving back at the campground road (2.1 mi.) **[12]**. You could turn right and retrace your steps to the parking area, but those stairs down to Lake Superior are calling. Take a left and indulge if you so choose.

1. Trailhead
2. Steps to Lake Superior
3. Trail begins next to campsite #6
4. Start hike up bluff
5. View of Lake Superior from bluff top
6. Red pine plantation
7. Trail bends
8. Fire scars
9. Start descending bluff
10. Interpretive sign
11. Nipissing beach bluff
12. Return to campground road

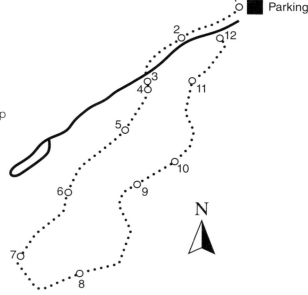

Au Sable Light Station

Distance Round-Trip: 3 miles
Estimated Hiking Time: 1.5 to 2 hours

Cautions: This hike takes you along the shore to the light station and along an old road back to the Hurricane River Campground. The walk is easy except for the climb up the dune on stairs in the sand that are made out of rope. This is bear country, so take proper precautions.

Trail Directions: Take Alger County H-58 to Hurricane River Campground, which is 12 mi. west of Grand Marais. The trail starts from the north end of the beach parking lot of the campground. Start from the lot near the bridge that crosses Hurricane River **[1]**. A path goes to the right near the bridge, but before you turn, step on the bridge to watch the river spill into Lake Superior. After viewing, take that path to the right and reach a gate for the Lakeshore Trail to Au Sable Point (.1 mi.) **[2]**. Look to the left to view a shipwreck along the shore. Ten notable shipwrecks are located near Au Sable Point. Like this one, three of them are near the shore.

The reef at Au Sable Point was dangerous for mariners. When traffic increased with the opening of the Soo Canal in 1855, the reef began to claim more victims. Ships that left St. Mary's River and rounded Whitefish Point typically traveled along the south shore of the lake in view of land. Over the years many hit the sandstone reefs that in some places were only a few feet below the surface of the water. The area was also infamous for fog—a result of warm air coming off the Grand Sable Dunes mingling with the cool air above Lake Superior. The shore from Au Sable Point to Pictured Rocks was a ship trap. Vessels risked being blown into the lee shore by strong north winds or being lost in fog. The area needed a lighthouse. In 1872 Congress appropriated funds for a lighthouse at Au Sable Point, and it was put into operation on August 19, 1874.

Stay straight along the old road for a bit. At 1 mi., an interpretive sign describes the "Graveyard Coast" **[3]**. Take the steps here left to the lake and see for yourself the red swirls in the sculpted Jacobsville Sandstone—that unscrupulous rock of the dangerous reef.

Follow along the shore to the right. At 1.1 mi., you reach the iron and wood wreckage of an old ship **[4]**. Continue enjoying your walk along the rocky shore. Perched on the bluff, the Au Sable Light Station is in view. Climb the 35 steps of the log rope (1.4 mi.) to reach the bluff top **[5]**. You reach the lighthouse at 1.5 mi. **[6]**. Tours are available in July and August for a $2 fee, which is money well spent to explore

the 87-foot-tall light station with its attached brick, two-story keeper's home. The view from the top is breathtaking, particularly of the Grand Sable Dunes. Afterward, visit the fog signal building for a history of the shipwrecks in the area.

After exploring the buildings, you can either take the road back to the campground under the shade of trees or descend the rope steps and return along the shore.

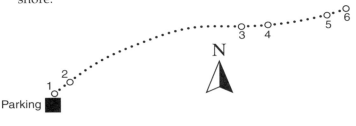

1. Trailhead
2. Gate and shipwreck
3. Interpretive board and steps to lake
4. Shipwreck
5. Rope steps
6. Au Sable Light Station

10. Grand Island National Recreation Area

- Escape to this 13,500-acre island of 300-foot cliffs, sandy beaches, inland lakes, and lush forests.
- Walk along bluffs high above Lake Superior.
- Dip your toes into the cold waters of Lake Superior as you stroll along a sandy beach.

Park Information

Situated in Lake Superior, this 13,500-acre island mirrors the Pictured Rocks National Shoreline that faces it from the mainland. Sandstone cliffs rising up to 300 feet rival those of Pictured Rocks. Sandy beaches, interior lakes, and forests of pine, beech, and hemlock combine to make this retreat a real treat.

The Cleveland-Cliffs Iron Company acquired the island in 1900 and used it as a corporate retreat. In 1990 the federal government purchased it.

Over 40 miles of trails embrace the ridges of the island or cut through its interior. Most run north to south and can be linked to form large loops. The north end of the island displays the cliffs. The trail along the tombolo, the bar of sand that ties the large island to its thumb, passes through dune swales.

Seventeen designated single campsites are located on Grand Island. Backcountry camping is also allowed. Drinking water is available at a few locations. Bring water along with you to the island. Given the limited ferry schedule, plan your time accordingly.

Directions: The island is about .5 mile from the mainland community of Munising. Grand Island Landing is on M-28, about 4 miles west of the blinking light at H-58 and M-28 in Munising.

Hours Open: Although the island is open year-round, weather limits use of the area. Unpredictable Lake Superior weather renders the island inaccessible at times. Ferry service is available only from the Friday before Memorial Day through October 9.

Facilities: Hiking, mountain biking, cross-country skiing, snowshoeing, snowmobiling, ATVs, swimming, canoeing, kayaking, fishing, hunting, camping (tent and backcountry), and picnicking.

Permits and Rules: The daily entrance fee of $2 is included in the passenger ferry fee. At this time, permits are not required for campsites. Random sites must not be on the tombolo and must be more than 100 feet from Lake Superior or its cliff edges, other campsites, roads, private property, trails, inland lakes and named creeks, and the research natural area.

Be careful; this is a primitive island. Rescues could take half a day. Bears inhabit the island; don't feed or harass them. Limited water is available. Advise someone on the mainland of your travel plans. Be prepared to spend at least an extra day in case bad weather fouls up boating schedules.

For Further Information: Hiawatha National Forest Visitor Center, Munising Ranger District, 400 E. Munising Avenue, Munising, MI 49862; 906-387-2512.

Other Points of Interest

Grand Island Ferry Service schedules trips to the island from the Friday before Memorial Day through October 9. The ferry leaves Grand Island Landing in Munising at 9:00 a.m., 12:00 p.m., and 3:30 p.m. up to June 30. From July 1 to Labor Day additional trips are added as follows: 10:00 a.m., 11:00 a.m., 4:30 p.m., 5:30 p.m., and 6:30 p.m. From the Tuesday after Labor Day to October 9, the schedule reverts to its early season timetable. The return trip leaves Williams Landing on the island 15 minutes later than the mainland departure time. But don't count on the ferry being there at these times unless you've made prior arrangements. For reservations, call 906-387-3503.

A shuttle service provided by ALTRAN offers **Grand Island Sightseeing Tours**. Tours leave at 12:00 p.m. daily, and an extra tour is added at 3:30 p.m. from July 1 through Labor Day. Arrangements must be made ahead of time. You can also make arrangements to be transported to the north end of the island so that you may hike back. Advance reservations must be made. Make arrangements at least a day ahead of time. For more information, contact ALTRAN, 530 E. Munising Avenue, P.O. Box 69, Munising, MI 49862; 906-387-4845; www.altranbus.com.

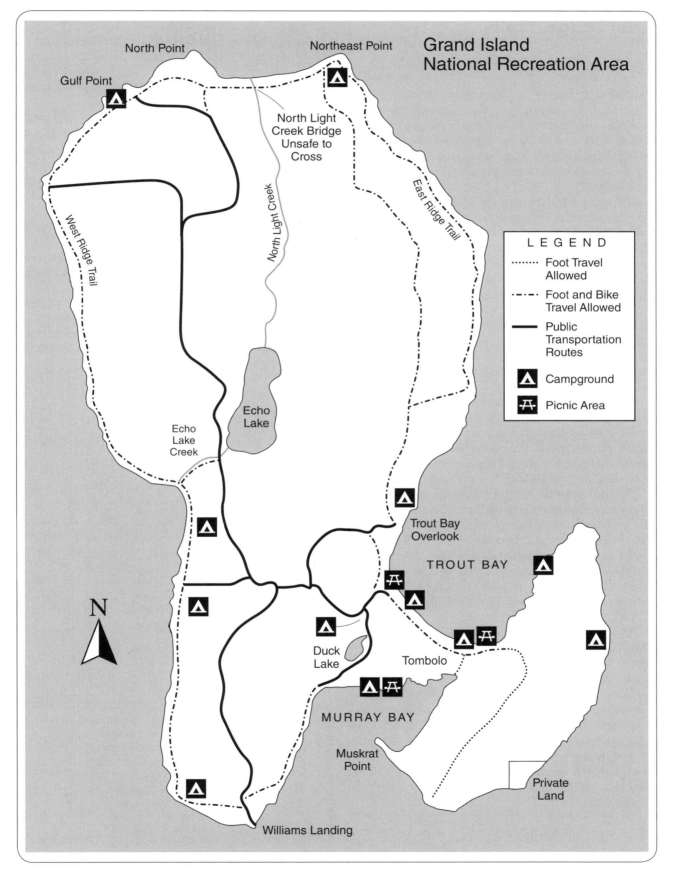

North Point

Northeast Point

Gulf Point

Grand Island
National Recreation Area

North Light
Creek Bridge
Unsafe to
Cross

North Light Creek

East Ridge Trail

West Ridge Trail

LEGEND

Foot Travel
Allowed

Foot and Bike
Travel Allowed

Public
Transportation
Routes

Campground

Picnic Area

Echo
Lake

Echo
Lake
Creek

Trout Bay
Overlook

TROUT BAY

N

Duck
Lake

Tombolo

Murray Bay

Muskrat
Point

Private
Land

Williams Landing

East Ridge Trail

Distance Round-Trip: 10.8 miles
Estimated Hiking Time: 5.5 to 6.5 hours

Cautions: Be careful on the cliffs. The bridge over North Light Creek is unsafe. Bears inhabit the island. Don't feed or harass them. Have plenty of water. Pack a lunch and all the gear that you need for a day. Wear proper footgear. Take insect repellent or netting. Advise the ferry service of your plans to return to the mainland.

Trail Directions: Arrange for ALTRAN to pick you up at the dock at Williams Landing and take you to the north end of the island [1]. From there, head east along the old carriage road through second-growth hardwoods. The trail winds north and takes you near the cliffs at about .2 mi.; this spot will give you a sense of the rim that you will be walking [2].

At .5 mi., a short spur leads down to the sandy beach along the Lake Superior shoreline [3]. Relax in the sand and listen to the waves rushing in as a breeze off the water brushes your cheeks. But don't get too comfortable. You've only just begun. Head back up to the trail.

Roll up your pant legs. North Light Creek dares you to cross it—by fording it, by stepping from stone to stone, or by balancing your body as you step across a log (.6 mi.) [4]. Just don't use the unsafe bridge. While you're down at the creek bed, look to the northwest at the tree-topped cliffs of North Point.

The trail ascends, at times drawing near the edge where fences keep you from getting too close. At 1.3 mi., the trail veers right, exposing a wall of sandstone that drops off to the lake below [5]. At 1.9 mi., look over a cove where a cave has been battered into the cliff [6]. The trail diverges from the lake, cuts through maples, and then swings back. Across Lake Superior you can see Pictured Rocks off in the distance (3.1 mi.) [7].

The cliff-hanger continues as the trail ebbs and flows near the lakeside ridge. At 3.9 mi., listen to the stream spilling over rocks in the rolling terrain to your right; you can also hear water gently rushing down the steep ravine on your left [8].

More lake views present themselves before the trail veers inland (4.9 mi.) [9] and cuts through woods as it subtly descends, passing streams, hills, and ravines. Under a canopy of darkness, the hill on your left looks like a fortress surrounded by a moat (5.8 mi.) [10]. The trail ascends to a small meadow at the junction (5.8 mi.) [11].

Stay to the left on the grassy two-track through mature hardwoods and descend in and out of tunnels of trees. Pass a dark pool littered with moss-covered logs. You continue rolling through woods before reaching the Trout Bay overlook (7.1 mi.) [12], where trees frame the blue waters of the bay.

At 7.4 mi., a trail board announces a footpath on the left [13]. Turn down this narrow, rolling, muddy path as it passes ephemeral pools. The trail descends gently, cuts across planked boards over a spring stream, and arrives at a dirt road (8 mi.) [14]. Follow the tree-lined road to the right to the next trail board (8.2 mi.) [15], where you veer left.

The dirt road passes through some large hemlocks. Duck Lake soon comes into view (8.4 mi.) [16]. Listen. Let the quiet envelop you like a warm blanket.

Soon the blue from Murray Bay comes into view. Relax at one of the picnic tables (9 mi.) [17] before continuing to the right, where you'll pass an old cemetery. The trail continues its gentle descent. Winding down, you pass some of the few remaining residences on the island before arriving at a road (10.6 mi.) [18]. Turn left and follow it back to Williams Landing.

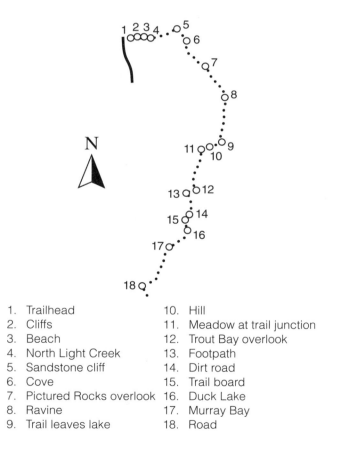

1.	Trailhead	10.	Hill
2.	Cliffs	11.	Meadow at trail junction
3.	Beach	12.	Trout Bay overlook
4.	North Light Creek	13.	Footpath
5.	Sandstone cliff	14.	Dirt road
6.	Cove	15.	Trail board
7.	Pictured Rocks overlook	16.	Duck Lake
8.	Ravine	17.	Murray Bay
9.	Trail leaves lake	18.	Road

West Ridge Trail

Distance Round-Trip: 10 miles
Estimated Hiking Time: 5.5 to 6.5 hours

Cautions: Be careful on the cliffs. Bears live on the island; don't feed or harass them. Have plenty of water. Pack a lunch and all the gear that you need for a day. Wear proper footgear. Take insect repellent or netting. Advise the ferry service of your plans to return to the mainland.

Trail Directions: You need to arrange with ALTRAN to pick you up at the dock at Williams Landing and take you to the north end of the island **[1]**. From there, head west along the old carriage road through second-growth hardwoods. You break out of the trees for a view of Lake Superior from behind the security of the safety fencing placed along the edge of the highest cliff of the hike (.3 mi.) **[2]**.

The trail takes you back into the woods, swings inland, and crosses a small stream. This section is prone to flooding. You soon see the lake and can hear it pounding the cliffs. Several small side paths lead from the trail to the edge of the cliff for adrenaline-pumping views from the edge (.7 mi.) **[3]**.

At 1 mi., you descend and cross an old bridge **[4]**. Here, through the ravine that the bridge spans, you get a peephole view of Lake Superior and a section of cliff. This sight is just a tease. Climb from the bridge to gain an unobstructed view from above a cove that has been carved out by the constant pounding of Lake Superior waters (1.1 mi.) **[5]**. This cove is the first of several that you will pass. Take time to enjoy the sights and sounds.

Not straying too far from the edge, where there are little step-out areas from which to view the cliff and Lake Superior, hang in there, because you soon reach the next cove (1.5 mi.) **[6]**. At 2.2 mi., you reach a third cove **[7]**, and then a fourth one only .1 mi. beyond that **[8]**. Notice that Wood Island and the mainland are now visible to the southwest.

Having moved inland and having hiked several straight sections of trail, you find yourself climbing as you pass an escarpment (rock cliff) on your left (3.2 mi.) **[9]**. The trail then levels off as you hike through the woods to a sign that cautions of an upcoming cliff area (4 mi.) **[10]**. The next 1.4 mi. contains a number of opportunities for stepping out to view the ragged edge of the island. Note the tenuous grasp of some trees as they cling to the edge of the cliff. At 5.4 mi., just before you swing left away from the edge, is a lookout point. Here, amid red pine, hemlock, and paper birch,

you can see a good portion of the western shore of the island to the south **[11]**.

Descending to cross Echo Lake Creek (5.7 mi.) **[12]**, the trail bypasses a private residence by cutting left at the post with a trail arrow. After looping around the private residence, through the hemlock trees on your right, you soon spot a wooden deck with steps down to a sandy Lake Superior beach (6.1 mi.) **[13]**. This, Mather Beach, is worth a short side trip. Did you bring your swimsuit? Can you spell C-O-L-D?

Continuing southward, the cliffs may be less dramatic, but watching your step is still necessary. As you approach the southwest end of the island, step out onto Merchandise Beach on a boardwalk. The beach is a magnet for driftwood and pebbles (8.9 mi.) **[14]**. The trail then swings left. You veer away from the lake and eventually pass through a gate near several large white pines before arriving at a road where there is a water pump (9.8 mi.) **[15]**. Turn right and follow the road back to Williams Landing.

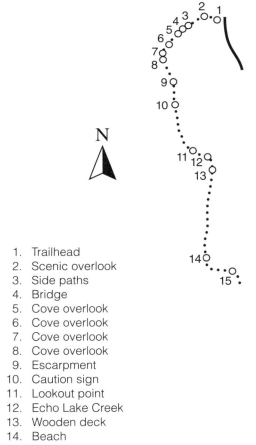

1. Trailhead
2. Scenic overlook
3. Side paths
4. Bridge
5. Cove overlook
6. Cove overlook
7. Cove overlook
8. Cove overlook
9. Escarpment
10. Caution sign
11. Lookout point
12. Echo Lake Creek
13. Wooden deck
14. Beach
15. Road

11. Fayette Historic State Park

- Hike along limestone bluffs that overlook a historic townsite.

- Walk amid the standing structures and ruins of a once-bustling industrial community.

- Drop by the visitor center for a glimpse into the life of a 19th-century company town.

Park Information

Once a bustling village of 500 people, the historic Fayette town site is preserved as a museum village within Fayette Historic State Park. This ghost town, made up of more than 20 of the original town buildings, some restored to their 1870s utility, rests along the Garden Peninsula on Big Bay de Noc. Old blast furnaces, the ruins of the company store, charcoal kilns, the town hall, and homes and lodging places stand in contrast to the 90-foot-high limestone cliffs that were essential to the town's success.

Limestone, plentiful hardwood forests for making charcoal, and a deep harbor once made this a profitable iron-smelting town, run by the Jackson Iron Company. But not for long. Coke iron became more efficient and cheaper to produce than charcoal iron, and in 1891 the company closed its smelting operations and left Fayette. The town took on a new life in the 1960s when it became part of a state park.

Self-guided tour maps allow visitors to stroll through the townsite on their own; guided tours are also available. The visitor center displays a representation of the once-bustling town.

This 700-acre park is more than a historic townsite. Hike along the limestone cliffs that line Snail Shell Harbor, where scuba diving is allowed. Camping, a sandy beach with picnic area, a boat launch, over 5 miles of hiking trails, cottage lodging, and boat camping at Snail Shell Harbor are also available.

Directions: Follow US 2 about 15 miles west of Manistique to M-183. Take M-183 south for about 15 miles.

Hours Open: The park is open year-round from 8:00 a.m. to 10:00 p.m.; the buildings are open from mid-May through mid-June and from Labor Day to mid-October from 9:00 a.m. to 5:00 p.m. From mid-June to Labor Day, they are open from 9:00 a.m. to dusk.

Facilities: Hiking, cross-country skiing, swimming, scuba diving, fishing, hunting, boat launch, camping (RV and tent), cottage lodging, picnicking, interpretive trail, and interpretive center.

Permits and Rules: A park fee is required for motor vehicles ($6 daily, $24 annually for residents; $8 daily, $29 annually for nonresidents). Fee and use permits are required for scuba diving. All submerged artifacts are to remain in place; nothing is to be removed from the harbor bottom.

For Further Information: Fayette Historic State Park, 13700 13.25 Lane, Garden, MI 49835; 906-644-2603; www.michigan.gov/fayette.

Other Points of Interest

Bay de Noc Grand Island Trail is a 40-mile trail that runs from Rapid River to Munising. The trail overlooks the Whitefish River basin. Although open for hiking and mountain biking, the trail is used primarily for horseback riding, so portions of the trail are sandy. For more information, contact the Hiawatha National Forest, 2727 N. Lincoln Road, Escanaba, MI 48289; 906-786-4062.

A 1.5-mile trail, **Peninsula Point Lighthouse Interpretive Trail**, points out historical and geographical features along Big Bay de Noc. The trail is about 19 miles south of Rapid River on County Road 513. For more information, contact the Hiawatha National Forest, 2727 N. Lincoln Road, Escanaba, MI 48289; 906-786-4062.

Twelve miles west of Manistique at **Palms Book State Park** is Kitch-iti-kipi, Indian for "big spring." Here you can ride a self-propelled observation raft that you pull along a cable from shore to shore over this crystal-clear spring where you can view the depths. The park has a picnic area and concession. For more information, contact Palms Book State Park, c/o Indian Lake State Park, 8970 W. County Road 442, Manistique, MI 49854; 906-341-2355. Or contact the Schoolcraft County Chamber of Commerce, 1000 W. Lakeshore Drive, Manistique, MI 49854; 906-341-5010; www.schoolcraftcountychamber.com.

Park Trails

Camp to Beach (🥾, .3 mile). Provides access from the campground to the sandy beach at the day-use area.

Camp to Townsite (🥾, .4 mile). Links the campground to the townsite and visitor center.

East Trail (🥾🥾, 1.8 miles). A connector from the campsite accesses this loop through a hardwood forest. Another connector accesses the northern loop that goes along the limestone cliffs.

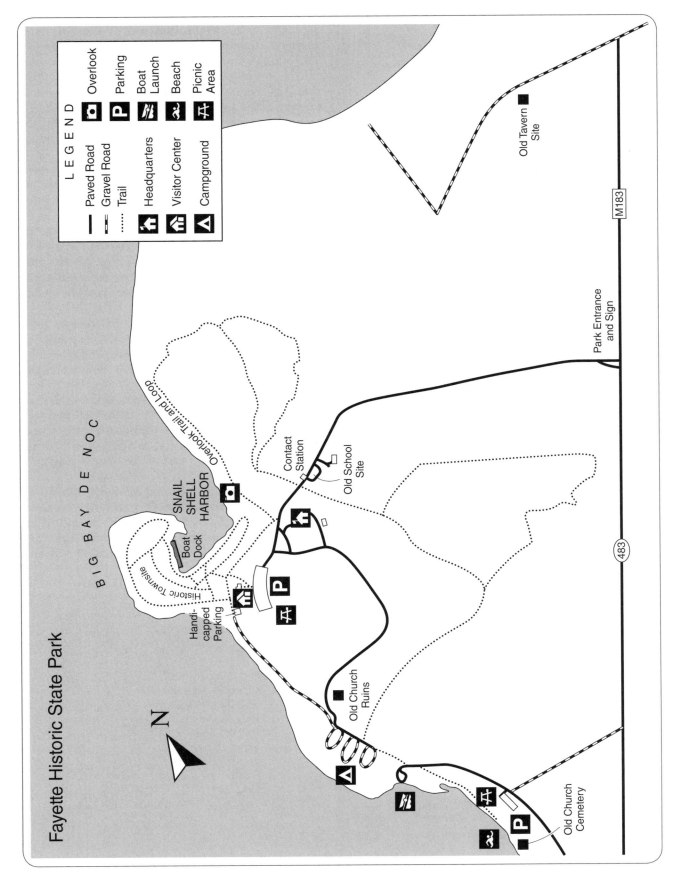

Fayette Historic State Park

LEGEND

—	Paved Road	◉	Overlook
⟊	Gravel Road	P	Parking
⋯	Trail	🏊	Boat Launch
🏛	Headquarters	🏃	Beach
🏠	Visitor Center	🛆	Picnic Area
△	Campground		

BIG BAY DE NOC

N

SNAIL SHELL HARBOR

Overlook Trail and Loop

Boat Dock

Historic Townsite

Handi-capped Parking

Contact Station

Old School Site

Old Church Ruins

Old Church Cemetery

Park Entrance and Sign

Old Tavern Site

M183

483

Townsite Trail

Distance Round-Trip: 1.7 miles
Estimated Hiking Time: 1.5 to 2 hours

Cautions: Bring insect repellent.

Trail Directions: Start in front of the visitor center [1]. Head down the hard-surfaced trail alongside the bluff. Take the gravel path at the bottom to the left, into the historic townsite nestled on a hook of land that juts out into Big Bay de Noc.

This ghost of a town has a haunting mix of walled remains and restored structures from its short-lived past as an industrial town. The deep, blue waters of Snail Shell Harbor form a backdrop to the townsite, and windows from crumbling structures frame the limestone cliffs that rise along the east shore of the harbor. Kilns and furnace complexes stand strong along the south end of the harbor.

Interpretive plaques describe the surroundings. For example, you can read about the 6 mi. railroad grade that serviced the townsite, or about the town's water system. Make your own path through the town or follow ours.

At .1 mi., follow the road to the left [2]. At the second road, walk over to the reconstructed working-class home on your left to get a sense of past lifestyles or continue to the plaque that overlooks beautiful Big Bay de Noc (.2 mi.) [3]. Listen to the waves as they roll onto the pebbled beach that was once a 19th-century industrial dump site for slag.

Turn around, head back to the middle road in front of the hotel, and take the north fork to the harbor. View the cliffs through the windows of the walled ruins of the company store (.3 mi.) [4].

Backtrack to the middle road by the hotel and follow it to the northwest as it takes you by the town hall, foundations and homes of company supervisors, and the foundation of a boardinghouse for workers (.4 mi.) [5]. Soon the road forks. Turn right and follow it between the houses to the harbor, where you get a first-class view of the cliffs (.5 mi.) [6], as did the superintendent who once lived in the large house that you just passed.

Follow to the left where trees shade the trail. Openings in the canopy and the resonating dong from the bell of a buoy remind you that you are on a ridge along the bay.

Stay on the bayside road as it takes you past the structural ghosts that house secrets from the past. At the end of this row of structures, a well-worn path cuts across the grass just before the hotel (.8 mi.) [7]. Take this back to the company store [4] and down to the road by the harbor (.9 mi.) [8].

Turn left and walk alongside the floating dock. Take in the cliffs of the harbor, the cool waters, and the exceptional remnants. Views are particularly striking from the tip of the land hook, where the warehouses once stood (1 mi.) [9].

Turn back and stroll along the harbor on the road behind the company store (1.2 mi.) [10]. Walk between the harbor and the furnace complex, past charcoal kilns, a limestone quarry, and to a lime kiln (1.4 mi.) [11]. This area was the heart of the town's industrial district.

Follow the path less traveled beside the kiln for an overview of the furnace complex and then continue to the plaque that describes an underground water system that the town once had (1.6 mi.) [12]. Turn left, retrace your steps to the asphalt-paved trail, and climb back up to the visitor center.

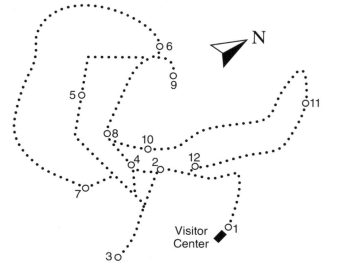

1. Trailhead
2. Left turn
3. Big Bay de Noc
4. Company store
5. Boardinghouse ruins
6. View of cliffs
7. Path by hotel
8. Road by harbor
9. Warehouses site
10. Road behind company store
11. Lime kiln
12. Plaque on underground water system

Overlook Trail and Loop 1

Distance Round-Trip: 2.6 miles
Estimated Hiking Time: 1.5 to 2 hours

Cautions: Mosquitoes and black flies could be a nuisance in the warmer months. Some sections of the trail have exposed roots and rocks. Wear appropriate footgear.

Trail Directions: Start from in front of the visitor center **[1]** and head down the asphalt walkway alongside the bluff. At the gravel path, turn right and climb past sumac and quaking aspen toward the drive into the visitor center. Turn left at the gate and follow the sign post for the trail.

You have just climbed Furnace Hill. In the old days this gravel path served as Fayette's primary link to the outside world during spring and late fall when the ice on the lake was either breaking up or forming. Escanaba, a three-hour trip by boat, took two days to reach by stage along this wagon road.

As you approach the first overlook of the townsite, you enter an open area where a 100-foot-long barn once stood. The Jackson Iron Company housed as many as 60 teams of horses and 5 yoke of oxen here (.2 mi.) **[2]**.

You soon find yourself leaning to look over the barrier at the first of two scenic overlooks that provide views of the ghost town, Snail Shell Harbor, and Lake Michigan (.4 mi.) **[3]**.

Walking near the edge of the cliff through cedars, you can hear the waves crashing and the bell on the buoy clanging in the harbor. Stop and look carefully over the edge to see how steep the cliff is. Also note the rock formations on your right that show the effects of wave action from an earlier period when Lake Michigan water levels were higher (.5 mi.) **[4]**. The formation resembles the mast of a ship protruding toward the lake.

The trail swings slightly right, and after a short distance you leave the mostly white cedar environment of the cliff and enter a beech-maple forest (.6 mi.) **[5]**. The change in the vegetation is dramatic. Watch your step on the roots and moss-covered rocks as songbirds welcome you into their home.

The trail climbs gradually, and you reach a junction with a trail post. Following the trail loop in a counterclockwise manner, you turn right (.9 mi.) **[6]**. Should you happen on this trail in the early morning you could be rewarded with a spiderweb-draped forest. A stroll on a dewy day would show off their lacy handiwork.

At 1.2 mi., make a sharp hairpin turn **[7]**. (An alternative would be to continue straight and return via the paved road to the visitor center.) This section of trail appears to get little use because moss carpeting and limestone slabs compete to guide your feet along the way. You complete the loop at 1.7 mi. **[6]**, where you turn right to retrace your steps to the visitor center. Listen as the bell of the buoy guides you back.

1. Trailhead
2. Barn site
3. Scenic overlooks
4. Limestone cliffs
5. Beech-maple forest
6. Trail junction
7. Trail junction

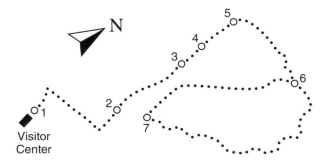

- Hike along an ancient Chippewa Indian portage route between Lake Michigan and Lake Superior.

- Find solitude in the two designated wilderness areas.

- Canoe a designated wild and scenic river into the heart of the Hiawatha.

Park Information

Named after Longfellow's celebrated poem "Song of Hiawatha," the Hiawatha National Forest includes water as a key element. Nearly 46 percent of the forest's 880,000 acres is wetland, featuring roughly 775 miles of rivers and streams, 413 lakes, and 100 miles of Great Lakes shoreline. Sandwiched between the Great Lakes, the Hiawatha's rolling hills are forested with northern hardwoods, white pine, and hemlock, and the flatter lands are more typically covered by red pine, jack pine, and aspen. The Hiawatha is separated into two large units. The West Unit stretches north from the towns of Rapid River and Manistique, along Lake Michigan, to Munising on Lake Superior. The East Unit (see park #6) extends north from St. Ignace, along Lakes Michigan and Huron, to the shore of Lake Superior west of Sault Ste. Marie. An abundance of recreational opportunities awaits fishermen, hunters, hikers, backpackers, mountain bicyclists, canoeists, kayakers, snowmobilers, and cross-country skiers.

Highlights within the West Unit are the Grand Island National Recreation Area (see park #10); two wilderness areas (Big Island Lake Wilderness and Rock River Canyon Wilderness); three designated national wild and scenic recreational rivers (Indian River, Sturgeon River, and Whitefish River); numerous waterfalls; around 150 miles of hiking trails; over 80 miles of cross-country ski trails; untold miles of snowmobile and ATV trails; mountain bicycling trails; and equestrian trails. In addition, 12 campgrounds provide serene and scenic camping opportunities. Two cabins are also available to rent. For those preferring a rustic camping experience, a number of dispersed campsites are available. These are generally in remote locations, many on inland lakes. Backcountry camping is another option.

Directions: Points of interest are spread out over a large area. Contact the forest supervisor's office or the individual district offices of the Hiawatha National Forest for more information.

Hours Open: Most facilities are open year-round.

Facilities: Hiking, mountain bicycling, cross-country skiing, snowshoeing, snowmobiling, ATV, swimming, equestrian, fishing, hunting, boat launch, canoeing, camping (tent and backcountry), picnicking, interpretive trails, and interpretive center.

Permits and Rules: Generally, no fees or permits are required for hikers, canoeists, or other users. A fee is required for using the day-use area at Little Bay de Noc and Camp 7. Fees are $3 per day per vehicle or $25 per year per family. Camping fees vary by site. No fee is required for backcountry camping. Motorized and mechanized vehicles or equipment are not allowed in the wilderness areas. Leave no trace. Carry out what you carry in. Most of the lands within the Hiawatha boundaries are federally owned, but small parcels of privately owned lands exist. Obtain permission to enter such lands.

For Further Information: Hiawatha National Forest, Forest Supervisor's Office, 2727 N. Lincoln Road Escanaba, MI 49829; 906-789-4062. Alternatively, you may contact the various district offices of the Hiawatha National Forest West Unit: Manistique Ranger District, 499 East Lake Shore Drive, Manistique, MI 49854; 906-341-5666; Munising Ranger District, 400 E. Munising Avenue, Munising, MI 49862; 906-387-2512; and Rapid River Ranger District, 8181 US 2, Rapid River, MI 49829; 906-474-6442.

Other Points of Interest

The Hiawatha National Forest West Unit covers a huge territory. For more information, contact the Upper Peninsula Travel and Recreation Association, P.O. Box 400, Iron Mountain, MI 49801; 800-562-7134; www.uptravel.com; Alger County Chamber of Commerce, P.O. Box 405 (501 M-28 East), Munising, MI 49862; 906-387-2138; www.algercounty.org; Bays de Noc Convention & Visitors Bureau, 230 Ludington Street, Escanaba, MI 49829; 906-789-7862; www.travelbaysdenoc.com; and Schoolcraft County Chamber of Commerce, 1000 W. Lakeshore Drive, Manistique, MI 49854; 906-341-5010; www.schoolcraftcountychamber.com.

Park Trails

The West Unit contains more than 150 miles of trails. Some trails are interpretive trails, such as the Bay Furnace Interpretive Trail. Some are historic, like the Maywood History Trail; others are for backpacking, like the 40-mile linear Bay de Noc–Grand Island National Recreation Trail or the 20 miles of the North Country National Scenic Trail. Finally, the potential in the wilderness is limitless.

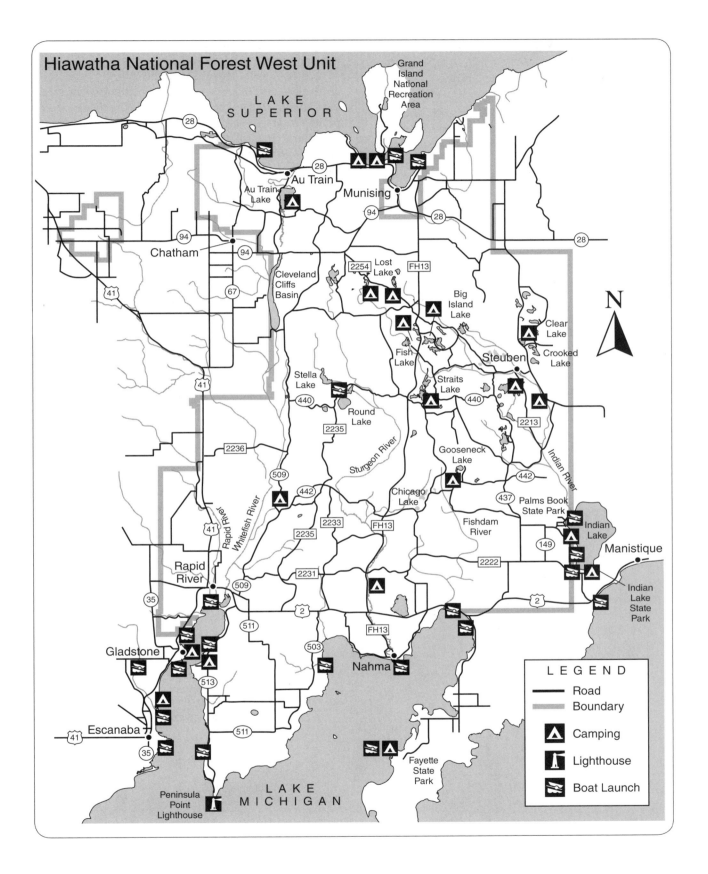

Hiawatha National Forest West Unit

LAKE SUPERIOR

Grand Island National Recreation Area

28

Au Train

Au Train Lake

Munising

94

28

28

Chatham

94

94

67

41

Cleveland Cliffs Basin

2254   Lost Lake

FH13

Big Island Lake

Clear Lake

Crooked Lake

Fish Lake

Steuben

Stella Lake

Straits Lake

440

2213

Round Lake

440

2235

Gooseneck Lake

2236

Sturgeon River

509

442

Chicago Lake

437   Palms Book State Park

442

Whitefish River

Rapid River

41

2235

2233

FH13

Fishdam River

149

Indian Lake

Manistique

Indian River

2222

Rapid River

2231

2

Indian Lake State Park

509

35

511

2

Gladstone

513

503

FH13

Nahma

511

Escanaba

41

511

Fayette State Park

35

Peninsula Point Lighthouse

LAKE MICHIGAN

N

LEGEND

— Road

— Boundary

⛺ Camping

🗼 Lighthouse

⚓ Boat Launch

Au Train Songbird Trail

Distance Round-Trip: 2 miles
Estimated Hiking Time: 1 to 1.5 hours

Cautions: Roots and rocks are exposed, and some areas are wet. Wear proper footgear. Use insect repellent in the warmer months. You are in bear country, so take care.

Trail Directions: With the help of a kit that can be picked up in Au Train at the A & L Grocery or the Au Train Grocery, this audio interpretive trail guides you along with a bird identification book, tape and tape player, and binoculars. The kit helps you to identify birds by their songs. Twenty bird species are featured along the trail. The Au Train Campground host also has a kit that you may check out. There is a $10 deposit; $8 will be refunded to you when you return the kit. The trail is located in the Au Train Lake Campground. From M-28 at Au Train, turn south on H-03 (Forest Lake Road) and drive about 4.5 mi. to FR-2276. Turn left (east) and go about .5 mi. to the campground access road. Take the first campground loop to the right and follow it to the parking spot that is across from the trail near campsite #11 **[1]**. Get the tape ready under the large hemlock at the trailhead. Besides learning about the birds that inhabit the area, be sure to enjoy the trail itself.

Although you may be eager to go straight for the main trail, head left over decking to the observation platform (.1 mi.) **[2]**. From the overlook you might catch a glimpse of ducks, shorebirds, or maybe an eagle or osprey in the Buck Bay habitat. Put the binoculars and field guide to use before heading back to the main trail.

The trail rolls through mixed woods. Intermittently stop and listen to the songs to identify the birds that belong in the varying habitats. Cross a series of planks to arrive at a bench (.3 mi.) **[3]**. Soon you pass a junction and follow a ridge with a wetland below on your left. The trail rolls, and you descend over a wet area on logs (.6 mi.) **[4]**. Soon afterward you hear running water and again climb onto a ridge. At .7 mi., you reach the crest, where you can see water flowing below **[5]**. A bench is nearby.

The trail falls and rises some more, often bringing you near Buck Bay Creek. At .8 mi., abundant ferns line the creek **[6]**. Another bench allows an overview of the creek before you descend to a huge stump that is a nursery to a good-size hemlock (.9 mi.) **[7]**. The fallen tree continues on the other side of the trail. The huge tree fell many years ago; notice the large size of the trees growing out of it.

You reach a meadow and a connector with the North Country Trail (1.1 mi.) **[8]**. Follow to the right and soon reenter the woods. You find many ferns here.

The trail rolls through wetlands to arrive at the Grass Pink Bog (1.3 mi.) **[9]**. Another bench is located at 1.4 mi. **[10]**, after which you find more trees growing out of a green-carpeted log. Continuing to pass through mixed woods, you wind down to cross planks (1.8 mi.) **[11]** and again roll along, crossing a two-track behind campsites (2 mi.) **[12]**. You soon reach a junction, where you turn left to return to the parking area. Rewind the tape for the next user.

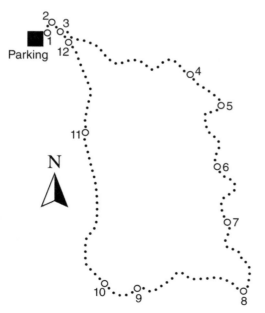

1. Trailhead
2. Platform overlooking Buck Bay
3. Bench
4. Logs over wet area
5. Overview of creek from crest
6. Ferns line the creek
7. Huge fallen nursery tree
8. Meadow
9. Grass Pink Bog
10. Bench
11. Planks
12. Cross two-track

13. Little Presque Isle Tract

- Enjoy sandy beaches along the rugged Lake Superior shoreline.
- Climb to spectacular overlooks.
- Find quiet solitude at a rustic log cabin retreat.

Park Information

Only 3.5 miles north of Marquette, sheer cliffs, sandy beaches, and old-growth forests of hemlock and red pine are accessible by the network of hiking, bicycling, and cross-country skiing trails that weave through 3,150 acres of Little Presque Isle Tract.

Four miles of Lake Superior shoreline, with rugged cliffs, rocky escarpments, and pockets of soft sand, are the focus of the tract—and an indicator of the diversity that lies in store inland. The 64-acre Harlow Lake provides for quiet contemplation and non-motorized boating. Hogback Mountain, 600 feet above Lake Superior, offers challenging hiking and a dramatic view of the lake and surrounding area.

Most of the public use is at Little Presque Isle Point, which overlooks the 8.6-acre island that the tract is named for, and Wetmore Landing. Both have sandy beaches, vault toilets, and parking.

More than 18 miles of trails cross Hogback Mountain, loop Harlow Lake, traverse ridges along Lake Superior, and link with other trails. Six rustic cabins are available along the Harlow Lake ski trail.

The tract, acquired by the state in three separate exchanges from 1976 through 1979, is managed by the Gwinn Management Unit for low-intensity recreational development and use. Camping is not permitted, and motorized vehicles are not allowed except in designated areas.

Directions: The tract is 3.5 miles north of Marquette. Three parking areas are located off County Road 550 at Wetmore Landing, Songbird Trail, and at Little Presque Isle Point.

Hours Open: The park is open year-round.

Facilities: Hiking, mountain bicycling, cross-country skiing, swimming, fishing, boat launch, cabins, picnicking, and interpretive trail.

Permits and Rules: No park fee is required. No camping is allowed. Fires must be contained in designated fire pits or grills. Motorized vehicles are permitted only on designated roads and parking areas.

For Further Information: Marquette Operation Services Center (OSC), 1990 US 41 South, Marquette, MI 49855; 906-228-6561 for the cabins. Contact either the Marquette OSC or the Gwinn Management Unit at 906-346-9201 for general information.

Other Points of Interest

The City of Marquette's 328-acre **Presque Isle Park** offers cliffed and sandy Lake Superior shoreline, dense northern forests, numerous vehicular turnouts for taking in panoramic views, short trails with overlooks, and a 160-foot water slide. In the evening, Sunset Point is an elegant spot in which to pull the shade down for the day. Follow Lakeshore Boulevard to the entrance of the park. For more information, call Marquette Parks and Recreation at 906-228-0460 or contact Marquette County Convention and Visitors Bureau, 800-544-4321 or www.marquettecountry.org.

Sugarloaf Recreational Trail winds up over .5 mile to the peak of Sugarloaf Mountain, where panoramic views of Lake Superior, its rugged shore, the city of Marquette, and its surrounding hills and forests abound. The trail is located north of the city off County Road 550.

Just south of Presque Isle Tract is the **Mead-Wetmore Pond Nature Trail**. Access is on the west side of County Road 550. Wetmore Pond is a floating bog on Mead Paper Company land. For more information, call 906-786-1660.

Get a taste of the history of the city's past at the **Marquette Maritime Museum**, open daily from 10:00 a.m. to 5:00 p.m. from late May through mid-October. The museum is located on East Ridge at Lakeshore Boulevard. For more information, call 906-226-2006.

Park Trails

Song Bird Trail (👟👟, 1.1 miles). This interpretive trail passes thickets, wetlands, and a river delta. It starts from the Little Presque Isle Point area parking lot. A brochure helps you identify the habitats and the various birds that are likely to inhabit them.

Harlow Lake Trail (👟👟, 6 miles). This trail is notable for its nordic use. Parking is near a gravel pit on the west side of County Road 550, near Wetmore Landing.

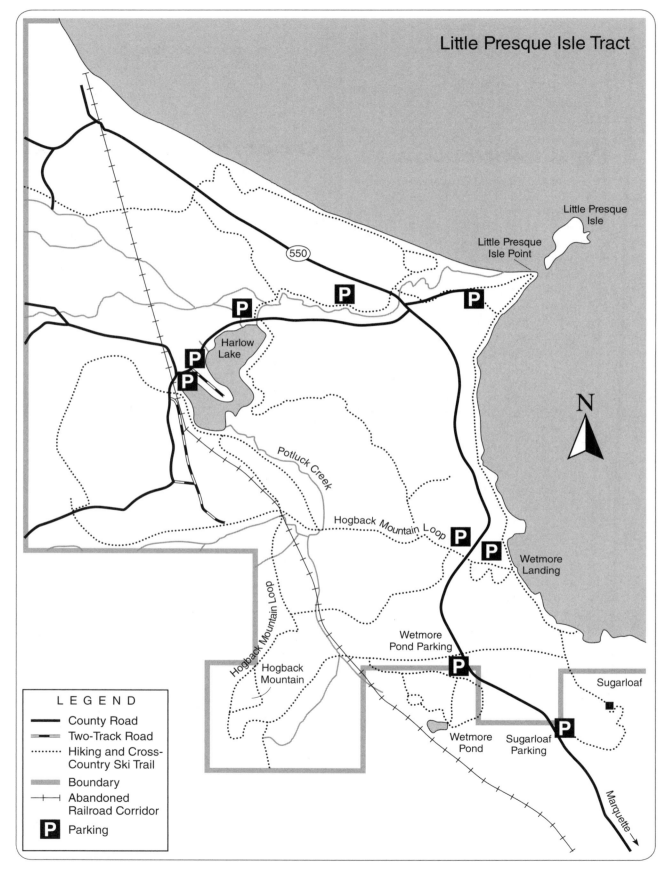

Little Presque Isle Tract

Little Presque Isle

Little Presque Isle Point

550

Harlow Lake

Potluck Creek

N

Hogback Mountain Loop

Wetmore Landing

Hogback Mountain Loop

Wetmore Pond Parking

Sugarloaf

Hogback Mountain

Wetmore Pond

Sugarloaf Parking

Marquette

LEGEND
County Road
Two-Track Road
Hiking and Cross-Country Ski Trail
Boundary
Abandoned Railroad Corridor
P Parking

Lake Superior—
Little Presque Isle Point to
Wetmore Landing

Distance Round-Trip: 3.6 miles
Estimated Hiking Time: 2 to 3 hours

Cautions: At times you are near the edge of the cliff. Be careful. Roots and rocks crop up along the trail, so watch your step. Bring along insect repellent.

Trail Directions: Start from the northwest side of the parking area at the Little Presque Isle Point area and head through the gate along the wide path **[1]**. Although the trail heads east along the Lake Superior shoreline, succumb to the temptation of the lake and head north for a short shoreline visit. The beach is an intriguing mix of sand and shore that is under the cover of red pines. You don't need to draw out the visit too long; this hike keeps you along the lake. Head back to the pine-carpeted trail toward the point, where you can see the island, Little Presque Isle.

A blue mark on a tree alerts you to follow the trail to the right, but go on out to the point for a closer view of the 8.6-acre island (.2 mi.) **[2]**. The view through pine and birch is tough to resist.

Follow to the right, and the trail eventually cuts near the lake. A few trails pass through here. Your path takes you under the cover of trees but near the shore. Follow the blue markings and stay near the line of the shore. From here you see the burnt-umber rock outcroppings along the shore ahead of you.

The trail ascends, and at about .4 mi. you walk along the sinuous line of coves that have been eroded into the ridge **[3]**. Gently rolling along the trail, you pass many more coves as you wind in and out of the trees. When you walk into darkness, notice the prevalence of hemlock. Some of them look as though they are about to dive off the cliff into the cold waters of Lake Superior (.6 mi.) **[4]**.

The shoreline continues, ragged, with a sawtooth edge of coves. Red cliffs drop to the depths of the lake below, only a few feet from your boots. Boulders pounded by waves below signal that you are near the steps that take you to a higher ridge (.8 mi.) **[5]**. Climb up and continue left through the mixed hardwoods. Notice that the forest floor is bright with foliage where uprooted trees expose a hole of sunlight (.9 mi.) **[6]**.

Roll along through the woods, passing an area with many fallen birches (1 mi.) **[7]**. This is your cue that a clear view of the lake is close, very close. Watch that edge; it's a sheer drop-off. Continue along, dipping down a small ravine and then crossing the footbridge over another (1.1 mi.) **[8]**. This section takes you to a viewing area with a seat and security railing. From here, past the steep escarpment (rock cliff), you view the sandy beach below.

Thereafter the trail gradually descends until you reach the nearly 100 steps that take you down to the boulder-strewn edge of the lake (1.4 mi.) **[9]**. Climb over and around these massive reminders of the cliffs of yesteryear. Wind among these giants and then pass along the pebble-stone shore, which gives way to the sandy beach at Wetmore Landing (1.8 mi.) **[10]**. A path leads less than .2 mi. to the parking area, but you may choose to rest in the sand before turning around and heading back to Little Presque Isle Point for a different perspective of the Lake Superior shoreline.

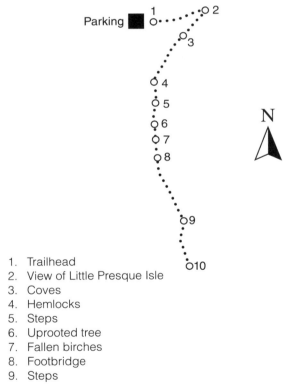

1. Trailhead
2. View of Little Presque Isle
3. Coves
4. Hemlocks
5. Steps
6. Uprooted tree
7. Fallen birches
8. Footbridge
9. Steps
10. Wetmore Landing

Hogback Mountain Loop

Distance Round-Trip: 5 miles
Estimated Hiking Time: 3.5 to 5 hours

Cautions: The trail includes steep climbs and descents on rock. Wear appropriate footgear. Bring insect repellent, a hat, and water.

Trail Directions: The parking area is 5 mi. north of Marquette on County Road 550. The trail begins on the west side of the parking area [1]. Cross County Road 550 and head west down an old road, past a sign for the Harlow Lake Pathway. When you reach the next trail junction, swing to the left and descend through red pine (.3 mi.) [2].

At .9 mi., you cross a footbridge [3] to reach the junction to Harlow Lake. Stay to the left and then go left again at the next junction to cross a culvert over running water (1 mi.) [4].

Turn left onto an abandoned railroad corridor and look for post #5. Head toward two boulders situated on the old railroad corridor and turn right between post #5 and the boulders (1.1 mi.) [5]. Then climb over a dirt mound to enter the woods and soon cross over a stream on a footbridge (1.2 mi.) [6]. You then climb into a hemlock grove, descend past a seasonal pond, and swing around a rock outcrop to find yourself in a stand of red pine at the junction for Hogback Mountain (1.5 mi.) [7]. Go right.

Cross a couple of muddy sections before starting to climb the Hogback. The trail is eroded, and many roots and rocks are exposed, making the climb treacherous (1.7 mi.) [8]. At 2 mi., you reach a trail sign [9]. Go left to the summit. This is the most difficult section of the trail. You may find that you need to use your hands to climb the steep grade over bare rock.

You are well rewarded for your effort when you reach the summit (2.2 mi.) [10]. A panoramic view of Lake Superior and the Marquette environs awaits you.

Getting down from the peak is no less difficult than the climb. Watch your step. Many blue marks along the summit indicate the route, but they are hard to follow over the bare rock. Take your time.

As you descend, you come upon a NCT post (2.5 mi.) [11]. Stay to the left and continue downward. Only when you reach a footbridge do you realize that the climb down has ended (3 mi.) [12]. You soon cross the abandoned railroad corridor again (3.1) [13].

Climb over the low end of a rock outcrop to the junction with the Mead Nature Trail (3.3 mi.) [14]. Stay left to climb along another rock outcrop. At the next outcrop take a look behind you for a scenic view of Hogback Mountain (3.5 mi.) [15].

Cross County Road 550 (3.8 mi.) [16] and start up another rock ridge. Snaking around the back side, you'll descend through a narrow ravine between rock outcrops. When the trail levels out, you swing right along the back side of an outcrop in a hemlock grove (4.2 mi.) [17].

At 4.3 mi., after hiking through a wet area, watch for a trail sign board [18]. Turn left toward Wetmore Landing and descend toward Lake Superior. A remnant walkway near the historical cabin site leads you from the ridge toward the beach (4.5 mi.) [19]. The trail now parallels the lake. As you periodically pass steps on your right that lead you down to the beach, keep an eye out for a trail on your left (5.4 mi.) [20] that leads you away from the beach and back to the parking area.

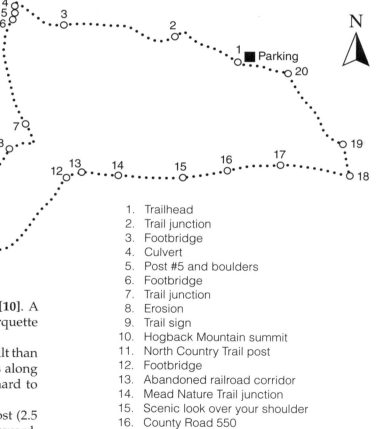

N

1. Trailhead
2. Trail junction
3. Footbridge
4. Culvert
5. Post #5 and boulders
6. Footbridge
7. Trail junction
8. Erosion
9. Trail sign
10. Hogback Mountain summit
11. North Country Trail post
12. Footbridge
13. Abandoned railroad corridor
14. Mead Nature Trail junction
15. Scenic look over your shoulder
16. County Road 550
17. Hemlocks
18. Trail sign board
19. Walkway to beach
20. Trail to parking area

- Explore a part of Negaunee closed off to the public for over 50 years.
- Visit the site where iron ore was first discovered in the region.
- Enter the cathedral-like setting of the Jackson Mine.

City Information

Known as the caving grounds, Old Town Negaunee is a 900-acre parcel of land that the City of Negaunee is resurrecting. Once a vital part of the community, Old Town Negaunee carries the scars of intense mining activity and the remains of a once-vibrant neighborhood. Acquired by the city in 2003, the site had been closed to the public since the 1950s. As the city makes plans to bring new life to the tract, a network of trails called the Miners Trail System now circulates visitors around Old Town Negaunee's unique historical features.

Visit the spot where the Chippewa Indian Marji Gesick led surveyors to a tree stump with iron ore clinging to its roots. View silent mine pits that once helped the region produce half of the country's iron ore supply between 1850 and 1900. Roam vacant city streets and imagine what life must have been like as you pass forgotten front steps and foundations. Walk the sidewalk to nowhere.

Stay tuned. The region is working to preserve and tell the story of its rich mining history through the establishment of an Iron Ore Heritage Area. Anchoring this effort is the establishment of the Iron Ore Heritage Trail, a 48-mile-long linear park that connects communities between the Cities of Republic and Marquette and preserves and tells the story of Marquette County's iron-mining heritage. The route between Ishpeming and Negaunee, which runs through Old Town Negaunee, was paved in 2008.

Directions: Old Town is located west of downtown Negaunee. From US 41/M-28, go south on M-28 BR (North Teal Lake Avenue) .5 mile, turn right to stay on M-28 BR (West Main Street) .2 mile, and go straight to stay on Jackson Street. Old Town starts where Jackson Street ends at Tobin Street. For now, parking is on city streets.

Hours Open: Old Town Negaunee is open all year.

Facilities: Hiking, bicycling, mountain bicycling, cross-country skiing, snowshoeing, snowmobiling, picnicking, interpretive trails, and historic sites.

Permits and Rules: There is no admission fee.

For Further Information: City of Negaunee, 906-475-7700 ext. 11; Negaunee Historical Museum, 906-475-4614; and Marquette Area Chamber of Commerce; 888-578-6489.

Other Points of Interest

The **Michigan Iron Industry Museum** overlooking Carp River occupies the site of the first iron forge in the Lake Superior region. Attractions include exhibits, outdoor interpretive paths, and a sound and slide program. For information, contact Michigan Iron Industry Museum, 73 Forge Road, Negaunee, MI 49866; 517-373-3559.

The **Cliffs Shaft Mine Iron Museum** sits on the site of what was the longest operating underground iron mine in the world. Take a guided tour of the tunnels and listen to the history of mining from those who worked the mines. For information, contact Cliffs Shaft Mine Iron Museum, 501 W. Euclid Street, P.O. Box 555, Ishpeming, MI 49849; 906-485-1882.

The **U.S. National Ski and Snowboard Hall of Fame and Museum** is located in Ishpeming, the birthplace of organized skiing in the United States. The museum exhibits an extensive collection of artifacts and archives relating to the history of skiing. Contact the U.S. National Ski and Snowboard Hall of Fame and Museum, 610 Palms Avenue, P.O. Box 191, Ishpeming, MI 49849; 906-485-6323.

Park Trails

Eight trails have been opened to the public. Trail signs are in the shape of old iron ore cars. The load in the ore car cleverly shows the profile of the trail.

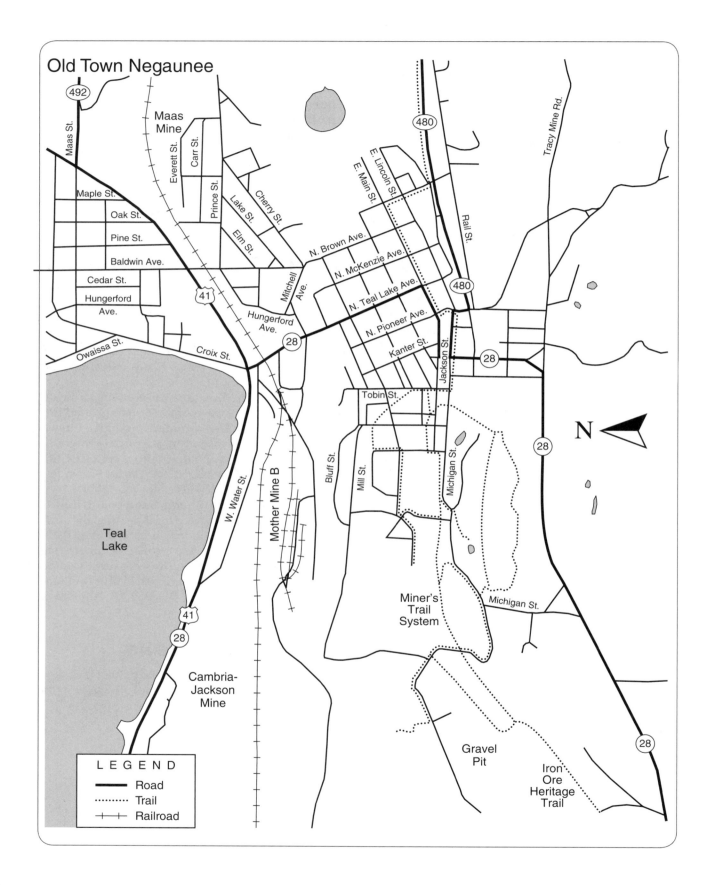

Old Town Negaunee

492

Maas St.

Maas
Mine

Everett St.

Carr St.

Prince St.

Lake St.

Cherry St.

Elm St.

Maple St.

Oak St.

Pine St.

Baldwin Ave.

Cedar St.

Hungerford
Ave.

Mitchell Ave.

41

Hungerford
Ave.

28

Owaissa St.

Croix St.

E. Lincoln St.

E. Main St.

N. Brown Ave.

N. McKenzie Ave.

N. Teal Lake Ave.

N. Pioneer Ave.

Kanter St.

480

Rail St.

Tracy Mine Rd.

480

28

Jackson St.

Tobin St.

Bluff St.

Mill St.

W. Water St.

Mother Mine B

Teal
Lake

41

28

Cambria-
Jackson
Mine

Michigan St.

Miner's
Trail
System

Michigan St.

28

N

Gravel
Pit

Iron
Ore
Heritage
Trail

28

LEGEND
——— Road
········ Trail
+—+—+ Railroad

Miners Trail Mix North

Distance Round-Trip: 2.4 miles
Estimated Hiking Time: 1.5 to 2 hours

Cautions: The Miners Trail System is new. Improvements are ongoing, so changes will occur. Do not enter fenced-off areas. This area was known as the caving grounds with good reason. Watch for the occasional vehicle as you walk the streets of Old Town.

Trail Directions: Begin at the signboard on the west side of Tobin Street, just north of Jackson Street [1]. Head west on the Heritage Trail across a grassy field. Turn right at the fence (.1 mi.) [2] to walk around the caving area, the Jackson Bowl. Turn left at Merry Street, cross a former railroad corridor, and turn right on Iron Street. Pass the location of Marquette County's first state police post before arriving at the Miners Trail (.5 mi.) [3]. Turn left, walk past the ruins of the Jackson Mine office, machine shop, and engine house for pit #1. Continue through a craggy wall of rock and arrive at the cathedral-like setting of the water-filled Jackson Pit #1 (.6 mi.) [4]. This is the site of the first iron mine in the region. Admire the setting before turning back. As you leave the mine site, cross the street and make a hard left onto the Heritage Trail, the former rail line (.7 mi.) [5].

You soon reach the junction with the Marji Gesick Trail (.8 mi.) [6]. Turn left to climb up a bank to Michigan Street (.9 mi.) [7]. This point is approximately where Chippewa Indian Marji Gesick led surveyors to the tree with iron ore in its roots. Turn right and climb toward the original site of the monument (now located on US 41/M-28) that was erected by the Jackson Mining Company in 1904 (1 mi.) [8]. On the left is the Everett Trail junction, and on the right is an overlook of the shining wall, an escarpment of specular hematite. Continue along the road, which bends to the right around the pit of the North Jackson Mine and deposits you at a junction (1.3 mi.) [9]. Turn right on the Heritage Trail and walk the old rail line. Pass the fenced pits of the North Jackson Mine and the junction with the Marji Gesick Trail to arrive at the junction with the Old Town Trail (1.7 mi.) [10]. Turn left and follow a two-track through the trees toward the site of an old railroad trestle. For a side trip to the sidewalk to nowhere, make a sharp left and walk about .7 mi. [11]. Because the top of the hill was cool during the heat of summer, it was a favorite gathering spot during the 1800s.

When you return from your side trip, make a left and then a right to enter the lost community as you head down Snow Street. You pass the remains of stairs that once served the houses long removed. The first school in Negaunee was located along this stretch. A sculpture of children playing is planned to commemorate the school site.

When you reach the intersection with Merry Street (2.1 mi.) [12], turn left and go to the end of the road. Turn right and follow an old railroad line back to Tobin Street. Turn right on Tobin to head back to where you started your hike.

1. Trailhead
2. Fence
3. Miners Trail
4. Jackson Pit #1
5. Heritage Trail
6. Marji Gesick Trail
7. Michigan Street
8. Old monument site
9. Junction
10. Old Town Trail
11. Sidewalk to nowhere
12. Merry Street

Upper
Peninsula

Miners Trail Mix South

Distance Round-Trip: 2.9 miles
Estimated Hiking Time: 1.5 to 2 hours

Cautions: The Miners Trail System is new. Improvements are ongoing, so changes will occur. Do not enter fenced-off areas. This area was known as the caving grounds with good reason. Watch for the occasional vehicle as you walk the streets of Old Town.

Trail Directions: Begin at the signboard on the west side of Tobin Street, just north of Jackson Street **[1]**. Head west on the Heritage Trail, cross a grassy field, and bear right at the fence (.1 mi.) **[2]** to walk around the caving area know as the Jackson Bowl. Turn left at Merry Street, cross a former railroad corridor, and turn right on Iron Street. On your left you pass the location of Marquette County's first state police post before arriving at the Miners Trail (.5 mi.) **[3]**. Turn left and walk past the ruins of the Jackson Mine office, machine shop, and engine house for pit #1. Continue through a craggy wall of rock and arrive at the cathedral-like setting of the water-filled Jackson Pit #1 (.6 mi.) **[4]**. This is the site of the first iron mine in the region. Revere in the setting before turning back. As you leave the mine site, cross the street and make a hard left onto the Heritage Trail, the former rail line (.7 mi.) **[5]**.

You soon reach the junction with the Marji Gesick Trail (.8 mi.) **[6]**. Continue straight, passing the fenced North Jackson Mine pits to arrive at the junction for the Ely Trail (1 mi.) **[7]**. Turn right and walk along the old road to Ishpeming. Turn left at the junction with the Frank Matthews Trail and leave the asphalt behind to walk in the shade along a ridge that is a former railroad grade. The trail soon swings left off the ridge to descend and then climb sharply, depositing you back at the Heritage Trail (1.4 mi.) **[8]**. Turn left, hike back to the start of the Ely Trail, and turn right onto the Marji Gesick Trail (1.7 mi.).

The trail swings around the North Jackson Mine pit before arriving at the original site of the monument (now located on US 41/M-28) that was erected by the Jackson Mining Company in 1904 (2 mi.) **[9]**. On the left is an overlook of a shining wall, an escarpment of specular hematite, and on the right is the Everett Trail junction that you will take after enjoying the overlook.

You are on the Everett Trail for only a short distance before you reach the Captain Merry Trail (2 mi.) **[10]**. Go straight and walk the wood-chipped trail as you descend, passing the location of Cornishtown on the right while a bluff rises on your left. The trail levels off at a park known as Jackson Grove, where there is a trail signboard (2.5 mi.) **[11]**. This location is the end of the Captain Merry Trail and the beginning of the Burt Trail, which will guide you past the site where iron ore was first discovered and back to the beginning of your hike.

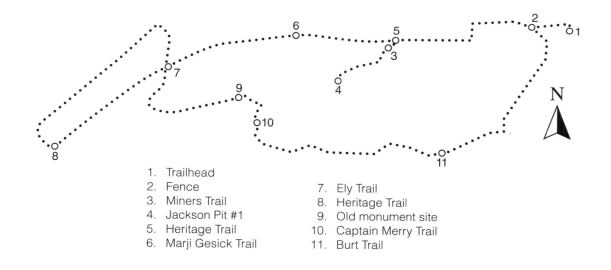

1. Trailhead
2. Fence
3. Miners Trail
4. Jackson Pit #1
5. Heritage Trail
6. Marji Gesick Trail
7. Ely Trail
8. Heritage Trail
9. Old monument site
10. Captain Merry Trail
11. Burt Trail

15. Estivant Pines Nature Sanctuary

- Experience a virgin forest.
- Catch a glimpse of what much of Michigan once looked like.
- Gaze skyward in awe at 100-foot-tall white pines.

Park Information

A visit to the Estivant Pines Nature Sanctuary is like stepping back in time. With 508 acres, it is the largest preserve of old-growth eastern white pine in Michigan. Scattered in a virgin forest of northern hardwoods, this sanctuary provides a sense of how Michigan looked when 130-foot-high white pine dominated much of the landscape.

The sanctuary is named after Edward A.J. Estivant, a French man who purchased 2,400 acres south of Copper Harbor in 1861. The land was held in the Estivant family until 1947, when it was sold to the Calumet and Hecla Mining Company. In 1970, when logging operations threatened the remaining old-growth forest, local citizens and the Michigan Nature Association organized a campaign to save the large trees. Three years later, 200 of the acres were purchased to establish the sanctuary; 177 acres were purchased in 1988 when logging operations encroached on the sanctuary property. In July 2005, 133 acres were added, creating a link to Fort Wilkins State Park.

Located on the spine of the Keweenaw Peninsula, the sanctuary is an area of rugged rock outcroppings and ragged hillsides. The sanctuary includes a softer side; 256 plant species and 10 species of orchids are found here. And at least 85 bird species nest in the sanctuary.

Maintained by the Michigan Nature Association, the sanctuary is intended to provide visitors with a true wilderness experience. The trails are rugged and are designed for foot traffic only.

Directions: From the junction of US 41 and M-26 in Copper Harbor, travel east .2 mile and turn south (right) toward Lake Manganese. Then follow the signs to Estivant Pines. The last leg of the drive into the sanctuary is over an improved backwoods road. The road is narrow and bumpy. Drive carefully.

Hours Open: Open year-round from dawn to dusk.
Facilities: Hiking and vault toilet.
Permits and Rules: No admission fee is charged, but donations are encouraged. Travel is by foot only; bicycles and motorized vehicles are strictly prohibited. Camping and fires are not allowed. Pack out all litter. To prevent damage to rare plants and maintain respect for the wildlife, pets are prohibited in the sanctuary.
For Further Information: Michigan Nature Association, 326 E. Grand River Avenue, Williamston, MI 48895; 517-655-5655; www.michigannature.org.

Other Points of Interest

Fort Wilkins State Park offers camping, hiking, and fishing, but the centerpiece of the park is the restored Fort Wilkins. Built in 1844 to keep the peace in Copper Country, the fort was abandoned two years later. One of the first lighthouses on Lake Superior was built on the site in 1866. Many original structures dating from the 1840s survive. Museum exhibits, audiovisual programs, and costumed interpretations show the rough life that soldiers had to endure here. This state park is located 1 mile east of Copper Harbor on US 41. For more information, contact Fort Wilkins State Park, 15233 US 41, Copper Harbor, MI 49918; 906-289-4215.

Brockway Mountain Drive ranks as one of the most scenic drives in America. This 9.5-mile roadway is one of the highest scenic drives between the Rockies and Alleghenies. To reach the drive, take M-26 .5 mile south from Copper Harbor or 5 miles north from Eagle Harbor. For more information, contact the Keweenaw Convention and Visitors Bureau, 56638 Calumet Avenue, Calumet, MI 49913; 800-338-7982; www.keweenaw.info.

Besides the Estivant Pines Nature Sanctuary, the **Michigan Nature Association** has more than a dozen other preserves in the Keweenaw Peninsula. To obtain a copy of the guidebook for the preserves, contact the Michigan Nature Association, 326 E. Grand River Avenue, Williamston, MI 48895; 517-655-5655; www .michigannature.org.

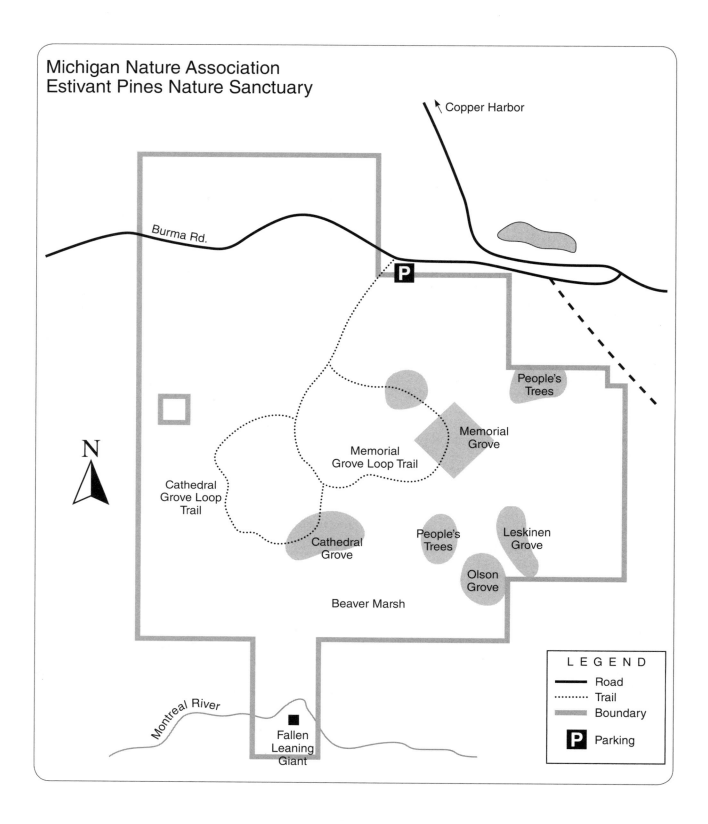

Michigan Nature Association
Estivant Pines Nature Sanctuary

↑ Copper Harbor

Burma Rd.

P

People's
Trees

Memorial
Grove

Memorial
Grove Loop Trail

Cathedral
Grove Loop
Trail

N

People's
Trees

Leskinen
Grove

Cathedral
Grove

Olson
Grove

Beaver Marsh

LEGEND
— Road
······ Trail
▬ Boundary
P Parking

Montreal River

Fallen
Leaning
Giant

Cathedral Grove Loop Trail

Distance Round-Trip: 1.5 miles
Estimated Hiking Time: 1 hour

Cautions: Roots and rocks are often exposed on the trail. Most wet areas are covered with boardwalks, but other areas are also prone to be wet or muddy. The trail includes steep climbs and descents. Proper footgear is a must. Another necessity is insect repellent and a hat or netting.

Trail Directions: The trail starts from the south end of the small parking area on Burma Road. A signboard here lists the sanctuary manners, or rules **[1]**.

The trail from the parking area is on an old mining road that dates back to the mid-1800s. If you are observant, you may see scars on the bases of the big trees; it has been said that the scars were left by wagons used for the small copper mine explorations that were conducted in the area.

After crossing a small stream, the trail swings right to skirt a hill on the left and climbs into the forest. You cross a number of boardwalks to arrive at a posted sign that shows the sanctuary's trails and your present location (.2 mi.) **[2]**. The Memorial Grove Loop goes to the left here. Go past this junction, cross another boardwalk, and walk through some large white pines before arriving at the junction for the Cathedral Grove Loop Trail (.4 mi.) **[3]**. Turn right, cross over wood planks, and climb a rocky, root-laden hill. The trail has been rerouted in this section to maneuver around a fallen giant (.5 mi.) **[4]**. Pay attention.

Although only a small percentage of the big pines are visible from the trail, take time to gaze skyward at the old giants that you encounter. Be careful though; the trail also commands your attention.

Shortly after a long descent to cross a boardwalk over a small stream (.7 mi.) **[5]**, you turn left where an unmarked trail goes to the right (.8 mi.) **[6]**. Climb into the area known as the Cathedral Grove (.9 mi.) **[7]**. Cloistered in this grove are some of the largest and oldest white pines in the sanctuary. Some of these 500-year-old trees measure over 4 feet in diameter and 125 feet in height.

Leaving the Cathedral Grove, you quickly reach the junction with the Memorial Grove Loop (1 mi.) **[8]**. Turn left and follow the old mining road for .5 mi. back to the parking area.

1. Trailhead
2. Memorial Grove Loop Trail junction
3. Cathedral Grove Loop Trail junction
4. Fallen giant
5. Boardwalk
6. Unmarked trail junction
7. Cathedral Grove
8. Memorial Grove Loop Trail junction

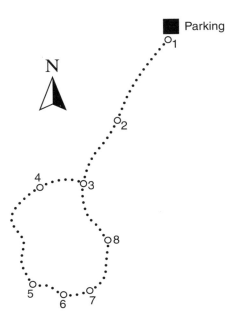

Memorial Grove Loop Trail

Distance Round-Trip: 1.5 miles
Estimated Hiking Time: 1 hour

Cautions: Roots and rocks are often exposed on the trail. Most wet areas are covered with boardwalks, but other areas may be wet or muddy as well. The trail includes steep climbs and descents. Proper footgear is a must, as are insect repellent and a hat or netting.

Trail Directions: The trail starts from the south end of the small parking area on Burma Road. A signboard here lists the sanctuary manners, or rules **[1]**. From the parking area, the trail follows the route of an old mining road that dates back to the mid-1800s. The road was used for small copper mine explorations conducted in the area. You may notice that some of the big trees have scars. It has been said that the scars were left by wagons used for the mine explorations.

The hike starts as you cross a small stream. Follow the trail as it veers right around a hill and climbs into the forest. After crossing a number of boardwalks, you arrive at a posted sign that shows the sanctuary trails and your present location (.2 mi.) **[2]**. To your left is where you will finish this hike.

Continue past the junction, cross another boardwalk, pass some large white pines, and arrive at the junction for the Cathedral Grove Loop Trail (.4 mi.) **[3]**. Keep going straight as the trail follows the old mining road to the second junction with the Cathedral Grove Loop Trail (.5 mi.) **[4]**. The Cathedral Grove is just a short distance away on your right and well worth the side trip. Some of the largest and oldest white pines in Michigan are clustered here, measuring over 4 feet in diameter and 125 feet in height. Some are 500 years old.

Beyond the junction, the trail rises and swings left. After it levels off, you find yourself walking along the edge of a ridge before swinging left and descending toward the area known as Memorial Grove (.9 mi.) **[5]**, an area of 200-year-old white pines. They filled in after a fire burned out all the competing hardwoods, exposing the thin soil. In this section, the trail is rugged and includes some steep descents and climbs. Take time to revere this remnant of the area as much of it looked before axes leveled the majestic trees. A trail sign at this spot commemorates the founder of the Michigan Nature Association, identifying this as the Bertha Daubendiek Memorial Trail.

At 1.2 mi., you come upon a large boulder ideal for sitting **[6]**. You then descend to complete the Memorial Grove Loop, arriving at the first junction (1.3 mi.) **[2]**. Turn right and follow the old mining road back to the parking area.

1. Trailhead
2. Map board and return point from Memorial Grove
3. Cathedral Grove Loop Trail junction
4. Side trip to Cathedral Grove
5. Memorial Grove
6. Large boulder

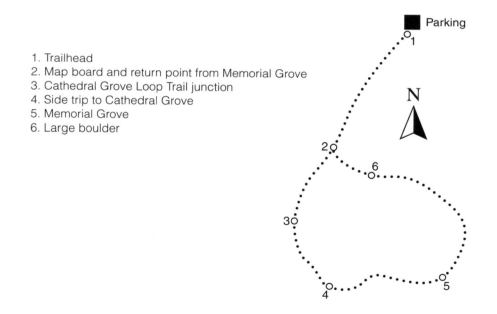

- Hike Copper Harbor's Isle Royale.
- Stroll a craggy, red-pebbled shoreline.
- Experience an intense spring bird migration.

Park Information

Hunter's Point, a finger of land that points in an easterly direction from the west end of Copper Harbor, serves as a natural barrier to Lake Superior's legendary storms. It has the distinction of being the northernmost projection in the state of Michigan.

The park, acquired by Grant Township in 2005 with the aid of a grant from the Michigan Natural Resources Trust Fund (MNRTF), is currently a modest 9.4 acres in size with 4,800 feet of shoreline. By the end of the decade the park is projected to grow by 122 acres and add 1,730 feet of shoreline, thanks to funding approved by the MNRTF. The expansion includes 49 acres at the west end of Copper Harbor connecting the park with the Copper Harbor Marina and 73 acres on the north side of Brockway Mountain connecting the park with the Michigan Nature Association's James Dorian Rooks Memorial Nature Preserve.

You might want to consider visiting Hunter's Point in spring, when thousands of migrating birds congregate before crossing Lake Superior. Peak activity is in late April and early May, especially on mornings when the night has been clear and the wind is out of the south-southwest.

Directions: The park is located west of Copper Harbor. From Copper Harbor, take M-26 west roughly .7 mile to North Coast Shores Road, where you head north (right) .7 mile to Harbor Coast Lane and drive east (right) to the parking area. The park is also accessible by trail from the west end of the Copper Harbor marina parking lot.

Hours Open: Open all year.

Facilities: Hiking, birding, snowshoeing, and fishing.

Permits and Rules: Check with Grant Township. No admission fee is charged.

For Further Information: Grant Township, 906-289-4292; Keweenaw Convention and Visitors Bureau, 906-337-4579; Copper Harbor Improvement Association, www.copperharbor.org; and Keweenaw Chamber of Commerce, 906-482-5240.

Other Points of Interest

Copper Harbor's Trail System has grown to over 25 miles of trails for mountain biking and hiking enthusiasts. For more information or a map of the trail system, contact the Keweenaw Adventure Company, LLC, 145 Gratiot Street (US 41), P.O. Box 70, Copper Harbor, MI 49918; 906-289-4303; www.keweenaw adventure.com.

Fort Wilkins State Park offers camping, hiking, and fishing, but the centerpiece of the park is the restored Fort Wilkins. This state park is located 1 mile east of Copper Harbor on US 41. For more information, contact Fort Wilkins State Park, 15233 US 41, Copper Harbor, MI 49918; 906-289-4215.

Brockway Mountain Drive ranks as one of the most scenic drives in America. To reach the drive, take M-26 .5 mile south from Copper Harbor or 5 miles north from Eagle Harbor. For more information, contact the Keweenaw Convention and Visitors Bureau, 56638 Calumet Avenue, Calumet, MI 49913; 800-338-7982; www.keweenaw.info.

Isle Royale National Park (see park #21), the only island national park, is located 50 miles off the Keweenaw Peninsula in Lake Superior. The park is reachable by boat from Copper Harbor and Houghton, or by seaplane from Houghton. The park has over 160 miles of trail. For more information, contact Isle Royale National Park, 800 East Lakeshore Drive, Houghton, MI 49931; 906-482-0984; www.nps.gov/isro.

Besides **Estivant Pines Nature Sanctuary** (see park #15), the **Michigan Nature Association** has more than a dozen other preserves in the Keweenaw. To obtain a copy of a guidebook for the preserves, contact the Michigan Nature Association, 326 E. Grand River Avenue, Williamston, MI 48895; 517-655-5655; www .michigannature.org.

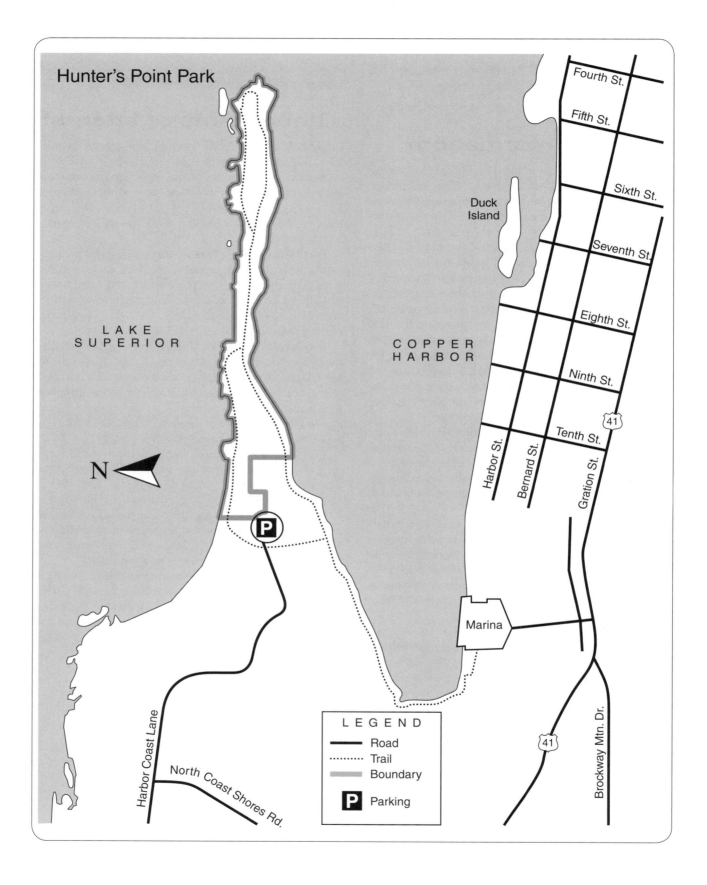

Hunter's Point Park

LAKE
SUPERIOR

COPPER
HARBOR

Duck
Island

N

P

Fourth St.

Fifth St.

Sixth St.

Seventh St.

Eighth St.

Ninth St.

41

Tenth St.

Harbor St.

Bernard St.

Gration St.

Marina

Brockway Mtn. Dr.

41

Harbor Coast Lane

North Coast Shores Rd.

LEGEND
Road
Trail
Boundary
P Parking

North and South Beach Loop

🐾 **Distance Round-Trip:** 1.3 miles
🐾 **Estimated Hiking Time:** 1 hour

Cautions: Exposed roots and rocks create hazards on the trail. Wear proper footgear and take along insect repellent.

Trail Directions: Head west on M-26 about .3 mi. from the Copper Harbor Marina and turn right on North Coast Shores Road. Then turn right on Harbor Coast Lane and drive east to the parking area. Start the trail at the south end of the parking lot **[1]**. An explosion of Shasta daisies envelops the lot. Head south through a mix of pine, birch, and maple trees, some draped with bearded moss. Descend through ferns to a junction (.1 mi.) **[2]**. Turn left along the South Beach Loop. Soon you walk a rock escarpment to arrive at a red-pebble beach where you have a fine view of the harbor. From here, the trail dips left under cover of trees and becomes braided with roots and covered with pine needles.

After you reach the second junction (.2 mi.) **[3]**, you enter the area that is now Hunter's Point Park. Go straight and enjoy the number of access points along the way that let you reach the shore. The next junction is at .3 mi. **[4]**. Go straight and cross red pebbles just before you get to the next junction (.4 mi.) **[5]**. Stay right to head out to the point; you'll loop back here.

From here you are on a finger of land; you can see water on both sides.

Red pebbles coat the trail. Watch for interesting root sculptures near the water. As you continue, red pebbles give way to red sand, which gives way to red needles. Verdant ground cover brushes up alongside the trail. You reach a boulder, which roughly marks the east end of the trail at .6 mi. **[6]**. Keep going east to the point, where you can view an island and sculpted rock. You can't beat this place for a break. Take one, take pictures, and then take yourself back to the boulder **[6]** so that you can head north to view huge, dark, boulders splattered with orange lichen and graced with tiny flowers growing from their cracks.

The trail winds through cedar and thimbleberry. Spurs to the lake tempt you. You could spend hours combing through the rocks. When done, head back along the trail to the next junction (1.3 mi.) **[5]**. Stay to the right to pick up the north loop on the east end (1.2 mi.) **[4]**. Soon you reach a spur that leads to a red-pebbled beach—one more temptation. Pass an outcropping that exposes the root structures of the trees on top to reach another outcropping on the beach that has colorful swirls. Pass another junction. Soon you see a field and a road on your left. This is the parking lot. Follow the well-worn, rocky path to the left to cut back to the lot.

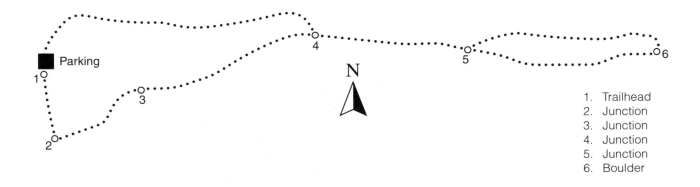

1. Trailhead
2. Junction
3. Junction
4. Junction
5. Junction
6. Boulder

Trail to Marina

🥾 **Distance Round-Trip:** .8 mile
🥾 **Estimated Hiking Time:** 30 minutes to 1 hour

Cautions: Exposed roots and rocks create hazards on the trail. Wear proper footgear and take along insect repellent.

Trail Directions: Head west on M-26 about .3 mi. from the Copper Harbor Marina and turn right on North Coast Shores Road. Then turn right on Harbor Coast Lane and drive east to the parking area. Start this point-to-point trail at the south end of the parking lot **[1]**. Shasta daisies and false lupines envelop the lot. Go south through a mix of pine, birch, and maple, some draped with bearded moss. Descend through ferns to a junction (.1 mi.) **[2]**. Turn right. The trail, which follows the shore of the bay, is littered with rocks and roots pocketed with copper-colored needles; large white pines hover above.

At about .2 mi., look southwest to view Brockway Mountain standing strong in the distance **[3]**. As you walk along, watch for evidence of pileated woodpecker. Plenty of trees provide places for feasting on insects.

Along the shore, many opportunities for hunting rocks present themselves. Look but don't take.

Bracken ferns up to your chin crowd the trail as you round the shore. A boardwalk winds you around the

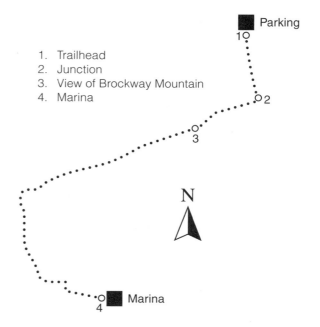

1. Trailhead
2. Junction
3. View of Brockway Mountain
4. Marina

harbor and deposits you into the shadows of dense cedar. Two more boardwalks hug the shore. You continue along the shore in a heavily wooded area with rocks strewn about to reach the parking lot for the marina at the Copper Harbor State Harbor (.4 mi.) **[4]**. The building there has a gift shop and restrooms. Stop in if it is open before you turn around to head back.

- Hike around lakes uncluttered with cabins or motorboats.
- Canoe the quiet waters of the pristine Fumee Lakes.
- Enjoy the call of a loon or the sight of an eagle soaring above the lakes.

Park Information

Tucked away within 5 to 10 minutes of three of Dickinson County's cities are 1,808 acres of serenity—the Fumee Lake Natural Area. This Dickinson County park has two pristine lakes, significant wetlands to recharge the water, and over 620 plant and wildflower species. The park provides a peaceful refuge for animals and other visitors to the area.

With 507 acres of surface water and numerous wetlands, the unique fishery is reserved for the birds and wildlife that call the natural area home. More than 5 miles of shoreline between the two lakes provide habitat for at least 150 species of birds. The bald eagle and common loon discover prime nesting habitat within the natural area.

From July through September, canoeists may enjoy the setting from their quiet watercraft in the lakes. Throughout the year, 18 miles of trails open the natural area to hikers, bicyclists, and cross-country skiers.

The two lakes, Little Fumee Lake and Fumee Lake, make up the bulk of this natural area. The area came about as a natural extension of what was once city-owned property. Around the turn of the century, the city of Norway needed a safe water source. In 1910 an underground pipeline was completed from Little Fumee Lake, so the lake and its watershed became important to the community. A 500-foot-long canal was dug between this lake and Fumee Lake so that lake levels could be regulated. This life source, the water and its surrounding area, was protected.

Newer well and groundwater systems paved the way for a change. Because the lakes and their surrounding watershed had been preserved in a natural state for many years, residents of Dickinson County voted in 1992 to purchase land to create the Fumee Lake Natural Area.

Directions: To reach this site located between Norway and Quinnesec, take Upper Pine Creek Road about 1 mile north from US 2 to the road in for the east end. It's about .25 mile west to the parking area. To access the west end, take Indiana Mine Road, east of Lake Antoine Park.

Hours Open: Open year-round.

Facilities: Hiking, mountain bicycling, cross-country skiing, and canoeing.

Permits and Rules: No park fee is required. This is a non-motorized area. No fishing or hunting is allowed. Canoeing is permitted from July through September.

For Further Information: Tourism Association of the Dickinson County Area, 600 South Stephenson Avenue, Iron Mountain, MI 49801; 800-236-2447; www.ironmountain.org.

Other Points of Interest

The **Merriman East Pathway** has almost 9.5 miles of trail for hiking and cross-country skiing. The pathway is northeast of Iron Mountain. From Iron Mountain, take M-95 6 miles north to Merriman East Truck Trail; then go east about 7 miles. For more information, contact Crystal Falls Management Unit, 906-875-6622.

Explore 400 feet below the ground in the tunnels and drifts of the **Iron Mountain Iron Mine**. Located on US 2 in Vulcan, the mine is open from June 1 through October 15, from 9:00 a.m. to 5:00 p.m. For more information, call 906-563-8077.

Park Trails

South Ridge Trail (👣, 2.8 miles). The trail starts from the northwest end of the parking area. This trail traverses the south portion of Little Fumee Lake, swings through forest, and skirts along a portion of Fumee Lake.

Fumee Mountain Trail Loop (👣👣👣, 4.4 miles). Start from either parking area. The trail climbs to an elevation of 1,520 feet, rewarding hikers and bicyclists with a view of Fumee Lake.

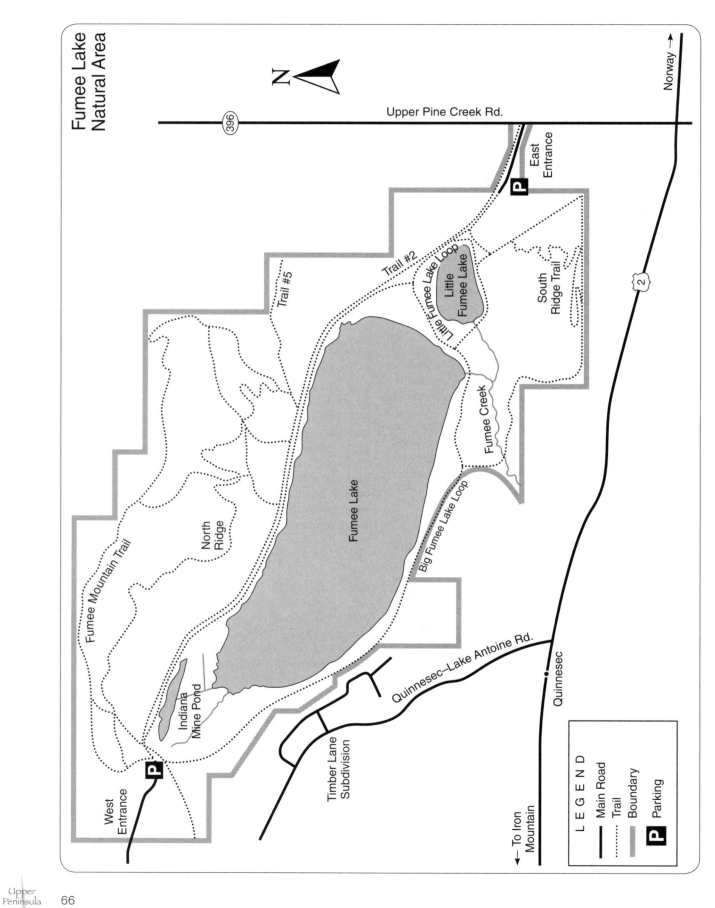

Fumee Lake
Natural Area

N

Upper Pine Creek Rd.

396

2

Norway →

East Entrance

P

Trail #2

Little Fumee Lake Loop

Little Fumee Lake

South Ridge Trail

Trail #5

Fumee Creek

Fumee Lake

North Ridge

Fumee Mountain Trail

Big Fumee Lake Loop

Indiana Mine Pond

West Entrance

P

Quinnesec–Lake Antoine Rd.

Quinnesec

Timber Lane Subdivision

To Iron Mountain →

LEGEND
Main Road
Trail
Boundary
P Parking

Little Fumee Lake Loop

Distance Round-Trip: 1.8 miles
Estimated Hiking Time: 1 hour

Cautions: Mosquitoes and black flies will be a problem in the warmer months. Bring insect repellent. Don't forget your binoculars.

Trail Directions: Start through the gate from the northwest corner of the eastern parking area **[1]**. The dirt road that you follow parallels the abandoned rail corridor that once serviced the Chicago and North Western Railroad. No motorized vehicles are allowed within the natural area, but this corridor, located just outside it, is a snowmobile trail in the winter.

Cattails wave in the breeze along the south side of the trail. On the other side, lily pads float in the channel between the old grade and the trail. Pass under the buzzing high wires, and you arrive at the trail junction where all three loops begin and end (.2 mi.) **[2]**.

Go straight, proceeding alongside the old rail corridor. Little Fumee Lake comes into view through a window of trees (.3 mi.) **[3]**. The small lake remains in view, passing in and out of the windows formed by the trees. Listen for the haunting cry of loons and watch for them as they float and dive in the water.

The trail passes through a dense mix of hardwoods and then veers left before arriving at the junction for the Big Fumee Lake Loop (.5 mi.) **[4]**. Follow the two-track to the left as it cuts through the hardwoods. As you draw nearer to Little Fumee Lake, grasses form the forefront to cattails, which precede the lake. Between the two lakes now, at times you have a view.

A stream crosses between the two lakes at .9 mi. **[5]**. This is also the canoe portage point. Near here, you can take in the big picture—both lakes—until you reach the next junction (1 mi.) **[6]**.

Follow to the left, where you walk between the cattails of Little Fumee Lake and the low, lush wetlands to your right. The trail flanks the lake as it wraps around to the northeast. Along this stretch, you get vivid views of this secluded little lake. Woods encircle the trail, which encircles the lake. A small concrete building, a relic from the natural area's water-provision days, stands strong along the shore (1.3 mi.) **[7]**. Have a seat on the bench to enjoy the scenery.

The trail curves left. You may be tempted to go right to access the South Ridge Trail (1.4 mi.) **[8]**. Follow the trail as it follows the lakeshore and heads under a canopy of trees. Soon afterward, a canoe route appears to your left near the lake. You turn right. Here, another building stands—a log cabin (1.5 mi.) **[9]** built after the Depression by the Works Progress Administration (WPA) as a warming shack for men engaged in other WPA projects. In this area, the project was the installation of 8 miles of gravel roads around the lakes. Turn left. Red pine needles cushion your steps until you arrive at the junction that closes the loop around Little Fumee Lake (1.6 mi.) **[2]**. Turn right and cut again through the wetlands, passing under the high wires and alongside the abandoned rail corridor until you return to the parking area.

1. Trailhead
2. Trail junction
3. Lake view
4. Big Fumee Lake Loop junction
5. Stream
6. Trail junction
7. Concrete building
8. South Ridge Trail junction
9. Log cabin

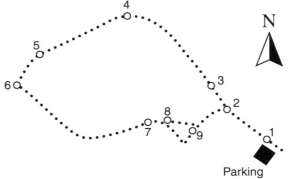

Big Fumee Lake Loop

Distance Round-Trip: 6.2 miles
Estimated Hiking Time: 2.5 to 3.5 hours

Cautions: Mosquitoes and black flies will be a nuisance in the warmer months. Bring insect repellent. Don't forget your binoculars.

Trail Directions: Start from the gate at the northwest corner of the eastern parking area **[1]**. The dirt road that you follow parallels an abandoned railroad corridor. No motorized vehicles are allowed within the natural area, but this corridor, located outside it, serves as a snowmobile trail.

To the south of the trail, moved by the breeze, cattails wave at you from a wetland. Look to the north. Lily pads float in the channel between the old rail grade and the trail. Pass under the buzzing high wires to arrive at a trail junction (.2 mi.) **[2]**. Stay to the right.

Little Fumee Lake comes into view through a window of trees (.3 mi.) **[3]**. Listen for the machine-gun "rat-a-tat-tat" of the kingfisher as it flies away, startled by your approach. The trail then passes a dense mix of hardwoods before arriving at the junction with the Little Fumee Lake Loop (.5 mi.) **[4]**. Follow the two-track to the right. Fumee Lake soon reveals itself, and the trail comes right up to the edge for an intimate viewing (1 mi.) **[5]**. Hiking along Fumee Lake, you will find that it is something of a tease, often hidden behind a veil of trees.

At 1.5 mi., you reach a trail junction and eagle viewing site **[6]**. Now is a great opportunity to use those binoculars that you were told not to forget. Boulders that lie partially buried in the soil along the edge of the water make fine seats. Farther down, the trail is again right up to the edge of the lake (1.8 mi.) **[7]**. The trail then climbs to reach another side path (1.9 mi.) **[8]**. Paper birch logs lie scattered and serve as a border along this walkway.

The trail rolls along past a stand of white cedar, and you find yourself at the lakeshore for your final views from the north side. Have a seat on the well-placed bench (2.3 mi.) **[9]**. You next enter the most recently acquired section of the park.

A barbed-wire fence separates you from the water-filled pit of the old Indiana Mine (2.7 mi.) **[10]**. The mine is now home to beavers, Canada geese, and other wild critters. Follow to the left, past the connector path to the western parking area, and descend to a small park for a chance to sit and drink from a natural spring (3.1 mi.) **[11]**.

White cedars now overshadow the landscape, and small creeks flow along both sides of the old corridor that the trail follows (3.3 mi.) **[12]**.

The south side of the lake is not as accessible as the north side. At 4.3 mi., at a clearing for a utility line, you get a good view of the lake and bluff to the north **[13]**. As you wind your way through the forest on the old road system, stay to the left at the junction with the South Ridge Trail (4.9 mi.) **[14]**. At 5.3 mi., you cross over a culvert with water rushing away from Fumee Lake **[15]**. Stop at the nearby bench and enjoy the view.

Just past the bench, stay left at the junction to reach the drain where canoeists portage between the two lakes (5.5 mi.) **[16]**. At the next junction you find that you have completed your loop of Fumee Lake (5.7 mi.) **[4]**. Turn right and retrace your steps to the parking area.

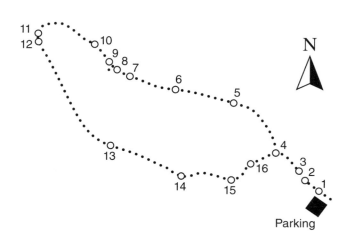

N

1. Trailhead
2. Trail junction
3. Lake view
4. Trail junction
5. Lake view
6. Eagle viewing site
7. Lake view
8. Side path
9. Lake view
10. Indiana Mine Pond
11. Natural spring
12. White cedars
13. Lake view
14. South Ridge Trail junction
15. Culvert
16. Canoe portage

Parking

18. Van Riper State Park

- See evidence of century-old mining ventures.
- Canoe, fish, or boat the Peshekee River and Lake Michigamme.
- Learn about moose.

Park Information

This park claims to be in the heart of moose country. It is. In 1985 and 1987, moose, once common in the region, were reintroduced 6 miles north of the park. (The mining of iron ore and copper and the harvest of timber near the turn of the century had devastated their habitat.) The park has an information kiosk with pictures and information about the reintroduction, a video story of the moose lifts, and maps and boards that show potential viewing areas.

The 1,200-acre park boasts a .5-mile stretch of frontage on Lake Michigamme. Visitors can swim at a sandy beach where lake temperatures are moderate. The park also has 1.5 miles of frontage on the Peshekee River.

The park is bisected by US 41/M-28. The developed part of the park south of the highway has modern and rustic campsites, a boat launch, a beach, a park store, and picnic shelters. North of the highway, the park is barely developed and has only a rustic cabin and group camping. About 4.5 miles of trails cut through rolling, forested woods, along and above the banks of the river, up to ridges with panoramic overviews, and to mine shafts abandoned long ago.

Directions: The park is located about 1.5 miles west of Champion. The entrance to the day-use and camping area is on the south side of US 41/M-28.

Hours Open: The park is open year-round, but the campground is open only from April 25 through November 3.

Facilities: Hiking, swimming, fishing, hunting, boat launch, canoeing, camping (tent and RV), sanitation station, picnicking, and cabins.

Permits and Rules: A park fee is required for motor vehicles ($6 daily, $24 annually for residents; $8 daily, $29 annually for nonresidents).

For Further Information: Van Riper State Park, 851 County Road AKE, Champion, MI 49814; 906-339-4461.

Other Points of Interest

Craig Lake State Park, administered by Van Riper State Park, offers rustic camping, canoeing, and hiking opportunities (see park #20). Access to the park is off an old logging road that is about 8 miles west on US 41/M-28.

The **McCormick Wilderness** (see park #19), a 27-square-mile preserve, serves as partial headwaters for four rivers and offers rocky cliffs, forests, waterfalls, and lakes, all in a rugged wilderness. Those who prefer a remote setting for hiking, backpacking, hunting, fishing, cross-country skiing, or snowshoeing are sure to enjoy this tract. The wilderness is located northwest of Van Riper State Park on County Road 607. For more information, contact Ottawa National Forest, Kenton Ranger District, 4810 E. M-28, Kenton, MI 49967; 906-852-3500.

Park Trails

Four trails, covering about 4.5 miles, may be combined to form various hikes. They may be accessed from the south unit by crossing the highway near the entrance road or from the loop that leads to the rustic cabin in the north section of the park.

Old Wagon Road Trail (🐾, 1.5 miles). This old wagon road starts on the north side of the highway near the south unit and moves through woods. It is a connector for other trails.

Main Trail (🐾🐾, .5 mile). This point-to-point trail is also a connector. It can be picked up from the Old Wagon Road Trail or at the campground trailhead. It climbs to a scenic overlook with a view of a beaver pond.

Miners Loop (🐾🐾, .3 mile). This loop, accessed from the Old Wagon Road Trail or the Main Trail, passes through an old mining area.

River Trail (🐾🐾🐾, 1.5 miles). This loop, accessed from the rustic cabin cul-de-sac, passes through woods, along the Peshekee River, and onto high ridges.

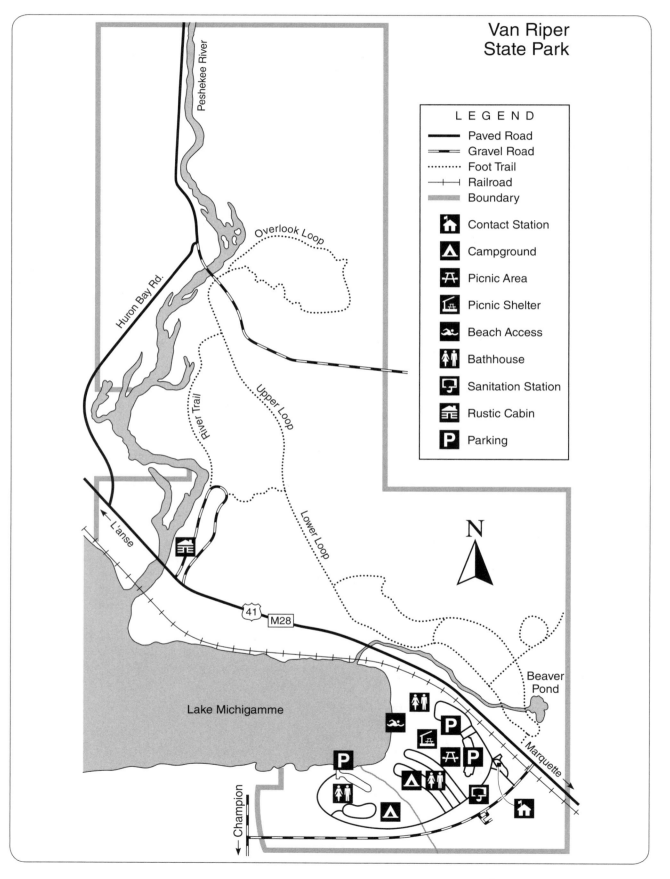

Van Riper
State Park

L E G E N D

——	Paved Road
—▪—	Gravel Road
········	Foot Trail
┼┼┼	Railroad
▬▬	Boundary

- Contact Station
- Campground
- Picnic Area
- Picnic Shelter
- Beach Access
- Bathhouse
- Sanitation Station
- Rustic Cabin
- Parking

Peshekee River

Overlook Loop

Huron Bay Rd.

River Trail

Upper Loop

Lower Loop

L'anse

N

41 M28

Lake Michigamme

Beaver Pond

Marquette

Champion

Upper Loop–River Trail With Old Wagon Road Trail Loop

Distance Round-Trip: 2.1 miles
Estimated Hiking Time: 1.5 to 2 hours

Cautions: Roots and rocks are exposed on the trail. Other areas are wet. The trail includes steep climbs and descents. Proper footgear is a must. Bring insect repellent during the warmer months.

Trail Directions: Start at the northwest end of the cul-de-sac that leads to the cabin north of the highway **[1]**. The trail forks, but don't worry; it merges back together. The left fork takes you to the edge of the river, where a bench invites you to sit and enjoy the sights and sounds of the river.

Cushioned with pine needles, the trail rolls along and then rises gently as it veers left, giving you an overview of the river and grasses below (.1 mi.) **[2]**. Soon the reddish brown, mottled bark of tall red pines surrounds you as you walk the ridge, gazing in duplicate at your surroundings—on a sunny day the reflection off the calm river is striking (.2 mi.) **[3]**.

As the trail nears the river bank, you leave the red pine monoculture and enter a mixed forest where bunchberries line the trail (.3 mi.) **[4]**. The trail ascends through ferns and enters the dark cover of conifers before descending to Old Wagon Road Trail (.5 mi.) **[5]**.

Turn left down this grassy way, pass high wires, and soon cross the small footbridge over a dammed pool. The trail veers left and becomes muddy, a precursor of what is to come. A footbridge keeps your feet dry over the foreshadowed wet stretch (.6 mi.) **[6]**.

At .7 mi., you reach a gravel road and a trail information board **[7]**. Cross the road and roll with the trail before arriving at the Overlook Loop (.8 mi.) **[8]**. Take the right fork and climb the steps up the steep ridge that serves as your lookout platform along this loop. A bench at the top lets you catch your breath. You'll need it—what a view of the Peshekee River and escarpments below!

This platform that you are on is not of flat form. The terrain undulates as you wind through woods and valleys of ferns. At .9 mi., you reach a spur (marked by a boulder) that takes you to an overlook **[9]**. From here you see a rolling green carpet of treetops for miles. Back on the trail, you come to another overlook. Rocks and outcroppings here make great seats. Use them.

The trail winds down steeply. Don't slip on the moss-covered rocks or roots that prevail along this stretch. At 1.3 mi., a large, mossy boulder with a flattop haircut of ferns **[10]** marks your entrance to a wet, rocky adventure lush with vegetation. Maneuver through the mud, the rocks, and the logs set in place over particularly wet spots, and enjoy this short but wild section.

Soon you reach a junction (1.4 mi.) **[11]**. Turn left and climb to a ridge overlooking the Peshekee River. You can see river grasses clumped on small islands. Downstream a steel bridge crosses the river. The views change as you continue to climb up the steep steps alongside a wall of rock. Wind steeply down to close the Overlook Loop (1.4 mi.) **[8]**.

Retrace your footsteps back to the junction with Old Wagon Road Trail (1.7 mi.) **[5]**. Stay straight. Your legs get a break on this gentle stretch. You can pamper them further if you choose at a bench located in a clearing.

After the clearing, enter the cool, dark shade of pines. Luxuriate in this section until you reach the closing spur to this trail at 2 mi. **[12]**. Turn right and enjoy the shade of the mixed forest as you wind your way back to the cul-de-sac where you left your vehicle.

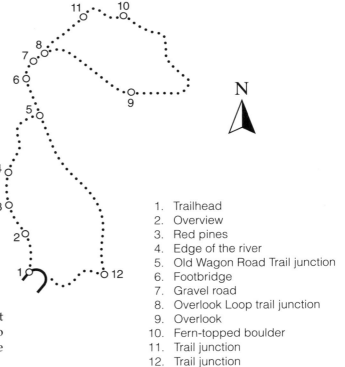

N

1. Trailhead
2. Overview
3. Red pines
4. Edge of the river
5. Old Wagon Road Trail junction
6. Footbridge
7. Gravel road
8. Overlook Loop trail junction
9. Overlook
10. Fern-topped boulder
11. Trail junction
12. Trail junction

Lower Loop—Old Wagon Road Trail, Main Trail, Miners Loop, River Trail Spur

Distance Round-Trip: 2.7 miles
Estimated Hiking Time: 1.5 to 2 hours

Cautions: Roots and rocks are exposed on some sections of the trail. Wear proper footgear. Take insect repellent during the warmer months.

Trail Directions: Start at the northeast end of the cul-de-sac that provides access to the rustic cabin north of US 41/M-28 [1]. A sign points in the direction of Old Wagon Road Trail.

This section of trail, a spur of the River Trail, leads you through a mix of hardwoods and pines to the Old Wagon Road Trail (.1 mi.) [2]. Turn right on the old wagon road and enjoy examples of large white pine, maple, and paper birch as you stroll down this old thoroughfare. At .4 mi., a bench waits for you at the junction with the Main Trail [3]. Stay right and pass a second junction with a bench and the first of many interpretive signs along the hike (.7 mi.) [4]. Swing left and enjoy the sounds of a babbling brook as it competes with the nearby highway for your attention.

Next, enjoy the aromatic pine as you approach the junction with the new Miners Loop (.9 mi.) [5]. Stay to the right and skirt a wetland (1 mi.) [6], just before arriving at the park's trail map board in an opening near the highway (1.1 mi.) [7]. This is the trailhead for people who camp at the park and the end of your hike on the Old Wagon Road Trail.

Proceed past the signboard to reenter the woods on a footpath, which is the Main Trail. Swing left, climb over a couple of small ridges, turn right, and climb steeply onto a ridge above Beaver Pond. Turn left to follow the ridge and emerge from the trees for a scenic overlook of the pond below (1.2 mi.) [8].

Leaving the ridge, you walk through lush ferns that take advantage of the additional light coming through a hole in the forest canopy. Then cross a footbridge over a stream that drains Beaver Pond (1.3 mi.) [9]. You pass several pits before turning right at the junction with the Miners Loop (1.4 mi.) [10]. Stay right where the trail splits and loop to the left. Eventually, you walk on an old corridor now lined by pine trees and arrive at a sign directing you to the left (1.5 mi.) [11]. You soon pass a small stone foundation, a relic from the mining that occurred in the area almost 100 years ago. Iron ore was first discovered in the Lake Superior region only a few miles east of here in 1845.

Proceeding past a pit in the center of a small open area, the trail swings left past a bench and descends back to the junction with the Main Trail. Turn right and descend to cross a footbridge (1.7 mi.) [12]. At 1.9 mi., after you have climbed and emerged into an open area, the view of Lake Michigamme is obscured by trees. At the junction, you have the option of taking the Lower Trail to the old wagon road or continuing right to complete the Main Trail (2 mi.) [13].

Staying right, you pass more pits before descending sharply to cross a footbridge (2.1 mi.) [14]. The trail then swings left and climbs up from the small stream. Follow it back to the Old Wagon Road Trail (2.3 mi.) [2]. From here, retrace your steps right to the River Trail spur that returns you to the parking area.

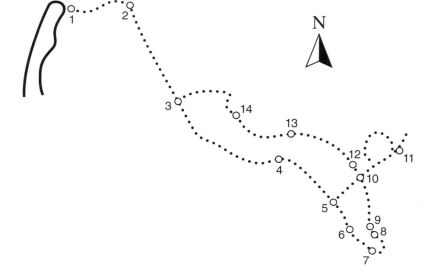

1. Trailhead
2. Old Wagon Road Trail junction
3. Bench and trail junction
4. Interpretive sign
5. Miners Loop junction
6. Wetland
7. Map board
8. Scenic overlook
9. Footbridge
10. Miners Loop junction
11. Mine pit
12. Footbridge
13. Lower Trail junction
14. Footbridge

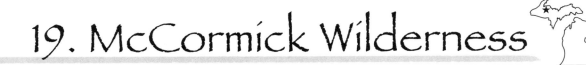

- Find solitude in the rugged yet peaceful wilderness.
- Discover varied landscapes—rocky cliffs, swamps, pristine lakes, islands, waterfalls, northern woods.
- Track moose whose release site was in the immediate area.

Park Information

The 16,850-acre McCormick Wilderness area is a part of the Ottawa National Forest. It offers rugged outdoor enthusiasts almost 27 square miles of glacially shaped landscape containing northern hardwoods, lowland conifers, rocky cliffs, swamps, streams, rivers, waterfalls, lakes, and plenty of wildlife.

Although the area was logged in the early 1900s, regenerated trees have been left undisturbed for at least 80 years. Patches of white pine somehow survived. Enthusiasts with acute survival skills may seek them out to view what few people have seen since before the logging era.

The wilderness serves as the divide between the Lake Michigan and Lake Superior watersheds. It also serves as partial headwaters for four rivers—Huron, Yellow Dog, Dead, and Peshekee—and cradles 18 lakes. Waterfalls are secretly tucked away on Yellow Dog River. A compass, boots, a good map, a GPS unit, and experience in orienteering can help you unearth these secrets.

This rugged, serene treat was once the vacation retreat of the McCormicks, descendants of Cyrus H. McCormick, who invented the reaping machine. Buildings of the estate once stood near White Deer Lake. It was the wish of the tract's last owner, Gordon McCormick, to donate the estate to the U.S. Forest Service upon his death, which occurred in 1967. In 1987 the unique property became part of the National Wilderness Preservation System.

Because this is a wilderness, few improvements are present. A parking area is located off County Road 607. An information board stands before a gated bridge, which forms part of the old road that once led to the estate on White Deer Lake. This 3-mile road and a portion of the North Country Trail are the only somewhat improved foot trails. Although over 100 miles of trails once weaved through the site in its heyday as a vacation retreat, these are overgrown.

One, the Bentley, weaves through the tract, but it is not maintained and is difficult to find in many places. The joy offered by this tract is for experienced hikers who like blazing their own trails.

In 1985 and 1987, moose were reintroduced near the wilderness. The moose were lifted by helicopter from the Algonquin Provincial Park in Ontario, Canada, carted by truck, and then dropped off nearby; 29 were released in 1985, and 30 were released in 1987. By 1995 their numbers were estimated to be about 378.

Directions: The park is located about 12 miles north of Champion. Take US 41/M-28 about 2 miles west of Champion to County Road 607. Take this road 9.3 miles north to the parking area, which is accessed by a drive on the east side of the road.

Hours Open: Open year-round, but Country Road 607 is not plowed in winter.

Facilities: Hiking, cross-country skiing, snowshoeing, fishing, hunting, canoeing, and camping (backcountry).

Permits and Rules: Although no fee is required for backcountry camping, you should fill out a registration card containing information about your intentions and deposit it in a container by the information board. Motorized or mechanized vehicles or equipment are not allowed. Leave no trace. Carry out what you carry in. Do not cut down live trees or other plants.

For Further Information: McCormick Wilderness, Ottawa National Forest, Kenton Ranger District, 4810 E. M-28, Kenton, MI 49967; 906-852-3500.

Other Points of Interest

Van Riper State Park (see park #18) provides modern camping facilities, a boat launch and swimming beach on Lake Michigamme, picnic facilities, and hiking trails. Here visitors can also look at a kiosk of information about the moose lifts. Contact Van Riper State Park, 851 County Road AKE, Champion, MI 49814; 906-339-4461.

Craig Lake State Park (see park #20), administered by Van Riper State Park, offers rustic camping, canoeing, and hiking opportunities. Access to the park is off an old logging road that is about 8 miles west on US 41/M-28.

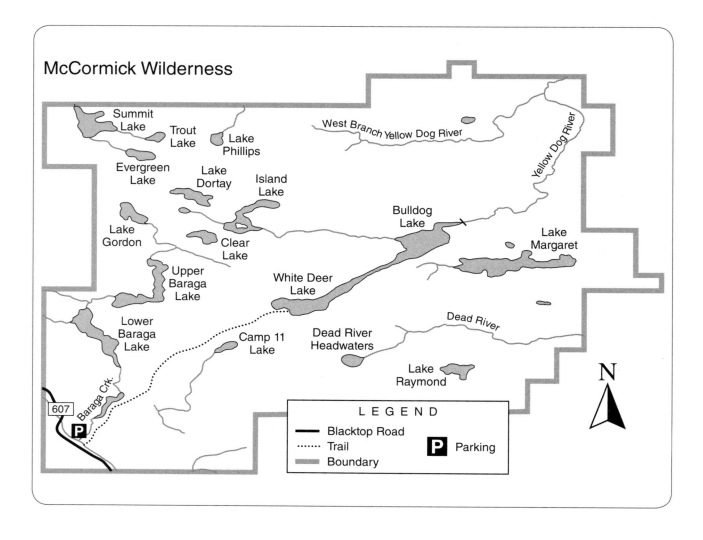

McCormick Wilderness

Summit Lake

Trout Lake

Lake Phillips

West Branch Yellow Dog River

Yellow Dog River

Evergreen Lake

Lake Dortay

Island Lake

Bulldog Lake

Lake Margaret

Lake Gordon

Clear Lake

Upper Baraga Lake

White Deer Lake

Dead River

Lower Baraga Lake

Camp 11 Lake

Dead River Headwaters

Lake Raymond

Baraga Crk.

607

P

N

LEGEND

— Blacktop Road

...... Trail

P Parking

▬ Boundary

White Deer Lake

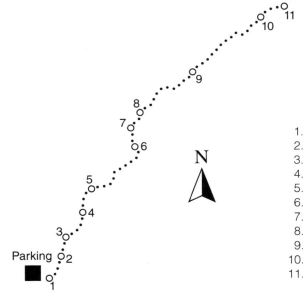 **Distance Round-Trip:** 6.6 miles
Estimated Hiking Time: 2 to 3 hours

Cautions: The trail is not marked, so follow the worn path carefully. Some sections are prone to flooding; wear appropriate footgear. At times you may need to maneuver over fallen trees. Take along insect repellent during the warmer months.

Trail Directions: Start by crossing the bridge over the Peshekee River next to the information board on the east side of the small parking area **[1]**. The trail, which follows the old access road to White Deer Lake where the McCormick estate once stood, parallels pristine Baraga Creek. You may hear the creek before you see it, but look for the beaver dam where the creek first comes into view on your left (.3 mi.) **[2]**.

Follow the trail to the right as it guides you around a small rock outcrop (.4 mi.) **[3]**, which hints at things to come. Having descended to cross a small stream, you soon arrive alongside the rocky cliffs of an escarpment (.6 mi.) **[4]**.

As if the cliffs themselves aren't sufficiently awesome, the creek reappears to complete the scene. You now walk on a trail nestled on a strip of land that is sandwiched between the flowing waters of Baraga Creek and the steadfast rock of the escarpment (.7 mi.) **[5]**. Hop on the rocks by the creek and take in the view.

You leave the creek and cliffs behind as you continue along the trail to the lake. You hike 1.2 mi. before you enter mature woods **[6]**. Enjoy the shade as you pass several large white pines before the trail makes what will be the steepest climb on the walk to the lake (1.3 mi.) **[7]**.

At 1.4 mi., the trail passes between a stream and an escarpment. As the stream opens to a large, grassy wetland, the trail hugs the escarpment and swings around the edge of the wetland **[8]**. This section of the trail is prone to flooding, so watch your step. At 2.1 mi., cattails surprise you **[9]**.

Snaking over a series of ridges, the trail finally emerges into the meadow that is slowly reclaiming the foundations of the McCormick estate (3.2 mi.) **[10]**.

Walk across this meadow and descend to the lake (3.3 mi.) **[11]**. Just offshore stands the island that once supported the estate's lodge. Stay and enjoy the serenity of the wilderness. Have a picnic. After all, you have a 3.3 mi. hike back to your vehicle.

N

1. Trailhead
2. Baraga Creek
3. Rock outcrop
4. Escarpment
5. Trail between creek and escarpment
6. Shaded trail
7. Steepest climb
8. Wetland
9. Cattails
10. Meadow
11. White Deer Lake

Parking

20. Craig Lake State Park

- Accept the challenges posed by this remote, rugged, primitive state park.
- Canoe, fish, or hike within this serene wilderness.
- Meet moose. Maybe.

Park Information

This park may not get much of a workout, but you and your vehicle will. Access to this wilderness area is over old logging roads that put your shocks to the test.

The only improvements in the park consist of two rugged cabins, a water pump, a yurt south of Teddy Lake, and outhouses near Craig Lake. Camping is for backpackers only; you may backcountry camp anywhere within the park.

Craig Lake State Park is primitive but rugged and serene. If you are willing to travel the 7.5 miles over beat-up roads to a park with minimal facilities, and are willing to haul your canoe, gear, or self over this non-motorized wilderness, then pristine lakes, quiet pine-perfumed forests, sparkling Peshekee River waters, and perhaps a chance meeting with a moose await you. Although two marked trails weave around Craig Lake for 8 miles of secure hiking, backcountry hiking potential throughout the park is limitless. Parts of the marked trail system are incorporated into the North Country Trail.

This is moose country. In 1985 and 1987, moose, once common in the region until the mining of iron ore and copper and the harvesting of timber devastated their habitat, were reintroduced near the park. The moose were lifted by helicopter from the Algonquin Provincial Park in Ontario, Canada, and dropped off about 5 miles from here.

Marked trails assist you over about 8 miles of terrain, but almost 7,000 acres are available for backcountry exploration. Eight lakes provide fishing and boating opportunities; three of these are connected by portages for broadened canoeing experiences.

Directions: The park is located about 10 miles west of Champion. The access road is about 8 miles west of the entrance to Van Riper State Park. Van Riper State Park administers Craig Lake State Park. Stop at Van Riper and pick up a map (and ask about the current road conditions to Craig Lake). Take US 41/M-28 about 8 miles west of Van Riper to Nelligan Road. This road is about .7 mile west of a gas station. Take this road about 2.7 miles north to Craig Lake Road (again not marked; turn left as shown on the map that you picked up at Van Riper) and take this corrugated road to the parking lot.

Hours Open: The park is open year-round. Cabins are available from May 15 through October 15 each year.

Facilities: Hiking, fishing, hunting, canoeing, camping (backcountry), and cabins.

Permits and Rules: A park fee is required for motor vehicles ($6 daily, $24 annually for residents; $8 daily, $29 annually for nonresidents). Camping is on a self-registration basis. Cabin users must check in at Van Riper State Park. You may backcountry camp as long as you set up camp at least 150 feet away from water and stay away from the immediate area of the cabins. No motors are allowed except on Lake Keewaydin. No live bait may be used for fishing. Carry out what you carry in.

For Further Information: Van Riper State Park, 851 County Road AKE, Champion, MI 49814; 906-339-4461.

Other Points of Interest

Van Riper State Park (see park #18) provides modern camping facilities, a boat launch and swimming beach on Lake Michigamme, picnic facilities, and hiking trails. A kiosk of information about the moose lifts is set up there.

The **McCormick Wilderness** (see park #19) is a 27-square-mile preserve that serves as the divide between the Lake Michigan and Lake Superior watersheds. In addition, it offers rocky cliffs, forests, waterfalls, and lakes, all in a rugged wilderness. The wilderness is located east of Craig Lake State Park on County Road 607. For more information, contact Ottawa National Forest, Kenton Ranger District, 4810 E. M-28, Kenton, MI 49967; 906-852-3500.

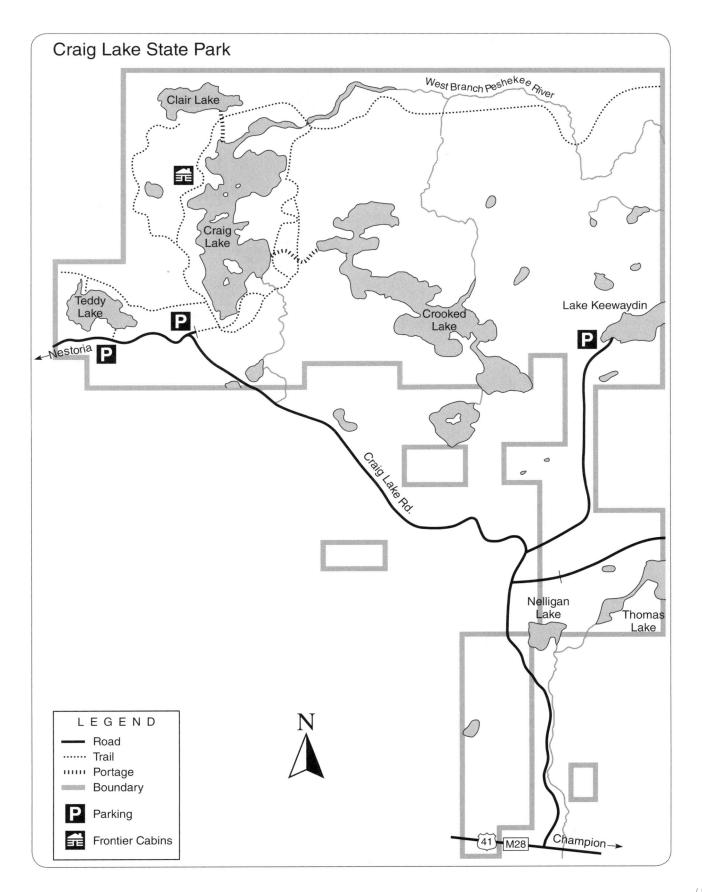

Craig Lake State Park

LEGEND

— Road
······ Trail
ıııııı Portage
█ Boundary
P Parking
🏚 Frontier Cabins

N

Crooked Lake Trail

Distance Round-Trip: 4 miles
Estimated Hiking Time: 2 to 2.5 hours

Cautions: Roots and rocks are found on the trail, and some areas are wet. Wear proper footgear. Take along insect repellent in the warmer months.

Trail Directions: The trail starts at the map board located at the east end of the Craig Lake parking lot **[1]**. Step through the gate and descend a remnant service road that flanks rolling hills, passes through mixed hardwoods, and proceeds past a bowl-shaped pool strewn with logs to arrive at the posted junction (.2 mi.) **[2]**.

Turn right and soon pass the spur that leads to campsites on Craig Lake. The trail rolls and snakes through hilly terrain, passing a moss-covered boulder before you notice a steep hill to your right. More noticeable is what is in front of the hill. A tree once grew on the huge boulder; now the root remnants cling to the boulder like huge talons of a bird of prey (.4 mi.) **[3]**.

Pass the other end of the campsite spur before crossing the footbridge (.8 mi.) **[4]**. The trail swings left to another junction (.9 mi.) **[5]**. Go right along the grassy trail as it passes the rigid, gray ghosts of trees; then duck under cover of pines.

At 1.1 mi., the portage between Crooked and Craig lakes crosses the trail **[6]**. Turn right and transport yourself over to Crooked Lake (1.3 mi.) **[7]**. The quiet lake enveloped with pines, boulders, and rock escarpments will have you whispering, "This is why I come to the wilderness." Enjoy the tranquility before returning to the trail (1.5 mi.).

Turn right and roll up and down the trail that is tightly embraced by pines. Climb up the trail, round the bend to the left past scattered boulders, and wind down to the junction (1.9 mi.) **[8]**. Turn left, pass through a muddy area, and stop at the large boulder (2 mi.) **[9]**. Now look up the trail at the steep hill that you will climb. Climb. The top of the hill is punctuated by a dead tree that has been pounded by woodpeckers. The trail rolls over a few small ridges and then begins a gradual descent that culminates where fallen trees line the trail (2.2 mi.) **[10]**.

Continue along, dipping in and out of the cool cover of trees. Descend sharply as the trail bends right. It rolls along through pine before reaching an area where many trees and logs are strewn about (2.3 mi.) **[11]**. Look closely for beaver activity. Soon you reach the portage. Turn right and stroll the couple of hundred feet to Craig Lake (2.4 mi.) **[12]**.

Back on the trail, cross a footbridge before arriving at the junction that closes the Crooked Lake loop

(2.8 mi.) **[5]**. Retrace your steps from earlier, over the footbridge **[4]**, and stop at the campsite spur (3 mi.) **[13]**. You can either continue straight or turn right for a hike along the lake. Turn right, winding through hardwoods until you get to the campsite trail junction (3.2 mi.) **[14]**. The spur continues left, and you hike along a ridge overlooking the lake. A steep hill is your backdrop to the left.

At 3.5 mi., follow the sharp bend to the right over a boardwalk **[15]**. Roll along and then descend to the main trail (3.8 mi.) **[16]**. Turn right and retrace your steps to the parking lot.

1. Trailhead
2. Trail junction
3. Roots on boulder
4. Footbridge
5. Trail junction
6. Canoe portage
7. Crooked Lake
8. Trail junction
9. Large boulder
10. Fallen trees
11. Forest massacre
12. Craig Lake
13. Campsite spur
14. Campsite trail junction
15. Boardwalk
16. Main trail junction

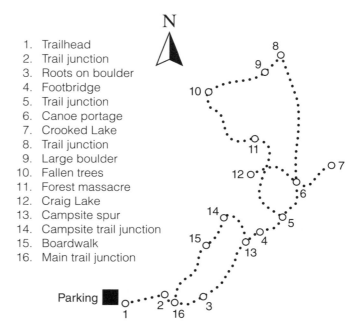

Craig Lake Trail

Distance Round-Trip: 6 miles
Estimated Hiking Time: 3 to 3.5 hours

Cautions: Roots and rocks are found on the trail, and some areas are wet. Wear proper footgear. Insect repellent is necessary during the warmer months.

Trail Directions: Start at the gate on the east end of the small parking area for Craig Lake **[1]**. Follow the orange diamond-shaped markers as you step out on an access road that doubles as the trail. Stay to the right at the first trail junction (.2 mi.) **[2]**, and again as you pass the two footpaths (.3 mi.) and (.7 mi.) that loop to the sandy beach campsites **[3]**. When you cross a footbridge (.8 mi.) **[4]**, the trail leaves the access road behind and becomes more of a footpath. Watch out for roots and rocks. Shortly the trail swings left and you reach a posted trail junction (.9 mi.) **[5]**. Go left.

At 1 mi., you pass a large white pine on the left **[6]** before descending into maples. Cross over a footbridge and pass a number of fallen trees before reaching the canoe portage between Craig and Crooked lakes (1.2 mi.) **[7]**. Craig Lake is only a couple of hundred feet down the portage and is well worth a peek. Otherwise, cross the well-worn portage and veer right to pass through another area of fallen trees. Note the evidence of beaver activity.

Cross a series of small ridges before descending sharply. Tread through a muddy stretch before you come to the second junction with the Crooked Lake Trail (1.6 mi.) **[8]**. Turn left. At 1.8 mi., the trail climbs sharply alongside trees that are perched on boulders, their roots gripping the rocks like talons of a predatory bird grasping its prey **[9]**. This is your cue that you are about to enter Mother Nature's rock garden. Rocks and boulders are strewn about erratically.

After the trail levels off, veer left near the large hemlock trees and begin a steep descent. Soon you reach a wet area; you cross it on moss-covered rocks and then swing right in a valley to cross it again (1.9 mi.) **[10]**. The trail climbs and then swings left to where the forest floor undulates with rocks, boulders, and fallen trees. Veering left again, the trail begins a steep descent near a large, rotting stump; it bottoms out in a valley of giant, moss-covered boulders (2.2 mi.) **[11]**.

Climbing again, you are teased by views of the lake through the trees. Listen for the call of the loon. As you approach a steep rock outcropping, the trail cuts sharply to the right. Thus you avoid another climb by crossing through a wet area on more moss-covered rocks. The trail veers left and descends before climbing through pine trees and swinging around the low side of a ridge, which directs you to a trail marker. Turn left and cross the West Branch Peshekee River on a single-log bridge (2.7 mi.) **[12]**.

Climbing away from the river, the trail crosses a series of rock outcroppings. At 3.4 mi., the effort expended to hike this section is rewarded when a steep climb takes you to a scenic overlook with a view of the lake **[13]**. Take a break here and enjoy the solitude.

At 3.6 mi., cross the portage between Craig and Clair lakes **[14]**. A short walk takes you over to Craig Lake. Go and enjoy it before continuing. Then climb to another scenic overview of the lake.

When you reach the rustic cabins, look for the road that doubles as the trail (4.3 mi.) **[15]**. After passing the North Country Trail junction (5.6 mi.) **[16]**, you soon reach the Craig Lake State Park camping area (5.7 mi.) **[17]**. From here, you have just a short hike back to where you parked.

1. Trailhead
2. Trail junction
3. Campsite trail junction
4. Footbridge
5. Trail junction
6. White pine
7. Canoe portage
8. Trail junction
9. Roots on boulders
10. Wet area
11. Moss-covered boulders
12. Single-log bridge
13. Scenic overlook
14. Canoe portage
15. Rustic cabins
16. North Country Trail junction
17. Camping area

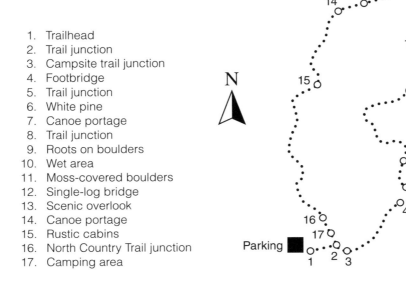

- Follow in the footprints of moose and wolf.
- Listen to the haunting cry of the loon.
- Enjoy a colorful sunset or a dazzling display of aurora borealis.

Park Information

Northwest Lake Superior is home to an 894-square-mile wilderness archipelago that features a 45-mile-by-9-mile island with unspoiled forests, rugged coast, and wild creatures. Isle Royale, a designated U.S. Biosphere Reserve, is the largest of Michigan's 14 wildernesses.

Over 165 miles of trails meander over the island, providing hiking opportunities that range considerably in difficulty. Most hikers strap on a pack and explore the island for days, spending the night gazing up at stars through unpolluted sky from one of 36 campgrounds.

Located 56 miles from Copper Harbor, the park is isolated. Its primitive nature and roadless backcountry prove challenging. Getting there is a challenge as well. Access the island by boat or seaplane. After visitors reach the island, they paddle the inland waterways, hike the trails, explore the coast, or dive to investigate shipwrecks.

No deer or bear inhabit the island, but you are likely to find beaver, otter, red squirrel, red fox, loon, eagle, and osprey. The crown jewels are the wolves and the moose—the subjects of the world's longest continuous study of a predator and its prey. Moose came to the island in the early 1900s; wolves crossed an ice bridge from Canada in the winter of 1948-49.

With isolation come other challenges. Potable water is available only on the east and west ends, at Windigo and Rock Harbor. Here you will also find camp stores, showers, modern restrooms, coin laundries, and visitor centers. The challenges of the park are well worth the effort. Arrange a day trip if you can, but to experience the island fully, plan to stay overnight.

Directions: The island is located in northwest Lake Superior. Arrange for ferry service in Copper Harbor or Houghton, Michigan, or in Grand Portage, Minnesota. You can also board a seaplane from Houghton.

Hours Open: Mid-April through mid-October.

Facilities: Hiking, interpretive trails, fishing, boating, canoeing, kayaking, camping, diving, and lodging.

Permits and Rules: For those 12 and over, the fee is $4 per day. This fee covers camping as well. An annual permit is $50 per person. For private boaters, a seasonal pass that includes all persons on board is $150. Leave no trace, plan ahead, stay on established trails, dispose of waste properly, leave what you find, minimize campfire impacts, and respect wildlife. Wheeled vehicles and pets are not permitted.

For Further Information: National Park Service, Isle Royale National Park, 800 E. Lakeshore Drive, Houghton, MI 49931; 906-482-0984; www.nps.gov/isro. Arrange ferry service from Houghton on *Ranger III* here as well. From Copper Harbor, arrange passage on *Isle Royale Queen IV* from the Isle Royale Line, Isle Royale Line Waterfront Landing, Copper Harbor, MI 49918; 906-289-4437; www.isleroyale.com. From Grand Portage, Minnesota, contact Grand Portage–Isle Royale Transportation Line, P.O. Box 10529, White Bear Lake, MN 55110; 218-475-0024 or 651-653-5872; www.grand-isle-royale.com.

Other Points of Interest

Rock Harbor Lodge and Marina offers accommodations on the island ranging from rooms in lodges to studio-type housekeeping cottages, and they provide a dining room and a grill. The marina rents boats, canoes, kayaks, and slips. You can rent a water taxi (but it will cost you). Contact Rock Harbor Lodge, Isle Royale National Park, P.O. Box 605, Houghton, MI 49931; 906-337-4993; www.rockharborlodge.com.

Park Trails

More than 165 miles of trails weave through the wilderness; most connect to form days-long hiking experiences. Paddle over to some of the smaller islands for a different adventure.

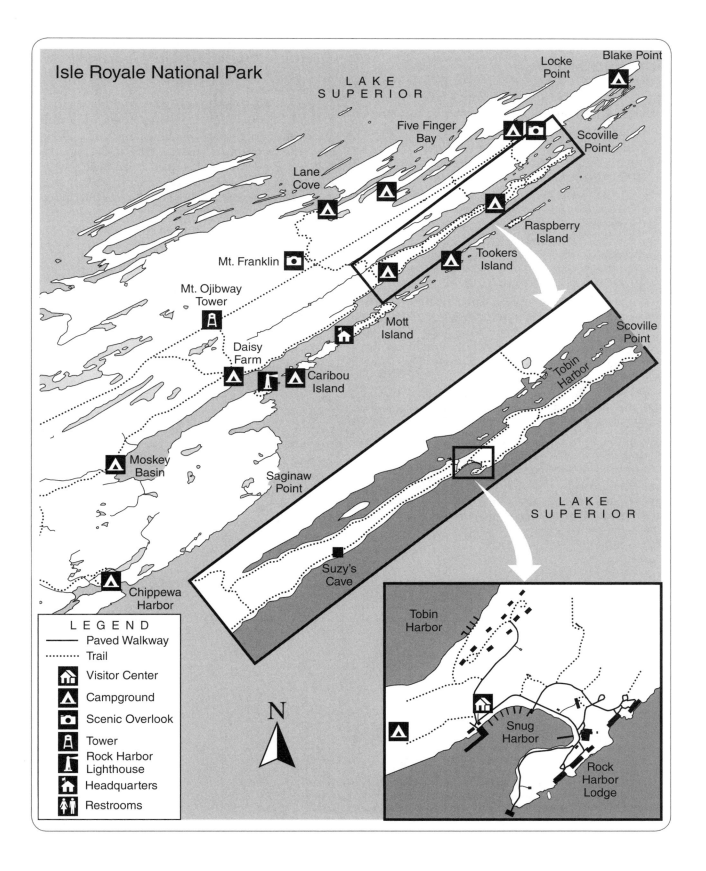

Isle Royale National Park

LAKE SUPERIOR

Locke Point

Blake Point

Five Finger Bay

Scoville Point

Lane Cove

Raspberry Island

Mt. Franklin

Tookers Island

Mt. Ojibway Tower

Mott Island

Scoville Point

Tobin Harbor

Daisy Farm

Caribou Island

Moskey Basin

Saginaw Point

LAKE SUPERIOR

Suzy's Cave

Chippewa Harbor

LEGEND
— Paved Walkway
.... Trail
Visitor Center
Campground
Scenic Overlook
Tower
Rock Harbor Lighthouse
Headquarters
Restrooms

N

Tobin Harbor

Snug Harbor

Rock Harbor Lodge

Stoll Memorial Trail to Scoville Point

Distance Round-Trip: 4 miles
Estimated Hiking Time: 1.5 to 2 hours

Cautions: Roots crop up along the trail. At times you walk along sheer rock walls, sometimes near edges with sharp drops. Wear proper footgear. Take insect repellent. Watch your time if you need to get back for the ferry. Watch for moose.

Trail Directions: Follow the wide road around the harbor east from the visitor center about .2 mi. Turn left at the trail in front of the grill and go about .1 mi. Head northeast down the pine trail that takes you through boreal forest along a cold, rocky shore **[1]**. Stay right where the trail splits.

As you walk a rocky ridge, Raspberry Island comes into view (.1 mi.) **[2]**. Soon a footbridge carries you over a small stream. Descend to an open view of islands, just a few of the over 400 that make up the archipelago. Read the interpretive board or rest on the bench there (.2 mi.) **[3]**.

A series of boardwalks guides you past marsh marigold and skunk cabbage. Roots and rocks compete to trip you before you swing right and climb onto a rocky overlook (.6 mi.) **[4]**. Enjoy the view before pressing on.

More interpretive boards educate you. One exhibits three small, shallow pits that were aboriginal copper mines (.7 mi.) **[5]**. You soon come to a spur to the shore. Go there and sit on the bench to marvel at the orange, lichen-covered islands.

Back on the trail you soon come to a junction. A left turn loops back for a shorter walk (not a bad idea if you need to rush for the ferry), but the spectacular part of the trail is yet to come. Go right to enter a designated wilderness.

The trail rolls and takes you down over other boardwalks and around rocks, giving you differing perspectives of the lichen-stained islands. Soon you walk along a rocky ridge mottled with lichen-covered cobblestones—a beach from the past when lake levels were higher. You reach a junction (1.4 mi.) **[6]**. Go right and climb onto the rock ridge for a clear vista of Lake Superior. Continue along this ridge.

Wind left off the rocks, only to climb back onto a rocky escarpment for more views of the lake and islands. You reach a plaque at 2 mi. that dedicates the Albert Stoll Jr. Memorial Trail **[7]**. From here you are a few hundred feet from Scoville Point. What a view! If you brought a lunch, you will find no better place to enjoy it before you turn back

Scramble over the rocks back to the junction (2.6 mi.) **[6]**. Follow to the right for a different route back and do a series of climbs. You begin to see Tobin Harbor at about 2.8 mi. **[8]**. The hike is gentler through here. Pass another junction and descend down to the water of Tobin Harbor (3.2 mi.) **[9]**. Rest on the bench in quiet contemplation as you overlook Tobin Harbor (3.4 mi.) **[10]**.

Swing away from the harbor and onto a ridge (3.5 mi.) **[11]**. Cross over piping before you reach the Smithwick Mine Site—one of the oldest on the island (3.9 mi.) **[12]**. At 4 mi., you are back to the blacktop road that loops the harbor.

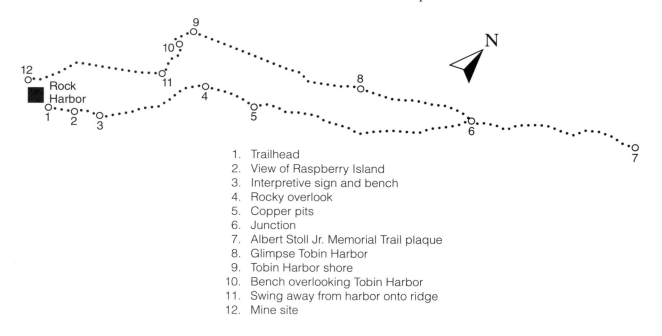

1. Trailhead
2. View of Raspberry Island
3. Interpretive sign and bench
4. Rocky overlook
5. Copper pits
6. Junction
7. Albert Stoll Jr. Memorial Trail plaque
8. Glimpse Tobin Harbor
9. Tobin Harbor shore
10. Bench overlooking Tobin Harbor
11. Swing away from harbor onto ridge
12. Mine site

Rock Harbor, Suzy's Cave, Tobin Harbor

Distance Round-Trip: 3.8 miles
Estimated Hiking Time: 2 to 2.5 hours

Cautions: Roots and rocks are found on the trail. At times you walk along sheer rock. Wear proper footgear and take care. Take insect repellent in the warmer months. Watch your time if you need to get back for the ferry. Watch for moose.

Trail Directions: Start just north of the Rock Harbor Visitor Center **[1]**. This trail starts or ends many of the longer hikes taken by backpackers as they set off for days of adventure. Set out for one of your own. Head west past park cottages, lean-tos, and the camp area (.2 mi.) to hike with the big packs **[2]**.

The rocky trail heads past pines draped with bearded moss. Thimbleberries crowd the trail. It winds and rolls, teasing you with views of the harbor. At .6 mi., step down the basalt stairs and experience the sights and sounds of the harbor before heading inland **[3]**. The trail brings you out again for a view of lichen-flecked islands and colorful canoes and kayaks in the harbor.

Pine needles soften your steps, and you have an open view of the rocky shore (.8 mi.) **[4]**. In about .2 mi. you are back on rock, soon crossing a footbridge (1 mi.) **[5]**. Cedar and spruce perfume the air. The trail is now a narrow, worn path along rock escarpment that winds and rolls through trees, over planks, and past boulders. A green wall of rock warns you that the junction for Suzy's Cave is not far off (1.8 mi.) **[6]**. An open view of the lake is at your side. Take a break on large boulders and consider the view.

After your respite, head right and up the escarpment. You have less than .1 mi. to go to reach Suzy's Cave. The cave was cut when Lake Superior's water levels were much higher. Explore it before wrapping around it and up and along a goatlike trail to arrive at the junction for Tobin Harbor Trail (2 mi.) **[7]**.

Turn right along this quieter, more contemplative trail. It follows a small, narrow harbor with its own small islands. Listen for loons as you walk along the water. At 2.2 mi., turn away from the water and into pines **[8]**. The trail climbs and descends along a ridge above the water where you have more rocks to contend with. The trail bottoms out at 3 mi., and you get an open view of the harbor **[9]**.

Start up a relatively steep climb (3.1 mi.) **[10]** and again walk a ridge above the water through scented pines. Steal peeks of the harbor before you start your descent from the ridge (3.4 mi.) **[11]** and roll through pines and thimbleberries. Climb over one more rock escarpment before arriving at a junction (3.7 mi.) **[12]**. Left goes to the seaplane dock; right takes you to the visitor center. Go right. You soon reach an asphalt path. Turn right here, which takes you back where you started.

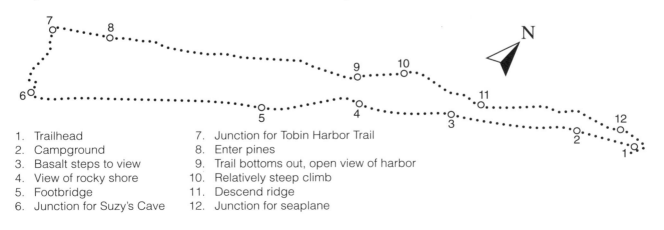

1. Trailhead
2. Campground
3. Basalt steps to view
4. View of rocky shore
5. Footbridge
6. Junction for Suzy's Cave
7. Junction for Tobin Harbor Trail
8. Enter pines
9. Trail bottoms out, open view of harbor
10. Relatively steep climb
11. Descend ridge
12. Junction for seaplane

- Find solitude in the wilderness for a day or plan to stay at a designated wilderness campsite.
- Hike through old-growth forests and along lakeshores.
- Canoe the pristine lakes.

Park Information

Part of the Ottawa National Forest, this 18,327-acre wilderness provides outstanding opportunities for outdoors enthusiasts. Combined with the Sylvania Recreation Area, which provides campgrounds and a lake that may be reached by vehicle, over 21,000 acres of pristine beauty await you.

More than 25 miles of trails and portages provide access to old-growth forests and to 34 named lakes. In keeping with its designation, this place is not to be controlled or modified by humans. Such a place offers outstanding opportunities for solitude and primitive recreation experiences, including wilderness camping, canoeing, fishing, and cross-country skiing. If you do not stay at one of the 48 auto-accessible camping sites, be prepared to be self-sufficient in this land of deer, bear, coyote, and loon.

The scars of past human interventions are fading. Buildings, roads, and trail markings will be allowed to revert to a wild state.

In 1895 A.D. Johnston bought 80 acres near Clark Lake with the intent of cutting the mature pines. Finding them too beautiful to cut, he made the tract his retreat. Friends and acquaintances found the area impressive, and they too bought land. Collectively, they formed the Sylvania Club. This jewel was well preserved by the time the U.S. Forest Service purchased it in 1967. It was designated a federal wilderness 20 years later.

Directions: From Watersmeet, go west on US 2 for about 4 miles to County Road 535. Turn south (left) and go about 4 miles to the entrance.

Hours Open: Open year-round.

Facilities: Hiking, cross-country skiing, swimming, fishing, hunting, boat launch, camping (tent and backcountry), and picnicking.

Permits and Rules: Visitors are required to register. Campers must register in person at the main entrance station between May 15 and September 30. All vehicles must have a facility pass. Passes are $5 daily or $20 annually. Motorized and mechanized vehicles or equipment are not allowed. Leave no trace. Carry out what you carry in and do not disturb live vegetation. Pets must be on a 6-foot leash. Fires are allowed in fire rings only; drown fires with water before leaving. Because of nesting loons, islands are off limits from ice-off to July 15.

For Further Information: Ottawa Visitor Center, Watersmeet, MI 49969; 906-358-4724. For campsite reservations, call 877-444-6777 or go online at www.recreation.gov. You may also contact the Watersmeet Ranger Station, Ottawa National Forest, Old US 2, P.O. Box 276, Watersmeet, MI 49969; 906-358-4551.

Other Points of Interest

The **Ottawa Visitor Center**, located on the corner of US 2 and US 45, has exhibits, interpretive materials, slide shows, and nature programs. For more information, contact Ottawa Visitor Center, Ottawa National Forest, Watersmeet, MI 49969; 906-358-4724.

Park Trails

More than 25 miles of trails weave through the wilderness. Trails build on each other, so innumerable combinations are possible. Access points with parking include the Clark Lake day-use area and at the campgrounds nearby; east of the entrance station between Katherine and Crooked lakes; at the north end of Crooked Lake; on the east side of Forest Road 6324; and south of Drone Lake, east of Forest Road 6320.

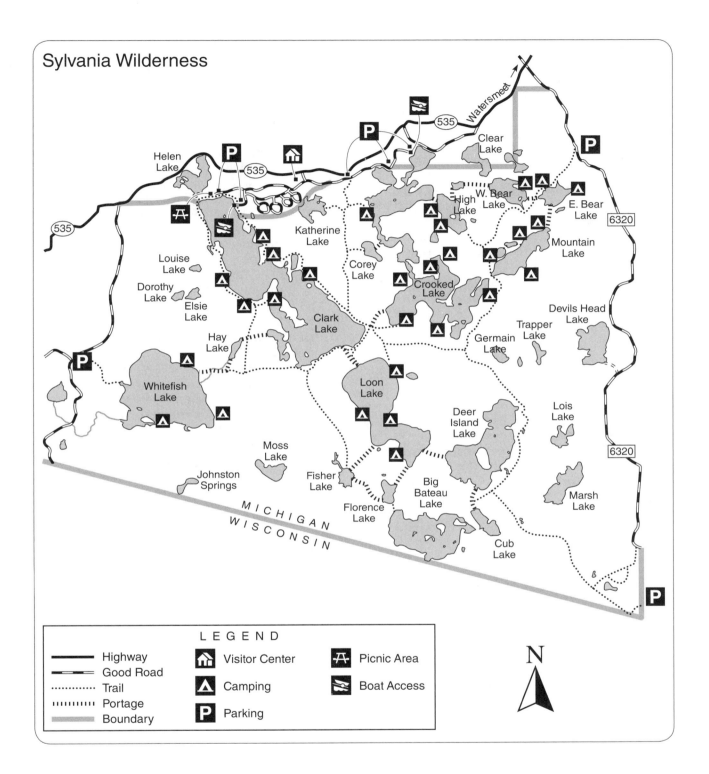

Sylvania Wilderness

LEGEND

Highway	🏠 Visitor Center	🛆 Picnic Area
Good Road	⛺ Camping	🛶 Boat Access
Trail	P Parking	
Portage		
Boundary		

N

Upper Peninsula

Clark Lake Trail

Distance Round-Trip: 8.1 miles
Estimated Hiking Time: 4 to 5 hours

Cautions: Remnant blue blazes appear on trees, but as these fade, new marks will not be made. Take along a map and compass. Wear appropriate footgear. Take insect repellent. You are in bear country, so take precautions.

Trail Directions: Park at the Clark Lake day-use area and head south to Clark Lake from the picnic shelter **[1]**. Follow to the right past the swimming beach, staying near the tree line. Cut through a small meadow and then swing left into the woods onto a cushion of pine needles (.2 mi.) **[2]**.

Get a taste of the wilderness as you step on stones to cross a small stream; then take the root stairs down, and then up, a small depression. Although surrounded by trees, you are near the lake and often get sneak previews through the trees. Several large trees, including many hemlocks, remind you that even lumbermen found value in keeping a tree standing.

The trail skirts the lake along a ridge and then passes through moss-covered lumps of fallen trees that look like rolling velvet. Test your balance at .8 mi., where you carefully cross logs and rocks that bridge a spillover from the pond that flanks the trail **[3]**. Pass over more rolling velvet and through more wet areas until you wind into Cedar Campground (1.2 mi.) **[4]**.

Just past the campgound you cross a small stream. The trail heads right and climbs to a bluff for a view overlooking the lake (1.4 mi.) **[5]**.

You need to cross another small stream bed. Use your ingenuity. The stream alerts you that you are near the Maple Campground (1.7 mi.) **[6]**. Soon the trail passes through another rolling stretch of green velvet that has burnt-umber pockets of pine needles. The trail veers away from the lake. Watch for a ridge on your right. The trail cuts up between it and the lake, heading into the woods.

At 2.3 mi., the portage from Glimmerglass Lake crosses your path **[7]**, signaling a stretch of trail with wetland foliage that brightens up the forest floor. Turn left at the junction (2.9 mi.) **[8]**. The grassy two-track passes through woods and wetlands and approaches the lake at 3.6 mi. **[9]**. The trail weaves on a ridge along the edge of the lake. Just after you enter a pine forest, the portage to Loon Lake crosses your way (4.5 mi.) **[10]**.

The path narrows and becomes grassy before you arrive at the junction for Loon and Crooked lakes (4.9 mi.) **[11]**. Go straight. At 5.2 mi., take a left at the junction **[12]**.

Pass a small bay. Several views of the lake open up before you enter the woods and wind down to the Pine Campground (6 mi.) **[13]**. Follow the trail around a small lake named Golden Silence and then climb to a vantage point where silence is golden.

The trail rolls, winds through woods, and then climbs again to an overlook of the lake before starting its descent. Pass through rolls of velvet and more wet areas to arrive at Balsam Campground (6.9 mi.) **[14]** and then Ash Campground (7.2 mi.) **[15]**. Roll along, dipping down streambeds and along ridges. At 7.7 mi., you arrive at the boat launch **[16]**. You are not far from the beach where you started. Continue following the trail near the beach, watching for the path up to the picnic shelter where you started.

1. Trailhead
2. Entrance to forest
3. Wet area
4. Cedar Campground
5. View of lake
6. Maple Campground
7. Canoe portage
8. Trail junction
9. Approach to lake
10. Canoe portage
11. Beach
12. Trail junction
13. Pine Campground
14. Balsam Campground
15. Ash Campground
16. Boat launch

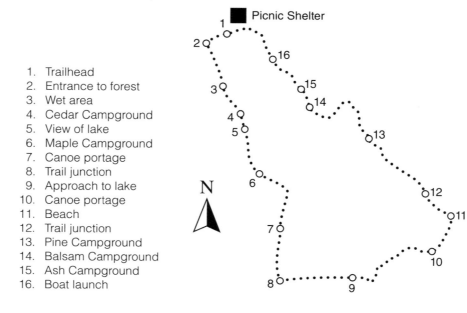

Unnamed Trail—
Loon Lake Access

Distance Round-Trip: 5.4 miles
Estimated Hiking Time: 2 to 3 hours

Cautions: The remnant blue blazes on trees along this trail are fading, and new marks will not be made. Take along a good map and compass. Wear appropriate footgear. Take insect repellent. This is bear country, so take proper precautions.

Trail Directions: From the Sylvania Wilderness entrance station, head east about .25 mi. to a small unmarked parking area on the north side of the road. Begin your hike by crossing the road, passing posts, and descending into the woods on what once was a single-lane road **[1]**.

This hike is not difficult, and it gives you a good opportunity to access the center of the wilderness, away from the Sylvania Recreation Area and the boat launch. You may want to pack a picnic lunch to enjoy at one of several lakes that can be reached from this trail. Loon Lake is your destination.

If you are really hungry, or just curious, you quickly reach a couple of side-trip opportunities. The first one heads east to the Porcupine Campground on Crooked Lake (.4 mi.) **[2]**. The second, less than .1 mi. farther, heads west to Katherine Lake **[3]**.

A large white pine stands guard at the trail junction to Corey Lake (.9 mi.) **[4]**. Note the number of large trees along this trail. At 1 mi., take pleasure as you pass more tall white pines **[5]**. Cross a tiny moss-covered footbridge (1.5 mi.) **[6]**. Watch for deer in this area. The trail then climbs into mostly hardwoods. Note the large maple on your right before you begin your descent to merge with the Clark Lake Trail (1.8 mi.) **[7]**.

Head left to follow along the edge of Clark Lake. Look for canoeists and loons and other waterfowl as they glide across the pristine water. At 2.2 mi., you reach a meadow and a sandy beach at the southeast end of the lake **[8]**. This area is a major unsigned junction. Two trails head left. Another goes to the beach on your right. A fourth trail parallels the beach on the right. This is the one to follow, and it may be hard to spot. It is the path least traveled.

Leaving the meadow behind, hike along an old lakeshore road past smaller meadows interspersed among the pines. The next junction is the canoe portage to Loon Lake (2.5 mi.) **[9]**. Turn left, climb the ridge through pines, cross a meadow, and descend through the woods to the small sandy beach at Loon Lake (2.7 mi.) **[10]**. Just in time for lunch. Take a break and enjoy the wilderness before packing up and heading back the way you came in. This different perspective sheds a whole new light on the scenery.

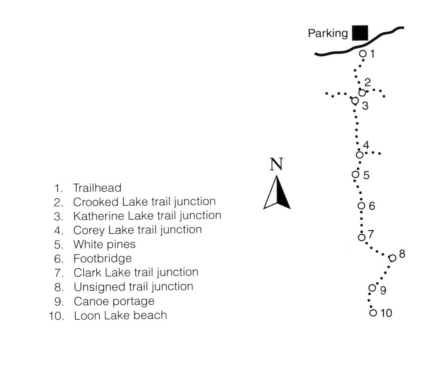

1. Trailhead
2. Crooked Lake trail junction
3. Katherine Lake trail junction
4. Corey Lake trail junction
5. White pines
6. Footbridge
7. Clark Lake trail junction
8. Unsigned trail junction
9. Canoe portage
10. Loon Lake beach

23. Ottawa National Forest

- Seek solitude in three designated wilderness areas.
- Visit some of the nearly 80 waterfalls located in or near the forest.
- Canoe on seven major river systems.

Park Information

The almost 1 million acres of the Ottawa National Forest have something for everyone. This mesh of forest that blankets Michigan's western Upper Peninsula has waterfalls; gorges; wilderness areas; nearly 2,000 miles of streams and rivers; over 500 lakes; forests of pine, maple, spruce, birch, and fir; and rugged terrain that was shaped by retreating glaciers thousands of years ago. A wealth of recreational opportunities awaits fishermen, hunters, hikers, backpackers, mountain bicyclists, canoeists, kayakers, snowmobilers, and cross-country skiers.

A few of the highlights within the forest are three wilderness areas (Sturgeon River Gorge, Sylvania Wilderness [see park #22], and McCormick Wilderness [see park #19]); a scenic drive (Black River National Scenic Byway); more than 50 waterfalls (Cascade, Agate, and the five falls along the Black River National Scenic Byway, to name a few); around 200 miles of hiking trails (Gogebic Ridge Trail, North Country National Scenic Trail, Sturgeon Falls, and Imp Lake Interpretive Trail, for example); over 1,000 miles of snowmobile trails; and mountain bicycling trails (the Pines and Mines Mountain Bike Trail System, which includes the Ehlco Mountain Bike Complex and the Henry and Pomeroy Lake Mountain Bike Complex). In addition, 22 campgrounds provide serene and scenic camping that ranges from rustic to semideveloped. Backcountry camping adds another dimension.

Directions: Facilities and points of interest are spread over a large area. Contact the forest supervisor's office or the individual district offices of the Ottawa National Forest for more information.

Hours Open: Most facilities are open year-round.

Facilities: Hiking, mountain bicycling, cross-country skiing, snowshoeing, snowmobiling, swimming, equestrian, fishing, hunting, boat launch, canoeing, camping (tent and backcountry), picnicking, interpretive trails, and interpretive center.

Permits and Rules: Generally, hikers, canoeists, and other users do not need permits and do not have to pay fees. No fee is required for backcountry camping, but campsites in campgrounds require fees. Motorized and mechanized vehicles or equipment are not allowed in the wilderness areas. Leave no trace. Carry out what you carry in, and don't cut down live trees and other plants. Don't feed the bears; keep food out of their reach.

For Further Information: Ottawa National Forest, Forest Supervisor's Office, E6248 US 2, Ironwood, MI 49938; 906-932-1330. Or you may contact the various district offices of the Ottawa National Forest: Bessemer Ranger District, E6248 US 2, Ironwood, MI 49938; 906-932-1330; Iron River Ranger District, 990 Lalley Road, Iron River, MI 49935; 906-265-5139; Kenton Ranger District, 4810 E. M-28, Kenton, MI 49967; 906-852-3500; Ontonagon Ranger District, 1209 Rockland Road, Ontonagon, MI 49953; 906-884-2085; and Watersmeet Ranger District, Old US 2, P.O. Box 276, Watersmeet, MI 49969; 906-358-4551. Contact the Ottawa Visitors Center at P.O. Box 276, Watersmeet, MI 49969; 906-358-4724.

Other Points of Interest

The Ottawa National Forest covers a huge territory. For more information about what is available in the area, contact Upper Peninsula Travel and Recreation Association, P.O. Box 400, Iron Mountain, MI 49801; 800-562-7134; www.uptravel.com; Iron County Tourism Council, 1700 County Road 424, Gaastra, MI 49927; 906-265-9244; Western U.P. Convention and Visitors Bureau, P.O. Box 706, Ironwood, MI 49938; 906-932-4850 or 800-522-5657; www.westernup.info; Ontonagon Tourism Council, 600 River Road, P.O. Box 266, Ontonagon, MI 49953; 906-884-4735; and Lake Gogebic Area Chamber of Commerce, P.O. Box 114, Bergland, MI 49910; 888-464-3242; www.lake gogebicarea.com.

Park Trails

Hiking opportunities within the forest seem endless. About 200 miles of trails range from easy to difficult. Some are interpretive trails, such as Deer Marsh Interpretive Trail at Lake Ste. Kathryn. Some are scenic, such as Sturgeon Falls or Wolf Mountain. Some are historic, like Gogebic Ridge Trail. Others are for backpacking, like the 108 miles of the North Country Trail that passes through the forest. The potential in the wilderness is inexhaustible.

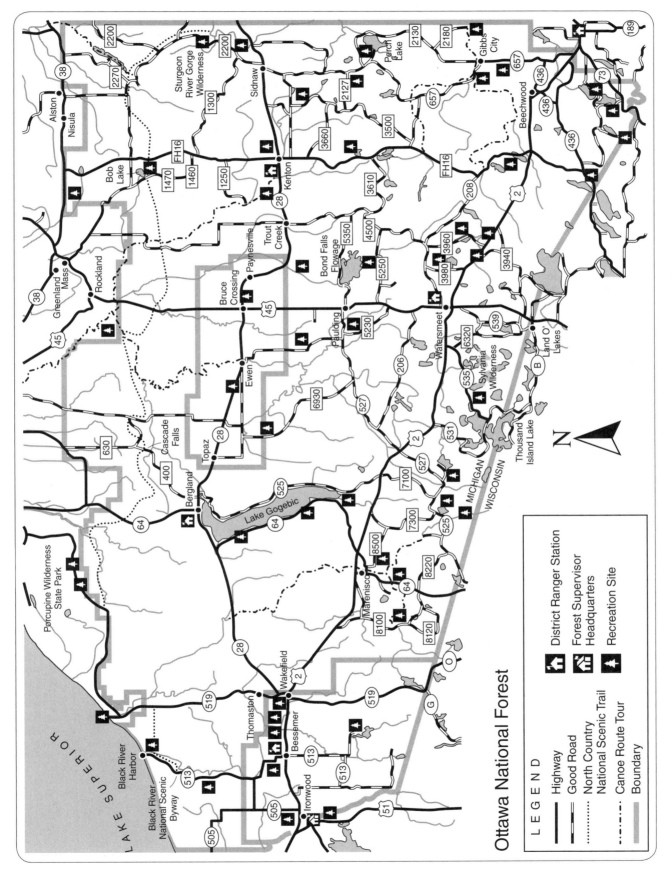

Ottawa National Forest

LEGEND

Highway	District Ranger Station
Good Road	Forest Supervisor Headquarters
North Country	Recreation Site
National Scenic Trail	
Canoe Route Tour	
Boundary	

Beaver Lodge Nature Trail

Distance Round-Trip: 1.3 miles
Estimated Hiking Time: 45 minutes to 1.5 hours

Cautions: Take along insect repellent during the warmer months. Be careful; you are in bear country.
Trail Directions: The trail is accessed from Bob Lake Campground, which is located north of Kenton and east of Greenland. From Kenton, take Forest Highway 16 north from M-28 to Pori Road. From Greenland, head west on M-38 to Forest Highway 16 and then south to Pori Road. Follow the signs west 4 mi. to Bob Lake; then turn left on Forest Road 1470 and proceed to Forest Road 1478. Travel 2 mi. to the campground.

The trail begins at the trail information board located at the parking lot for the beach and picnic area on the east end of the campground [1]. Located along the trail are 24 high-quality interpretive stops. The trail also has its own trail marker. White on brown, the square marker depicts a beaver gnawing a tree.

The trail starts out level, skirts a floating bog, and swings southward. The first .1 mi. contains a number of interpretive stops, so take your time. That odd-looking device that you come upon is a tree finder. Take aim at a nearby tree, and the tree finder will identify it [2].

When you reach the trail junction next to the yellow birch interpretive stop, turn left (.1 mi.) [3]. This section is part of the North Country National Scenic Trail, and it once was a railroad grade for the logging activities carried out in this area earlier in the 1900s.

As you cross the road to the beach and picnic area, veer right to climb a series of steps along the side of a steep hill. At the top is a bench. Rest if you need to catch your breath (.2 mi.) [4]. The forest floor here is literally littered with maple saplings. Just past a large white pine stump, the trail swings left to skirt a small pond that is labeled a pothole (.3 mi.) [5]. Potholes result from pits that formed in glacial deposits and filled with water. These areas brighten up a dark forest by allowing sunlight to break through the otherwise dense canopy.

At .5 mi., while descending, stay straight where the North Country Trail cuts off to the left [6]. Soon you reach a pond. Step across the single-plank boardwalk to a series of three interpretive boards that describe how this locale has changed over time. Rest on a bench before crossing another boardwalk, skirting a wetland, and swinging right to cross a footbridge at the beaver dam and large, lakelike pond (.6 mi.) [7]. The trail then takes you left; from a ridge, follow along the pond to the next interpretive stop with a bench (.7 mi.) [8], which educates you on the beaver, "the furry woodsman."

From here, the trail turns right and climbs away from the beaver pond. At .8 mi., you cross a small footbridge, swing right around another wetland, and then climb into a hemlock grove [9]. Note the shade from the cover and the lack of growth on the forest floor.

After descending the steps on your way down to the campground road, look back at the ravine that was on your left to notice that it is shaped like a natural amphitheater (1 mi.) [10]. Then cross the road and turn right at the trail junction to find yourself again walking along the old logging railroad corridor. Turn left at the next trail junction by the yellow birch interpretive stop (1.2 mi.) [3], and retrace your steps to the parking area. Before leaving the campground, walk down to the beach area and enjoy the small, pristine lake in one of the most serene settings that you can drive to. You may even want to set up camp.

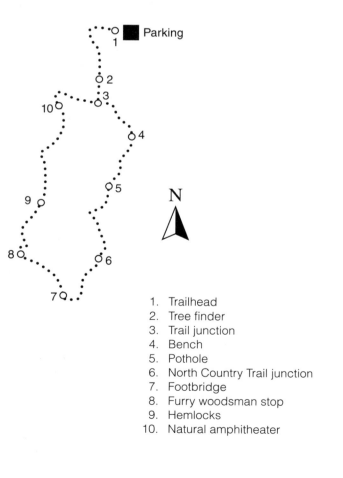

1. Trailhead
2. Tree finder
3. Trail junction
4. Bench
5. Pothole
6. North Country Trail junction
7. Footbridge
8. Furry woodsman stop
9. Hemlocks
10. Natural amphitheater

Cascade Falls Hiking Trail

Distance Round-Trip: 1.7 miles
Estimated Hiking Time: 1 to 1.5 hours

Cautions: The trail includes steep climbs and descents, has you stepping over roots and rocks, and passes through areas that are prone to be wet. Wear appropriate footgear. Take along insect repellent during the warmer months. Poison ivy lines the trail in some places. Be careful: This is bear country.

Trail Directions: The Cascade Falls Hiking Trail is located northeast of Bergland. From M-28, take Forest Road 400 north for about 7 mi. to the sign for the falls and turn right to access the drive into the parking area. The trail starts at the information board on the south end of the small parking area **[1]**.

This hike consists of two trails that, when looped together, create an unforgettable hiking experience. Near the trailhead, stay to the right to bypass the Bluff Trail as it climbs that rocky escarpment on your left. Take the Valley Trail to seek the falls.

The trail swings left to head east, roughly paralleling the ridge to your left and Cascade Creek flowing unseen on your right. Aspens are prevalent as you snake along on the gravel trail. You cross a series of three boardwalks before reaching the junction with the other end of the Bluff Trail (.4 mi.) **[2]**. Turn right and descend to cross a small footbridge.

At .5 mi., you cross another footbridge over a small stream **[3]**. The forest canopy soon opens, and the trail becomes grassier and wetter as you hike through the shrubs and small trees toward the increasing roar of the falls.

At the falls, the scene changes to water cascading over rocks, which drowns out the silence of the stoic pines that crowd the edge of the creek (.7 mi.) **[4]**. Take your time and scramble over the exposed rock to gain different vantage points from which to witness the water of Cascade Creek tumbling over rock.

Leaving the falls behind, retrace your steps to the second junction with the Bluff Trail (1 mi.) **[2]**. Continue straight as you climb past the junction and then swing to the left. Don't be fooled into thinking that you have reached the top after you start descending. You are soon climbing steeply to reach an overlook with a view of the surrounding forest (1.2 mi.) **[5]**. When you finish huffing and puffing, you may hear the roar of the falls off in the distance.

Turn right at the blue diamond trail marker and descend, only to climb another escarpment. Again, a scenic overlook awaits you—this time a view of forested hills to the north (1.4 mi.) **[6]**. The trail then descends slightly and swings left to provide a panoramic view of the surrounding area **[7]**. Stop to enjoy the incredible view of the area known as the Trap Hills. It's all downhill from here.

The descent is steep and often on bare rock that can be slippery. Take your time and watch your step. At 1.6 mi., you emerge at another lower overlook **[8]** before making the last steep descent to the first trail junction. Turn right and return to the parking area.

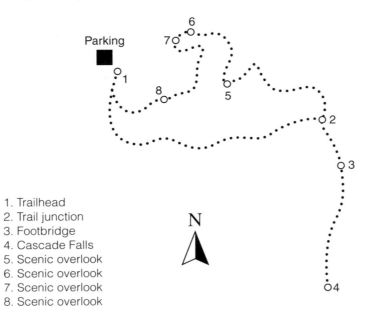

1. Trailhead
2. Trail junction
3. Footbridge
4. Cascade Falls
5. Scenic overlook
6. Scenic overlook
7. Scenic overlook
8. Scenic overlook

- Enjoy panoramic views from the Lake of the Clouds overlook and from Summit Peak Tower.

- Explore the wilderness in the park on more than 90 miles of hiking trails.

- Visit the impressive Presque Isle waterfalls.

Park Information

More than 25 miles of Lake Superior shoreline stretch along this 60,000-acre wilderness, Michigan's largest state park. Across its vast, rugged terrain are over 90 miles of trails that open up the park's remote interior of secluded lakes, streams, rivers, waterfalls, and virgin timber. The ruggedness and remoteness helped spare the timber from the saw.

Although the network of point-to-point trails encourages backcountry exploration, day users have much to see and do. The Wilderness Visitor Center, located near the junction of South Boundary Road and M-107, has wildlife exhibits and a relief map of the park. A multi-image slide program gives information on the history of the park and provides data on the myriad recreational opportunities that the park offers. For example, Summit Peak Tower, a 40-foot observation structure, provides a view of the park and the surrounding area. The ski area has a 640-foot drop over a 5,800-foot run for alpine skiing. In addition, over 26 miles of groomed cross-country ski trails weave through the area.

Two campgrounds provide ample accommodations for visitors. The park also offers 19 rustic trailside cabins, backcountry campsites, three yurts, a lodge, and trailside camping sites. Trailside camping is allowed throughout the park as long as campers set up at least .25 mile from cabins, scenic areas, shelters, or roads.

Directions: The east entrance to the park is about 17 miles west of Ontonagon on M-107. The Wilderness Visitor Center is located just south of M-107 on South Boundary Road. About 15 miles north of Wakefield, at the end of County Road 519, is the Presque Isle River Unit.

Hours Open: The park is open year-round, but the campgrounds are open only from early May through mid-October. The Wilderness Visitor Center is open daily from late May through October. Some of the roads are limited seasonally. South Boundary Road is plowed only through the end of November. M-107 is plowed to the ski area.

Facilities: Hiking, cross-country skiing, snowshoeing, snowmobiling, fishing, hunting, boat launch, camping (tent, RV, and backcountry), sanitation station, picnicking, cabins, lodge, yurts, interpretive trails, and interpretive center.

Permits and Rules: A park fee is required for motor vehicles ($6 daily, $24 annually for residents; $8 daily, $29 annually for nonresidents). Overnight hikers must register. Motorized vehicles are not allowed on the trails. Pack out what you pack in. Fires are allowed in designated areas only. No fires are allowed if a high-fire-danger alert is in effect. Burn only downed trees; do not cut down live trees.

For Further Information: Porcupine Mountains Wilderness State Park, 33303 Headquarters Road, Ontonagon, MI 49953; 906-885-5275.

Other Points of Interest

The **Ehlco Mountain Bike Complex** of the Pines and Mines Mountain Bike Trail System is located south of the park. Access is from Forest Road 360, which is west of M-64. For more information, contact the Ottawa National Forest, Supervisor's Office, E6248 US 2, Ironwood, MI 49938; 906-932-1330.

Park Trails

Most of the trails are point-to-point trails that can be connected to form innumerable loops. Although most of these form longer loops that appeal to the backpacker, shorter options are possible.

Summit Peak Tower Trail (👣👣, .5 mile). Midway along South Boundary Road is Summit Peak Road. From this, a .5-mile trail, with benches for resting, leads the way to the 40-foot-high Summit Peak Tower.

Lake of the Clouds (👣👣, .3 mile). A paved trail from the parking lot at the end of M-107 leads up to the rocky escarpment that serves as the overlook for Lake of the Clouds. From here, you get a view of the Big Carp River Valley hundreds of feet below.

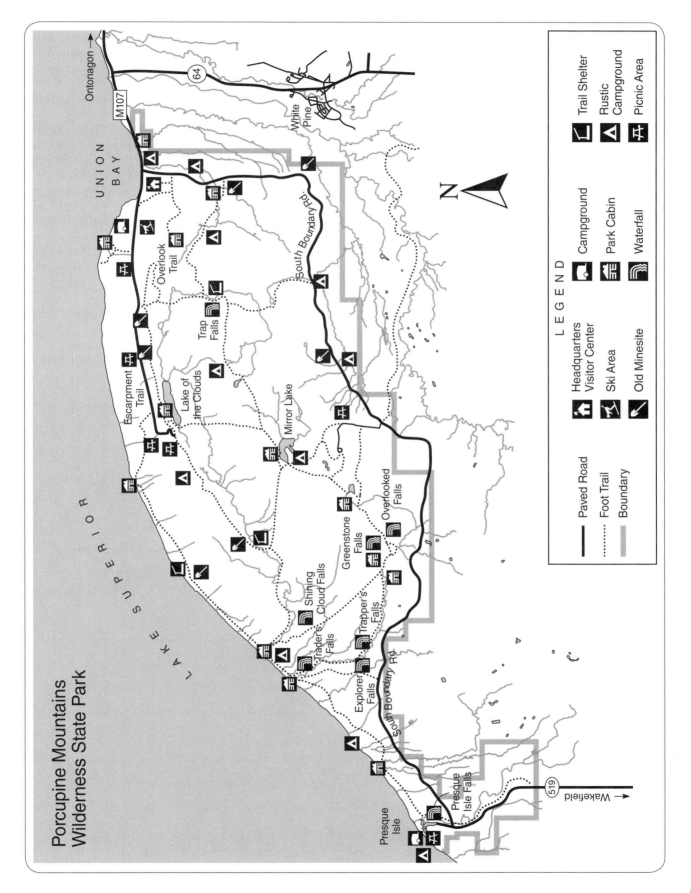

Porcupine Mountains
Wilderness State Park

LEGEND

Paved Road	Headquarters Visitor Center	Campground	Trail Shelter
Foot Trail	Ski Area	Park Cabin	Rustic Campground
Boundary	Old Minesite	Waterfall	Picnic Area

LAKE SUPERIOR

UNION BAY

Escarpment Trail

Overlook Trail

Lake of the Clouds

Trap Falls

Mirror Lake

South Boundary Rd.

Shining Cloud Falls

Trader's Falls

Greenstone Falls

Trapper's Falls

Overlooked Falls

Explorer's Falls

South Boundary Rd.

Presque Isle

Presque Isle Falls

White Pine

N

Ontonagon →

M107

64

519

Wakefield →

Upper Peninsula

Overlook Trail

Distance Round-Trip: 3.4 miles
Estimated Hiking Time: 2 to 3 hours

Cautions: This trail has some steep climbs and descents; it goes through what can be long, muddy stretches; and it has roots and rocks. Wear proper footgear. Mosquitoes and black flies can be a problem in the warm months. Take water. Be careful; this is bear country.

Trail Directions: The trail starts at the Government Peak parking area off M-107 **[1]**. Head south, through the hardwoods and up the stony path of the Government Peak Trail. The cobblestones mark an ancient beach line from a time when lake waters were much higher. Climb past the junction for the Escarpment Trail and past what will be your return loop on the Overlook Trail, until the hill crests and you notice more hemlocks (.3 mi.) **[2]**. Start heading down and to the left; then cross by a small stream. Notice the huge hemlocks here.

Follow along through mud, cross over planks, and continue through another stand of hemlock before arriving at the south junction for the Overlook Trail (.6 mi.) **[3]**. Turn left onto the needle-carpeted trail and wind along under the cover of hemlock.

At .8 mi., the trail climbs **[4]** and then veers to the left up and around through more hemlock. The climb gets steeper until you reach the crest at 1.2 mi. **[5]**. From here you can see light through the trees. Follow the light to an overlook that offers a somewhat obscured view of the interior of the park. Foliage from trees may block an otherwise bird's-eye view.

The trail descends as a narrower path, leaving the hemlock behind. At times, with maple saplings hugging your knees, you may think that you have strayed off the trail. You haven't. Just make sure that you watch for the blue marks on the trees.

Although the trail dips down to an ephemeral stream (1.7 mi.) **[6]** and then up, its general tendency is a climb—sometimes gentle, sometimes steep—until it reaches another crest (1.8 mi.) **[7]**. Here a bench faces to the west. On a clear day, this vista overlooks the rugged interior of the park and the Big Carp River Valley.

The trail swings left, cutting through hardwoods, and merges with a wide cross-country ski path (1.9 mi.) **[8]**. Keep to the left, heading down through maple saplings. Your steep descent culminates at a

small streambed (2 mi.) **[9]**. Climb again and dip to another streambed (2.2 mi.) **[10]**. Start up again. After you notice that you are on a ridge, the trail rolls down, steeply, and you step from rock to rock to cross a stream lined with moss-covered rocks (2.3 mi.) **[11]**.

Large conglomerates along the trail make hard but secure seats, useful if you need a break. The scattering of large boulders continues, even when you reenter the darkness of hemlocks (2.4 mi.) **[12]**. The trail rolls through the dark forest, past huge boulders that look as though they had been strewn about by an angry giant. The path continues past moss-covered logs, along a web of exposed roots through huge thimbleberry leaves, and then down a moderately steep slope (2.8 mi.) **[13]**. Now roll up your pant legs. You will be trudging over roots and rocks through a section that may be seasonally muddy.

At 3.2 mi., the trail descends steeply to a stream that you can probably jump over **[14]**. Climb up the bank, and you soon see the sign for the Government Peak Trail ahead. At its junction (3.3 mi.) **[15]**, turn right and head down on the cobblestones back to where you left your vehicle.

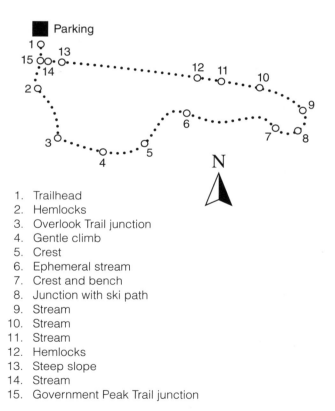

■ Parking

1. Trailhead
2. Hemlocks
3. Overlook Trail junction
4. Gentle climb
5. Crest
6. Ephemeral stream
7. Crest and bench
8. Junction with ski path
9. Stream
10. Stream
11. Stream
12. Hemlocks
13. Steep slope
14. Stream
15. Government Peak Trail junction

Escarpment Trail

Distance One-Way: 4.2 miles
Estimated Hiking Time: 2.5 to 3.5 hours

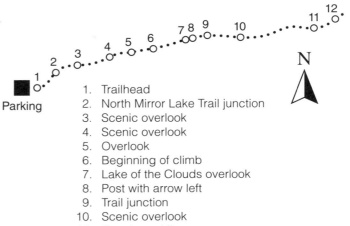

Parking

1. Trailhead
2. North Mirror Lake Trail junction
3. Scenic overlook
4. Scenic overlook
5. Overlook
6. Beginning of climb
7. Lake of the Clouds overlook
8. Post with arrow left
9. Trail junction
10. Scenic overlook
11. Cuyahoga Mine
12. Government Peak Trail junction

Cautions: This trail includes some steep climbs and descents. You will step over roots and rocks and hike through rough areas prone to wetness. Wear proper footgear. Take insect repellent and water. This is bear country, so be careful.

Trail Directions: Begin by Lake of the Clouds Scenic Overlook **[1]**. You start on a surfaced path and soon make a brief walk on rock before making a rather steep descent. At .3 mi., you reach a posted junction. The North Mirror Lake Trail splits off to the right; the Escarpment Trail continues straight **[2]**.

M-107 is the other end of this point-to-point trail, so plan your hike accordingly. Options include arranging to be dropped off or picked up at either end, using two vehicles, or simply turning around at any point to return to where you started. However you make your plans, you don't want to miss this hike. Many think the Escarpment Trail is the most scenic trail in the park.

At .5 mi., you have climbed to your first scenic peek at the interior of the park **[3]**. Follow the blue blazes as you step over rocks and roots, and then swing left to descend into the woods. You soon make a steep climb before breaking out to a spectacular view of the Lake of the Clouds and its surrounding area (.9 mi.) **[4]**. Stop, sit down on a rock, catch your breath, and enjoy the view.

After following along the open escarpment, you slip back into the woods and descend before reemerging

at another overlook (1.2 mi.) **[5]**. At 1.6 mi., after a particularly long descent, you start the climb up Cloud Peak **[6]**. When you complete the climb, you are rewarded with a view from the site of the original overlook for the Lake of the Clouds (2 mi.) **[7]**. Before the road was extended and the current overlook was opened, visitors had to hike .5 mi. from M-107 to enjoy this view.

You soon reach a post (2.1 mi.) **[8]** that leads you away from the rocks and toward the woods for a long descent. At 2.3 mi., you reach a trail junction **[9]**. If you go left, the halfway turnoff to M-107 allows you to hike out to the road and return to the parking area along that route. To the right is a side trip to the site of the Carp Lake Mine, established in 1858.

Continue straight—a short cutoff to the right takes you to a fenced-off cistern—and start your steep climb up Cuyahoga Peak. With an elevation of just over 1,600 feet, it is the tallest hill along the trail. At 2.7 mi., having completed the climb, enjoy views of the Carp River Valley below as you walk along the edge of the escarpment **[10]**.

The last mile of the trail is a long descent, so you may want to turn around here if you plan to hike back to the start-ing point. If not, you descend sharply before leveling out to walk over the scattered tailings, remnants of the Cuyahoga Mine of 1856 (4 mi.) **[11]**.

Cross a boardwalk and turn left at the junction with Government Peak Trail (4.1 mi.) **[12]**. You finish by hiking down the steep slope to M-107. This is the end of the trail, but not the end of your hike if you must head back to the Lake of the Clouds parking area for your vehicle.

East and West River Trails

Distance Round-Trip: 2.5 miles
Estimated Hiking Time: 1 to 1.5 hours

Cautions: This trail has many stairs to climb and a considerable amount of boardwalk, which can be slippery when wet. Roots and rocks obstruct the east trail. Take insect repellent and water. Be careful; this is bear country.

Trail Directions: Take 519 north of South Boundary Road to the northeastern parking area [1]. Start out on a level trail flanked by timbers and turn left at the first junction. Mature hemlocks and cedars soar over a floor lush with ferns and maple saplings. At .1 mi., you arrive at the steps down to the falls [2]. From here you can see the frothy Presque Isle River. Midway down the steps, follow the boardwalk to the right for your trek along the West River Trail. You will see several potholes in the river, the result of eddies scouring the shale in a circular manner.

Still on the boardwalk, you reach a viewing platform (.2 mi.) [3] before climbing more than 40 stairs to walk another boardwalk higher above the river. Interpretive plaques describe the environment. Some of the trees are nearly four centuries old.

At .3 mi., you climb more than 30 steps to a viewing area [4] and then reach Manabezho Falls. Manabezho was a powerful Ojibwa spirit god. A bench allows you to watch the falls spill from mossy escarpment. When rested, climb almost 50 more steps to another bench. The trail is now flat and outlined by timbers.

You reach the junction for the Manido Falls viewing platform at .4 mi. [5]. Go left and down about 70 steps to reach another trail. Keep going about 30 additional steps to reach various view platforms and finally Manido Falls (.5 mi.) [6]. Watch the spilling amber water before climbing the steps to reach the trail. Soon you are back on a boardwalk, where you can sight bald eagles from a scope at a viewing platform (.5 mi.) [7].

You leave the boardwalk and climb a rooty, steep trail to walk the ridge high above the river (.6 mi.) [8]. Watch for eagles here before descending steeply and to the right along the river.

At .8 mi., steps guide you up the ridge where you find a groomed trail on top [9]. Keep to the left and roll over to the viewing platform for Nawadaha Falls (.9 mi.) [10].

Now you leave the boardwalks and platforms behind. At 1.2 mi., climb up to South Boundary Road to cross the bridge over the river so that you can return on the East River Trail for a different perspective of the falls [11].

This side of the trail is natural, and it undulates along the river through mature trees. You view Nawadaha Falls while standing on the edge of a steep cliff (1.5 mi.) [12]. Take care here. The trail climbs steeply over roots and follows along the ridge before descending steeply (1.7 mi.) [13]. At 1.8 mi., you are across the river from the Manido Falls platform [14].

Although the trail rises to the right, a bench beckons you to sit and view the falls (1.9 mi.) [15]. Take a break before you climb up the ridge high above the river. Go straight at the junction and descend the ridge just before swinging left to cross the rock bed of Nonesuch shale to get to the west side of the river (2.2 mi.) [16]. From here you get a great view of the falls as the river tumbles past you.

At 2.3 mi., a suspension bridge carries you over the river [17]. To your left are clear examples of the potholes where the water from an unnamed falls spills over them before joining Lake Superior, which you see to your right.

Soon you climb almost 100 steps to pass the board-walk of the West River Trail, which you traveled on at the beginning of the hike. You then return on the timber-framed trail that you started on and head back to the parking area.

1. Trailhead
2. Steps down
3. Viewing platform
4. Viewing area
5. Manido Falls overview
6. Manido Falls
7. Bald eagle viewing platform
8. Ridge
9. Steps up to ridge
10. Nawadaha Falls
11. South Boundary Road
12. View of Nawadaha Falls from cliff edge
13. Steep descent
14. View of Manido Falls platform
15. Bench
16. Rock bed crossing
17. Suspension bridge

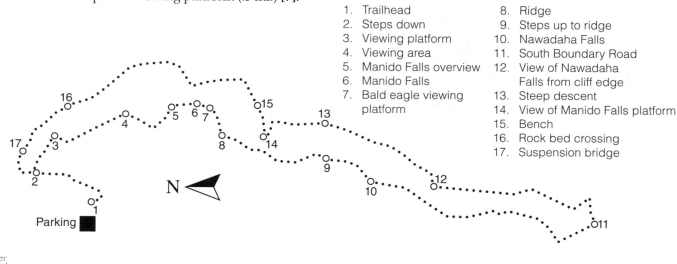

Upper Peninsula

Summit Peak Trail and South Mirror Lake

Distance Round-Trip: 4.8 miles
Estimated Hiking Time: 2 to 2.5 hours

Cautions: This trail has many stairs to climb, planks, and a boardwalk. These can be slippery when wet, as can the roots and rocks elsewhere on the trail. Mosquitoes and black flies can be a problem in the warm months. Take water. Be careful; this is bear country.

Trail Directions: Take Summit Peak Road 1.9 miles north from South Boundary Road to the north end of the parking area for the Summit Peak scenic area [1]. This spot is a hub for a couple of trails. Take the right trail and start climbing toward Summit Peak. You will find respite in a bench along the way. At .6 mi., steps to a platform take you over a rock escarpment [2]. Climb more steps to reach a boardwalk. You eventually get a view of Lake Superior and the Porcupine Mountains. Have a seat at the bench or keep climbing until you reach the tower at Summit Peak (.7 mi.) [3]. Now climb more than 50 steps to get a grand view of Lake Superior and the Little Carp River Valley. On a clear day, you might see Minnesota, Wisconsin, the Apostle Islands, or Copper Peak. At 1,958 feet, this is the highest point in the park.

The trail makes a rocky descent. At 1 mi., you cross planks, coming off the escarpment. Shortly afterward, planks keep your feet dry over a low wet area [4].

A bench sits at a trail junction (1.1 mi.) [5]. Follow to the left and down the wide, stone path. Keep descending. At 1.4 mi., a series of planks directs you over potentially wet areas [6]. Another bench awaits you at 1.5 mi. [7]. The trail narrows, is planked, and then winds and rolls. You cross logs and planks over ephemeral wet areas while passing through hemlock and then maple and birch.

Ferns announce a junction to the camp area (2.3 mi.) [8]. Stay left and cross a wood footbridge over a creek that spills into Mirror Lake (2.4 mi.) [9]. Planking carries you through the wet environment, and you soon reach a junction. Turn left and follow the Little Carp River Trail, which takes you over more planking and into the darkness of hemlocks. The trail undulates, puts you on a ridge with a stream below, passes a campsite and through giant hemlocks, and takes you to another campsite (3.5 mi.) [10]. Go straight over the small planks and leave the hemlocks behind.

At 3.7 mi., go left at the junction [11] and continue along a series of planks through cattails. In .1 mi., you step down to a plank bridge that carries you over a wetland and pond [12]. Be on the lookout for bees, bullfrogs, and fish along this wetland trail as it winds through beaver meadows and alder thickets.

Steps lead back up into the woods at 3.9 mi. [13]. Soon you cross another bridge and more planking before arriving at another bridge (4 mi.) [14].

More planking, rocky streambeds, and undulating climbs with wetlands visible below prepare you for the beaver pond (4.4 mi.) [15]. Rest on the bench there before heading back to the parking area.

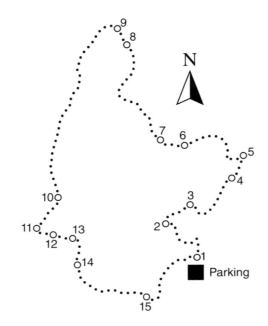

1. Trailhead
2. Rock escarpment
3. Summit Peak viewing tower
4. Planks
5. Junction
6. Series of planks
7. Bench
8. Junction to camp area
9. Bridge over creek
10. Campsite
11. Junction
12. Bridge
13. Steps
14. Bridge
15. Beaver pond

25. Black River Harbor
National Forest Recreation Area

- Explore five scenic waterfalls on the Black River as it plunges toward Lake Superior.
- Drive the Black River National Scenic Byway.
- Hunt for agates along the Lake Superior shore.

Park Information

Take one harbor at the mouth of the Black River where it spills into Lake Superior, add a succession of waterfalls with ample access points, provide a sprinkling of campsites, link this all together with a scenic byway, and you have a recipe for recreation success. Spice this up with a hiking trail that links the scenic waterfalls for invigorating viewing, and this recreation area is a splash.

Five picturesque waterfalls may be viewed from County Road 513, otherwise known as Black River Road. Because of the area's beauty, in 1992 the area was dedicated as a national scenic byway. Short trails from a series of parking areas lead to viewing platforms for all the falls: Rainbow, Sandstone, Gorge, Potawatomi, and Great Conglomerate.

The harbor, the only active harbor owned and managed by the USFS, provides access to Lake Superior with a boat ramp that can accommodate most crafts that are trailered in. There is no launching fee. A concessionaire offers limited supplies for boaters and picnickers, provides fuel for boaters, and regulates boaters who need transient docking. A picnic shelter, picnic area, Rainbow Falls, and Lake Superior beach are accessible from the harbor.

A .25-mile hike away is the Black River Harbor Campground, which provides 39 sites, offers a scenic overlook of the Lake Superior Apostle Islands, and has a trail down to Lake Superior.

Several short hikes from various parking stops lead to the observation decks of the falls. All of these are linked by the North Country Trail, which passes through the recreation area.

Directions: The harbor and campgrounds are located about 15 miles north of Bessemer. Access is from Black River Road, or County Road 513. Parking areas for the falls are off this road as well.

Hours Open: The trails have no posted hours, but the campground is open from mid-May through October

1. At the harbor, the concessionaire offers services from Memorial Day through September.

Facilities: Hiking, boat launch, camping (tent and RV), and picnicking.

Permits and Rules: There is no trail fee, but there is a charge for camping. Keep pets on a leash. Do not cut or carve any live trees. When hiking to the falls, keep children nearby.

For Further Information: Ottawa National Forest, Bessemer Ranger District, E6248 US 2, Ironwood, MI 49938; 906-932-1330. The Black River Harbor Campground is located at 500 N. Moore Street, Bessemer, MI 49911.

Other Points of Interest

With rugged hills and rocky bluffs, the area is a mecca for winter skiing. **Big Powderhorn Mountain** is nearby, as are several lodges and resorts. Also nearby is the **Copper Peak International Ski Flying Facility**, the largest ski flying facility in the Northern Hemisphere. For more information on these attractions or for information on canoeing, horseback riding, fishing, and other recreational activities, contact Bessemer Chamber of Commerce, US 2, P.O. Box 243, Bessemer, MI 49911; 906-663-0026; Ironwood Chamber of Commerce, 150 North Lowell, Ironwood, MI 49938; 906-932-1122; www.ironwoodmi.org; Western U.P. Convention and Visitors Bureau, P.O. Box 706, Ironwood, MI 49938; 906-932-4850 or 800-522-5657; www.westernup.info.

Park Trails

Black River Harbor Recreation Area Self-Guided Neotropical Breeding Bird Tour (👣, 1 mile). This interpretive trail, part of a watchable-wildlife site, starts just beyond the gate into the campground.

North Country Trail (👣👣, 12.5 miles). The trail is a segment of what will be a 4,600-mile trail that links the Lewis and Clark Trail in North Dakota to the Appalachian Trail in New York State. About 5 miles of the North Country Trail traverses the Black River and its waterfalls.

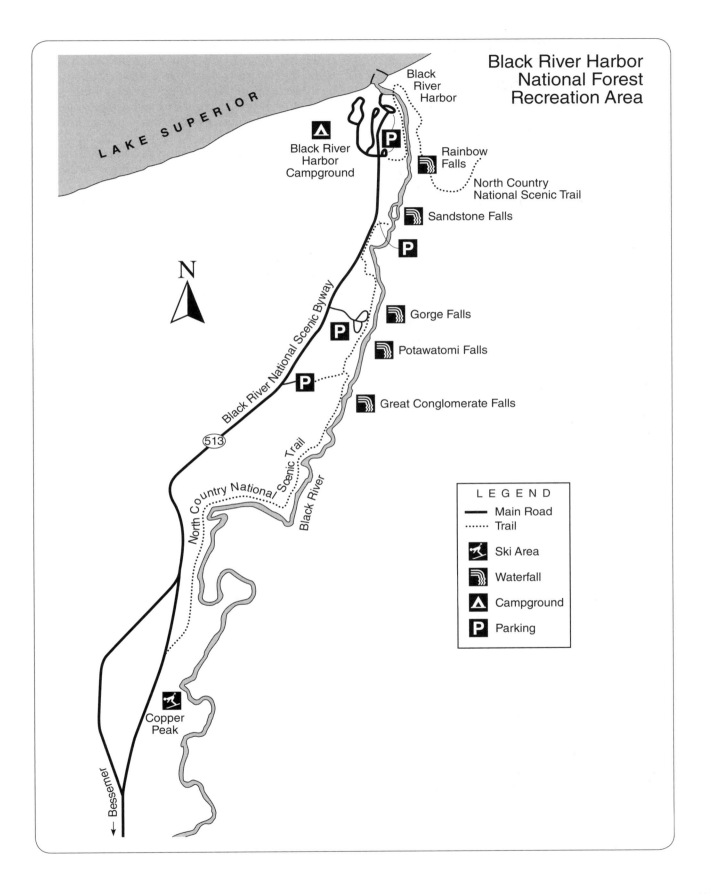

Black River Harbor National Forest Recreation Area

LAKE SUPERIOR

Black River Harbor

Black River Harbor Campground

Rainbow Falls

North Country National Scenic Trail

Sandstone Falls

Gorge Falls

Potawatomi Falls

Great Conglomerate Falls

N

Black River National Scenic Byway

513

North Country National Scenic Trail

Black River

LEGEND
Main Road
Trail
Ski Area
Waterfall
Campground
Parking

Copper Peak

Bessemer

North Country Trail to Sandstone, Gorge, Potawatomi, and Great Conglomerate Falls

Distance Round-Trip: 3.6 miles
Estimated Hiking Time: 2 to 3 hours

Cautions: This trail has steep climbs and descents. Hikers encounter muddy stretches, step over roots and rocks, and move along ridges that at times are near the edge of the river. Carefully watch the blue blazes on trees for your way. Wear proper footgear. In warm months, mosquitoes and black flies can be a nuisance. Take care; this is bear country.

Trail Directions: Although parking areas provide access to all of the falls, this trail begins at the Sandstone Falls parking lot. Start at the east end of the lot **[1]**. Enter the woods and descend steps to the falls. The steep slopes can be extremely slippery. Switch back and forth down to the edge of the river and then head north. A platform offers a view of the water as it drops over sandstone and then rushes between conglomerate cliffs to plunge about 20 feet (.2 mi.) **[2]**.

Head back to the parking lot to pick up the North Country Trail, which will weave you around to the other falls. The trail is located near the road (.3 mi.) **[3]**. Go south through the hardwoods. The trail parallels the road for about .1 mi. and then swings away through old hemlocks.

The trail cuts down ravines and crosses a footbridge over a stream flowing into the Black River (.8 mi.) **[4]**. As you follow the river ridge, cross more steep ravines while catching glimpses of the caves cut into the river canyon. Hear the thunder of the falls before you arrive at the Gorge Falls parking junction (1.1 mi.) **[5]**.

Go down the steps to the viewing platform. Through a narrow canyon, the water drops 24 feet, stirring up foam in the amber waters below. Go downstream to another viewing platform to see the deep gorge cut by the river.

Continue south on the main trail. It winds around for more views and then cuts down stairs and a steep slope to arrive at another platform (1.2 mi.) **[6]**. This section, between Gorge Falls and Potawatomi Falls, because of its design that includes a series of stairways and observation platforms, has been designated a national recreation trail. As an alternative, an asphalt trail connects the Gorge Falls parking area to the viewing overlook at Potawatomi Falls.

Go down the next stairway off the main trail to view Potawatomi Falls. Water, spread over a width of 130 feet, rushes over rock rubble as it drops 30 feet. Head back up to the main trail and continue south to an information board. Read about the geology of the river before pressing on. More viewing platforms await you.

At 1.4 mi., an overview shows you the full breadth of the falls **[7]**. Go up more stairs, merge with the trail, and then reach another overview.

Climb down, then up, steep root steps (1.5 mi.) **[8]**. At 1.6 mi., cross a stream by stepping from stone to stone **[9]**. The trail is muddy here, and you soon cross another stream, this time over logs. Then climb to a challenging overlook.

You are in for more challenges. Cross a stream on slippery logs and then climb a mountain of roots to a point where you get a glimpse of the next falls. Round a bend, maneuver down a steep, treacherous web of roots, and then cross the footbridge over a stream to arrive at Great Conglomerate Falls (1.8 mi.) **[10]**. From a natural platform of rock, view the water as it splits around a mass of rock into two waterfalls and plunges about 40 feet. Then follow the North Country Trail back to Sandstone Falls.

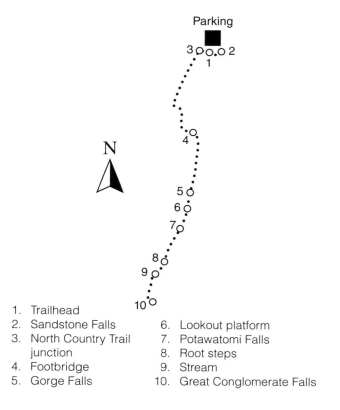

1. Trailhead
2. Sandstone Falls
3. North Country Trail junction
4. Footbridge
5. Gorge Falls
6. Lookout platform
7. Potawatomi Falls
8. Root steps
9. Stream
10. Great Conglomerate Falls

North Country Trail to Rainbow Falls—West and East

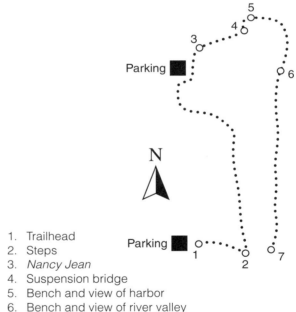

Distance Round-Trip: 3.2 miles
Estimated Hiking Time: 2 hours to 2.5 hours

Cautions: This trail has some steep climbs and descents, on stairs and slopes. Some stretches are muddy, some have roots and rocks to step over, and some are along ridges near the edge of the river. Take care and wear proper footgear. Keep children close by. Take insect repellent. You are in bear country, so be careful.

Trail Directions: Start from the information board at the parking area for Rainbow Falls [1]. Head into the woods for a short, level walk. About halfway to the falls, cross a footbridge over calm water as you move rapidly toward the thunderous roar of the falls ahead of you.

You reach the stairs down to the falls in less than .2 mi. [2]. To see a display of the falls' awesome power up close, climb down the nearly 200 steps to the observation deck below. The noise is deafening as you come almost close enough to touch the frothing water as it tumbles over the rock.

Look to the top of the cliff on the opposite bank of the river. That observation area is a better place from which to see the falls, and you are headed that way. Climb up the steps, catch your breath, and then turn right to follow the North Country National Scenic Trail. Watch your feet as you walk along the edge of the gorge and step over roots and around fallen hemlock trees. Gradually the roar of the falls dies down, and you find yourself descending steeply toward the parking area for the Black River Harbor. Head for *Nancy Jean*, anchored behind the information board in front of you (.7 mi.) [3]. *Nancy Jean* is a restored commercial fishing vessel that once served the fishing village located here at the harbor.

Follow the paved path through the picnic area to cross the Black River on a pedestrian suspension bridge (.8 mi.) [4]. From the bridge, enjoy your view of the harbor as the frothy Black River empties into Lake Superior.

Stepping off the bridge, you head left to where the trail splits. Going left takes you to the Lake Superior beach. Veer to the right and climb the steps through paper birch. Where the trail makes a hairpin turn to the right, rest and take in the view of the harbor (.9 mi.) [5].

Completing the climb, a side trail cuts off to the left, and you get a view of Lake Superior from your perch on the ridge. Turn right and continue along overlooking the river valley (1.1 mi.) [6]. You should hear a dull roar off in the distance. This scenic section of the trail snakes its way along the edge of the river valley, crosses a number of footbridges and boardwalks, heads down steps, and passes large white pines and hemlocks. The roar of the falls becomes louder as you approach them.

At 1.6 mi., you arrive at the falls [7]. If the sun is shining, look for a rainbow in the mist emanating from the water as it tumbles more than 40 feet over the rock. Hence the name—Rainbow Falls. Enjoy the sights and sounds before retracing your steps to your vehicle. You may even want to take a side trip over to the Lake Superior beach.

1. Trailhead
2. Steps
3. *Nancy Jean*
4. Suspension bridge
5. Bench and view of harbor
6. Bench and view of river valley
7. Rainbow Falls overlook

Upper Peninsula

Northern Lower Peninsula

The northern section of the Lower Peninsula extends from the knuckles
of the mitten (roughly north of a line from Pentwater to Saginaw Bay)
to the Straits of Mackinac at the tip of the mitt.

Glaciers created much of the state's general topography. Large sections of broad plains are covered with rocky glacial deposits. In many areas, the glacial plains are level to gently rolling, with occasional higher hills. Specific features include belts of morainic hills, ridges, kames, terraces, sinkholes, hollows, and kettle-shaped depressions. A ridge of glacial deposit extends from Mackinac to central Michigan, approximately bisecting the northern Lower Peninsula. The highest point is near Cadillac, where the morainic mass reaches over 1,700 feet above sea level.

Two Great Lakes, Michigan and Huron, border the northern Lower Peninsula and join at the Straits of Mackinac. It is here, too, that Michigan's two peninsulas were joined by the completion of the Mackinac Bridge in 1957. Dubbed the Big Mac, it was the second-longest suspension bridge in the world when it was built.

Michigan's unique sand dunes reach their peak along Lake Michigan at the Sleeping Bear National Lakeshore. Here, sand is perched on top of glacial features that had been near the edge of the water at a time when the lake was higher. The top of Sleeping Bear Dune towers 450 feet above Lake Michigan. Less than 4,500 years old, Michigan's coastal dunes are relative topographical youngsters.

Major Rivers and Lakes

Lakes Michigan and Huron define the tip of Michigan's mitten. Among inland water bodies, Houghton Lake is the state's largest lake. Other large lakes include Crystal, Torch, Charlevoix, Burt, and Mullet. Burt and Mullet lakes are part of the 40-mile Inland Waterway.

Most of Michigan's rivers are "extended." As the levels of the Great Lakes dropped, the rivers lengthened their channels to reach the lakes. Along Lake Michigan, sand dunes tended to block the rivers' openings to the lake. As a result, most of the rivers empty first into a natural impoundment before flowing into the lake. Pentwater, Pere Marquette, and Manistee are examples of these natural reservoirs.

Ocqueoc Falls in Presque Isle County is the only significant waterfall in the Lower Peninsula. The Au Sable River, a favorite with canoeists, is the swiftest river, dropping over 600 feet along its length, which stretches from near Grayling to Lake Huron. Close to the town of Frederick, the upper Au Sable is only a few miles away from the upper Manistee River (another favorite of canoeists). For centuries, Native Americans portaged through the area, using the two rivers to canoe across the peninsula.

Common Plant Life

The northern Lower Peninsula lies between the needleleaf boreal forest of Canada and the broadleaf trees that stretch south. Known as the north woods, here the species of both forest communities flourish. Sugar maple, basswood, beech, and red maple reach northward into the territory of the white spruce, balsam fir, tamarack, and quaking aspen. Also found in this zone are red pine, eastern hemlock, yellow birch, and eastern white pine.

During the logging era, the best of Michigan's pines—in both quality and quantity—came from the center of the Lower Peninsula. Today, a small stand of virgin white pine, preserved at Hartwick Pines

State Park, serves as a reminder of Michigan's natural beauty before it was logged over.

Among the state's wildflowers a popular spring bloom to look for is the dwarf lake iris, which grows around the shores of Lakes Michigan and Huron near the Straits. Others to see include trillium, bird's-eye primrose, pitcher's thistle, Houghton's goldenrod, ram's-head orchid, yellow lady's slipper, marsh marigold, and the scented trailing arbutus. In May, seek out morel mushrooms near Mesick, the capital of Michigan's morel mushrooms; then head for the National Morel Mushroom Hunting Championship, held in Boyne City.

Common Birds and Mammals

Elk is the northern Lower Peninsula's exotic mammal. It was reintroduced into the Pigeon River Area in 1918. Today the elk herd numbers about 800 to 1,000 animals. Other mammals to look for include white-tailed deer, black bear, red fox, coyote, bobcat, raccoon, opossum, porcupine, beaver, mink, and weasel.

Northern Michigan is the only nesting area in the world for the endangered Kirtland's warbler. This bird enjoys nesting under 8- to 20-year-old jack pines that grow in the coarse Grayling sand. Wild turkeys have become plentiful since they were reintroduced to the region in the 1950s. These large birds are often seen along roadsides in numbers varying from small groups to large flocks. Other birds in the region include ruffed grouse, bald eagle, spruce grouse, upland sandpiper, eastern bluebird, herring gull, and various shorebirds and waterfowl.

Climate

Michigan is divided into the humid continental mild and humid continental hot summer climatic regions. The transition zone between them occurs along a line roughly parallel to the line used here to divide the Lower Peninsula into two regions. The mild-summer zone corresponds to the northern Lower Peninsula and is similar to the area around Moscow, Russia, in having short, cool summers and long, cold winters. Temperatures are tempered by the presence of Lake Michigan. A climatic subregion exists one to two counties inland. In the so-called fruit belt, temperatures are altered by the slower cooling of the lake water compared with the adjacent land. Because warm spring temperatures are delayed, the blossoming of the fruit trees does not occur until after the danger of frost has passed. Later, warmer temperatures linger into fall, allowing the fruit time to ripen.

The average maximum temperature in January ranges between 25 and 29 degrees Fahrenheit, while the low averages between 9 and 16 degrees. In July the average maximum temperature ranges from 77 to 81 degrees Fahrenheit, and the low average ranges between 53 and 59 degrees. Annual snowfall totals range from 51 inches at Gladwin to nearly 100 inches at Pellston. The moraine highlands of Crawford, Otsego, and Kalkaska counties receive an average annual snowfall of over 130 inches.

Best Natural Features

- Lakes Michigan and Huron
- Straits of Mackinac
- Sleeping Bear Dunes National Lakeshore
- North and South Manitou islands
- Pigeon River Country elk range
- Virgin white pine at Hartwick Pines State Park
- Au Sable, Manistee, and Pere Marquette rivers
- Ocqueoc Falls
- Sinkholes Natural Area
- Grand Traverse Bay
- Beaver Island Archipelago

- Enjoy a state park without crowds.
- Walk along a secluded Lake Huron beach.
- Hike to South Point for scenic views of the Lake Huron shoreline.

Park Information

This isolated park offers natural beauty to hikers who are willing to trade convenience for quiet, contemplative walks along 8 miles of sinuous Lake Huron shoreline, forests of birch and cedar, and more than 2,400 acres of nearly undeveloped splendor.

Challenging access has helped keep this park a serene retreat. Park brochures warn that Sand Hill Road, leading to the park's gravel road entrance, is so sandy that most two-wheeled vehicles are likely to become stuck. Our rear-wheel-drive minivan made it through, but we were probably lucky. And we were lucky enough to be one of only two vehicles parked in the gravel lot.

The limited development of the park includes an information board with park data and trail maps, vault toilets, and a continually flowing water spigot. Around the spigot are telling footprints; if you take along a good guide on tracking, you can probably identify the tracks here from most of the types of animals found in the park. All that you are likely to miss in the mud are human tracks. Precisely this lack of noticeable human interaction enhances the beauty of this nature retreat.

Chippewa Indians once inhabited the area, and the park is named after Chief Negwegon, one of their leaders. Three hiking trails (covering more than 10 miles) are named after Indian tribes: the Algonquin, Chippewa, and Potawatomi.

This facility has no camping sites or picnic tables. If you want a picnic, spread out a blanket and enjoy the remote serenity of the beach. This unspoiled quiet may not last: Plans have been suggested for rustic accommodations.

Directions: From Harrisville, take US 23 north for 12 miles to Black River Road, where you head east for about 1.5 miles to Sand Hill Road. This unmarked dirt road is by a cemetery, a good landmark. Go north (left) on Sand Hill Road about 2.5 miles to a gravel road and sign that identifies Negwegon State Park. Turn right here and follow the road about 1.3 miles to the parking lot.

Hours Open: Open year-round.

Facilities: Hiking, swimming, fishing, hunting, and picnicking.

Permits and Rules: A park fee is required for motor vehicle ($6 daily, $24 annually for residents; $8 daily, $29 annually for nonresidents). There is no station here. The park is administered by Harrisville State Park.

For Further Information: Negwegon State Park, c/o Harrisville State Park, P.O. Box 326, 248 State Park Road, Harrisville, MI 48740; 989-724-5126.

Other Points of Interest

Harrisville State Park provides modern camping facilities with shaded sites, a sandy Lake Huron beach with picnic area, and a nature trail. The park is about 1 mile south of Harrisville on US 23. For more information, contact Harrisville State Park (address earlier).

One mile east of the Village of Ossineke, which is about 10 miles north of Black River Road, the **Ossineke Campground** has 42 rustic campsites and offers boating, fishing, and swimming on Lake Huron. Hiking and cross-country skiing enthusiasts can enjoy the Ossineke Pathway. For more information, contact the Atlanta Forest Management Unit, 13501 M-33, Atlanta, MI 49709; 989-785-4251.

Sturgeon Point Lighthouse, located north of Harrisville, offers tours of the 70-foot-high museum. For more information, contact the Huron Shores Chamber of Commerce at 989-724-5107 or www.huronshorescc.com.

Park Trails

Chippewa Trail (🐾🐾, 4.8 miles). This trail is an inner loop of the Algonquin Trail. You can begin hiking at either the north or northwest end of the parking area. The trail loops through a hardwood forest of aspen, maple, and paper birch.

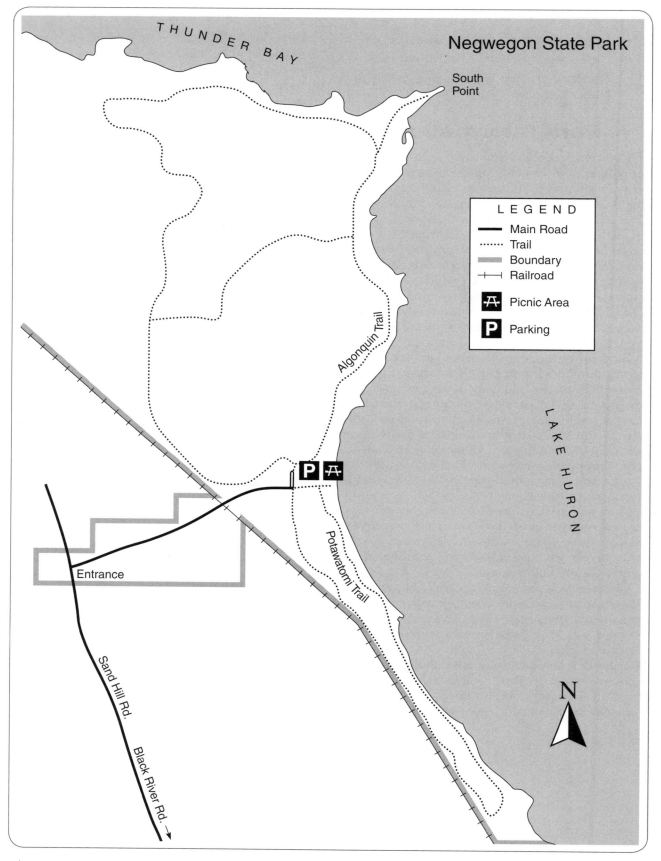

THUNDER BAY

Negwegon State Park

South
Point

LEGEND
Main Road
Trail
Boundary
Railroad
Picnic Area
Parking

Algonquin Trail

LAKE HURON

Potawatomi Trail

Entrance

Sand Hill Rd.

Black River Rd.

N

Potawatomi Trail

Distance Round-Trip: 3.3 miles
Estimated Hiking Time: 1.5 to 2 hours

Cautions: An occasional root crosses this mostly sandy trail, so watch your footing. Some areas are apt to be muddy, depending on the weather or season; prepare accordingly. Take along insect repellent in warm months.

Trail Directions: Start from the southeast end of the parking area and head through the gate toward the beach **[1]**. About half of this trail follows near Lake Huron, giving access to the beach, so you may want to bring along a blanket, towel, bathing suit, and lunch.

After you pass the water spigot, you will see the post for the trail, which directs you to the right. But straight ahead, framed in the silhouette of a tree, are the aqua waters of Lake Huron rolling onto the sandy beach, beckoning to you. Give in!

Head south at the post along the grassy trail. The shore is often unmasked by openings in the trees that form a line between you and the lake. Reach the first unveiling at .1 mi. **[2]**. Walking through cedars on a carpet of pine needles entertains your nose and feet. Soon you pass a post with a blue triangle. Notice that the trail is sandier than it had been.

White pine and cedar trees seem noticeably larger when you listen to the song of the beach here—waves gently breaking onshore (.3 mi.) **[3]**. Red pine mix in to frame the beach scene; white birch trees dominate along your right side. Pine perfumes the air as you peek again at the lake at .5 mi. **[4]**. The beach music

intensifies, and at .7 mi., the trees open wide, allowing the cool breeze off the lake to brush past you **[5]**.

A trail post in the sand near the beach marks .9 mi. **[6]**. Weave into more pines and then break out to a prime beach access point (1.2 mi.) **[7]**. More breaks come, but they taper off. Soon you enter the shade of the woods as the trail veers away from the lake. Walk through the tunnel of leaning cedars and a swampy area strewn with debris from fallen trees (1.4 mi.) **[8]**.

The trail takes you over roots and through several cedars (1.5 mi.) **[9]**. The forest becomes a mix of pines; their needles carpet the floor. Bunchberries inform you that the trail will become grassy. Soon you enter an opening along the corridor of an active rail line (1.7 mi.) **[10]**. Turn right and follow alongside the iron tracks. Look for deer tracks here. The narrow opening lets in sunlight, encouraging meadowlike vegetation for browsing, yet the forest also provides easily reached cover at its edges for the deer who picnic here.

The trail swings away from the tracks. You'll pass through large white pines and under a mixed canopy. As you roll along, the strong perfume of pine mingles with the oily scent of the creosote from the railroad ties, never quite blending as one aroma.

You pass through a dazzling display of white birches (2.3 mi.) **[11]**. A mixed forest appears, with plentiful aspens, and you pass through a wet area highlighted by irises (2.4 mi.) **[12]**. The trail becomes sandy and then presents some pine-needle carpeting. A mound of dirt with a gate marks the end of the trail (3.3 mi.) **[13]** and takes you to the southwest end of the parking lot.

1. Trailhead
2. View of lake
3. White pines, cedars
4. View of lake
5. View of lake
6. Trail post
7. Beach access
8. Leaning cedars and swampy area
9. Trail veers right
10. Rail corridor
11. White birches
12. Wet area
13. End of trail

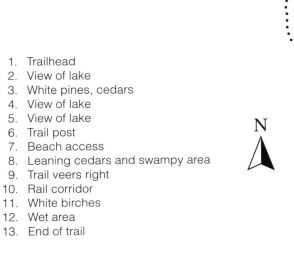

Algonquin Trail

Distance Round-Trip: 6.7 miles
Estimated Hiking Time: 3 to 4 hours

Cautions: The trail has exposed roots and rocks, and some sections are apt to be wet and muddy. Wear appropriate footgear. Bring insect repellent in warm months.

Trail Directions: Start from the information board hidden at the northwest end of the parking area **[1]**. You can orient yourself to the trails in the park by using the large map on the back of the board. Then head west into the mixed hardwood forest, crossing several small dune ridges and water-filled, swalelike features. This part of the trail does not get the traffic that the Lake Huron end does, and after you enter the interior of the park, you may have the trail to yourself. Enjoy the solitude.

At 1.1 mi., hike through a striking forest of white paper birch and young firs **[2]**. Watch your step on the rocks. As the forest canopy opens to the delight of the local ferns and lichen, hike past the Chippewa Trail where it splits off to the right (1.4 mi.) **[3]**. Continue your hike north through red pine and then aspen. Continue past some oak trees and across an abandoned forest road (1.6 mi.) **[4]**. Watch your step as you pass through a wet area and cross over loose rocks at the culvert (2.1 mi.) **[5]**.

Keep going to pass through a striking forest of white birch. At 2.8 mi., turn right with the trail to avoid private property **[6]**. Pass a large aspen, turn

right again, and cross a footbridge (3 mi.) **[7]**, which brings you to a series of old dune ridges. Lake Huron soon becomes visible through the trees.

Cross a footbridge over a small stream (3.5 mi.) **[8]** and skirt a large, open area on the right as you walk through tall grass. Cross on yet another footbridge over a small stream (3.7 mi.) **[9]** and pass an old field on the left before walking the edge of another old field to arrive at the trail junction to South Point (4 mi.) **[10]**.

Turn left and hike the .5 mi. out to the tip of the rocky South Point for scenic views of the Lake Huron shoreline **[11]**. To the north are two islands. Bird Island is the closer one; Scarecrow Island, the farther one, is part of the Michigan Island National Wildlife Refuge. Enjoy the isolated splendor before retracing your steps back to the trail junction (5 mi.) **[10]**.

Turning left, you travel along an old road leading through maple, oak, and paper birch to arrive at the junction with the Chippewa Trail and a trail to the beach (5.4 mi.) **[12]**. Although you now hike parallel to the lake, you won't see much of it. Look for opportunities to take jaunts over to the shore. Cross a couple of footbridges. At 5.8 mi., a narrow, worn path beckons you to follow it over to a sandy beach **[13]**.

The remainder of the hike along the trail is fairly level despite some sand and wet areas with footbridges. When you reach the parking area (6.1 mi.) **[14]**, head over to the southeast end for a thirst-quenching drink from the constantly running spigot or continue out to the beach for a refreshing swim.

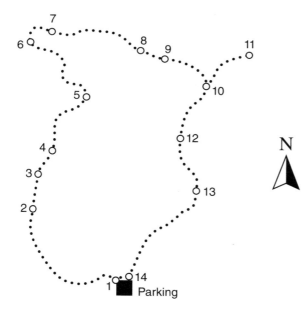

1. Trailhead
2. Forest of white birch
3. Chippewa Trail junction
4. Forest road
5. Culvert
6. Private property
7. Footbridge
8. Footbridge
9. Footbridge
10. South Point Trail junction
11. South Point
12. Chippewa Trail junction
13. Side path to beach
14. Parking area

N

- Enjoy the peace and quiet of an undeveloped park.
- Walk a rugged, cobbled Lake Huron shoreline.
- Catch glimpses of the rare dwarf lake iris in spring.

Park Information

Other than one latrine, 6 miles of hiking trails, and a gravel parking area, this rustic park offers no facilities or improvements. But that's going to change—about 2.6 miles of trail will be improved for universal accessibility and a rustic cabin will be available in 2009. Then the visitor will share the peaceful and quiet environment of this rugged retreat with more than just naturalists, hikers, hunters, fishermen, and seekers of solitude. Wait. Maybe there will just be more of them.

Over 7 miles of cobbled Lake Huron shoreline skirt the 5,300-acre park. About 304 acres is a designated natural area. E. Genevieve Gillette, an early Michigan conservationist responsible for conserving and creating two lakeshores, donated the acres for the natural area. The natural area harbors a dune-swale complex—one with a series of approximately parallel sandy ridges and low, wet swales formed during irregular cycles of high and low water.

Other unique features include fens, marshes, and woodlands. Six miles of hiking trails outline the shore and dip into second-growth forests. Early spring brings wildflower blooms, including the rare dwarf lake iris. In winter, challenge yourself with the ungroomed cross-country ski trails. Portions of the park are open to hunting seasonally.

Directions: The park is located 12 miles southeast of Rogers City via US 23. Go north on the park road about a half mile to the unmarked road to the parking lot located about .7 mi. to the east.

Hours Open: Open year-round.

Facilities: Hiking, fishing, hunting, and cross-country skiing. A rustic cabin will be available in 2009.

Permits and Rules: A park fee is required for motor vehicles ($6 daily, $24 annually for residents; $8 daily, $29 annually for nonresidents). There is no station here.

For Further Information: Cheboygen Field Office, 120 A Street, Cheboygan, MI 49721; 231-627-9011.

Other Points of Interest

P.H. Hoeft State Park offers modern camping facilities in a 300-acre, wooded park that features a sandy Lake Huron beach and four hiking trails. The park is about 5 miles north of Rogers City via US 23. For more information, contact P.H. Hoeft State Park, 5001 US 23 North, Rogers City, MI 49779; 989-734-2543. Located on the southeast shore of Black Lake, **Onaway State Park** provides modern camping set amid virgin pines. Contact the park at 3622 N. M-211, Onaway, MI 49765; 989-733-8279.

The **Herman Vogler Conservation Area** combines 7 miles of trails with hardwood highlands, cedar thickets, marshes, and 3,500 feet along the Trout River for biking, hiking, hunting, and cross-country skiing. For information, contact Presque Isle Soil Conservation District, 658 S. Bradley Highway, Rogers City, MI 49779; 989-734-4000.

Park Trails

Three loops weave through the park, covering 6 miles of terrain.

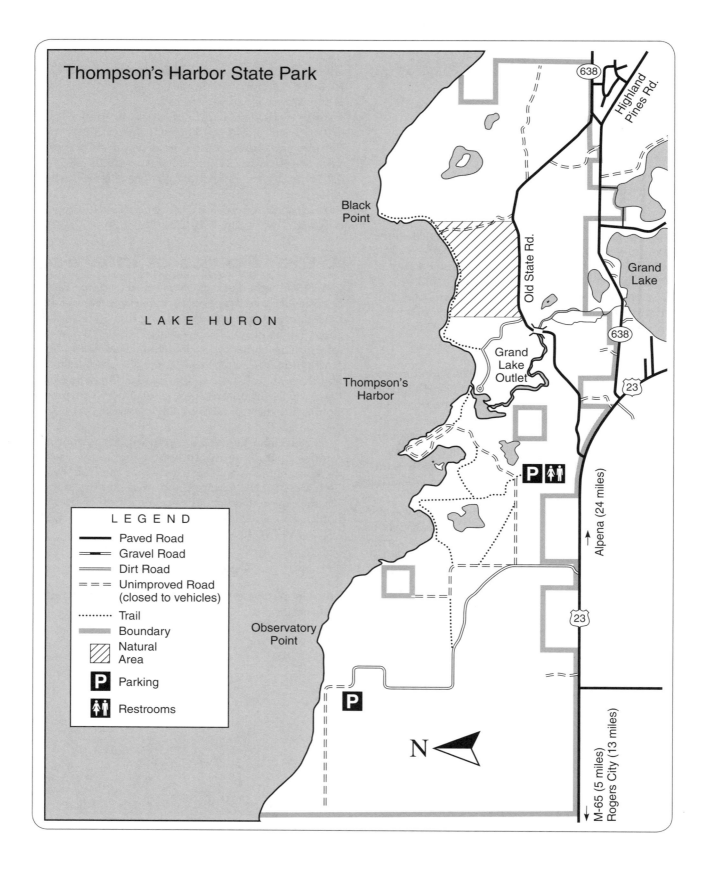

Thompson's Harbor State Park

Black Point

LAKE HURON

Thompson's Harbor

Grand Lake Outlet

Observatory Point

Old State Rd.

Grand Lake

638

638

23

Highland Pines Rd.

Alpena (24 miles)

M-65 (5 miles)
Rogers City (13 miles)

LEGEND
Paved Road
Gravel Road
Dirt Road
Unimproved Road (closed to vehicles)
Trail
Boundary
Natural Area
P Parking
Restrooms

N

Loops 1 and 2

☙ **Distance Round-Trip:** 2.9 miles
☙ **Estimated Hiking Time:** 1 to 1.5 hours

Cautions: Loop 2 has a smooth crushed limestone surface, but Loop 1 has roots and large cobblestones to walk on. Wear proper footgear and take along insect repellent.

Trail Directions: Start from the northeast end of the parking area **[1]**. The path is wide and cuts through cedar, fir, and spruce.

The trail veers right (.1 mi.) **[2]** and passes by plumes of grasses and tamaracks. Watch for small snakes sunning themselves on the trail.

Climb and find yourself in a mix of trees with more birch and aspen before you reach the junction for Loop 1 (.4 mi.) **[3]**. From here you get an open view of the harbor in the distance. Stay to the right along what is now a two-track. The cover of trees is less dense, but the fragrance from them is powerful. You reach the junction that will loop you up to the harbor at .7 mi. **[4]**. Don't be tempted to go straight to the water; you'll be coming back that way. Turn left and wrap around the finger of land that protrudes out into the harbor.

Cedars grow alongside the grassy two-track. You can hear the waves rushing the shore as you stroll the rolling trail.

A picture window of green, blue, and turquoise water opens to your left (.9 mi.) **[5]**. Venture off to the cobbled shore to enjoy the colorful display. You pass a number of similar openings as you move along the trail, and you may want to explore them all.

At 1.1 mi., you reach the peak of the finger and the greenish blue expanse of the harbor opens before you **[6]**. Follow the now-cobbled trail lined with cedars to the right as it follows the rocky shore. Snags, or standing dead trees, point up like sharpened pencils on your right.

The trail bends right to loop back along the finger of land (1.2 mi.) **[7]**. On this side, you are farther removed from the water, but you can make out the old beach line.

You close the finger loop at 1.7 mi. **[4]**. Stay straight and follow back to the junction for Loop 1 (2 mi.) **[3]**. Here you can take one last look into the harbor before turning right and following along the crushed stone.

At 2.4 mi., fallen trees litter the cedar swamp **[8]**. Stay left of the Loop 3 junction (2.5 mi.) **[9]** and pass through red pines. Later, leaves on aspen saplings flutter as you walk by. Mixed woods then surround you as you wind your way back to the lot.

1. Trailhead
2. Trail veers right
3. Loop 1 junction
4. Junction to loop finger of land
5. Opening to water
6. Reach the harbor
7. Loop back along finger of land
8. Fallen trees in cedar swamp
9. Junction with Loop 3

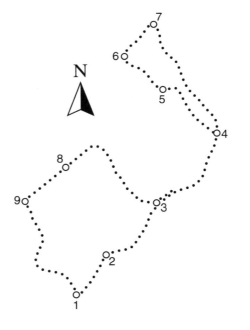

N

Loop 3

🐾 **Distance Round-Trip:** 2.9 miles
🐾 **Estimated Hiking Time:** 1 to 1.5 hours

Cautions: Loop 2 and the portion of Loop 3 that leads out to Lake Huron have a smooth crushed limestone surface, but Loop 3 has roots and large cobblestones to walk on. Wear proper footgear and take along insect repellent.

Trail Directions: Start this trail from the northwest end of the parking area **[1]**. The trail winds through spruce, then small aspen, and then red pine before reaching the junction (.4 mi) **[2]**. Turn left and wind through red pine, fir, and aspen. Although the trail undulates, the general trend is downward.

You leave the red pine, and the trees become more of a mix. At .6 mi., dense fir trees line the trail like a wall **[3]**. The light at the end of the tunnel—the blue water of the harbor—beckons you. You reach it at .9 mi. **[4]**. A bench set on decking waits for you to rest. Watch the waves rolling ashore from Lake Huron or stop for lunch before going on to the left.

From here on, the trail is not developed. The cobbled path with roots and large rocks takes you through more cedar. Cobbles give way to a lush carpet of moss and grasses (1 mi.) **[5]**, and you break out along the lake on an old, cobbled beach ridge. Walk near the shore, moving in and out of trees for breathtaking views of the lake.

Take one last look at the lake before turning left and moving away over a grassy trail (1.3 mi.) **[6]**. Walking planks hint of a wetter time.

The trail transforms to cobble and then two-track while rolling and winding, largely through cedar. Soon after you pass a post and the trail veers left and down into a mix of tamarack and cedar, you come to a two-track (1.6 mi.) **[7]**. Turn left and follow along through smaller trees. Notice the cobble around them—an old beach from when Lake Huron water levels were higher. After you pass a large boulder, you'll see a rusted barrier on the left (1.8 mi.) **[8]**. This is the junction; follow through it. You pass mostly small cedar and cross planking. Red pine and young aspen alert you that you are approaching a barricade (2.4 mi.) **[9]**. This obstacle stops you at the road that you drove in on. Turn left to return to the lot.

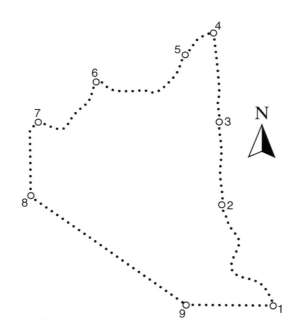

1. Trailhead
2. Junction for Loop 3
3. Wall of trees
4. Lake and bench
5. Moss trail
6. Turn left inland
7. Two-track
8. Barrier junction
9. Barricade and road

- Enjoy panoramic views from bluffs overlooking the Au Sable River Valley.
- Experience the 22-mile River Road Scenic Byway.
- Visit three monuments memorializing the area's rich past.

Park Information

Originally called the Michigan National Forest, the Huron National Forest was created in 1909 from the abandoned farms and wastelands surrounding the heavily logged areas of the Au Sable River. The forest contains 437,287 acres spreading 70 miles east to west and 30 miles north to south across the northeast Lower Peninsula, offering an abundance of recreational opportunities.

The Lumberman's Monument, erected in 1931, is a tribute to the lumbermen who harvested Michigan's white pine in the 1800s. The 14-foot bronze statue depicts three figures who represent various stages of a lumbering operation—the timber cruiser, sawyer, and river rat. The visitor center, added in 1981, provides exhibits, interpretive displays, educational programs, trails, and picnic facilities. You may be content with enjoying scenic views from the observation deck overlooking the Au Sable River, or you can take the 280-step plunge to view the river up close at the wanigan, or floating cook shack, display. A rustic campground is adjacent to the visitor center.

Directions: Facilities and points of interest are spread out over a large area. Contact the forest supervisor's office or the individual district offices of the Huron National Forest for more information. The Lumberman's Monument is located at the center of the River Road National Scenic Byway, 15 miles west of Oscoda.

Hours Open: Many facilities are open year-round. The Lumberman's Monument Visitor Center is open May through October.

Facilities: Hiking, mountain biking, cross-country skiing, snowshoeing, snowmobiling, ATV, swimming, fishing, hunting, boat launch, canoeing, camping (tent and backcountry), picnicking, interpretive trails, and visitor center.

Permits and Rules: There are no fees for the Lumberman's Monument Visitor Center. Recreation passes are required at sites that provide specific amenities ($3 daily, $5 weekly, $20 annually). Camping fees vary by site. No fee is required for backcountry camping.

For Further Information: Huron-Manistee National Forest, Supervisor's Office, 1755 S. Mitchell Street, Cadillac, MI 49601; 800-821-6263. Alternatively, contact the two district offices of the Huron National Forest: Huron Shores Ranger Station, 5761 North Skeel Road, Oscoda, MI 48750; 989-739-0728; Mio Ranger Station, 107 McKinley Street, Mio, MI 48647; 989-826-3252. For the Lumberman's Monument Visitor Center, call 989-362-8961 or go to www.fs.fed.us/r9/hmnf.

Other Points of Interest

The **Iargo Springs Interpretive Site** and **Canoer's Memorial**, just west of the Lumberman's Monument, offer spectacular views of the Au Sable River Valley. For more information, contact the Huron Shores Ranger Station at 989-739-0728.

The Huron National Forest covers a huge territory. For information about what is available in the area, contact Oscoda Area Convention and Visitor's Bureau; 877-8-OSCODA; www.oscoda.com; or Tawas Bay Area Chamber of Commerce; 800-55-TAWAS; www.tawas.com.

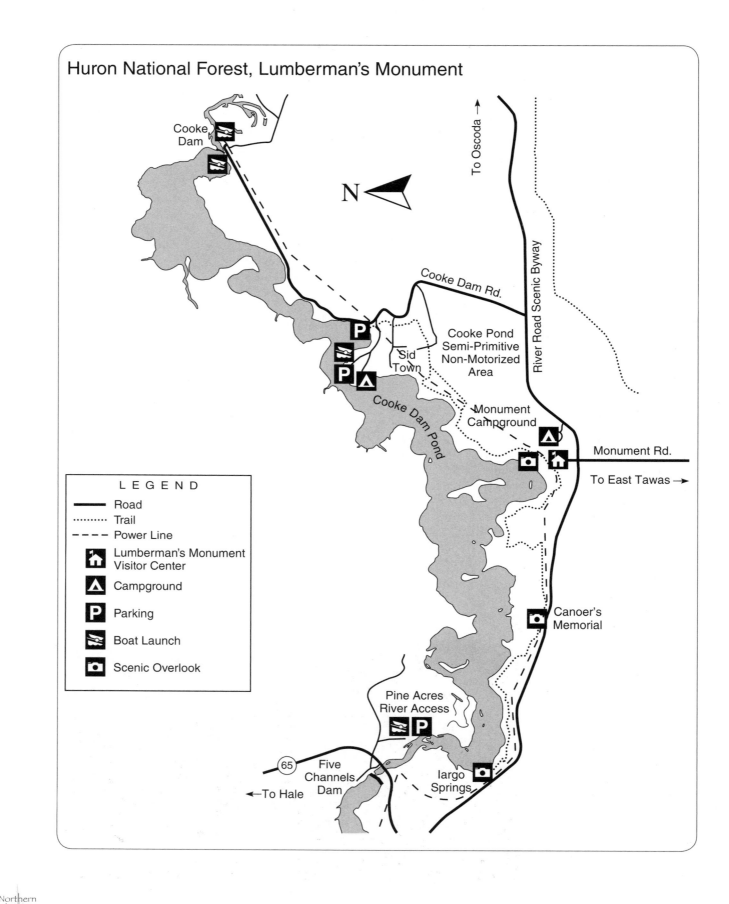

Huron National Forest, Lumberman's Monument

Cooke Dam

N

To Oscoda →

Cooke Dam Rd.

River Road Scenic Byway

Cooke Pond
Semi-Primitive
Non-Motorized
Area

Sid Town

Cooke Dam Pond

Monument
Campground

Monument Rd.

To East Tawas →

LEGEND

—— Road

.... Trail

– – – Power Line

Lumberman's Monument
Visitor Center

Campground

Parking

Boat Launch

Scenic Overlook

Canoer's
Memorial

Pine Acres
River Access

65

Five
Channels
Dam

Iargo
Springs

← To Hale

Highbanks—Sid Town to Lumberman's Monument

Distance One-Way: 2.7 miles
Estimated Hiking Time: 1.5 to 2 hours

Cautions: The trail goes over exposed roots; portions cut through sand and over dunes. Watch for poison ivy. Wear proper footgear. Take water and insect repellent.

Trail Directions: From the Lumberman's Monument, head east about 1.4 mi. to Cooke Dam Road. Then turn left for about 1.6 mi. (go past the Old Sid Town and campground entrances). The parking lot is on the left. Start by the information board **[1]**. For a tease of what to expect, from your high bank, view the river valley where Cooke Dam Pond widens it. Then veer left away from the river and enter the forest through a wooden fence opening. Blue blazes direct you, and you soon cross the campground road and start to climb into the woods.

Cross the road into Sid Town, go under a utility line, and climb past many fallen trees. At the crest, make a hairpin right turn and enter a red pine plantation.

At .8 mi., cross a dirt road **[2]**. Your hike through the woods brings you to a junction (1.1 mi.) **[3]**. Stay right for more high-bank views of the river valley. At the utility corridor, turn left and cross diagonally, climbing through sand.

Be sure to take a side trip to the right along the worn path for a stunning view of the river valley (and maybe a soaring bald eagle) (1.3 mi.) **[4]**. Better yet, sit down and take a break. You don't find many scenes like this one without getting off the beaten path.

Go back and continue along the corridor, where you get a number of peeks of the scenic valley below. At 1.6 mi., the alternate trail merges **[5]**. Veer right into the trees to follow along the bluff.

When you move away from the high bank, firs and other pines perfume the air. The trail descends (1.9 mi.) **[6]** and then winds and rolls through dunes. You pass a number of blowouts. Sandy trails that lead up the dunes offer opportunities for further exploration of the valley. At a particularly large one, the trail veers left (2.2 mi.) **[7]**.

After you are back at the utility corridor, the trail follows along the edge of trees until you reach the junction for the Forest Discovery Trail (2.3 mi.) **[8]**. Turn right along this interpretive trail, pass large dunes, and then reach the Sand Dune Overlook (2.4 mi) **[9]**.

On your left is the trail; on the right, decking with benches provides yet another scenic overview of the river valley. Sit a spell before heading up the trail past the rock wall along the crushed limestone surface.

Veer right at the junction and follow the blue blazes along the utility line (2.6 mi.) **[10]**, which guide you to the stairs for the overlook at the Lumberman's Monument. The 280-step descent to the river is worth the trip. Then come up and explore the Lumberman's Monument Visitor Center.

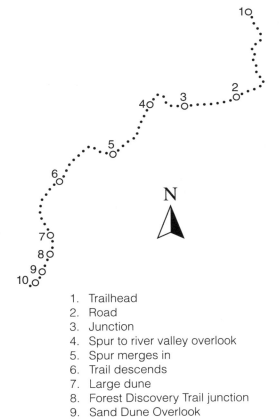

N

1. Trailhead
2. Road
3. Junction
4. Spur to river valley overlook
5. Spur merges in
6. Trail descends
7. Large dune
8. Forest Discovery Trail junction
9. Sand Dune Overlook
10. Junction

Highbanks–Iargo Springs to Lumberman's Monument

Distance One-Way: 3.6 miles
Estimated Hiking Time: 2 to 2.5 hours

Cautions: The trail goes over exposed roots; portions cut through sand and over dunes. Watch for poison ivy. Wear proper footgear. Take water and insect repellent.

Trail Directions: From the Lumberman's Monument, head about 3.5 mi. west and park at the Iargo Springs Interpretive Site. Before you hike, take the more than 300 steps down to the river and walk the extensive system of boardwalks that show off the river, streams, and small falls. Then come up and start the hike by the information board at the east end of the lot [1]. Follow to the right through the woods high above the river. Pass through a barrier and soon reach a fork (.1 mi.) [2].

Stay right. The trail breaks across a utility corridor and then flows along the south side of it as it wraps around the steep river valley. Scenic overlooks of the valley break out now and again, but after the trail veers left, stop for a spectacular overview [3]. Watch as kayakers silently paddle the river as it snakes through wetlands enveloped by thick forest. Tiny islands add texture to the river.

Pass through fragrant pines as the trail gently rolls and winds. A fork on the left leads to another view. Turn right along the trail after you take a peek. Other views unveil themselves from the trees as you press on.

Pass through another barrier and then enter the darkness of a canopy of hemlocks (1 mi.) [4]. The trail continues through a mix of trees, offering views of the river valley as you go along. Later, hemlock, pine, and fir perfume the air. Soon after you pass through a wood barricade, you reach the parking area for the Canoer's Memorial (1.6 mi.) [5]. Visit the memorial for yet another spectacular view of the river valley.

Continue past the memorial. Look for the skinny Highbanks trail sign and continue to walk along the forested ridge. The trail banks near the road and then takes you for a walk along the utility corridor, ascending gradually in sand (1.8 mi.) [6]. You are rewarded or teased with glimpses of the river valley. Gradually, the trail works its way across the utility corridor after a short descent. Roll along and turn left off the corridor into red pines and oaks (2.2 mi.) [7].

At 2.4 mi., climb along the back side of a dune [8]. Soon, the trail veers left, and you begin to see water on the left through trees. The trail winds and rolls, leading you to a scenic overlook (2.7 mi.) [9]. The trail veers right and descends. More views of the valley open to you.

Pass through a red pine plantation and then find yourself walking along the edge of a wooded bluff (3 mi.) [10].

You are teased again by swinging right to the utility line (3.1 mi.) [11]. Cross under the lines and turn right again into red pines. Although still in red pines at 3.3 mi., you can see and hear the road, your sign that the end is near [12]. Pass a parking lot and picnic area to arrive at the steps of the Lumberman's Monument. Take the 280 steps down to the river for another view. Then visit the Lumberman's Monument Visitor Center.

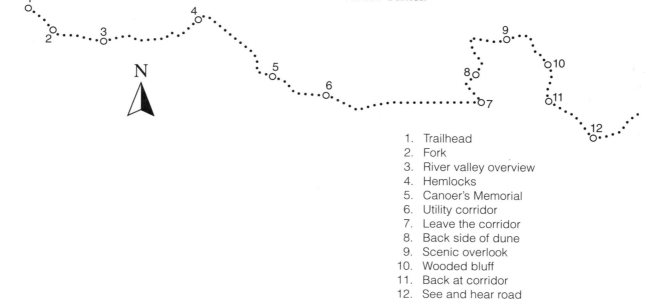

1. Trailhead
2. Fork
3. River valley overview
4. Hemlocks
5. Canoer's Memorial
6. Utility corridor
7. Leave the corridor
8. Back side of dune
9. Scenic overlook
10. Wooded bluff
11. Back at corridor
12. See and hear road

29. Hoist Lakes Foot Travel Area

- Enjoy 10,600 acres set aside as a refuge for foot travel.
- Hike a day or longer on 20 miles of trail that wander the backcountry.
- Camp on ridges overlooking pristine lakes.

Park Information

As its name implies, the Hoist Lakes Foot Travel Area, comprising some 10,600 acres of the Huron National Forest, is for pedestrian recreational travel only. Those who hike, snowshoe, or cross-country ski have this area all to themselves.

Scattered among the forested hills of the area are seven lakes and numerous wetlands, including some created by beaver. More than 20 miles of trails wander through this mix, providing many opportunities to enjoy the backcountry. The trails, marked with blue diamonds, are relatively easy to follow.

Primitive campsites and beaches are located at Byron and North and South Hoist lakes. Pack in your own water; the campsites don't have potable water.
Directions: Reach the east parking area on M-65 about .5 mile south of M-72. It is 7 miles north of Glennie. You can reach the west parking area by taking M-65 south from the east parking lot about 2 miles to Sunny Lake Road. Head west about 5 miles to Au Sable River Road and turn north for about 3 miles to the parking area.
Hours Open: Open year-round.
Facilities: Hiking, cross-country skiing, snowshoeing, swimming, fishing, hunting, and camping (backcountry).
Permits and Rules: The fee is $3 daily, $5 weekly, or $20 annually. No motorized vehicles, pack animals, or bicycles are permitted on the trails. Camping and fires are not permitted closer than 200 feet to trails or waterways. If you do make a fire, use fallen wood only; do not cut standing timber. Hunting and fishing are permitted in season; all Michigan Department of Natural Resources regulations apply. Parking for hunters is located along the boundary of the area.

For Further Information: Huron Shores Ranger Station, 5761 N. Skeel Road, Oscoda, MI 48750; 989-739-0728.

Other Points of Interest

Reid Lake Foot Travel Area offers 6 miles of trail for non-motorized recreation. The area is located on M-72, east of the Hoist Lakes Foot Travel Area. For more information, call the Huron Shores Ranger Station at 989-739-0728.

Take the **Jack Pine Wildlife Viewing Tour**—a self-guided, 58-mile auto tour that loops through the jack-pine ecosystem, home to the endangered Kirtland's warbler. Special signs mark the route. Pick up a tour brochure from the U.S. Forest Service Mio Ranger Station, 107 McKinley Road, Mio, MI 48647; 989-826-3252.

A 22-mile drive, the **River Road Scenic Byway**, parallels the scenic and historic Au Sable River. Stop along the way for its hiking trails, campsites, and numerous scenic overlooks. Other points of interest include **Iargo Springs Interpretive Site**, **Canoer's Memorial**, **Lumberman's Monument and Visitor Center** (see park #28), and the **Kiwanis Monument**. For more information, call the Huron Shores Ranger Station at 989-739-0728.

Park Trails

Twenty miles of trails weave through the Hoist Lakes Foot Travel Area. Although the park has five basic loops, they build on one another from the two access points. Innumerable combinations can be created, ranging from day hikes and cross-country ski excursions to backpacking and overnight wilderness experiences.

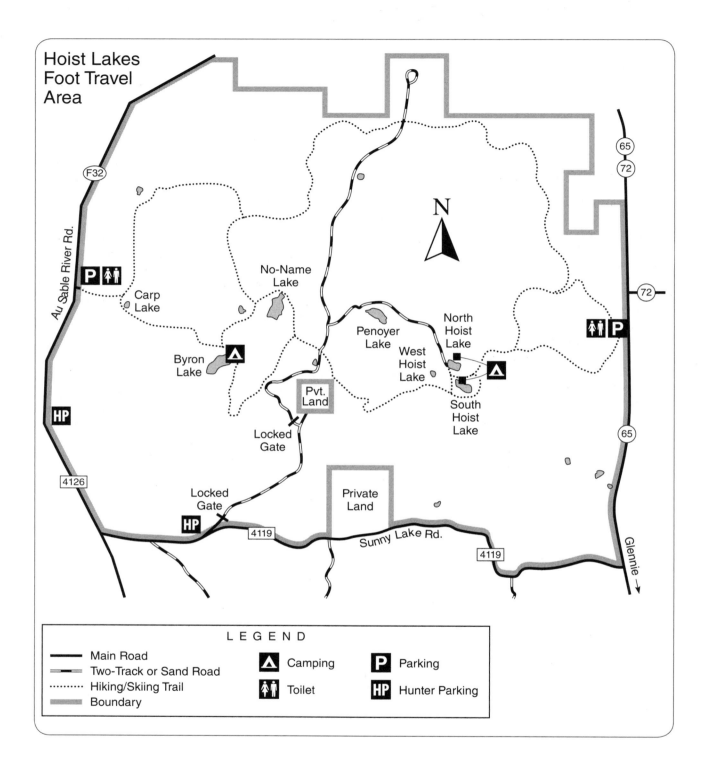

Hoist Lakes Foot Travel Area

F32

Au Sable River Rd.

P 👫

Carp Lake

No-Name Lake

N

Byron Lake

🏕️

Penoyer Lake

West Hoist Lake

North Hoist Lake

🏕️

👫 P

Pvt. Land

Locked Gate

South Hoist Lake

HP

4126

Locked Gate

HP

4119

Private Land

Sunny Lake Rd.

4119

65
72

72

65

Glennie →

LEGEND

—— Main Road		🏕️ Camping		P Parking
=== Two-Track or Sand Road		👫 Toilet		HP Hunter Parking
⋯⋯ Hiking/Skiing Trail				
▬ Boundary				

Hoist Lakes Little East Loop

Distance Round-Trip: 4.8 miles
Estimated Hiking Time: 2 to 2.5 hours

Cautions: Many roots are exposed on the trail, and you hike through wet areas. Wear proper footgear. Take water and insect repellent.

Trail Directions: Park on the west side of M-65, just south of M-72. Start from the parking area, immediately west of the information board **[1]**. Take the trail to the right of the metal gate to post #1. Turn right.

Although the trail starts out rolling through a mix of aspen and pine, it generally descends. Pass some blueberries before the trail bottoms out (.3 mi.) **[2]** and then head back up. Red and jack pine prevail here, and a reddish brown carpeting of pine needles rolls down the trail and through a red pine plantation (.4 mi.) **[3]**. At .5 mi., where the trail veers left, notice the corrugated landscaping, with red pines lined up in the furrows like soldiers standing in formation **[4]**.

After the plantation you pass through a thicket before arriving at post #2 and a bench and water pump (.7 mi.) **[5]**. Go straight, or west, following the now moss-covered trail as it veers left and passes a marsh and a stand of paper birch (.9 mi.) **[6]**.

The trail continues its undulations, narrowing until ferns hug your knees (1.1 mi.) **[7]**. Ferns give way to saplings, and you veer left, beginning an ascent (1.2 mi.) **[8]** that continues for .1 mi. Your descent is gentle, ending at a wetland with a lawn of cattails and grasses (1.5 mi.) **[9]**. Start back up and then head back down, past where the white bark of birch trees lights up the woods. Continue down the mossy trail until you reach the junction at post #14 (1.7 mi.) **[10]**.

Turn right. As you walk along, enjoy the views of the low-lying areas off to the west. The trail gently ascends through the hardwoods and reaches a fork (1.9 mi.) **[11]**. You can go either way. To the left is the high road, and the right is the low road. A boulevard of trees separates them. The paths meet again at the campsite spur (2.1 mi.) **[12]**.

Stay left to go south of South Hoist Lake. The trail rolls, passing through hardwoods softened by a feathering of pines (2.2 mi.) **[13]**. On one of the ascents, you get a peek at the lake through the trees (2.3 mi.) **[14]**. The trail winds down to post #13 (2.7 mi.) **[15]**.

Turn right and hike the narrow, eroded trail until South Hoist Lake is at your side (2.8 mi.) **[16]**. The lake mirrors protruding logs and lily pads on its crystal surface. Birches envelop the lake. Listen. The only sounds are of birds, frogs, and the wind whispering in the trees.

Turn right at the junction at the north end of the lake (2.9 mi.) **[17]**. View North Hoist Lake to the left before passing a primitive latrine in the rustic campground and reentering the woods. Rejoin the trail **[12]** and take the low road back to post #14 (3.5 mi.) **[10]**. Go right, passing a beaver dam and recent cuttings. We saw a live tree with the signature gnaw marks. Continue past downed trees and a wet area before starting a gradual descent.

Roll through hardwoods, then red pine, back into hardwoods, and then red pine again. You pass through cut rubble and into youthful stubble where young aspens have taken hold (4.7 mi.) **[18]**. Wildflowers lattice the trail before the edging becomes shrubby—a clue that you are near the end of the trail. Take the right fork up to the parking lot.

1. Trailhead
2. Low area
3. Red pine plantation
4. Furrows of red pines
5. Post #2
6. Paper birch
7. Ferns
8. Begin ascent
9. Wetland
10. Post #14
11. Fork in trail
12. Spur to campsites
13. Pines mixed with hardwoods
14. View of lake
15. Post #13
16. South Hoist Lake
17. Trail junction
18. Young aspen

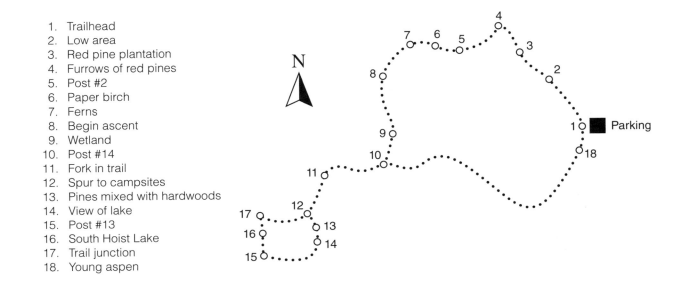

Hoist Lakes Little West Loop

Distance Round-Trip: 6.4 miles
Estimated Hiking Time: 3 to 3.5 hours

Cautions: Wear appropriate footgear: You encounter loose stones on the steeper climbs and descents. Other sections of the trail may be wet or have roots or loose sand. Take along insect repellent and water.

Trail Directions: Begin your hike at the information board in the west parking area [1]. Follow the well-worn path, which leads you east over gentle hills and past aspen, oak, and mixed pines. You quickly reach the junction with post #6 (.4 mi.) [2]. Turn right and descend on a carpet of pine needles.

Skirt Carp Lake, which lies hiding at the bottom of a small, bowl-shaped landform to your left. You barely see the lake through the trees before it finally pops into view (.6 mi.) [3]. Climb through aspen and maple to arrive at post #8 and a water pump (.7 mi.) [4].

Veer right and climb through saplings to reach a mixed forest of oak and maple. Then descend into an area of fallen trees, surrounded by growth on the forest floor fueled by the light that now penetrates (1.2 mi.) [5]. Descend again to a stand of paper birch (1.3 mi.) [6]. You soon circle a ravine on your left. Roll through the hills until you reach post #9 at the north end of Byron Lake (1.6 mi.) [7].

A side trail to the right provides the opportunity to explore the west shore of the lake. Stay left until post #10 and then turn right (1.6 mi.) [8]. You can easily miss this marker if you've mistakenly followed the trail that splits to the right to access the campsites on the ridge between the lake and the trail. If you have missed post #10, you know that you are still headed in the right direction if the trail that you are on swings behind the campsites, a primitive latrine, and past the small, sandy beach at the northeast end of the lake (1.7 mi.) [9].

Continue along the ridge on the east side of the lake. A path leads down to the lake and a campfire site. The trail climbs and then makes a steep descent, only to climb again. When you think that you are at the top of the hill, the trail veers and you climb some more. At the top, go left.

For the next .8 mi., you are heading mostly downhill. During the descent the dominant tree changes from oak to maple. The forest canopy is now denser, and the trees, which include some red pines, are larger. At the bottom of a descent is a meadow opening from which you then climb to pass a small pond on your left (3.1 mi.) [10]. Look carefully and you might see a beaver dam and lodge in the distance.

The trail is fairly level as you pass fire-scarred stumps, trees toppled by the wind, and several bowl-shaped wetlands to arrive at post #12 (3.6 mi.) [11]. Turn left and descend into the woods.

At 3.8 mi., you reach No-Name Lake [12] and cross an opening of ferns, milkweed, and aspen saplings. You then walk between the lake and a swamp before swinging left to climb away from the lake and reach post #11 (4.3 mi.) [13]. Stay left to return to Byron Lake.

You soon find yourself walking between two small ponds. Climb into the woods and then descend past a red pine plantation. Continue past a couple of wetlands to arrive back at post #10 (4.8 mi.) [8]. Linger and enjoy your second stop at sandy-bottomed Byron Lake. Then retrace your steps to post #6 [2] to turn left and follow the trail back to the parking area.

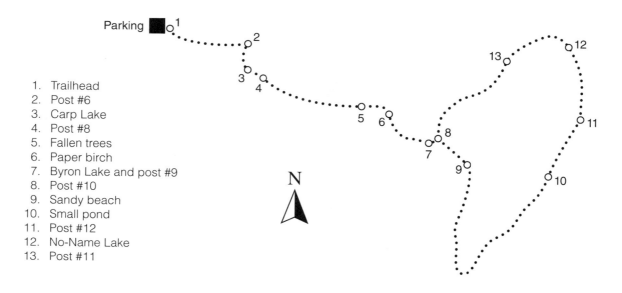

1. Trailhead
2. Post #6
3. Carp Lake
4. Post #8
5. Fallen trees
6. Paper birch
7. Byron Lake and post #9
8. Post #10
9. Sandy beach
10. Small pond
11. Post #12
12. No-Name Lake
13. Post #11

N

- Swim in small pools as water cascades over the rocks around you.
- Picnic on a grassy riverbank along the falls.
- Hike or ski through forest or along the riverbank.

Park Information

Although waterfalls flow freely in Michigan's Upper Peninsula, the Lower Peninsula has only two waterfalls. One of them is Ocqueoc Falls. Not exactly the Niagara of northern Michigan, these falls make up with their personal touch what they lack in height and thunder. Jump in the river and let the waters caress you as they gently cascade about 10 feet down a series of three steps. You find no drama, no foam, no thunder—only the laughter and splashes of children intermingled with the comforting music of the falls.

Ocqueoc Falls Bicentennial Pathway was built, as the name implies, in 1976. About 6 miles of trails in the form of concentric loops provide recreational pathways for hiking, mountain bicycling, cross-country skiing, and snowshoeing.

Although the falls are the focal point, the woods, banks along the Ocqueoc River, and abundant blueberry patches along the pathway present other reasons to recreate here.

Directions: The pathway is about 11.5 miles west of Rogers City. Take M-68 west. Where it curves sharply south, stay straight onto Ocqueoc Falls Road. The entrance is a few hundred feet farther on the north side of the road. The campgrounds are south of the entrance.

Hours Open: Open year-round.

Facilities: Hiking, mountain bicycling, cross-country skiing, snowshoeing, swimming, fishing, hunting, camping (tent), and picnicking.

Permits and Rules: There is a camping fee but no fee for otherwise using the park. Motorized use is prohibited on the pathway.

For Further Information: Atlanta Forest Management Unit, 13501 M-33, Atlanta, MI 49709; 989-785-4251.

Other Points of Interest

Black Mountain Forest Recreation Area has a network of more than 30 miles of trails for hiking and cross-country skiing. Mountain bikers and equestrians may use trails and roads that are not posted as being specifically closed to them. All-terrain vehicles have their own system of trails—about 60 miles of them.

In winter some 80 miles of trails are groomed for snowmobiles. Stay at one of two nearby state campgrounds. For more information, contact the Atlanta Forest Management Unit, 13501 M-33, Atlanta, MI 49709; 989-785-4251.

Located on the shores of Black Lake about 6 miles north of Onaway is the **Onaway State Park**. It has a small swimming beach, boat launch, picnic area, and campgrounds. Contact the park at 3622 N. M-211, Onaway, MI 49765; 989-733-8279.

P.H. Hoeft State Park, about 5 miles north of Rogers City, has campsites and a picnic area, over a mile of sandy Lake Huron shoreline, rolling sand dunes, and hiking trails. For more information, contact P.H. Hoeft State Park, 5001 US 23 North, Rogers City, MI 49779; 989-734-2543.

Seagull Point Park is on Lake Huron, just north of Rogers City. Foot trails weave along the shore, through a forest, and past wildflowers and dunes. For more information, contact City of Rogers City, 193 E. Michigan Avenue, Rogers City, MI 49779; 989-734-2191.

The **Herman Vogler Conservation Area** offers more than 7 miles of nature study trails. For more information, contact the Presque Isle Soil Conservation District, 658 S. Bradley Highway, Rogers City, MI 49779; 989-734-4000. This park and Seagull Point Park are on Forest Avenue, off US 23.

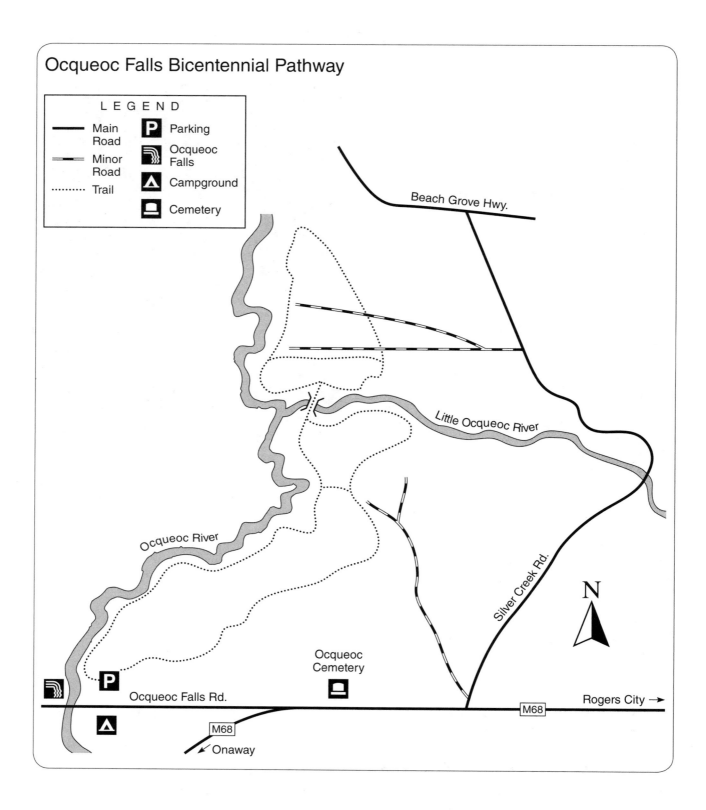

Ocqueoc Falls Bicentennial Pathway

LEGEND

—— Main Road	**P** Parking
⊨ Minor Road	Ocqueoc Falls
········ Trail	▲ Campground
	☐ Cemetery

Beach Grove Hwy.

Little Ocqueoc River

Ocqueoc River

Silver Creek Rd.

N

Ocqueoc Cemetery

P

Ocqueoc Falls Rd.

▲

M68

M68   Rogers City →

↙ Onaway

Ocqueoc Falls Bicentennial Pathway—Medium Loop

Distance Round-Trip: 4.6 miles
Estimated Hiking Time: 2 to 2.5 hours

Cautions: Roots are exposed, some areas are riddled with holes, slopes have loose stones, and some areas are wet. Wear appropriate footgear. Take insect repellent.

Trail Directions: Start from the northeast corner of the parking lot, near the map board [1]. Turn right at the junction, post #1, and head up the grassy trail through mixed hardwoods and then red pines (.1 mi.) [2]. The undulating trail is lined with a soft carpeting of pine needles and pine cones.

Although the land rolls, it trends upward; soon you are on a ridge (.6 mi.) [3]. Other trails cut through, so watch for blue blazes on trees. At .9 mi., you pass an old road with a cul-de-sac [4].

Red pines stand straight in their planted rows as you round the curve to the left (1.1 mi.) [5]. Continue to watch for blue blazes as you wind through the forest; old roads cross the trail. At 1.4 mi., an opening in the trees allows you to look to your left at the grassy valley below [6].

Continue past a bench and junction #2 (1.5 mi.) [7], crossing a couple of wide paths and following the arrow at the fork, which directs you to the right. At 1.7 mi., another arrow directs you to do a hairpin turn left [8]. Walk the ridge with the valley of the river below to the right.

The trail winds and rolls along the ridge. At the junction, follow the arrows to the right (2.1 mi.) [9]. Soon you pass a gate, and the trail becomes a single-track (2.2 mi.) [10]. Cross the bridge over Little Ocqueoc River at 2.3 mi. [11] and climb up to the junction. Turn right on this extension trail. Look closely for the next junction (2.5 mi.) [12]. Seeing through the tall ferns is difficult. Turn left and follow through the red pines to post #4 (2.7 mi) [13]. The post and a bench sit high overlooking the river. Take a break and enjoy the view.

Follow along to the left to the junction with the bridge (2.8 mi.) [14]. Turn right and cross the bridge to go back to the gate (3.1 mi.) [10]. Pass the junction and go straight, following the blue blazes.

You soon ascend and descend a steep incline that has loose stones. Another trail crosses your path. By the time you notice that you are walking a ridge, the trail descends through a mixed forest, and you wind down to junction #5 (3.3 mi.) [15].

Go straight, down into the meadow; then wind along through the forest, cross a small culvert, and ascend with the trail. The river now winds to and from your side. At 3.7 mi., notice a large, sandy hill across the calm waters of the river [16]. Enjoy your riverside stroll before climbing up a steep hill, finding yourself on a small ridge over the bend of the river (3.9 mi.) [17]. Rest on the bench there.

As you wind along, notice the stumps and fallen logs—evidence of beavers. Pass a junction where you can listen as the falls grow louder. At 4.4 mi., a path cuts down to a small set of stairs. Here you can head down to the bank and look upstream at the falls as they tumble down their short, rocky steps [18].

A grassy picnic area with tables and grills awaits you. First, however, take a few more steps over to the falls, kick off your boots, and sink your toes into the refreshing water. Enjoy the moment. You have only a short walk back to your vehicle.

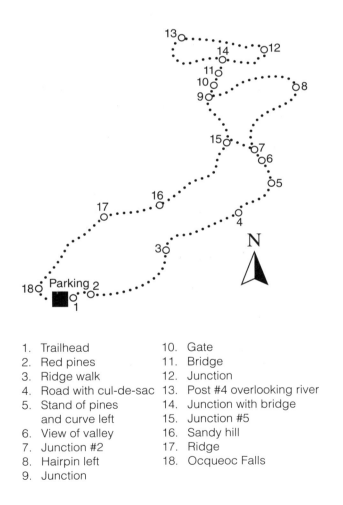

1. Trailhead	10. Gate
2. Red pines	11. Bridge
3. Ridge walk	12. Junction
4. Road with cul-de-sac	13. Post #4 overlooking river
5. Stand of pines and curve left	14. Junction with bridge
6. View of valley	15. Junction #5
7. Junction #2	16. Sandy hill
8. Hairpin left	17. Ridge
9. Junction	18. Ocqueoc Falls

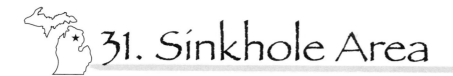

- Hike the rim of five major sinkholes.
- Descend more than 100 feet to the bottom of a sinkhole.
- Enjoy 2,600 acres of non-motorized serenity.

Park Information

This 2,600-acre tract of state forest is an open textbook for hands-on geology. Its subject is glacial terrain; more specifically, karst topography. Don't close this book. The area is fascinating! Sinkholes are not mere holes; some are deep, conical depressions more than 100 feet deep and wide enough for you to jog around the periphery at the bottom (almost .1 mile around one). Some sinkholes are awesome—you can look down at the tops of trees growing in them.

A *karst* is topography created when groundwater erodes the underlying bedrock (limestone, in this area). Water dissolves the rock into subterranean caves. Eventually these caves collapse, or sink. The glacial *till*, or *overburden*, which is composed of sediments left over from the glaciers, collapses in as well, forming cones or depressions. Some of the holes become clogged so that water does not drain away; they become lakes. Shoepac and Tomahawk are two such lakes.

Although you may explore the area with a compass and good map in hand, the Sinkholes Pathway leads you around five impressive sinkholes, one of which has a staircase down to the bottom. You'll also find old logging roads and forest trails to explore.

Directions: The area is about 10 miles south of Onaway. Take M-33 south to Tomahawk Lake Highway. Turn east, following the signs to Shoepac Lake Campground. Parking for the pathway is less than a mile past the campground, on the west side of the road by Shoepac Lake. The pathway begins on the east side of the road.

Hours Open: Open year-round.

Facilities: Hiking, mountain bicycling, cross-country skiing, snowshoeing, and hunting.

Permits and Rules: No fee is required. Motor vehicles are prohibited. Pack out whatever you pack in.

For Further Information: Department of Natural Resources, Onaway Field Office, 2321 North M-211, Onaway, MI 49765; 989-733-8774; or Atlanta Management Unit, 13501 M-33, Atlanta, MI 49709; 989-785-4251.

Other Points of Interest

Shoepac Lake Campground is located immediately south of the Sinkhole Area. Besides campsites, it offers the lake for boating and fishing, the nearby Sinkholes and High Country pathways, as well as off-road vehicle trails. **Tomahawk Lake Campground** on Tomahawk Lake Highway is less than a mile south of the Sinkholes Pathway. There you may camp, fish, boat, or swim. **Tomahawk Creek Flooding Campground** is south of Tomahawk Lake Road, about 1 mile east of M-33. The shallow waters of the area, which afford fishing and boating, are also great for canoeing and wildlife viewing. For more information on the three campgrounds, contact the Atlanta Management Unit, 989-785-4251.

The **High Country Pathway** provides more than 70 miles for extended backpacking in the remote Pigeon River Area. Make one long adventure out of the single-loop trail or break it into numerous shorter segments. The Shingle Mill, Sinkholes, and Clear Lake–Jackson Lake pathways all connect with or run close to the High Country Pathway. For more information, contact the Pigeon River Country Management Unit at 9966 Twin Lakes Road, Vanderbilt, MI 49798; 989-983-4101.

Clear Lake State Park (park #32) is about 10 miles north of Atlanta on M-33. The park has campsites, a swimming beach, a boat launch, and hiking trails. For more information, contact Clear Lake State Park, 20500 M-33, Atlanta, MI 49709; 989-785-4388.

For other things to do in the area, contact the Onaway Chamber of Commerce, 20774 State Street, Onaway, MI 49675; 989-733-2874; www.onaway chamber.com.

Sinkhole Area

Loon Lake

634

High Country Pathway

Sinkholes Pathway

Shoepac Lake

Shoepac Lake Rd.

Tomahawk Lake Hwy.

M33

Tomahawk Lake

LEGEND
— Main Road
···· Pathway
━ Boundary

Camping
Sinkhole
P Parking

N

Northern Lower Peninsula

Sinkholes Pathway—
Short Loop

Distance Round-Trip: .9 mile
Estimated Hiking Time: 30 minutes
to 1 hour

Cautions: Roots and loose stones are exposed, particularly on the steeper slopes. Take insect repellent in warm months. Don't overexert yourself climbing the steps out of the sinkhole.

Trail Directions: Cross the dirt road from the parking area at Shoepac Lake and head northeast to the barren information board, where the trail begins [1]. Walk down the woodchip path. The rustic, split-rail fence at your right side protects you from stepping too close to the depths and protects the sensitive slopes of the sinkholes from you.

Round the bend of the trail. In less than .1 mi., descend the few steps on the slope that take you to the staircase of the observation deck, which overlooks the first of five sinkholes [2]. Climb down the nearly 30 steps to the overlook for an awesome sight. You peer down at the tops of trees growing within this massive hole more than 100 feet deep. Awesome, too, is the erosion that occurred in the underlying limestone to produce a cave large enough that its collapse resulted in the interesting terrain that you are about to descend. Take a deep breath and then start down the 181 steps to the bottom of the sinkhole. Take your time. Benches are positioned along the way down the slope and another awaits you at the bottom, help for your shaky knees (.1 mi.) [3]. Look up. Yes, you've come a long way!

A small trail loops through the brush and trees along the periphery of the hole. Stroll around this green cone. In less than .1 mile you can loop it, getting your knees in shape to climb back up. Those benches start to look golden as you climb. The observation deck has benches, too (.3 mi.) [2].

Head back to the trail, turn right, and continue down the steps of the slope. Wind left with the trail,

around the fencing that skirts the edge of the sinkhole. Soon you reach the overlook for the second sinkhole (.4 mi.) [4], not as deep as the first but no less interesting.

The trail continues through red pine, jack pine, and oak. At .5 mi., you wind down to junction #2 [5]. This is your turnoff. Winding to the left with the trail would take you around the other three sinkholes. Turn right at this junction, descending along the trail before steeply ascending a land bridge that has you teetering between sinkholes #2 and #3.

Turn right onto the trail and stroll along the south side of the sinkholes (.7 mi.) [6]. Tall, slender aspens surround the trail as you hike westward toward Shoepac Lake. The trail descends. At .8 mi., if you look across the gaping hole, you can see the steps and observation deck that you were on earlier [7]. Continue down the straight path. A tunnel of aspens frames the lake that lies straight ahead of you. Step out onto the dirt road at about .9 mi. [8]. To the right in only a few steps is the parking area where you left your vehicle. After seeing the sinkholes, think about Shoepac Lake. The lake is a sinkhole, too, one filled with water. Swimming anyone?

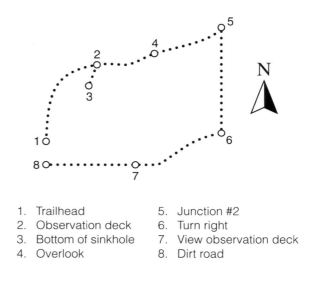

1. Trailhead
2. Observation deck
3. Bottom of sinkhole
4. Overlook
5. Junction #2
6. Turn right
7. View observation deck
8. Dirt road

Sinkholes Pathway—
Long Loop

Distance Round-Trip: 2.2 miles
Estimated Hiking Time: 1 to 1.5 hours

Cautions: Roots and loose stones are exposed, particularly on the steeper slopes. Take insect repellent. Don't overexert yourself climbing out of the sinkhole.

Trail Directions: Cross the dirt road from the parking area by Shoepac Lake and head northeast to the information board where the trail begins **[1]**. Head along the path with a rustic fence at your side separating you and the sinkhole. In less than .1 mi., descend to the observation deck that overlooks the first of five sinkholes **[2]**. Climb down 28 steps to the platform and view the tops of trees that grow within the massive hole more than 100 feet deep. You can go to the bottom; 181 steps await you. Step down, passing benches along the way. Another bench awaits you at the bottom (.1 mi.) **[3]**. Look up—way up. Take the short stroll that loops through the brush and trees around the bottom of this hole before climbing back up. Then rest at one of the benches on the observation deck at the top (.3 mi.) **[2]**.

Follow along to the observation deck for the second sinkhole (.4 mi.) **[4]**. Pass through red pine, jack pine, and oak. At .5 mi., you wind down to junction #2 **[5]**, the turnoff for a shorter hike. Wind around to the left, through the occasional blueberry patches, and then walk onto the observation deck for the third sinkhole (.6 mi.) **[6]**.

You descend along the trail through, over, and around a number of dead pines. Trudge along the sandy trail as it ascends and deposits you at a point where you have an open view of the fourth sinkhole (.9 mi.) **[7]**. In less than .1 mi., you get a different perspective of this fourth hole, with eroded, sandy slopes. From here, the trail descends, passing through an area of pines affected in 1939 by one of Lower Michigan's major forest fires (it scorched nearly 40,000 acres). Soon after the pines, you are at the overlook for the fifth sinkhole, which is steeper than the last one (1 mi.) **[8]**.

Climb away from this overlook, through a mix of silvery green lichen, moss, and blueberries. After leading you through a meadow, the trail descends, leveling out into a mix of grass and crunchy lichen. The trail is not well defined here; watch for blue blazes. Keep your eyes open for an old trail post, where you see the turnoff to the right (1.2 mi.) **[9]**. Turn right and climb through jack pine, past aspen growth, and then through paper birch as the trail becomes steeper before it levels out (1.4 mi.) **[10]**.

You reach the south point of the junction, where you turn right (1.4 mi.) **[11]**. The trail descends through hardwoods, passes boulders (as you walk the rim), and descends through aspen and then jack pine, regenerated after the 1939 fire (1.7 mi.) **[12]**. At about 1.9 mi., you meet the junction from the shortcut trail **[13]**. The trail descends as you look through the tunnel of aspens framing the lake straight ahead of you. Step out onto the dirt road by the lake at 2.2 mi. **[14]**; it's only a few steps to the right to your vehicle.

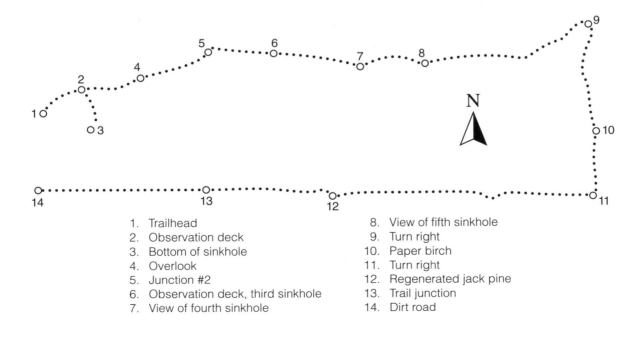

1. Trailhead
2. Observation deck
3. Bottom of sinkhole
4. Overlook
5. Junction #2
6. Observation deck, third sinkhole
7. View of fourth sinkhole
8. View of fifth sinkhole
9. Turn right
10. Paper birch
11. Turn right
12. Regenerated jack pine
13. Trail junction
14. Dirt road

- Swim the crystal clear waters of Clear Lake.
- Listen for the majestic bugling of a bull elk.
- Gain access to more than 70 miles of hiking trails.

Park Information

Aptly named, spring-fed Clear Lake is the centerpiece of Clear Lake State Park. Embracing more than half of the lake's shoreline, the park's 300 acres are accessed by two separate entrances. One serves the modern campground facilities on the north shore; the second serves the day-use area on the south shore.

The modern, year-round campsites are within easy walking distance of the sandy beach and swimming area. Two restroom and shower buildings are located nearby. A minicabin that sleeps four is also available for rental.

The day-use beach and swimming area includes a pavilion, picnic areas, playgrounds, and horseshoe pits. You can reach the Clear Lake–Jackson Lake Trail from the day-use area. Stocked with a variety of fish species, Clear Lake itself is noted for its excellent smallmouth bass and trout fishing. Two paved boat launches provide boaters with access to the lake.

If you are lucky, you may spot an elk—or hear one bugling in the distance. Your best chance at an encounter is in the early morning or evening hours during spring or fall. Elk disappeared from Michigan more than 100 years ago, but 24 elk were reintroduced in 1918. A sizable herd now lives in the area.

Directions: The park is located 10 miles north of Atlanta on M-33. The day-use entrance is on the south side of Clear Lake, and the campgrounds are on the north side of the lake.

Hours Open: The park is open year-round from 8:00 a.m. to 10:00 p.m., but the campsites are open only from April through November.

Facilities: Hiking, mountain bicycling, cross-country skiing, swimming, fishing, boat launch, camping (tent and RV), sanitation station, picnicking, and cabin.

Permits and Rules: A park fee is required for motor vehicles ($6 daily, $24 annually for residents; $8 daily, $29 annually for nonresidents).

For Further Information: Clear Lake State Park, 20500 M-33, Atlanta, MI 49709; 989-785-4388.

Other Points of Interest

Jackson Lake Campground, located about 4 miles south of the Clear Lake State Park on M-33, has 18 campsites. The Clear Lake–Jackson Lake Trail loops through the camp. For more information, call the Atlanta Management Unit, 13501 M-33, Atlanta, MI 49709; 989-785-4251.

The **High Country Pathway** provides more than 70 miles of extended backpacking opportunities in the heart of Michigan's northern Lower Peninsula. Make one long adventure of the single-loop trail or break it into shorter segments. The Shingle Mill, Sinkholes, and Clear Lake–Jackson Lake pathways all connect with or run close to the High Country Pathway. For more information, call the Pigeon River Country Management Unit at 989-983-4101.

A 48.5-mile **Scenic Drive** begins 3 miles north of Atlanta at the corner of M-33 and Voyer Lake Road. Marked by yellow-topped posts, the scenic route is especially beautiful in fall. For more information, call Clear Lake State Park at 989-785-4388.

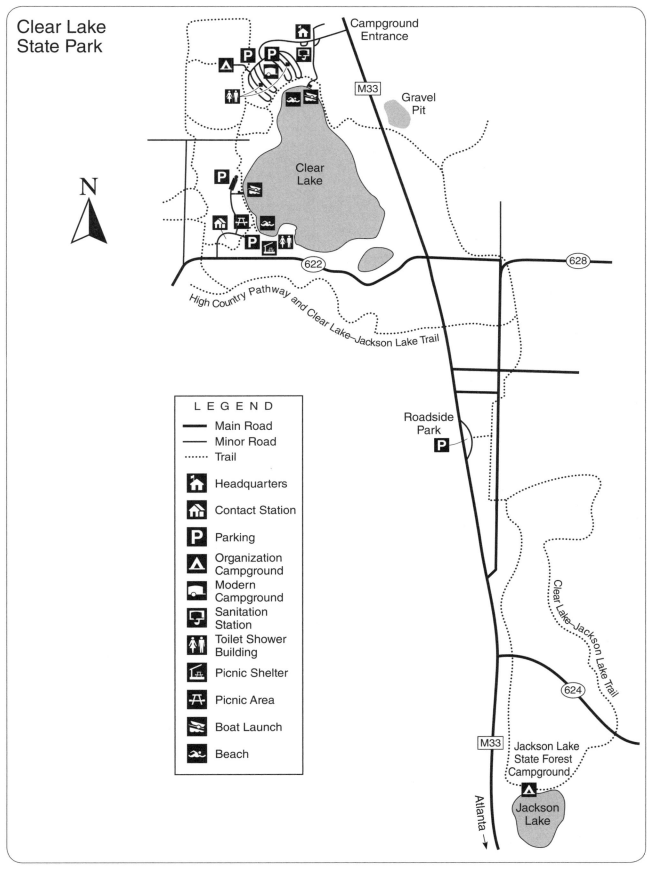

Clear Lake State Park

LEGEND
— Main Road
— Minor Road
···· Trail

Headquarters
Contact Station
P Parking
Organization Campground
Modern Campground
Sanitation Station
Toilet Shower Building
Picnic Shelter
Picnic Area
Boat Launch
Beach

Campground Entrance

M33

Gravel Pit

Clear Lake

622

High Country Pathway and Clear Lake–Jackson Lake Trail

628

Roadside Park
P

Clear Lake–Jackson Lake Trail

624

M33

Jackson Lake State Forest Campground

Atlanta

Jackson Lake

N

Clear Lake Nature Trail

Distance Round-Trip: 4.7 miles
Estimated Hiking Time: 2 to 2.5 hours

Cautions: Be prepared to walk over roots and rocks. Take along insect repellent in the warm months.

Trail Directions: The trail mostly follows around Clear Lake, but it also combines with the High Country Pathway. The access point (one of several) starts at the north end of the day-use parking area **[1]**. Head north through the picnic area. Stop and enjoy the clear, green waters that are so crystalline that you can see the rippled sandy bottom. Continue walking along near the shore. Go straight past the boat launch (.2 mi.) **[2]**.

Eventually the trail meanders away from the lake, and you pass behind a handful of cottages (.3 mi.) **[3]** and cross a road. Other trails merge or cross; follow the blue marks and stay straight. The trail swings near the lake again past some benches before you enter the campground. You soon reach a path to the lake (.7 mi.) **[4]**. Turn right and then follow left and along the shore. This beach has benches, picnic tables, and a volleyball court. Stay along the shore to the boat launch (.9 mi.) **[5]**. Notice how the lake displays a palette ranging from light green to aqua and bluish purple. Colors blend where they meet, like a rainbow. Enjoy the canvas before cutting back into woods.

The trail veers away from the lake into a mix of oak, white pine, and gnarled jack pine before crossing under a high wire and winding to merge with another trail, old M-33 (1.2 mi.) **[6]**.

Head right. Eventually you swing around to the present M-33 (1.3 mi.) **[7]**. Cross it to a dirt road that leads to a gravel pit heavily used by all-terrain vehicles. Don't go that far! The hiking trail swings right, into the woods, and skirts the pit. You come into the open, crunching over gravel. Keep heading straight and reenter the woods. Under the cool cover of trees, you'll wind up and around to a junction with the High Country Pathway (1.6 mi.) **[8]**.

Turn right, descend to cross a dirt road, and then climb to the crest of a hill. Swing down to where you catch a glimpse of a small valley before winding through white pines and several aspens to emerge onto another dirt road (2.1 mi.) **[9]**. An arrow directs you left. Follow the road for about .1 mi. and turn right at the next dirt road.

Soon another road curves around from your left. At this point, look to your left across the road for blue marks that will lead you diagonally back into the woods (2.2 mi.) **[10]**. Look carefully because the trail is easy to miss. You pass utility lines and reach a junction (2.6 mi.) **[11]**. Turn right and within a couple of hundred feet, cross the road.

Stay left and follow through hardwoods and under high wires. Then wind back down to M-33 (2.9 mi.) **[12]**. Cross back, meandering through mixed hardwoods and then red pine, generally descending to a meadow, which is an old rail grade (3.1 mi.) **[13]**. The Valentine Branch of the Detroit Mackinac Railroad cut through here during the logging era, 1880 through 1902.

As a trail merges in, stay right. Descend and cross crushed stone over an ephemeral stream (3.3 mi.) **[14]**. Take a sharp right at post #11 (3.5 mi.) **[15]**. This spot overlooks a pond holding the skeletal remains of trees. When you reach the dirt road (3.9 mi.) **[16]**, follow left and pick up the trail again on the other side. Continue west through a grassy area and then past the ghost of a baseball diamond built by the Civilian Conservation Corps (4.1 mi.) **[17]**. Follow to the right at the junction for the Clear Lake Trail past new aspen growth before crossing County Road 622 (4.3 mi.) **[18]**. Red pine and blueberries are prominent along the next stretch, with silvery green lichen adding pockets of color and texture. Follow to the right at the junction with a nature trail (4.4 mi.) **[19]** and cross the day-use area road. Stay left at a fork to cross another road to take you to the parking area, where you left your vehicle.

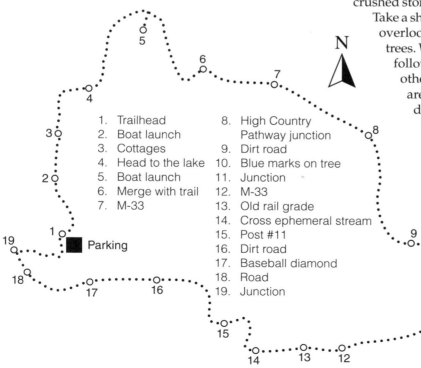

N

1. Trailhead
2. Boat launch
3. Cottages
4. Head to the lake
5. Boat launch
6. Merge with trail
7. M-33
8. High Country Pathway junction
9. Dirt road
10. Blue marks on tree
11. Junction
12. M-33
13. Old rail grade
14. Cross ephemeral stream
15. Post #11
16. Dirt road
17. Baseball diamond
18. Road
19. Junction

Parking

- View the largest elk herd east of the Mississippi River.
- Camp the backcountry along the High Country Pathway.
- Explore "the Big Wild."

Park Information

Pigeon River Country boasts two major distinctions. With 112,962 nearly contiguous acres, it is a large block of relatively undeveloped public forest land. The area is also the center of Michigan's elk herd, the largest free-roaming elk herd east of the Mississippi River.

Logged out between 1860 and 1910, much of the forest area came to the state through tax reversion when later attempts at farming failed. Designated a state forest in 1919, tree planting began soon afterward. The Civilian Conservation Corps built the forest headquarters in the 1930s, which has served also as a state fish research station and as the state's first conservation school.

Michigan's native elk disappeared about 1875, but in 1918, 24 western elk were released at three sites near the Pigeon River area. Your best opportunities to spot the elk are in September and early October and from late April through early May.

This beautiful area includes seven campgrounds (one that caters to equestrians and has horse trails); over 90 miles of trails for hiking, biking, and cross-country skiing; and excellent fishing and hunting locations.

Directions: Located primarily in Otsego and Cheboygan counties, Pigeon River Country has many access points. The headquarters are located about 13 miles east of Vanderbilt. Take Sturgeon Valley Road east to Twin Lakes Road. Turn left and continue north about a mile to the headquarters.

Hours Open: Open year-round.

Facilities: Hiking, mountain bicycling, cross-country skiing, snowshoeing, swimming, fishing, hunting, camping (tent, RV, and backcountry), equestrian camping, and visitor center.

Permits and Rules: In state forest campgrounds, you must camp at a designated site, register, and pay the camping fee. Wilderness camping on state forest land along the High Country Pathway is permitted. Camp no closer than 100 feet from any body of water or the pathway. You must post a camp registration card at the campsite or register at a forestry field office. Pack out what you pack in. In established campgrounds, pets must be on a leash. Operating licensed vehicles on any roads not designated as open is illegal.

For Further Information: Pigeon River Country Management Unit, 9966 Twin Lakes Road, Vanderbilt, MI 49795; 989-983-4101.

Other Points of Interest

North Central State Trail, a 62-mile multiuse trail of packed, crushed limestone surface, is open to all nonmotorized uses year-round and to snowmobiles from December 1 to March 31. For more information, contact the Gaylord Management Unit at 989-732-3541.

Park Trails

Shingle Mill Pathway (🐾🐾 to 🐾🐾🐾). This pathway provides for hiking, mountain bicycling, cross-country skiing, and snowshoeing along five loop trails that build on each other from the Pigeon Bridge Campground. The loops range in difficulty and in length from .75 mile to 11 miles.

High Country Pathway (🐾 to 🐾🐾🐾🐾). This pathway, which begins and ends at the Pigeon Bridge Campground, features more than 70 miles for extended backpacking in the heart of Michigan's northern Lower Peninsula. The single-loop trail can be hiked as one long adventure or broken into shorter segments of varying difficulties.

Northern Spur of the Michigan Shore-to-Shore Riding and Hiking Trail (🐾 to 🐾🐾🐾). This spur extends through the forest and gives equestrians access to the Pigeon River Country. The trail stretches from Oscoda on the Lake Huron side of the state to Empire on the Lake Michigan side.

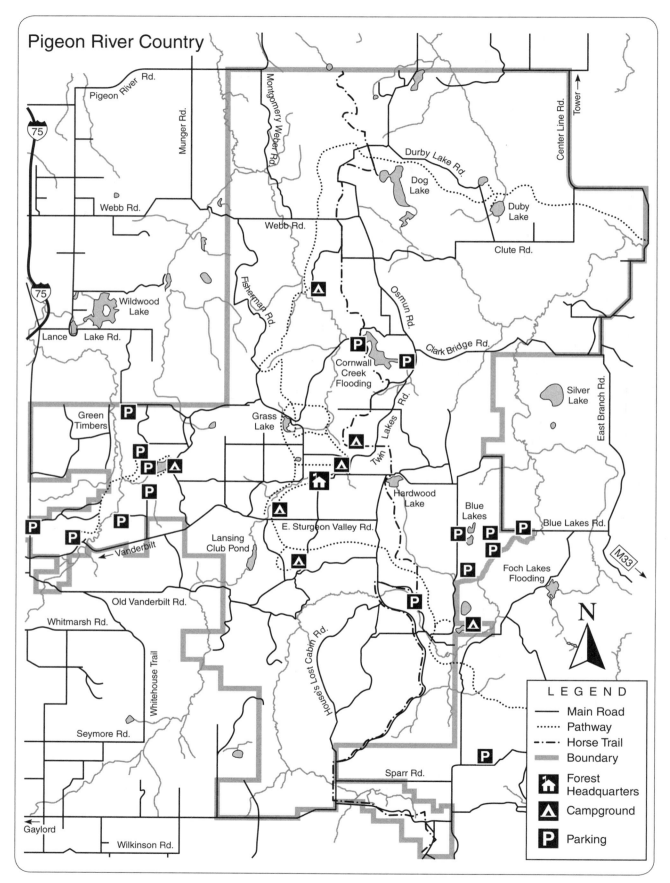

Pigeon River Country

Shingle Mill Pathway— Upper Loop

Distance Round-Trip: 6 miles
Estimated Hiking Time: 3 to 3.5 hours

Cautions: Prepare for roots, rocks, and wet areas. Wear proper footgear. Take water and insect repellent.

Trail Directions: Start at the Pigeon River Management Unit Campground, which is less than 1 mi. north of the headquarters. Take Sturgeon Valley Road east to Twin Lakes Road. Turn left and go north about 1 mi. to the headquarters. Continue north. Turn west into the campground and follow Pigeon Bridge Road, crossing the Pigeon River. Park near the bridge and follow the path through red pines **[1]** along the river to post #6 (.2 mi.) **[2]**.

Turn right and travel along the river, where blueberries and ferns intermingle along the trail. Ascend to walk the ridge overlooking the river plain and then pass through brush along the first crest. Follow the ridge. At .5 mi., an equestrian trail crosses your path **[3]**. Continue on the ridge and pass the end of a dirt road (.8 mi.) **[4]**. Then descend into birch, aspen, and pine (1.1 mi.) **[5]**. The trail gently undulates through red pines and then veers left to arrive at post #7 (1.3 mi.) **[6]**.

Head right through ferns, winding down to cross a boardwalk over a stream; then wind up to a junction (1.4 mi.) **[7]**. Turn right through a mixed forest. At the clearing is post #8 (1.6 mi.) **[8]**. Cornwall Flats, a former lumber mill, sat here. Its old millpond is now the alder swamp.

Cross another boardwalk, brush through lush ferns, and then wind and climb through hardwoods before heading back down and over another boardwalk (2 mi.) **[9]**. Get ready for an arduous, two-tiered climb over roots and loose stones as the trail winds its way into a dark forest. Expect more undulations; after a two-track crosses your path, another steep climb awaits you (2.5 mi.) **[10]**. The trail levels out and then gently descends to the dirt road (2.8 mi.) **[11]**.

After you cross this road, you'll cross many logging roads; thinning pockets in the forest indicate that logging has occurred in the past dozen years or so. The trail winds up to the junction at post #10 (3.2 mi.) **[12]**. You have three choices here: Go right to post #11, go left to post #9 (which you will do momentarily), or climb a few steps and go left to the overlook. If you like, head to the overlook for a stunning view of the Pigeon River Valley. Even on a hazy day, the smoky fog rolling from the backdrop of hills and wafting over the valley is breathtaking. Or go back and head down the trail as it descends steeply through the woods, bottoming out at about 3.4 mi. **[13]**.

Cross a dirt road (3.6 mi.) **[14]** and soon cross it again. Youthful aspens and maples cluster near the road. The trail traverses boardwalks. Pass between beaver-dammed pools filled with the white ghosts of birches (3.9 mi.) **[15]**. Soon, you wind into the campground at post #9 (3.9 mi.) **[16]**.

Turn left, passing through red pines. Descend, cross the dirt road again (4.3 mi.) **[17]**, pass a clearing, and continue to descend to a junction near a lake (4.4 mi.) **[18]**. Swing left and walk along Section 4 Lake—a nondescript name for a beautiful lake.

Murky aqua and sea-foam green waters mottle this bowl-shaped lake; fallen trees break up the surface like spokes in a wagon wheel. The colors (some as vibrant as spearmint mouthwash) vary with the depths within this watery sinkhole yet still throw off crystalline reflections of the surrounding forest.

The trail continues rolling through the woods, follows along a ridge, and returns you to post #7 (4.8 mi.) **[6]**. From here, retrace your steps to your vehicle.

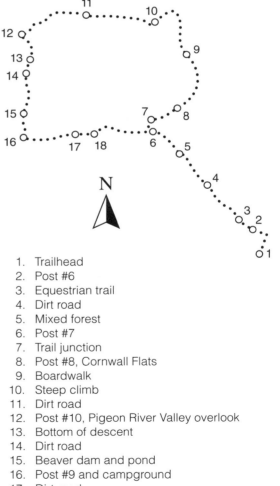

1. Trailhead
2. Post #6
3. Equestrian trail
4. Dirt road
5. Mixed forest
6. Post #7
7. Trail junction
8. Post #8, Cornwall Flats
9. Boardwalk
10. Steep climb
11. Dirt road
12. Post #10, Pigeon River Valley overlook
13. Bottom of descent
14. Dirt road
15. Beaver dam and pond
16. Post #9 and campground
17. Dirt road
18. Trail junction

Northern Lower Peninsula

Shingle Mill Pathway—
Middle Loop

Distance Round-Trip: 6.3 miles
Estimated Hiking Time: 3 to 3.5 hours

Cautions: Watch for roots and rocks. Wear proper footgear. Take water and insect repellent.
Trail Directions: Start at the Pigeon River Management Unit Campground, which is less than 1 mi. north of the headquarters. Take Sturgeon Valley Road east to Twin Lakes Road. Turn left for about 1 mi. to the headquarters. Keep going north and then turn west into the campground. Follow Pigeon Bridge Road, crossing the Pigeon River Park at the bridge. Follow the pathway through red pines along the river [1] to post #6.

Go right and follow along the river. The trail ascends to a ridge overlooking the grassy river plain and then passes through brush at the first crest.

Follow along the ridge. At .5 mi., an equestrian trail crosses your path [2]. Continue on the ridge and pass the end of a dirt road (.8 mi.) [3]. Then descend into birch, aspen, and pine (1.1 mi.) [4]. The trail gently undulates through red pines and winds down to arrive at post #7 (1.3 mi.) [5].

Head left and soon arrive at beautiful Section 4 Lake, a small, bowl-shaped body with jade-shaded water (1.4 mi.) [6]. The colors vary with the depths within this watery sinkhole yet it still throws off crystalline reflections of the surrounding forest. A number of trees, enamored of their reflections on the lake, appear to have met their demise by leaning over too far to look at their images. The trail veers right away from the lake.

At 1.6 mi., cross a dirt road [7]; then hike through a mixed forest to arrive at the campground at post #9 (2.1 mi.) [8]. Turn right to cross a land bridge and then descend through saplings to cross a boardwalk and a footbridge. Alongside to your left is an old beaver dam (2.2 mi.) [9].

Cross a dirt road (2.3 mi.) [10] and soon cross it again. You pass through an area of spindly legged saplings and climb through a beech-maple forest to arrive at post #10 (2.8 mi.) [11]. Turn left at the junction for a magnificent view of the Pigeon River Valley. Enjoy the view before you backtrack. Then head left to reach post #11 (3 mi.) [12].

Turn left and descend steeply through the woods before you skirt the Devil's Soup Bowl on your right (3.2 mi.) [13]. Grass Lake comes into view after you cross a road and walk through a small parking area (3.3 mi.) [14]. Cross a footbridge (3.7 mi.) [15] and then cross another.

Stay right when the trail splits. Go through a clear-cut area now overgrown with ferns and grasses (4.6 mi.) [16]. Cross a two-track into areas at various stages of recovery from logging. Descend and skirt a small, bowl-shaped wetland (4.7 mi.) [17] before passing Ford Lake (4.8 mi.) [18]. Then climb to post #12 (4.9 mi.) [19], turn left, and make a steeper climb. Descend and climb again before the trail levels out to cross Ford Lake Road (5.1 mi.) [20].

A dozen years ago this area looked like the clear-cut area that you previously traveled. At 6.1 mi., you reach the bluff overlooking the Pigeon River and a campground [21]. The trail swings left, away from the bluff. Stay to the right away from the trail to take the steep slope down to the bridge where you parked.

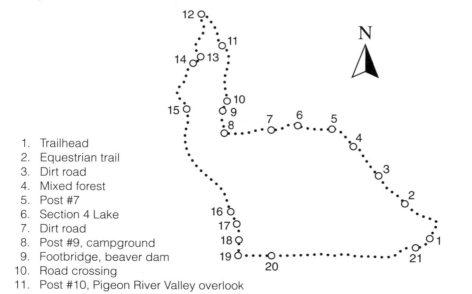

1. Trailhead
2. Equestrian trail
3. Dirt road
4. Mixed forest
5. Post #7
6. Section 4 Lake
7. Dirt road
8. Post #9, campground
9. Footbridge, beaver dam
10. Road crossing
11. Post #10, Pigeon River Valley overlook

12. Post #11
13. Devil's Soup Bowl
14. Road crossing, parking area
15. Footbridge
16. Overgrown clear-cut
17. Wetland
18. Ford Lake
19. Post #12
20. Road crossing
21. Bluff

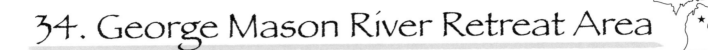

- Canoe the scenic South Branch Au Sable River.
- Try your luck at fly-fishing for trout.
- Visit the remains of Durant's Castle.

Park Information

The people of Michigan might thank the late George W. Mason as they fish, canoe, or hike along this stretch of the South Branch Au Sable River. Mason so loved this area that he bequeathed 1,500 acres to the state for preservation in 1954. Subsequent land acquisitions brought the holding up to 4,493 acres. Previously known as the South Branch Au Sable River Area, the site now is called the George Mason River Retreat Area, bearing the name of its benefactor.

Recognized for excellent trout fishing, the South Branch is also popular with canoeists. Canoe landings are located at Chase Bridge on the south end and, 11 miles to the north, at Smith Bridge. A third landing is located at the Canoe Harbor Campground, the only campground in the area.

Directions: To reach the northern trailhead on M-72, head east from Grayling about 15 miles and turn south on Canoe Harbor Campground Road. Parking is on the left. To reach the southern trailhead from M-72, head east from Grayling about 12 miles and turn south on Chase Bridge Road. Go about 8 miles to the parking area. From Roscommon, take M-18 east 2.5 miles and turn left on Chase Bridge Road. Parking is 2 miles up the road on the right.

Hours Open: Open year-round.
Facilities: Hiking, cross-country skiing, fishing, hunting, canoeing, and camping (tent).
Permits and Rules: There is no visitor fee for the park. In state forest campgrounds, however, you must camp at a designated site, register, and pay the camping fee.
For Further Information: Grayling Management Unit, 1955 N I-75 BL, Grayling, MI 49738; 989-348-6371.

Other Points of Interest

Canoe all or portions of the Au Sable River between Grayling and Oscoda. For canoe rental information, call the Grayling Visitors Bureau at 800-937-8837; www.grayling-mi.com.

The **Wakeley Lake Semi-Primitive Non-Motorized Area** (see park #35), located on M-72 about 2 miles west of the Mason Tract Pathway, offers an extensive trail network for non-motorized recreation. Contact the Mio Ranger Station at 989-826-3252.

The **Midland–Mackinac Trail** passes just east of the Mason Tract Pathway. The trail was built by the Boy Scouts and approximates the old migratory route used by Native Americans. For maps, contact the Lake Huron Area Council Boy Scouts of America, P.O. Box 129, Auburn, MI 48611-0129; 989-662-4464; www.lhacbsa.org.

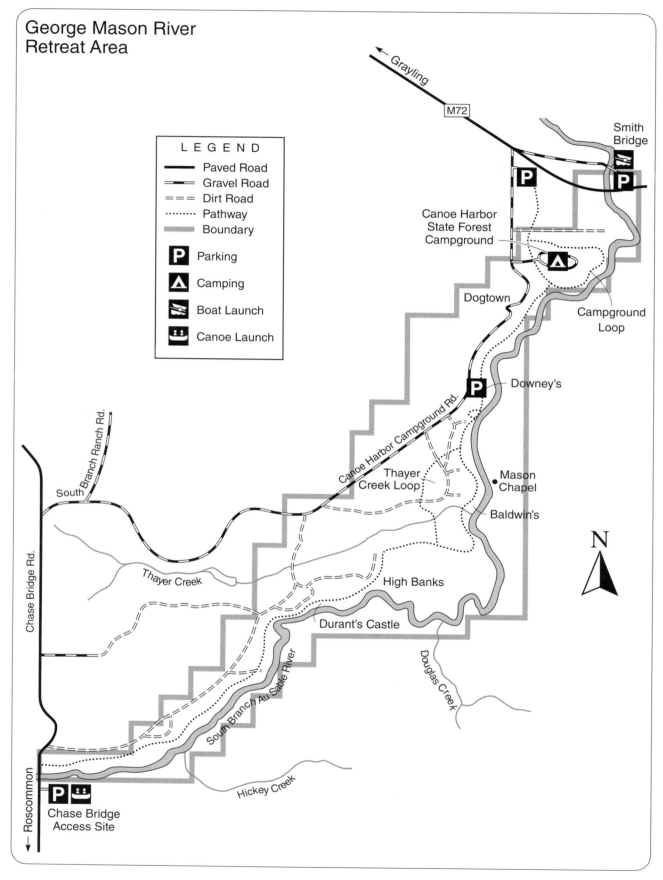

George Mason River Retreat Area

Grayling

M72

Smith Bridge

P

P

Canoe Harbor State Forest Campground

Dogtown

Campground Loop

Downey's

P

Canoe Harbor Campground Rd.

Thayer Creek Loop

Mason Chapel

Baldwin's

High Banks

Durant's Castle

Douglas Creek

South Branch Ranch Rd.

South

Chase Bridge Rd.

Thayer Creek

South Branch Au Sable River

Hickey Creek

Roscommon

P

Chase Bridge Access Site

N

LEGEND

———	Paved Road
—•—•—	Gravel Road
===	Dirt Road
······	Pathway
▬▬▬	Boundary
P	Parking
▲	Camping
🚤	Boat Launch
🛶	Canoe Launch

Mason Tract Pathway—North

Distance One-Way: 2.4 miles
Estimated Hiking Time: 1 to 1.5 hours

Cautions: Some sections of the trail have exposed roots and stumps. Wear appropriate footgear. Take along insect repellent in the warm months.

Trail Directions: The hike starts at the north trailhead, which is on the east side of Canoe Harbor Campground Road, just south of M-72. This access covers the northern end of the trail as a point-to-point hike and provides an out-and-back day hike of reasonable length.

Start at the east end of the parking area **[1]** and head south along the narrow path lined with blueberries and silvery gray lichen. Jack pines sparsely cover the landscape, and the dry, gray trunks of long-dead trees lie scattered about. The area looks as though it had been cleared in the past. Some standing dead trees still spike above second growth. Carcasses of fallen trees lie gray and brittle, their branches turned upward to form what look like giant rib cages picked clean and left to dry.

At .5 mi., cross a sandy two-track **[2]** and pass jack pines before arriving at the Campground Loop (.7 mi.) **[3]**. If you are inclined to take a side trip, you could follow this trail, which loops around the campground for almost a mile and skirts the river before rejoining the main trail. You will see the river soon, however, if you continue straight. The trail passes the road into the campground at .8 mi. **[4]** and then gently rolls through ferns, jack pines, scrubby oaks and maples, and finally white pines. Just before you reach post #3 (1.1 mi.) **[5]**, a path cuts across your trail. You can sit on a bench at the post, watching the river below from this ridge. From here, the trail swings right and begins to climb. Perched on a ridge, you view the river below (1.2 mi.) **[6]**.

As you continue, a feathering of white pines softens the scene. Listen to the quiet. Strain to hear even the aspen leaves shimmering in the breeze. Pass through red pines and a small parking area. Just before you reach the parking area known as Dogtown (1.5 mi.) **[7]**, the river comes into view. Several paths lead from here down to the river. The trail undulates along the river. You are on a ridge, often overlooking river debris; trees and stumps pose minor obstacles to canoeists paddling down the river.

Your ridge walk ends, and the trail veers away from the river, continuing its gentle undulations until it presents you with a steep climb at 1.9 mi. **[8]**. At the crest is a seat, a small lot for parking, and a sign that states "Quality Fishing Area." Pass a couple of meadows and then ascend a red carpet of needles to walk the ridge above the river (2.2 mi.) **[9]**.

After another meadow, silvery lichen introduce you to a mixed forest before you pass an old fence post with a rusty bale of wire (2.3 mi.) **[10]**. The trail dips and then climbs up through the trees to another grassy area. Listen in the woods to the boughs moaning and creaking like a hinge on an old door. At 2.4 mi., a grassy path on the right leads you to the parking area, Downey's Access Site, the end of this trail **[11]**. If you have not arranged for a driver to pick you up here, continue along the south end of the trail or turn and hike the 2.4 mi. back to the north parking lot.

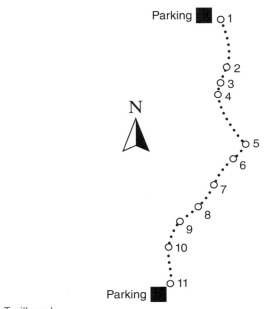

1. Trailhead
2. Sandy two-track
3. Campground Loop and trail junction
4. Campground road
5. Post #3
6. View of river
7. Post #4, parking area
8. Steep climb
9. Ridge above river
10. Old fence post
11. Path to Downey's Access Site

Mason Tract Pathway—South

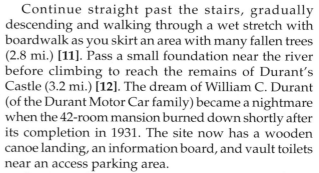

Distance One-Way: 6.4 miles
Estimated Hiking Time: 3 to 4 hours

Cautions: Wear appropriate footgear. Carry water and insect repellent.

Trail Directions: Start at Downey's parking area, 2.5 mi. south of the north trailhead [1]. The hike covers the southern end of the trail. Out and back makes for a long day hike.

Pass an overgrown foundation as you follow the trail that many anglers use to reach the river. Take the less-worn trail that soon splits to the right. The trail undulates through grass and past rows of red pine, crosses an old field, and skirts a dirt cul-de-sac to arrive at a stairway down to the river (.3 mi.) [2]. Go past the stairway to walk along a pine plantation. After entering an aspen stand, you reach post #6 (.5 mi.) [3]. Go left.

View the river as you walk the banks. At 1 mi., you reach post #7 [4]. Step to the left to stand alongside the river; then follow the trail away from the river, walking over a boardwalk through a wet area. Cross a footbridge over Thayer Creek (1.1 mi.) [5] and climb for an obstructed view of the river from a bluff (1.2 mi.) [6]. The trail swings right and onto an overgrown forest road (1.3 mi.) [7] that snakes past a number of large red and white pines.

At 1.7 mi., you reach post #8 and a bench [8]. Swing left past the bench and climb to cross a meadow. Pass by more large red and white pines and eventually skirt a dirt cul-de-sac (2.3 mi.) [9].

When you reach an old two-track, turn right and follow it briefly before veering left along the edge of a wooded ravine. You soon see the river below as you approach a stairway with 75 steps down to the river. This is High Banks (2.6 mi.) [10]. During the logging era, logs were rolled into the river here and floated downstream to the sawmills.

Continue straight past the stairs, gradually descending and walking through a wet stretch with boardwalk as you skirt an area with many fallen trees (2.8 mi.) [11]. Pass a small foundation near the river before climbing to reach the remains of Durant's Castle (3.2 mi.) [12]. The dream of William C. Durant (of the Durant Motor Car family) became a nightmare when the 42-room mansion burned down shortly after its completion in 1931. The site now has a wooden canoe landing, an information board, and vault toilets near an access parking area.

Continue along a two-track that runs through the woods across from the information board. Look for blue blazes and then walk through an area recovering from a fire (3.3 mi.) [13]. At 3.6 mi., you reach a bench along a bluff [14], just before you swing left.

At 4.2 mi., walk the edge of an area that is recovering nicely from logging [15]. Swing left at post #11 (4.3 mi.) [16]. The trail descends to a cul-de-sac, and you eventually cross a boardwalk (4.8 mi.) [17]. Pass the bench while walking through maple, aspen, and mixed pine. The trail levels out, and you proceed through a number of wet areas with the river in view on the left. Swing right to cross several more boardwalks. Walk through mixed pine to arrive at post #12 (5.5 mi.) [18].

The trail here parallels a two-track. Skirt another parking area (5.7 mi.) [19] and follow the edge of a bluff. At 6.2 mi., cross a small opening with a bench [20] before swinging left past a number of fallen trees to arrive at Chase Bridge Road (6.4 mi.) [21]. Turn left and walk .2 mi. to the southern trailhead parking area.

1. Trailhead
2. Stairway to river
3. Post #6
4. Post #7
5. Footbridge over Thayer Creek
6. Bluff
7. Old forest road
8. Post #8 and bench
9. Cul-de-sac
10. High Banks
11. Fallen trees
12. Durant's Castle
13. Recovering burned area

14. Bench on bluff
15. Recovering logged area
16. Post #11
17. Boardwalk
18. #12 posted to tree
19. Parking area
20. Grassy opening
21. Road

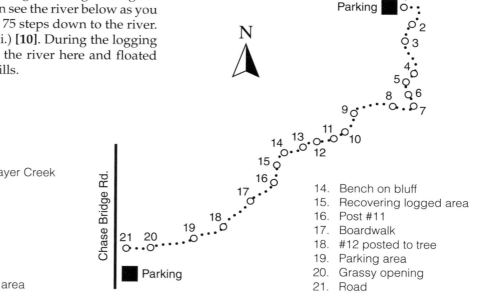

- View nesting loons.
- Watch bald eagles and ospreys fish the lake.
- Camp in the tall pines overlooking the lake.

Park Information

As the name implies, the Wakeley Lake Semi-Primitive Non-Motorized Area, comprising some 2,100 acres of the Huron National Forest, is for non-motorized recreational travel only. This area has been set aside for those who enjoy hiking, mountain bicycling, snowshoeing, or cross-country skiing.

The shallow, marshy lake provides good wildlife viewing opportunities. Common loons can be seen nesting here during the spring and summer. Watch as bald eagles and ospreys fish the lake. Spot beaver, river otter, mink, and over 115 species of birds. See trumpeter swans when they visit the lake in late winter and early spring.

The lake also sports a walk-in campground with four rustic campsites, a hand pump, and vault toilet. The campground is a short hike from the parking area.

Directions: The parking area is located on M-72, 10 miles east of Grayling and 1 mile east of Wakeley Bridge–Chase Bridge Road.

Hours Open: Open year-round.

Facilities: Hiking, cross-country skiing, mountain bicycling, snowshoeing, bird watching, fishing, hunting, and camping (backcountry).

Permits and Rules: The fee is $3 daily, $5 weekly, or $20 annually. The area is closed to motorized recreation, including boat motors. Catch-and-release fishing is permitted from June 15 through August 31. Camping is not permitted closer than 200 feet from the lake or trail system. Carry out what you carry in. Hunting is permitted in season.

For Further Information: Mio Ranger Station, 107 McKinley Street, Mio, MI 48647; 989-826-3252.

Other Points of Interest

Canoe all or portions of the Au Sable River between Grayling and Oscoda. For canoe rental information, contact the Grayling Visitors Bureau at 800-937-8837 or www.grayling-mi.com.

George Mason River Retreat Area (see park #34), offers over a dozen miles of trail for non-motorized recreation. It is located on M-72, 2 miles east of the Wakeley Lake Semi-Primitive Non-Motorized Area. For more information, call the Grayling Management Unit at 989-348-6371.

Hartwick Pines State Park (see park #36), located northeast of Grayling, is home to the largest stand of virgin white pines in the Lower Peninsula. Visit the Michigan Forest Visitor Center to learn about forest management now and in the logging era. For more information, call Hartwick Pines State Park at 989-348-7068 or the Michigan Forest Visitor Center at 989-348-2537.

Park Trails

About 10 miles of trails weave through the Wakeley Lake Semi-Primitive Non-Motorized Area. A number of loops build on one another. Innumerable combinations can be created, ranging from day hikes and cross-country ski excursions to backpacking and overnight wilderness experiences.

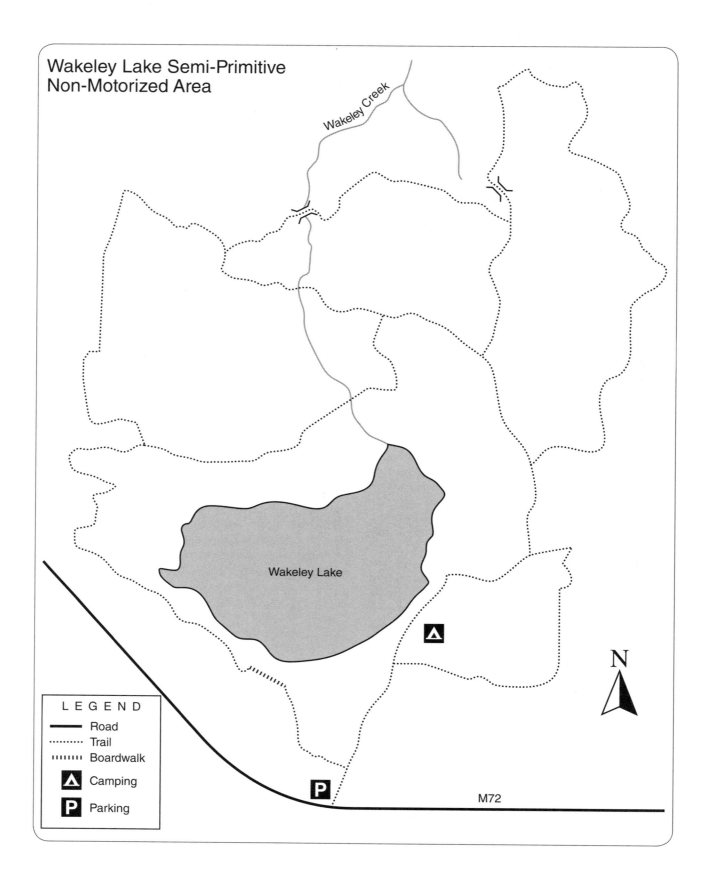

Wakeley Lake Semi-Primitive
Non-Motorized Area

Wakeley Creek

Wakeley Lake

LEGEND
—— Road
······· Trail
ııııııı Boardwalk
▲ Camping
P Parking

M72

N

Wakeley Lake—Inner Loop

Distance Round-Trip: 3.6 miles
Estimated Hiking Time: 1.5 to 2 hours

Cautions: The trail goes over roots, through sand, and over dikes. Wear proper footgear. Bring insect repellent and binoculars.

Trail Directions: Start at the north end of the parking lot **[1]**. You soon pass the junction where you will return. Stay straight through mixed woods fragrant with white pine and reach the junction for the Beaver Pond Trail (.3 mi.) **[2]**. Stay straight. Soon you reach Wakeley Lake (.4 mi.) **[3]**. If you brought the gear, you can try fishing, which is allowed from June 15 through August 31.

An outhouse announces the camping area (.5 mi.) **[4]**. A handful of campsites line up along the lake. The trail makes a sharp right through young white pines and tall red ones. Veer left along with the wide, now-grassy path and pass the junction where the Beaver Pond Trail comes back in (.7 mi.) **[5]**.

Roll and wind with the trail through maples and ferns. Stay left at the junction (.9 mi.) **[6]**. Descend to a large wetland area and then climb and swing left around the wetland to another junction (1.2 mi.) **[7]**.

Stay left and gradually climb for a view of the lake and wetland. Descend to another junction (1.4 mi.) **[8]**. Turn left to cross a land bridge between wetlands.

Climb onto what looks like an island. Look for evidence of beaver. Note the dam (1.5 mi.) **[9]** on your left. Was it made by beavers or humans?

Leave the island setting to cross a long land bridge between the lake and wet area. Climb up a sandy slope and around it to the left. Watch for ospreys flying over the lake.

The trail swings right on a ridge. It begins to undulate and offers a view of the wetland west of the lake (2 mi.) **[10]**. Continue along the ridge to the junction (2.2 mi.) **[11]**. Keep to the left and climb sharply over roots on the sandy, eroding slope. Watch for a number of large ant mounds.

Head east after swinging a wide left (2.4 mi.) **[12]**.

Catch a glimpse of water to the left as the trail winds right, climbs a ridge, swings left, and descends to a junction (2.6 mi.) **[13]**. Go right to avoid the steep hill.

You get more peeks at the lake as you walk the ridge. Descend away from the lake and bend left to approach a lush wetland. Cross the land bridge. Ferns lace the edge of the wetland. Plumes of grasses and sedges brush your knees as you pass over the boardwalk that separates the lake from the wetland (3.2 mi.) **[14]**. Stags, stumps, and lily pads pepper the lake. Turn right at the end of the boardwalk to reach the main trail junction (3.5 mi.) **[15]**. Turn right back to the parking lot.

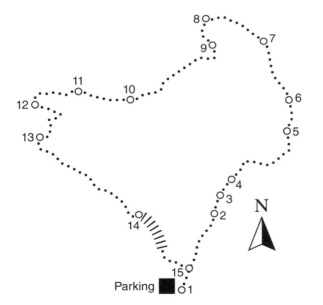

1. Trailhead
2. Beaver Pond Trail junction
3. Wakeley Lake
4. Camping area
5. Beaver Pond Trail junction
6. Junction
7. Junction
8. Junction
9. Dam and dike
10. View of wetland
11. Junction
12. Trail swings left
13. Junction
14. Boardwalk
15. Junction

Beaver Pond Loop

Distance Round-Trip: 1.7 miles
Estimated Hiking Time: 45 minutes to 1 hour

Cautions: The trail goes over roots and over land bridges with holes. Wear proper footgear. Bring insect repellent during warm months. Don't forget your binoculars.

Trail Directions: Start this trail at the north end of the parking lot **[1]**. In less than .1 mi., pass a junction for one of the Wakeley Loops. Stay straight along the path through mixed woods fragrant with white pine and reach the junction for the Beaver Pond Trail (.3 mi.) **[2]**. Turn right through a mixed forest of maple, oak, aspen, jack pine, red pine, birch, and fir.

As you walk, notice the explosion of ferns in the openings (.6 mi.) **[3]**. The trail swings left away from private property and then on to the beaver pond (.7 mi.) **[4]**, which is littered with stumps, grasses, lily pads, and standing dead trees, known as stags. A nesting box awaits birds. Look for great blue herons in the pool. And don't miss the beaver lodge off in the distance.

Continue on the land bridge that dikes the pond, with a fencerow accompanying you to the right. The trail veers right and then quickly left for a wide swing through ferns and myrtle. Arrive soon at the junction (1 mi.) **[5]**.

Go to the left along the wide, grassy path. The trail soon veers right through small white pines and stately red ones. An inviting campsite on your left lies under towering pines where the trail makes a sharp left and passes a handful of additional campsites that line the eastern shore of Wakeley Lake.

Stately pines shadow campsites, picnic tables, a fishing lake, and even an outhouse (1.2 mi.) **[6]**. You'll be wishing that you had packed a tent along on your hike so that you could stay the night. You could. It's only .5 mi. back through mixed woods. You pass the junction that you took for the Beaver Pond Trail at 1.4 mi. **[2]**. Then you have only .3 mi. to retrace your steps to the parking lot. If you brought fishing and camping gear, what's another .5 mi. back to the campsites for some secluded camping?

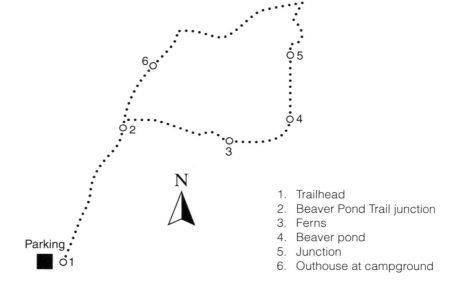

N

1. Trailhead
2. Beaver Pond Trail junction
3. Ferns
4. Beaver pond
5. Junction
6. Outhouse at campground

- Hike in the shadows of the largest stand of virgin white pine in the Lower Peninsula.
- Learn about the life of a lumberjack at the Logging Camp Museum.
- Pay your respect to the regal Monarch.

Park Information

Mrs. Karen B. Hartwick donated this 9,672-acre park to the state in 1927 in memory of her husband, Major Edward E. Hartwick. The park is home to the largest stand of virgin white pine in the Lower Peninsula. The park memorializes a 49-acre tract of white pine that survived the state's logging era from 1840 to 1910. Remembered as well are the men who logged the trees. A reconstructed logging camp with bunkhouses, a mess hall, and other structures gives a sense of how those men lived.

Four interpretive trails provide more than 6 miles for hiking. Ten miles of trails are available for cross-country skiing and mountain biking.

The park's Michigan Forest Visitor Center offers hands-on exhibits, dioramas, and a "Living Tree" that tells the story of Michigan's forests. Visit the towering trees on the Virgin Pines Trail. Most notable among them was the Monarch, which stretched upward 155 feet before gusty winds trimmed 30 to 40 feet from it in 1992, eventually causing it to perish in 1996.

Directions: The park entrance is located 7 miles north of Grayling. Take I-75 to exit 259. Head north on M-93 about 3 miles to the park entrance.

Hours Open: The recreation area is open daily from 8:00 a.m. to 10:00 p.m. The Michigan Forest Visitor Center is open from 9:00 a.m. to 7:00 p.m. daily from Memorial Day through Labor Day, and from 9:00 a.m. to 4:00 p.m. daily except for Mondays from Labor Day through Memorial Day. The Logging Camp Museum is open from 9:00 a.m. to dusk daily, June through Labor Day. Call for hours at other times of the year.

Facilities: Hiking, mountain bicycling, cross-country skiing, fishing, hunting, camping (RV and tent), sanitation station, picnicking, cabin, interpretive trails, and interpretive center.

Permits and Rules: A park fee is required for motor vehicles ($6 daily, $24 annually for residents; $8 daily, $29 annually for nonresidents). Motorized traffic is prohibited on trails; bicycles are permitted only on designated trails and roads.

For Further Information: Hartwick Pines State Park, 4216 Ranger Road, Grayling, MI 49738; 989-348-7068; or Michigan Forest Visitor Center, 989-348-2537.

Other Points of Interest

Grayling is the midpoint of the **Michigan Shore-to-Shore Riding-Hiking Trail**. The trail stretches from Oscoda on Lake Huron to Empire on Lake Michigan. Contact the Grayling Management Unit, 1955 N I-75 BL, Grayling, MI 49738; 989-348-6371.

Park Trails

Mertz Grade Foot Trail (🥾, 2 miles). This trail starts in the picnic area. It follows an abandoned railroad grade in an area where wildflowers and blueberries are prolific and then loops through second-growth forest.

Bright and Glory Nature Trail (🥾, .5 mile). This trail starts near site #15 in the campground. It heads through aspen, twists through a blowdown area where a tornado cut a swath in 1994, and cuts through dense swamp stands of northern white cedar near Bright and Glory lakes.

Trailheads for skiing and biking are located at the north end of the visitor center parking area and the north end of the day-use parking area.

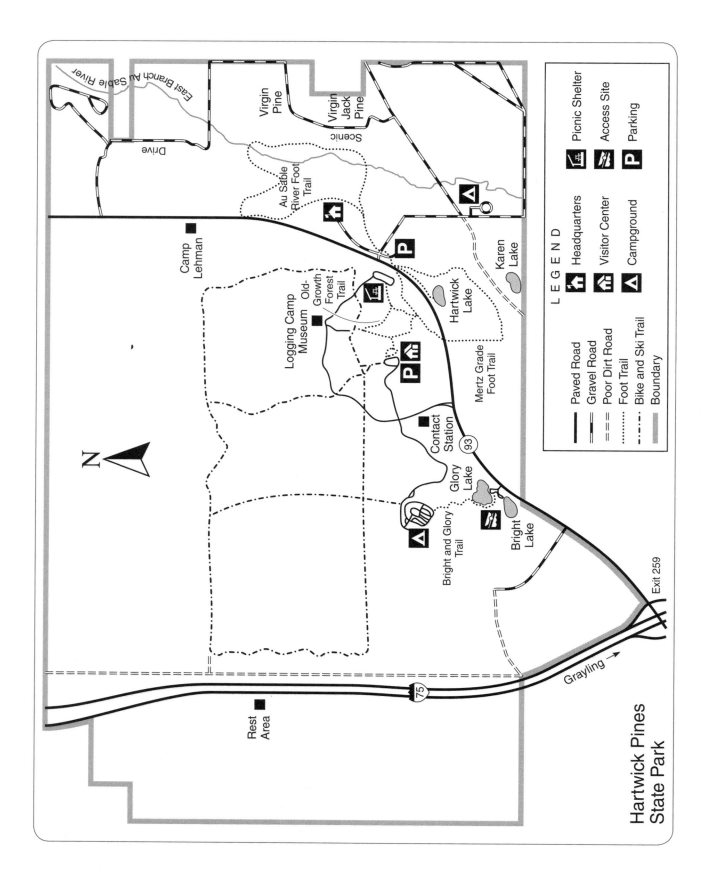

Hartwick Pines
State Park

LEGEND

Headquarters	Picnic Shelter	
Visitor Center	Access Site	
Campground	Parking	

Paved Road
Gravel Road
Poor Dirt Road
Foot Trail
Bike and Ski Trail
Boundary

East Branch Au Sable River

Drive

Virgin Pine

Virgin Jack Pine

Scenic

Karen Lake

Au Sable River Foot Trail

Camp Lehman

Old-Growth Forest Trail

Logging Camp Museum

Hartwick Lake

Mertz Grade Foot Trail

Contact Station

Glory Lake

Bright and Glory Trail

Bright Lake

Rest Area

Grayling

Exit 259

93

75

N

Old-Growth Trail

Distance Round-Trip: 1.2 miles
Estimated Hiking Time: 1 to 1.5 hours

Cautions: To ensure a pleasant stroll along this paved trail, bring insect repellent during warm months.

Trail Directions: Start behind the visitor center, off the northeast deck **[1]**. Pick up an interpretive map so that you can enjoy the stops along this trail through a primeval pine forest and a logging camp museum.

Head down the trail, thick with beech, maple, and hemlock—the trees of a climax forest, as you learn at post #1 (.1 mi.) **[2]**. Continue descending as you pass under big, beautiful trees set in the rolling hillsides around you. Learn about beech trees and then round the corner to learn about sugar maples before strolling through this forest. Savor the old growth that towers above you. Admire their stately stature. A bench at .2 mi. lets you do just that **[3]**.

At the bench is post #3, which describes the hemlocks among the pines. Pass the explosion of growth on the forest floor among old logs strewn about like fallen soldiers. At .3 mi., a wood railing drapes around a majestic tree **[4]** like a courtier holding a robe and attending to his king, giving space for subjects to stand back and revere. This tree, known as the Monarch, reigned supreme here, having reached a height of 155

feet. Its reign ended on its death in 1996 after it lost its crown in a windstorm four years earlier.

Wind through the old growth and storm damage. Pass a deer fence study area just before a junction for the Mertz Grade Foot Trail (.4 mi.) **[5]**. Turn left and make your way through the youthful growth of the 1950s and 1960s. Ferns carpet the floor, growing over the rolling terrain and nature's plowing—fallen, rotting trunks of yesteryear.

You reach a junction with a bench at .6 mi. **[6]**. A right leads to the day-use area. Turn left instead and climb up to the log church (.7 mi.) **[7]**. Benches await you at the top if you want to rest before visiting the Chapel in the Pines. Head down, up, and down again to the Logging Camp (.9 mi.) **[8]**, built in 1935 by the Civilian Conservation Corps as a memorial to those who labored in the Michigan forests. Turn right; wander through the mess hall and view the equipment (like the snow roller and sled) or investigate the mill. The buildings are open from June through Labor Day.

Turn around and head back up the trail past the big wheels that were once used to move the logs (1 mi.) **[9]**. Stroll through the undulating woods, reaching the trail back to the visitor center at 1.1 mi. **[10]**. Turn right and visit inside to enjoy the exhibits and hands-on displays of Michigan's forests.

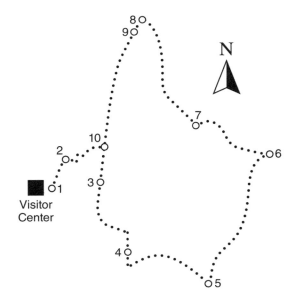

1. Trailhead
2. Post #1
3. Bench
4. Monarch
5. Mertz Grade Foot Trail junction
6. Junction
7. Chapel in the Pines
8. Logging Camp
9. Big wheels
10. Trail junction back to visitor center

Au Sable River Foot Trail

Distance Round-Trip: 3.9 miles
Estimated Hiking Time: 1.5 to 2 hours

Cautions: This interpretive trail has exposed roots and areas that flood. Wear appropriate footgear. Take insect repellent during warm weather.

Trail Directions: Start at the information board in front of the old Civilian Conservation Corps building at the south end of the day-use area parking lot **[1]**. Cross M-93, heading to the junction with the Mertz Grade Foot Trail and a pathway that leads down to Hartwick Lake. Continue straight through the former park campground (.3 mi.) **[2]**. Cross a dirt parking area and a dirt road (.4 mi.) **[3]**.

Here you find a narrow, worn goat trail that widens when it enters a red pine plantation. At post #3, stay right as you follow the posts with blue boot prints and deer tracks (.6 mi.) **[4]**. Cross a two-track and go under a power line. Watch for exposed roots along the path otherwise cushioned by pine needles. You leave the pine plantation and enter a mix of trees just before arriving at a bench along the clear water of the East Branch Au Sable River (.9 mi.) **[5]**.

Cross two footbridges that sandwich a small island at the tip of a bend in the river. On the other side, you pass the old swimming hole used by the Civilian Conservation Corps in the late 1930s and early 1940s. The trail swings north through a mixture of pines and hardwoods. One type of tree stands out—not because of size but for its wonderful, fresh scent—the balsam fir that dominates the forest here (1.2 mi.) **[6]**.

At 1.6 mi., go under a large white pine **[7]**. You soon cross another footbridge over the East Branch Au Sable River (1.7 mi.) **[8]**. When this area was logged in the late 1800s, the logs were hauled out by sled across another bridge that existed at this location.

As you walk past the white cedar near the river, the trail is likely to be damp or muddy. At 2 mi., you enter a hemlock grove marked by a notable lack of growth on the rolling forest floor **[9]**. Pass between large, white pines and the utility corridor and enter a red pine plantation (2.2 mi.) **[10]**.

At 2.4 mi., you reach a sign and an option. You can continue straight to make a steep climb to an overlook or turn left to take the less difficult alternate route **[11]**. Go for the challenge. Climb steeply, switchbacking up the side of a moraine (built with debris deposited by the glaciers), through beech and maple, over roots and sand, and under a power line. When you reach the top, unfortunately, trees seasonally obscure the overlook (2.6 mi.) **[12]**. Don't trip on the roots as you descend from the glacial hill into a red pine plantation. You cross the utility corridor again (2.7 mi.) **[13]**. Cross a road at 3.1 mi. **[14]**. Pick up the trail on the left. You soon wind your way back to the first trail junction (3.3 mi.) **[4]**. Having completed the loop, retrace your steps to the parking area.

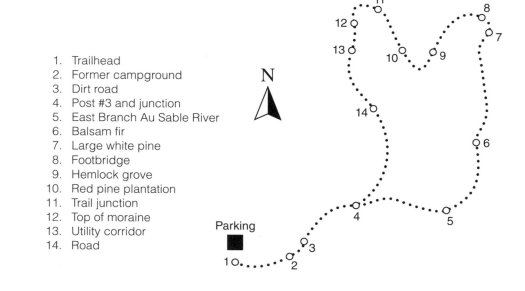

1. Trailhead
2. Former campground
3. Dirt road
4. Post #3 and junction
5. East Branch Au Sable River
6. Balsam fir
7. Large white pine
8. Footbridge
9. Hemlock grove
10. Red pine plantation
11. Trail junction
12. Top of moraine
13. Utility corridor
14. Road

N

Parking

37. Historic Mill Creek Discovery Park

- Rediscover early log-cutting techniques at a reconstructed, 18th-century sawmill that uses water power.
- See the log-cutting and construction techniques of the beaver along Mill Creek.
- Climb to view Mackinac Island in the distance.

Park Information

This park combines groomed nature trails, beaver dams, and scenic overlooks of the Straits of Mackinac and Mackinac Island with a historic site that depicts an industrial complex of the late 1700s.

The 625-acre park features a working replica of an ...ntury, water-powered sawmill. Archaeological ...tion in 1972 revealed that this site had housed ...mill two centuries earlier.

...ch the water-powered saw bite through fresh ...ust as its predecessor did in the late 18th and ...19th centuries. You can also see costumed inter... depict the tedious method used to cut lumber ...e the water-powered saw was invented.

...ew in 2008: Soar like an eagle down the Eagle's ...t Zip Line. Walk through treetops on the Forest ...opy Bridge. Youngsters can explore the Water ...er Station and interact in the Forest Friends Chil...n's Play Area.

...Trails loop through aspen, along a bluff, around ...nds, over footbridges and dams, and to overlooks ... views of the Straits of Mackinac. Pack a lunch ...d picnic at a spot overlooking Mill Pond or visit ...e park pavilion.

Directions: The park is located on US 23, about 3 miles southeast of Mackinaw City. From I-75 take exit 337 to US 23 and drive east to the park.

Hours Open: The park is open daily from early May through mid-October. Hours from May 5 through June 6 and from August 24 through October 12 are 9:00 a.m. to 4:00 p.m. From June 7 through August 23, the park is open from 9:00 a.m. to 5:00 p.m.

Facilities: Hiking, picnicking, interpretive trails, interpretive center, and historic demonstrations.

Permits and Rules: The fee is $10.00 for adults and $6.25 for children 5 to 17. Combination packages, which allow seasonal access to Fort Mackinac, Colonial Michilimackinac, and Historic Mill Creek are available at $59.00 for a family.

For Further Information: Mackinac State Historic Parks, 207 W. Sinclair Street, P.O. Box 873, Mackinaw City, MI 49701; 231-436-4100; www.mackinacparks .com.

Other Points of Interest

Other historic state parks are nearby: **Fort Mackinac** (see park #4) and **Colonial Michilimackinac State Historic Park.** Colonial Michilimackinac provides an overview of British, French, and Indian life in the 18th century. For more information, contact Mackinac State Historic Parks, P.O. Box 873, Mackinaw City, MI 49701; 231-436-4100; www.mackinacparks.com.

From the glimmering beauty of the Straits of Mackinac to the history of Fort Michilimackinac, and, yes, even to the fudge, **Mackinaw City** has much to offer. For information, contact the Mackinaw City Chamber of Commerce, 231-436-5574 or 888-455-8100, www.mackinawchamber.com; or the Mackinaw City Chamber of Tourism, 800-577-3113, www.mackinaw citychamber.com.

About 11 miles west of Mackinaw City, **Wilderness State Park** (see park #39) offers 25 miles of Lake Michigan shoreline, modern campsites, sandy beaches, and hiking trails. For more information, contact Wilderness State Park, 903 Wilderness Park Drive, Carp Lake, MI 49718; 231-436-5381.

Park Trails

Five trails covering 3.5 miles loop through the park and flow along the Mill Creek. Three of them build on one another; the other two are appendages off the longest loop.

Mill Pond Trail (🐾, .5 mile). This loop takes you up to an overlook of the pond and historic buildings below. It then goes down and across Mill Creek, over to another overlook, and through the main exhibit area.

Aspen-Wildlife Forest Trail (🐾, .5 mile). Accessed off the west end of the Beaver Pond Trail, this extension loops through aspen forest and exhibits aspen management techniques.

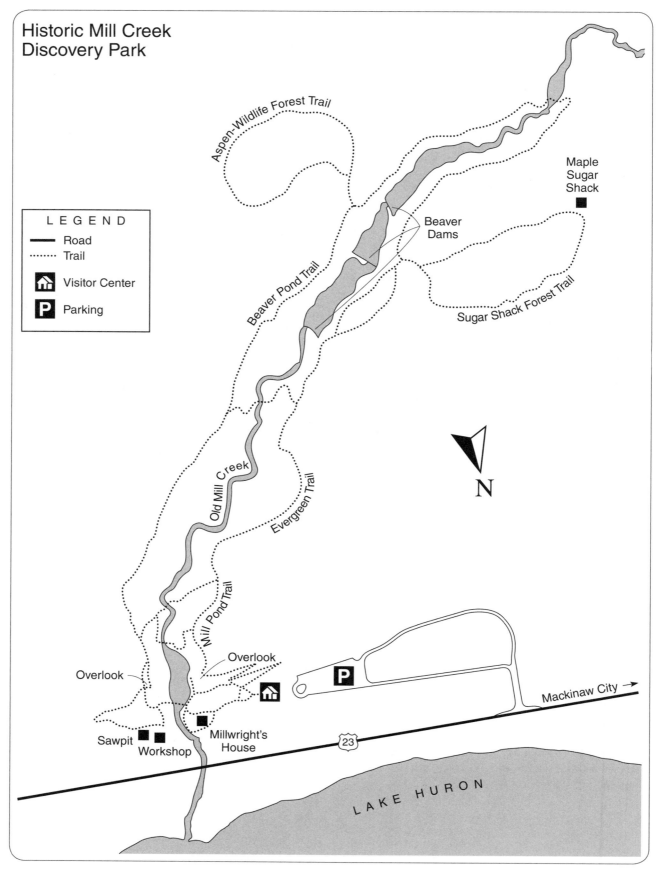

Historic Mill Creek
Discovery Park

LEGEND
— Road
···· Trail
🏠 Visitor Center
🅿 Parking

Aspen-Wildlife Forest Trail

Maple Sugar Shack

Beaver Dams

Beaver Pond Trail

Sugar Shack Forest Trail

N

Old Mill Creek

Evergreen Trail

Mill Pond Trail

Overlook

Overlook

🏠

🅿

Mackinaw City →

Sawpit Workshop

Millwright's House

23

LAKE HURON

Evergreen, Beaver, and Sugar Shack Forest Trails

Distance Round-Trip: 1.9 miles

Estimated Hiking Time: 45 minutes to 1 hour

Cautions: This trail follows along decking, boardwalk, or crushed limestone, making it highly accessible. Insect repellent is a must.

Trail Directions: Start this interpretive trail behind the visitor center at the kiosk **[1]**. Go to the right up the decking (.1 mi.) **[2]**. From the deck you overlook the mill site, pond, and grassy picnic area below. You can see Mackinac Island in the distance.

Follow to the right on crushed limestone through mixed forest and over a bridge. Signs along the way help you identify trees as you stroll along, arriving at the junction for the Mill Pond Trail at .2 mi. **[3]**. A bench is located at the junction where steps lead down the short route. Continue straight under a canopy of trees. With a bit more sunlight, ferns and foliage carpet the floor. You reach the Evergreen Trail junction (.4 mi.) **[4]**. Stay straight.

Soon you reach a fork that leads to a bench and overlook at the creek. Listen to the trickle of the water as you view the creek with its debris of logs. Move along through the birch and maple trees.

You cross more decking and a bridge to arrive at a spur (.4 mi.) **[5]**. Stay straight to arrive at a creek overlook with benches. At .5 mi., go right at the spur **[6]**. Pass an interpretive board by a pond that discusses beavers and dams. Then climb the trail a couple of hundred feet, pass a huge boulder, and arrive at the junction for the Sugar Shack Forest Trail (.6 mi.) **[7]**.

Turn right. You soon see large boulders beside the trail. These rocks are not limestone like most rocks in the area. Transported from Canada by glaciers, they are called erratics. Near them, the trail forks. It is a loop. Follow to the right through sugar maple, beech, oak, basswood, ash, and hemlock. Interpretive boards coach you on how the forest is managed.

Before you arrive at the sugar shack, read about maple syrup and how trees are tapped (.9 mi.) **[8]**. Visit the building and get a taste for how maple syrup is made. Follow the trail to the left after the sugar shack.

Rocks and boulders line the trail. Pass the huge Canadian imports again and arrive back at the Beaver Trail at 1.2 mi. **[7]**. Head left, past the beaver dam, and past the junctions, spurs, and overlooks to reach the decking that takes you down to the visitor center (1.8 mi.) **[1]**. Wander through the center, and then, if you are so inclined, head over to the mill site for a demonstration.

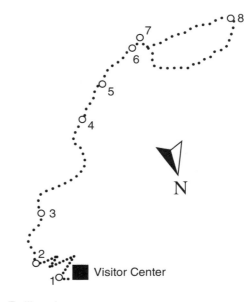

1. Trailhead
2. Overlook
3. Mill Pond Trail junction
4. Evergreen Trail junction
5. Spur
6. Spur
7. Junction for sugar shack
8. Sugar shack

Beaver Pond Trail

Distance Round-Trip: 1.8 miles
Estimated Hiking Time: 45 minutes to 1 hour

Cautions: Although the western portion is handicapped accessible, elsewhere the trail takes you over exposed roots and rocks. Take along insect repellent in warm months.

Trail Directions: Start at the kiosk behind the visitor center **[1]**. Follow the sign to the mill on the left. As you walk along the tranquil Mill Pond, you can decide whether you want to visit the reconstructed mill now or when you return here. As you cross the bridge at the end of Mill Pond, water rushing over the milldam below drowns out the sound of your footsteps. On the far bank, a left turn takes you past the sawmill and saw pit where log-cutting demonstrations take place. Check at the visitor center for the schedule of activities. A right turn has you climbing steeply to another kiosk (.1 mi.) **[2]**. Here, enjoy an overlook of Mill Pond and the bluffs on the west side of the creek.

Pass the junction with the Mill Pond Trail and then cross a series of boardwalks designed to keep your feet dry on this lush, wet section of the trail. An interpretive board explains what caused the formation of the small sinkhole that you are peering into (.3 mi.) **[3]**. Take a deep breath to savor the fresh pine scent of the forest before you pass the junction with the Evergreen Trail (.4 mi.) **[4]**.

Some large boulders at .5 mi. **[5]** signal (like the slap of a beaver's tail on water) that you are entering beaver country. Just past the rocks, a bench overlooks an old beaver dam. After the Aspen-Wildlife Forest Trail splits off to the left, you reach an overlook of a large beaver dam and then an interpretive sign about these industrious engineers (.7 mi.) **[6]**. Have a seat on the bench overlooking the beaver pond.

At .8 mi., you reach an overlook and interpretive sign that highlights the beaver lodge **[7]**. Cross a boardwalk, swing right, and descend to the edge of the creek where there is an old beaver dam. As you reach the far end of the loop, you cross a boardwalk and a footbridge over Mill Creek (.9 mi.) **[8]**. Yet another interpretive stop here describes the abandoned beaver dam. Abandon this site and climb the steps to reach the top of the embankment on the west side of the creek.

Turn right, back toward the visitor center. At 1.1 mi., you reach the junction with the Sugar Shack Forest Trail **[9]**. Pass a large boulder and descend to the next interpretive sign for the beaver dam (1.2 mi.) **[10]**.

Climb back onto the bluff and reach a fork in the trail (1.3 mi.) **[11]**. To the right is an observation deck overlooking the creek. Listen to the trickle of water as you view the creek with its debris of logs and surrounding trees. Follow the trail as it snakes along. You pass the junction with the Evergreen Trail, cross two footbridges, stop to view the creek from an observation deck, and pass the junction with the Mill Pond Trail to arrive at the overlook of Mill Pond (1.7 mi.) **[12]**. From the deck you can see not only the mill site but also the Grand Hotel on Mackinac Island across the straits.

Turn left and descend down to the visitor center. From here you can leave, hit the refreshment stand, or visit the historic sites if you missed them earlier.

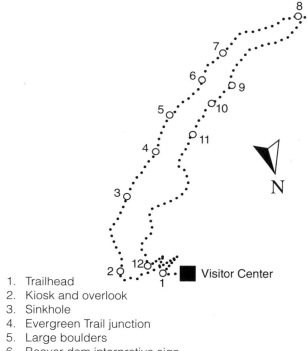

1. Trailhead
2. Kiosk and overlook
3. Sinkhole
4. Evergreen Trail junction
5. Large boulders
6. Beaver dam interpretive sign
7. Beaver lodge interpretive sign
8. Footbridge
9. Sugar Shack Forest Trail junction
10. Beaver dam interpretive sign
11. Fork, bench, and overlook
12. Mill Pond overlook

- Stroll along the rocky shores of the Straits of Mackinac.
- Experience spectacular Lake Michigan sunsets.
- Stay at the Beach House or the Guest House.

Park Information

The Headlands date back to the late 1950s when Roger McCormick dropped 50-pound flour sacks from a helicopter to mark the boundaries of the property that he intended to purchase. Today, at nearly 600 acres, and with more than 2 miles of undeveloped rocky Lake Michigan shoreline, the Headlands represents the largest and least disturbed forest tract near Mackinaw City.

Situated as it is on the Straits of Mackinac, the park is an important resting spot for migratory birds. Other wildlife commonly seen includes bald eagle, osprey, white-tailed deer, and, less commonly, black bear and coyote. Forest types include mature upland hardwoods, upland conifers, swamp hardwoods, swamp conifer, mixed upland conifer and hardwoods, and mixed swamp conifer and hardwoods. The park also hosts a number of rare or endangered plant species including the threatened dwarf lake iris, Michigan's state wildflower.

Marked trails lead hikers, bird watchers, nature lovers, mountain bicyclists, and cross-country skiers throughout the park. Two facilities are available for public rental. The Beach House has two bedrooms that accommodate 18 people dorm style, with two restrooms and a kitchen. The Guest House has four bedrooms that handle 22 people dorm style, with three restrooms and a kitchen. Linens and table service are available at both facilities.

Directions: The park is located west of the Village of Mackinaw City. From I-75 northbound, take exit 338 and go north on Nicolet Avenue to Central Avenue. Turn left and go to Wilderness Park Road. Turn left and go .5 mile to the park entrance. From I-75 southbound, take exit 339 to Louvingny Street. Turn left and go one block to Central Avenue. Turn right and go to Wilderness Park Road. Turn left and go .5 mile to the park entrance.

Hours Open: The park is open year-round. The Beach House is open from May 1 to October 31.
Facilities: Hiking, cross-country skiing, mountain bicycling, bird watching, and picnicking.
Permits and Rules: There is no admittance fee. Motorized vehicles, including snowmobiles, are prohibited on the foot trails.
For Further Information: Emmet County Parks and Recreation—Headlands, 7725 E. Wilderness Park Drive, Mackinaw City, MI 49701; 231-436-4051; www.co.emmet.mi.us.

Other Points of Interest

East of the park are the four Mackinac State Historic Parks: **Fort Mackinac** and **Mackinac Island State Park** (see park #4), **Historic Mill Creek Discovery Park** (see park #37), and **Colonial Michilimackinac State Historic Park**. For more information, contact Mackinac State Historic Parks, P.O. Box 873, Mackinaw City, MI 49701; 231-436-4100; www.mackinacparks.com.

Southwest of the park, **Wilderness State Park** (see park #39) offers 25 miles of Lake Michigan shoreline, modern campsites, sandy beaches, and about 12 miles of hiking trails. For more information, contact Wilderness State Park, 903 Wilderness Park Drive, Carp Lake, MI 49718; 231-436-5381.

Also southwest of the park, 800-acre **Cecil Bay**, with more than 1 mile of Lake Michigan shoreline, offers fishing at the Carp River, a boardwalk, and sandy beaches for swimming. For more information, call Emmet County Parks and Recreation at 231-347-6536.

Park Trails

Roughly 5 miles of trails guide you through the park's diverse habitats.

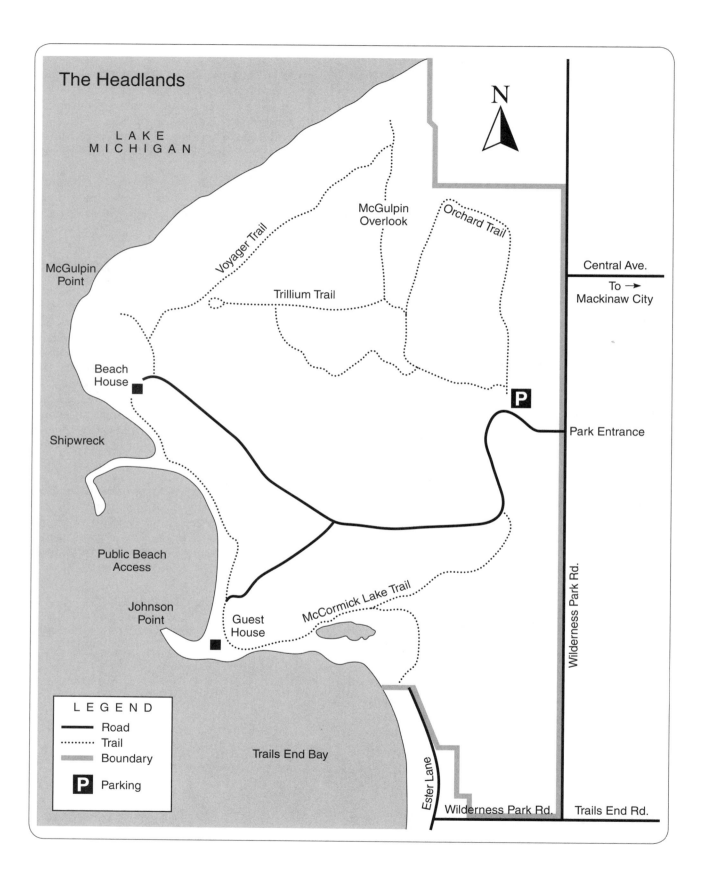

The Headlands

LAKE MICHIGAN

McGulpin Point

Shipwreck

Public Beach Access

Johnson Point

Beach House

Voyager Trail

Trillium Trail

McGulpin Overlook

Orchard Trail

Central Ave.

To →
Mackinaw City

Park Entrance

Wilderness Park Rd.

Guest House

McCormick Lake Trail

Trails End Bay

Ester Lane

Wilderness Park Rd.

Trails End Rd.

LEGEND
—— Road
······ Trail
▬▬ Boundary
P Parking

Trillium Trail

🐾 **Distance Round-Trip:** 1.6 miles
❄ **Estimated Hiking Time:** 45 minutes to 1 hour

Cautions: Watch for roots and poison ivy. Portions of the trail take you over stone; wear proper footgear.

Trail Directions: Spring is the perfect time to hike this trail if you wish to appreciate its namesake. Park in the main lot near the entrance. The trail starts at the north end of the lot **[1]**. Head north along the grassy path surrounded by wildflowers and reach a junction with the orange (Voyager) trail (.1 mi.) **[2]**. Turn left and follow along through the mixed hardwoods and past your return junction (.3 mi) **[3]**.

Stay straight along this wide trail that then bends right and passes clumps of fern, trillium, false Solomon seal, and a smattering of fallen trees. It veers left, and you see a flagpole just before the blue (Orchard) trail junction (.4 mi.) **[4]**. Keep straight on the trail that becomes soft with moss and grass until you reach the green junction for the Trillium Trail (.5 mi.) **[5]**. You've already passed trilliums to get here. Turn left among the many ferns that line the trail. You soon wonder why this wasn't called the Fern Trail.

Gently climbing and then undulating, the trail passes through a forest with a lush understory. Watch for huge holes in dead trees from pileated woodpeckers.

You reach a junction before long (.7 mi) **[6]**. The spur leads to a loop high on a bluff overlooking the lake; you want to take it. Stay straight.

Raspberries show themselves sporadically along the trail. The canopy opens a bit, and more shrubs appear. When you reach the junction, notice the thick understory (.9 mi.) **[7]**. Stay right to circle this bluff loop where you catch glimpses of the lake, as well as the Voyager Trail far below. Close the loop in less than .1 mi. and turn right to head back **[7]** to the spur junction (1 mi.) **[6]**.

Turn right. The trail winds through mostly maples. Birds welcome you with their songs. Ferns again feather the forest floor. Soft moss carpets the trail. More sun shines through, and the trail becomes grass. Raspberries are more abundant. The trail veers left and becomes mossy again. After the trail swings left, listen. The birds just won't let up on their singing.

At the orange junction (1.5 mi.), you end the green Trillium Trail **[2]**. Turn right and retrace your steps to the parking lot.

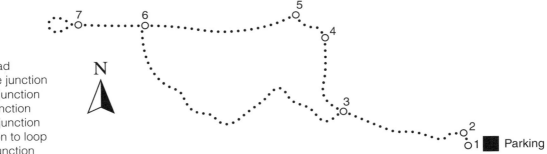

1. Trailhead
2. Orange junction
3. Green junction
4. Blue junction
5. Green junction
6. Junction to loop
7. Loop junction

N

Voyager–Beach–McCormick Lake Trail Loop

Distance Round-Trip: 3.4 miles
Estimated Hiking Time: 1.5 to 2 hours

Cautions: Watch for roots and poison ivy. Portions of the trail take you over stone; wear proper footgear.
Trail Directions: Park in the main lot near the entrance. The trail starts at the north end of the lot **[1]** and heads north along a grassy path enveloped by wildflowers to a junction with the orange (Voyager) trail (.1 mi.) **[2]**. Turn left and follow along through the mixed hardwoods. Go straight at the junction (.3 mi.) **[3]**.

The wide trail bends right and passes clumps of fern, trillium, false Solomon seal, and a smattering of fallen trees. It veers left, and you see a flagpole just before the blue trail junction (.4 mi.) **[4]**. Keep straight. The trail softens with moss and grass until you reach the green junction for the Trillium Trail (.5 mi.) **[5]**.

Stay to the right along the orange (Voyager) trail, which gently descends through beech and maple and then passes through several downed trees and branches. The canopy thins, and grasses spread around the trail.

Descending, wrap to the left around a wooded bluff (.7 mi.) **[6]**. Follow the short path straight when you reach the spur junction (.8 mi.) **[7]**. The narrow trail descends past large, eerie cedars. A number of branches or trees have fallen or are twisted. You see a light up ahead and then come out onto the rocky shore of the Straits of Mackinac—your own secluded beach. From here you can see the Upper Peninsula and the Mackinac Bridge. Sit back and relax or listen to the cry of the loon before heading back to the junction **[7]**.

Turn right and follow along the base of the tall, wooded beach ridge. The mossy trail winds along the back side of the ridge. When devoid of its moss carpeting, the trail moves away from the ridge and winds down to a junction, another spur to the lake (1.5 mi.) **[8]**. Turn right and head down through mostly wildflowers and grass to reach the rocky beach at McGulpin Point. Listen again for the loon before returning to the junction (1.7 mi.) **[8]**.

Head right through cedars to end the orange (Voyager) trail at the drive to the Beach House (1.8 mi.) **[9]**. For now, head for the beach to the right of the house. Plans call for the trail to pass to the left of it eventually. Reach the rocky shore again at 1.9 mi. **[10]**.

Turn left and walk the rocky shore in the direction of the spit. At 2.2 mi., climb left up a spur **[11]** and then right to follow along the bluff to the yellow (Beach) trail marker at the road (2.3 mi.) **[12]** (here a spur leads back to the lake).

Stay to the right on the road, which is now the red (McCormick Lake) trail, and round the bend past guest houses to pick up the trail at the end of the road. The grassy trail, shaded by young trees, perches on a bluff overlooking the lake.

Enter the darkness of small cedars, veer away from the bluff along the shore, and wind past a bench at McCormick Lake (2.7 mi.) **[13]**. A dense cedar swamp darkens the left side of the trail—the site of a catastrophe. Fallen debris and undulations are scattered about.

You reach another spur at 2.8 mi. **[14]**. Stay straight and enjoy the fragrances of fir and cedar before you enter more mixed woods. You see the road up ahead before you reach it (3.2 mi.) **[15]**. Turn right and follow it back to the parking lot.

1. Trailhead
2. Orange junction
3. Green junction
4. Blue junction
5. Green junction
6. Bluff
7. Spur to lake
8. Junction
9. Beach House
10. Rocky beach
11. Spur
12. Road
13. McCormick Lake
14. Spur to bay
15. Road

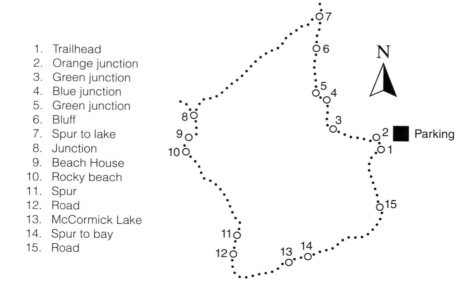

- Hike through stands of virgin hemlock trees.
- Enjoy scenic views of Lake Michigan, the Straits of Mackinac, and the Mackinac Bridge.
- Swim or walk along a sandy Lake Michigan beach.

Park Information

Combine sandy beaches and rocky shores with rugged backcountry, add views of Lake Michigan, and you get a general picture of Wilderness State Park. Throw in camping facilities, a boat launch, rustic cabins, and a habitat suitable for bobcat, beaver, and bear, and you have plenty of reasons to visit this 10,500-acre park.

Directions: The park is located about 10 miles west of Mackinaw City. Follow County Road 81 and continue west along Wilderness Park Drive.

Hours Open: Open daily.

Facilities: Hiking, mountain bicycling, cross-country skiing, snowmobiling, swimming, fishing, rustic cabins, hunting, camping (tent and RV), picnicking, boat launch, and interpretive trails.

Permits and Rules: A park fee is required for motor vehicles ($6 daily, $24 annually for residents; $8 daily, $29 annually for nonresidents). No hunting is allowed within the marked safety zone. Snowmobiles and bikes are allowed only on certain trails (the contact station can tell you which trails these are).

For Further Information: Wilderness State Park, 903 Wilderness Park Drive, Carp Lake, MI 49718; 231-436-5381.

Other Points of Interest

East of the park are the four Mackinac State Historic Parks: **Fort Mackinac** and **Mackinac Island State Park** (see park #4), **Historic Mill Creek Discovery Park** (see park #37), and **Colonial Michilimackinac State Historic Park**. For more information, contact Mackinac State Historic Parks, P.O. Box 873, Mackinaw City, MI 49701; 231-436-4100; www.mackinacparks.com.

From the glimmering beauty of the Straits of Mackinac to the history of Fort Michilimackinac and, yes, even to the fudge, **Mackinaw City** has much to offer. For information, contact the Mackinaw City Chamber of Commerce, 231-436-5574 or 888-455-8100, www.mackinawchamber.com; or the Mackinaw City Chamber of Tourism, 800-577-3113, www.mackinaw citychamber.com.

Park Trails

Big Stone (, .75 mile). Starting across from the picnic area, this trail links up with the Red Pine and Pondside Trails.

East Boundary (, 2 miles). Start on the south side of Park Drive Road and head south to access the North Country Trail and the South Boundary Trail.

East Ridge (, 1.4 miles). Beginning near the East Boundary Trail off Park Drive Road, the trail links with the North Country Trail and Nebo Trail.

Hemlock (, .6 mile). You can reach this trail, which loops Mount Nebo, either by continuing east along the Red Pine Trail or from the Nebo Trail.

Nebo (, 2 miles). This trail heads south from the access road and descends through woods to the South Boundary trail.

Pondside (, .5 mile). Starting across from the Pines Campground to the southeast, the Pondside Trail loops around Goose Pond.

Red Pine (, 1.3 miles). This trail starts from the Pondside Trail, south of the dam. The trail links with the Nebo and Hemlock trails.

South Boundary (, 1.5 miles). This trail starts from the Sturgeon Bay, Swamp Line, Nebo, and East Boundary Trails.

Sturgeon Bay (, 2.25 miles). This trail starts south of Park Drive Road, east of the Station Point Cabin. It crosses the Big and Little Sucker creeks and provides access to the west portion of the North Country Trail, Swamp Line Trail, and South Boundary Trail.

Swamp Line (, 2 miles). This trail follows south from the access road to the Pines Campground. It passes through cedar and aspen and overlooks beaver ponds.

North Country National Scenic Trail (, 5.5 miles). This trail incorporates sections of the others on its planned trek through Michigan.

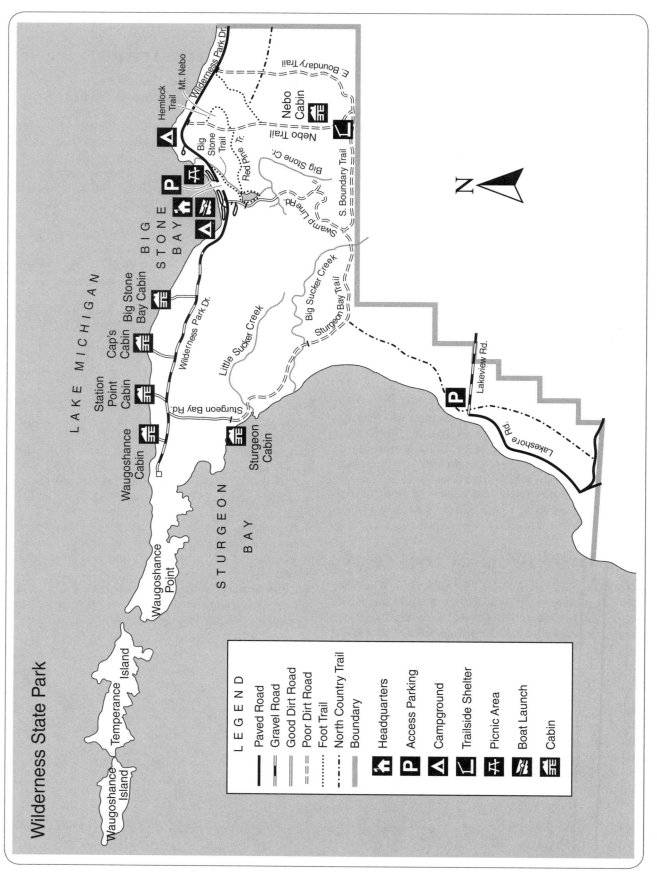

Wilderness State Park

LAKE MICHIGAN

Temperance Island

Waugoshance Island

Waugoshance Point

STURGEON BAY

Waugoshance Cabin

Station Point Cabin

Cap's Cabin

Big Stone Bay Cabin

Wilderness Park Dr.

Little Sucker Creek

Big Sucker Creek

Sturgeon Bay Rd.

Sturgeon Cabin

Sturgeon Bay Trail

B I G   S T O N E   B A Y

Hemlock Trail

Mt. Nebo

Big Stone Trail

Red Pine Tr.

Big Stone Cr.

Nebo Trail

Nebo Cabin

E. Boundary Trail

Wilderness Park Dr.

S. Boundary Trail

Swamp Line Rd.

Lakeview Rd.

Lakeshore Rd.

L E G E N D

——	Paved Road
═══	Gravel Road
═══	Good Dirt Road
= = =	Poor Dirt Road
· · · ·	Foot Trail
—·—·—	North Country Trail
▬▬	Boundary

Headquarters
Access Parking
Campground
Trailside Shelter
Picnic Area
Boat Launch
Cabin

N

East Ridge–Nebo– South Boundary– East Boundary Trails Loop

Distance Round-Trip: 5.4 miles
Estimated Hiking Time: 2.5 to 3 hours

Cautions: This trail has exposed roots. A good chunk of the East Boundary Trail may be extremely wet. Wear proper footgear. Don't even think of hiking this trail without insect repellent during warm months.

Trail Directions: Park on the south side of Wilderness Park Drive to access the East Ridge and East Boundary trails. The hike starts along the East Ridge Trail, which is to the right of the parking area. Head southwest into the designated wilderness area **[1]** and roll through a forest carpeted with pine needles. The dark forest, hills, and low, lush areas give this area a wilderness feeling.

Leave pine perfume behind and blaze along a trail overgrown with vegetation. A tree stump presages the logs that soon litter the trail. Eventually you reenter the cover of trees, and later you pass moss-covered logs while crossing a boardwalk (.3 mi.) **[2]**. The trail narrows, and the forest darkens. Maples mingle with varied floor foliage. Velvety moss-covered logs and lush foliage draping the trail create an eerie feeling.

A lowland (.5 mi.) **[3]** accompanies you on the left as you hike along a ridge, announcing the arrival of a junction for the North Country Trail, which you reach at .6 mi. **[4]**. The trail veers right and has you climbing.

Break out of the hills to an open area to your right and climb again. You encounter much the same terrain through ferns, mud, darkness, and wet areas. Wind your way up the trail, most likely not meeting a soul, and reach the Nebo Trail at 1.4 mi. **[5]**. Head left along this tree-lined two-track. Mostly level here, it cuts through wetlands and hills. At 2 mi., a silvery green hill of lichen on your left precedes the Nebo Cabin, where you'll find a latrine and water pump **[6]**.

The trail winds before breaking into sunlight, only to reenter the shade of the forest. When you see a barrier to keep snowmobiles off the trail, you are near the trailside shelter (2.4 mi.) **[7]**. Soon the trail winds down to the South Boundary Trail junction (2.5 mi.) **[8]**.

Turn left and soon walk along a narrow meadow filled with wildflowers. This lovely little stretch of trail apparently receives little use. Darkness looms in the shadows of the forest that envelops the bright meadow corridor of wildflowers.

At 2.8 mi., the trail curves left and into the shadows of the East Boundary Trail **[9]**. The trail cuts through hardwoods that grow dense, and foliage becomes noticeably lush, a tip that you are nearing a wet area

(3.2 mi.) **[10]**. Did you remember your insect repellent? If not, run! Your arms will be flapping above you as you swat off clouds of mosquitoes while you race through cattails, their leaves scraping at your pants as you pass.

Still moving quickly, because you have likely gathered a crowd, pass 4- to 5-feet-tall ostrich ferns just before you reach the North Country Trail junction (4.8 mi.) **[11]**. The trail widens. For a stretch, grasses and wildflowers grow in it. Pass through more pines before the trail takes you through the gate and back to your vehicle.

1. Trailhead
2. Boardwalk
3. Lowland
4. North Country Trail junction
5. Nebo Trail junction
6. Nebo Cabin
7. Trailside shelter
8. South Boundary Trail junction
9. East Boundary Trail junction
10. Lush foliage
11. North Country Trail junction

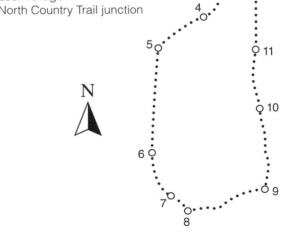

Big Stone–Pondside–Red Pine–Hemlock Trails Loop

Distance Round-Trip: 4.2 miles
Estimated Hiking Time: 2 to 2.5 hours

Cautions: This hike takes you through areas prone to flooding or with exposed roots. Wear appropriate footgear. Take along insect repellent. Watch traffic while hiking along Wilderness Park Drive.

Trail Directions: Park at the picnic area, northeast of the Lakeshore Campground on the north side of Wilderness Park Drive. The trailhead is across the road, where a sign and map board are posted **[1]**.

Step into the woods and onto a cushion of pine needles. Turn right and walk parallel to the little stream called Big Stone Creek. Numerous trees have fallen into and around the creek, to the delight of the ferns now thriving in the sunlight. Shortly after a sign for the Big Stone Trail, you reach a point where the trail splits, providing a short alternate route useful when the main trail is wet (.2 mi.) **[2]**. The main trail follows along the edge of the creek and has you stepping through mud, over roots and fallen trees, and past wildflowers.

Shortly after the alternate route rejoins the trail, note the white cedar on your left that fell years ago and whose individual branches have grown from the trunk to become trees (.3 mi.) **[3]**. Cross a clearing, go under a power line, pass a graveyard of standing trees, and swing left back to the creek. You soon reach the dam at Goose Pond (.6 mi.) **[4]**. Turn right and circle the lily-covered pond on the .5 mi. Pondside Trail.

You pass interpretive posts that help identify some of the features hidden in the trees. Follow south, away from the Pines Campground; you pass between the pond and a parking area with a large map board of the park's trails (.7 mi.) **[5]**. The North Country Trail merges where you swing left to cross a series of three footbridges at the south end of the pond. At the first two bridges, beavers have built dams to complement the man-made dam on the north side of the pond (1 mi.) **[6]**.

Back at the manmade dam, turn right and start down the interpretive Red Pine Trail (1.1 mi.) **[7]**. The trail crosses a low-lying wet area, and you soon walk through mud and over boardwalks and cut logs for nearly .5 mi. You then climb onto a ridge, passing the remains of several old, large trees (1.6 mi.) **[8]**.

The hike has been mostly level until now. The trail undulates, and you snake along the spine of the ridge. You finally reach the red pine plantation, which gives the trail its name (2.1 mi.) **[9]**. Eventually, after several ups and downs, descend to skirt a small, bowl-shaped wetland (2.2 mi.) **[10]** and pass through a white cedar swamp to reach a trail junction (2.3 mi.) **[11]**. The North Country Trail splits right, while you go left and climb.

At 2.4 mi., you cross the roadlike Nebo Trail and continue on the Hemlock Trail **[12]**. Climb gradually to reach the top of Mount Nebo (2.6 mi.) **[13]**, where the foundation of an old lookout tower remains. The trail then descends steeply, and you enter a forest with large hemlock trees (some of them 200 years old) that survived the lumber era (2.7 mi.) **[14]**.

When you reach the Nebo Trail again, turn right (3 mi.) **[15]**, arriving at the Nebo Trail parking area on Wilderness Park Drive (3.3 mi.) **[16]**. Turn left and follow the road, passing a big stone, a glacial erratic (3.4 mi.) **[17]**, on the hike back to the picnic area parking lot.

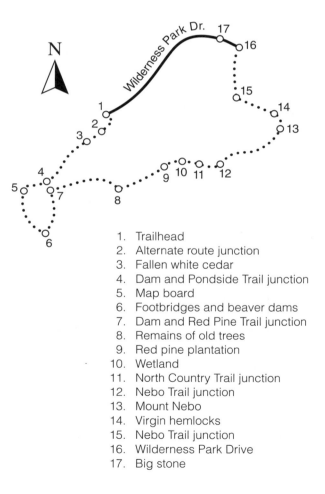

1. Trailhead
2. Alternate route junction
3. Fallen white cedar
4. Dam and Pondside Trail junction
5. Map board
6. Footbridges and beaver dams
7. Dam and Red Pine Trail junction
8. Remains of old trees
9. Red pine plantation
10. Wetland
11. North Country Trail junction
12. Nebo Trail junction
13. Mount Nebo
14. Virgin hemlocks
15. Nebo Trail junction
16. Wilderness Park Drive
17. Big stone

40. Gaylord Forest Management Unit

- Canoe the Inland Waterway.
- Hike, bike, or ski over hundreds of miles of trails.
- Ferry to Beaver or Bois Blanc Islands.

Park Information

Michigan's nearly 3.9 million acres of state forest land, the largest dedicated state forest system in the United States, are divided into 15 forest management units. No longer do state forest lands carry the official title of "state forest." Gone are state forest names like Copper Country, Escanaba River, Lake Superior, Mackinaw, Pere Marquette, and Au Sable. These names have been replaced by management units that carry the name of the town in which the office is located.

The Gaylord Forest Management Unit manages 315,000 acres of state forest land located in Cheboygan, Emmet, Charlevoix, Antrim, and Otsego counties. Besides 18 campgrounds, 12 pathways, and hundreds of miles of rail-trail, snowmobile, and ATV trails, the Gaylord Forest Management Unit offers a diverse collection of natural resources that provide enjoyment for a variety of public uses. Five world-class trout streams originate here: the Au Sable, Manistee, Sturgeon, Pigeon, and East Branch of the Black. The unit features many miles of Lake Michigan and Lake Huron shoreline, including Beaver Island (see park #45) in Lake Michigan and Bois Blanc Island (see park #3) in the Straits of Mackinac. Special management areas include the Jordan River Valley Management Area (see park #41), which carries the distinction of having the first designated natural and scenic river in the state, and the Crapo Lake Kirtland's Warbler Management Area, composed of 3,200 acres of jack pine plains.

Directions: Facilities and points of interest are spread out over a large area. Contact the Gaylord Forest Management Unit.

Hours Open: Many facilities are open year-round.

Facilities: Hiking, cross-country skiing, snowshoeing, snowmobiling, ATV, swimming, fishing, hunting, boat launch, canoeing, camping (tent and backcountry), and picnicking.

Permits and Rules: No fee is required to use pathways. State forest campgrounds remain open all year, but access is limited by snow. There is no charge for undesignated or dispersed camping, but a camp registration card is required. Registration cards may be obtained at any DNR office.

For Further Information: Gaylord Forest Management Unit, 1732 West M-32, Gaylord MI 49735; 989-732-3541.

Other Points of Interest

The Gaylord Forest Management Unit covers a huge territory. For more information about what is available in the area, contact the Gaylord Area Convention and Tourism Bureau, 101 W. Main Street, Gaylord, MI 49735; 800-345-8621; www.gaylordmichigan.net; Charlevoix Area Convention and Visitors Bureau, 100 Michigan Avenue, P.O. Box 388, Charlevoix, MI 49720; 800-367-8557; www.charlevoixlodging.com; Cheboygan Area Chamber of Commerce, 124 North Main Street, Cheboygan, MI 49721; 800-968-3302; www.cheboygan.com; Petoskey Area Visitors Bureau, 401 East Mitchell Street, Petoskey, MI 49770; 800-845-2828; www.boynecountry.com; Mackinaw Area Visitors Bureau, 10800 W. US 23, Mackinaw City, MI 49701; 800-666-0160; www.mackinawcity.com; or Indian River Tourist Bureau, 3435 S. Straits Highway, P.O. Box 57, Indian River, MI 49749; 231-238-9325; www.irtourism.com.

Northern
Lower
Peninsula

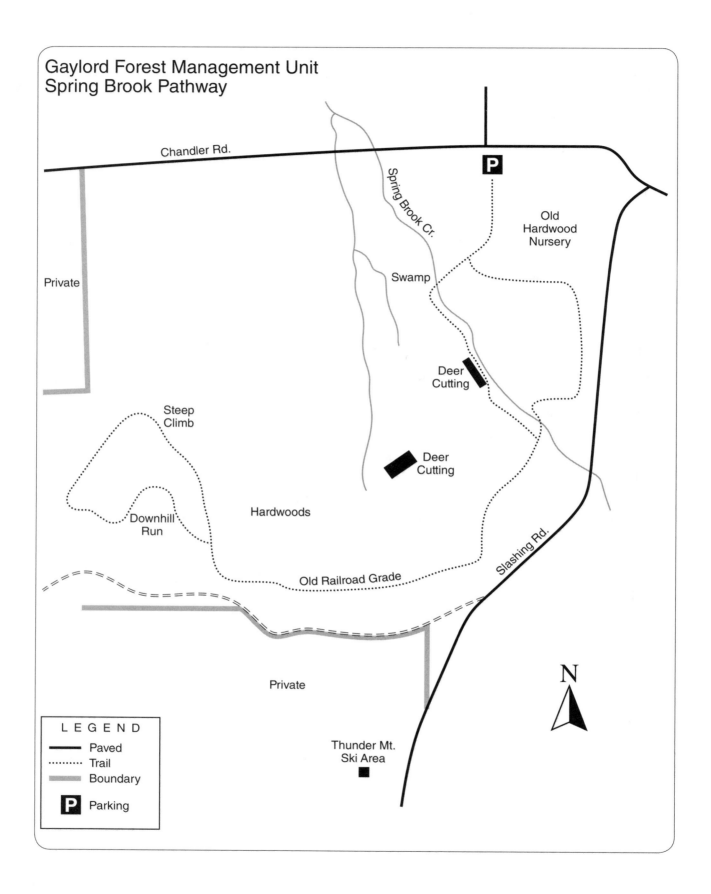

Gaylord Forest Management Unit
Spring Brook Pathway

Chandler Rd.

Spring Brook Cr.

Private

Old
Hardwood
Nursery

Swamp

Deer
Cutting

Steep
Climb

Deer
Cutting

Downhill
Run

Hardwoods

Slashing Rd.

Old Railroad Grade

Private

N

Thunder Mt.
Ski Area

LEGEND
Paved
Trail
Boundary
P Parking

Spring Brook Pathway— East Loop

🌀 **Distance Round-Trip:** 1.6 miles
🌿 **Estimated Hiking Time:** 1 to 1.5 hours

Cautions: This hike takes you over roots and rocks and through areas that are often wet. Wear proper footgear. Take insect repellent in the warm months and watch for poison ivy.

Trail Directions: Take M-131 north from Boyne Falls to Thumb Lake Road. Head east about 5 mi. to Slashing Road. Head north for about 2 mi. to Chandler Hill. Turn left; the lot is about .4 mi. farther on the south side. Start the trail at the southwest end of the lot by the post **[1]**. Follow the blue blazes along the two-track through an old hardwood nursery. The trail passes through large trees and swings left (.3 mi) **[2]**.

Pass through red pines and then a power line. Notice the crisp browse line on the cedar along the trail (.5 mi.) **[3]**. Not far afterward, the trail turns right through a small open area with young aspen. Moss covers the trail, and you pass through a meadow. Listen; you can hear a spring. Cut through bracken fern and then cross a footbridge (.8 mi.) **[4]**.

Pass what looks like a trail and through a utility corridor. Running water sounds clearer. It is, and so is the water of Spring Brook Creek. Step onto the bridge and watch the water meander around logs, fallen trees and branches, and tiny islands of grasses (1 mi.) **[5]**. At the junction on the other side of the bridge, turn right and wind through a mixed forest so moist that roots of trees fan out from their bottoms, giving the trees the illusion that they are standing on their tiptoes.

So tangled are the roots, so sporadic is the placement of the dense trees, that it seems as if there is no trail, but there is. Blue blazes on trees guide you through the swamp as you follow the creek. Logs embedded in the trail aid your steps through a wet area. Pass through an old lumber cut of graying stumps that contrast with the soft and green ferns, mosses, and sphagnum of the rolling forest floor. Ancient fallen trees are thick with verdant moss. The floor rolls like a putting green at a miniature golf course.

Pass through a cedar swamp. Large trees, alive and long gone, crisscross and tangle above textures of vegetation on the floor. You leave the textured, verdant wonderland and the creek (1.1 mi.) **[6]** on a now-spongy green trail through cedar. You soon return to the creek and cross it on a log bridge (1.2 mi.) **[7]** before winding away for good. Pass through waist-high ferns and out to a junction (1.3 mi) **[8]**. Turn left to head back to the parking lot.

1. Trailhead
2. Trail swings left
3. Browse line on cedar
4. Footbridge
5. Spring Brook Creek bridge
6. Leave creek
7. Log bridge
8. Junction

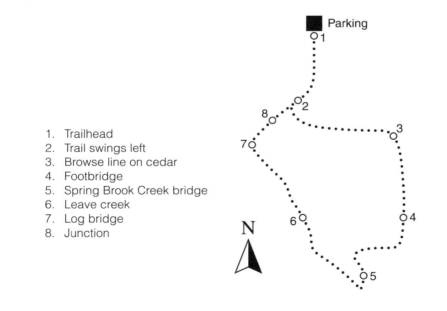

Spring Brook Pathway— West Loop

Distance Round-Trip: 4.8 miles
Estimated Hiking Time: 2.5 to 3 hours

Cautions: This hike takes you over roots and rocks and through areas that are often wet. Wear proper footgear. Take insect repellent in the warm months and watch for poison ivy.

Trail Directions: Take M-131 north from Boyne Falls to Thumb Lake Road. Head east about 5 mi. to Slashing Road. Head north about 2 mi. to Chandler Hill. Turn left; the lot is about .4 mi. farther on the south side. Start the trail at the southwest end of the lot by the post [1]. Follow blue blazes along the two-track through an old hardwood nursery. The trail passes through large trees; look for an opening on the right (.3 mi) [2] and follow it through tall ferns.

Pass through cedars; the creek soon meets you, and you cross over on a bridge (.4 mi.) [3], and then on a log footbridge. Moss softens everything. Ferns and sphagnum texture the rolling floor in this incredible, verdant environment. Cedar dominates as you walk along the creek, past stumps, and through a tangle of trees and roots until you reach the bridge and junction (.6 mi.) [4].

Stay right of the bridge and enter the darkness of woods, broken up by light in openings. A trail merges in (.7 mi.) [5]. Stay right again. The trail makes some abrupt curves as if turning on old roads.

Shortly after you meet a small stream, cross it on a footbridge (1 mi.) [6]. Soon you find yourself on an old rail grade that passes through mixed hardwoods. Ferns caress the trail, and you notice more spruce, fir,

and cedar trees—your cue that you are in for a thick, lush, mossy carpet to walk on (1.2 mi.) [7]. Tread quietly by the beaver dam on your right (1.3 mi.) [8]. A stream trickles just as quietly along the left side of the trail.

Moss gives way to pine carpeting, and now streams run along both sides until they meet under the trail (1.4 mi.) [9]. Farther on, hardwoods again prevail, and you reach a junction (1.6 mi.) [10]. Go right along the grassy way and start to climb to an old road (1.7 mi) [11].

Turn right on the two-track; a forested hill is at your left side. The road veers left, and you soon see a trail junction on your left (2 mi.) [12]. Follow this up the narrow path and up into darker woods. Then climb. Climb some more. When you think you have leveled off, climb more. You walk high along a ridge that slopes steeply away. You reach the crest at an opening (2.3 mi.) [13].

Cut straight across the grass opening back into the woods and head down to close the loop at the road (2.7 mi.) [11]. Cross the road and head back to the bridge and junction (3.9 mi.) [4]. Turn right to cross the bridge and then turn left on the other side.

The trail turns away from the creek and under a power line to pass through a meadow and later waist-high ferns. Cross a footbridge over a stream (4.1 mi.) [14]. Enter a tunnel of trees before breaking out into a meadow. Red pines alert you to watch for the junction (4.3 mi.) [15]. Turn left but first notice the crisp browse line on the cedar along the trail.

You pass the power line and then reach the junction where you started the first loop (4.5 mi) [2]. Continue back to the parking lot.

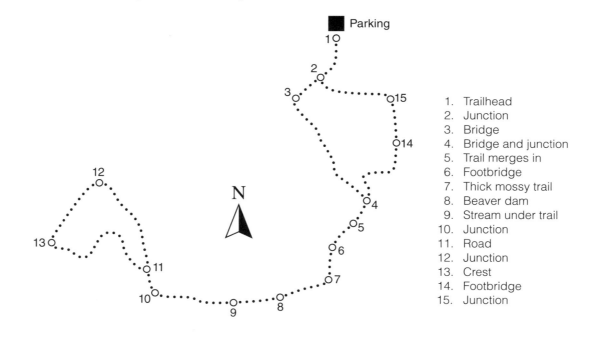

1. Trailhead
2. Junction
3. Bridge
4. Bridge and junction
5. Trail merges in
6. Footbridge
7. Thick mossy trail
8. Beaver dam
9. Stream under trail
10. Junction
11. Road
12. Junction
13. Crest
14. Footbridge
15. Junction

- View the spectacular Jordan River Valley from Deadman's Hill Overlook.
- Hike the pathway to appreciate why the Jordan River is a dedicated wild and scenic river.

Park Information

Michigan's first waterway to be classified a wild and scenic river, the Jordan River unveils its natural beauty to viewers from the overlook at Deadman's Hill. To gain more than a glimpse of the scenic river valley, you can hike all or part of the 18-mile Jordan River Pathway, which winds through an 18,000-acre block of state-owned forest land, providing hikers an opportunity to become more intimate with the river and valley. The path traverses hills and spring-fed streams, low-lying wet areas, old logging railroad grades, and northern hardwoods and mixed pines. The North Country National Scenic Trail uses a portion of this trail for its route through the Jordan River Valley.

The pathway begins and ends at the parking area for Deadman's Hill. Backpacking the entire 18-mile trail takes two days. For shorter hikes, try the Deadman's Hill Loop or the half-mile round-trip hike to Deadman's Hill Overlook. You can customize your hike by using local county roads or the 3.7-mile Warner Creek Pathway.

Directions: On US 131 go north 11.5 miles from Mancelona or south about 1.5 miles from M-32. Turn west on Deadman's Hill Road and drive about 2 miles to the parking area of the Jordan River Pathway. Warner Creek Pathway is north on M-32, west of US 131.

Hours Open: Open year-round.

Facilities: Hiking, snowshoeing, fishing, hunting, camping (backcountry), picnicking, and interpretive trail.

Permits and Rules: All hikers are asked to register. Campers are required to register and pay the fee. The maximum length of stay in any calendar week is two days. No more than eight persons may occupy a campsite. Fires are prohibited except in designated fire circles in the campground. Do not bury garbage or refuse. No camping is allowed outside the designated campground.

For Further Information: Gaylord Operations Service Center, 1732 West M-32, Gaylord, MI 49735; 989-732-3541.

Other Points of Interest

The North Country National Scenic Trail, which uses portions of both the Jordan River and Warner Creek pathways, connects them with a 1-mile section of trail. For more information, contact the Gaylord Operations Service Center.

Graves Crossing Campground is accessible from M-66 or from the Jordan River. Contact the Gaylord Operations Service Center to obtain more information and to find out whether the **Pinney Bridge Hike-In Campground** is open.

The **Grass River Natural Area** (see park #42) contains 10 interpretive trails bedecked with boardwalks, observation platforms, and footbridges with built-in benches, all designed to help visitors observe wetland flora and fauna. For more information, contact Grass River Natural Area, Inc., P.O. Box 231, Bellaire, MI 49615; 231-533-8314; www.grassriver.org.

Park Trails

Deadman's Hill Overlook (🥾, .5 mile round-trip). This trail takes you from the parking area to the Deadman's Hill Overlook for scenic views of the Jordan River Valley.

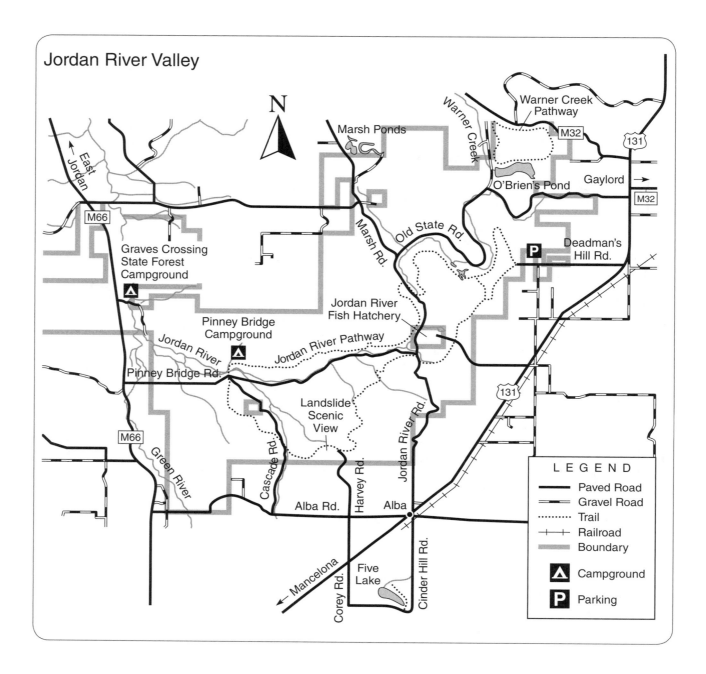

Jordan River Valley

N

Warner Creek Pathway

Marsh Ponds

M32

131

East Jordan

Warner Creek

O'Brien's Pond

Gaylord

M32

M66

Old State Rd.

P

Deadman's Hill Rd.

Graves Crossing State Forest Campground

Marsh Rd.

Jordan River Fish Hatchery

Pinney Bridge Campground

Jordan River Pathway

Jordan River

Pinney Bridge Rd.

131

Landslide Scenic View

Jordan River Rd.

M66

Green River

Cascade Rd.

Harvey Rd.

Alba Rd.

Alba

L E G E N D

——	Paved Road
—•—	Gravel Road
·····	Trail
+++	Railroad
▬▬	Boundary
▲	Campground
P	Parking

Mancelona

Corey Rd.

Five Lake

Cinder Hill Rd.

Three Mile Pathway Loop—Deadman's Hill

🐾🐾🐾🐾🐾 🐾🐾🐾🐾🐾 **Distance Round-Trip:** 3 miles
Estimated Hiking Time: 1.5 to 2 hours

Cautions: This hike takes you over roots and rocks and through areas that are often wet. Wear proper footgear. Take insect repellent in the warm months. At one time this trail had 25 numbered posts that corresponded with an interpretive brochure. These posts have fallen into disrepair

Trail Directions: Start the hike at the north end of the parking area at the end of Deadman's Hill Road **[1]** and begin a long, steep descent, passing several tree identification markers before you reach the valley floor (.5 mi.) **[2]**. From a small clearing at the bottom, the North Country National Scenic Trail splits off to the right toward the Warner Creek Pathway. Turn left, however, and walk over sand and roots to reenter the woods. Climb along the edge of the hill before descending to a rickety observation platform that overlooks a small stream flowing down to the Jordan River (.8 mi.) **[3]**.

Step over a log bridge; watch your step as you follow the sloppy trail, which undulates between the base of Deadman's Hill and the valley floor. Here, the trail takes you over gnarly roots, through mud, across trail logs, and teetering along the edge of eroded slopes. A swing right into ferns and aspen is your cue to look for the trail junction at 1.2 mi. **[4]**.

Turn left for a steep climb through ferns and an open area dominated by the silver and green patchwork of lichens. As you climb back up Deadman's Hill, notice that the trail is not as worn as the section of trail that you descended when you started. You pass increasingly larger beech and maple trees as the climb becomes steeper. Stoop under some fallen trees. When you pass a large boulder on the left, you have almost completed your climb. At the top, turn left at the trail junction, where a sign points you back to the starting point (1.8 mi.) **[5]**.

The remainder of the hike is fairly level; you snake through a forest of primarily beech and maple. At 2.7 mi., stay left to head over to the overlook **[6]**. You reach the overlook where a bench lets you sit and enjoy a panoramic vista of the Jordan River Valley (2.8 mi.) **[7]**. In less than .1 mi., you reach another overlook with an interpretive sign. Here, you are 435 feet above the Jordan River. The interpretive board gives the sad tale of the unfortunate lumberjack Big Sam and the event that cost him his life and gave this site its name.

Go to the right past boulders; you are about .1 mi. from the parking lot where you left your vehicle.

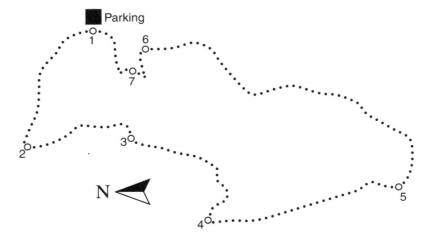

1. Trailhead
2. Valley floor and trail junction
3. Observation platform
4. Trail junction
5. Trail junction, top of climb
6. Stay left
7. Deadman's Hill Overlook

Warner Creek Pathway

Distance Round-Trip: 3.7 miles
Estimated Hiking Time: 1.5 to 2 hours

Cautions: This hike takes you over roots and rocks and through areas that are often wet. Wear proper footgear. Take insect repellent in the warm months.

Trail Directions: On US 131 go north about 13.5 miles from Mancelona. Turn west on M-32 and travel less than 2 miles to the parking lot for the Warner Creek Pathway. Head through the gate at the southwest end of the lot **[1]** along the wide path into the woods.

After passing through an open area, the trail swings south; the trees are more a mix of hemlock and white pine. The trail passes huge fallen trees. Ferns line the trail now pocketed with moss.

The trail winds around the flank of a steep hill (.3 mi.) **[2]**. Continue along the winding trail through mixed woods. As you walk the pine-needle trail, a dark pool in a swamp lies below you on your right (.5 mi.) **[3]**, a precursor of the creek to come. Warner Creek mirrors through the trees (.6 mi.) **[4]**.

Still in the woods, the trail winds between the low area of the creek and the ridge beside you. The trail narrows to a path; it is wetter through here (.8 mi) **[5]**. Veer left with the trail and pass an ephemeral pond. Shortly after you notice that you are in a valley, you reach a junction (1.1 mi.) **[6]**.

The North Country Trail continues straight. If you wish to get a view of O'Brien's Pond or connect with the Jordan River Pathway, head straight. But your trail turns left here. It continues as a narrow path, passing through fragrant fir and cedar. After you catch a glimpse of O'Brien's Pond through the trees, the trail becomes grassy, wet, and spongy (1.2 mi.) **[7]**. You reach dry land at about 1.4 mi. **[8]**, but the firmness is just a tease. Soon, your boots make a sucking sound as you pull them from mud. Pass a small pond where you might catch glimpse of critters. Continue along, squishing through the grass.

The trail veers left to climb up and up onto dry land (1.6 mi.) **[9]**. Pass through a small meadow, ferns, and youthful trees to rise over a ridge. Descend through bracken ferns and past a small open area to renter the woods (1.9 mi.) **[10]**. Stay right along a wide path that gradually climbs.

Soon you see a road. Stay left on the path less traveled. You again climb through a valley and begin to rise above the road on your right. The climb becomes more serious, and you soon reach the top (2.2 mi.) **[11]**. Rolling terrain surrounds the trail. Swing left and descend. Stay left when what looks like a trail merges in. Continue descending. At the fork, stay right (2.4 mi.) **[12]** and descend back into a valley.

Follow the blue blazes to the left (2.6 mi.) **[13]**. The trail bottoms out, winds through mostly maples, and reaches a junction with the North Country Trail (3 mi.) **[14]**. Go straight and pass the utility corridor. Young maples crowd the trail; small pockets open occasionally elsewhere, and you see a gate near the highway (3.5 mi.) **[15]**. Turn left between the woods and the road, and head back to the parking area.

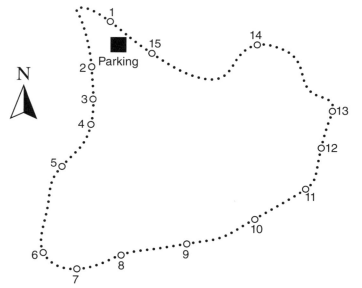

N

1. Trailhead
2. Flank of hill
3. Dark pool
4. Warner Creek
5. Trail narrows
6. Junction
7. Wet area
8. Dry tease
9. Veer left to high ground
10. Reenter woods
11. Crest
12. Fork
13. Follow to left
14. North Country Trail junction
15. Gate

42. Grass River Natural Area

- Hike an extensive system of boardwalks to observe wetland flora and fauna.
- View wildlife from wooden observation platforms.
- Sit atop Finch Creek on benches built into wooden decks that double as bridges.

Park Information

The 1,325 acres within this natural area produce diverse habitats: creeks, rivers, and wetlands; upland and marsh forests; and sedge meadows. These habitats are home to a diverse collection of plants, birds, reptiles, and mammals. Deer, beaver, loons, and eagles are seen here frequently.

The Grass River Natural Area is a huge wetland drained by the Grass River and its tributaries. It lies midway on Antrim County's Chain of Lakes waterway, a connector of Torch and Clam lakes and Lake Bellaire. Ten interpretive trails, bedecked with boardwalks, observation platforms, and footbridges, flaunt the scenery and wildlife within the 225 acres of the education zone. Visit the Grass River Natural Area Interpretive Center, which has displays and area information.

Directions: The natural area is located about 8 miles west of Mancelona. Go west on M-88 about 2.5 miles until the road bends north. Stay west on Alden Highway for another 5.5 miles to the access road, which is about .5 mile west of Comfort Road. Head north less than a mile to the parking lot.

Hours Open: The natural area is open daily from dawn until dusk. The interpretive center is open daily from 10:00 a.m. until 4:00 p.m., June through Labor Day. In May, September, and October, it is open on weekends from 10:00 a.m. until 4:00 p.m.

Facilities: Hiking, cross-country skiing, snowshoeing, fishing, hunting, canoeing, equestrian, interpretive trails, and interpretive center.

Permits and Rules: No fee is required, but donations are accepted. Hunting and horses are not allowed within the educational area. Please stay on trails and do not disturb plants. Do not litter, and leave pets at home. Open fires and alcoholic beverages are prohibited.

For Further Information: Grass River Natural Area, Inc., P.O. Box 231, Bellaire, MI 49615; 231-533-8314. Call the interpretive center at 231-533-8576.

Other Points of Interest

Antrim County has two chains of lakes—an upper and a lower chain. Some of these lakes are **Lake Bellaire**, **Clam Lake**, **Torch Lake**, **Lake Skegemog**, and **Elk Lake**. For information on canoe rentals or other interests in the area, contact the Bellaire Chamber of Commerce at 231-533-6023 or www.bellairechamber.org.

South of Torch Lake and about 9 miles west of Kalkaska is the **Skegemog Lake Wildlife Area**. Here, the Skegemog Lake Pathway, via a rail-trail and an elaborate system of boardwalks, passes through a cedar swamp to an observation tower. For more information, contact the Traverse City Management Unit, 970 Emerson, Traverse City, MI 49686; 231-922-5280.

Park Trails

Cabin Trail (👣, .1 mile). Passes through an upland forest and an abandoned field. It leads to the Sedge Meadow, Tamarack, and Fern trails.

Sedge Meadow Trail (👣, .7 mile). Loops through wetlands and has a spur that leads you to the dock on Grass River.

Tamarack Trail (👣, .3 mile). This barrier-free trail starts at the cabin and loops through wetlands. Use this trail to reach the Sedge Meadow and Fern trails.

Fern Trail (👣, .5 mile). Begins off the Tamarack Trail and winds along Finch Creek, crosses it, and heads back.

Glacial Plain Trail (👣, 2 miles). Follows the rail-trail less than a mile, crosses a boardwalk, and ends at a meadow. Here you can explore the terraced hills, remains from the wave action of higher waters.

Grass River Natural Area Nature Trail (👣, 4 miles). This rail-trail curves along the south end of the natural area.

Chippewa Trail (👣, .75 mile). Loops through a variety of forest types and skirts clear areas where new growth provides food and shelter for wildlife.

Nipissing Trail (👣, 1 mile). Crosses the Chippewa Trail and heads out to the rail-trail.

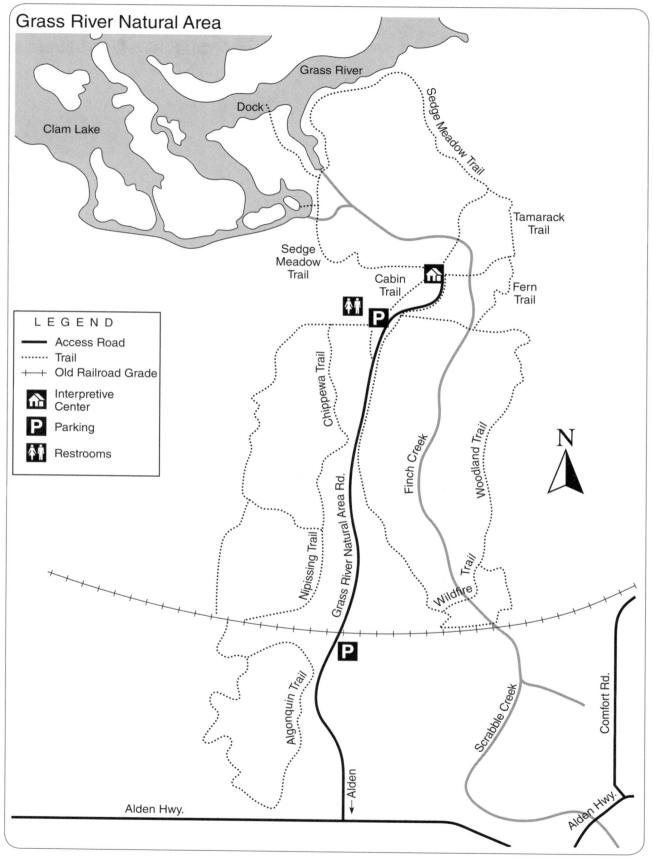

Grass River Natural Area

Grass River

Clam Lake

Dock

Sedge Meadow Trail

Tamarack Trail

Sedge Meadow Trail

Cabin Trail

Fern Trail

LEGEND
— Access Road
····· Trail
+—+ Old Railroad Grade
🏠 Interpretive Center
🅿 Parking
🚻 Restrooms

Chippewa Trail

Finch Creek

Woodland Trail

N

Nipissing Trail

Grass River Natural Area Rd.

Wildfire Trail

Algonquin Trail

Scrabble Creek

Comfort Rd.

Alden

Alden Hwy.

Alden Hwy.

Woodland/Wildfire Trail

Distance Round-Trip: 1.3 miles
Estimated Hiking Time: 30 minutes to 1 hour

Cautions: Stumps and roots protrude from the trail. Watch for low branches and fallen trees. Some boardwalk boards give a bit; keep your balance. Take insect repellent in warm months.

Trail Directions: Start from the northeast corner of the north parking lot **[1]**. Head east through the tall ferns (this portion is shared with the Fern Trail). Your soft steps on woodchips are soon hardened on wood boards, and you cross a boardwalk that evolves into an ornate footbridge over Finch Creek. Have a seat on one of the benches of this observation deck over the creek. Small islands of grass have trees growing from them.

At the junction (.1 mi.) **[2]**, continue straight and pass moss mounds with trees sprouting from them. Walk a stretch with scented trees tightly embracing the trail. At the end of the boardwalk, veer left. Soon you see moss draped over roots and fallen logs. Cross one short boardwalk and then another overlooking grass plumes that provide a feathery softness against the darker draping moss and logs (.2 mi.) **[3]**.

The trail veers right, and you may notice more aspen, hemlock, and maple saplings. On another short boardwalk, view the vernal pond (.3 mi.) **[4]**. Pass by uprooted trees, dodging any stumps as the trail winds through the upland forest. Near .4 mi., you pass a number of nursery stumps **[5]**; from the stumps new trees grow.

Pass more nursery stumps and walk along a small ridge. Forested hills envelop the trail. At .5 mi., you reach the shortcut junction **[6]**. Continue straight, winding your way through aspen, hemlock, and then white pine. At about .6 mi., reenter a wetland environment, take the steps down to the boardwalk, and pass by lush grasses, moss, and ferns **[7]**. This boardwalk curves and leads to another elaborate footbridge with an observation deck. An old wooden railroad trestle bridges Finch Creek to your left. Plumes of grass islands sprouting trees decorate this stretch of the creek.

The boardwalk soon ends, and the natural trail winds around, leading you to steps that take you up to the railroad grade. After reaching the grade (.7 mi.) **[8]**, follow to the right along the raised ridge. Around you, maple gives way to aspen and then white pine. Listen—you might hear Scrabble Creek as you walk over it. At .8 mi., turn right at the sign and abandon the rail corridor **[9]**.

Blaze down through a wall of ferns and back under maple cover. Cedars grow near the creek to your right. Pass the shortcut junction at .9 mi. **[10]** as the trail veers left and begins to undulate before passing through low ferns.

The trail winds through woods and then passes through spindly young maples before it reaches the access road (1.2 mi.) **[11]**. Turn right and follow the road through its canopy of hardwoods to reach the parking area.

1. Trailhead
2. Fern Trail junction
3. Grass plumes and moss
4. Boardwalk at pond
5. Nursery stumps
6. Shortcut trail junction
7. Steps down to boardwalk
8. Abandoned rail corridor
9. Turn right at sign
10. Shortcut trail junction
11. Access road

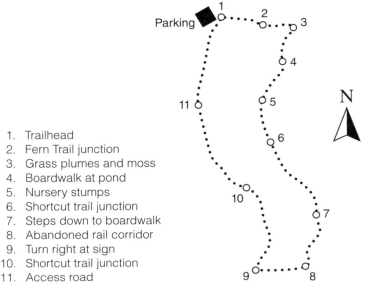

Cabin–Sedge Meadow–Tamarack–Fern Trails Loop

Distance Round-Trip: 1.3 miles
Estimated Hiking Time: 30 minutes to 1 hour

Cautions: Some boardwalk boards give a bit when you walk on them. Watch for low branches and trees leaning over the trail. Take insect repellent. Don't touch the poison sumac and poison ivy.

Trail Directions: Start at the north end of the parking lot and head toward the interpretive center [1]. Follow the woodchip path as you traverse an abandoned field and pass fragrant pines to arrive at the center (.1 mi.) [2].

The Sedge Meadow Trail starts west of the center and heads into the woods. As you hike you see the habitat change from upland forest to swamp. Soon, step onto a boardwalk where white cedar dominates (.2 mi.) [3]. At Finch Creek, the boardwalk evolves into an ornate footbridge (.3 mi.) [4]. Sit on a bench on the observation deck over the creek. If you're patient, you may see brook, brown, or rainbow trout.

Past the bridge, a spur boardwalk splits off to the left, taking you to an observation platform [5]. From it, view the open waters of Finch Creek, Grass River, and Clam Lake as well as portions of the sedge meadow and the scrubby swamp forest. With such a diversity of habitat in view, this is a prime site from which to view wildlife.

Back on the main boardwalk, you reach another spur in less than .1 mi. that leads you across the sedge meadow to another observation platform [6] and a dock along the Grass River (.5 mi.) [7]. See how the Grass River got its name as you walk among the grass-like plants—reeds, rushes, and sedges—that are not really grasses at all. Return to the main boardwalk, turn left, and cross a footbridge over a small branch of Finch Creek (.6 mi.) [8]. Look for marker post #10 where a white cedar blew over. Each of its upraised branches is becoming a separate tree.

You pop out onto a section of sedge meadow before reentering the scrubby swamp forest to arrive at another observation platform situated along the Grass River (.7 mi.) [9]. The platform provides an opportunity to view marsh hawk, osprey, and bald eagle.

Continuing along the boardwalk through the swamp, you reach a covered bench (.9 mi.) [10] at the junction with the Tamarack Trail. Turn left and follow the boardwalk for a short distance before you veer left to pick up the Fern Trail (1 mi.) [11].

Pass moss mounds with trees sprouting from them before you reach the bench along Finch Creek (1.1 mi.) [12]. Turn right at the trail junction to cross the creek. The boardwalk evolves into an ornate footbridge with enticing benches (1.2 mi.) [13]. Leaving the bridge behind, you soon step off the boardwalk for the first time in just over .1 mi. Wood chips lead you to the road, which returns you to the parking lot.

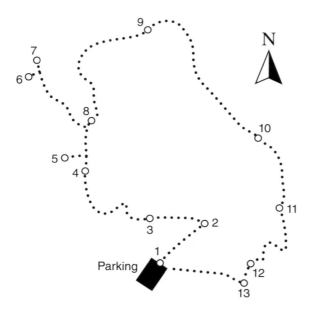

1. Trailhead
2. Interpretive center
3. Start boardwalk
4. Ornate footbridge
5. Observation platform
6. Observation platform
7. Dock
8. Footbridge
9. Observation platform
10. Covered bench and Tamarack Trail junction
11. Fern Trail junction
12. Bench
13. Ornate footbridge

43. Wm. Mitchell State Park

- Learn about Michigan's hunting and fishing heritage.
- Fish Lakes Mitchell and Cadillac for walleye, pike, crappie, bluegills, perch, and largemouth and smallmouth bass.
- In springtime head for the woods in search of the morel mushroom.

Park Information

Nestled between Lake Mitchell and Lake Cadillac, with a historic canal running through it, this 334-acre park is a popular destination for people looking to camp, fish, or boat. The canal, built during the logging era to float timber from Lake Mitchell to the sawmills on Lake Cadillac, now serves as a connector between the two popular fishing lakes. Together the lakes offer more than 3,700 acres of prime fish habitat. Also popular are the swimming beaches provided in the campground and day-use areas of the park. For landlubbers, the scenic 7-mile paved Lake Cadillac Bike Path awaits those more interested in walking, running, biking, or inline skating.

The park also sports the Carl T. Johnson Hunting and Fishing Center. The center promotes awareness of Michigan's hunting and fishing heritage, management, and recreation potential. Exhibits, interactive displays, multi-image slide shows, a wall-size aquarium, and outdoor pellet and archery ranges await the visitor. The Heritage Nature Trail starts from the center and accesses a nature study area that supports a variety of plants and animals such as white-tailed deer, great blue heron, osprey, wild turkey, beaver, painted turtles, and various species of waterfowl.

Directions: From M-55, go northwest on M-115 .25 mile and look for the state park entrance just south of the canal bridge. The visitor center and entrance to the nature study area are another .1 mile north on M-115. Look for the sign on the east side of the road. From US 131 take M-115 north 3 miles.

Hours Open: The park is open year-round. The Carl T. Johnson Hunting and Fishing Center is open daily from 10:00 a.m. to 6:00 p.m., May 1 to November 30; from December 1 to April 30 it is open Friday from noon to 5:00 p.m. and Saturday through Sunday from 10:00 a.m. to 5:00 p.m.

Facilities: Hiking, cross-country skiing, snowshoeing, swimming, fishing, hunting, boat launch, bicycling, canoeing, camping (tent and RV), minicabins, playground, picnicking, and visitor center.

Permits and Rules: A park fee is required for motor vehicles ($6 daily, $24 annually for residents; $8 daily, $29 annually for nonresidents). There is no admission fee for the Carl T. Johnson Hunting and Fishing Center.

For Further Information: Wm. Mitchell State Park, 6093 E. M-115, Cadillac, MI 49601; 231-775-7911; Carl T. Johnson Hunting and Fishing Center, 231-779-1321.

Other Points of Interest

Canoe all or portions of the Pine and Manistee rivers. The Pine River is ideal for the experienced canoeist. The Manistee is a wide, deep river with an easy current, making it a good choice for families or those learning to canoe. For canoe rental information, contact the Cadillac Area Visitors Bureau at 800-22-LAKES or www.cadillacmichigan.com.

Northern Lower Peninsula

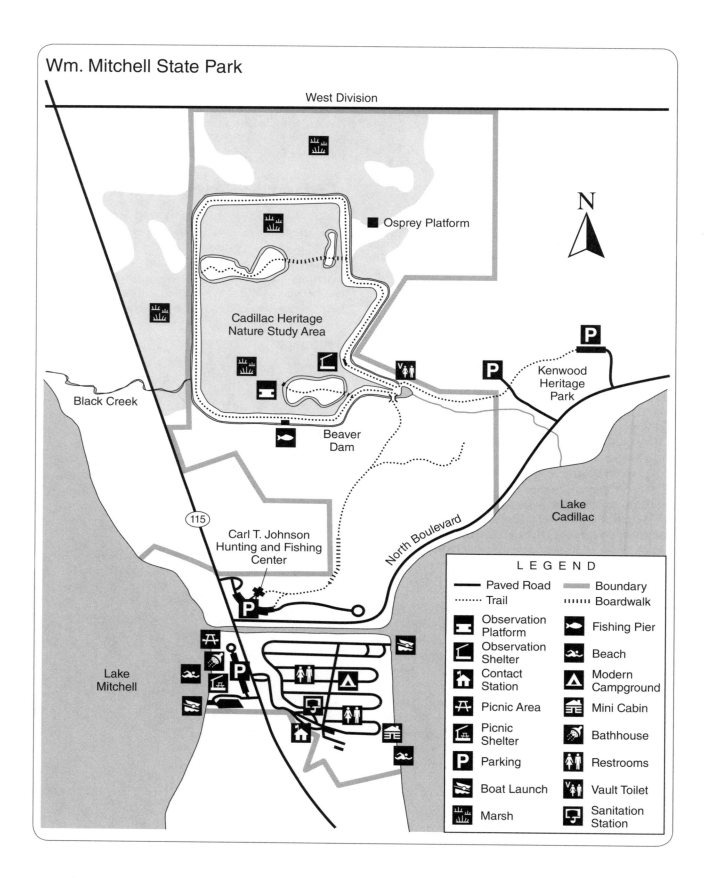

Wm. Mitchell State Park

West Division

Osprey Platform

Cadillac Heritage
Nature Study Area

Black Creek

Beaver
Dam

115

Carl T. Johnson
Hunting and Fishing
Center

Kenwood
Heritage
Park

Lake
Cadillac

North Boulevard

Lake
Mitchell

LEGEND

—— Paved Road		Boundary	
······· Trail		۱۱۱۱۱۱ Boardwalk	

Observation Platform — Fishing Pier

Observation Shelter — Beach

Contact Station — Modern Campground

Picnic Area — Mini Cabin

Picnic Shelter — Bathhouse

P Parking — Restrooms

Boat Launch — Vault Toilet

Marsh — Sanitation Station

N

Heritage Nature Trail

🐾 **Distance Round-Trip:** 2.5 miles
🐾 **Estimated Hiking Time:** 1 to 1.5 hours

Cautions: Bring your binoculars and insect repellent to maximize the experience.

Trail Directions: Begin this interpretive trail either from behind the visitor center or from the parking area **[1]**. Enter the mixed woods along a crushed limestone trail. You soon arrive at post #2 to cross a footbridge into a gathering of hemlock trees and then reach an L-shaped boardwalk into another gathering of hemlock trees (.2 mi.) **[2]**.

As you walk through the forest here, be sure to stop and read the interpretive sign to learn what trees are found in this woodland zone. The stately large pine that you pass shortly before you arrive at post #3 (.4 mi.) **[3]** is a white pine. Stay left past the post and soon enter a meadow with a row of bluebird houses strung along the tree line. You then cross a footbridge to arrive at post #4 (.5 mi.) **[4]**. Turn left and begin your hike on the dike system for the Cadillac Heritage Nature Study Area. Be observant. You are bound to see something in, on, over, or alongside the water found on both sides of the trail. Now where are those binoculars?

You don't go far before you reach post #5 (.6 mi.) **[5]** and the chance for a side trip. Go right, cross a footbridge onto a small island, and walk a natural pathway through the trees to arrive at an observation deck (.7 mi.) **[6]**. Climb up onto the deck for a chance to view the emergent zone. Then turn around and retrace your steps to post #5. Turn right at the dike.

When the trail veers right, have a seat on the bench and look for evidence of beaver (.9 mi.) **[7]**. If you happened to have brought a fishing pole, the next stop is for you—a fishing pier (1 mi.) **[8]**. If not, continue and soon make a wide turn to the right to arrive eventually at post #7 for a chance to do a little island hopping (1.4 mi.) **[9]**. Turn right, cross a small footbridge, and enter the shade of Hemlock Island to learn about wetland evergreens. Then cross a long boardwalk (1.6 mi.) **[10]** before hopping across a small island and footbridge to arrive at post #9 (1.7 mi.) **[11]**. Turn right.

The trail swings left, right, and then left again to arrive at an observation platform (1.9 mi.) **[12]**. Pull out those binoculars and look for wetland waterfowl before continuing. At post #10 is a vault toilet (2 mi.) **[13]**. Turn right, cross two footbridges, and begin your return hike to the visitor center.

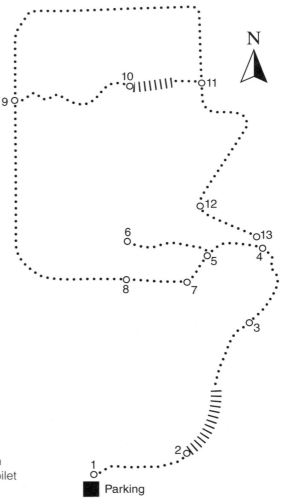

1. Trailhead
2. L-shaped boardwalk
3. Post #3
4. Footbridge
5. Side trip
6. Observation deck
7. Bench
8. Fishing pier
9. Post #7
10. Long boardwalk
11. Post #9
12. Observation platform
13. Post #10 and vault toilet

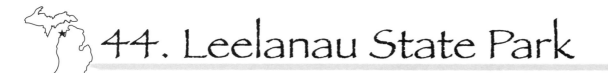

44. Leelanau State Park

- Climb to enjoy a scenic overlook of Lake Michigan.
- Tour the Grand Traverse Lighthouse and Museum.
- Stroll a Lake Michigan beach and hunt Petoskey stones.

Park Information

If a quiet, sandy, Lake Michigan shoreline; secluded walks over wooded terrain; and inland lakes with views of migrating waterfowl pique your interest, this is the place to visit. Its two separate sections include the popular day-use, camping, and lighthouse–museum area in the north and the undeveloped southern tract, woven with lightly used trails through woods and over dunes, marshes, and interdunal wetlands.

Leelanau, the Native American word for "a land of delight," aptly describes the 1,350-acre park. The northern section is at the tip of the little finger of Michigan's Lower Peninsula, where Lake Michigan meets Grand Traverse Bay. Lake Michigan yields a rocky shoreline for those who can take advantage of rustic campsites, enjoy picnic areas, or enlighten themselves at the Grand Traverse Lighthouse, an interpretive maritime museum. Many people enjoy sifting through rocks along the shoreline for Michigan's state stone, the Petoskey stone.

Four miles south of the developed section, the larger southern section provides about 1.5 miles of

sandy Lake Michigan shoreline. More than 8.5 miles of trails loop through this tranquil part of the park. Climb the stairway to the top of a dune and an observation deck overlooking Lake Michigan. Or head inland to Mud Lake and view waterfowl during their spring and fall migrations.

Directions: The southern section of Leelanau State Park is about 3 miles north of Northport. Take County Road 629 north from Northport 3 miles to Densmore Road (Airport Road) and then go left to the parking lot. The northern section is another 4 miles north on County Road 629.

Hours Open: The park is open daily from 8:00 a.m. to 10:00 p.m. The Grand Traverse Lighthouse is open daily from 10:00 a.m. to 6:00 p.m. during the summer.

Facilities: Hiking, cross-country skiing, swimming, fishing, hunting, camping, picnicking, minicabins, and interpretive and historic centers.

Permits and Rules: A park fee is required for motor vehicles ($6 daily, $24 annually for residents; $8 daily, $29 annually for nonresidents).

For Further Information: Leelanau State Park, 15310 N. Lighthouse Point Road, Northport, MI 49670; 231-386-5422.

Other Points of Interest

For information on attractions, contact the Northport-Omena Chamber of Commerce at 231-386-9809 or the Leelanau Peninsula Chamber of Commerce at 231-271-9895 or www.leelanauchamber.com.

Hike along the Boardman River in the **Grand Traverse Natural Education Preserve**. This 420-acre preserve is 2 miles south of Traverse City. For more information, contact the Grand Traverse Conservation District, 1450 Cass Road, Traverse City, MI 49684; 231-941-0960.

Two area trails incorporate active or abandoned rail lines. The **Traverse Area Recreation Trail** (TART) is an asphalt-paved route within view of the Grand Traverse Bay. The 15-mile **Leelanau Trail** stretches from Traverse City to Suttons Bay. For more information, contact TART Trails, Inc., 415 S. Union Street, P.O. Box 252, Traverse City, MI 49685; 231-941-4300; www.traversetrails.org.

Park Trails

The park's one loop has cutoff spurs that allow you to divide the large loop into four smaller ones. Two spurs lead to the beach on Lake Michigan and to an overlook.

Leelanau State Park

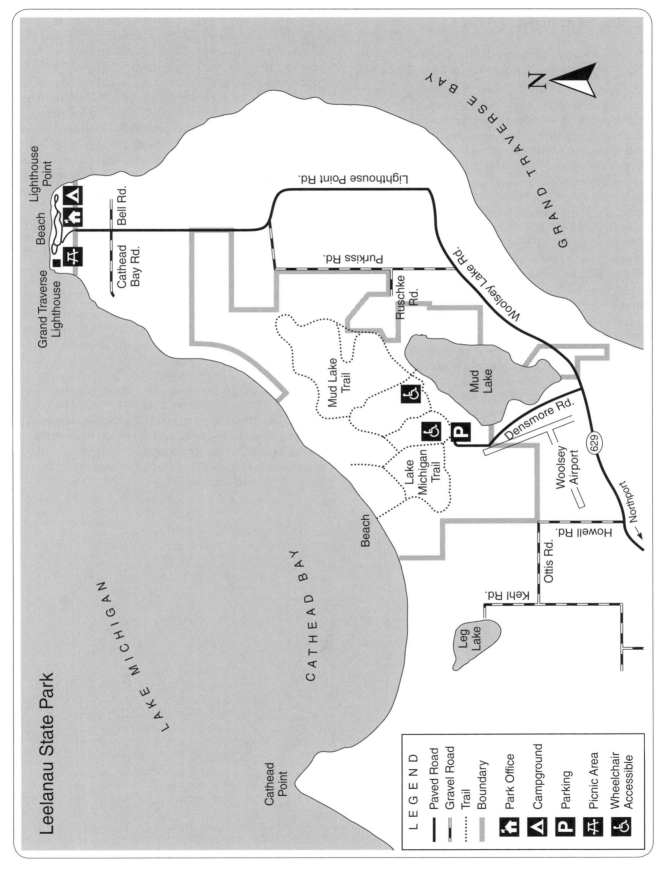

Grand Traverse Lighthouse

Lighthouse Point

Beach

Lighthouse Point Rd.

Bell Rd.

Cathead Bay Rd.

Purkiss Rd.

Ruschke Rd.

Mud Lake Trail

Mud Lake

Woolsey Lake Rd.

Densmore Rd.

Woolsey Airport

629

Lake Michigan Trail

Beach

Northport

Howell Rd.

Ottis Rd.

Kehl Rd.

Leg Lake

LAKE MICHIGAN

CATHEAD BAY

Cathead Point

GRAND TRAVERSE BAY

N

LEGEND

	Paved Road
	Gravel Road
	Trail
	Boundary
	Park Office
	Campground
P	Parking
	Picnic Area
	Wheelchair Accessible

Lake Michigan Trail

Distance Round-Trip: 2.2 miles
Estimated Hiking Time: 1 to 1.5 hours

Cautions: Watch for exposed roots and poison ivy. You pass through dense woods, dunes, and open, rolling sand; layer your clothing for the variations. Take sunscreen and insect repellent.

Trail Directions: All the trails start from the parking area off Densmore Road, about 4 mi. southwest of the campground. A map board shows the trails in various colors. The Lake Michigan trail, light blue, starts and ends at the northwest end of the parking lot [1]. The orange Mud Lake Trail has an access point there as well, so the entry post that you see is tipped with orange. After a few steps, you notice a blue post off to the left. Follow it into the cool, dark shadows of the mixed forest. Under this thick canopy, the trail rolls through undulating terrain.

The canopy breaks open at .4 mi., where a bench marks your entry to the flat, open area that the trail will encircle [2]. Reenter the cool cover of trees at .5 mi. [3] and continue along as the trail passes between wooded ridges.

After sliding through dunes resembling a bobsled bank, you reach the junction for the beach access. A map board shows your location, and a bench awaits your return from the beach (.6 mi.) [4]. Turn left and roll along the trail as it descends through steep dunes. Your beacon to the beach is an arch of sunshine through a tunnel of trees. Step through the tunnel into the sunlight of the hot, sandy beach (.8 mi.) [5].

Stroll down another .1 mi. over gently rolling sand and then stop and enjoy the solitude at Cathead Bay. Kick off your shoes and lie back awhile before returning to the junction. Your trip back is uphill through open sand, so rest now and enjoy sunshine and the gentle rush of waves rolling onto the shore. Then head back through the tunnel and wooded dunes to the junction [4] where that bench is waiting. Next, hike on straight, going through the forest. The trail bends left to cut over a footbridge that crosses over a small ravine (1.3 mi.) [6]. Shortly after walking over a small ridge braided with roots, you reach the overlook junction (1.4 mi.) [7].

Turn left for a bird's-eye view of the bay. The trail along this spur rises (often over a series of stairs), culminating at the top of an observation deck (1.8 mi.) [8]. From this perch you look over rolling sand against a backdrop of the bay and sky—blue splashed with white. On a clear day, the Fox Islands add the final touches to the temporal canvas that you view. Sit on a bench before you head back down the spur and continue straight past the junction (1.9 mi.) [7].

Continue straight past the next junction as well, through the rolling woods. Pass birch logs strewn about like fallen bowling pins, cluttering the forest floor. A trail merges in at 2 mi. [9]. Stay to the right. Soon after, the trail swings left and begins to climb. A steep hill flanks the trail, and you then begin to wind down and reach the junction that brings your hike to a full circle (2.2 mi.) [10]. Turn left and walk the few steps back to the parking lot.

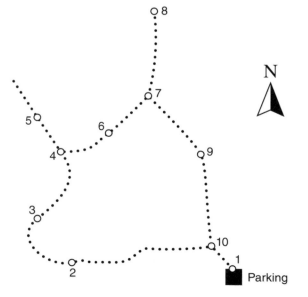

1. Trailhead
2. Bench
3. Cover of trees
4. Beach trail junction and bench
5. Beach
6. Footbridge
7. Overlook trail junction
8. Observation deck
9. Strewn logs
10. Trail junction to parking lot

Northern
Lower
Peninsula

Mud Lake Trail

Distance Round-Trip: 3.2 miles
Estimated Hiking Time: 1.5 to 2 hours

Cautions: Low areas, especially along Mud Lake, are prone to flooding. Be careful walking among exposed roots and bring your insect repellent.

Trail Directions: Start from the trail map board at the northeast end of the parking area and turn right **[1]**. All the trails, spurs, and cutoffs are color coded and marked by wooden posts with tips painted in the corresponding color. The Mud Lake Trail follows orange-tipped posts.

Your right turn takes you along crushed limestone through a field of ferns; then the trail quickly breaks into the woods. Forested dunes are on your left. To your right is Mud Lake, evidenced by many dead trees (most notably paper birch). You may have noticed these ghost trees as you drove to the trailhead along Densmore Road.

At .2 mi., you reach the Maple Ridge Cutoff **[2]**. Each trail junction has a map board showing your location, a bench, and color-coordinated trail posts that lead you in the right direction. Just before the Tamarack Cutoff (.5 mi.) **[3]**, the crushed stone ends. The trail is sliced to a thin track that runs along the edge of the lake and the base of a forested dune. You soon leave this catwalk and may think that you are venturing backstage at what appears to be a huge natural amphitheater (.7 mi.) **[4]**. Enjoy the show before you swing right to stay near the lake and avoid a steep climb up a ridge.

After reaching the Pot-Hole Ridge junction (.8 mi.) **[5]**, the trail twists past fallen paper birch trees to climb a small ridge. When descending, swing left and inspect the neat rows of red pine standing at attention like wooden soldiers (.9 mi.) **[6]**.

Just beyond the second Pot-Hole Ridge junction, you reach a footbridge (1.2 mi.) **[7]** that carries you over a swamp and deposits you onto a pine needle–covered bank. Turn left, and, with the needles cushioning your steps, follow along the swamp. The trail swings right, away from the swamp, and climbs to a peak high above a natural bowl-shaped depression (1.4 mi.) **[8]**. Rest on the bench here.

You reach the halfway point of your hike when you spot the trail marker near a bench at the hairpin turn (1.6 mi.) **[9]**. Turn left and continue your hike through the dense beech-maple forest as the trail snakes through the dune environment. A bench at 2 mi. beckons you to stop and enjoy the solitude of the forest **[10]**. Sit back and enjoy the quiet.

Not long before you reach the northern end of the Tamarack Cutoff (2.4 mi.) **[11]**, the many fallen trees allow in the light; the trail seems to brighten. Bask in this rare window of sunshine. Pass the Maple Ridge junction (2.7 mi.) **[12]**. At 2.9 mi., you can turn right at the junction with the Lake Michigan Trail **[13]**. This route, with its light-blue-tipped posts, takes you to the scenic overlook of Cathead Bay and the Fox Islands and to a spur down to the beach. Go ahead; the side trip will add only .6 mi. to your hike. Or turn left to head back. The Mud Lake Trail completes its loop and winds back to the parking area.

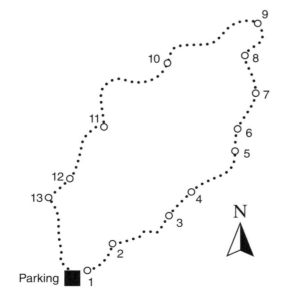

1. Trailhead
2. Maple Ridge Cutoff
3. Tamarack Cutoff
4. Natural amphitheater
5. Pot-Hole Ridge junction
6. Red pine stand
7. Footbridge
8. Natural bowl
9. Halfway point
10. Bench
11. Tamarack Cutoff
12. Maple Ridge junction
13. Lake Michigan Trail junction

45. Beaver Island

- Catch a sunrise and a sunset over Lake Michigan.
- Visit Big Rock.
- Explore the other islands of the Beaver Archipelago.

Park Information

Billed as America's Emerald Isle, this 58-square-mile island is the largest in Lake Michigan. About 45 miles of shoreline encircle 37,000 acres; the State of Michigan owns more than one-third of the island. A small community of 550 to 600 full-time residents occupies the island.

Thirteen miles long, 6 miles wide, and shaped like a beaver's tail, Beaver Island is crisscrossed by a network of dusty roads and two-track trails that lead you through a diverse environment of rolling farm fields, dense forests, cedar swamps, isolated Lake Michigan beaches, and a number of inland lakes worthy of a visit. Keep a watchful eye for white-tailed deer, wild turkey, common loon, and beaver. It isn't called Beaver Island for nothing.

The island has two rustic campgrounds, with hand water pumps and pit toilets but no electricity or showers. The St. James Township Campground, located 1 mile from the dock, sits on a bluff overlooking Garden Island. The Peaine Township–Bill Wagner Campground, located 7 miles south of the dock, lies level with Little Sand Bay with views of mainland Michigan.

Directions: Beaver Island is connected to the mainland by ferry or plane. Pick up the ferry in Charlevoix at 103 Bridge Park Drive. From US 31, turn east onto Bridge Park Drive, just south of the bridge. Although the ferry transports vehicles, cars can be rented on the island. Contact the Beaver Island Boat Company at 888-446-4095 or www.bibco.com. Flights originate from Charlevoix. Contact Island Airways at 800-524-6895 or www.islandairways.com, or Fresh Air Aviation at 888-FLY-RGHT or www.freshairaviation.net. Cars can be rented from Beaver Island Car Rental at 231-448-2300 or www.beaverislandmarina.com, or Gordon's Auto Rental and Clinic at 231-448-2438.

Hours Open: The ferry runs from April into December, weather permitting. Flights are available year-round. The campgrounds are open April 1 through November.

Facilities: Hiking, biking, camping, swimming, cross-country skiing, dogsledding, snowmobiling, ATV, ORV, canoeing, kayaking, hunting, fishing, golfing, sightseeing, picnicking, skydiving, scuba diving, snorkeling, boating, boat tours, and cruises.

Permits and Rules: No charge is levied for day use of the trails, although fees are required for the campgrounds. Ferry service each way costs $21 per adult, $70 per vehicle up to 16 feet long, or $9 per bicycle. Reservations are not accepted for passengers but are required for vehicles. No camping is allowed on state land between May 15 and September 10 except in areas specifically designated for camping. Beaver Island is part of a state wildlife research area. For complete rules and regulations, contact the Gaylord Management Unit at 1732 West M-32, Gaylord, MI 49735; 989-732-3541.

For Further Information: Beaver Island Chamber of Commerce, P.O. Box 5, Beaver Island, MI 49782; 231-448-2505; www.beaverisland.org.

Other Points of Interest

Visit the **Old Mormon Print Shop Museum** and learn about the Mormon King, Doctor Protar, Father Gallegher, and much more about the interesting history of the island. For more information, contact the Beaver Island Historical Society, P.O. Box 263, Beaver Island, MI 49782; 231-448-2254; www.beaverisland.net/history.

Beaver Island Ecotours offer custom or packaged ecotours. Explore the various communities on Beaver Island by foot, boat, vehicle, or mountain bike. For more information, contact Beaver Island Ecotours at 231-448-2194 (late May through early August) or www.beaverislandecotours.com.

Park Trails

Various trails weave around the island. Contact the Beaver Island Chamber of Commerce for a map.

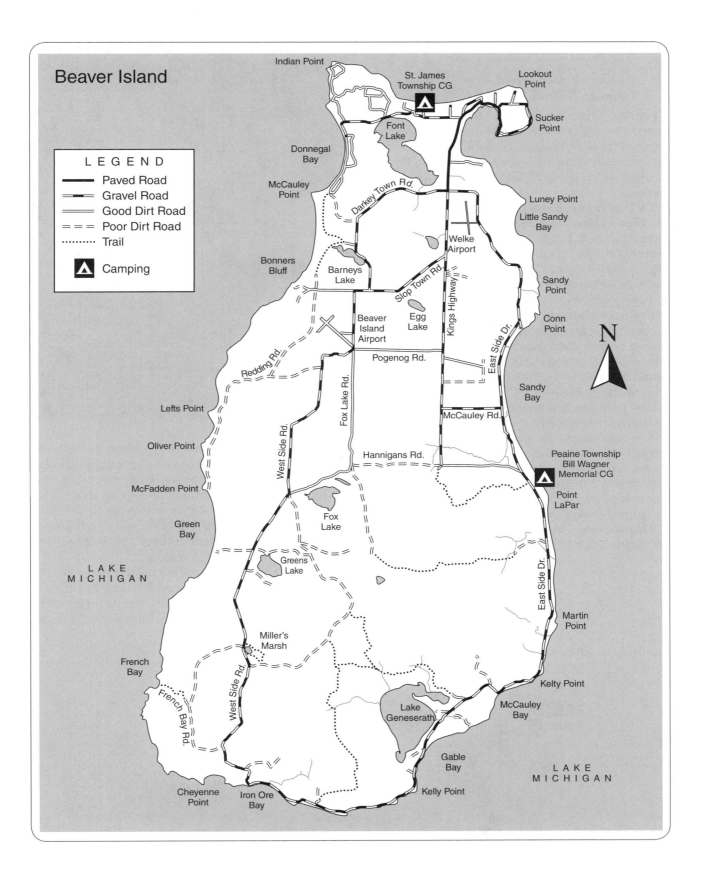

Beaver Island

LEGEND
— Paved Road
— Gravel Road
— Good Dirt Road
— — — Poor Dirt Road
········· Trail
▲ Camping

Indian Point

St. James Township CG ▲

Lookout Point

Sucker Point

Font Lake

Donnegal Bay

McCauley Point

Darkey Town Rd.

Luney Point

Little Sandy Bay

Welke Airport

Bonners Bluff

Barneys Lake

Slop Town Rd.

Sandy Point

Conn Point

Beaver Island Airport

Egg Lake

Kings Highway

East Side Dr.

Redding Rd.

Pogenog Rd.

Sandy Bay

Lefts Point

Oliver Point

West Side Rd.

Fox Lake Rd.

McCauley Rd.

N

McFadden Point

Hannigans Rd.

Peaine Township Bill Wagner Memorial CG ▲

Point LaPar

Green Bay

Fox Lake

LAKE MICHIGAN

Greens Lake

East Side Dr.

Martin Point

Miller's Marsh

West Side Rd.

French Bay

Kelty Point

French Bay Rd.

McCauley Bay

Lake Geneserath

Cheyenne Point

Iron Ore Bay

Kelly Point

Gable Bay

LAKE MICHIGAN

Miller's Marsh Nature Trail

🐾 **Distance Round-Trip:** 1 mile
🐾 **Estimated Hiking Time:** 30 to 45 minutes

Cautions: Bring your binoculars to maximize the experience, and don't forget insect repellent. Watch for exposed roots and daggerlike sapling stumps honed by the beavers that call the marsh home. Portions of the trail are prone to flooding. Wear appropriate footgear.

Trail Directions: Owned and managed by Central Michigan University, the 230-acre Miller's Marsh Natural Area is located 6.3 mi. south of the county airport on West Side Road. The interpretive trail begins from the south side of the parking area [1]. Interpretive brochures are available here.

Hike past the vault toilet and large red maple tree to begin your hike around the marsh. The red maples bordering the marsh are some of the largest found on Beaver Island. Watch out for the gnarly roots, which look much like what you might find on a tropical island. This portion of the trail is prone to flooding, so plan accordingly.

The trail goes left near an old well dug long ago by early homesteaders (.3 mi.) [2]. Just beyond the well a bench waits for you to have a seat and enjoy the sights, sounds, and smells of this lowland forest (.4 mi.) [3]. The plants here that look like miniature pine trees are really club moss, commonly called the princess pine. The Mormon King may be dead, but the princess pine lives on as a protected species in Michigan. Note that a trail is proposed in this area to connect to Doty's Trail.

You are now in the toughest stretch of this short hike and find yourself veering left to walk on a beaver dam (.5 mi.) [4]. You soon arrive at a tree blind from which to observe the local wildlife from an elevated position (.5 mi.) [5]. When you continue you should be able to recognize the effect that the beaver is having in shaping the environment of the marsh. You will also see the beaver's lodge (.7 mi.) [6].

You will have almost completed the loop when the trail swings left to avoid the road (.8 mi.) [7], although the road is a handy option during periods of flooding. Have a seat on the bench (.9 mi.) [8] to savor the marsh environment again.

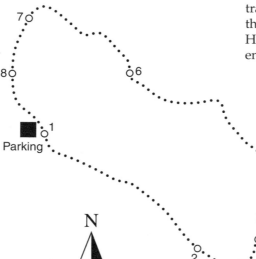

1. Trailhead
2. Old well
3. Bench
4. Beaver bam
5. Tree blind
6. Beaver lodge
7. West Side Road
8. Bench

Buffalo's Camp, Doty's, and North Lake Trails

Distance Round-Trip: 6.7 miles
Estimated Hiking Time: 2.5 to 3.5 hours

Cautions: Watch for exposed roots, rocks, and low branches. Portions of the trail may be wet. Wear appropriate footgear. Bring insect repellent. Beavers are active in this area. Walk around felled trees and be prepared for a rearranged trail.

Trail Directions: From the dock, take the Kings Highway south for about 6 mi. to Hannigans Road. Go east about 1 mi. to East Side Drive and head south about 5 mi. to the Lake Geneserath boat launch. Turn right and park. Walk the launch drive northeast to the trailhead and head northwest along the old rutted two-track [1].

Trees generally line the trail. The area appeals to ruffed grouse; don't jump as they explode in a flurry of feathers as you pass. Stay left past the blue arrow (.8 mi.) [2].

A stream joins you on the left, and you descend to a beaver dam where trees lean over the pool (1 mi.) [3]. The stream flows away on the other side of the trail.

Now on the trail less traveled, notice the larger beech and maple trees. At 1.5 mi., larger hemlocks are prevalent [4]. Trees and branches lean on one another, moaning.

The trail ascends through bracken ferns, small pines, and firs before descending to a narrow bridge for you to cross (1.7 mi.) [5]. Head back up through ferns to the junction (1.8 mi.) [6]. Go left on this loop. The trail is a mix of grass and moss. You soon cross another small bridge and enter a burst of sunshine and wildflowers.

The trail appears to be seasonally wet. It undulates over roots, ruts, and rocks. Cedars appear. Take care to duck under low branches. When the forest darkens, watch for the MASH sign (2.5 mi.) [7] and turn right on the West Lake Trail.

At 2.6 mi., leave the cedar behind [8]; maple, beech, and birch accompany the trail as it descends. Watch for tracks in the muddy area (2.7 mi.) [9]. Pass again through open areas with wildflowers and grasses, then young maples, and then dense maples. Enjoy the quiet, perhaps interrupted only by the creaking of trees. You soon pass large fallen trees on this path less traveled (2.9 mi.) [10].

At the junction, stay right (3 mi.) [11] on the much-less-traveled path through more fallen trees and pass through four poles to the junction for Doty's Trail (3.2 mi.) [12]. Turn right on the two-track for an easy trek.

Turn right at the junction for the North Lake Trail (3.7 mi.) [13] and descend to a muddy area that is home to skunk cabbage, tall grasses, fir, and cedar. Logs in the mud help somewhat. The trail is lightly traveled.

Pass through a graveyard of fallen trees and burned trunks. Moss, bunchberries, and grass pocket the trail. It veers right through ferns, an open grassy area, standing dead trees, and a seasonal bog. Beavers may leave an obstacle course of trees for you to work around. A dam (4.2 mi.) [14] makes use of the downed trees. Other aspects are interesting as well: Trees are uprooted, rocks interfere with your steps, and the trail, inundated with grasses and plants, is nearly indistinguishable from the surrounding area.

Move on into ferns and aspens. Swing left into pines around and past beaver ponds (4.7 mi.) [15]. Reenter mixed woods and then close the loop (5 mi.) [6]. Turn left and go back over the small bridges, past the beaver dam (5.8 mi.) [3] to where you started your venture into beaver country.

1. Trailhead
2. Blue arrow
3. Beaver dam
4. Large hemlocks
5. Narrow bridge
6. Junction
7. West Lake Trail junction
8. Leave cedar
9. Mud
10. Fallen trees
11. Junction
12. Doty's Trail junction
13. North Lake Trail junction
14. Beaver dam
15. Swing left

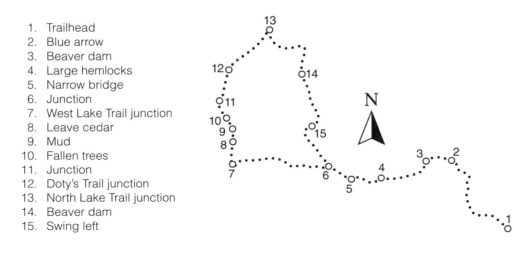

- Ascend the 110-foot Dune Climb.
- Ferry over to explore the Manitou Islands.
- Enjoy panoramic views of the dunes and lakes along the Pierce Stocking Scenic Drive.

Park Information

Composed of 35 miles of mainland Lake Michigan shoreline, the North and South Manitou islands, inland lakes, forests, rivers, cliffs, and towering dunes, Sleeping Bear Dunes is a national treasure. Several routes open up the treasures of the park.

One of them, the 7.4-mile Pierce Stocking Scenic Drive, opens up views of the Lake Michigan shoreline. Besides more than 50 miles of mainland trails, an additional 60 miles of trails are found on South Manitou Island (see park #48) and North Manitou Island (see park #47). The visitor center houses a slide program and exhibits.

Try canoeing the Platte or Crystal rivers, swimming in Glen Lake, or visiting the Sleeping Bear Point Maritime Museum. And there's always the main attraction—the Dune Climb.

Directions: The park follows the Lake Michigan shoreline in Benzie and Leelanau counties, about 20 miles west of Traverse City. From US 31 you can access M-22, which is the main north–south road through the park. If you're coming from the east, M-115 and M-72 also lead to M-22. The visitor center is on M-72, just east of M-22.

Hours Open: The park is open year-round. The visitor center is open daily from 8:00 a.m. to 6:00 p.m. in summer; hours are shorter in the off-season. It is closed on Christmas and New Year's Day. The Sleeping Bear Point Maritime Museum in Glen Haven has varied hours. Call ahead. The Pierce Stocking Scenic Drive is open from mid-April through mid-November.

Facilities: Hiking, bicycling, cross-country skiing, snowshoeing, swimming, fishing, hunting, canoeing, canoe rental, picnicking, hang gliding, camping (tent, RV, and backcountry), bridle path, boat launch, sanitation station, interpretive trails, and interpretive center.

Permits and Rules: The fee for individuals is $5 per week; the fee for vehicles is $10 per week. The annual fee is $20. Dunes are unstable; don't venture onto them. Vehicles, including bicycles, are not allowed on the trails. Pets must be kept on a leash; they are prohibited on the Dune Climb and on North and South Manitou islands. Do not collect plants or historical features.

For Further Information: Sleeping Bear Dunes National Lakeshore, 9922 Front Street, Empire, MI 49630; 213-326-5134; www.nps.gov/slbe. For ferry service to North and South Manitou islands, contact Manitou Island Transit, P.O. Box 1157, Leland, MI 49654; 231-256-9061; www.leelanau.com/manitou.

Park Trails

Old Indian Trail (🐾 to 🐾🐾🐾, 2.5 miles). Located north of Crystal Lake off M-22 at the south end of the park, this trail has two loops, one that builds on the other.

Platte Plains Trail (🐾🐾, 14.7 miles). This network of trails has many loops that are mostly level (except for some steep hills on the Lasso Loop). There are two trailheads: (1) Trail's End Road, west of M-22, and (2) Esch Road, west of M-22.

Empire Bluff Trail (🐾🐾, 1.5 miles round-trip). This one-way interpretive trail cuts over hilly terrain through beech-maple forest and over fields and dunes to a boardwalk with an overview of Lake Michigan. The trail is located in Empire, south of the visitor center off M-22.

Dunes Hiking Trail (🐾🐾🐾🐾, 3.5 miles round-trip). This one-way trail starts with the Dune Climb and then rolls over open dunes to Lake Michigan. Access is from the Dune Climb off M-109, north of Empire.

Duneside Accessible Trail (🐾, .9 mile round-trip). Designed for visitors in wheelchairs and those with visual impairments, the trail goes through fields and woods. Start at the north end of the Dune Climb.

Cottonwood Trail (🐾🐾, 1.5 mile round-trip). This trail takes you through perched dunes above the Dune Climb. Additionally, several miles of ski trails may be used for hiking.

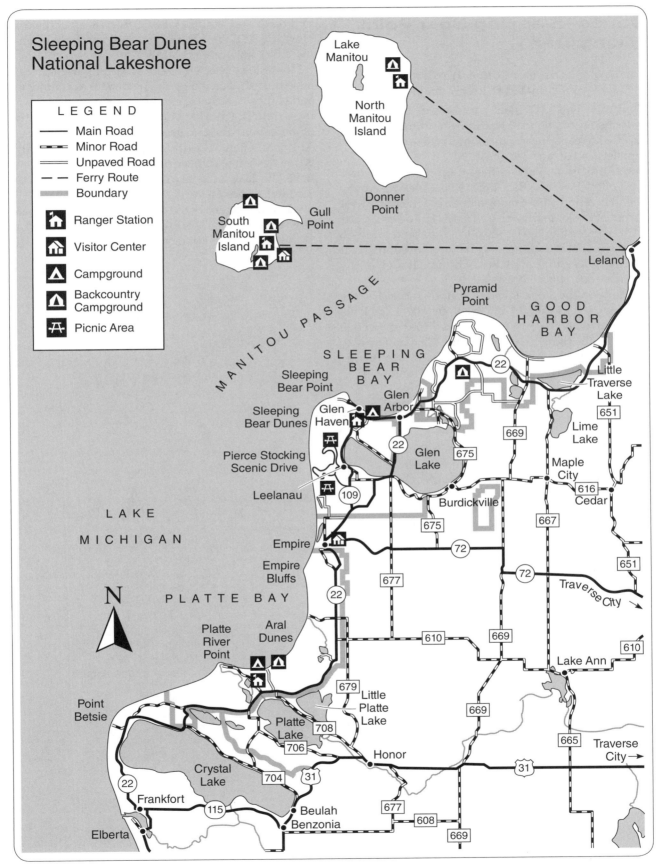

Sleeping Bear Dunes National Lakeshore

LEGEND

— Main Road
--□-- Minor Road
═══ Unpaved Road
- - - Ferry Route
▐▌ Boundary

🏠 Ranger Station
🏠 Visitor Center
⛺ Campground
⛺ Backcountry Campground
🏕 Picnic Area

Lake Manitou

North Manitou Island

Donner Point

South Manitou Island

Gull Point

Leland

MANITOU PASSAGE

Pyramid Point

GOOD HARBOR BAY

SLEEPING BEAR BAY

Sleeping Bear Point

Little Traverse Lake

Glen Arbor

Lime Lake

Sleeping Bear Dunes

Glen Haven

Glen Lake

Maple City

Cedar

651

675

669

616

Pierce Stocking Scenic Drive

Leelanau

109

Burdickville

675

667

651

LAKE MICHIGAN

72

651

Empire

72

Traverse City

Empire Bluffs

677

669

610

610

N

PLATTE BAY

22

Lake Ann

Aral Dunes

669

Platte River Point

679

Little Platte Lake

Point Betsie

708

Platte Lake

706

665

Traverse City →

Crystal Lake

704

31

Honor

US 31

22

Frankfort

115

Beulah

Benzonia

677

608

Elberta

669

Dunes—Sleeping Bear Point Hiking Trail

Distance Round-Trip: 2.5 miles
Estimated Hiking Time: 1.5 to 2 hours

Cautions: This trail blazes across steep dunes and hot, open sand. Sand shifts. Roots and rocks may be exposed. Wear appropriate footgear. Take along insect repellent, a hat, and sunscreen.

Trail Directions: Park in the lot off the gravel road, west of the Sleeping Bear Point Maritime Museum in Glen Haven. An information board at the northwest corner of the lot marks the trailhead [1]. The trail starts with firm footing, but it soon turns to sand and you get the first hint that this may be a trail of contrasts. It is. Open, desertlike stretches of dunes later give way to lush, cool, shady forests.

Plow up the slope through soft, deep sand to the first junction (.1 mi.) [2] and ask yourself, "Cool Lake Michigan waters or hot, open dunes?" Go for the cool. A spur to the right takes you to Lake Michigan by way of a climb up the sandy slope, past a blowout (the saucer-shaped depression in the sand, hollowed out by wind), and gently down past one of many walls of sand that characterize this dune environment (.3 mi.) [3].

Kick off your shoes, pour out the sand, and dip your toes into the cool waters before heading back up to the junction [2], where you round the curve and blaze through grassy dunes.

At .6 mi., a large blowout opens up a turquoise and deep lavender blue Lake Michigan framed by a grassy dune [4]. Move on, and the view gets better. Below you lies a large, flat, sandy basin shaped by wind and water; the Manitou Islands are off in the distance behind you.

The trail veers left; blue-tipped posts guide you on your southwesterly trek. As you come down the dune, skeletons of trees lie before you. These trees were buried by shifting sands, creating ghost forests (.8 mi.) [5].

Pass through the ghosts standing upright like pencils in the sand and step onto the sandy stripe that winds over the grassy dunes before you (1 mi.) [6]. Climb to the right through rolling dunes blanketed by grasses and wildflowers. You pass an occasional blowout. At 1.3 mi., the grassy, rolling terrain is reminiscent of an alpine meadow [7].

The trail curves left again, wrapping itself around a crescent-shaped blowout. The trail takes another left and climbs to a crest that offers a panoramic view of the terrain (1.4 mi.) [8]. You get a different perspective of the barren sand and grassy dunes that you crossed. At 1.6 mi., Glen Lake comes into view [9]. Although it is not a volcanic caldera filled with water, like Crater Lake, this lake looks like one as it nestles beneath the wooded slopes that give it a bowl shape.

The trail rolls over the dunes. At 1.8 mi., you head down into the cool shadows of a forest [10]. Break out of the woods back to the parking lot [11].

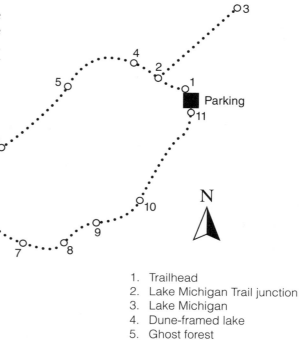

1. Trailhead
2. Lake Michigan Trail junction
3. Lake Michigan
4. Dune-framed lake
5. Ghost forest
6. Grassy dunes
7. Alpine-like meadow
8. Panoramic view
9. View of wooded dunes
10. Forest
11. Parking lot

Pyramid Point Hiking Trail

Distance Round-Trip: 2.7 miles
Estimated Hiking Time: 1.5 to 2 hours

Cautions: At the scenic overlook, watch your step—it is a long drop to the lake. The hike finishes on Basch Road, where you should watch for traffic. Take insect repellent.

Trail Directions: Heading northeast of Glen Arbor on M-22, turn left on Port Oneida Road. Continue north for 2 miles and turn right on Basch Road. In .3 mi., you reach the parking area and trailhead on the left. A vault toilet is located at the parking area, but no water source is present. The trail begins at the northeast end of the parking area to the right of the trail board and map box **[1]**.

Your crushed-stone path angles northeast from the parking area across a meadow and climbs into woods loaded with paper birch. You quickly reach the posted junction to the scenic Lake Michigan lookout (.3 mi.) **[2]**.

From the junction the trail climbs .2 mi. through the woods before it breaks out onto the sandy edge of a dune towering high over Lake Michigan. Take your time to soak in the view. You should be able to see North Manitou and South Manitou islands in the distance (.5 mi.) **[3]**.

Leaving the overlook, retrace your steps and descend to the marked trail junction, where you turn left and leave the crushed-stone surface behind. The trail continues to descend into the beech-maple forest; gradually it swings left along the back side of the dune. At 1.1 mi., the trail turns sharply right away from the dune **[4]**. You'll see that many people before you have been tempted to turn left and climb the steep sandy slope before moving on. Do the dune a favor; don't cave in to temptation.

At the next posted junction, one option is to take a shortcut back to the trailhead (1.2 mi.) **[5]**. The other is to continue on the trail, which descends sharply and then levels out to deposit you at the edge of a meadow (1.4 mi.) **[6]**. You turn right and follow along the tree line before bursting into the open meadow. After you cross the meadow and as you approach new tree growth at the edge of the forest, stop and look behind you. You should be able to see the top of the dune peeking over the vegetation (1.7 mi.) **[7]**.

Back in the woods, the trail swings right and climbs back onto the ridge that you previously descended to reach the meadow. Don't turn left until you meet the junction at the other end of the shortcut (2.1 mi.) **[8]**. Turn left here and make a steep climb along a ravine to Basch Road (2.3 mi.) **[9]**. Turn right on Basch Road and make a steep descent. Be alert for traffic on this narrow dirt road. You reach the parking area in .4 mi.

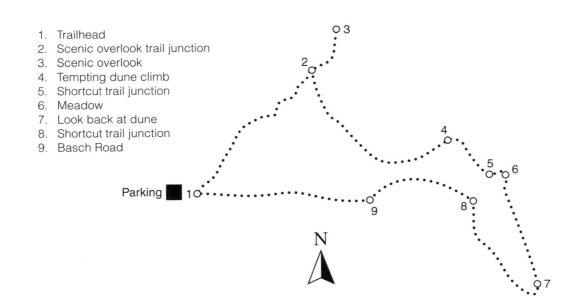

1. Trailhead
2. Scenic overlook trail junction
3. Scenic overlook
4. Tempting dune climb
5. Shortcut trail junction
6. Meadow
7. Look back at dune
8. Shortcut trail junction
9. Basch Road

N

47. North Manitou Island

- Find solitude in this 15,000-acre wilderness.
- Plan to camp at least one night.
- Perch atop spectacular sand dunes.

Park Information

North Manitou, with 15,000 acres and 20 miles of shoreline, is the larger of the two Manitou Islands; both are part of the Sleeping Bear Dunes National Lakeshore. Except for the village area around the dock, the island is managed as a wilderness area. Day hiking here takes some preparation but is well worth the effort. Please note that the ferry does not lay over, so you must plan to camp at least one night.

Roughly 8 miles long and 4 miles wide, North Manitou's terrain varies from low open sandy dunes, to rolling hills, to impressive bluffs and sand dunes that tower 300 feet above Lake Michigan. The islands' wilderness includes miles of Lake Michigan shore, wetlands, two inland lakes, and thousands of acres of deciduous trees, and it is slowly reclaiming abandoned townsites, old logging camps, empty cottages, deserted farm fields, and orchards—the skeletons of human activity.

One rustic campground on the island—the Village Campground—provides a handful of designated campsites, two fire rings, and one outhouse. The wilderness has no designated campsites. Potable water is available only at the ranger station. Watch out for poison ivy and chipmunks, a.k.a. microbears. They are numerous and a nuisance. Hang your food.

Directions: Access the island by ferry, which you pick up at the Fishtown Dock in Leland. Take M-22 north to Leland. Cross the bridge and take the first left. The ticket office is down the hill in the last building on the left. Plan to arrive 45 minutes before departure for check-in. Contact Manitou Island Transit at 231-256-9061 or www.leelanau.com/manitou.

Hours Open: The ferry runs from May 1 to early October. During summer the ferry is daily except on Tuesday and Thursday. Check with Manitou Island Transit for the trip schedule for the remainder of the season. All trips are weather permitting.

Facilities: Hiking, backpacking, backcountry camping, swimming, canoeing, and hunting.

Permits and Rules: Wilderness camping regulations are in effect on the island. A national park entrance pass is required for any use of the island, and a backcountry permit and camping fee payment must be completed before camping. Call 231-326-5134 for fee information. Pick up passes and permits at the ferry ticket office before boarding. Camping is prohibited within 300 feet of the Lake Michigan high-water mark, lakes, streams, ponds, springs, buildings, other camps, or on any trail. Open fires are prohibited in the wilderness area. All trash must be packed off the island. All human waste and toilet paper must be buried at least 6 inches deep. Washing is not permitted at or in any water source. Pets are not allowed. Do not enter abandoned buildings. No wheeled vehicles are allowed. Round-trip ferry service costs $30 per adult and $16 for children under 12; transport of a canoe or kayak costs $30.

For Further Information: Sleeping Bear Dunes National Lakeshore, 9922 Front Street, Empire, MI 49630; 231-326-5134; www.nps.gov/slbe.

Other Points of Interest

Sleeping Bear Dunes National Lakeshore (see park #46) and **South Manitou Island** (see park #48) complement and complete your trip to this unique part of the world. Contact information for the Sleeping Bear Dunes National Lakeshore was provided earlier.

Park Trails

Roughly 22 miles of signed, designated trails weave around this island wilderness. The three basic loops build on one another. When combined with the untold miles of unmaintained trails on the island, innumerable combinations can be created, ranging from day hikes and side trips to backpacking and extended overnight wilderness experiences.

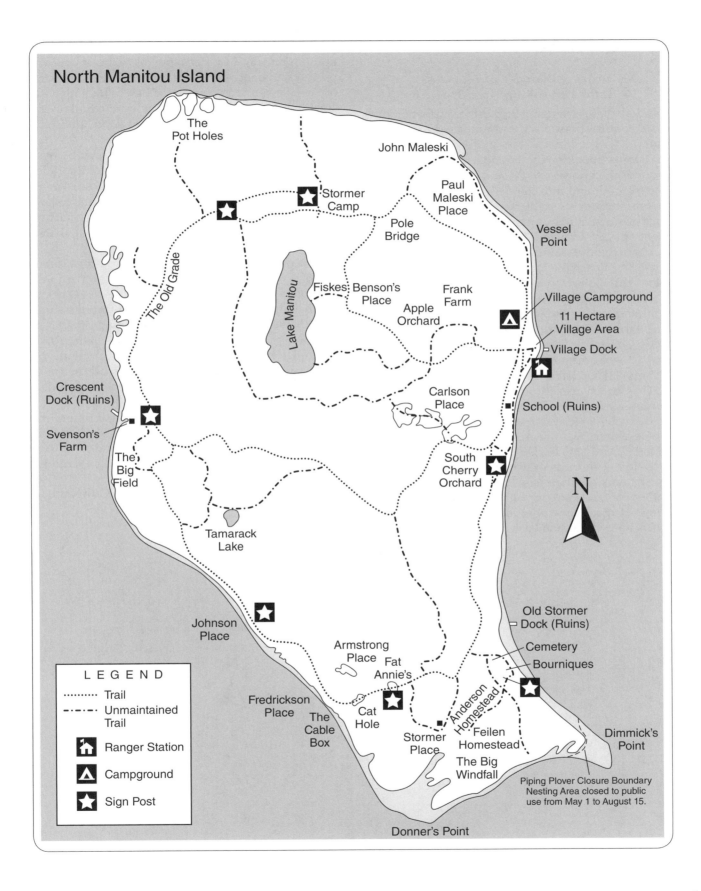

North Manitou Island

The Pot Holes

John Maleski

Paul
Maleski
Place

Vessel
Point

Stormer
Camp

Pole
Bridge

The Old Grade

Lake Manitou

Fiskes
Benson's
Place

Frank
Farm

Village Campground

Apple
Orchard

11 Hectare
Village Area

Village Dock

Crescent
Dock (Ruins)

Carlson
Place

School (Ruins)

Svenson's
Farm

The
Big
Field

South
Cherry
Orchard

N

Tamarack
Lake

Old Stormer
Dock (Ruins)

Johnson
Place

Cemetery

Bourniques

Armstrong
Place

Fat
Annie's

Anderson
Homestead

Dimmick's
Point

Fredrickson
Place

The
Cable
Box

Cat
Hole

Feilen
Homestead

Stormer
Place

The Big
Windfall

Piping Plover Closure Boundary
Nesting Area closed to public
use from May 1 to August 15.

Donner's Point

LEGEND

.... Trail

–·–·– Unmaintained
Trail

🏠 Ranger Station

🔺 Campground

⭐ Sign Post

Small Northeast Loop

Distance Round-Trip: 6.4 miles
Estimated Hiking Time: 3 to 3.5 hours

Cautions: Take insect repellent in the warmer months. Watch out for poison ivy and roots and rocks in the trail.

Trail Directions: Start at the end of the Village Campground by campsite #8 **[1]** and head out along the narrow path and into the dark woods. Soon, a trail merges in from the right. Keep straight and pass the rundown structures along the bluff. Break out of the woods by an old field. The trail is now a grassy two-track. Bergamot paints the meadow with lavender splotches. Reach the junction for the wilderness area (.4 mi.) **[2]**. Follow to the left at the edge of the field.

Again the path darkens, and you gently climb. Boulders are scattered about among fallen trees. The trail narrows. You pass ridges, and moss softens your steps. Continue rolling past ferns and maple saplings and arrive at the junction for the Paul Maleski Place (1.7 mi.) **[3]**. Go left to head for Lake Manitou.

This stretch goes through woods, but the trees are not as large as before. Where there are pockets of light, an explosion of ferns bursts out. You reach a junction where a sign gives mileages to various points on the island (2.3 mi.) **[4]**. Go left.

Listen as the birds welcome you. Ferns blanket the forest floor. You then pass through youthful maples, and an old field joins on your left. Another bright spot allows bergamot, raspberries, and grasses to texture the meadow. You enter back into darkness. Small trees

again alert you that the junction to Fiskes Landing is near (3.1 mi.) **[5]**. Turn right and follow this spur down past an abundance of ground cover. You see the glisten of the lake before you reach it (3.4 mi.) **[6]**. Enjoy the small sandy beach before picking up the trail on the left about 20 feet from shore. Head south along the goat path and into the cedars.

Get ready for a beautiful roll through cedars, over root steps, and past lush, thick clumps of avocado-colored moss that contrast with the red needles. Waves lap gently below you. Large hemlocks join the cedars. Eventually, the rolling stops, and you reach a narrow trail on your left that is near a couple of old shacks (4 mi.) **[7]**.

Follow it back. Stay left at the fork and climb through mixed woods where at times you are in a small valley. Keep climbing and then descend back to the main trail (5.2 mi.) **[8]**. Head right through small maples, past open areas and grass, and past areas of regrowth to reach Frank Farm, where a small secondary trail heads left (5.4 mi.) **[9]**. Stay straight along the wide, gently undulating trail that eventually becomes a valley between hills. At 6.2 mi., you leave the wilderness (6.2 mi.) **[10]**.

The terrain opens. Soon you see the lake and the flag flapping in the wind on the ranger's office. Pass a house, the Frank Farm secondary trail loop (6.3 mi.) **[11]**, and a row of trees that stand as sentinels to the past.

Turn left at the junction for the Village Campground (6.4 mi.) **[12]** and head back to camp.

1. Trailhead
2. Junction for wilderness area
3. Junction for Paul Maleski Place
4. Junction
5. Junction to Fiskes Landing
6. Lake Manitou
7. Trail inland
8. Junction
9. Frank Farm junction loop
10. Leave the wilderness
11. Frank Farm and loop
12. Junction for Village Campground

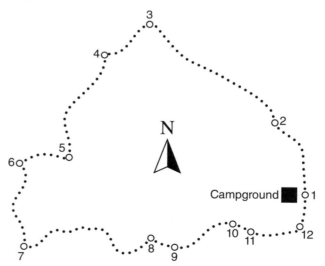

Waiting for the Ferry

🐾 **Distance Round-Trip:** 2.3 miles
❄ **Estimated Hiking Time:** 45 minutes to 1 hour

Cautions: If you are really waiting for the ferry, take a watch. Insect repellent is needed in the warmer months. Keep an eye out for poison ivy. Watch the time.

Trail Directions: Begin at the trailhead [1] west of the dock and head west on the old road as if you were going to Lake Manitou. But don't. Instead, go left at the first junction to cross an old farm field. This is a level hike, and you soon enter the wilderness area and a beech-maple forest with scattered large hemlock trees (.3 mi.) [2]. Briefly interrupt your pleasant hike through the woods when you skirt an old field (.6 mi.) [3].

When you reach the next junction you will have hiked just over a mile (1.1 mi.) [4]. To the right, it is 4.4 mi. to Svenson's Farm, which is too far. Straight, it is 4 mi. to Fredrickson Place, again too far. Behind you, it is 1.1 mi. back to the village. Go left to see where that trail goes. You soon find out after you descend and reach another trail (1.3 mi) [5]. Go left again. Straight takes you to a habitat restoration area closed to the public. Heading north now, you can soon hear Lake Michigan waves lapping or gulls shrieking. You walk the edge of a forest and through an occasional sandy area, with views of the lake to your right.

When you reach an open area you pass by the ruins of the old school (1.8 mi) [6] and soon enter a forest. Grassy undergrowth gives it the look of an unkempt park.

Eventually the trail becomes a sidewalk that leads you away from the wilderness area and back into the village (2 mi.) [7]. Cottage Row is on your left. Please note that some of the cottages are still private residences. As you continue along the grass in front of the cottages, you have the option of taking the stairs on the right down to the ranger station (2.2 mi) [8] or continuing straight to the trailhead. Now gather all your gear together and head down to the dock for your trip back to the mainland.

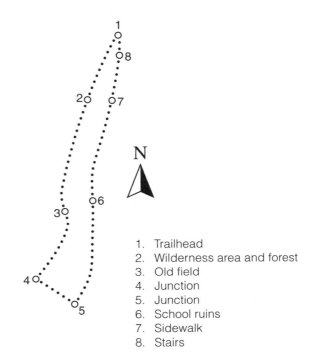

N

1. Trailhead
2. Wilderness area and forest
3. Old field
4. Junction
5. Junction
6. School ruins
7. Sidewalk
8. Stairs

48. South Manitou Island

- Hike to giant white cedars.
- View an old shipwreck.
- Enjoy panoramic views atop the South Manitou lighthouse.

Park Information

South Manitou Island, part of the Sleeping Bear Dunes National Lakeshore and roughly one-third the size of North Manitou Island, is more conducive to day hiking than its larger neighbor. The ferry lays over for four and one-half hours, allowing you time to explore, but you'll probably want to plan to camp at least one night just to take in the island. Another option is to arrange for a motorized tour of portions of the island.

The island has much to offer the day hiker. Walk through the old village, pass the old schoolhouse and farmsteads, explore isolated Lake Michigan beaches, tour the old lighthouse, view the wreck of the *Francisco Morazon*, experience some of the largest white cedars you'll see anywhere in Michigan, and climb to stand on a sand dune where you can see Lake Michigan in every direction.

Three designated campgrounds are located on the island. Low-impact camping is the rule, and you will have to pack in all your gear. Water is available at two of the three campgrounds, at the village, and at the old schoolhouse (which is the best tasting). You need to watch out for poison ivy and chipmunks, a.k.a. microbears. They are numerous and a real nuisance; keep food away from them.

Directions: Pick up the ferry at the Fishtown Dock in Leland. Take M-22 north to Leland. Cross the bridge and take the first left. The ticket office is down the hill in the last building on the left. Plan to arrive 45 minutes before departure for check-in. Contact Manitou Island Transit at 231-256-9061 or www.leelanau.com/manitou.

Hours Open: The ferry runs from late May to early October. During summer the ferry is daily. Check with Manitou Island Transit for the trip schedule for the remainder of the season. All trips are weather permitting.

Facilities: Hiking, backpacking, camping, swimming, canoeing, guided tours, lighthouse tours, and visitor center.

Permits and Rules: A national park entrance pass is required for any use of the island, and a backcountry permit and camping fee payment must be completed before camping. Call 231-326-5134 for fee information. Pick up passes and permits at the ferry ticket office before boarding. Camp only in a designated campground. Fires are permitted only in the campground community rings. Washing is not permitted at or in any water source. Pets are not allowed. Do not enter abandoned buildings. No wheeled vehicles are permitted. Round-trip ferry service costs $30 per adult and $16 for children under 12; transport of a canoe or kayak costs $30.

For Further Information: Sleeping Bear Dunes National Lakeshore, 9922 Front Street, Empire, MI 49630; 231-326-5134; www.nps.gov/slbe.

Other Points of Interest

Sleeping Bear Dunes National Lakeshore (see park #46) and **North Manitou Island** (see park #47) complement and complete your trip to this unique part of the world. Contact information for the Sleeping Bear Dunes National Lakeshore was provided earlier.

Park Trails

You may want to get a copy of the South Manitou Island brochure that contains a map showing key features on the island and suggested hikes with round-trip distances from the ranger station. This information helps you plan your visit so that you get back to the dock in time for departure.

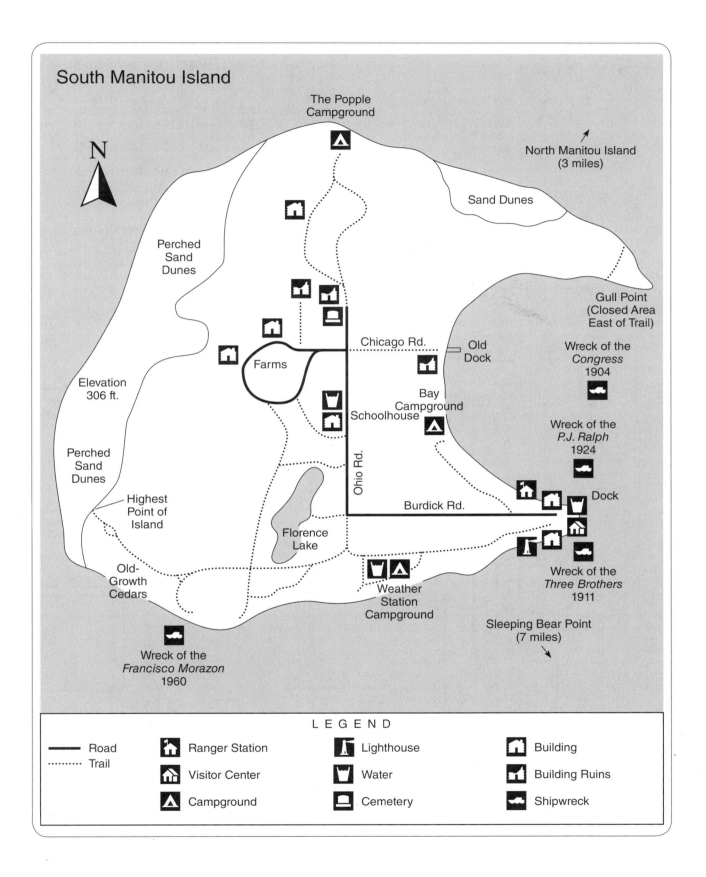

South Manitou Island

The Popple
Campground

N

North Manitou Island
(3 miles)

Sand Dunes

Perched
Sand
Dunes

Gull Point
(Closed Area
East of Trail)

Chicago Rd.

Old
Dock

Wreck of the
Congress
1904

Farms

Bay
Campground

Schoolhouse

Wreck of the
P.J. Ralph
1924

Elevation
306 ft.

Ohio Rd.

Dock

Perched
Sand
Dunes

Highest
Point of
Island

Burdick Rd.

Florence
Lake

Wreck of the
Three Brothers
1911

Old-
Growth
Cedars

Weather
Station
Campground

Sleeping Bear Point
(7 miles)

Wreck of the
Francisco Morazon
1960

LEGEND

——	Road	Ranger Station		Lighthouse		Building
····	Trail	Visitor Center		Water		Building Ruins
		Campground		Cemetery		Shipwreck

Lighthouse, Shipwreck, Cedars, Dunes

Distance Round-Trip: 10.3 miles
Estimated Hiking Time: 4 to 5.5 hours

Cautions: Take insect repellent in the warmer months. Watch out for poison ivy and roots and rocks in the trail. If returning to the ferry, plan your time accordingly.

Trail Directions: Start at the welcome center straight past the restrooms and drinking fountain to the trail sign for the Weather Station Campground **[1]**. On the old road, pass the Coast Guard building and old residences from the past that are now a staff home and visitor center. The trail veers closer to the water and over wood planking in the sand, past the Underwater Preserve of the *Three Brothers* Shipwreck (.3 mi.) **[2]**, past a junction to which you will return (.4 mi.) **[3]**, and to the steps of the lighthouse (.5 mi.) **[4]**. Take a tour if a guide is present and get a panoramic view from atop the lighthouse.

Head back to the junction **[3]** and turn left through jack pine along a rolling trail. When you enter an area of more maples, notice the abundance of yew around you. Thanks to the lack of deer on the island, this plant (and poison ivy) proliferates (1 mi.) **[5]**.

Stay straight when you pass the Weather Station Campground junction (1.7 mi.) **[6]**. Pass through rolling grounds of trees fallen long ago to pass the other camp junction (2.1 mi) **[7]** and go on to a third junction (2.2 mi.) **[8]**. Stay left. The trail, wide like an old road, passes through less dense woods and then into older growth. At the small spur to Florence Lake (2.8 mi) **[9]**, turn right for a peek at the small lake. Then continue to pass the junction for the Florence Lake Trail to the junction to the farms (3.2 mi.) **[10]**.

Go straight; the trail becomes rocky. In the beech and maples, birds sing. At the junction to the shipwreck (4.1 mi.) **[11]**, go left and descend to the bluff, where you get an overview of the cormorant-encrusted shipwreck (4.4 mi.) **[12]**. Listen to gulls as you take care around the steep bluff.

Head back to the junction **[11]** and continue to the junction to the old-growth cedars (4.9 mi.) **[13]**. Turn left and enter the old cedars, some of which have toppled over the trail. Weave around and up this trail. You go around a huge cedar carcass that, on its side, towers over you. Continue up a narrow path until it is overgrown (5.5 mi.) **[14]** and turn back to the junction **[13]**.

Turn left and head for the dune. Climb and climb some more. The trail veers left, and you reach the dune vista, where you can see water all around the island (6.6 mi.) **[15]**. Sit back in the sand for a spell before heading back to the farms junction (8.2 mi.) **[10]**. If you are headed back to the ferry, continue straight. If you are staying at the Bay Campground or still have time to spare, turn left on the wide grassy road through maple and beech. You then pass old fields and apple trees before reaching the junction to Florence Lake (9 mi.) **[16]**. Turn right. Stay straight at the junction for a view of the lake (9.3 mi.) **[17]**.

At the road (9.5 mi.), turn left **[18]**. Stroll down to a path on the right (9.7 mi.) **[19]**. You'll be heading down that path, but first visit the old schoolhouse a few steps ahead on the road.

Now head down the path, through a bright area of old farmland and back into dark forest. Stay right at the fork (9.9 mi.) **[20]**. This path leads to a post along the Bay Campground. Find your campsite or turn right to head back to the dock.

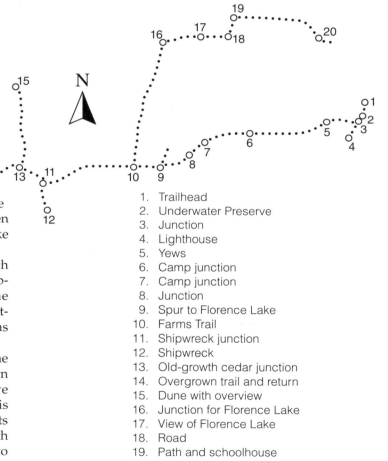

1. Trailhead
2. Underwater Preserve
3. Junction
4. Lighthouse
5. Yews
6. Camp junction
7. Camp junction
8. Junction
9. Spur to Florence Lake
10. Farms Trail
11. Shipwreck junction
12. Shipwreck
13. Old-growth cedar junction
14. Overgrown trail and return
15. Dune with overview
16. Junction for Florence Lake
17. View of Florence Lake
18. Road
19. Path and schoolhouse
20. Fork

Farm Loop

Distance Round-Trip: 5.9 miles
Estimated Hiking Time: 2 to 3 hours

Cautions: Take insect repellent in the warmer months. Watch out for poison ivy and roots and rocks in the trail. If returning by ferry, plan your time accordingly.

Trail Directions: Start at the welcome center straight past the restrooms and drinking fountain to the trail sign for the Weather Station Campground **[1]**. On the old road, pass the old residences from the past that are now a staff home and visitor center. The trail veers closer to the water and over wood planking in the sand, past the Underwater Preserve of the *Three Brothers* Shipwreck (.3 mi.) **[2]**, and to a junction (.4 mi.) **[3]**. Turn right through jack pine along a rolling trail. When you enter an area of more maples, notice the abundance of yew around you. Thanks to the lack of deer on the island, this plant (and poison ivy) proliferates (.7 mi.) **[4]**.

Stay straight when you pass the Weather Station Campground junction (1.4 mi.) **[5]**. Pass through rolling grounds of trees fallen long ago to pass the other camp junction (1.8 mi.) **[6]** and go on to a third junction (1.9 mi.) **[7]**. Turn right through ferns, old fields, and young trees—an area progressively filling in from past practices.

Pass a road junction (2.2 mi.) **[8]** and a spur into Florence Lake (2.6 mi.) **[9]**. The woods are dense—mostly hemlock and then a mix. Just after you pass a shortcut route back to camp on the right, you reach the schoolhouse (2.7 mi.) **[10]**. If you brought a lunch, you can use a picnic table, and the pump offers the sweetest water on the island.

Continue along this old road. The canopy opens, and you walk through a tunnel of trees and past a foundation, farming implements, and fruit trees—a natural location for the junction for the Farm Loop (3.2 mi.) **[11]**.

Turn left, passing farm relics. You can see the forest slowly reclaiming the fields. Past farmers were able to grow hybrids for seeds because the island is far from other influences.

At the junction, go straight to visit the historic Anderson Farm. Enter the darkness of woods and wind through until sandy ridges are on both sides of you. Birds sing their pleasure of this area. Pass the Hass Farm in the rolling woods (3.8 mi.) **[12]**. A field is up the way—and another house and a barn. Sit at the picnic table under the old maple and ponder what life on an island was like in the mid-1800s.

Wind around, pass a path, and come to a farm with a house and several barns (4.2 mi.) **[13]**. The old field at G.C. Hutgler's farm, loaded with bergamot and grasses, sets a perfect foreground to the abandoned rural setting.

Stay straight at the next junction (4.6 mi.) **[14]** and soon enter woods. When the forest darkens, watch for the junction to the schoolhouse (4.7 mi.) **[15]**. Turn right through young growth and then an older forest. At the junction to Florence Lake, stay left (5 mi.) **[16]** and follow the trail back to the schoolhouse (5.2 mi.) **[10]**.

Turn right and follow the road back to the road junction (5.6 mi.) **[8]**. Turn left to go back to the village. Close the loop at the staff houses, veering left to go back to the welcome center.

1. Trailhead
2. Underwater Preserve
3. Junction
4. Yews
5. Camp junction
6. Camp junction
7. Junction
8. Road junction
9. Spur to Florence Lake
10. Schoolhouse
11. Farm Loop junction
12. Hass Farm
13. G.C. Hutgler Farm
14. Junction
15. Junction to schoolhouse
16. Junction for Florence Lake

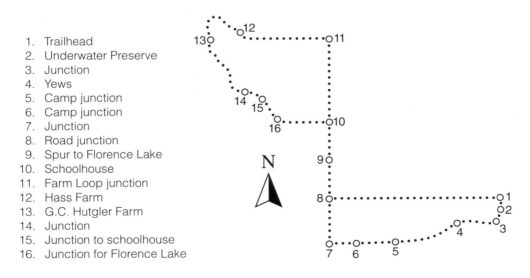

- Camp in the backcountry on bluffs overlooking Lake Michigan.
- Swim or stroll along miles of sandy Lake Michigan beach.
- Enjoy almost 3,450 acres set aside as wilderness.

Park Information

Distinguished as the only federally designated wilderness in Michigan's Lower Peninsula, the Nordhouse Dunes Wilderness has miles of isolated Lake Michigan beach, dunes towering 140 feet high, extensive interdunal wetlands, and vegetation ranging from dune grass that tolerates desertlike conditions to northern hardwood beech-maple forest.

The wilderness has no designated campgrounds, but you may camp almost anywhere in the backcountry. Pack in your own water or purify what you need. Well-equipped regular camping facilities can be found at the Lake Michigan Recreation Area that borders the northern end of the wilderness.

Roughly 15 miles of trails provide access to the varied habitats found at Nordhouse Dunes. Designation as a wilderness area provides unique recreation experiences for visitors. The trail system is no longer maintained with signs or markers, although the trails still exist and maps of the wilderness highlight their locations. Carry a map and compass.

Directions: Nordhouse Dunes Wilderness lies between Manistee and Ludington. To reach the southern trailhead from US 31, turn west on West Forest Trail (FR 5629) for about 3 miles and then head south on Quarterline Road for a generous mile to Nurnberg Road. Head west about 6 miles to a small parking area. The Lake Michigan Recreation Area, at the northern boundary, is accessed from US 31 by following the Lake Michigan Recreation Road west about 8 miles to its end.

Hours Open: Open year-round.

Facilities: Hiking, cross-country skiing, snowshoeing, swimming, fishing, hunting, and camping (backcountry).

Permits and Rules: Fees for vehicles are $3 per day, $5 per week, or $20 per year. Motor vehicles and mechanized equipment, including mountain bikes and wheeled carts, are not permitted. Pack animals, including horses, are not allowed. Campfires and campsites must be more than 400 feet from Lake Michigan; no beach fires are allowed. Do not burn driftwood or remove it from the wilderness. Campsites along roads must be 400 feet from the wilderness boundary. Maximum group size is 10 people. Pack out what you bring in.

For Further Information: Manistee National Forest, Manistee Ranger Station, 412 Red Apple Road, Manistee, MI 49660; 231-723-2211.

Other Points of Interest

Bordering the Nordhouse Dunes Wilderness to the north, the **Lake Michigan Recreation Area** provides campsites, observation decks, an interpretive trail, mountain bike trails, and a swimming beach. Access the Nordhouse Dunes Wilderness from here. Contact the Manistee Ranger Station.

East of the Nordhouse Dunes Wilderness trailhead on Nurnberg Road sits the 100-acre **Hamlin Lake Marsh**. From Nurnberg Road, take Forest Road 5540 south to this little-used spot on the northern tip of Hamlin Lake. A small boat launch is located at this site. Contact the Manistee Ranger Station.

Ludington State Park (see park #50) borders the Nordhouse Dunes Wilderness on the south. This park provides modern camping facilities, an interpretive center, beaches on two lakes, paved bicycling paths, and many miles of hiking paths. For more information, contact Ludington State Park, 8800 W. M-116, Ludington, MI 49431; 231-843-2423.

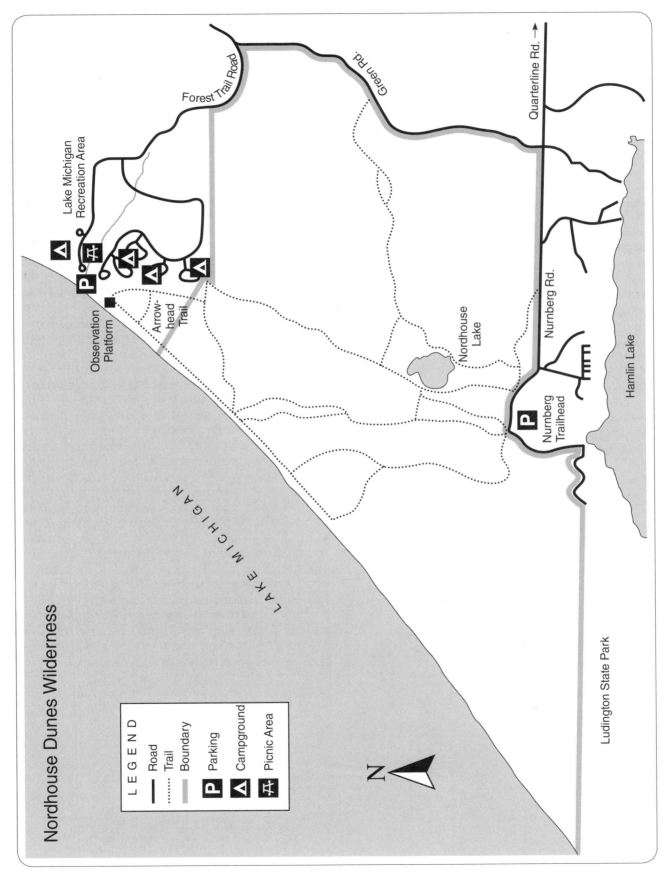

Nordhouse Dunes Wilderness

LEGEND

— Road
⋯⋯ Trail
▬ Boundary
P Parking
▲ Campground
🛆 Picnic Area

N

Forest Trail Road

Green Rd.

Quarterline Rd. →

Lake Michigan Recreation Area

Observation Platform

Arrow-head Trail

LAKE MICHIGAN

Nordhouse Lake

Nurnberg Rd.

Nurnberg Trailhead

Hamlin Lake

Ludington State Park

Four-Mile Loop

Distance Round-Trip: 3.9 miles
Estimated Hiking Time: 2 to 3 hours

Cautions: The trails are worn and usually easy to follow, but they are not marked. Carry a map and a compass. You travel through sand and mud, over roots and rocks, and along ridges. Wear appropriate footgear. Take water and insect repellent.

Trail Directions: Park on Nurnberg Road 6 mi. west of Quarterline Road. Start at the north end of the parking area, taking the left trail to the north [1]. Climb into the forest.

Wind around, gently ascending (.2 mi.) [2] the back side of a dune. Go through forested hills while ascending, passing grassy slopes that line troughs and the fern- and tree-lined slopes along the ravines. At .5 mi., a trail that leads to Nordhouse Lake cuts in on the right [3]. Go straight.

The trail narrows, continuing its ascent. At 1.3 mi., moss carpeting flanks the trail [4], tipping you off that dunes will soon appear. When the trail swings noticeably to the right, a gully begins to accompany you (1.4 mi.) [5]. Birch trees occasionally light up the wooded dunes that you pass through.

At 1.6 mi., you reach a ravine [6]. Blaze your way down the right side of the steep slope to the sandy shores of Lake Michigan. Kick off your shoes and stroll to the southwest. Play tag with the water as it ebbs and flows. Listen to the waves and seagulls. The next .6 mi. is yours to enjoy as you head southwest along the shore before reaching the point of reentry back inland (2.2 mi.) [7].

Watch for an opening in the sandy dunes. Head inland. Go straight. The trail passes through a valley between dunes. You go by a graveyard of stumps; then hardwoods, cedar, and hemlock perfume the way. A massive dune advances to your right, following along the edge of the trail. Pass through a valley of ferns, roll along through hemlock, and reach a main trail junction at 2.8 mi. [8].

Head left. You pass wetlands, ferns, maples, oaks, and hemlocks. A trail merges in from the left; stay to the right. The trail winds down around a wetland (3.5 mi.) [9] and down even further to the parking area where you left your vehicle.

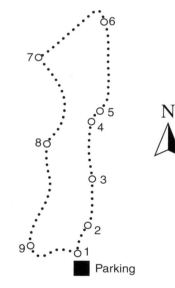

N

1. Trailhead
2. Gentle ascent
3. Trail junction
4. Moss on trail
5. Gully
6. Ravine at lake
7. Reenter inland
8. Main trail junction
9. Wetland

Six-Mile Loop

Distance Round-Trip: 5.9 miles
Estimated Hiking Time: 3 to 4 hours

Cautions: The trails are worn but not marked. Carry a map and a compass. Wear appropriate footgear. Take water and insect repellent.

Trail Directions: Start near the information board at the west end of the parking area on Nurnberg Road, about 6 mi. west of Quarterline Road **[1]**. Climb gently into the forest along a wide, sandy path. A large wetlands follows on your right. Swing around and climb to end up hiking north (.4 mi.) **[2]**.

Trudging along the sandy trail, shaded by mixed woods, you pass several small wetlands and an occasional side path. The trails are not marked, so you are on your own for any side trips (which is, after all, in the spirit of a wilderness experience).

At 1 mi., turn right off the main trail and onto a less-used pathway **[3]**. You soon skirt a large wooded dune on your left. Continuing north, you pass through cedar and hemlock that give way to maple. You also pass old stumps that stand like tombstones, a reminder of the forest that stood here long ago.

As you undulate along the trail, you eventually come to a small valley between a dune and a ridge. Follow the sometimes moss-carpeted trail to reach the edge of the Lake Michigan beach. Go right and climb the natural root steps onto a ridge (1.6 mi.) **[4]**. You could walk the Lake Michigan beach, but instead walk the ridge high above the lake.

Watch your step as you climb up the bluff, stopping now and then to enjoy a scenic view through the trees of Lake Michigan's white, sandy beach. At 1.9 mi., after a steep climb, you descend on dilapidated steps. A trail merges from the right (2.1 mi.) **[5]**. Descend and skirt an eroded section of the bluff. A second trail merges from behind the bluff at a ravine (2.2 mi.) **[6]**. Continue north past the ravine. Pass the Nordhouse Dunes Wilderness sign to enter the Lake Michigan Recreation Area (2.7 mi.) **[7]**. You reach the junction with the southern leg of the Arrowhead Trail at 2.9 mi. **[8]**. Continue along the bluff.

At 3 mi., you pass steps and arrive at a bench that overlooks Lake Michigan **[9]**. Continue straight as the east leg of the Arrowhead Trail merges in. Keep straight past the observation tower **[10]** (you will get back to it) to go on to enjoy the observation platforms, boardwalks, trail to the beach, and interpretive markers at the Lake Michigan Recreation Area (3.2 mi.) **[11]**.

Turn back and climb the observation tower (3.3 mi.) **[10]**. Catch your breath and then catch the trail back by heading southeast off the back end of the platform. After the Arrowhead Trail splits, you pass a water-storage tank (3.6 mi.) **[12]**.

Soon reenter the Nordhouse Dunes Wilderness and pass a junction (3.6 mi.) **[13]**. Passing the back side of the dunes, the trail tunnels through velvet moss.

As the trail gradually descends, look for glimpses of Nordhouse Lake through the trees on the left. At about 5.2 mi., you have the option of turning left to descend to the lake or turning right to head back. Turn right **[14]** and hike the short distance to another trail. Turn left and descend to the parking lot.

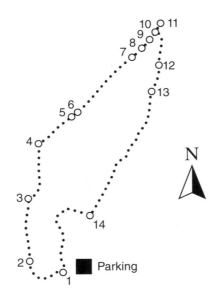

N

1. Trailhead
2. Wetland
3. Trail junction
4. Trail junction; steps to ridge
5. Trail junction
6. Trail junction and ravine
7. Leave wilderness area
8. Trail junction
9. Bench and overlook
10. Observation tower
11. Lake Michigan Recreation Area
12. Water-storage tank
13. Trail junction
14. Trail junction

- Take in almost 6 miles of dune-lined Lake Michigan shoreline.
- Canoe or tube along the Big Sable River between Hamlin Lake and Lake Michigan.
- Follow the beacon—a number of trails guide you to the impressive Big Sable Point Lighthouse.

Park Information

This park's attendance ranks in the top 10 of all Michigan state parks, with good reason. Miles of Lake Michigan shoreline, rolling dune terrain, and a historic lighthouse provide the ingredients to satisfy any number of appetites for recreation. Two beaches—one on Lake Michigan and one on Hamlin Lake—encourage fishing, swimming, canoeing, and boating. Paved pathways along the river endow bicyclists with grounds for enjoyment. Some areas of the park are open to in-season hunting. Moreover, this 5,300-acre park is home to the Great Lakes Interpretive Center for exhibits, interpretive programs, and multimedia shows.

Although the camp and day beaches are usually crowded, plenty of acreage supplies opportunities to escape. Wilderness abounds to the north, extend-

ing from the park's own acreage to the neighboring Nordhouse Dunes Wilderness (see park #49). A hike-in campground offers 10 wilderness sites. About 16 miles of cross-country ski trails glide over the park during winter.

Directions: Ludington State Park is 8 miles north of Ludington. Take US 10 west into Ludington. Head north on M-116 about 8 miles to the park entrance.

Hours Open: The park is open year-round from 8:00 a.m. to 10:00 p.m. The lighthouse is open daily from 10:00 a.m. to 6:00 p.m. May through October.

Facilities: Hiking, bicycling, cross-country skiing, swimming, fishing, hunting, canoeing, picnicking, camping (RV and tent), cabins, boat launch, boat and canoe rentals, sanitation station, and interpretive center.

Permits and Rules: A park fee is required for motor vehicles ($6 daily, $24 annually for residents; $8 daily, $29 annually for nonresidents). Snowmobiles are not allowed in the park. Bicycles are allowed only on paved roads and paths.

For Further Information: Ludington State Park, 8800 W. M-116, Ludington, MI 49431; 231-843-2423.

Other Points of Interest

To find other activities in the area, contact the Ludington Area Convention and Visitors Bureau, 5300 W. US 10, Ludington, MI 49431; 877-420-6618; www .ludingtoncvb.com; or the Ludington Area Visitors Guide at www.visitludington.com.

Park Trails

Coast Guard Trail (🥾, 1.5 mile). The trail starts on the northwest end of the day-use area on Hamlin Lake and takes you to a scenic viewpoint along Lake Michigan.

Ridge Trail (🥾🥾, 2.7 miles). The trail starts from behind the park store at the southwest end of the Cedar Campground and traverses a ridge, following through woods.

Logging Trail (🥾🥾, 3 miles). Access this trail from the north end of the Pines Campground. The trail is the remnant of an old logging road that climbs a ridge, descends into lowlands, and reaches hills and woods.

Skyline Trail (🥾🥾, .5 mile). A scenic trail along a boardwalk, it loops around the visitor center and offers panoramic views of Lake Michigan and the Big Sable River.

Dune Trail (🥾🥾, .7 mile). This trail starts behind the park store in the Cedar Campground.

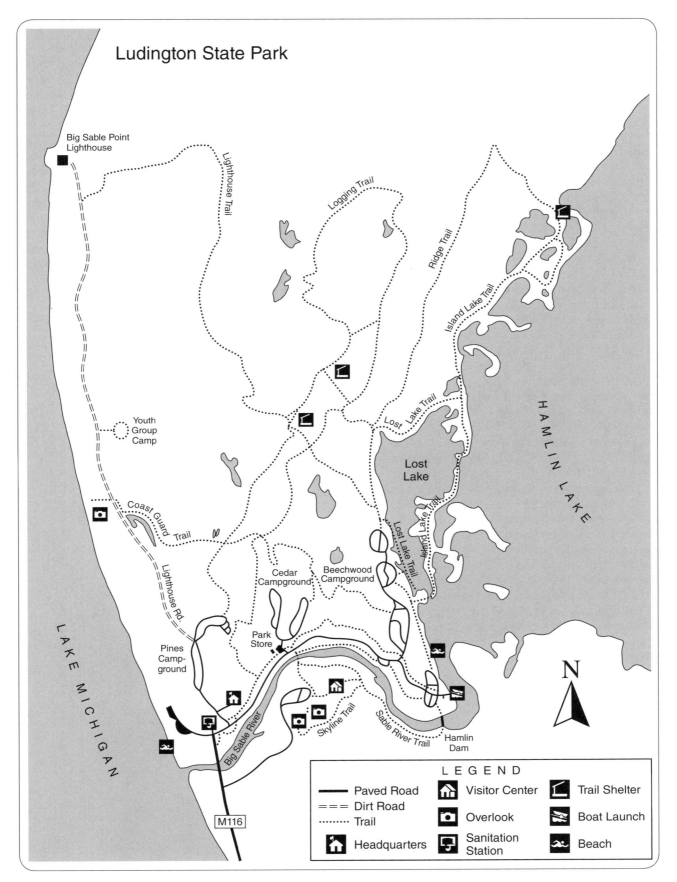

Ludington State Park

Big Sable Point Lighthouse

Lighthouse Trail

Logging Trail

Ridge Trail

Island Lake Trail

HAMLIN LAKE

Lost Lake Trail

Youth Group Camp

Lost Lake

Coast Guard Trail

Island Lake Trail

Lost Lake Trail

LAKE MICHIGAN

Cedar Campground

Beechwood Campground

Pines Camp-ground

Park Store

Lighthouse Rd.

Skyline Trail

Big Sable River

Sable River Trail

Hamlin Dam

N

M116

LEGEND

——	Paved Road	🏠 Visitor Center	🏠 Trail Shelter	
===	Dirt Road	📷 Overlook	🛶 Boat Launch	
······	Trail			
🏠	Headquarters	🚻 Sanitation Station	🏖 Beach	

Skyline–Sable River–Island Lake–Lost Lake Trails

Distance Round-Trip: 3.5 miles
Estimated Hiking Time: 1.5 to 2 hours

Cautions: Exposed roots and rocks can be slippery. Insect repellent is a must during the warm months.

Trail Directions: The hike combines several trails to offer overviews from boardwalks on bluffs, river walking, island hopping, and dock strolling. Start from the southwest end of the visitor center parking lot **[1]** to pick up the Skyline Trail, which takes you up a series of steps to a boardwalk on the bluffs, affording you a view of Lake Michigan.

At .1 mi., you see the Big Sable River **[2]**. Watch for the flotilla of resident Canada geese. At .3 mi., pass the staircase that leads down to the visitor center **[3]**. Walk along the boardwalk to the Sable River Trail (.4 mi.) **[4]**. Turn right. The trail gradually takes you along the bank of the river on a boardwalk along the side of a wooded hill. Then it climbs and swings left over Hamlin Dam and the Big Sable River (.7 mi.) **[5]**.

On the other side, cut through the Hamlin Lake day-use area. Pass right through the parking lot to the concrete walk near the beach. Go by the concession stand and after you pass the swing set, swing near the beach and follow along the shore of Hamlin Lake (1 mi.) **[6]**. Soon you reach the junction for the Island Lake Trail (1.1 mi.) **[7]**.

Turn right onto the boardwalk through the cattails. At 1.2 mi., a footbridge crosses to one of the narrow islands separating Hamlin Lake and Lost Lake **[8]**. Notice the vast openness of Hamlin Lake and the narrow, riverlike quality of Lost Lake. Follow the narrow strip of land and boardwalks over to another narrow strip. Because of the irregular shape of the island, lagoonlike pools are at your side. The irregularities continue to play, and you seem to pass open lakes, rivers, ponds, and lagoons. At times, the burnt orange carpeting of pine needles underfoot offers a striking contrast with the dark-green canopies. Both lakes open wide. Continue along the strip of land between them, cross another bridge, and then sit on the bench overlooking the lake (1.6 mi.) **[9]**. More boardwalks await you before you arrive at the junction for the Lost Lake Trail (1.8 mi.) **[10]**.

Turn left, head down between wetlands, and then climb to a ridge where you reach an overlook of Lost Lake (1.9 mi.) **[11]**. Roll along through the woods and arrive at a blowoutlike slope that opens up another view of Lost Lake. Here, the trail veers right and soon takes you to a junction (2.1 mi.) **[12]**. Although you should veer left here, the observation deck to your right is enticing, so catch the view there before continuing your left turn along the Lost Lake Trail.

The Lost Lake Trail passes along a ridge above Lost Lake. At the junction, go left (2.2 mi.) **[13]**. Soon, a platform of steps assists you down to the lake level. You can see the campgrounds up ahead as the Lighthouse Trail merges in (2.4 mi.) **[14]**. Just before the campground, turn left along the boardwalk–dock that carries you along Lost Lake. At 2.6 mi., the boardwalk gives access to a small island where benches nestled under pines, hemlocks, and maples invite you to rest **[15]**. At the end of the boardwalk, turn left and soon close the Island Lake–Lost Lake Loop. Retrace your steps to the Hamlin Lake day-use area, but instead of cutting across the park road back to the dam, turn right to the bike path and follow along the north side of the river (3 mi.) **[16]**.

Just before you reach the Cedar Campground, you reach the bridge that crosses over the river (3.4 mi.) **[17]**. Turn left and cross the bridge. Pass the Sable River Trail junction in a small stretch of woods before arriving back at the parking lot.

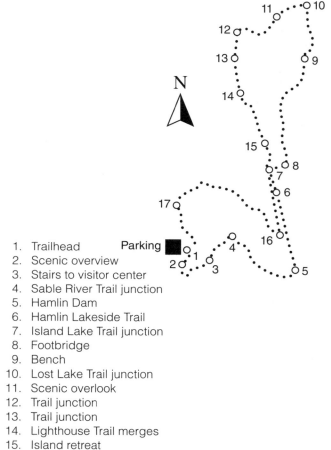

1. Trailhead
2. Scenic overview
3. Stairs to visitor center
4. Sable River Trail junction
5. Hamlin Dam
6. Hamlin Lakeside Trail
7. Island Lake Trail junction
8. Footbridge
9. Bench
10. Lost Lake Trail junction
11. Scenic overlook
12. Trail junction
13. Trail junction
14. Lighthouse Trail merges
15. Island retreat
16. Bike path
17. Bridge

Northern
Lower
Peninsula

Big Sable Point Lighthouse Loop

Distance Round-Trip: 4.4 miles
Estimated Hiking Time: 2 to 3 hours

Cautions: The trail takes you through varied terrain, over roots, and may be hard to follow in the dunes. Take insect repellent, sunscreen, and a hat for the dunes and Lake Michigan shore.

Trail Directions: Park north of the Big Sable River at the fish-cleaning station at the day-use area. Start at the fish-cleaning station **[1]** and head west along the drive to the bathhouse and beach.

North of the swimming area, the beach is wide and often covered with sun worshippers or people intent on using lake breezes to fly colorful kites. Hiking along the beach, you may even feel the pull of the lake and, depending on the weather, an uncontrollable urge to jump in. Plan ahead and wear your swimsuit. You can jump in now or wait until you've completed your hike.

Just after passing a shipwreck, the Big Sable Point Lighthouse comes into view (1.2 mi.) **[2]**. As you approach, its dark top rises above the light dune; it becomes your beacon, as it has been to others since it was first illuminated in 1867 (2 mi.) **[3]**. Owned by the Coast Guard, the lighthouse is maintained by the Sable Point Lighthouse Keepers Association. The top of the lighthouse provides a spectacular view of the surrounding Lake Michigan shoreline and dunes environment. If you brought your lunch, eat at one of the picnic tables.

When you leave the lighthouse, start out on the service drive and turn left by the toilets at post #15 (2.1 mi.) **[4]**. (Brown arrows designate the Lighthouse Trail.) Head east into the dunes. Locating the trail in the open sand may be difficult, so look ahead for trail markers across the open dunes. At 2.2 mi., after climbing a dune, take a close look at the lighthouse nestled between the dunes and Lake Michigan **[5]**.

At the map sign post, stay to the right (2.5 mi.) **[6]** and hike through pines. After climbing a small dune, look behind for your last glimpse of the lighthouse. Climb out of the pines to walk across open, grassy dunes (3 mi.) **[7]**. The trail swings right and descends sharply into a forest. You soon leave the loose sand behind. Turn right onto the Logging Trail (3.4 mi.) **[8]**. Follow the green arrows past the stone CCC shelter as the trail rolls and snakes through the trees and past many old stumps left over from the logging era.

After passing two wetlands, you cross the junction for the Coast Guard Trail, post #3 (3.8 mi.) **[9]**. Climb over a ridge and enter an area with fallen trees. Soon, you pass the Dune Trail and enter the Pines Campground next to site #41 (4.1 mi.) **[10]**. Turn right and hike through the campground to return to the parking area at the fish-cleaning station.

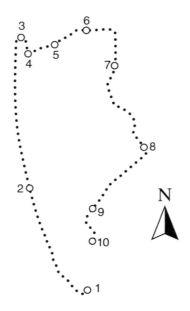

1. Trailhead
2. First view of lighthouse
3. Big Sable Point Lighthouse
4. Lighthouse Trail junction
5. View of lighthouse
6. Map sign
7. Open dune
8. Logging Trail junction
9. Coast Guard Trail junction
10. Campground

Southern Lower Peninsula

Michigan's south extends from the Indiana and Ohio borders to the imaginary line that corresponds to the knuckles of Michigan's mitten and includes the thumb.

Topography

The southern Lower Peninsula roughly includes the part of Michigan that used to be referred to as the industrial core of the United States and Canada. It contains the bulk of the state's population, all its major urban areas, and its prime agricultural lands. Interestingly, it is the only part of the state where the fossil remains of elephant-like mammals—the mastodons and mammoths—are found. As the glaciers receded, herds of these huge animals roamed southern Michigan. People believe that these now extinct mammals were looking for life-sustaining salt seeps. An imaginary line called the Mason-Quimby Line marks the northernmost occurrence of mastodon and mammoth fossil finds and all the recorded salt seeps, or shallow saline waters, in the state. The line also corresponds to the area of transition between the north woods and the southern agricultural lands.

The present form of Michigan owes its shape to the last glacial retreat, which occurred between 10,000 and 35,000 years ago. The massive ice sheets transported large amounts of soil and rock, depositing them as moraines, serpentine eskers, elliptically shaped drumlins, kames, valleys, and hills of many shapes. An area of striking morainic development is found in Oakland and Washtenaw counties, where two lobes of glacial ice collided and left a jumble of hills and lakes. Michigan's lowest elevation of 572 feet above sea level occurs along the shoreline of Lake Erie.

Famous for its sand dunes along the Great Lakes, Michigan also has dunes that lie far inland from the present shores. These inland dunes formed when the levels of the Great Lakes were higher. Many of these inland dunes are located well away from the shore of Lake Michigan. Another group of inland dunes stretches west of Saginaw Bay almost as far as Clare. These dunes are less than 13,000 years old.

Major Rivers and Lakes

Lake Michigan borders the southern Lower Peninsula on the west; Lake Huron and Lake Erie are on the east. Canada shares the border with Michigan along Lake St. Clair and the St. Clair and Detroit rivers. The Detroit River is the state's widest river, the Grand is the longest, and the Saginaw, with a length of 20 miles, is the shortest. Paradoxically, the Saginaw, with its tributaries—the Tittabawassee, Shiawassee, Flint, and Cass rivers—has the largest drainage basin in the state. Other significant rivers include the Muskegon, Kalamazoo, St. Joseph, and Huron.

Material carried by a river and deposited in a relatively quiet body of water forms a delta, which gradually grows outward from the shore. The St. Clair River delta, where the St. Clair River empties into Lake St. Clair, is the largest freshwater delta in the country.

As the glaciers receded, blocks of ice were left stranded. When these blocks finally melted, they left behind pits, or what are termed *kettle holes*. Many of these kettles holes filled with water and today are lakes. One of the greatest concentrations of kettle-hole lakes in Michigan occurs in a broad belt that stretches from just north of Pontiac and heads southwest to Jackson. This region contains many recreation sites important to the Detroit metropolitan area.

Common Plant Life

Michigan is a forest state. What early explorers noted first were the trees. Of the state's 37 million acres of land, 35 million were once forest. All of Europe has only 8 kinds of trees; Michigan has 83. The southern Lower Peninsula differs from the rest of the state in that it is not part of the transitional north woods. It is an area where hardwoods such as oak, hickory, maple, beech, ash, and elm dominate. Of the 83 tree types native to Michigan, 27 are found throughout the state. Thirty-three are abundant only in the southern half, and another dozen, like the paw paw, are considered unusual and are found only in the southernmost counties.

Beginning as early as April, wildflowers blanket the forest floor. The blue hepatica and bloodroot are among the early bloomers. Later, the trillium and yellow-flowered trout-lily bloom. In the summer, common meadow flowers like bergamot, brown-eyed susan, teasel, chicory, and goldenrod are prominent.

Common Birds and Mammals

In southern Michigan, spring arrives when the state's bird, the robin, arrives. Other birds to look for include the red-winged blackbird, various warblers, eastern bluebird, chickadee, goldfinch, nuthatch, tufted titmouse, junco, tree sparrow, cardinal, blue jay, red-tailed hawk, marsh hawk, kestrel, turkey vulture, sandhill crane, great blue heron, egret, woodcock, wood duck, mallard, Canada geese, great horned owl, swans, and various shorebirds.

Resident mammals include the white-tailed deer, raccoon, skunk, opossum, woodchuck, cottontail rabbit, red fox, coyote, muskrat, beaver, thirteen-lined ground squirrel, and chipmunk.

Climate

Michigan's south is in a climatic region identified as humid continental hot summer. *Humid continental* signifies that Michigan is a snow-forest region affected by a continental land mass and is constantly moist with enough precipitation to support trees. *Hot summer* refers to the warmest summer month, averaging above 71.6 degrees Fahrenheit.

Lake Michigan tempers the climate. A climatic subregion exists one to two counties inland from the lake. In this subregion, called the fruit belt, the temperatures are altered by the warm lake waters that cool more slowly than the adjacent land does.

The average maximum January temperature ranges between 28 and 32 degrees Fahrenheit, while the low averages between 13 and 18 degrees. In July the average maximum temperature ranges from 78 to 84 degrees Fahrenheit, and the low averages between 56 and 62 degrees. Annual precipitation ranges from 31 to 39 inches in the southwest to between 28 and 33 inches in the northeast. Annual snowfall totals vary from 93 inches at Muskegon to 29 inches at Ann Arbor. The longest growing season, 187 days, occurs in the southwest, near Benton Harbor.

Best Natural Features

- Three Great Lakes—Michigan, Huron, and Erie
- Sand dunes and sandy beaches along Lake Michigan
- Lake St. Clair
- St. Clair River delta—largest freshwater delta in the country
- Rolling landscape of the Irish Hills
- Glacial features—kettles, kames, moraines, and glacial erratics
- Remnant pockets of prairie landscape

- Study the petroglyphs—the only known rock carvings ascribed to prehistoric Native Americans in Michigan.
- Contemplate the history that the park offers.
- Enjoy a quiet retreat.

Park Information

Sanilac Petroglyphs State Historic Park is a historic site that features petroglyphs, or aboriginal rock carvings. Archaeologists estimate that these carvings were chipped into exposed sandstone between 300 and 1,000 years ago. Fires that swept through the region in 1881 cleared the vegetation that had been protecting these sandstone impressions over the years. Today, a pavilion protects the large slab of sandstone that features dozens of carvings of animals, animal tracks, birds, and a bowman with arrow.

The Michigan Archaeological Society raised private funds to purchase the 240-acre site; in 1970 it transferred the land to the State of Michigan. Although short on mileage, the 1.4-mile interpretive trail that weaves through the park is long on amenities. The nature trail not only educates you about the many historic facets within the park, including petroglyphs, Indian villages, and logging camps, but also cuts across a branch of the Cass River, weaves through woods and open meadows, and meanders along a stream through rugged, scenic terrain. Beaver dams and animal prints abound along the banks of the stream.

Directions: The park is located about 13 miles south of Bad Axe. Take M-53 to the Bay City–Forestville Road. Head east about 4 miles to Germania Road. Turn south. The park entrance is about .5 mile south of this intersection, on the west side of the road.

Hours Open: The hiking trail is open daily. You may view the petroglyphs from approximately Memorial Day weekend to Labor Day weekend on Wednesdays through Sundays from 10:00 a.m. to 5:00 p.m. Call ahead.

Facilities: Hiking, interpretive trail, and historic features.

Permits and Rules: No admission fee is charged. This cultural resource is fragile. Keep off the rock carvings.

For Further Information: Michigan Historical Museum, 702 W. Kalamazoo Street, Lansing, MI 48909; 517-373-3559.

Other Points of Interest

Located on the shores of Saginaw Bay, **Port Crescent State Park** (see park #52), offers camping, white sand beaches, dunes, and hiking trails. The Pinnebog River flows through the park and on to the bay. For more information, contact Port Crescent State Park, 1775 Port Austin Road, Port Austin, MI 48467; 989-738-8663.

The **Huron County Nature Center Wilderness Arboretum** is located between Caseville and Port Austin, south of M-25 and east of Oak Beach Road on Loosemore Road. This 280-acre nature center has rolling dune ridges and shallow, wet depressions (swales), traversed by an interpretive trail system. For more information, call the Huron County Nature Center Wilderness Arboretum at 989-453-2426; www.huronnaturecenter.org.

The **Albert E. Sleeper State Park**, 5 miles east of Caseville, provides white sand beaches, camping and picnicking facilities, an outdoor center with 13 cabins and a dining hall, and about 4 miles of hiking trails. A good portion of this park is wild, attractive to those interested in blazing their own trail. For more information, contact Albert E. Sleeper State Park, 6573 State Park Road, Caseville, MI 48725; 989-856-4411.

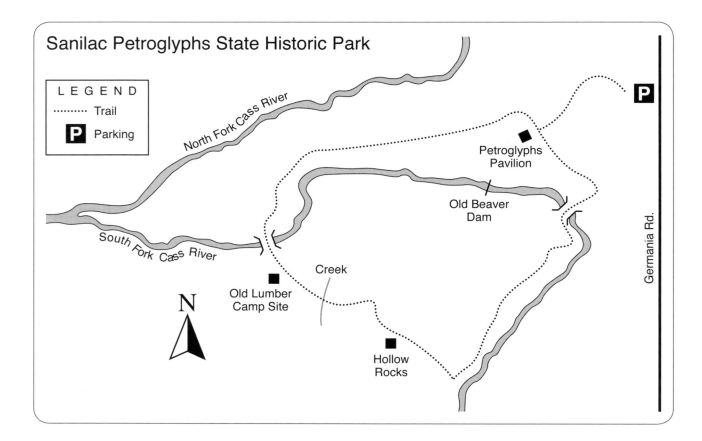

Sanilac Petroglyphs State Historic Park

LEGEND
········· Trail
P Parking

North Fork Cass River

South Fork Cass River

P

Germania Rd.

Petroglyphs Pavilion

Old Beaver Dam

Creek

N

Old Lumber Camp Site

Hollow Rocks

Petroglyphs Park Nature Trail

Distance Round-Trip: 1.4 miles
Estimated Hiking Time: 30 minutes to
1 hour

Cautions: Portions of the trail have exposed roots, are wet, or are strewn with rocks and boulders. Watch your step.

Trail Directions: Start at the map board on the west end of the parking lot [1]. Wind through scrubby trees along the crushed limestone trail and into a field of wildflowers with reddish orange petals and hairy stems. No, the flowers are not Indian paintbrush; they're hawkweed, or the devil's paintbrush. And they're the only devil's paintbrush that the legacy within this park needs. Respect the fragile artwork here and don't add any of your own.

Look for rocks that have bowl-shaped holes in them (.1 mi.) [2]. You will see many more of these potholes along the trail. Glacial waters scoured the soft sandstone about 12,500 years ago to produce them. Up the trail, the pavilion shades the sandstone that bears the petroglyphs (.2 mi.) [3]. On the weathered stones, try to pick out the outlines of human figures, birds, and animal tracks. The crushed limestone ends at the pavilion.

Now follow to the right. You soon pass another outcrop of art and then reach a path on the left (.3 mi.) [4]. A short walk through lush foliage takes you to the river and the remains of a beaver dam.

Continue along the main trail, stepping over rocks and blazing through brush that tunnels around the trail. You soon reach marker #5 and more potholes in the rocks. Lichen on many of the rocks look like mint green and white paint splatters from nature's palette.

The trail swings left through ferns, and you then climb over large slabs of bedrock (.4 mi.) [5]. The trail now flows along a stream. Fallen trees lie across the stream, and more huge outcrops of bedrock are exposed. Stroll along the stream banks. At .5 mi., cross the wooden footbridge over the stream, hanging on as it swings and bounces with your steps [6].

Climb to the right. The trail, laden with rocks, winds through ferns and young maples, which give way to mature maples and birches as you walk farther. Pass several low-lying depressions. Keep an eye out for animal tracks in the muddy trail.

Pass through a field of ferns and duck under the cover of mixed brush. Pass through mature maples, cross a boardwalk over a seasonal pool (.8 mi.) [7], and climb over boulders. Along this last stretch, you pass by what was once a Native American village. Several paths off to your left lead to a massive bedrock of sandstone; some forms look like sculptures in an open-air museum (.9 mi.) [8].

Cut through the ferns and across more rocks scattered along the trail until you reach post #8 at a large pine that survived the 1881 fire (1 mi.) [9]. Another bridge takes you back over the stream (1.1 mi.) [10]. The rocky, rooty trail winds back to the pavilion (1.2 mi.) [3]. Retrace your steps to the parking lot.

1. Trailhead
2. Potholes
3. Petroglyphs under pavilion
4. Path to beaver dam
5. Bedrock
6. Footbridge
7. Boardwalk
8. Sandstone sculptures
9. Fire survivor
10. Footbridge

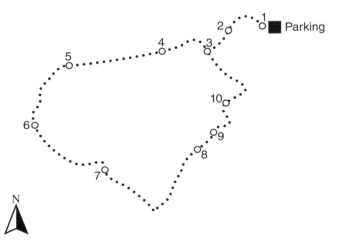

- View the spring hawk migration.
- Traverse the crest of dunes from a 1,000-foot boardwalk.
- Canoe the winding Pinnebog River.

Park Information

This 565-acre state park gets a thumbs-up. Several picnic decks, interconnected by a 1,000-foot boardwalk, show off almost 3 miles of fine, white sand along the Lake Huron shoreline of Saginaw Bay. Dunes, impressive for the east side of Michigan, roll down to the shore. The winding Pinnebog River provides additional water frontage as it carves the park into two major areas for camping and day use.

The east side of Port Crescent State Park is for camping. Here, a 3-mile figure-eight trail winds over wooded dunes, overlooks scenic viewpoints of Saginaw Bay, and crosses bluffs above the banks of the Pinnebog River. The day-use area on the west side of the park has 3.5 miles of trails over wind-blown dunes. Each of the two major trail systems, one in the camping area and one in the day-use area, has spurs for shorter routes. These spurs cut across from the southern and northern portions of each outer, or main, loop.

From March through April, broad-winged hawks and other birds of prey congregate in the area to feed and rest before they continue on to their northern breeding grounds.

Directions: Port Crescent State Park is located in the thumb area of Michigan, about 5 miles southwest of Port Austin on M-25.

Hours Open: Open daily.
Facilities: Hiking, cross-country skiing, swimming, canoeing, fishing, hunting, camping (tent and RV), picnicking, sanitation station, camper-cabin, and boat launch.
Permits and Rules: A park fee is required for motor vehicles ($6 daily, $24 annually for residents; $8 daily, $29 annually for nonresidents).
For Further Information: Port Crescent State Park, 1775 Port Austin Road, Port Austin, MI 48467; 989-738-8663.

Other Points of Interest

Five miles northeast of Caseville on M-25 is **Albert E. Sleeper State Park**, a heavily forested state park with a .5-mile beach on Saginaw Bay. The park features camping, swimming, bicycling, cross-country skiing, and more than 4 miles of nature trails. For more information, contact Albert E. Sleeper State Park, 6573 State Park Road, Caseville, MI 48725; 989-856-4411.

The **Huron County Nature Center Wilderness Arboretum** is 9 miles east of Caseville. This tract with sand ridges and swales offers a network of trails. Enjoy one of the self-guided trails within the park. Take M-25 east from Caseville to Oak Beach Road and turn right to Loosemore Road. Turn left and continue to the park entrance. For more information, call the Huron County Nature Center Wilderness Arboretum at 989-453-2426; www.huronnaturecenter.org.

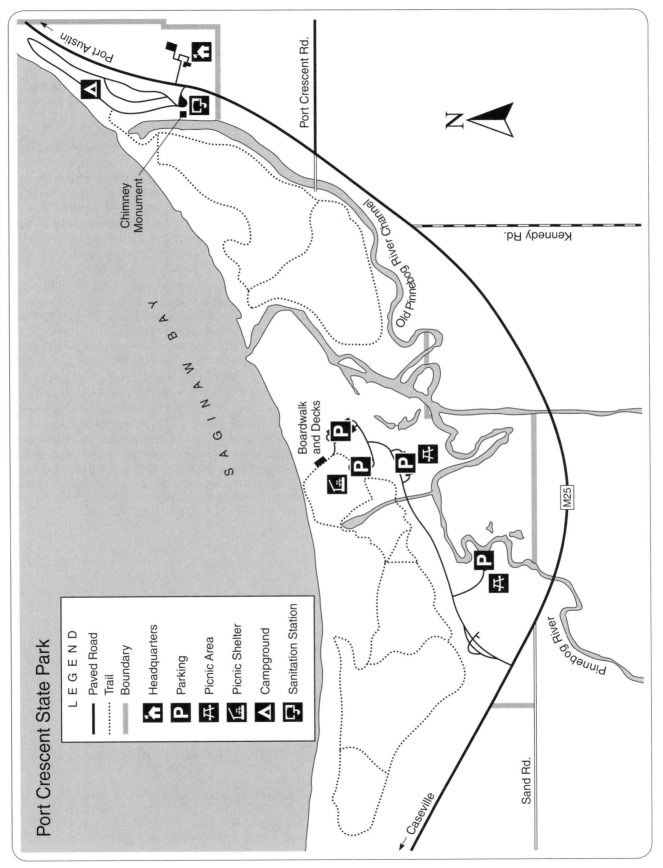

Port Crescent State Park

LEGEND

——	Paved Road
......	Trail
▬	Boundary
[Headquarters icon]	Headquarters
P	Parking
[Picnic Area icon]	Picnic Area
[Picnic Shelter icon]	Picnic Shelter
▲	Campground
[Sanitation Station icon]	Sanitation Station

SAGINAW BAY

Chimney Monument

Boardwalk and Decks

Old Pinneboog River Channel

Port Austin

Port Crescent Rd.

Kennedy Rd.

Sand Rd.

M25

Caseville

Pinnebog River

N

Camping Area Trail

Distance Round-Trip: 1.8 miles
Estimated Hiking Time: 1 to 1.5 hours

Cautions: Several unofficial paths cross the trail, particularly on the western portion of the trail. Keep an eye out for posts or paint marks on trees. The outer loop is made of two trails; blue marks the east side, and red marks the west side. Take insect repellent.

Trail Directions: Start by the iron bridge on the northwest side of M-25, right across from Port Austin Road [1]. A tiny lot, located about .3 mi. southwest of the campground entrance, provides a few parking spaces. Another trailhead may be reached from the beach area within the campground.

Head west over the bridge that crosses the Old Pinnebog River Channel. Just past the bridge is the junction for the trail. Go right and follow the outer loop, which mostly flows along with the three major water bodies that define this area of the park—Saginaw Bay, the Pinnebog River, and the Old Pinnebog River Channel. The Old Pinnebog River Channel is the first to accompany you through the canopy of trees along the narrow, gently rolling trail. Listen for splashes in the channel and look for what may be making them. Every so often, a break in the foliage allows a view of the channel.

At .4 mi., you reach your turnoff (.4 mi.) [2]. You want to turn here, but wait. A few steps ahead, a bench overlooks the channel below. Have a seat. East of this, a spur links the trail with the campground.

Return to the junction and follow the trail through the ravinelike trough in the hardwoods. Corrugated hills covered with trees envelop you as you wind your way. You pass between two large trunks poised tightly on either side of the trail like sentinels guarding their post (.6 mi.) [3]. The post, with a blue diamond, reassures you that you are on the right trail. Watch for more such posts with blue diamonds as the trail winds again through undulating terrain before veering sharply to the north (right). Soon the trail winds left, and you get a view of Saginaw Bay (.8 mi.) [4].

A trail enters from the left. Stay right, however, and the trail reaches another well-worn path. A right takes you to another overlook of the bay; a bench and another junction mark this spot, which separates the red and blue trails (1 mi.) [5]. You could shorten your hike by taking a left here to go back to the bridge but continue walking along the westerly route, where the trail will veer right. You reach a bluff where you see the bay and, in a few more steps, the Pinnebog River spilling into the bay (1 mi.) [6].

The trail climbs steeply, and many paths cut through this area. Watch for red paint marks on the trees and try to follow the worn trail. The trail follows along the ridge over the Pinnebog River. The trail swings east, and you're hiking through woods. When the path gets close to where the organization camp had been, you will know it—several trails cut through. Just watch ahead for the trees marked red. At 1.7 mi., you reach the blue trail [7]. Turn right and soon you will come back to the iron bridge where you left your vehicle.

1. Trailhead
2. Channel overlook; trail turnoff
3. Tree sentinels at post
4. Bay overlook
5. Short loop junction
6. Bay and Pinnebog River overlook
7. Blue trail junction

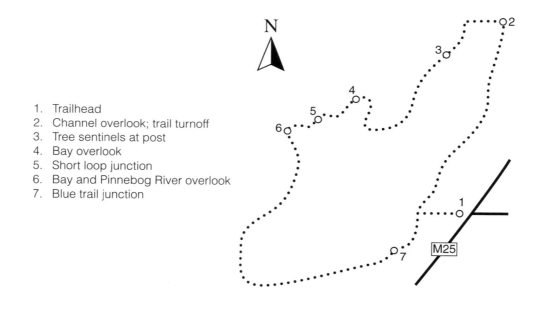

Day-Use Area Trail

Distance Round-Trip: 2.7 miles
Estimated Hiking Time: 1.5 hours

Cautions: Low areas are prone to flooding. Wear appropriate footgear. Stay on marked trails when you hike in the dunes. Take insect repellent.

Trail Directions: The trail begins at the fitness trail sign board at the west side of the day-use area's west parking lot **[1]**. Heading right, along the crushed stone of the old fitness trail—the exercise stations have been removed—you reach the first missing station on a rise overlooking the Pinnebog River Drain (.1 mi.) **[2]**. The trail swings right, following the drain through dune grass, providing scenic overlooks of Lake Huron. Descending the dune, you arrive at the 1,000-foot boardwalk covered with sand that dominates the eastern end of the day-use area (.2 mi.) **[3]**. Continue past the boardwalk.

At .3 mi., the trail cuts to the right, away from the fitness trail **[4]**. Denoting the hiking trail is a hard-to-spot brown post. Now a hiking trail, the surface is made of sandy or natural material, and it guides you through jack pines.

Continue past an old two-track at a brown post. The trail enters a sandy section and makes a hairpin turn to the right, along the back side of a dune (.8 mi.) **[5]**. Be sure to follow the brown posts because the trail can be hard to spot in the sand. Plow a short distance through the sand and then follow the trail as it cuts left and climbs into a hardwood forest (.9 mi.) **[6]**. Stop to enjoy the view of Lake Huron.

Shortly after you enter the woods, turn left to parallel the Lake Huron shoreline. As you walk through the woods along old beach ridges, the lake is often not visible. You will notice, however, a number of paths that provide access to the lake. Brown posts now have white triangles. Keep straight at a trail junction (1.1 mi.) **[7]**. At 1.3 mi., the trail swings left, almost reaching the westernmost end of the park **[8]**. As the trail loops back, it runs at an angle to the lake, parallel to M-25. Stay straight at a junction (1.4 mi.) **[9]**. The trail takes you up and over a series of old dune ridges and down into shallow areas called swales that may be seasonally wet. A footbridge is located over one such swale (1.6 mi.) **[10]**.

A notable bend takes you along the back side of a ridge that you have already climbed. Watch next for the trail markers at 2 mi. that lead you left (the ones to the right lead you to the gatehouse at the day-use entrance) **[11]**. Soon you reach a junction. Turn right.

At 2.2 mi., keep right at the pole **[12]**. The trail leaves the shelter of the woods and snakes its way along the perimeter of an open dune. Soon you rejoin the fitness trail for the last leg of your journey (2.4 mi.) **[13]**. Turn right. The boardwalk over the Pinnebog River Drain is a gentle reminder of the boardwalk at the beach (2.6 mi.) **[14]**. Grab your swimsuit and head for the beach before returning to the day-use parking area.

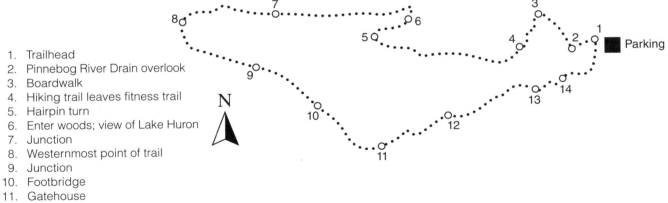

1. Trailhead
2. Pinnebog River Drain overlook
3. Boardwalk
4. Hiking trail leaves fitness trail
5. Hairpin turn
6. Enter woods; view of Lake Huron
7. Junction
8. Westernmost point of trail
9. Junction
10. Footbridge
11. Gatehouse
12. Pole
13. Fitness trail
14. Boardwalk

53. Detroit International Riverfront

- Ride the carousel.
- Watch freighters.
- Frolic in the fountain.
- Look south to Canada.

Park Information

A riverfront pathway, the RiverWalk, spanning about 5.5 miles from the Ambassador Bridge on the west to Gabriel Richard Plaza beyond the MacArthur Bridge on the east, is the central focus of the nonprofit Detroit Riverfront Conservancy. Created in 2003, the conservancy is charged with the cleanup and improvement of the Detroit riverfront.

The coming-out party for the East Riverfront portion of the RiverWalk was a grand six-day celebration held in June 2007—the first annual International River Days. Two new plazas were unveiled. The Rivard Plaza features a one-of-a-kind carousel that has sculpted creatures both mythical and native to the Detroit River, an inlaid granite map of the Detroit River system, and a standing glass map of the St. Lawrence Seaway. The Gabriel Richard Plaza features fishing platforms, butterfly gardens, and a meditative labyrinth. Both plazas have concessions, restrooms, water fountains, and canopy-like pavilions.

But stay tuned. More is to come. At this writing, one-quarter of the East Riverfront is unfinished, work on the West Riverfront has yet to begin, and two more plazas are planned.

Directions: Park at a free lot off Atwater and Rivard. From Jefferson turn south on Rivard and then turn east onto Atwater. For other parking options, call the conservancy at the number provided later.

Hours Open: The RiverWalk is open year-round. Call the conservancy for the carousel schedule.

Facilities: Hiking, biking, inline skating, fishing, dog walking, sightseeing, picnicking, boating, and boat tours.

Permits and Rules: The RiverWalk is free. The carousel costs $1 per ride. Bike riders and inline skaters must yield to pedestrians. Fish only in designated areas. Pets must be on a leash. Pick up and properly dispose of pet waste. Swimming, camping, campfires, grills, and alcoholic beverages are not permitted. Unauthorized motor vehicles are not allowed. Do not climb on guardrails. Vagrancy, vending, and solicitation are not permitted. Put all trash in the trash receptacles.

For Further Information: Detroit Riverfront Conservancy, Inc., 600 Renaissance Center, Suite 1720, Detroit, MI 48243-1802; 313-566-8200; www.detroit riverfront.org.

Other Points of Interest

Designed by Frederick Law Olmsted, 983-acre **Belle Isle Park** is the largest city-owned island park in America. Visit the Nancy Brown Peace Tower, the Belle Isle Casino, Dossin Great Lakes Museum, Scott Memorial Fountain, and Anna Scripps Whitcomb Conservatory; enjoy 200 acres of woodlands; or cool off at the Belle Beach and water slide. For more information, contact the Detroit Recreation Department, 18100 Meyers, Detroit, MI 48235; 313-224-1158; www .ci.detroit.mi.us/recreation; or contact the Friends of Belle Isle, 8109 East Jefferson, Detroit, MI 48214; 313-331-7760; www.fobi.org.

Tri-Centennial State Park and Harbor, the first urban state park, offers several covered picnic areas, shoreline fishing, and a 52-slip harbor of refuge. A scaled-down replica of the lighthouse at Tawas Point marks the harbor entrance. Further developments will highlight the natural habitats found throughout Michigan's state parks. For more information, contact Tri-Centennial State Park and Harbor, 1900 Atwater Street, Detroit, MI 48207; 313-396-0217.

Park Trails

When completed, the 3.5-mile East RiverWalk will link parks, plazas, and greenways from Hart Plaza to Gabriel Richard Plaza east of Belle Isle. The West RiverWalk will extend to Riverside Park, west of the Ambassador Bridge. The Dequindre Cut is a rails-to-trails project that when completed will connect the RiverWalk to the neighborhoods to the north and to Gratiot near Eastern Market. The conservancy will maintain it.

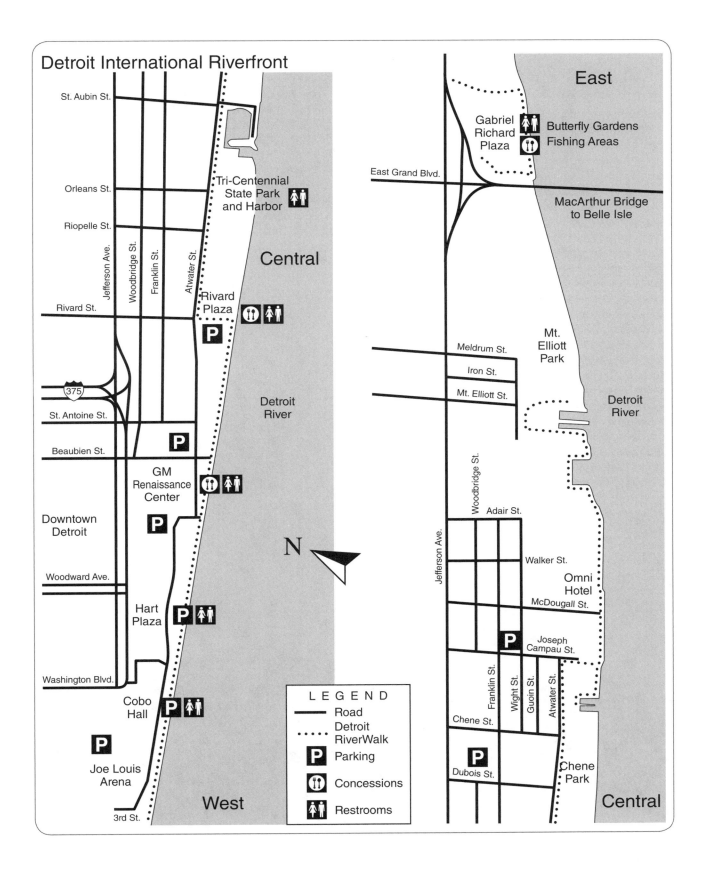

Detroit International Riverfront

St. Aubin St.

Orleans St.

Riopelle St.

Jefferson Ave.
Woodbridge St.
Franklin St.
Atwater St.

Rivard St.

Tri-Centennial
State Park
and Harbor

Central

Rivard
Plaza

375

St. Antoine St.

Beaubien St.

Detroit
River

GM
Renaissance
Center

Downtown
Detroit

Woodward Ave.

N

Hart Plaza

Washington Blvd.

Cobo
Hall

Joe Louis
Arena

West

3rd St.

East

Gabriel
Richard
Plaza

Butterfly Gardens
Fishing Areas

East Grand Blvd.

MacArthur Bridge
to Belle Isle

Mt.
Elliott
Park

Detroit
River

Meldrum St.

Iron St.

Mt. Elliott St.

Woodbridge St.

Jefferson Ave.

Adair St.

Walker St.

Omni
Hotel

McDougall St.

Joseph
Campau St.

Franklin St.
Wight St.
Guoin St.
Atwater St.

Chene St.

Chene
Park

Dubois St.

Central

LEGEND
Road
Detroit
RiverWalk
Parking
Concessions
Restrooms

East RiverWalk

🐾 **Distance Round-Trip:** 2.5 miles
🐾 **Estimated Hiking Time:** 45 minutes to 1 hour

Cautions: You will be in the open along the river. Bring sunscreen and a hat.

Trail Directions: Start from the Rivard Plaza parking lot located at 1340 E. Atwater Street **[1]**. This is a popular spot. Watch children's faces light up as they go 'round on the sculpted creatures of the carousel. Become a kid yourself. Stroll past the fountain and the people seated under the tent canopy. Step lightly on the inlaid granite map of the Detroit River system before pausing to admire the standing glass map of the St. Lawrence Seaway. Scan the river for freighters and waterfowl. Look south at the Windsor, Canada, skyline. Then head west toward the towering GM Renaissance Center under the watchful eyes of seagulls.

As you walk downstream, you can go just as fast as the water, 1 to 3 feet per second, but what's the rush? Stop and watch as children play in the multispout fountains at the big public plaza at the GM Renaissance Center (.4 mi.) **[2]**. Become a kid yourself.

After leaving the tiled walk at the Ren Cen, the trail makes a jog. This is the general area where Great Lakes cruise ships will be allowed to dock in the future. You then pass Diamond Jack's River Boat Tours to arrive at Hart Plaza and the Gateway to Freedom Sculpture (.8 mi.) **[3]**. Stop and admire this International Under-

ground Railroad Memorial. Study the figures and the map identifying the routes to Detroit and safe house locations. Stop, too, and admire local artists' work.

You pass the docked *Detroit Princess* just before you reach Cobo Hall, where the people mover moves noisily above you (1.1 mi.) **[4]**. Check the luck of those who are fishing as you reach the end of the trail by the spiral tower behind the Joe Louis Arena (1.3 mi.) **[5]**. If you walk up and around the spiral tower, you can add .3 mi. to your walk. Go ahead and take it for a spin. At the top you get a good look downstream at the Ambassador Bridge. In the future the RiverWalk will stretch that far. For now this is as far as you can go, so turn around and retrace your steps upstream to the Rivard Plaza.

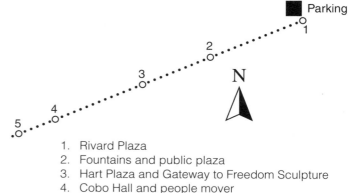

1. Rivard Plaza
2. Fountains and public plaza
3. Hart Plaza and Gateway to Freedom Sculpture
4. Cobo Hall and people mover
5. Spiral tower

54. Wm. C. Sterling State Park

- Visit the only state park on Lake Erie.
- View migratory birds at this major flyway.
- Enjoy recreational opportunities within an hour of Detroit.

Park Information

Enjoy boating, shore fishing on Lake Erie and fishing lagoons, lakeside camping, wildlife viewing, and 6 miles of paved trails—all within an hour's drive of Detroit. Wm. C. Sterling State Park has the distinction of being the only state park on Lake Erie.

The day-use area of the 1,300-acre park includes a .5-mile sandy beach. The new campground, located on the shore of Lake Erie, provides lake views and a sandy beach. A 2.8-mile paved trail loop circles one of the three lagoons in the marshland; another .6-mile trail flows along the shoreline. About 320 acres of globally significant Great Lakes marsh and lake-plain prairie habitat are being restored to what grew in the park over 200 years ago.

Launch your boat to enjoy Lake Erie, fish onshore at one of three fishing piers, or access the River Raisin. Birdwatchers find the park a great place to see waterfowl; it is a major flyway for many migratory birds.

Although it is not a natural park as most are—it has paved trails and some unquestionably urban views, such as one of the Detroit Edison plant—the park offers a quick getaway from the confines of urban life.

Directions: The park is near Monroe on the south side of Dixie Highway, less than a mile east of I-75, exit 15.

Hours Open: The park is open daily.

Facilities: Hiking, interpretive stations, biking, playground, fishing, swimming, camping (RV), boat launch, and picnicking.

Permits and Rules: A park fee is required for motor vehicles ($6 daily, $24 annually for residents; $8 daily, $29 annually for nonresidents). Alcohol is prohibited in the day-use areas from April 1 through September 30 except with the written permission of the park manager.

For Further Information: Wm. C. Sterling State Park, 2800 State Park Road, Monroe, MI 48162; 734-289-2715.

Other Points of Interest

Bird watchers can take delight in two other freshwater marshes nearby. **Pointe Mouillee State Game Area** is one of the largest freshwater marsh restoration projects in the world. Enjoy the waterfowl, shorebirds, and other wetland wildlife that visit the wetlands, diked marshes, and river bayous of the 4,000-acre game area. For more information, contact the Pointe Mouillee State Game Area headquarters, 37205 Mouillee Road, Route 2, Rockwood, MI 48173; 734-379-9692. Weaving islands, shoals, coastal wetlands, marshes, and waterfront lands along 48 miles of Detroit River and western Lake Erie shoreline, the **Detroit River International Wildlife Refuge** is the only international wildlife refuge in North America. Near the park, it incorporates the **Humbug Marsh** and **Erie Marsh Preserve**. For more information, contact Detroit River International Wildlife Refuge, Large Lakes Research Station, 9311 Groh Road, Grosse Ile, MI 48138; 734-692-7608.

For information about the Monroe area, contact the Monroe County Convention and Tourism Bureau at www.monroeinfo.com.

Southern
Lower
Peninsula

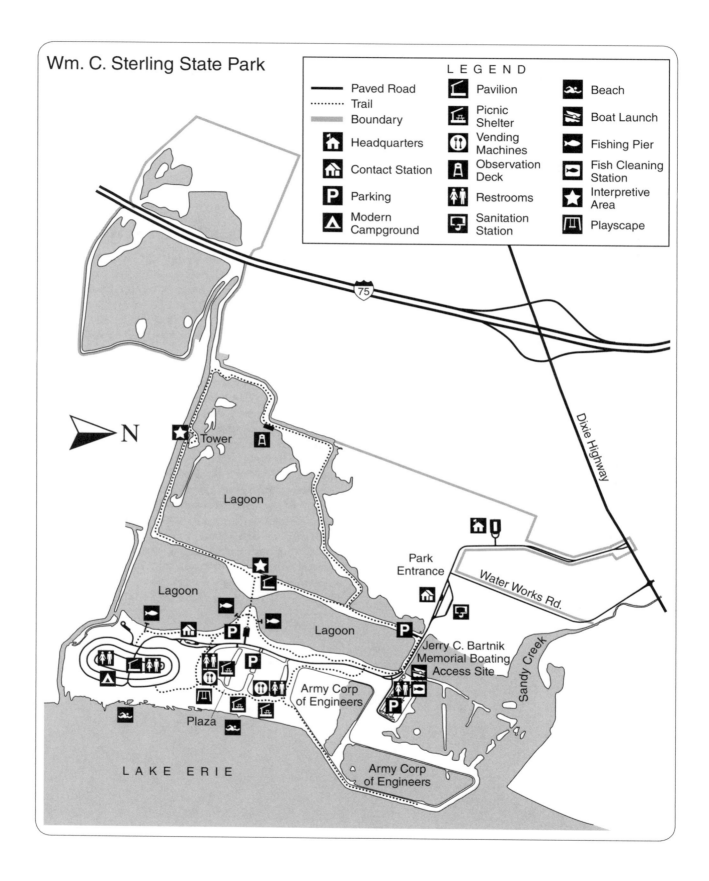

Wm. C. Sterling State Park

LEGEND

— Paved Road
····· Trail
Boundary

Headquarters
Contact Station
P Parking
Modern Campground

Pavilion
Picnic Shelter
Vending Machines
Observation Deck
Restrooms
Sanitation Station

Beach
Boat Launch
Fishing Pier
Fish Cleaning Station
Interpretive Area
Playscape

75

Dixie Highway

Tower

Lagoon

Lagoon

Lagoon

Park Entrance

Water Works Rd.

Jerry C. Bartnik Memorial Boating Access Site

Sandy Creek

Army Corp of Engineers

Plaza

Army Corp of Engineers

LAKE ERIE

N

Sterling Marsh Trail

Distance Round-Trip: 3.1 miles
Estimated Hiking Time: 1 to 1.5 hours

Cautions: Watch for poison ivy along the asphalt-paved trail. You share the trail with bicyclists. Bring binoculars and a bird identification book. Take insect repellent in warm months.

Trail Directions: Park in the small lot north of the day-use area parking lot. Head along the asphalt path toward the lagoons [1]. Don't let the view of the power plant off in the distance to your left fool you. This restorative trail makes amends. A sign on this interpretive trail describes the 320 acres here as globally significant Great Lakes marsh and lake-plain prairie. An ecological restoration is under way to convert the area back to the habitat that existed over 200 years ago.

Cross the bridge between the two lagoons (.1 mi.) [2] and go on to the interpretive pavilion at the third lagoon (.2 mi.) [3]. Learn about the marsh habitat and the innumerable birds in it. Break out your binoculars or use the spotting scope. Off-season, the lagoon is host to a plethora of birds. One can only imagine what spring and fall migrations bring.

Follow to the left. Trees shade the trail as you stroll on the dikes between lagoons. Swallows swoop past you. You see power lines in the distance, a reminder of why restoration is needed. Egrets splash offshore.

Benches rest at the trail curve (.6 mi.) [4]. Follow the curve. Now you walk between a creek and lagoon. Urbanization crackles overhead as you pass beneath power lines that contrast with the natural environment around them. Songs of birds compete with the buzzing of automobiles.

Swing right over a small footbridge (.9 mi.) [5]. Soon afterward, you reach a viewing tower. Be careful climbing up.

Stay on the asphalt at the curve (1.3 mi.) as you again mix nature with urban appurtenances [6]. Soon pass again under power lines and then by a sea of cattails waving at you in the breeze. An observation deck at 1.6 mi. provides an overlook for the waves of green cattails and of phragmites, the tall invasive reed that can grow to 15 feet [7].

The trail becomes more shaded. Soon you pass a golf course, a bench, and then another. A marsh separates you from the subdivision on the left. A doe and her fawn hide in the grasses as herons stab at the water and swans glide softly away. Swallows ornament the branches of a dead tree. Forget about that power plant off in the distance.

Stay right at the junction (2.6 mi.) [8] and walk between the grasses and cattails that veil the lagoons on either side. When you reach the pavilion (2.9 mi.) [3], get those glasses out again to view the ever-changing occupants of the marsh. Then turn left to head back to the parking lot.

1. Trailhead
2. Bridge
3. Pavilion
4. Benches at curve
5. Footbridge
6. Trail curves
7. Observation deck
8. Junction

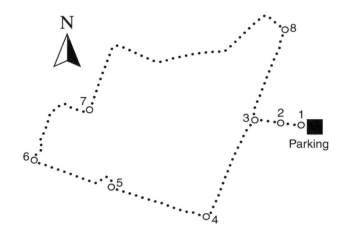

55. William P. Holliday Forest and Wildlife Preserve

- Visit a forest of towering beech, maple, and oak trees.
- Look for signs of deer and other wildlife.
- Enjoy a quiet moment along Tonquish Creek.

Park Information

Established in the late 1950s, this site of more than 500 acres served for decades as southeast Michigan's only dedicated wildlife preserve. The park was a gift to the citizens of Wayne County from the late Arthur J. Richardson in honor of his uncle, William P. Holliday.

The preserve is long and slender, like Tonquish Creek, which it hugs. It contains 10 miles of trails that wind through the varied habitats, including upland forests, meadows, wetlands, and thickets. The trails that follow the creek date back to the days of the Potawatomi Indians. Chief Tonquish was killed and buried on the lands within the preserve.

Not all the trails are well marked. Stop in Nankin Mills Interpretive Center to pick up a map. While there, visit displays of the natural and cultural history of the Rouge River watershed. Plan to be surprised by the natural beauty preserved in the park.

Directions: To reach the east trailhead, south of Nankin Mills, exit on Farmington Road from I-96. Head south about 2 miles on Farmington Road to Joy Road. Turn right on Joy Road and then left to access Hines Drive. Parking is available at Nankin Mills.

Hours Open: The park is open one-half hour before sunrise to one-half hour after sunset. Nankin Mills Interpretive Center is open Mondays through Saturdays from 9:00 a.m. to 4:00 p.m.

Facilities: Hiking, interpretive center, and picnicking.

Permits and Rules: There is no admission fee. Visitors are not permitted to possess alcoholic beverages; injure, deface, or disturb any structure; remove any trees, flowers, or natural objects; hunt, trap, or molest animals; have firearms, slingshots, or any other dangerous weapons; dispose of refuse; wander off established roads and trails; or disturb the peace. No swimming is allowed. Only pedestrian travel is allowed. Respect that any part of the park may be closed at any time.

For Further Information: Wayne County Department of Parks and Recreation, 33175 Ann Arbor Trail, Westland, MI 48185; 734-261-1990.

Other Points of Interest

The east end of the preserve is connected to the **Hines Parkway**, which spans 17 miles and offers varied recreational facilities. For more information, contact the Wayne County Department of Parks and Recreation.

Two driving tours highlight the mills that Henry Ford converted or established between 1919 and 1944. For information on the **Ford Heritage Trails**, contact the Wayne County Department of Parks and Recreation.

You can spend hours walking through the many buildings and artifacts collected at Greenfield Village and Henry Ford Museum. For more information call the **Henry Ford Museum** at 313-982-6001 or 800-835-5237; www.hfmgv.org.

Park Trails

Ellsworth and Acorn Trails (👣👣, .6 miles). Start across the street from Nankin Mills. The trail follows the Middle Rouge River and loops through upland oaks.

Wildflower Trail (👣👣, 1.5 mile). Start from the Central City Parkway entrance. The trail comes alive with color in the spring.

Fox Trail (👣, 1 mile). Park at the Koppernick entrance. The trail loops through field and forest.

William P. Holliday Forest and Wildlife Preserve

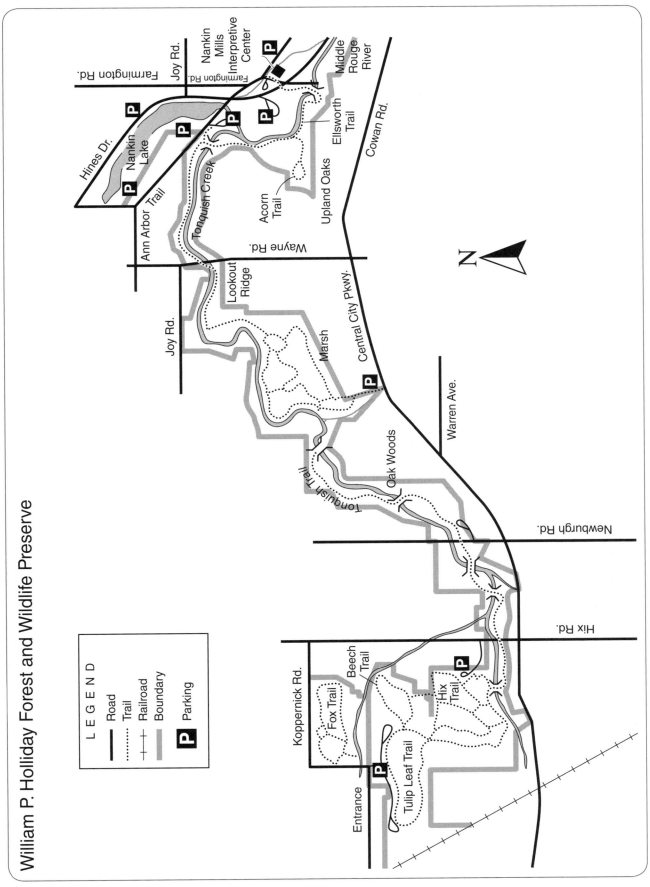

LEGEND
- Road
- Trail
- Railroad
- Boundary
- **P** Parking

N

Farmington Rd.

Joy Rd.

Nankin Mills Interpretive Center

Nankin Lake

Hines Dr.

Ann Arbor Trail

Tonquish Creek

Ellsworth Trail

Middle Rouge River

Cowan Rd.

Acorn Trail

Upland Oaks

Wayne Rd.

Joy Rd.

Lookout Ridge

Marsh

Central City Pkwy.

Warren Ave.

Oak Woods

Tonquish Trail

Newburgh Rd.

Hix Rd.

Koppernick Rd.

Fox Trail

Beech Trail

Tulip Leaf Trail

Hix Trail

Entrance

Tulip Leaf–Beech Trails

Distance Round-Trip: 1.9 miles
Estimated Hiking Time: 1 hour

Cautions: Watch for exposed roots, slippery logs, loose boardwalks, and poison ivy. Take insect repellent in warm months.

Trail Directions: Park west of Hix Road on Koppernick Road in the lot on the south side of the road **[1]**. Start from the southern barricade and head southwest through something remarkable—an old-growth forest with beautiful giants; namely, beeches, maples, and oaks.

Follow the wide path that was once a drive to the picnic area. Crane your neck at the awesome beeches and maples. You may wonder if you are really in Wayne County. Violets and ferns soften the trail edges. Marvel at the smooth, smoky gray bark of the beeches. An occasional oak tree towers above you (.1 mi.) **[2]**. Through the woods, you see residences. OK, you are in Wayne County, but at least you are in rolling woods, where the massive elders of the forest seem to keep the outside world at bay.

The fork at .3 mi. **[3]** is an old cul-de-sac that led to the now overgrown and rusting picnic shelter. Whichever way you go, the trail winds up at the post for the Tulip Leaf Trail. Embark on the narrow trail through the forest. Depressional pockets envelop the trail as you continue through the hardwoods, littered in places with fallen comrades (.4 mi.) **[4]**.

Veer left and pass another pocket of civilization. Pass a short stretch of mobile homes before veering away from them to reenter solitude. Pass more downed trees; large, sinuous vines drape from those that remain standing (.5 mi.) **[5]**. Cross logs in the seasonal low-lying wet areas that the trail winds through.

In the dense woods, boughs moan. Before, and especially after, you reach the junction for the Tonquish Trail (.9 mi.) **[6]**, you pass beech trees—the unfortunate graffiti boards of the lovelorn. Their size and smooth bark seem to invite the scarring of initials and hearts. Turn left.

Veer left where ferns soften the turn. A post and bench announce the Beech Trail (1.1 mi.) **[7]**. To your left, posts that once supported a picnic shelter now stand rusting and bare, like the lifeless ghosts of trees.

Turn right into the woods past a small stand of white pines. Sassafras trees with mitten-shaped leaves grow beneath beeches, oaks, and maples. Loop around, pass another junction, and descend to a fence line of twigs. Soon you cross a narrow footbridge over a stream (1.3 mi.) **[8]**.

The trail veers sharply left (1.4 mi.) **[9]**; a drainage ditch to your right delineates the forest from commercial properties. Keep rounding the curve as your veiled view through the trees shows residences and then woods. Pass more beech graffiti boards. Large vines snake over the trail before you cross some logs strewn over the wet-prone path. Then walk the footbridge with a bench back over the stream (1.6 mi.) **[10]**.

A dilapidated boardwalk of patchwork materials assists you through the wetland. Reeds line the trail, and large vines drape from the canopies like sinuous netting. Brushy foliage closes in on the trail to form a tunnel, but you break into the open at 1.7 mi. where restrooms once stood (only a ceramic tile floor remains) **[11]**. Cut over to the wide path and turn right back to the small parking lot.

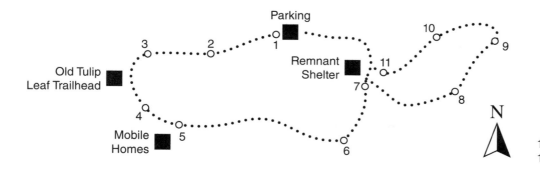

1. Trailhead
2. Large oak
3. Cul-de-sac
4. Fallen trees
5. Fallen trees, sinuous vines
6. Tonquish Trail junction
7. Beech Trail junction
8. Cross stream
9. Veer left
10. Recross stream
11. Ceramic tile floor

Ellsworth–Tonquish–Wildflower Trails

Distance Round-Trip: 3.5 miles
Estimated Hiking Time: 2 to 3 hours

Cautions: The trail may be unmarked in places. Watch for poison ivy. Portions may be wet or flooded. Take insect repellent.

Trail Directions: Begin your adventure across the road from Nankin Mills. A sign at the tree line identifies the starting point **[1]**.

Step into the woods and cross a new bridge over the Middle Rouge River. Turn right as the trail splits to follow the Ellsworth Trail and soon teeter along the edge of the river. Walking up and down along the floodplain in the shade of a mix of trees, you pass what looks like an overflow channel at .1 mi. **[2]**. Swing left and onto a ridge. Continue through upland oaks to cross a small feeder stream on a footbridge. Make a hairpin curve to the right down steps (.2 mi.) **[3]** and over a small footbridge that crosses Tonquish Creek. The trail is confusing here—follow the worn path as best you can.

Veer left to follow the creek and cross another new bridge at .6 mi. **[4]**. Go left after crossing to walk along the bank. Fallen trees dam up the waterway. At 1 mi., you reach a dilapidated trail shelter **[5]**. Continue along the creek bend and walk along the eroding bank to cross a small footbridge.

Ahead, vehicles intrude on your solitude as they rush by. Swing left over rocks to cross beneath the road and then cross the creek on an old bridge that stands in the shadow of its larger replacement (1.2 mi.) **[6]**. Turn right and follow the south side of the creek.

After edging along the creek, climb to walk along Lookout Ridge (1.4 mi.) **[7]**. The trail undulates and dips down to the edge of the creek. When you reach the missing bridge, turn left and climb a steep bluff to hike a section of the Wildflower Trail (1.6 mi.) **[8]**. Stay to the right as the trail splits, high above the creek, and walk through mixed hardwoods. Stay left when the trail splits and teeter along the eroding edge of a ravine (1.7 mi.) **[9]**. You soon make a left hairpin turn to skirt some apartments. The trail passes through a small white pine grove; needles cushion the trail.

Turn left at the next junction and soon close the Wildflower Trail loop (1.9 mi.) **[8]**. Turn right to descend to the missing bridge. Follow to the right along the Tonquish Trail and retrace your steps to Nankin Mills.

1. Trailhead
2. Overflow channel
3. Steps
4. Bridge
5. Old trail shelter
6. Old road bridge
7. Lookout Ridge
8. Wildflower Trail junction
9. Trail splits

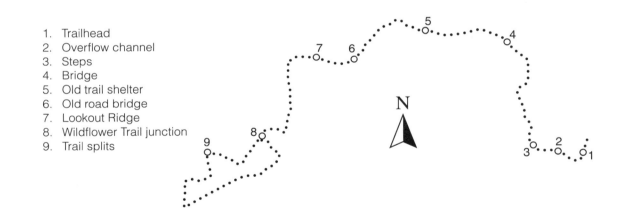

N

56. West Bloomfield Woods Nature Preserve

- View great blue herons nesting from a deck overlooking a rookery.
- Hike through the first site in Michigan recognized as an urban wildlife sanctuary.
- Stroll a trail where trains once rolled.

Park Information

Wandering over steep hills blanketed with oak and hickory and past lush, wooded wetlands in this 162-acre site, you may find it hard to believe that you are only 20 miles from downtown Detroit. More amazing are the sights and sounds preserved at the great blue herons' rookery here, a major reason that West Bloomfield Woods Nature Preserve gained recognition as the first urban wildlife sanctuary in the state.

A 2.1-mile interpretive trail meanders through the preserve, allowing visitors to seek nature on their own. Brochures direct you to the 16 interpretive sites located along the trail. A .5-mile section of the trail is designed for those with physical disabilities.

The preserve also serves as the western trailhead for the 4.3-mile West Bloomfield Trail Network, which follows the route of the Michigan Air Line Railroad, built in the 1870s. The trail cuts through several natural and man-made habitats. The trail has a surface of crushed limestone and is lined with 21 interpretive sites; pick up interpretive brochures at the kiosk near the parking area.

Directions: From I-696, take Orchard Lake Road north about 6 miles to Pontiac Trail. Turn left and go 1.5 miles to Arrowhead Road. Turn left and go about .5 mile to the preserve entrance.

Hours Open: Open from 8:00 a.m. to sunset daily.

Facilities: Hiking, bicycling, and picnicking.

Permits and Rules: No fee is required. All pets must be on a 6-foot leash; clean up after them. Refrain from smoking. No bicycles or horses are permitted in the preserve, although bicycles may use the rail-trail. Motor vehicles, hunting, weapons, fireworks, golf activity, and alcohol are prohibited. Don't remove plants.

For Further Information: West Bloomfield Parks and Recreation, 4640 Walnut Lake Road, West Bloomfield, MI 48323; 248-451-1900; www.westbloomfieldparks.org.

Other Points of Interest

West of the preserve, along a stretch of the Huron River, is the **Proud Lake Recreation Area**. Over 20 miles of hiking, biking, and bridle trails wander through the 4,700-acre park, which provides camping, canoeing, fishing, cross-country skiing, and picnicking facilities. For more information, contact Proud Lake Recreation Area, 3500 Wixom Road, Commerce Township, MI 48382; 248-685-2433.

At the tip of a peninsula that extends into Cass Lake is the **Dodge No. 4 State Park**, an area that has a popular sandy beach and swimming area but no camping facilities or trails. For more information, contact Dodge No. 4 State Park, 4250 Parkway Dive, Waterford, MI 48327; 248-682-7323.

To the northwest lie some 5,900 acres of the **Highland Recreation Area**. Seventeen miles of hiking trails and 12 miles of bridle trails traverse the hilly terrain. The area has a riding stable and facilities for camping, fishing, swimming, cross-country skiing, and picnicking. For more information, contact the Highland Recreation Area, 5200 E. Highland Road, White Lake, MI 48383; 248-889-3750.

West Bloomfield Woods Nature Preserve

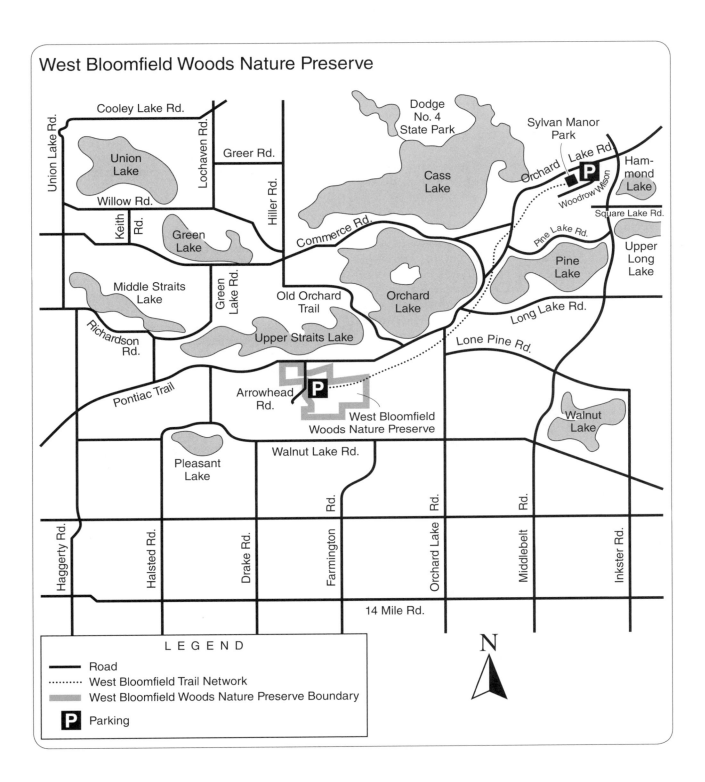

LEGEND

— Road

.... West Bloomfield Trail Network

▬ West Bloomfield Woods Nature Preserve Boundary

P Parking

West Bloomfield Woods Nature Preserve Trail

Distance Round-Trip: 2.1 miles
Estimated Hiking Time: 1 to 1.5 hours

Cautions: Poison ivy lines the trail, so be careful. Take insect repellent in warmer months.

Trail Directions: Start at the information kiosk **[1]** and pick up an interpretive brochure before heading down the crushed limestone path to reach interpretive stop #1. Look carefully at the specimen—it's poison ivy.

A canopy of trees shades you, a pine-lined ridge accompanies you, and a green pool lies low to your right. Pass a large oak, one of many in this preserve, which has one of the oldest oak stands in southeast Michigan. Get a closer look at a wetland after you reach the junction at .2 mi. **[2]**. A boardwalk extends to an overlook for the pond; here you can watch and listen from one of the benches built into the platform.

Continue east. The trail ascends. On your left, look for a blanket of wildflowers in spring. Climbing through oak, hickory, and maple, the trail veers right and over a short boardwalk (.3 mi.) **[3]**. Gently rolling woods envelop the trail.

You reach a junction with a bench at .4 mi. **[4]**. Stay straight, walking through an old-growth forest of oak and hickory, past boulders and fallen trees, and down and left, bypassing post #8 and the vernal pond that it highlights. Planks keep your feet dry through a wetland. A bench gives you a quiet place to stop, or you may choose to rest your elbows on the railing of the bridge that crosses a small stream (.7 mi.) **[5]**.

The trail rolls through wooded hills. Round the curve to a lush green pool (.8 mi.) **[6]**. Residences stand dignified on a distant hill, a reminder that the preserve is an urban one. Rest on the bench at an overlook and enjoy the vista of the river below, its narrow valley, and the dense cover of trees hugging the slopes (.9 mi.) **[7]**. Pass through spruce trees along the trail. The single ridgeline becomes a terrace briefly; you then descend to a bowl-like depression before ascending to a junction (1 mi.) **[8]**. Straight ahead, you can see a building. Turn left and wind down over a carpet of reddish gold needles. Your descent culminates at the bridge (1.1 mi.) **[9]**.

Pause as you cross. Listen to the water and enjoy the irises and other foliage clumped together like green, feathery islands in the channel. The winding trail climbs before halting at another junction (1.2 mi.) **[10]**. Turn left and follow the ridge amid the hardwoods.

Reach post #15 (1.4 mi.) **[11]**, which refers your gaze over the ridge, beyond the trees, to the great blue heron rookery. These elegant birds have a haunting beauty, silhouetted in the trees with their scraggly nests. You won't see them from here, though, although you might hear their squawks in springtime.

At 1.5 mi., a bench lets you contemplate the hill; the interpretive brochure informs you that this hill, a moraine, was shaped by mile-high ice **[12]**. This loop of the trail comes full circle just after 1.6 mi. **[13]**. Head right, retracing your steps to the pond overlook (1.8 mi.) **[2]**. Make the hairpin turn right and climb up and around to the West Bloomfield Trail Network (1.9 mi.) **[14]**. If you want, follow the line about .3 mi. to the right to reach the great blue heron rookery.

Otherwise, go straight to walk through second-growth trees—quite a contrast to the forest that you just exited. Wind around; the trees and brush gradually thin out, acclimating you to urban reality before you reach the parking lot.

1. Trailhead
2. Junction at overlook
3. Boardwalk
4. Junction
5. Bridge
6. Bench near pool
7. Overlook of river
8. Junction
9. Bridge
10. Junction
11. Post #15
12. Bench, moraine
13. Trail junction
14. West Bloomfield Trail Network

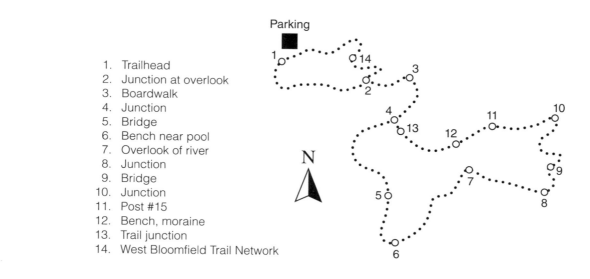

West Bloomfield Trail Network

Distance One-Way: 4.3 miles

Estimated Hiking Time: 1.5 to 2 hours

Cautions: The trail crosses busy Orchard Lake Road three times. On this linear trail, you may turn around at any point to make your hike as short or long (up to 8.6 miles) as you choose.

Trail Directions: Start at the trail kiosk on the south side of the parking area for the West Bloomfield Woods Nature Preserve **[1]**. An alternative starting point is the Sylvan Manor Park on Woodrow Wilson, south of Orchard Lake Road **[11]**. There are 21 interpretive sites along this former railroad corridor. Pick up a guide at the kiosk and head down the crushed limestone path. Imagine a time when trains thundered along on tracks here.

Chug up the slight grade, noting the nature preserve on your right. Picking up speed, pass the first four interpretive sites and the junction with the nature trail at .1 mi. **[2]**. Stop at the decked overlook of the great blue heron rookery (.4 mi.) **[3]**. Spring is a time of great activity here.

Back on the line, pass the stand of spruce that buffers the rookery. Standing like a tombstone is a replica of a railroad mile marker (.6 mi.) **[4]**. This one is W.B. 42, representing the mileage to the terminal.

You soon reach a land bridge through a wet area (.9 mi.) **[5]**. Look for blue heron, hunting patiently. The trail crosses a dirt road where ducks and egrets explore green pools. At about 1.1 mi., the trail skirts an aqua green pond surrounded by palatial homes **[6]**. Pass another tombstone (W.B. 41) before you reach the urban corridor along Orchard Lake Road (1.7 mi.) **[7]**. Jog left to cross at the light.

Beyond the urban corridor, the rail-trail becomes a land bridge and seems to sink below grade as you approach a culvert tunnel (2.2 mi.) **[8]**. Listen to your footsteps echo with metallic pings as you crunch through this safe passage and proceed to an area with an overlook deck on both sides (2.4 mi.) **[9]**. To your left, besides the traffic whizzing by, is an overlook above a small wetland with Orchard Lake in the distance. On the right, a large cattail marsh sprawls between you and Pine Lake.

Cross Orchard Lake Road again and pass your third tombstone (W.B. 40) at 2.6 mi. **[10]**. Pass a ball field before crossing a dirt road and skirting the grounds of St. Mary's College. Arrive at Orchard Lake Road for your last crossing (3.3 mi.) **[11]**.

The corridor opens up on the left for a play lot and picnic area. Press on and reach the last tombstone, W.B. 39 (3.6 mi.) **[12]**. Pass another playground and then enter a tunnel of trees (3.9 mi.) **[13]**. The canopy opens, and the trail takes you behind a small commercial area.

You reach the end of the line here—Sylvan Manor Park (4.3 mi.) **[14]**. If you left a second car or arranged to be picked up, your hike is over. If not, put your engine in reverse and head back to the preserve.

1. Trailhead
2. Nature trail junction
3. Rookery
4. Mile marker 42
5. Wetland
6. Aqua green pond
7. Orchard Lake Road
8. Culvert tunnel
9. Overlook decks
10. Mile marker 40
11. Orchard Lake Road
12. Mile marker 39
13. Tunnel of trees
14. Sylvan Manor Park

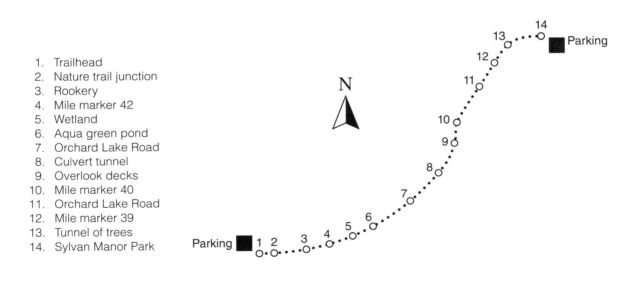

- Visit the Huron Swamp—headwaters of the Huron River.
- Wind along a boardwalk through the swamp and past towering maple trees.
- Explore the 20,000-square-foot Environmental Discovery Center.

Park Information

One of 13 metroparks under the administration of the Huron-Clinton Metropolitan Authority, this 2,217-acre park stands out from the rest in that a large portion of it is dedicated to preserving and interpreting one of southeast Michigan's last great natural areas—the Huron Swamp. From the Huron Swamp flow the headwaters of the Huron River.

The solar-heated nature center at the park offers displays, exhibits, and programs that help explain this unique wetland environment. The center features live and mounted pond creatures, and park naturalists are on hand. Stop by and pick up maps or information about the services provided. The center is the focal point for the three nature trails. Six miles of trails weave through swamps, meadows, fields, and woodlands, offering hikers an intimate experience with the area.

The Environmental Discovery Center also has displays. It features 60 acres of restored or created native ecosystems—ponds, wetlands, and prairies. The building has classrooms, a biology lab, and a 200-person event room. Three short discovery trails branch out from it.

Additional features include an 18-hole public golf course, picnic facilities with grills and shelters, and an 8-mile, barrier-free hike or bike trail for exploring the greater expanses of this exceptional environment. The Meadowlark Picnic Area has a tot lot and a spray 'n' play area.

In winter, 12 miles are groomed for cross-country skiing, and the nature center has a parking lot for sledding.

Directions: The park is about 9 miles northwest of Pontiac. From M-59, take Teggerdine Road north about 3 miles to White Lake Road. Head west for a little more than a mile to the entrance.

Hours Open: The park is open from 8:00 a.m. to 10:00 p.m. during summer. The nature trails are open from daylight until dusk. Hours at the nature center are 10:00 a.m. to 5:00 p.m. daily during summer. During the school year, the center is open from 1:00 to 5:00 p.m. weekdays and from 10:00 a.m. to 5:00 p.m. on weekends. The Environmental Discovery Center is open from 10:00 a.m. to 7:00 p.m. daily from Memorial Day to Labor Day; after that, hours are shortened to 10:00 a.m. to 5:00 p.m.

Facilities: Hiking, bicycling, picnicking, golfing, cross-country skiing, sledding, and interpretive center.

Permits and Rules: A motor vehicle permit is required. Fees are $4 daily and $20 annually. Adhere to posted regulations. If kept on a leash, pets are allowed in the park except at nature areas. Motor vehicles are allowed only on designated park roads and parking areas. Remain on the nature trails when hiking them and picnic only at designated sites. Bicycles, horses, and motorized vehicles are not allowed on the nature trails. Leave natural things where they are.

For Further Information: Indian Springs Metropark, 5200 Indian Trail, White Lake, MI 48386; 248-625-7280. For information on all the metroparks, contact Huron-Clinton Metropolitan Authority, 13000 High Ridge Drive, Brighton, MI 48114-9058; 810-227-2757 or 800-477-2757.

Other Points of Interest

Just south of Indian Springs, and adjacent to it, **Pontiac Lake Recreation Area** opens up 3,745 recreation-packed acres for bicycling, hiking, horseback riding, fishing, hunting, swimming, cross-country skiing, and camping. For more information, contact Pontiac Lake Recreation Area, 7800 Gale Road, Waterford, MI 48327; 248-666-1020.

Park Trails

Pondside Trail (, .3 mile). Start behind the nature center. The hard-surfaced trail loops around a pond. Benches allow visitors to sit and enjoy the setting.

Turkeyfoot Trail (, .5 mile). This discovery trail wanders through tall prairie grasses.

Lupine Loop (, .7 mile). This discovery trail goes through prairies.

Pond Promenade (, .2 mile). This discovery trail circles a pond and passes a marsh and through tall-grass prairie.

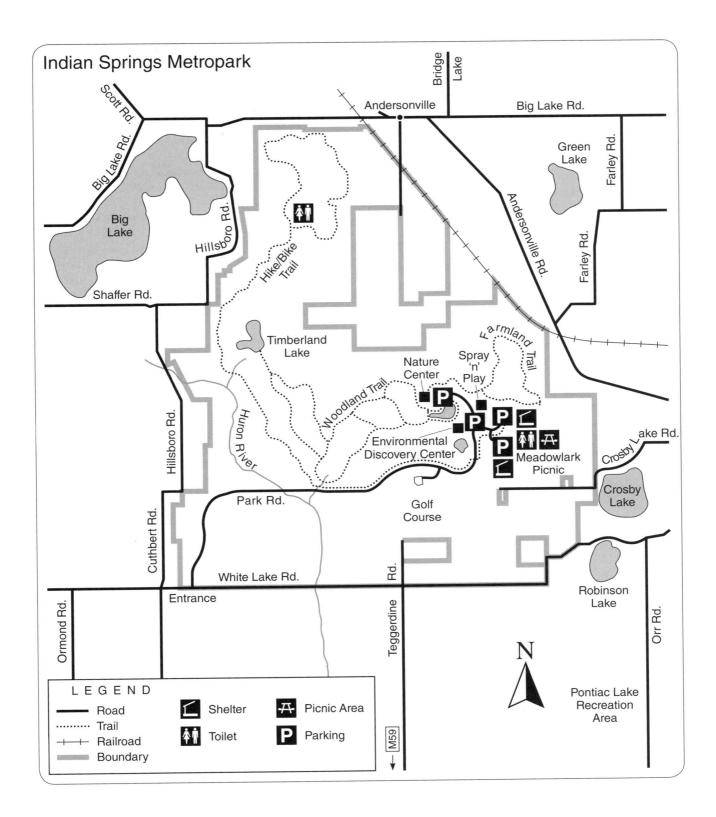

Indian Springs Metropark

Scott Rd.

Big Lake Rd.

Bridge Lake

Andersonville

Big Lake Rd.

Big Lake Rd.

Hillsboro Rd.

Big Lake

Green Lake

Farley Rd.

Shaffer Rd.

Farley Rd.

Hike/Bike Trail

Andersonville Rd.

Timberland Lake

Farmland Trail

Nature Center

Spray 'n' Play

Hillsboro Rd.

Huron River

Woodland Trail

P

Environmental Discovery Center

P **P**

P

Crosby Lake Rd.

Crosby Lake

Meadowlark Picnic

Cuthbert Rd.

Park Rd.

Golf Course

White Lake Rd.

Rd.

Robinson Lake

Ormond Rd.

Entrance

Teggerdine Rd.

N

Orr Rd.

Pontiac Lake Recreation Area

LEGEND

— Road
••••• Trail
+ + Railroad
▬▬ Boundary

▟ Shelter
👫 Toilet

🛖 Picnic Area
P Parking

M59

Woodland Trail

🐾 **Distance Round-Trip:** 3.5 miles
🐾 **Estimated Hiking Time:** 1.5 to 2 hours

Cautions: Stay on the boardwalks. Wet environments are home to Michigan's only poisonous snake—the massasauga. Leave this small, shy rattler alone. Take insect repellent. Boardwalks are slippery when wet.

Trail Directions: Start behind the nature center [1]. Head west. The asphalt trail soon becomes a mowed swath through a meadow; it then goes under a canopy of trees.

An interpretive sign identifies the scraggly looking conifer with eyelash starbursts of needles as a tamarack. This tree serves as a sentinel posted at the bridge. Cross the Huron River, which is streamlike here at its headwaters (.1 mi.) [2]. The bridge evolves into a boardwalk.

A series of boardwalks takes you through luxuriant foliage and past green logs, softened with moss, that lie atop corrugated soil—the effects of the uprooting of trees, nature's way of plowing. More boardwalks carry you along. You reach the Crosscut Shortcut at .4 mi. [3]. Stay right. Sweet woodruff lines the trail. High above you, the canopy is thick.

Pass Hunter's Ridge Shortcut (.6 mi.) [4] and cross between two pools littered with logs, grassy clumps, and green algae. The next stretch alone is worth the hike. Tall stately trunks stretch high above you, silhouettes against the lighter greens of foliage in the background (.7 mi.) [5]. Maples. Huge. Impressive.

Wind through more pools and reach the Sawmill Shortcut at .8 mi. [6]. Stay right, curving along a boardwalk that makes a U-turn through the reeds and pools. Sinuous turns take you under remarkable beech and maple trees and over a boardwalk that wraps around a pool. Boardwalks lace through the wetland; one curves around to the junction for the Timberland Lake Walk (1.5 mi.) [7].

Follow the curving boardwalk through lush foliage that hugs its sides. You see the small, intimate lake up ahead as you follow the boardwalk over a bog. The boardwalk becomes an overlook with benches at the edge of the lake (1.7 mi.) [8].

On the main trail, wind around onto a crescent-shaped boardwalk. Pass through woods, small clearings, and pools. At 2.1 mi., a bench announces the beginning of a long, S-shaped boardwalk that crosses a particularly large swampy area [9]. More boardwalks await you.

Large maples again grace you before you reach the Sawmill Shortcut (2.3 mi.) [10]. Stay right. Youthful growth follows.

Wind along and cross a footbridge over the Huron River (2.6 mi.) [11]. At 3 mi., a bench overlooks a small meadow [12].

Cross the Hunter's Ridge Shortcut (3.1 mi.) [13], passing through second-growth trees. More grasses and reeds envelop you, and then you pass the Crosscut Shortcut (3.3 mi.) [14]. The trail is now a mowed path. At the junction, veer left and walk by a wildflower garden. Pass the Pondside Trail, cross a small bridge, and arrive at the intersection of trails where you started.

1. Trailhead
2. Bridge
3. Crosscut Shortcut junction
4. Hunter's Ridge Shortcut junction
5. Maples
6. Sawmill Shortcut
7. Timberland Lake Walk junction
8. Timberland Lake
9. Boardwalk
10. Sawmill Shortcut
11. Bridge
12. Bench
13. Hunter's Ridge Shortcut
14. Crosscut Shortcut

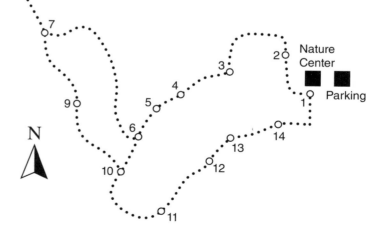

Farmland Trail

Distance Round-Trip: 1.6 miles
Estimated Hiking Time: 30 minutes to
1 hour

Cautions: The park is home to the massasauga rattlesnake. Leave this small, shy snake alone. Poison ivy lines the trail. Use insect repellent in warm months.
Trail Directions: This interpretive trail starts at a map board near a shelter at the north end of the nature center parking lot **[1]**. Head east between the park driveway and a wetland.

After descending slightly, veer left, pass a large oak, and enter a fencerow of trees. Ascending, you cut through an old fence line, the first of many that you cross, before winding left to walk along an old drive.

The trail veers right to skirt the edge of a forest. Walking along the forest boundary, you make a wide left, pass an erratic (a boulder transported by a glacier) (.2 mi.) **[2]**, descend sharply around a wetland burrowed in among the trees, and cross a footbridge.

Undulating along the transition area between forest and field, you cut through shrubs and skirt past blackberry, aspen, and gray dogwood. Then cross a land bridge between two wetlands before climbing to a junction (.4 mi.) **[3]**. Stay left to hike the loop in a clockwise direction.

Following an old fence line, jog right and enter a field of goldenrod. A bench allows you to sit and enjoy the golden moment, and provides a base from which to identify types of goldenrod found here.

Cross the field; then cut through mixed hardwoods to reach a larger field. Stay along the edge of forest and field. Don't sit down on that mound to your right. The ants won't appreciate it. Stop to investigate a rusting piece of farm equipment, where there is a bench under a pine tree (.6 mi.) **[4]**.

Pass more ant mounds. The trail winds, skirting a wetland, and takes you to a bench shaded by a green canopy (.8 mi.) **[5]**.

Pass more ant mounds. At 1 mi., a bench is situated to overlook a field to the southwest **[6]**. Beyond this, discover an old plow. Then walk along a line of old oaks that witnessed the work of a relic farm implement when it was in its prime.

The trail makes a sharp right, crossing the fence line of large trees and fieldstones, to arrive at another collection of retired farm equipment (1.1 mi.) **[7]**. Roll with the landscape and veer left to cross a fallow field emerging into a meadow. Unlike the implements, keep plowing on. You don't want to rust like this fourth collection of farm equipment (1.2 mi.) **[8]**.

From here you have only to descend into some trees and shrubs and cross another old fence line to arrive back at the junction that closes the loop (1.3 mi.) **[3]**. Turn left and retrace your steps along the transition area to the nature center.

1. Trailhead
2. Glacial erratic
3. Trail junction
4. Bench
5. Bench
6. Bench
7. Farm equipment
8. Farm equipment

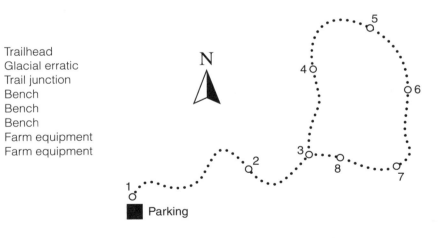

- Discover fresh air and sunshine.
- Explore the history of a tuberculosis sanatorium.
- Relive history at the rebuilt Maybury Farm.

Park Information

The 944-acre Maybury State Park is more than the 5 miles of mountain bike trails, more than 6 miles of hiking trails, more than the 4 miles of paved biking trails, and more than the 11 miles of equestrian trails. The rolling terrain of woods and open meadows offers people in the surrounding metropolitan area wonderful opportunities with these trails, but there is more.

At the beginning of the 20th century, tuberculosis infected a large percentage of the population. The City of Detroit, at the behest of William H. Maybury, purchased eight farms in Northville to construct a sanatorium that emphasized providing fresh air and sunshine to help with the long healing process of tuberculosis. Construction began in 1919 of what was to become a self-contained community of more than 40

buildings, including infirmaries, staff homes, a power plant, water plant, pasteurization plant, fire protection, and even a farm to produce the food and milk consumed there. In the late 1940s, effective antibiotic treatment became available for tuberculosis. The last patient at the sanatorium transferred in August 1969. Aside from a handful of homes, the buildings were destroyed before the park took ownership. Today a Heritage Trail weaves around to empty sites that housed the buildings. Interpretive plaques give their histories.

In 2003 Maybury Farm suffered a tragic loss as fire destroyed barns, animals, and machinery. The farm has since been rebuilt and offers tours. The farm has a separate entrance from the park. If you don't own a horse, the Maybury Riding Stable off Beck Road does, so get out and enjoy the trails.

Directions: The farm is located on 8 Mile Road between Napier and Beck roads in Northville. The farm entrance is west of the park entrance. Equestrians enter off Beck Road. The farm is 5 miles west of I-275 or 4 miles south of I-96.

Hours Open: The park is open daily from 8:00 a.m. until dusk. The horse stable is open from April through November from 9:00 a.m. until 6:00 p.m. It is closed Mondays. The farm is closed for the winter season.

Facilities: Hiking, bicycling, mountain biking, equestrian trails, riding stable, picnicking, fishing pond, playground, picnic shelter, and cross-country skiing.

Permits and Rules: A park fee is required for motor vehicles ($6 daily, $24 annually for residents; $8 daily, $29 annually for nonresidents). The farm has no fee. Alcohol is prohibited from all areas of the park from April 1 through Labor Day except with written authorization of the park manager. Horses are permitted only on marked trails.

For Further Information: Maybury State Park, 20145 Beck Road, Northville, MI 48167; 248-349-8390. Maybury Farm is administered by the Northville Community Foundation. Contact them at 248-374-0200. Contact the Maybury Riding Stable at 20303 Beck Road, Northville, MI 48167; 248-347-1088.

Other Points of Interest

Island Lake Recreation Area, a 4,000-acre park in Livingston County, provides plenty of room for canoeing, biking, hiking, swimming, and picnicking. For more information, contact Island Lake Recreation Area, 12950 E. Grand River Avenue, Brighton, MI 48116; 810-229-7067.

Maybury State Park

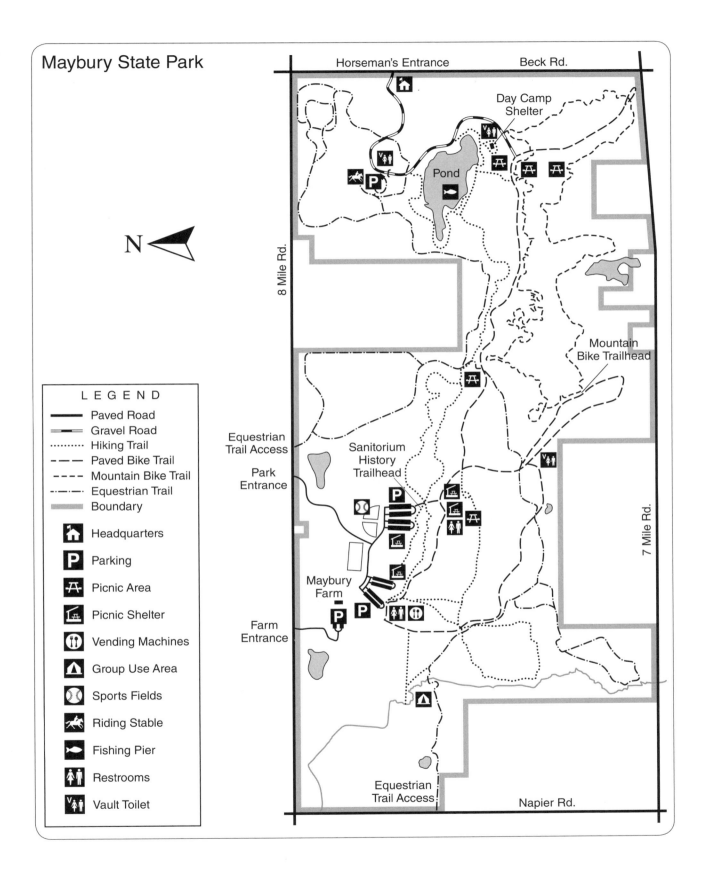

LEGEND

———	Paved Road
⊐═⊐	Gravel Road
········	Hiking Trail
– – –	Paved Bike Trail
- - -	Mountain Bike Trail
-·-·-	Equestrian Trail
▬▬▬	Boundary

Headquarters
P	Parking
Picnic Area
Picnic Shelter
Vending Machines
Group Use Area
Sports Fields
Riding Stable
Fishing Pier
Restrooms
V	Vault Toilet

N

Horseman's Entrance
Beck Rd.

Day Camp Shelter

Pond

8 Mile Rd.

Mountain Bike Trailhead

Equestrian Trail Access

Park Entrance

Sanitorium History Trailhead

7 Mile Rd.

Maybury Farm

Farm Entrance

Equestrian Trail Access

Napier Rd.

History Trail

Distance Round-Trip: 1.2 miles

Estimated Hiking Time: 30 minutes to 1 hour

Cautions: Watch for poison ivy. Take insect repellent.

Trail Directions: Start this interpretive trail from the southeast end of the east parking lot near the Maybury Sanatorium arbor and interpretive board [1]. Get a lesson on the history of the sanatorium and its namesake, William H. Maybury, who himself contracted tuberculosis and later died in the farmhouse on November 4, 1931. The farm provided dairy and fresh food for the patients of the sanatorium. The City of Detroit bought farms for the facility. For its work, Detroit was ranked one of the leading cities in the world in facilities for the treatment of tuberculosis.

Cut down the asphalt path through good-sized maples. Stay straight past the first junction that merges in and soon arrive at the next one, #3. Turn left. Interpretive boards tell the story of the lost buildings. You pass the long-gone doctor's house and then the very real bench and Maple Picnic Shelter to reach another junction (.1 mi.) [2].

Turn right along the old, broken concrete path and walk along a remnant of the old sanatorium. What woeful souls once walked along the sidewalk to experience the fresh air in these woods? Now you are behind the tot lot. In days of old, the administration building took up space here.

At .3 mi., stay west (straight) to cut through a grassy path near where the ambulatory building was and on through rolling woods [3]. You reach the path that leads to the remains of the old water tower (.5 mi.) [4].

Stay straight. At the next junction, turn right along the natural trail (.6 mi.) [5]. Again you find yourself in some larger maples, and the Water Tower Trail merges in (.7 mi.) [6]. When you reach the junction for the asphalt trail (.8 mi.) [7], turn right and wind through woods with impressive hardwoods, especially maples. Trees tower above you and their lush understory. Continue your shaded stroll until you come to the spur where you started the loop. Turn left and head back to your vehicle.

1. Trailhead
2. Junction #3
3. Grassy path
4. Path to water tower
5. Junction
6. Trail merges in
7. Junction for paved trail

Trail to Pond

Distance Round-Trip: 3.1 miles
Estimated Hiking Time: 1 to 1.5 hours

Cautions: Watch for poison ivy. Take insect repellent.

Trail Directions: Start from the southeast end of the east parking lot near the Maybury Sanatorium arbor and interpretive board [1]. Get a lesson on the history of the sanatorium and its namesake, William H. Maybury.

Head down the asphalt path through large maples. Stay straight past the first junction that merges in and soon reach the next one, #3. Turn left. Interpretive boards tell the story of the lost buildings. You pass the long-gone doctor's house and then the very real bench and Maple Picnic Shelter to reach another junction (.1 mi.) [2].

Stay straight on the wide path and pass the ghosts of the nurse's house and the men's annex. Farther on is a picnic area with grills (.3 mi.) [3]. The trail winds and crosses an equestrian path (.4 mi.) [4]. Soon you see the rugged mountain bike path to your right (.5 mi.) [5]. The trail winds and rolls to reach the drive that remains, where there is now the ghost of the children's unit (.8 mi.) [6].

At the junction for the fishing pond loop (1 mi.), turn left and leave the ghosts and asphalt trail behind [7]. Keep straight until the trail reaches the T at post #9 (1.1 mi.) [8]. Turn right and wind down to the fishing dock (1.2 mi.) [9]. From here, follow around the profuse pond on the boardwalk.

In less than .1 mi., you reach a gravel road at post #8. Stay to the left along the road to junction #7 (1.4 mi.) [10]. Go left along the narrow, wood-chipped path on the opposite side of the pond. Cross a couple of small bridges and rest on the bench under the maples before following alongside the wet area to cross a footbridge (1.7 mi.) [11].

Continue around the pond to another dock (1.8 mi.) [12]. Have a seat on the bench to admire the textured pond and then head over to junction #6 (1.9 mi.) [13].

Turn right along the chipped path through the woods. The trail winds; stay left at the fork and climb up the root steps. Wind and roll with the trail. Stay left when a trail merges in and then step down the root steps (2.2 mi.) [14]. Stay right at the next junction, which appears to be a shortcut to the main trail. You come to a multiple junction [15]. Stay on the narrow path straight and soon reach junction B. Take the path on the left and soon reach junction #5 (2.5 mi.) [16]. Turn right to take the northern route along a narrow path through mixed hardwoods.

Cattails appear on your left in the wetland (2.8 mi.) [17]. The trail becomes rocky. Stay left when a trail merges in. You still skirt the wetland and then enter an area with much taller trees. Fallen trees litter the rolling floor.

Ascend to a T and turn right to wind and climb a rocky slope to a ridge (3 mi.) [18]. Walk the ridge with a meadow below on your right. At the junction, you have a choice to turn left down to the main asphalt trail or to stay right to continue to the parking lot.

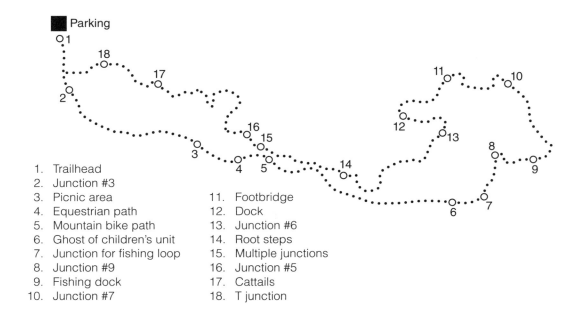

■ Parking

1. Trailhead
2. Junction #3
3. Picnic area
4. Equestrian path
5. Mountain bike path
6. Ghost of children's unit
7. Junction for fishing loop
8. Junction #9
9. Fishing dock
10. Junction #7
11. Footbridge
12. Dock
13. Junction #6
14. Root steps
15. Multiple junctions
16. Junction #5
17. Cattails
18. T junction

Southern
Lower
Peninsula

59. For-Mar Nature Preserve and Arboretum

- View live reptiles housed in the interpretive center.
- Visit an Audubon bird exhibit with over 600 specimens.
- Hike the scenic and varied terrain along Kearsley Creek.

Park Information

About 383 acres, stitched together in a patchwork of woodlands, restored prairies, open fields, meadows, ponds, edges, and Kearsley Creek, provide the main ingredients for the preserve. An arboretum cultivates interesting trees, shrubs, and vines. Seven miles of hiking trails weave through the diverse habitat. The preserve is named in recognition of the previous owners, Forbes and Martha Merkely.

The Forbes and Martha Merkely Interpretive Center offers educational and interpretive programs, displays, live animals and reptiles, and bird-viewing areas. The Corydon E. Foote Bird Collection contains more than 600 mounted birds that can be seen at limited viewing times. The exhibit building is located from the north entry off Potter Road.

Directions: The preserve is located about 1 mile east of Flint. From I-75, head east on I-69 about 7 miles to Belsay Road. Take this road north about 1 mile to Davison; then turn west for 1 mile to Genesee Road. Go north for about .2 mile. The main entry for most of the trails and for the interpretive center is located here, on the east side of Genesee Road. The entrance for the bird exhibit is about .2 mile farther north of this entrance.

Hours Open: The preserve is open Wednesdays through Sundays from 8:00 a.m. until sunset. The interpretive center is open Wednesdays through Sundays from 8:00 a.m. to 5:00 p.m. Hours for the bird exhibit are limited to Sundays from 2:00 to 4:00 p.m. from June through August. In April, May, September, and October, the bird exhibit is open on the first Sunday from 2:00 to 4:00 p.m.

Facilities: Hiking and interpretive center.

Permits and Rules: There is no fee at this Genesee County park. Please stay on the trails and leave pets, radios, and toys at home. Don't smoke, jog, or bicycle on the trails, and don't disturb plants or animals.

For Further Information: For-Mar Nature Preserve and Arboretum, 2142 North Genesee Road, Burton, MI 48509; 810-789-8568. You may also call Genesee County Parks at 810-736-7100.

Other Points of Interest

For a trip to the past, visit **Crossroads Village** and **Huckleberry Railroad**. Crossroads Village offers a collection of 34 historic structures that, with the help of costumed interpreters, recreate the small-town days of early Michigan, circa 1800s. A train of the Huckleberry Railroad leaves the Crossroads Depot for 40-minute excursions. The train, powered by a historic Baldwin steam locomotive, carries up to 500 passengers.

For fees, hours, and other information, call Genesee County Parks at 810-736-7100 or 800-648-PARK; www.geneseecountyparks.org.

Park Trails

The 7 miles of trails form an intricate web of loops made up of wood-chipped paths, mowed swaths through grasses, service roads, and naturally beaten-down tracks. All are relatively easy.

Trail names reflect what they pass through: Ground Water Pond, Young Woods, Succession, Hawthorn, Edge of Woods, Woodlot, and Sugar Bush. There are also Maple and Lilac walks. Variations of the trails circle ponds, meander along Kearsley Creek, cross wooden suspension bridges, or cut through woods, wetlands, or prairies.

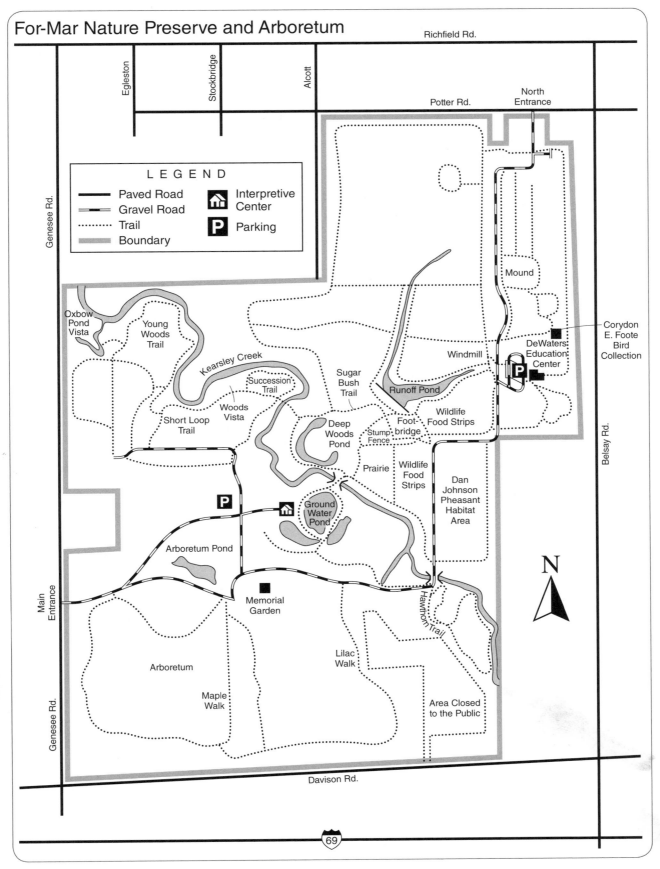

For-Mar Nature Preserve and Arboretum

LEGEND

—— Paved Road	🏠 Interpretive Center
—·— Gravel Road	🅿 Parking
···· Trail	
▬▬ Boundary	

Richfield Rd.

Egleston

Stockbridge

Alcott

Potter Rd.

North Entrance

Genesee Rd.

Mound

Oxbow Pond Vista

Young Woods Trail

Kearsley Creek

Succession Trail

Woods Vista

Short Loop Trail

Sugar Bush Trail

Windmill

DeWaters Education Center

Corydon E. Foote Bird Collection

Runoff Pond

Wildlife Food Strips

Deep Woods Pond

Foot-bridge

Stump Fence

Belsay Rd.

Prairie

Wildlife Food Strips

Dan Johnson Pheasant Habitat Area

🅿

🏠

Ground Water Pond

Arboretum Pond

Memorial Garden

Main Entrance

Hawthorn Trail

N

Arboretum

Maple Walk

Lilac Walk

Area Closed to the Public

Genesee Rd.

Davison Rd.

69

Ground Water Pond and Hawthorn Trail

🥾 **Distance Round-Trip:** 1.2 miles
🥾 **Estimated Hiking Time:** 30 minutes to 1 hour

Cautions: Poison ivy lines the trail and winds up into trees. Take insect repellent.

Trail Directions: Start from the east side of the interpretive center on the Ground Water Pond Trail **[1]**. Pass a black locust tree, the one with many small oval leaves drooping from one stalk. In spring its fragrant flowers perfume the air.

Almost immediately, you reach a quiet area of benches. Behind them is Ground Water Pond. The Hawthorn Trail goes right, past briers flowing down the trail like prickly veils and through a blockade of trees. The trail passes between two ponds. A bright green cover shields the pond on the right. On your left, the pool is clear; plumes of grasslike reeds clump in islands. Watch for waterfowl making Vs in the water.

The ponds end at a circle of grass (.1 mi.) **[2]**. Leave the Ground Water Pond Trail by cutting right to an open field. Turn left along the mowed swath that flanks the low-lying, grasslike wetland. Grasses stretch out in the field on your right.

The trail wraps around the wetland, winding past goldenrod and shrubs, and then approaches an edge of trees before reaching a service road (.2 mi.) **[3]**. Turn left. This road serves as your trail.

Woods edge the trail on your left; a field of grasses and goldenrod stretches out on your right. Multiple trail choices await you (.3 mi.) **[4]**. The Hawthorn Trail is the grassy trail that cuts through shrubby growth on the other side of the road. It takes you up for a sneak preview of Kearsley Creek and then winds down to the junction for the trail's loop (.4 mi.) **[5]**. Stay right and follow the loop counterclockwise. A ridge rises tall and strong along the narrow channel, like a fortress wall that encloses this preserve; the trail follows along its bounds. Untamed roses, long and spindly, weave their own wall along the trail.

Soon the trail curves north to meet the creek that will follow along with you. At .6 mi., the trail bends left **[6]**. The creek is in full view. Here, the corrugated spine of a culvert spills its contents into the creek. Now stroll with the creek flowing at your side before you wind back along the trail to close the loop. Head out onto the service road and turn right toward the bridge. Pass the intersection of trails **[4]** and step onto the wood planks to cross Kearsley Creek (.8 mi.).

Soon after you cross the creek, you reach an open prairie. Take the trail on your left that skirts through the trees edging the creek. A prairie opens up to the north. You pass a mowed path that follows through it. Continue straight through a tunnel of trees and reach another junction (1 mi.) **[7]**.

Turn left and soon reach another junction. Follow left near the creek; the trail directs you to a wooden suspension bridge. Hold on to the railing; the arched bridge sways and wobbles as you cross over the water.

In a few steps you reach Ground Water Pond. Follow the north side of the pond to the right and wind up to the circle of benches. From here, retrace your steps to the interpretive center.

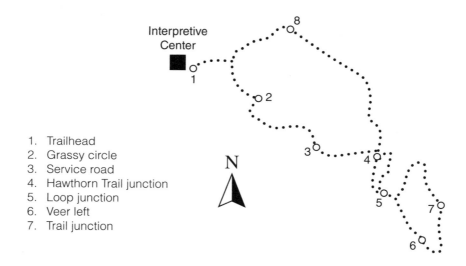

Interpretive Center

1. Trailhead
2. Grassy circle
3. Service road
4. Hawthorn Trail junction
5. Loop junction
6. Veer left
7. Trail junction

N

Ground Water Pond and Sugar Bush Trail

Distance Round-Trip: .7 mile
Estimated Hiking Time: 30 minutes

Cautions: Sections of this trail may be muddy. Wear appropriate footgear. Take insect repellent in the warmer months.

Trail Directions: Start from the east side of the interpretive center and enter the quiet area—a small grassy area with a bench **[1]**. Stay left under a canopy of trees and descend onto a ridge above Ground Water Pond.

You soon arrive at an observation dock where you can investigate the environment surrounding the murky brown waters of the pond. Keep an eye out for ducks, frogs, kingfishers, and other local residents that might be making a fuss over your presence.

Turn left at the dock and enter the woods to arrive at a pedestrian suspension bridge over Kearsley Creek (.1 mi.) **[2]**. Hold on to the railing as the arched bridge bounces as you cross to the other side. Back on solid ground, turn left at the trail junction to parallel the creek. Pass an old stone barbecue that looks out of place among the ferns and horsetail; then walk up to the edge of the vernal pond. A creek is a few feet away.

Snake between the creek and pond, duck under vine-draped trees, and arrive at another junction (.2 mi.) **[3]**. Turn right and cross a bridge. Watch your step, both on the bridge and as you wind around the small pools nestled here on the forest floor.

Pass an odd, casket-shaped, concrete structure near a large oak. Don't worry. No one is missing. This structure was used back in the days when maple syrup was made from the sugar bush—the maple.

Farther on, walk past a fallen oak left to decay. Reach the junction (.3 mi.) **[4]** just past a sign that announces the Sugar Bush Trail. Turn right, pass a bench, and start to climb a ridge.

You reach another junction with a bench before you reach the top of your climb. Stay right and skirt an old field on your left. Descend through small trees and shrubs, where the trail becomes grassy. Pass another junction and descend to cross over a small creek on a footbridge (.4 mi.) **[5]**.

Stay right as the trail splits. Hike through brush and small trees until you pass yet another junction. This one is near a stump fence. Follow along the old tree stumps and begin to descend along the edge of a bluff overlooking the vernal pond (.5 mi.) **[6]**. Large oak and beech trees line the ridge. A white fence separates you from the edge. Stay to the right at the junction there.

Railroad ties edge the bluff, and you descend past rustic log benches. Soon, reach another trail junction, turn right past an erratic—a boulder transported by a glacier—and then cut between the large fallen oak and another erratic to arrive back at the pedestrian suspension bridge (.6 mi.) **[2]**. Cross the bucking-bronco bridge and retrace your steps to the interpretive center.

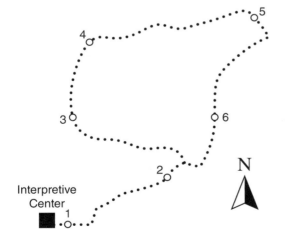

1. Ground Water Pond Trail sign
2. Suspension bridge
3. Trail junction
4. Trail junction
5. Footbridge
6. Bluff overlook

60. Parker Mill Park

- Tour a restored 19th-century gristmill.
- Walk the boardwalk along scenic Fleming Creek.
- Observe wildlife from a blind along the Huron River.

Park Information

Located along Fleming Creek just above its confluence with the Huron River, this Washtenaw County park preserves 44 acres of the original 1863 Parker family homestead. The county owns 26 acres, which include historic Parker Mill, the old millpond site, Fleming Creek forestlands, and a remnant tract of prairie-fen habitat. The remaining 17 acres, known as Forest Park, provides access to the Huron River.

The renovated gristmill, which began operation in 1873, is one of the oldest surviving sites in Washtenaw County.

For day hikers, the park includes the Hoyt G. Post Trail, a barrier-free boardwalk trail complete with wheelchair curbs and state-of-the-art self-guided interpretive stations. A second, shorter trail is called the Sugarbush. An asphalt trail that accommodates bikers, skaters, and joggers connects the park with Ann Arbor's Gallup Park along the Huron River.

Directions: From US 23, east of Ann Arbor, take Geddes Road east just past Dixboro Road. The park is on the south side of Geddes Road.

Hours Open: The park is open May through September from 7:00 a.m. to 8:00 p.m. and October through April from 7:00 a.m. to 6:00 p.m. You can tour the mill most September and October weekends. Call ahead to confirm.

Facilities: Hiking, bicycling, fishing, picnicking, interpretive trail, and historic site.

Permits and Rules: No admittance fee is required. The following are not permitted: fires; swimming; picking or removing plants or animals; fishing except in designated areas; skateboarding; alcohol; hunting; pets, food, and smoking in the buildings. Dog walking, jogging, and bicycling are prohibited on Hoyt G. Post Trail. Elsewhere in the park, dogs must be on a leash.

For Further Information: Washtenaw County Parks and Recreation Commission, 2230 Platt Road, Ann Arbor, MI 48104; 734-971-6337.

Other Points of Interest

North of the park, **Matthaei Botanical Gardens** offer a greenhouse with desert, temperate, and tropical rooms, and the garden has trails that pass through marsh, prairie, and forest. For more information, contact Matthaei Botanical Gardens, 1800 N. Dixboro Road, Ann Arbor, MI 48105; 734-647-7600.

West of the park, Ann Arbor's **Gallup Park** has several miles of trails as well as canoe rentals, picnic shelters, and boat launch. Adjacent to Gallup Park, the 48-acre natural area called **Furstenberg Park** features the most diverse flora of any park in the city. North of Matthaei Botanical Gardens is the 87-acre **Marshall Park**. One of the wilder parks in the area, it includes a meadow, pine stands, and virgin oak-hickory forest. **Bird Hills Nature Area** has 147 acres of wooded hills and ravines with trails weaving through it. For more information on all four parks, call the City of Ann Arbor, Department of Parks and Recreation, 734-994-2780.

West of Gallup Park, **Nichols Arboretum** features over 500 species of trees and plants and offers scenic trails for walking and nature study. For more information, contact Nichols Arboretum, 1600 Washington Heights, Ann Arbor, MI 48104; 734-647-7600.

Park Trails

Main Trail (🥾, .7 mile). This asphalt trail provides access to the Sugarbush Trail, the Hoyt G. Post Trail, and Ann Arbor's Gallup Park.

Sugarbush Trail (🥾, .2 mile). This trail starts southeast of Parker Mill and crosses over Fleming Creek.

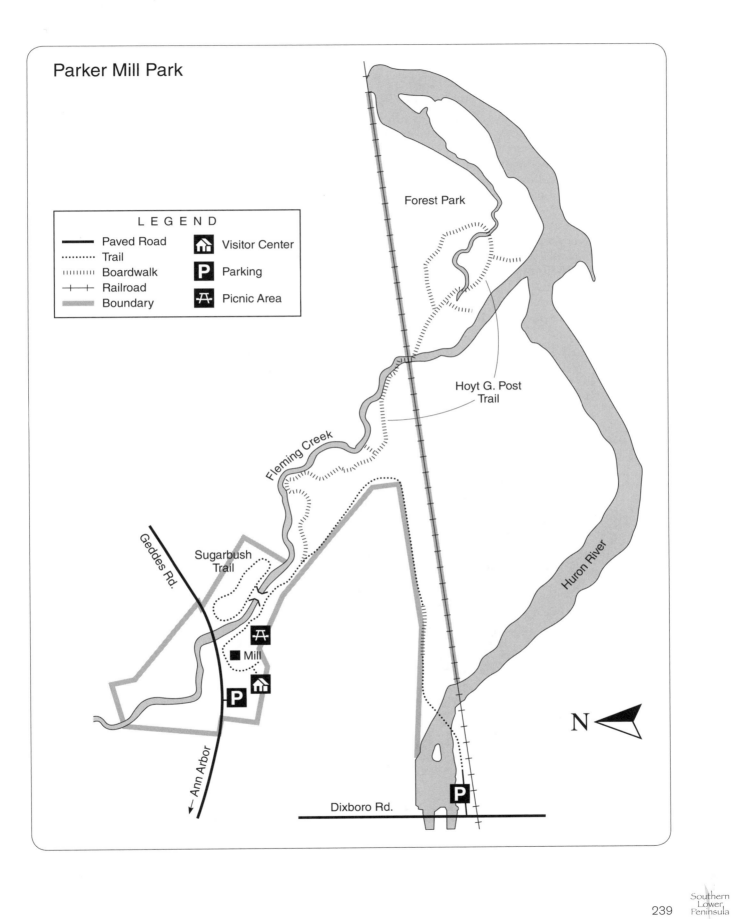

Parker Mill Park

LEGEND

—— Paved Road	🏠 Visitor Center
···· Trail	🅿 Parking
⊪⊪⊪ Boardwalk	🅰 Picnic Area
+—+ Railroad	
▬▬ Boundary	

Forest Park

Hoyt G. Post Trail

Fleming Creek

Geddes Rd.

Ann Arbor

Sugarbush Trail

■ Mill

🅰

🏠

🅿

Huron River

🅿

Dixboro Rd.

N

Hoyt G. Post Trail

Distance Round-Trip: 1.3 miles
Estimated Hiking Time: 30 minutes to 1 hour

Cautions: Poison ivy grows along the trail. The boardwalk is slippery when wet. Take insect repellent during the warm months.

Trail Directions: Start by the sign at the east end of the parking lot **[1]**. Follow the asphalt trail and swing right around the mill site, descending sharply to parallel Fleming Creek. Pass a junction with the Sugarbush Trail (.1 mi.) **[2]**. Soon you arrive at the trailhead for the Hoyt G. Post Trail (.2 mi.) **[3]**. Turn left onto the boardwalk. The trail leads you to an orientation deck, and you soon reach the first interpretive station, which explains the link between the Fleming Creek Watershed and the postglacial landscape. From here you get a scenic view of the creek and then another.

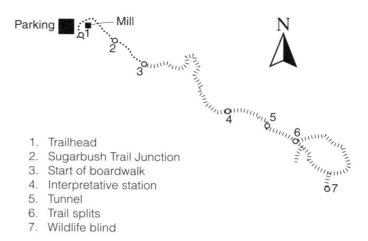

1. Trailhead
2. Sugarbush Trail Junction
3. Start of boardwalk
4. Interpretative station
5. Tunnel
6. Trail splits
7. Wildlife blind

Pass an area invaded by nonnative species of plants; this area will be managed to reestablish native flora. Shortly afterward, you reach the spur to the next interpretive station, which takes you to a creek-side platform with an interpretive board.

Continuing along the boardwalk, you pass large deadfalls, cross the overflow channel again, and arrive at a large, moss-covered deadfall next to another interpretive station (.4 mi.) **[4]**, which explains the fallen trees in this floodplain environment. Winds topple whole trees over.

Arrive back at the creek for another interpretive station. Soon, you reach a fascinating section of the trail. The boardwalk swings over Fleming Creek and runs under a limestone-arched railroad bridge that forms a shaded tunnel around the boardwalk (.5 mi.) **[5]**. When trains are overhead, the weight of the cars exerts enough pressure to cause air bubbles to fizz in the water. In winter, icicles form, hanging like stalactites from the limestone blocks of the bridge.

Beyond the bridge, you enter the Huron River floodplain and walk through a sunny opening before entering a climax black maple forest. Stay to the right as the boardwalk splits (.6 mi.) **[6]** and soon reach the spur to an interpretive station. This station is perched on a 100-foot-wide dome of peat that is being gently lifted by several artesian springs. Don't leave the deck; the mud may be up to 17 feet deep in places.

Beyond this stop you wander through a backup depression to a lagoon of the Huron River. This area floods when it rains. At .7 mi., you reach a spur to a wildlife blind on the Huron River **[7]**. In spring, fall, and winter, you can view large congregations of waterfowl at this location.

From the blind, continue your hike along the boardwalk to complete your loop through this unique floodplain forest (.8 mi.) **[6]**. Now retrace your steps to the parking area.

- Revere nature from extensive boardwalks through wetlands.
- View waterfowl from 30-foot towers that overlook marshes and lagoons.
- Wade the shallow waters of Saginaw Bay.

Park Information

Situated on the shores of Saginaw Bay, the Bay City State Recreation Area is home to one of the largest remaining freshwater, coastal wetlands on the Great Lakes—Tobico Marsh. Besides a mile of sandy shoreline, the area embraces 2,100 acres of wetland woods, wet meadows, oak savannah prairies, and cattail marshlands that create an ideal staging area for migratory birds.

The recreation area offers modern camping, Saginaw Bay access, fishing opportunities, picnic shelters, more than 7 miles of trails, and, for children, the Come Play by the Bay playscape. The park has 30-foot observation towers, boardwalks, and observation docks over wetlands.

For year-round programs, hands-on learning, and interpretive events, stop in at the Saginaw Bay Visitor Center. The facility is a combination of laboratory, museum, and classroom. Two trails are accessed from the center. One, designed for people with visual and physical disabilities, forms a loop just outside the visitor center. The other, a 1-mile hard-surface loop, encircles the Tobico Lagoon.

The Andersen Nature Trail allows a contemplative transition as you stroll from recreation to reverence in the refuge. The hard-surface trail follows an abandoned rail grade. It has interpretive plaques, observation decks, and benches to enhance your enjoyment of the surroundings. Its extension connects with Bay City's Riverwalk–Rail Trail Loop.

Directions: The recreation area is located about 5 miles north of Bay City. Take I-75 to exit 168 and head east along Beaver Road for about 6 miles.

Hours Open: The area is open daily. Saginaw Bay Visitor Center is open Tuesday through Sunday from noon to 5:00 p.m.

Facilities: Hiking, bicycling, cross-country skiing, swimming, fishing, camping (tent and RV), sanitation station, picnicking, interpretive trails, and interpretive center.

Permits and Rules: A park fee is required for motor vehicles ($6 daily, $24 annually for residents; $8 daily, $29 annually for nonresidents).

For Further Information: Bay City State Recreation Area, 3582 State Park Drive, Bay City, MI 48706; 989-684-3020; Saginaw Bay Visitor Center, 989-667-0717.

Other Points of Interest

The **Riverwalk–Rail Trail Loop** connects with the south end of the Bay City State Recreation Area and takes you along the banks of the Saginaw River to a pier, crosses a pedestrian bridge to a small island in the river, and passes through Veterans' Memorial Park and the Liberty Harbor Marina. The hard-surface trail accommodates walking, inline skating, bicycles, strollers, and wheelchairs. For more information, contact the Bay Area Community Foundation, 703 Washington Avenue, Bay City, MI 48708; 989-893-4438.

Park Trails

Chickadee Trail (🥾, .5 mile). This paved trail loops behind the visitor center and features colorful displays with recorded messages.

Tobico Lagoon Trail (🥾, 1 mile). This hard-surface trail circles around a lagoon and meanders along the shores of Saginaw Bay.

Andersen Trail Extension (🥾, 1 mile). This paved trail extends the Andersen Nature Trail to the south to link up with the Riverwalk–Rail Trail Loop.

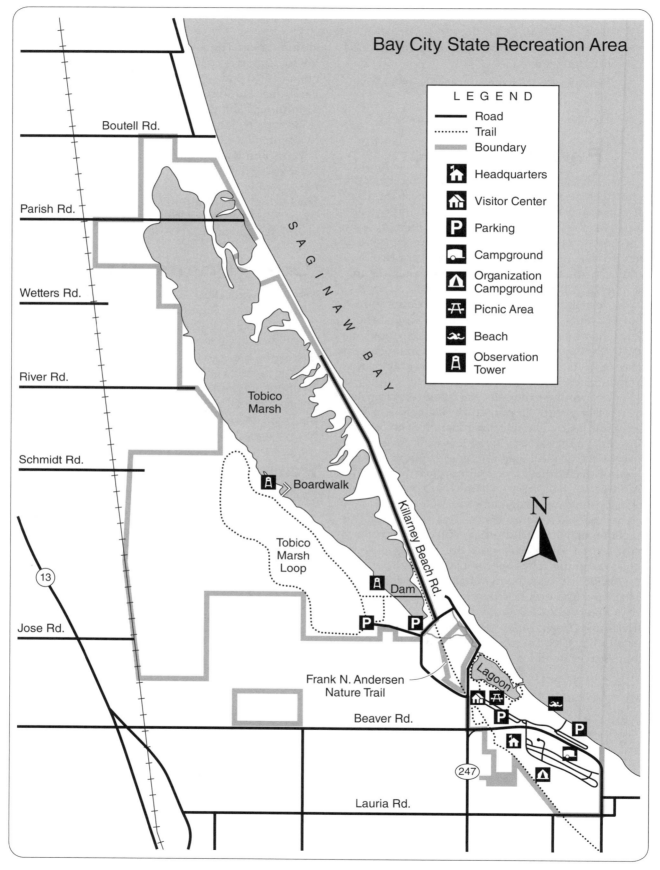

Bay City State Recreation Area

LEGEND
— Road
···· Trail
▬ Boundary

🏠 Headquarters
🏠 Visitor Center
P Parking
🚐 Campground
⛺ Organization Campground
🪑 Picnic Area
🏊 Beach
🗼 Observation Tower

Boutell Rd.

Parish Rd.

Wetters Rd.

River Rd.

Schmidt Rd.

(13)

Jose Rd.

Beaver Rd.

(247)

Lauria Rd.

SAGINAW BAY

Tobico Marsh

Tobico Marsh Loop

Boardwalk

Dam

Killarney Beach Rd.

Frank N. Andersen Nature Trail

Lagoon

N

Frank N. Andersen Nature Trail

🐾 **Distance Round-Trip:** 3.2 miles
🐾 **Estimated Hiking Time:** 1 to 1.5 hours

Cautions: Take insect repellent, a hat, and sunscreen. Bring binoculars (and a bird identification book) for wildlife viewing while you are on the observation decks.

Trail Directions: Start behind the Saginaw Bay Visitor Center, located at the northwest end of the park's day-use area **[1]**.

Behind the visitor center, go past the large sign announcing the trail and immediately cross Euclid Road. The asphalt trail follows the route of an abandoned Detroit and Mackinac Railway corridor for 1.2 mi.

You enter into a wooded area where a nature observation deck awaits (.2 mi.) **[2]**. The covered deck has benches and interpretive plaques that describe the plants and animals in the surrounding habitat. This one features the trees and birds that might be found here in the woodland zone. Have a seat and wait to see what might fly in to feast at the feeders.

Leaving the woods, you enter a large marsh area and arrive at a second covered observation deck (.3 mi.) **[3]**. Here, the plants and animals of the marsh environment are highlighted.

You soon cross a small wood-decked bridge built on the back of the old railroad trestle. Then stop to read about the important role that reptiles play in Michigan's wetlands. At .5 mi., cross Killarney Beach Road as it swings to parallel the trail **[4]**.

When the trail splits (.7 mi.) **[5]**, stay along the corridor for exceptional views of Tobico Marsh. Take your time and look for waterfowl floating or feeding in the water. When the asphalt ends (1.3 mi.) **[6]**, double back, return to the junction **[5]**, and turn right to cross on the weir (1.9 mi.).

You quickly reach a wooden bridge with interpretive plaques at both ends. Then, in the cattails to your right, look for the beaver lodge (2 mi.) **[7]**. If you are lucky, you may spot a beaver swimming in the water. Learn more as you pass a couple more interpretive plaques. Get another great view of the marsh and then arrive at an observation deck on your right (2.1 mi.) **[8]**.

After crossing the marsh, you arrive at a large, two-story observation tower (2.2 mi.) **[9]**. Make the climb up the steps of the tower, catch your breath, and enjoy the sweeping view of the area. You will be glad that you brought your binoculars. Without them, those specks in the water will remain just that, specks in the water. So lift up your glasses. What is that out there? Your bird identification book will be useful here.

When you've had enough, descend and retrace your steps to the visitor center. If you still want to hike, turn the page to read about the Tobico Marsh Loop. You can pick up this loop by heading west past the vault toilet and into the woods.

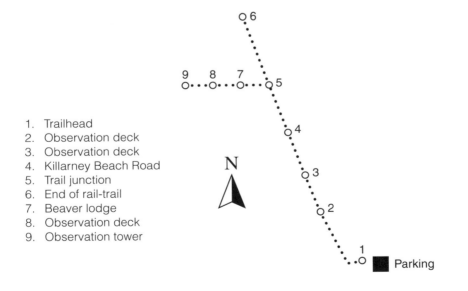

1. Trailhead
2. Observation deck
3. Observation deck
4. Killarney Beach Road
5. Trail junction
6. End of rail-trail
7. Beaver lodge
8. Observation deck
9. Observation tower

Tobico Marsh Loop

🐾 **Distance Round-Trip:** 4.7 miles
🐾 **Estimated Hiking Time:** 1.5 to 2.5 hours

Cautions: Take insect repellent during the warmer months. Bring binoculars for wildlife viewing at the nature observation decks.

Trail Directions: Start behind the Saginaw Bay Visitor Center, located at the northwest end of the park's day-use area **[1]**. Take the asphalt-surfaced Andersen Nature Trail, which you will follow for 1 mi.

Cross Euclid Road and you are on the route of an abandoned Detroit and Mackinac Railway corridor. This corridor transports you to a nature observation deck. Look around and learn about the trees and birds found in this woodland zone (.2 mi.) **[2]**. Your next scheduled stop is at the second nature observation deck (.3 mi.) **[3]**, which highlights the plants and animals of the marsh.

Cross Killarney Beach Road (.5 mi.) **[4]**. Turn left at the junction (.7 mi.) **[5]** to cross on a weir to the other side of the marsh. While crossing the wooden bridge, look to your right for evidence of a beaver lodge or dam (.8 mi.) **[6]**. Then pass more interpretive plaques, view more marsh scenes, and arrive at an observation platform with viewing scopes (.9 mi.) **[7]**. Then pass another.

After you cross the marsh, you will see a two-story observation tower overlooking the area (1 mi.) **[8]**. Climb the steps, catch your breath, and enjoy the view. If you brought binoculars, this is a place to use them.

With your feet back on the ground, head past the vault toilet and into the woods where the asphalt ends;

now your feet really are back on the ground (actually crushed stone). Soon the trail splits (1.1 mi.) **[9]**, and you have the option of going either clockwise or counterclockwise. Turn right and head north through mixed hardwoods and an occasional pine.

At 1.7 mi., cross a clearing that exposes a vault toilet and arrive at the second observation tower **[10]**. At the foot of the tower is a boardwalk that leads you out for a more intimate interaction with the marsh. Have a seat on one of the benches and enjoy the setting.

The trail continues north from the tower. At 2.1 mi., the northernmost point of the hike, the trail swings left **[11]**. Now headed south, you pass between two wetlands where you view cattails through trees (2.2 mi.) **[12]**. Hiking the lightly used west side of the trail, you pass through an open area (2.8 mi.) **[13]**. Continue strolling through woods and then cross a small wooden bridge (3.2 mi.) **[14]**.

Eventually a footbridge takes you over the pool that has been paralleling the trail. Soon you arrive at the parking area that served as the original trailhead when this section of the park was on its own as the Tobico Marsh State Game Area (3.5 mi.) **[15]**. Besides a shelter and vault toilets, a rock with a plaque commemorates the 1976 designation of Tobico Marsh as a registered natural landmark.

Continue north past the shelter. Turn right where the trail splits to cross the first of the three bridges that carry you over a series of old Lake Huron beach ridges. After crossing the last bridge (3.6 mi.) **[16]**, turn left and you will soon be back at the weir (3.7 mi.) **[17]** that is east of the first observation tower. From here, retrace your steps for 1 mi. to the visitor center parking area.

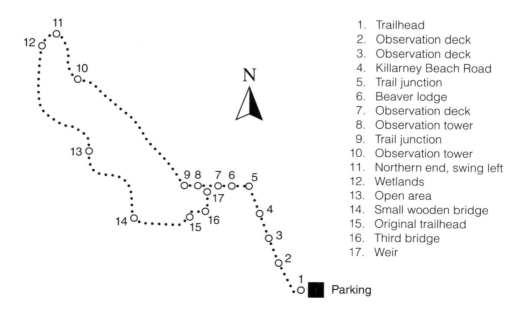

1. Trailhead
2. Observation deck
3. Observation deck
4. Killarney Beach Road
5. Trail junction
6. Beaver lodge
7. Observation deck
8. Observation tower
9. Trail junction
10. Observation tower
11. Northern end, swing left
12. Wetlands
13. Open area
14. Small wooden bridge
15. Original trailhead
16. Third bridge
17. Weir

62. Shiawassee Nat'l. Wildlife Refuge/ Green Point Environmental Learning Center

- Enjoy a designated United States Important Bird Area (IBA)
- Hike along dikes through forest, farm fields, and wetlands.
- View an abundance of diverse wildlife.

Park Information

Although the Shiawassee National Wildlife Refuge and the Green Point Environmental Learning Center are separate entities, they share a location near the confluence of four rivers—the Flint, Tittabawassee, Cass, and Shiawassee—all of which combine to form the Saginaw River.

The refuge, with over 9,000 acres, was established in 1953 to restore a historically significant wetland area for the benefit of migrating waterfowl. During peak populations in late October, up to 25,000 geese and 40,000 ducks may be seen at the refuge. Songbirds, wading birds, owls, hawks, and even bald eagles either call the refuge home or pass through at some time.

An observation deck and a wheelchair-accessible observation blind are strategically placed for prime wildlife viewing. Dikes, pumps, and gravity-flow structures flood and drain various areas, promoting the growth of seeds and invertebrates that wildlife use for food. Sharecrop farmers leave a certain percentage of their crops in the field, providing wildlife with a winter food source.

Adjacent to the refuge is the Green Point Environmental Learning Center. Owned by the City of Saginaw but operated under a cooperative agreement with the U.S. Fish and Wildlife Service, this natural area provides another 76 acres of diverse habitat and has an interpretive center for learning about nature.

Directions: The refuge headquarters are located about 4 miles south of Saginaw. From M-13, turn west onto Curtis Road for about .5 mile. Green Point Environmental Learning Center is located at the end of Maple Street in Saginaw. Take M-46 to South Michigan Avenue. Turn south, go about 1.5 miles to Maple Street, and turn left. Go about .5 mile to the Center at 3010 Maple Street.

Hours Open: The refuge is open from dawn until dusk, seven days a week year-round. During hunting periods the hours are limited. Refuge headquarters are open from 7:30 a.m. to 4:00 p.m., Mondays through Fridays throughout the year except on federal holidays. Floods are a possibility any time. Call ahead to check conditions. At the Green Point Environmental Learning Center, the trails are open daily during the daylight hours. They too may be flooded. Center hours are generally Monday through Friday from 8:30 a.m. to 4:00 p.m. Call ahead.

Facilities: The refuge has hiking, biking, cross-country skiing, hunting, and interpretive trails. The Green Point Learning Center has hiking, cross-country skiing, fishing, and an interpretive center.

Permits and Rules: No fee is charged at either facility. Stay on the established trails. No pets or motorized vehicles are allowed. Leave all plants and animals as you found them and pack out your litter. At the refuge, observe the "Closed Area" signs. At the learning center, no bicycling is allowed on the trails.

For Further Information: Shiawassee National Wildlife Refuge, 6975 Mower Road, Saginaw, MI 48601; 989-777-5930; Green Point Environmental Learning Center, 3010 Maple Street, Saginaw, MI 48602; 989-759-1669.

Park Trails

Woodland Trail (🥾, 4.5 miles). This trail is in the north portion of the refuge. Drive west on M-46 from Saginaw to Center Road and turn south. Go about 2 miles to Stroebel Road. Turn left to the parking lot. This rustic trail travels largely through bottomland hardwoods and at times draws close to the Tittabawassee River.

Wildflower, Turtle, Hawk, and Deer Trails (🥾, .2 to 1 mile). These trails are smaller loops off the longer Songbird Trail at the Green Point Environmental Learning Center. They all start with the Songbird Trail behind the center and wander through bottomland hardwoods.

Duck and Beaver Trails (🥾, .4 and 1 mile). These trails are extension loops at the southern end of the Songbird Trail, where a boardwalk continues the trail across a wetland. They provide wildlife-viewing opportunities along the Tittabawassee River.

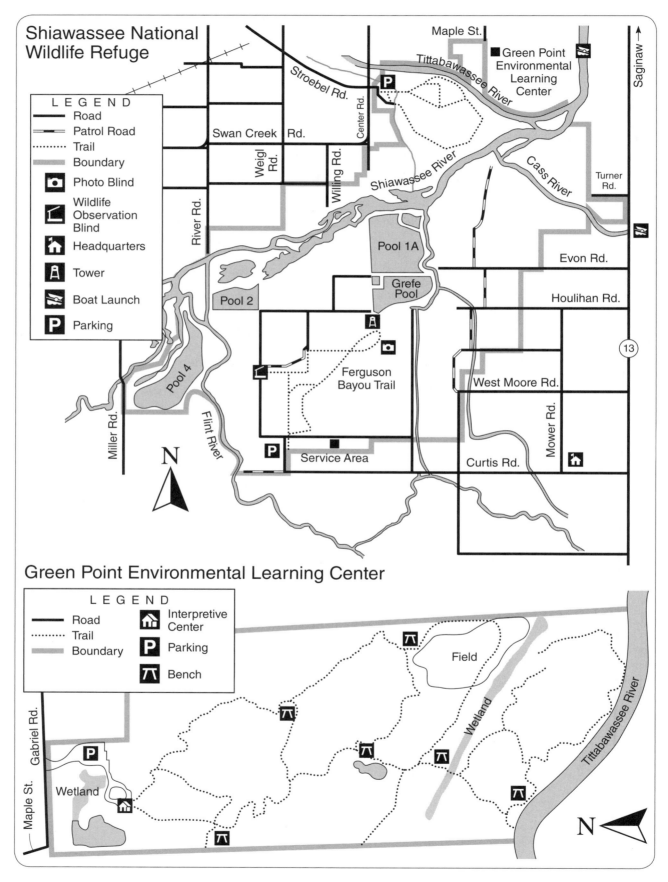

Shiawassee National Wildlife Refuge

LEGEND
— Road
⊣⊢ Patrol Road
···· Trail
▬ Boundary
📷 Photo Blind
🏠 Wildlife Observation Blind
🏠 Headquarters
🗼 Tower
🚤 Boat Launch
🅿 Parking

Maple St.
Stroebel Rd.
Swan Creek Rd.
Center Rd.
Weigl Rd.
Willing Rd.
River Rd.
Miller Rd.
Flint River

Tittabawassee River
Green Point Environmental Learning Center
Saginaw →
Shiawassee River
Cass River
Turner Rd.
Evon Rd.
Houlihan Rd.
West Moore Rd.
Mower Rd.
Curtis Rd.
13

Pool 1A
Grefe Pool
Pool 2
Pool 4
Ferguson Bayou Trail
Service Area

N

Green Point Environmental Learning Center

LEGEND
— Road
···· Trail
▬ Boundary
🏠 Interpretive Center
🅿 Parking
🔱 Bench

Gabriel Rd.
Maple St.
Wetland
Field
Wetland
Tittabawassee River

N

Ferguson Bayou Trail

🐾 **Distance Round-Trip:** 5.2 miles
🐾 **Estimated Hiking Time:** 2 to 3 hours

Cautions: The trail is prone to flooding. Take insect spray and call ahead for trail conditions. Keep an eye out for holes that have developed on the trail and for poison ivy.

Trail Directions: From M-13, take Curtis Road west about 4 mi. The trail starts at the northwest end of the parking lot by the information board **[1]**. Grass cushions your steps as you head out through cultivated fields. Just before you reach the service road, if the season is right, listen for bullfrogs in the pond to your right (.2 mi.) **[2]**. Follow the road to the right and then left as it carries you above pools of water until you arrive at a posted junction (.3 mi.) **[3]**. This marks the beginning and ending point for both the short loop and the long loop. Turn right along the gravel service road perched along the dike. Scan the field to your left for deer; the refuge is inundated with them.

Stop and take notice of your surroundings. You don't often have the opportunity to hike along a dike. From this elevated embankment, look to the pools below to your right and the marsh to your left. Your adventure on this trail will occur atop these linear mounds.

A new environment awaits you at the upcoming junction—wooded wetlands (.5 mi.) **[4]**. Trees wade in dark pools occasionally lit by moss-green algae floating on the surface of the water. Turn left; this wet, wooded wonderland flanks the trail as you walk to a bench at .8 mi. **[5]**. A nest box is placed in the pool in front of it. Wood ducks or hooded mergansers are likely users of these nests.

The trail continues its wide, gravely way until you reach a posted junction at the edge of the water (.9 mi.) **[6]**. Turn right and follow along this moatlike spur that is bordered by trees standing in pooled channels. Another bench and nest box (1.2 mi.) **[7]** await you just before the trail winds back to the main trail; there the spur for the short loop continues straight.

Turn right; the long loop continues on to a viewing tower. At 1.8 mi. is the junction for the tower loop **[8]**. Follow to the right under the dark canopy of trees along this swamplike corridor. At 2 mi., head over to the photo blind **[9]**. Wind around this loop and, after stepping out of the shadows, climb the observation tower (2.3 mi.) **[10]** for a panoramic view of the Shiawassee River wetlands and its agricultural fields. A magnification scope helps to focus in on any wildlife that is near.

Head southwest past the field on your right that displays sharecropping. A sign interprets its benefits

to wildlife. At 2.7 mi., a bench and vault toilet mark where the trail veers left **[11]** and continues a short stretch until it returns to the tower loop junction (2.8 mi.) **[8]**. Turn right down the shaded corridor of the wooded wetland and emerge from the den of darkness at 3.1 mi. **[12]**. When you notice a bench ahead, look closely to your left. Growths on either side of a maple tree give the impression that a bear and her cub are starting to climb it (3.3 mi.) **[13]**.

The trail turns left through grass and then right until you get to the spur to the wildlife observatory site (3.8 mi.) **[14]**. Head out to observe; then return and turn right to continue along the main trail.

Pass a bench and the short-loop spur at 4.5 mi. **[15]**. It is a straight line back to the junction where you started the loop (5 mi.) **[3]**. Retrace your steps along the trail to the parking lot or follow the service road back.

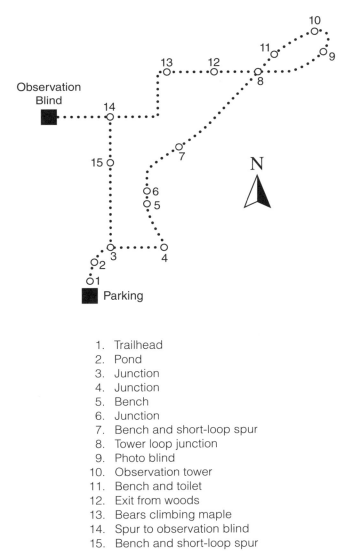

1. Trailhead
2. Pond
3. Junction
4. Junction
5. Bench
6. Junction
7. Bench and short-loop spur
8. Tower loop junction
9. Photo blind
10. Observation tower
11. Bench and toilet
12. Exit from woods
13. Bears climbing maple
14. Spur to observation blind
15. Bench and short-loop spur

Southern
Lower
Peninsula

Songbird–Duck Trails

🌀 **Distance Round-Trip:** 1.4 miles
🍃 **Estimated Hiking Time:** 45 minutes

Cautions: Located in the floodplain of the Tittabawassee River, the trails at Green Point are prone to flooding. Wear appropriate footgear. Insect repellent is a must during spring and early summer. Poison ivy is widespread along the trail.

Trail Directions: All trails start from behind the interpretive center building. The trails can be accessed from either the east or the west end of the building. Start from the east end of the building at the signboard listing the rules and regulations [1].

Just follow the blue songbird symbol located on the trail posts. Your first steps take you into the woods along the wood-chipped path. You will soon realize why the center's educational programs are based on the theme "Water, Wildlife, and You."

Soon after the beginning of the hike through this bottomland hardwood forest, the Wildflower Trail branches off to the right (.1 mi.) [2]. Stay straight. Shortly afterward, you come upon a large maple tree (.1 mi.) [3]. Here a wealth of moneywort lines the trail; notice the coin-shaped leaves deposited along the forest floor.

At .2 mi., you reach a bench where the Turtle Trail heads off to the right [4]. Stay on the Songbird Trail; the trail soon narrows. You then pass dead trees standing vigil over their fallen comrades. After rounding a bend, you pass the junction with the Deer Trail (.4 mi.) [5]. A bench is near the opening to a field nearby. This is a good spot to stop and watch for wildlife. When you resume your hike, you walk parallel to a drainage area before swinging right, along the other side of the field.

At about .6 mi. is the trail junction for the two River Trail loops [6]. Turn left and take the shorter of the two, the Duck Trail, which has a light blue symbol. Walking this loop takes you across a boardwalk to a bench anchored securely on the bank of the Tittabawassee River (.8 mi.) [7]. A floating dock was once located here, but it floated off to freedom in the flood of 1986.

When you return to the Songbird Trail at the junction with the River Trail [6] turn left and then veer right. You are now walking alongside a pond. Beyond the pond, the trail enters the woods that you started in. You encounter several large oak and maple trees and the junction to all the other woodland trail loops before you return to the interpretive center.

N ◀

1. Trailhead
2. Wildflower Trail junction
3. Large maple and moneywort
4. Turtle Trail junction
5. Junction
6. River Trail junction
7. Tittabawassee River

63. Pinckney Recreation Area

- Traverse the rugged landscape shaped by glaciers.
- Climb to scenic overlooks.
- Hike past numerous inland lakes, ponds, and creeks.

Park Information

The park encompasses over 11,000 acres and is composed of three major use areas—Halfmoon day-use area, Silver Lake day-use area, and Bruin Lake Campground. The rolling topography of hills and ridges interspersed with numerous inland water bodies is typical of a landscape shaped by glacial activity. Seven lakes, connected by streams and channels, form a chain that provides extended boating opportunities. The rolling, shaded landscape is popular with equestrians.

Six hiking trails weave through the park. All start from the Silver Lake day-use area. Although the older trails are popular with mountain bikers, the three Losee Lake Loops are closed to bicycles. The park also serves as the eastern terminus of the Waterloo-Pinckney Hiking Trail (see park #64).

Directions: The park headquarters, located at the Silver Lake day-use area, is 15 miles northwest of Ann Arbor. From US 23, head west on North Territorial Road about 10 miles to Dexter-Townhall Road, turn north for 1.2 miles, and then turn left at Silver Hill Road where the park entrance is located. From I-94, head north on M-52 for 6 miles to North Territorial Road and turn right (east) for 6 miles to Dexter-Townhall Road; turn north for 1.2 miles and then left at the park entrance.

Hours Open: Open daily from 8:00 a.m. to 10:00 p.m.

Facilities: Hiking, bicycling, horseback riding, swimming, hunting, fishing, canoeing, boating, cross-country skiing, camping (tent and RV), yurt, and picnicking.

Permits and Rules: A park fee is required for motor vehicles ($6 daily, $24 annually for residents; $8 daily, $29 annually for nonresidents). Motor vehicles are permitted on established roads only.

For Further Information: Pinckney Recreation Area, 8555 Silver Hill Road, Pinckney, MI 48169; 734-426-4913.

Other Points of Interest

Washtenaw County's **Park Lyndon**, traversed by the Waterloo-Pinckney Hiking Trail, has its own system of nature trails that features a variety of habitats including fens, marshes, bogs, ponds, forest, and prairie. The park is located on North Territorial Road, 1 mile east of M-52. Contact Washtenaw County Parks and Recreation for more information at 734-971-6337.

Park Trails

Waterloo-Pinckney Hiking Trail (🥾🥾🥾, 36 mi.). This trail links the Waterloo and Pinckney recreation areas. The eastern end of the 36-mile trail, at the Silver Lake day-use area, is typically the endpoint for people hiking the entire trail from its starting point at the Portage Lake day-use area in the Waterloo Recreation Area (see park #64). Excellent day-hike opportunities exist on this point-to-point trail. Park at Green Lake in the Waterloo Recreation Area, at Washtenaw County's Park Lyndon, or on several of the dirt roads that the trail crosses.

Potawatomi Trail (🥾🥾🥾, 17 miles). Start at the Silver Lake day-use area. This trail is popular with mountain bikers, who are are required to travel clockwise. Hikers should travel counterclockwise. Through hikers can camp at a walk-in campground on Blind Lake, roughly the halfway point of the trail.

Silver Lake Trail (🥾🥾, 1.9 miles). This trail starts at the Silver Lake day-use area. You share this scenic trail with mountain bikers.

Pinckney Recreation Area

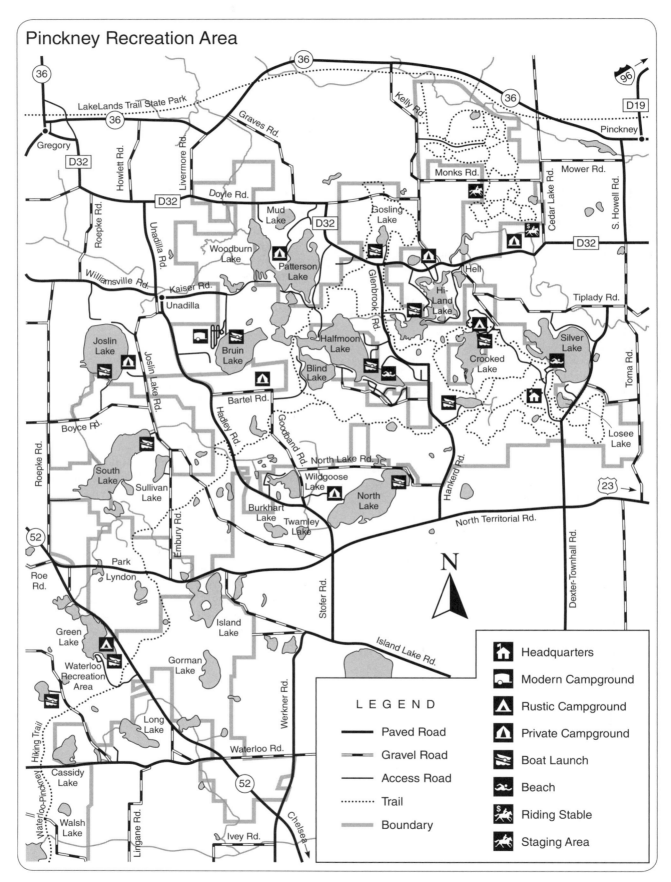

LEGEND

— Paved Road

┤├ Gravel Road

— Access Road

····· Trail

━━ Boundary

🏠 Headquarters

🚐 Modern Campground

⛺ Rustic Campground

⛺ Private Campground

🚤 Boat Launch

🏊 Beach

🏇 Riding Stable

🏇 Staging Area

Crooked Lake Trail

Distance Round-Trip: 5.1 miles
Estimated Hiking Time: 2 to 3 hours

Cautions: Hiking and mountain biking are allowed. Hike counterclockwise to avoid conflicts. Use insect repellent during the warmer months.

Trail Directions: Start behind the wooden map board located at the northeast end of the north parking lot of the Silver Lake day-use area **[1]**.

Head northwest following the shore of Silver Lake. A long boardwalk takes you over a wet area. After you step from the boardwalk and make a short climb, you come to mile marker #36 (.1 mi) **[2]**. This marker is for hikers who have finished the Waterloo-Pinckney Hiking Trail (see park #64).

Shortly thereafter, the Silver Lake Trail splits off to the left (.2 mi.) **[3]**. Stay right. Your trail eventually loops back here.

At .5 mi., the trail swings west and climbs away from the lake **[4]**. Just before crossing Silver Hill Road, you pass a sign directing cross-country skiers to the right. The trail undulates, and you cross the Crooked Lake access road and climb steeply to a veiled overlook of Crooked Lake and the surrounding countryside (1.1 mi.) **[5]**. Rest on the bench here.

Descend from the overlook. At the bottom, you briefly skirt the bank of a creek before turning sharply left and crossing a small footbridge (1.5 mi.) **[6]**. Roll through the woods to another trail junction (2.4 mi.) **[7]**. Here, turn left and head south, away from the Potawatomi Trail. You then cross a wooden footbridge, climb a sandy slope, and cross Glenbrook Road.

On the other side of the road you pass through what had been a mature oak-hickory forest that was leveled by the destructive winds of a tornado that touched down here in 1994. Then pass an area that shows evidence of burn (2.8 mi.) **[8]**. This was a prescribed burn, one planned to manage the habitat. Continue past the trail split on the right that goes to the Halfmoon Lake beach, a 1 mi. round-trip.

Reenter the woods and begin to veer left. Heading east, you pass Pickerel Lake (3.3 mi.) **[9]**. At the east end of the lake, cross a footbridge over a channel that connects Crooked and Pickerel lakes (3.6 mi.) **[10]**.

After climbing a couple of hills, you reach a junction with the Silver Lake Trail (3.9 mi.) **[11]**. Continue straight, or east, and soon you will be on a ridge that rises above kettle ponds, first to your right and then to your left. Negotiate a couple of steep climbs and descents before dropping sharply and then climbing to cross Silver Hill Road (4.7 mi.) **[12]**. Turn right at the next junction to return to the parking lot

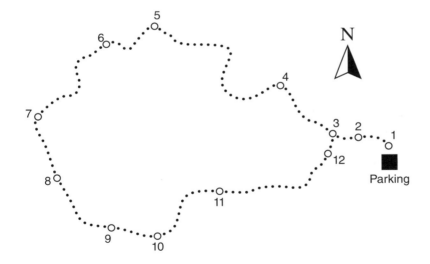

1. Trailhead
2. Mile marker #36
3. Trail junction
4. Turn west
5. Scenic overlook
6. Footbridge
7. Trail junction
8. Tornado destruction
9. Pickerel Lake
10. Channel
11. Trail junction
12. Silver Hill Road

Losee Lake Hiking Trail— Large Loop

Distance Round-Trip: 3.3 miles
Estimated Hiking Time: 1 to 1.5 hours

Cautions: Watch for rocks, roots, and small stumps. Some sections may be wet. Wear appropriate footgear. Take insect repellent in warm months.

Trail Directions: Start at the information board at the southeast end of the lower parking lot near Silver Lake. Watch for the information board located between the parking lot and the lake **[1]**.

Head south past the information board, skirt the lake, and follow the edge of the mowed lawn up the side of a hill. Pass a bench before reaching a defined pathway cut through small shrubs and cedars. Still ascending, you soon make a sharp left that takes you past small cedars and a bowl-shaped wetland (.2 mi.) **[2]**. Hike through a stand of red pine to arrive at a bench in a clearing (.4 mi.) **[3]**.

Now an old two-track, the trail splits left at a marker, and you begin a descent. Turn left just before reaching the park's driveway and descend sharply to junction #2 (.5 mi.) **[4]**. Stay right.

Skirting a wetland, you cross boardwalks before climbing a cedar-covered ridge. Descend to junction #3 (.8 mi.) **[5]**. Stay right and cross Dexter-Townhall Road. You soon walk a boardwalk between two wetlands. Then swing right and climb onto a ridge of red pine (1 mi.) **[6]**. Turn left and approach a power-line corridor. Don't cross here; swing left back into the woods and approach it a second time. Cross near the large utility pole (1.1 mi.) **[7]**.

Descend sharply and veer right to climb steeply. A bench and a scenic vista of the rolling landscape to the south await you (1.2 mi.) **[8]** at junction #4.

Stay right and descend into the shade of an oak-hickory forest. Swing left and find yourself alongside a wetland. Veer right and step down a small ridge to cross a boardwalk onto what is best described as a small island in a large wetland. Enjoy the setting at the bench (1.5 mi.) **[9]**.

Turn left and then left again to cross a boardwalk through cattails. Veer right past red pine, through cedar, and past a busy ant mound. After crossing a line of fieldstones, veer left to cross a boardwalk. Then climb a steep pine-needle-covered hillside to a bench (1.8 mi.) **[10]**.

Roll along open landscape through shrubs and small trees. Pass a bench overlooking a small pond (1.8 mi.) **[11]** and then begin a descent that leads you under the power lines (2.1 mi.) **[12]**. After bottoming out near several large cottonwood trees, the trail veers left into an oak-hickory forest.

Heading west, you can see Silver Lake through the trees to the north. Wind around a bowl-shaped wetland and pass through aromatic cedars to junction #5 (2.4 mi.) **[13]**. Stay right and descend to a large wetland (2.6 mi.) **[14]**. Across the road is Losee Lake.

Climb a small ridge to get a fine view of Losee Lake. The trail descends to cross Dexter-Townhall Road; then a boardwalk supports your steps through a wetland (2.6 mi.) **[15]**. Pass a bench overlooking the lake before junction #6 (2.7 mi.) **[16]**. Stay right and step onto a boardwalk that flows along the marsh perimeter of Losee Lake (2.8 mi.) **[17]**. From the boardwalk you climb to a bench, near a large oak tree, that faces the lake (2.9 mi.) **[18]**. Descend from the small ridge and wind around a wetland to junction #2 **[4]**. Turn right and retrace your steps to the parking lot.

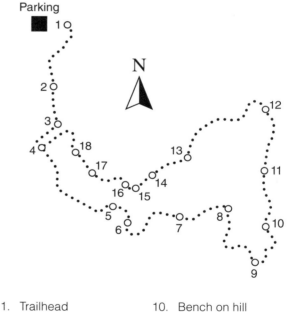

1. Trailhead
2. Wetland
3. Bench at clearing
4. Junction #2
5. Junction #3
6. Red pine
7. Utility pole
8. Bench and junction #4
9. Bench in wetlands
10. Bench on hill
11. Bench overlooking pond
12. Utility corridor
13. Junction #5
14. Wetland
15. Boardwalk
16. Junction #6
17. Boardwalk
18. Bench at oak

- Experience geology hands-on at the Gerald E. Eddy Discovery Center.
- Discover nature along interpretive trails.
- Escape to scenic overlooks, inland lakes, and deep woods.

Park Information

Covering over 20,000 acres, this patchwork quilt of private and public landholdings is the largest state park in Michigan's Lower Peninsula. The landscape was shaped more than 10,000 years ago in the last glacial period. Receding ice, often more than 1 mile thick, formed the moraines (ridges), kames (hills), and kettles (lakes, ponds, and low-lying areas) that characterize the area, providing an abundance of recreational opportunities today. The area includes remnant fields, upland oak-hickory forests, lowland beech-maple woods, and bogs.

The recreation area contains 17 lakes, numerous ponds and streams, four campgrounds, the Gerald E. Eddy Discovery Center, several hiking trails, a 22-mile portion of the Waterloo-Pinckney Hiking Trail, a riding stable, bridle paths, and mountain bike trails.

Directions: West of Chelsea, head north from any of the six exits along I-94 that access the Waterloo Recreation Area. Take M-52 5 miles north to the Green Lake Campground. Follow Pierce Road north to the Cedar Lake Outdoor Center; go north from there and west on Bush Road to reach the Gerald E. Eddy Discovery Center.

To reach park headquarters, go north on Kalmbach Road, jog west on Cavanaugh Lake Road, and go north on Glazier Road, which curves west to Lowry. Head north to McClure Road; the headquarters is west on McClure.

Access Sugarloaf Lake Campgrounds via Clear Lake Road north to Seymour Road. Turn east to Loveland Road and then go south about .5 mile to the campground entrance. Horseman's Camp is about .25 mile south from there.

Big Portage Lake Campground is located between Race and Mt. Hope roads. Head north from either of these exits and turn onto Seymour.

Hours Open: Open daily.

Facilities: Hiking, bicycling, horseback riding, cross-country skiing, snowmobiling, swimming, fishing, hunting, boat launch, camping (tent and RV), picnicking, interpretive trails, and an interpretive center.

Permits and Rules: A park fee is required for motor vehicles ($6 daily, $24 annually for residents; $8 daily, $29 annually for nonresidents). Camping and horseback riding are permitted in established areas only.

For Further Information: Waterloo Recreation Area, 16345 McClure Road, Chelsea, MI 48118; 734-475-8307.

Other Points of Interest

The **Gerald E. Eddy Discovery Center** features slide shows, hiking trails, and interpretive programs to help visitors appreciate the geologic history of the region. From April through August, hours are from 10:00 a.m. to 5:00 p.m. on Tuesdays through Sundays. Hours are reduced thereafter. For more information, contact the Gerald E. Eddy Discovery Center, 17030 Bush Road, Chelsea, MI 48118; 734-475-3170.

The **Waterloo Area Farm Museum**, situated at 9998 Waterloo-Munith Road, serves as a memorial to Michigan pioneer farmers. For more information, call 517-596-2254.

The **Waterloo Riding Stable and Dude Ranch** offers guided trail rides. It is located at 12891 Trist Road, Grass Lake, MI 49240. For more information, call 517-522-8920.

View the fall migration of sandhill cranes at the **Phyllis Haehnle Audubon Sanctuary**, which adjoins the recreation area. The sanctuary is located on the north side of Seymour Road, about 1.5 miles west of Race Road in Jackson County. For more information, contact the Michigan Audubon Society at 517-886-9144.

Park Trails

Dry Marsh Nature Trail (🥾, .5 miles). This trail starts from the Portage Lake campground area and encircles a marsh.

Waterloo Discovery Center Trails (🥾 to 🥾🥾🥾, 14 miles). Various trails emanate from the discovery center, providing many hiking options.

Waterloo-Pinckney Hiking Trail (🥾🥾🥾, 36 miles). This linear trail links the Waterloo and Pinckney Recreation Areas.

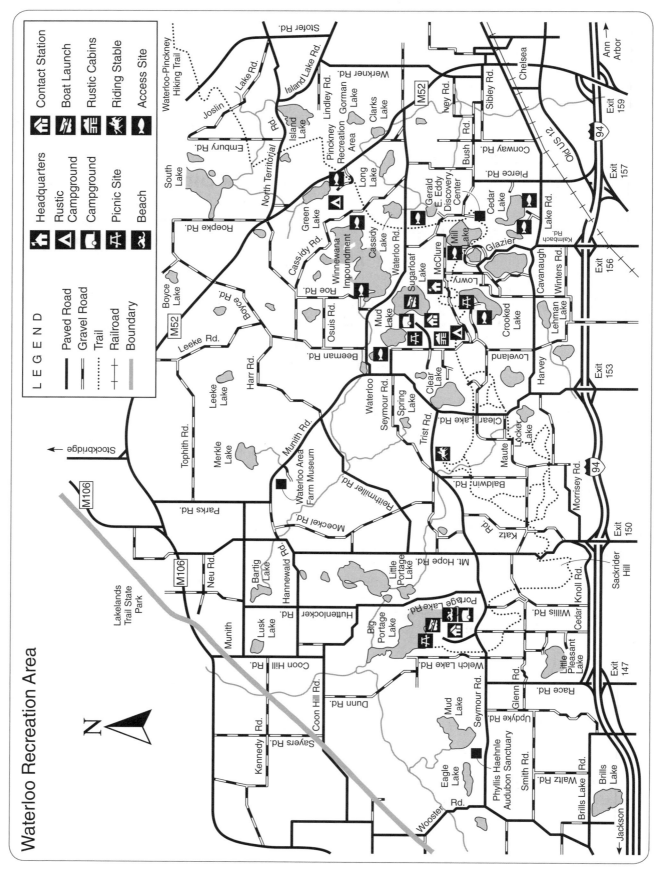

Waterloo Recreation Area

N

Southern Lower Peninsula

LEGEND

Paved Road
Gravel Road
Trail
Railroad
Boundary

Headquarters	Contact Station
Rustic Campground	Boat Launch
Campground	Rustic Cabins
Picnic Site	Riding Stable
Beach	Access Site

Waterloo-Pinckney Hiking Trail—Portage Lake to Sackrider Hill

Distance: 5.8 miles one-way
Estimated Hiking Time: 2.5 to 3 hours

Not many people hike the Waterloo-Pinckney Hiking Trail from end to end, but day-hike opportunities are numerous. You may park at a number of crossroads. Hiking this trail offers as close to a wilderness experience as you will find in southeast Michigan.

Cautions: Some areas are wet, steep, rocky, or have roots, so wear proper footgear. Take insect repellent. Various unmarked trails weave across this one. Follow posted markings and watch for the well-worn path.

Trail Directions: Start in the northwest end of the Portage Lake boat launch parking area **[1]**. The trail takes you along a ridge overlooking the lake, dips to cross a stream on wood planks, and then flows westward in gentle undulations until it bears south, away from the lake, climbing into the woods (.4 mi.) **[2]**.

At the fork (.8 mi.) **[3]**, stay right. The trail makes an S-curve. Follow the trail signs. The trail descends and climbs steeply just before Seymour Road (1.4 mi.) **[4]**. Continue somewhat parallel to the road, pass a power line, angle left past the pole, and weave through grassy clearings before reentering the woods in an undulating pattern of hills and ridges, marshes, wetlands, and ponds.

After you cross List Road (2.5 mi.) **[5]**, the area is predominantly low lying and wet until you reach an old road, now a two-track (2.8 mi.) **[6]**. Turn left on the now single-track trail. Veer right when the trail splits (3.2 mi.) **[7]** and continue on to Willis Road, which has space for parking (3.3 mi.) **[8]**.

Across the road, a concrete dam carries you over a stream that drains the cattail-covered wetland. Climb steeply back into the woods. The trail intermittently dips into marshy and wet areas. At 3.7 mi., a footbridge passes over a soggy stretch of lowland **[9]**. Follow as the trail snakes around the rolling terrain and then descends onto Glenn Road (4.2 mi.) **[10]**. Steep hills, blanketed by hardwoods and an occasional large oak, envelop the trail as you climb. Ascents are difficult and steep; eroded down-sloping sections require extra precaution. A trail merges in at 4.6 mi. **[11]**.

Take a dizzying look over the edge of the steep, wooded ravine when you reach the crest (5 mi.) **[12]**. About .1 mi. farther, veer left at the fork and continue along a land bridge above the forest floor. Descend at a steep angle before you wind around to begin a serious climb up Sackrider Hill. Stay right when the trail splits. A white cross marks the top (5.7 mi.) **[13]**, and a decked platform provides a well-deserved but somewhat obscured panorama of rolling farm fields, hedgerows, barns, and woodlands. If you have arranged to be picked up at the end of your hike, descend steeply to the parking area at Mt. Hope Road (5.8 mi.) **[14]**. Otherwise, turn back here.

1. Trailhead
2. Entrance to woods
3. Fork in trail
4. Seymour Road
5. List Road
6. Two-track
7. Split in trail
8. Willis Road, parking
9. Planked wetland
10. Glenn Road
11. Merging trail
12. Crest overlooking ravine
13. Sackrider Hill
14. Mt. Hope parking lot

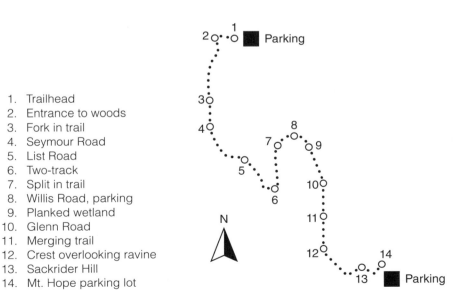

Oak Woods–Waterloo-Pinckney Hiking Trail–Hickory Hills Nature Trail

Distance: 4.7 miles round-trip
Estimated Hiking Time: 1.5 to 2 hours

Cautions: The trail goes over roots, rocks, and poison ivy. Wear appropriate footgear. Take insect repellent during the warm months.

Trail Directions: Start from the northwest end of the Gerald E. Eddy Discovery Center parking lot at post #5 **[1]**. The trail skirts along a ridge through the woods and then descends to a bench that overlooks a wetland (.2 mi.) **[2]**. Continue through the woods, primarily oak and hickory, to junction #8 (.4 mi.) **[3]**.

Stay straight on the narrow path across a land bridge where water embraces both sides. The level trail widens, crosses a culvert, crosses another land bridge (.9 mi.) **[4]**, and then ascends to junction #9, where a bench is nestled in the small opening (1 mi.) **[5]**.

Stay straight, passing a house whose residents are fortunate enough to live near the wooded recreation trail, and then descend, only to climb to a strip of land that bridges two wetlands. You soon reach junction #10 (1.2 mi.) **[6]**. The now-wide trail climbs through the woods to enter an area that is open to hunting. Soon afterward, you cross Ridge Road and descend gradually (1.5 mi.) **[7]**. Enter a grassy area where parking is available at junction #12 (1.6 mi.) **[8]**. The park headquarters is across the road.

Cross the road. Left of the headquarters building is a brown Hickory Hills Nature Trail sign. Pick up an interpretive brochure and then climb through the brush to piles of rocks and stairs to continue climbing (1.7 mi.) **[9]**. At the top is a concrete slab with a hidden bench that has an obscured view of the area below.

This location was once part of the Sylvan Estates Country Club. The slab had been part of a pavilion for picnicking. As late as 1935, visitors could see seven lakes from this point. The forest now obscures the view.

Stay left of the pad, descend the stairs, and enter the woods that you looked down on. The trail swings right along an old fencerow and makes an S curve. The trail descends sharply along the hillside, passing a gully to cut through wetlands (1.9 mi.) **[10]**. The trail swings right for you to climb more stairs (2 mi.) **[11]**.

Turn left at the top and swing around a drying marsh. Stay left at junction #13 to descend and cross McClure Road by angling left past Crooked Lake Road. Climb the stairs onto the ridge where you find a bench and an overview of Crooked Lake (2.2 mi.) **[12]**. Descend sharply, switchbacking along the hillside to wind down to the lake (2.3 mi.) **[13]**. Rest on the bench there before climbing over loose stones. Pass a field that had been a golf course in a prior life and climb to junction #12 (2.6 mi) **[8]**.

Turn right and retrace your steps to junction #8 (3.8 mi.) **[3]**. Turn left along the Oak Woods Trail and climb into the woods, a wetland at your side. The trail rolls, steeply at times, and takes you down to an overlook of Mill Lake (3.9 mi.) **[14]**. Turn right and walk along the edge of a ridge with the lake on your left, veiled by trees. Roll down to a bench, descend more, and swing away from the lake and around and past a wetland.

Stay left when the trail splits (4.2 mi.) **[15]**. Climb more stairs to a bench with a view of Mill Lake (4.5 mi.) **[16]**. Turn right on the paved trail to head back to the center, passing Rock Cycle Trails. You get more overviews of the lake. Pass the picnic shelter and the front door of the discovery center to the overlook, where you get the best views yet of Mill Lake (4.6 mi.) **[17]**. Stop in the center or turn back to the parking lot.

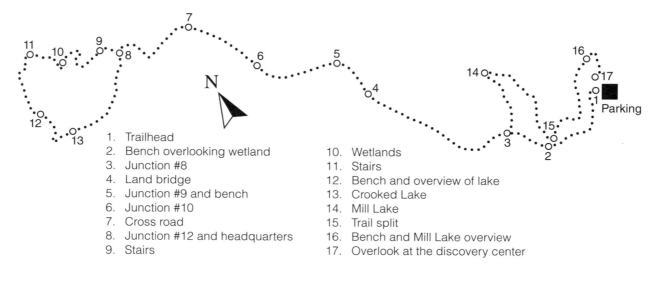

1. Trailhead
2. Bench overlooking wetland
3. Junction #8
4. Land bridge
5. Junction #9 and bench
6. Junction #10
7. Cross road
8. Junction #12 and headquarters
9. Stairs
10. Wetlands
11. Stairs
12. Bench and overview of lake
13. Crooked Lake
14. Mill Lake
15. Trail split
16. Bench and Mill Lake overview
17. Overlook at the discovery center

65. Hidden Lake Gardens

- View the gardens from winding, hilly drives.
- Visit tropical and arid plants in the conservatory.
- Test your plant identification skills.

Park Information

The 755-acre garden exhibits valuable plant collections and creates landscape pictures, fulfilling the objective of the Michigan State University–owned Hidden Lake Gardens. Open woodlands, native meadows, rolling hills, public gardens with natural and designed landscapes, and thousands of plants labeled for identification offer an incredible variety of landscapes for anyone interested in the outdoors.

Set in the glacially sculpted Irish Hills, this unique property has a plant conservatory that features tropical and arid plants. The visitor center features an auditorium, exhibits, a gift shop, and a reference library. Some of the many plantings that color the landscape include a hosta collection, the Harper dwarf and rare conifer collection, a hill planted with various junipers, and a demonstration garden. Directing visitors to these and numerous other features are 6 miles of drives. Five trails weave over 6 miles through woods and meadows, offering visitors a chance to get close to the natural environment.

Directions: The gardens are located 2 miles west of Tipton, or 8 miles west of Tecumseh. From M-52 head west on M-50 about 6 miles. The gardens are on the north side of M-50.

Hours Open: The gardens are open from 8:00 a.m. to dusk in April through October and from 8:00 a.m. to 4:00 p.m. in November through March.

Facilities: Hiking, picnicking, visitor center, and scenic drives.

Permits and Rules: The fee is $3 per person. Please preserve property and natural resources. Pets must be leashed, and children must be kept under supervision. Do not swim or boat; hunt or fish; park or drive vehicles or bicycles on grass, walks, or trails; picnic outside designated area; consume intoxicants; sunbathe; litter; ride bicycles on Sundays or holidays; have horses on the property; or use inline skates.

For Further Information: Hidden Lake Gardens, 6214 Monroe (M-50), Tipton, MI 49287; 517-431-2060.

Other Points of Interest

Bicentennial Woods contains the last stand of virgin beech-maple forest in Lenawee County. A short trail winds through the park. The park is on the west side of Tipton Highway, about 5 miles southwest of Tipton.

For information, contact Building and Grounds Department, Lenawee County, 320 Springbrook Avenue, Adrian, MI 49221; 517-264-4738.

Northwest of the gardens on US 12 is the **Walter J. Hayes State Park**, which offers boating, swimming, fishing, and camping. For information, contact Walter J. Hayes State Park, 1220 Wamplers Lake Road, Onsted, MI 49265; 517-467-7401.

At the junction of US 12 and M-50 is the **Walker Tavern Historic Complex**. The tavern once served weary travelers along a stagecoach road connecting Detroit and Chicago. Exhibits, guided tours, and programs revisit that time. For information, contact Walker Tavern Historic Complex, 13220 M-50, Brooklyn, MI 49230; 517-467-4401; or Michigan Historical Museum, 702 W. Kalamazoo Street, Lansing, MI 48909; 517-373-3559.

Park Trails

Kettle Hole Trail (, .4 mile). Start from the Kettle Hole parking lot. The trail loops through plantings.

Sassafras Trail (, .7 mile). Start from the north end of the parking lot north of Hidden Lake. The trail loops through woods.

Handicapped Access Trail (, .3 mile). Start from the northwest loop of the Sassafras Trail and wind through rejuvenating fields and woods.

Hikers' Trail

Distance Round-Trip: 2.8 miles
Estimated Hiking Time: 1.5 to 2 hours

Cautions: The trail takes you over roots and rocks, and along narrow paths on ridges that angle down slopes. Watch your footing. Poison ivy grows along the trail. Take insect repellent.

Trail Directions: Start from the north end of the parking lot that lies north of Hidden Lake **[1]**. Head up the asphalt trail.

The trail curves, and you pass a junction (.1 mi.) **[2]**. Leave the asphalt and climb the wood-chipped path. Glacial boulders show themselves erratically.

You pass the Sassafras Trail junction, where the woodchips end. The trail winds down and up to the junction for the Pine-Tree Trail (.3 mi.) **[3]**. Stay straight, ascend slightly into an open area, and then descend to the lip of a deep wooded depression, the Butter Bowl (.4 mi.) **[4]**. This formation resulted from the melting of a huge hunk of buried glacial ice. Walk around the large bowl and then descend along a narrow path into it. Making a wide right, you pass moss-covered boulders as you skirt a rise on your left. Climb and follow along the lip of the bowl before making a sharp left (.6 mi.) **[5]**.

Heading east, wind and roll with the trail until it heads north and then west along the northern boundary. Trees block you from the grassy field on your right.

Winding your way through the woods, make a wide left to skirt a large, wooded depression (1 mi.) **[6]**. Start a gradual descent that becomes steeper and veers to the right. You bottom out at a gathering of fieldstones (1.2 mi.) **[7]**. The trail dips and climbs, taking you past purple coneflowers and a pasture, through lush foliage, and then back into woods to wind a hill.

After you circle the hill, the trees become more impressive and the hills more demanding. Descend sharply toward the drive and then climb steeply to top out in the myrtle that spills down the slopes (1.7 mi.) **[8]**.

Roll through the oak upland forest and wind around a couple of depressions before breaking out into a field (2.1 mi.) **[9]**. Stay close to the tree line. Follow the mowed path. The trail descends through the rolling landscape. Veer left behind several white pines; then wind down before again climbing. Through here, you may see a path for the Kettle Hole Planting on your left.

Descend sharply to cross the drive to Juniper Hill (2. mi.) **[10]**. Keep descending, cross the road, and reach the path at Hidden Lake (2.6 mi.) **[11]**.

Turn left and follow along the lake. Cut past myrtle to a small parking area on the north end of the lake (2.7 mi.) **[12]**. Stop and watch the swans before returning to the parking area north of the lake.

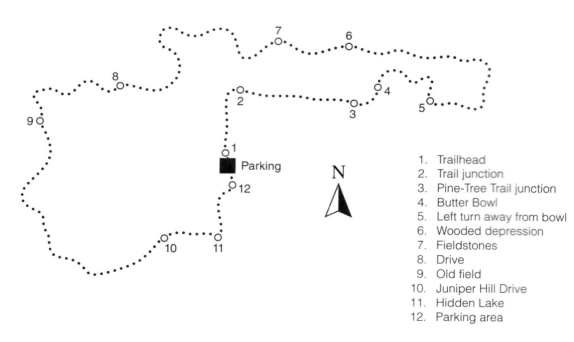

1. Trailhead
2. Trail junction
3. Pine-Tree Trail junction
4. Butter Bowl
5. Left turn away from bowl
6. Wooded depression
7. Fieldstones
8. Drive
9. Old field
10. Juniper Hill Drive
11. Hidden Lake
12. Parking area

66. Chippewa Nature Center

- Explore almost 900 acres of woods, fields, rivers, ponds, and wetlands.
- Learn about the history and wildlife of the area at the visitor center.
- Discover various ecosystems along 15 miles of trails.

Park Information

Start with a location at the confluence of the Pine and Chippewa rivers; add a visitor center with a museum, wildflower walkway, and wildlife-viewing area; sprinkle in wetlands; and you have only skimmed the surface of programs and amenities available at the Chippewa Nature Center.

Fifteen miles of trails wind along the rivers, through forests and fields, and over wetlands (including remnant bog, oxbow, ponds, and marshes). Visit the Homestead Farm area of restored buildings—a cabin, log schoolhouse, and sugarhouse. These attractions are open seasonally. The center offers school programs, a nature day camp, and nature walks.

Directions: From Midland, take Poseyville Road south. Turn right on St. Charles and left onto Whitman. Follow the signs. Turn right off Badour to the center. From US 10, take Business 10 west to Cronkright (Poseyville Road). Turn left on Cronkright and go over Poseyville Bridge to St. Charles Street. Turn right and follow the signs to the center. From M-47, head northwest on Midland Road and turn left at Gordonville Road. Take this to Poseyville Road, turn right, and go to Ashby. Turn left on Ashby to Badour, where you turn right to reach the center.

Hours Open: The visitor center is open Monday through Friday from 8:00 a.m. to 5:00 p.m., Saturdays from 9:00 a.m. to 5:00 p.m., and Sundays from 1:00 to 5:00 p.m. Call to find out holiday hours. The trails are open from dawn to dusk daily.

Facilities: Hiking, cross-country skiing, and interpretive center.

Permits and Rules: There is no admission fee for the visitor center or trails. No pets, smoking, alcohol, fishing, or hunting is allowed. Bicycles are permitted only on the Chippewa Trail. Leave all plants, animals, and artifacts as you found them.

For Further Information: Chippewa Nature Center, 400 S. Badour Road, Midland, MI 48640; 989-631-0830; www.chippewanaturecenter.com.

Other Points of Interest

Dow Gardens, located in Midland, features over 100 acres of various plants. The founder of Dow Chemical Company, Herbert Henry Dow, started the gardens in the late 1800s as part of the landscaping for his home. The gardens are open daily from 9:00 a.m. until sunset, except on major holidays. For more information, contact the Dow Gardens, 1809 Eastman Avenue, Midland, MI 48640; 989-631-2677; 800-362-4874; www.dowgardens.org.

The **Pere Marquette Rail-Trail of Mid-Michigan** is a 30-mile, asphalt-paved trail that runs from Midland to Clare. For information, contact Midland County Parks and Recreation Department, 220 W. Ellsworth Street, Midland, MI 48640; 989-832-6874. Information is also available from Friends of the Pere Marquette Rail-Trail at www.lmb.org/prmt.

Park Trails

Sugar Bush Trail (🐾, 1 mile). Start at the visitor center. The trail follows along the Chippewa River and then heads through sugar bush and beech-maple woods.

Homestead Trail (🐾, .6 mile). The trail starts off the River Trail and takes you through the Homestead Farm.

Arboretum Trail (🐾, .4 mile). The trail starts off the River Trail, follows the river, and then cuts through an area near the arboretum.

Wetlands Trail (🐾, 1.7 miles). This trail weaves through the wetlands area, which is located off the east side of Badour Road, south of Pine River Road.

Arbury Trail (🐾, .4 mile). This paved trail starts at the southwest portion of the visitor center parking area. It loops through pines, goes over a boardwalk near Arbury Pond, and overlooks the Pine River.

Meadow Mouse Trail (🐾, .6 mile). This trail is accessed from the parking area along Hubert Road, which is northwest of the Pine River. It passes primarily through a meadow.

Ridge Trail (🐾, 1.5 miles). This trail starts off Grey Road and follows an ancient beach ridge into young woodlands.

River Point Birch Trail (🐾, 1 mile). This trail starts from the parking area at Hubert Road and cuts through mixed woods.

Field and Wood Duck Trail (🐾, .1 mile to .4 mile). These trails are spurs off other loops.

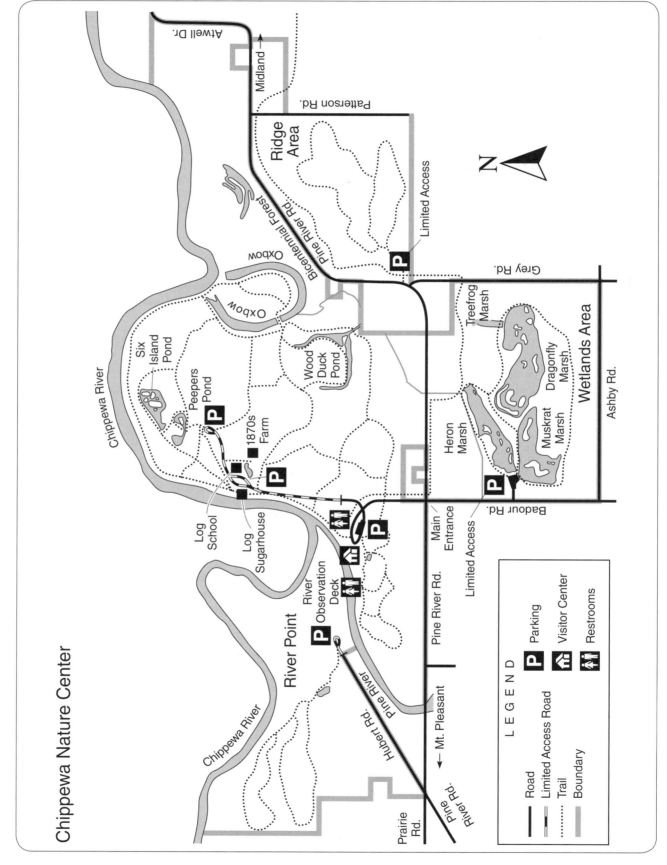

Chippewa Nature Center

River Point

Chippewa River

Chippewa River

Six Island Pond

Peepers Pond

1870s Farm

Log School

Log Sugarhouse

River Observation Deck

Oxbow

Oxbow

Wood Duck Pond

Bicentennial Forest

Pine River Rd.

Heron Marsh

Treefrog Marsh

Dragonfly Marsh

Muskrat Marsh

Wetlands Area

Ridge Area

Atwell Dr.

← Midland

Patterson Rd.

Limited Access

Grey Rd.

Ashby Rd.

Main / Entrance

Limited Access

Badour Rd.

Hubert Rd.

Pine River

← Mt. Pleasant

Prairie Rd.

Pine River Rd.

L E G E N D

Road

Limited Access Road

Trail

Boundary

P Parking

Visitor Center

Restrooms

River Point Woodland Trail

🐾 **Distance Round-Trip:** 1.5 miles
🐾 **Estimated Hiking Time:** 30 to 45 minutes

Cautions: Watch out for poison ivy, as well as for small stumps that may be protruding from the trail. Some sections of the trail are prone to flooding. Take insect repellent during warmer months.

Trail Directions: The trail is located about .6 mi. northwest of the visitor center. Take Pine River Road west to Hubert and turn northeast. Hubert ends at a cul-de-sac. There are a few parking spaces here. The trail, along with the Meadow and Birch trails, begins northwest of the parking area. Watch for the "Trail Head" sign; then cut through the mowed path of grass **[1]**.

Don't let this grassy feeder trail that passes under transmission lines dissuade you. Soon the trail bends, and you enter a canopy of trees, your gateway to a secluded environment (.1 mi.) **[2]**. The trail goes through a mix of mostly hardwoods and arrives at a footbridge by a pond (.2 mi.) **[3]**.

Shortly, you pass the first junction for the Birch Trail. A vernal stream parallels the trail to your right. Depending on the season, you may hear flowing water.

Just after the second Birch Trail junction, pass a small clearing bright with the foliage of ferns to arrive at a bench overlooking the Chippewa River (.3 mi.) **[4]**.

After a short walk along the river, the trail arrives at the junction for the Woodland Trail (.4 mi.) **[5]**. Go to the right where the slightly undulating trail veers away from the river, descends, and then veers left under the cover of trees before approaching intermittent clearings of ferns.

Cutting through mature woods, the trail, cushioned by a carpet of moss and pine needles, veers right. You pass a number of large hemlocks (.8 mi.) **[6]**. The trail turns left, rolling gently before it passes through an area prone to flooding (.9 mi.) **[7]**. Taking another left, it then undulates through seasonally wet, wooded lowlands. Look into the dark shadows of the trees. Is wildlife that you can't see lurking there, waiting for you to pass? Listen for the gentle sound of foliage being torn from a plant or the light snapping of a twig.

Continue rolling and winding through the mix of pine and hardwoods to arrive at the close of the Woodland Loop (1.1 mi.) **[5]**. From here, retrace your steps for the .4 mi. hike back to the starting point of the trail.

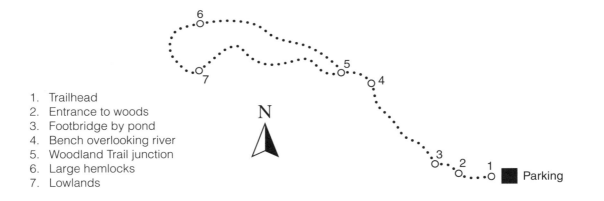

1. Trailhead
2. Entrance to woods
3. Footbridge by pond
4. Bench overlooking river
5. Woodland Trail junction
6. Large hemlocks
7. Lowlands

N

River Trail

🌿 **Distance Round-Trip:** 2.9 miles
🌿 **Estimated Hiking Time:** 1 to 1.5 hours

Cautions: Much of the trail is near water; bring insect repellent. The trail is prone to flooding. Watch for roots and rocks; wear appropriate footgear. Steer clear of poison ivy.

Trail Directions: The trail begins east of the flagpole next to the visitor center **[1]**. Look for the River Trail sign and pick up a trail guide. The first .3 mi. is a guided trail with six stops. The first is a seasonal camp that Native Americans used about 1,100 years ago.

Leave the pavement behind and head north to the Pine River. You follow the river a short distance to the point at which it converges with the Chippewa River. Benches are located along the bank so that you can sit and watch the waters of the two rivers flow together (.1 mi.) **[2]**. When you continue your hike, the Chippewa River is at your side.

After passing a number of trail junctions that all go to the right, you reach an old oak with a bench (.7 mi.) **[3]**.

The river soon swings to the right, and a number of houses come into view on the other bank. Along this stretch look for geese, kingfishers, and muskrats.

At 1.3 mi., turn left at the trail marker and enter what once was the river channel **[4]**. A bench has been positioned nearby to allow you to sit and watch the river flow by in its current channel. Beyond the bench, pass a large oak before you reach the still waters of the old river channel, or oxbow lake (1.5 mi.) **[5]**. An oxbow lake is formed when the main channel is cut off, most likely during a flood event, as the river seeks a straighter or more direct path. The cutoff section forms the oxbow lake.

As you walk through the woods along the inside bend of the oxbow lake, look for snakes and turtles sunning themselves on exposed logs. Swinging right, you eventually reach a land bridge that takes you across the oxbow and starts you on your journey back to the visitor center (1.8 mi.) **[6]**. After crossing, turn left at the trail junction.

Walk along what looks like another old river channel. A wooden bridge provides a good platform from which to take in this interesting location at Wood Duck Pond (2.1 mi.) **[7]**. Note the contrast of dead trees on the right. A bench at 2.2 mi. gives you a chance to sit and view the stags **[8]**. Turn left at the trail marker and enter an area where younger hardwood trees mix with pine. Not confined by water, the trail snakes its way through the trees and over a couple of boardwalks before reaching a trail sign that reads "Short Cut" (2.7 mi.) **[9]**. Resist temptation, stay to the left, and follow the trail over the driveway, past the trailhead to the Arbury Trail, and back to the parking lot at the visitor center.

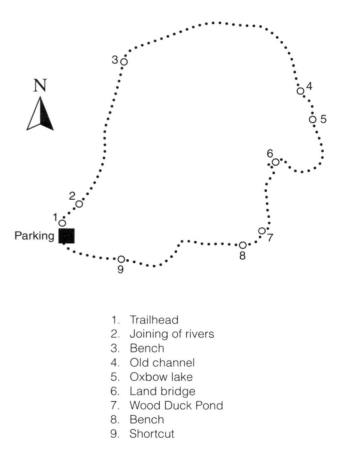

1. Trailhead
2. Joining of rivers
3. Bench
4. Old channel
5. Oxbow lake
6. Land bridge
7. Wood Duck Pond
8. Bench
9. Shortcut

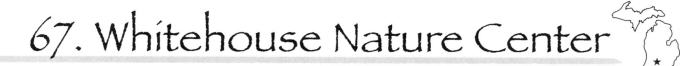

- Hike five self-guided nature trails.
- Explore a tallgrass prairie restoration area.
- Visit an arboretum that features Michigan trees and shrubs.

Park Information

Situated along the East Branch Kalamazoo River, only .25 mile from the main campus of Albion College, are the diverse lands of the Whitehouse Nature Center. Five self-guided interpretive trails wind through a variety of natural and manmade habitats.

Dedicated in 1972, this 144-acre nature center, although owned and maintained by Albion College, is available for more than just college activities. People of all ages are encouraged to use the center's facilities and to participate in its educational programs and activities. Call the center for information about adult education courses or public hikes that feature seasonal wildflowers, birds, autumn trees and shrubs, and more.

Pick up a trail guide at the interpretive building. No, the building is not a white house. The facility is named in honor of the 10th president of Albion College, Dr. William W. Whitehouse. While at the interpretive building, visit the observation room to see what might be feasting at the feeders. More than 168 bird species have been sighted at the center.

Directions: From I-94, take exit 124 to Albion. Go to the traffic light at Clark Street. Turn left and continue to a T-intersection at East Erie Street. Turn right and proceed to Hannah Street. Turn left, cross the railroad tracks, and immediately turn left into a parking lot. Follow the signs through the parking lot to the nature center at the end of the athletic field.

Hours Open: The nature center is open daily from dawn until dusk. The interpretive building is open weekdays from 9:30 a.m. to 4:30 p.m. and weekends from 10:30 a.m. to 4:30 p.m. Call ahead for holiday hours.

Facilities: Hiking, interpretive trails, and interpretive center.

Permits and Rules: There is no admittance fee. Not allowed are bicycling, horseback riding, picnicking, camping, fire building, hunting, unattended dogs, consumption of alcoholic beverages, or motorized vehicles. Please do not take any natural materials or leave any unnatural materials.

For Further Information: Whitehouse Nature Center, 517-629-0582; www.albion.edu/naturecenter.

Other Points of Interest

If it is history that you seek, a trip to **Marshall** is in order. Noted for its outstanding Greek and Gothic revival homes from the 1840s and 1850s, the Marshall Historic Homes Tour is conducted annually the weekend after Labor Day. For information, call the Marshall Area Chamber of Commerce, 800-877-5163, www.marshallmi.org.

Park Trails

History Trail (🐾). Not a separate trail, the History Trail consists of nine sites scattered throughout the nature center that are listed in a printed guide.

Main Trail (🐾, .5 mile). The route of the old interurban trail bisects the nature center. Trails loop off this historic corridor.

McIntyre Marsh Trail (🐾, .5 mile). This trail is a boardwalk path through the marsh on the west side of the river. The interpretive theme of the trail is marshland ecology.

Beese Ecology Trail (🐾, 2.4 miles). This trail features wildlife-viewing areas where various species occupy their open-field and fencerow habitats.

Stowell Arboretum Trail (🐾, 1 mile). This trail passes through an area that features Michigan trees and shrubs.

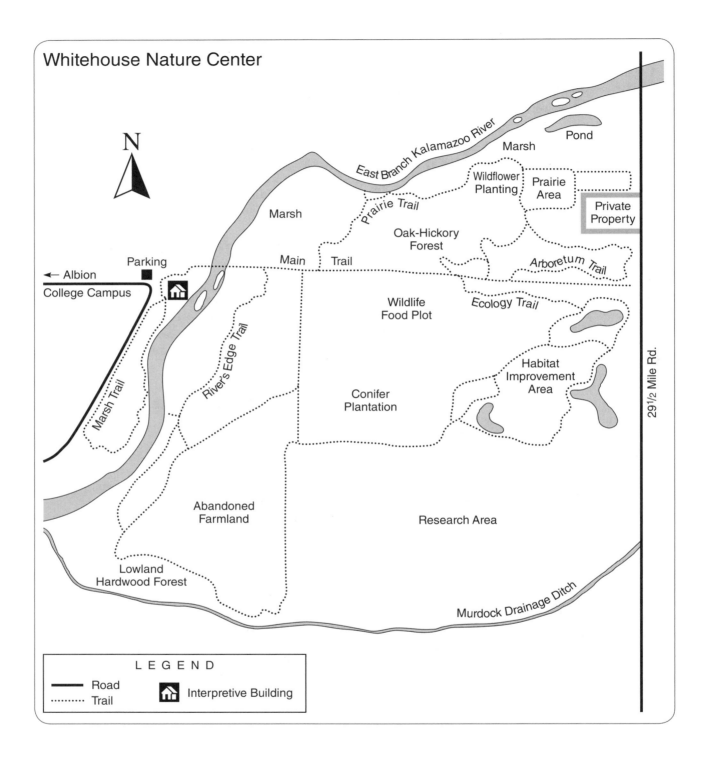

Whitehouse Nature Center

N

← Albion
College Campus

Parking

East Branch Kalamazoo River

Pond

Marsh

Wildflower
Planting

Prairie
Area

Private
Property

Marsh

Prairie Trail

Oak-Hickory
Forest

Main   Trail

Arboretum Trail

Ecology Trail

Wildlife
Food Plot

River's Edge Trail

Habitat
Improvement
Area

Marsh Trail

Conifer
Plantation

Abandoned
Farmland

Research Area

29½ Mile Rd.

Lowland
Hardwood Forest

Murdock Drainage Ditch

LEGEND

——— Road
········· Trail

Interpretive Building

River's Edge Trail

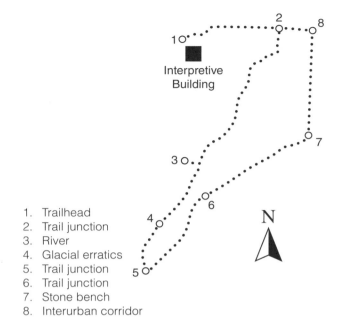

Distance Round-Trip: .9 mile
Estimated Hiking Time: 30 minutes

Cautions: Take insect repellent during the warm months. Some sections of the trail may be wet or muddy. Wear appropriate footgear.

Trail Directions: The hike starts at the information board located at the east end of the parking lot near the interpretive building **[1]**. Stop in at the building for a trail guide.

Proceed to the left of the information board and follow a gravel and then wood-chipped path past various wildflowers and the chatter of feeding birds. You then find yourself looking over the railing of a footbridge that spans the scenic East Branch Kalamazoo River.

The green corridor that stretches out before you once served as the rail bed for the interurban Michigan Electric Railway, which operated between Detroit and Kalamazoo from 1904 to 1929. The corridor now transports visitors, under their own power, to the center's various nature trails.

The River's Edge Trail is the first stop (.1 mi.) **[2]**. Turn right and you will be on a narrow path that gives you a more intimate moment with nature than the old corridor did. The canopy here is dense, an indicator of a floodplain forest where mucky soils promote luxuriant growth. Winding through the lush vegetation, you pass a number of interpretive stops that cover topics varying from wood-rotting fungi to wild yams to wild plant communities. After you walk through a natural fernery, a spur trail splits off to take you to see what is happening at the edge of the river (.3 mi.) **[3]**.

When you are back at the trail, you have the option of taking a shortcut through the woods or following the trail markers to the right. The shortcut saves you only about .3 mi. Either way, keep an eye out for blueberries. As you continue, a small ridge that has glacial erratics scattered among its vegetation rises on your left. At .4 mi., you can sit on one of the larger glacial boulders and watch the river flow by **[4]**.

Soon, turn left and climb away from the river to reach a trail junction (.5 mi.) **[5]**. Turn left and pull out your History

1. Trailhead
2. Trail junction
3. River
4. Glacial erratics
5. Trail junction
6. Trail junction
7. Stone bench
8. Interurban corridor

Trail guide. You pass a place where Native Americans winter camped about 500 to 1,000 years ago. You also pass the site of a sandstone quarry that was in operation in the 1840s.

The shortcut trail merges back in from the left (.6 mi.) **[6]**.

At the next trail junction, a stone bench waits (.7 mi.) **[7]**. Turn left and wind through the woods back to the old interurban (.8 mi.) **[8]**. Turn left and retrace your steps to the parking area.

Prairie Trail

🐾 **Distance Round-Trip:** 1 mile
🐾 **Estimated Hiking Time:** 30 minutes

Cautions: Take insect repellent if you visit during the warm months. Some sections of the trail may be wet or muddy, so wear appropriate footgear.

Trail Directions: The hike starts at the information board located at the east end of the parking lot near the interpretive building **[1]**. Stop in at the building for a trail guide. Proceed to the left of the information board and follow the gravel and then wood-chipped path past various wildflowers and the sounds of birds feeding. Turn right and you soon will then be looking over the railing of a footbridge that spans the scenic East Branch Kalamazoo River (.1 mi.) **[2]**.

Follow along the green corridor that bisects the nature center. It once served as the rail bed for the interurban Michigan Electric Railway, which connected Detroit and Kalamazoo from 1904 to 1929. Now the corridor is a path that visitors take to the nature center's various nature trails.

The Prairie Trail is the first stop on the left (.2 mi.) **[3]**. Turn left. The trail swings right and winds through the forest to arrive at the river (.3 mi.) **[4]**. Within the nature center, marsh typically borders the river. Here the river has a sandy, rocky bank that enables you to get close for wildlife viewing.

Continue east right alongside the river and then enter the native wildflower garden (.4 mi.) **[5]**. Most of the wildflowers that you see here have been brought from other natural areas that face destruction. Because many of these wildflowers bloom before the trees leaf out and block the sunlight, try to visit this area in spring. A small rock-bordered pathway loops through the garden to help you across the wildflowers. Just don't pick or remove any of them.

Just east of the wildflower garden is the Prairie Restoration Area. Dominated by grasses, this tallgrass prairie is best visited in the fall. Two loops from which you may view the prairie plants weave through the area. Although they may look like weeds, prairie plants differ from weeds in that they are native plants; most weeds are plants that have been introduced into an area.

Go ahead and weave through the inner loop. Back at the main trail, head south to the junction with the Ewell A. Stowell Arboretum Trail (.6 mi.) **[6]**. Turn right. Soon another junction gives you two options for getting back to the Main Trail. One is as good as the other. If you choose the one on the right, you weave through the woods. After you are back to the Main Trail (.7 mi.) **[7]**, turn right and follow the old interurban corridor back to the parking area.

1. Trailhead
2. Footbridge
3. Prairie Trail
4. River
5. Wildflower garden
6. Trail junction
7. Old corridor

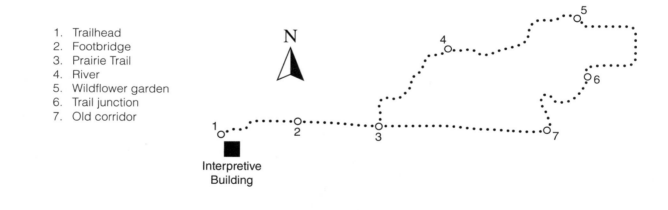

N

Interpretive
Building

- Hike over rugged moraines to the Devil's Soup Bowl.
- Enjoy nine lakes, meandering streams, and numerous bogs.
- View wildlife in this recreation area and the adjoining Barry State Game Area.

Park Information

Almost 5,200 acres of diverse terrain, once the hunting grounds of the Algonquian Indians, provide varied recreation experiences. Nine lakes within the park boundaries offer opportunities for fishing, boating, swimming, and wildlife viewing. The largest, Gun Lake, exceeds 2,500 acres. The site of Yankee Springs was established in 1835. Yankee Bill Lewis made the village famous by owning and operating an inn along the stagecoach run between Kalamazoo and Grand Rapids.

As with most of Michigan, the glacial period left its mark here. Features like the Devil's Soup Bowl, an old, dried-out kettle lake formation, and Graves Hill, a scenic overlook and one of the most popular of the rugged moraines that make for challenging hiking within the park, remind us of that period long ago.

Over 15 miles of hiking trails wind through the park to various points of interest. Additionally, the park has 12 miles of biking trails and 8 miles of bridle trails.

Directions: The park is halfway between Kalamazoo and Grand Rapids, about 12 miles west of Hastings. From US 131, take exit 61 (County Road A42) east, following the signs for about 8 miles to the headquarters. From Hastings, take M-37 west to Gun Lake Road.

Hours Open: Open daily from 8:00 a.m. to 10:00 p.m.

Facilities: Hiking, mountain bicycling, cross-country skiing, snowmobiling, swimming, bridle trails, fishing, hunting, boat launch, camping (tent and RV), equestrian camping, picnicking, cabins, and interpretive trails.

Permits and Rules: A park fee is required for motor vehicles ($6 daily, $24 annually for residents; $8 daily, $29 annually for nonresidents).

For Further Information: Yankee Springs Recreation Area, 2104 S. Briggs Road, Middleville, MI 49333; 269-795-9081.

Other Points of Interest

Barry State Game Area, which offers 17,000 acres for wildlife viewing, adjoins the park. For more information, contact the Barry Field Office, 1805 South Yankee Springs Road, Middleville, MI 49333; 616-795-3280.

Park Trails

Chief Noonday (🥾🥾, 4 miles). This trail begins off Chief Noonday Road and takes you to the Devil's Soup Bowl. Get a panoramic view of the area from the McDonald Lake overlook.

Deep Lake (🥾🥾, 5 miles). This trail begins and ends across from the campground office. It meanders around the bog area at Deep Lake, trudges across open fields and old farmsteads, and winds around the smaller of the kettles at the Devil's Soup Bowl.

Sassafras Nature (🥾, 1 mile). This trail begins by the Gun Lake Campground office and heads through woods.

Gun Lake (🥾, .5 mile). This accessible trail connects the Gun Lake Campground and the day-use area. It crosses a boardwalk through a bog and goes to the fishing pier on Gun Lake.

A portion of the North Country National Scenic Trail winds through this park, beginning south of Gun Lake Road. This 4,600 mile-long trail follows sections of the Chief Noonday and Hall Lake trails.

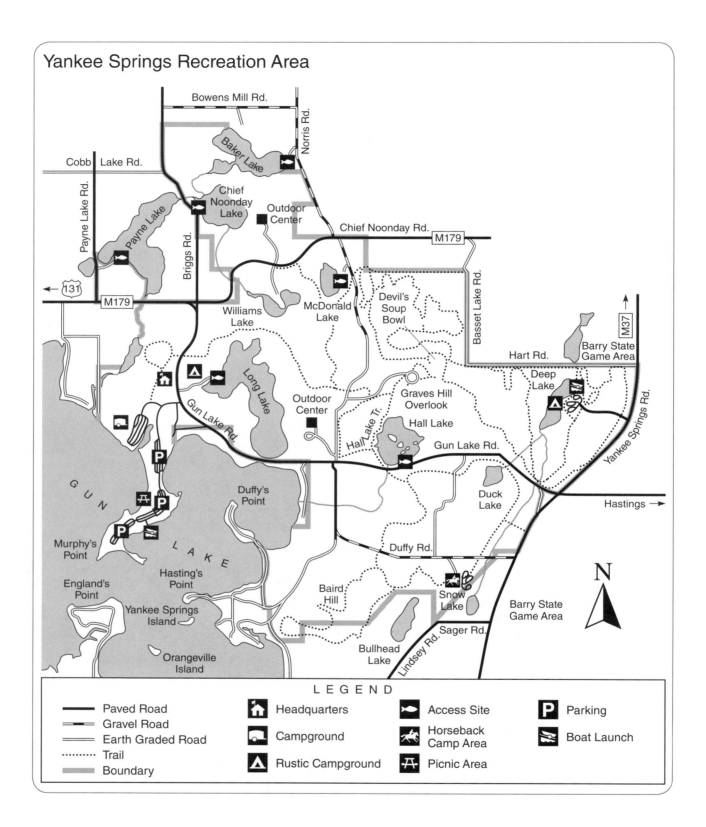

Yankee Springs Recreation Area

Bowens Mill Rd.

Norris Rd.

Cobb Lake Rd.

Baker Lake

Payne Lake Rd.

Chief Noonday Lake

Outdoor Center

Chief Noonday Rd. M179

Payne Lake

Briggs Rd.

← 131

M179

Williams Lake

McDonald Lake

Devil's Soup Bowl

Basset Lake Rd.

M37

Hart Rd.

Barry State Game Area

Deep Lake

Long Lake

Gun Lake Rd.

Outdoor Center

Graves Hill Overlook

Hall Lake Tr.

Hall Lake

Gun Lake Rd.

P

Duffy's Point

Yankee Springs Rd.

A P

Duck Lake

Hastings →

P

Murphy's Point

G U N   L A K E

England's Point

Hasting's Point

Yankee Springs Island

Baird Hill

Snow Lake

Barry State Game Area

Duffy Rd.

Orangeville Island

Bullhead Lake

Lindsey Rd.

Sager Rd.

N

L E G E N D

—— Paved Road	🏠 Headquarters	🐟 Access Site	P Parking
⊶ Gravel Road	🚐 Campground	🐎 Horseback Camp Area	🛶 Boat Launch
═ Earth Graded Road	▲ Rustic Campground	🪑 Picnic Area	
···· Trail			
▬ Boundary			

Southern Lower Peninsula   270

Hall Lake Trail

Distance Round-Trip: 2.5 miles
Estimated Hiking Time: 1 to 2 hours

Cautions: Watch for poison ivy, roots, and rocks along the trail. Take insect repellent.

Trail Directions: The trail starts across from the entrance drive of the Long Lake Outdoor Center, north of Gun Lake Road **[1]**.

Just after embarking, you come to a posted junction that points the way to either Hall Lake or Graves Hill. Head to the right into the pines toward Hall Lake. Soon the trail veers left, and you walk through small pines intermixed with mature hardwoods. The trail winds through rolling terrain until it enters an area of more mature pines. After a short trek, look ahead to your left, where you catch your first glimpse of Hall Lake. Thereafter, the trail swings left to begin traversing Hall Lake. A post guides you over a footbridge that positions you between lake and wetland (.4 mi.) **[2]**.

Stay to the right of a trail junction and walk along the lake (.5 mi.) **[3]**.

Logs placed over a small stream remind you that you are still in a wetland environment (.6 mi.) **[4]**. Watch for turtles or other wildlife in the pond to your left or gaze out over Hall Lake to your right.

Now the trail begins its climb into beeches and maples. Stop along the way and take in a view of the lake from a high point (.7 mi.) **[5]** before swinging left away from the lake. Soon the trail begins a steep climb along an eroding route. Near the top is a junction (.8

mi.) **[6]**. Head straight to Graves Hill, a moraine (a hill created from an accumulation of glacial deposits) (.9 mi.) **[7]**.

To experience kettles, or glacier-made depressions, continue straight. Follow as the trail descends, winds around, and then heads left to a parking area at a posted junction (1 mi.) **[8]**. The trail continues to the right of the parking area and then goes left at the junction. Follow this path up to the Devil's Soup Bowl (1.2 mi.) **[9]**. From here you can look deep down into the kettle created thousands of years ago from the weight of ice that broke off from glaciers. Do not be tempted to advance down the steep slope. Instead, follow the trail to the left as it traverses the steep kettle and takes you to an unmarked junction along the ridge. Turn left and descend to the parking area (1.4 mi.) **[8]**. Look to the left—to where you first came out onto the parking area. Go back that way and retrace your steps to Graves Hill and then to the junction (1.6 mi.) **[6]**.

Turn right and head down the slope. At the bottom, stay left at the posted junction with the Long Lake Trail. Soon you will see a vernal pond to your left (1.9 mi.) **[10]**, just before you climb a short, steep hill and come to a posted fork (2 mi.) **[11]**. Stay to the right. The trail descends; then it veers left around a wetland and takes you to another post (2.1 mi.) **[12]** before heading left through woods. Ski trails weave throughout this area, so be sure to stay on the main trail until you finally reach the junction that introduced you to the loop along the Hall Lake Trail. Turn right to head back to your vehicle.

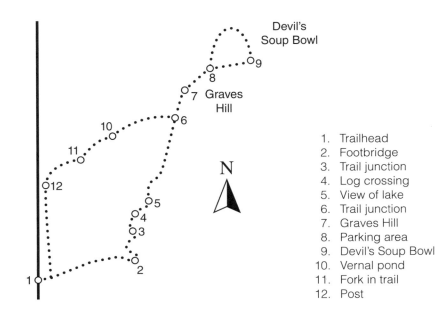

1. Trailhead
2. Footbridge
3. Trail junction
4. Log crossing
5. View of lake
6. Trail junction
7. Graves Hill
8. Parking area
9. Devil's Soup Bowl
10. Vernal pond
11. Fork in trail
12. Post

Long Lake Trail

Distance Round-Trip: 5.2 miles
Estimated Hiking Time: 2.5 to 3 hours

Cautions: Watch for poison ivy. Ski trails weave through the area. Take care to stay on the main hiking trail. Boardwalks may be slippery when wet.

Trail Directions: Start on the east side of Gun Lake Road, just north of park headquarters **[1]**. The trail is posted. You may park alongside Gun Lake Road.

Head east through a mixed forest until you come to a posted junction (.2 mi.) **[2]**. Veer left and soon follow along past stately white pines until you reach the boardwalk that will support your steps through a beautiful forested wetland (.5 mi.) **[3]**. In spring this area lights up with the foliage and flowers from skunk cabbage, fiddleheads, and marsh marigolds—a stunning contrast to the dark, rich soil in this wet area and to the shaded woods at its periphery. The boardwalk winds around for almost .3 mi. before it ends (.8 mi.) **[4]**. Continue to the right as you traverse between a small stream and rolling hills. Just after crossing a small footbridge over the stream (.9 mi.) **[5]**, the trail ascends into a mixed forest.

The trail comes to a post (1 mi.) **[6]**, where you are directed to the right for Graves Hill, your destination.

The path, now wide, is a remnant of an old wagon road that is believed to have been part of a stagecoach run from Kalamazoo to Grand Rapids.

At about 1.1 mi., a junction **[7]** directs you left to follow along a wetland. The trail swings left off the wagon road and descends across a meadow (1.4 mi.) **[8]**. At about 1.6 mi., your path merges with a ski trail **[9]**. Swing left and begin a climb into pine-covered hills. Ski trails weave throughout the area. Stay straight on the main trail. At about 1.7 mi., you come to a posted junction **[10]**. Stay straight and soon you will see another junction. Turn right and then cross the dirt road at about 1.8 mi. **[11]**.

The trail climbs into hardwoods and comes to another post (1.9 mi.) **[12]**. Stay right and follow the trail south to cross another dirt road. You soon reach a junction (2 mi.) **[13]**. Go left and climb the moraine to reach another junction at the crest (2.2 mi.) **[14]**. Turn left. Within a few steps you arrive at Graves Hill.

From this overlook, turn right on the first trail and descend to a post (2.3 mi.) **[15]**. Cross a small boardwalk where a sign informs that you are 6 minutes from the Devil's Soup Bowl (2.4 mi.) **[16]**. Make a left turn at the junction and follow it quickly with a right turn, which takes you to the Devil's Soup Bowl (2.6 mi.) **[17]**. From here look deep down the glacier-created depression before turning around and heading back.

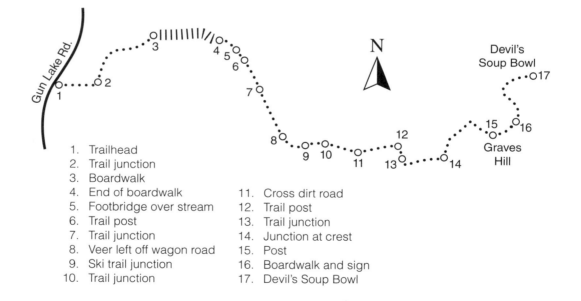

1. Trailhead
2. Trail junction
3. Boardwalk
4. End of boardwalk
5. Footbridge over stream
6. Trail post
7. Trail junction
8. Veer left off wagon road
9. Ski trail junction
10. Trail junction
11. Cross dirt road
12. Trail post
13. Trail junction
14. Junction at crest
15. Post
16. Boardwalk and sign
17. Devil's Soup Bowl

- Explore 1,100 acres of thickets, meadows, farm fields, ponds, woodlands, and marshlands.
- Stroll through a hummingbird and butterfly garden
- Enjoy 140 acres of native tallgrass prairie.

Park Information

With a mission to inspire people to care for the environment by providing experiences that help them understand their connection to the natural world, the Kalamazoo Nature Center has much to offer. Its Interpretive Center features displays, a nature library, and a bookshop. Field trips, training for teachers and naturalists, school curriculum programs, preschool programs, and family activities (nature walks and summer camps) are a few of the opportunities offered.

Wander the grounds and visit the DeLano Homestead, a restored 1858 homestead where activity demonstrations help visitors interpret the history of rural Michigan. Learn how a pioneer farm functioned, explore the arboretum, and walk through a hummingbird and butterfly garden. Eleven miles of nature trails wind through mature beech-maple forest; past ponds, marshes, and streams; and over open fields. If you take time to explore the area, you are sure to leave with a better appreciation of the environment.

Cooper's Glen, as the area used to be known, is named after James Fenimore Cooper, who visited the area in 1847 and 1848. While he pursued business interests in the vicinity, he collected information on natural features for a novel, *Oak Openings*.

Directions: The nature center is 5 miles north of Kalamazoo. From US 131, take D Avenue 3 miles east to Westnedge Avenue. Go south 1 mile to the entrance.

Hours Open: The center is open Monday through Saturday from 9:00 a.m. to 5:00 p.m. and Sundays from 1:00 p.m. to 5:00 p.m. The center is closed on the Fourth of July, Thanksgiving, Christmas Eve, Christmas Day, and New Year's Day.

Facilities: Hiking, interpretive trails, and Interpretive Center.

Permits and Rules: Members pay no admission fee. The fee is $6 for nonmember adults, $4 for nonmember children, and $5 for nonmember senior citizens. No pets are allowed.

For Further Information: Kalamazoo Nature Center, 7000 N. Westnedge Avenue, Kalamazoo, MI 49009; 269-381-1574; www.naturecenter.org.

Other Points of Interest

Northwest of Battle Creek is the **Kellogg Bird Sanctuary**, at 12685 East C Avenue in Augusta, which is between Kalamazoo and Battle Creek. A unit of the Kellogg Biological Station of Michigan State University, the sanctuary is host to a variety of waterfowl. Stroll along the landscaped paths. For more information, call Michigan State University at 269-671-2510 for the sanctuary.

The **Kal-Haven Trail Sesquicentennial State Park** is a 33.5-mile rail-trail between Kalamazoo and South Haven. Contact the Van Buren County Road Commission at 269-674-8011 or visit www.kalhaventrail.org..

Park Trails

Pioneer Woods (👣👣, 1 mile). This trail begins at the parking area south of West E Avenue and goes through a beech-maple forest and on to Source Pond.

Habitat Haven, Barn, and Prairie Pathway (👣, .6 mile, .2 mile, and .5 mile, respectively). The first trail is interpretative. The others go through an old farm field or a reconstructed prairie.

Cooper's Overlook, Ridge Run, Blue Bird, and Trout Run (👣👣, .2 mile, .6 mile, 2.7 miles, and .4 mile, respectively). The first overlooks Trout Run Stream. The next goes through young woodlands, while the third allows you to explore a gravel pit. The last passes through mature forest and overlooks Trout Run Stream.

Green Heron Ravine, Pioneer Woods, and Source Pond (👣👣, .7 mile, 1 mile, and .7 mile, respectively). The first trail passes through young forest and past ponds. The next takes you through young forest and along farm fields. The last leads to Source Pond.

Raptor Ridge (👣👣👣, .4 mile). Climb to a high point and watch birds soaring over the Kalamazoo River Valley.

Kalamazoo Nature Center

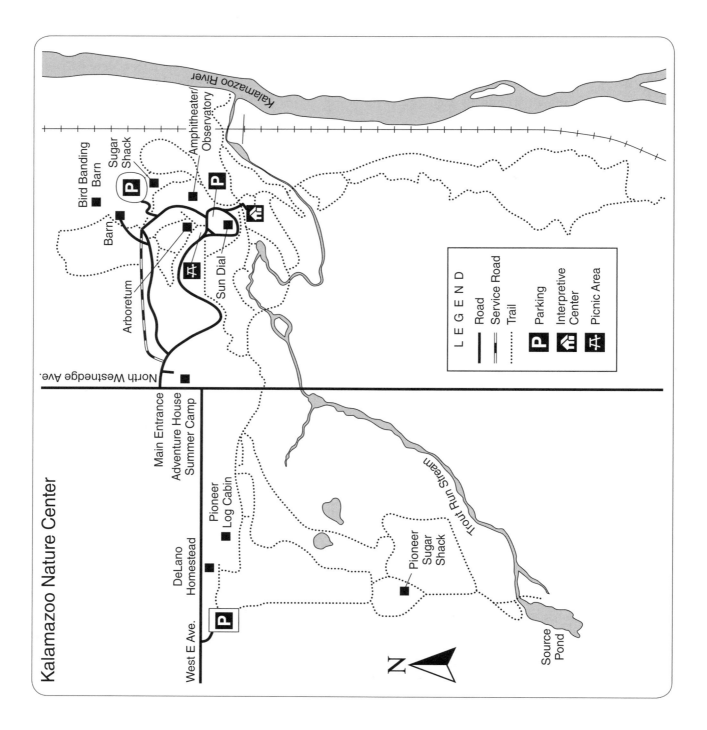

Kalamazoo River

Amphitheater/
Observatory

Bird Banding
Barn

Sugar
Shack

Barn

Arboretum

Sun Dial

North Westnedge Ave.

Main Entrance
Adventure House
Summer Camp

DeLano
Homestead

Pioneer
Log Cabin

Pioneer
Sugar
Shack

Trout Run Stream

Source
Pond

West E Ave.

N

L E G E N D

	Road
	Service Road
	Trail
P	Parking
	Interpretive Center
	Picnic Area

Beech Maple–Riverwalk Trail

Distance Round-Trip: 1.1 mile
Estimated Hiking Time: 30 minutes to 1 hour

Cautions: Watch out for poison ivy, as well as for small stumps that may protrude from the trail. The boardwalk is slippery when wet. Take along insect repellent.

Trail Directions: The trail starts from the back deck of the Interpretive Center **[1]**. Enter the darkness of thick woods and veer right at the first fork to the start of the loop. Take the southernmost trail down the crushed-stone path that winds through rolling hills and mature sugar maples.

Step down stony stairs of railroad ties, wind down more, and soon you see the stream up ahead, Trout Run Stream. The trail makes a hairpin bend to the left (.1 mi) **[2]**. Trout Run Stream flows along to the right of the trail. At about .2 mi., a bridge fords the stream **[3]**, and another trail, Raptor Ridge, heads off there to the right, rolling through the wooded hills. It offers an overview of the Kalamazoo Valley.

Continue straight on the Beech Maple Trail, walking in the small valley that Trout Run Stream cuts through. Impressive hills rise steeply from its banks. Just before you reach .3 mi., the trail winds left and up, soon rising above the stream **[4]**.

Shortly, the stream widens to include wetland vegetation. When you come to a planked bridge, watch the small stream of water spilling down the hillside to your left. The stream and surrounding wetland vegetation widen subtly as you continue. Watch for the horseshoe-shaped turn in the stream. Evidence of recent overflows suggest that a shorter, straighter path is being cut by the stream, perhaps eventually to cut off the horseshoe bend (or oxbow, as it is called).

So steep is the slope to the stream now that railroad ties are used to prevent the embankment from eroding into the stream. Just before the trail makes a sharp curve left up the hill, look down at the small valley. This area, once known as Cooper's Glen, was a favorite picnic and hiking stop of interurban and railroad passengers; a rail corridor remains (.4 mi.) **[5]** with a corrugated tunnel under it. This is the junction for the Riverwalk Trail. Head right and duck under the tunnel. The trail breaks out onto a boardwalk that crosses the stream and then heads out to the Kalamazoo River (.6 mi) **[6]**. Have a seat on the overlook deck to enjoy the river before turning back to the junction to close the small loop (.8 mi) **[5]**.

Stay straight and begin your steep climb up the moraine, or glacier-created hill. You pass the junction with the Fern Valley Trail and come to the drive near the parking lot at the interpretative center. Stop inside to explore the center.

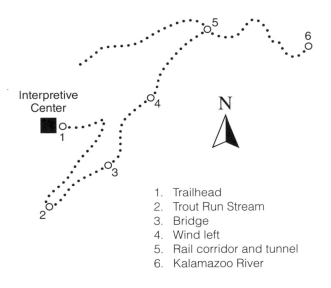

1. Trailhead
2. Trout Run Stream
3. Bridge
4. Wind left
5. Rail corridor and tunnel
6. Kalamazoo River

Fern Valley Trail

Distance Round-Trip: .6 mile
Estimated Hiking Time: 15 to 30 minutes

Cautions: Watch out for poison ivy, as well as for roots and rocks that may be exposed along the trail. Take along insect repellent in warm months.

Trail Directions: Start the trail at the northeast corner of the eastern parking lot for the Interpretive Center (although you could also start this off the Beech Maple Trail near the Interpretive Center) **[1]**. After only a few steps, veer right and stroll down through mixed hardwoods.

The trail ascends, curves to the right, and then winds down and around through the wooded hills. For the most part, a canopy shades out any intense sunlight, but small clearings occasionally let in streams of sunshine.

After bottoming out, the trail climbs, taking you through large beeches and maples. It veers left and parallels the rail track below to your right (.2 mi.) **[2]**. Your loop continues to wind left. At .3 mi., steps made of railroad ties lead down the slope to a deck overlooking a small, verdant pond **[3]**.

The trail wraps around the pond, which connects to a pool on your right. Listen. You can hear the passage of water as you step over the drainage stream. Wind up and around to get a perspective of the pond.

Continue ascending and step up the rail-tie staircase past boulders—erratics transported here by the glaciers. Keep climbing and get another view of the pond. Go straight and ascend the hill to the sugar shack (.4 mi.) **[4]**. Sugar maples sweeten your climb with their cooling canopies.

From behind the shack, the trail veers sharply to the left, ascends, and rolls through the forested terrain. At .5 mi., on your left, trees stand cloistered together to create a cathedral **[5]**. One type of tree—small, with a spindly trunk and huge leaves—is noticeable through this stretch of trail. With its thin trunk and enormous leaves, the tree resembles an awkward, big-eared, long-legged colt. The tree—the paw paw—is native to the area.

Soon you walk around a large tree of many trunks. Thereafter, the trail turns grassy, warning you that you are near the end of your journey. Pass the junction with the Barn Trail. Break out onto the grassy, narrow area where you started and return to your starting point. Turn into the parking area or stop by the Interpretive Center if you haven't already done so.

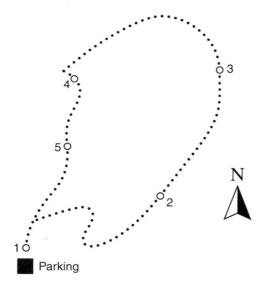

1. Trailhead
2. View rail corridor
3. Pond overlook
4. Sugar shack
5. Cathedral of trees

N

■ Parking

- Hike through the rolling, wooded terrain shaped by Sand Creek.
- Enjoy a quiet corner of Grand Rapids far removed from the bustling urban center.
- View a spectacular springtime display of wildflowers.

Park Information

Although there is more history than meets the eye in how Jacob Aman's property ended up as part of Grand Rapids, it was his wish that the land belong to the city after his death. In a nutshell, that is why Grand Rapids has this city park located about 6 miles west of the city limits.

Sand Creek has cut a narrow valley through the park's 331 acres. Trails wander ridges high above the valley. Other trails cut through marshes, bogs, forests, and fields. The six trails that weave over the rugged yet peaceful environment offer a beautiful and stark contrast with the boisterous city nearby.

Wildflowers are spectacular in spring, and the diverse terrain and varied plants of the park produce continual showings throughout the year, from skunk cabbage and marsh marigold to beech and aspen, and even to the gray of leafless branches pocketed with ice crystals. All seasons show off something in this retreat.

Directions: From I-196, take M-45 west about 6 miles. The park is on the north side of M-45, or Lake Michigan Drive.

Hours Open: The trails are open year-round from dawn until dusk.

Facilities: Hiking, fishing, cross-country skiing, and picnicking.

Permits and Rules: There is no fee. Enjoy the natural setting but build no fires and pick no wildflowers or other plants.

For Further Information: Grand Rapids Department of Parks, 201 Market Avenue, Grand Rapids, MI 49503; 616-456-3696.

Other Points of Interest

Pigeon Creek Park provides more than 10 miles of trails for hiking, mountain biking, cross-country skiing, and horseback riding. The park is about 12 miles west of Aman Park on Stanton Road. For more information, call Ottawa County Parks and Recreation at 616-738-4810.

Explore the **Frederik Meijer Gardens and Sculpture Park**, home of the state's largest tropical conservatory. Besides plants from around the world, the gardens feature waterfalls, streams, sculptures, and winding, barrier-free pathways. For more information, contact the Frederik Meijer Gardens, 888-957-1580 or www.meijergardens.org.

Walk, skate, ski, or pedal along the 15 miles of the linear **Kent Trails**. Running partly along the abandoned Lakeshore and Michigan Southern Railway grade, the northern end of the trail can be reached from John Ball Park. For more information, call the Kent County Parks Department at 616-336-PARK.

Hidden within Grand Rapids is the 143-acre **Blandford Nature Center**. Miles of trails wind around the center's woods, fields, ponds, and streams. The center joined forces with Mixed Greens to share a vision of inviting the community to connect to the land, to food, and to their surroundings. Contact Mixed Greens at 616-735-6240 or www.mixedgreens.org.

Park Trails

The trails that loop through the park build on one another, weaving to Sand Creek or along the ridges high above the creek's valley.

Blue Trail (🐾🐾, 1.2 miles). Access this trail from the Red Trail. It heads into the north end of the park along the west side of Sand Creek.

Green Trail (🐾🐾, .9 mile). Reach this trail from the Red Trail. It loops over to the southwest side of the park, climbs out of the valley, and makes for an extended Red Trail walk.

Orange Trail (🐾, .8 mile). This trail starts from the trail board north of the small parking area off the access road. It follows an edge separating field and forest, and culminates at Sweet's Monument overlooking Sand Creek and its valley before it heads back.

Creek Trail (🐾, 1 mile). Access this trail from the Red Trail. It follows along Sand Creek.

Aman Park

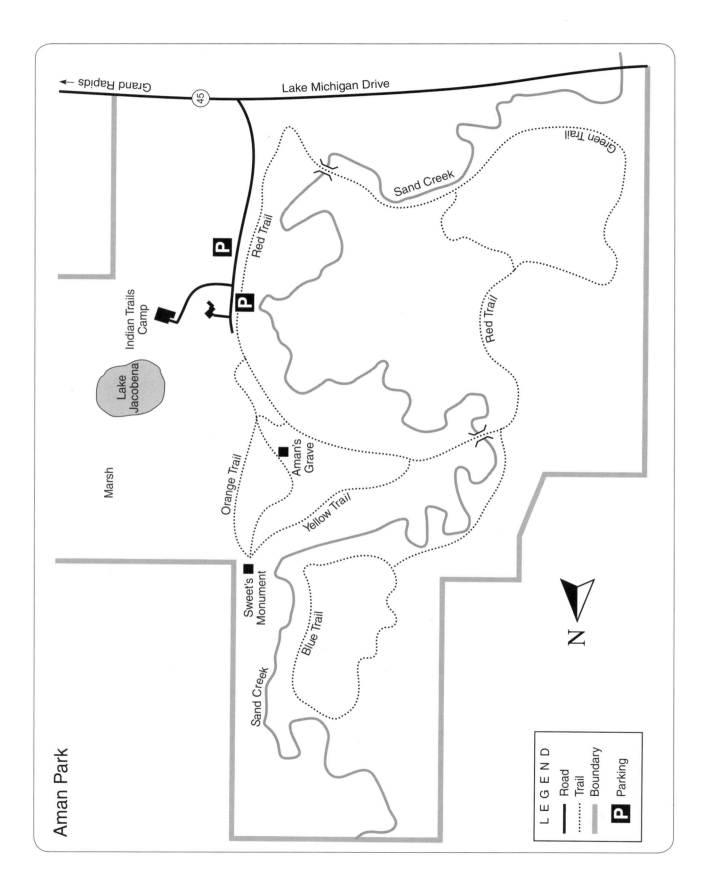

Grand Rapids ← 45 Lake Michigan Drive

Green Trail

Sand Creek

Red Trail

Red Trail

P

Indian Trails Camp

P

Lake Jacobena

Orange Trail

Aman's Grave

Yellow Trail

Marsh

Sweet's Monument

Sand Creek

Blue Trail

N

L E G E N D
— Road
.... Trail
— Boundary
P Parking

Yellow Trail

Distance Round-Trip: 1.1 miles
Estimated Hiking Time: 30 minutes

Cautions: Parts of the trail are eroded and parts have roots or rocks. Poison ivy is present. Take insect repellent in warm months.

Trail Directions: Park in the small northern lot on the west side of the access drive, south of the trailhead. Start at the end of the access road, to the left of where it bends right **[1]**. Your trail is the Yellow Trail. Your path is wide as you head through a canopy of mixed hardwoods. A ravine is at your side as the trail winds around and passes a junction, which will be your return route (.2 mi.) **[2]**.

Still level, wide, and winding, the trail cuts through beech and maple and gently descends just before you arrive at a junction (.3 mi.) **[3]**. Turn right at this junction and follow along the trail as it takes you high on a ridge that overlooks a green pool in the valley below. On the ridge you walk through more hardwoods, oak, and maple. The trail subtly ascends.

Pass some trees that have leaned too far over the slope and have fallen. (Now they lean on one another.) From your perch on the ridge, you can see green pools of water below. The creek below teases as you walk along the ridge high above it; you hear the gentle ripples of the water before you catch the glisten of its surface (.6 mi.) **[4]**. The slope down to it is steep.

Enjoy the sights and sounds. This point on the ridge is near a posted junction for you to follow. But if you follow straight up the trail about 100 feet, you reach Sweet's Monument, where a plaque on a boulder commemorates Edwin F. Sweet. Additional park plaques memorialize other honorable members of the Grand Rapids community. Head back to where you listened to the music of the creek and follow the junction there to the southeast **[4]**.

Again the path is wide as you pass through large oaks, beeches, maples, and some pines. Although you are among giants here, no commemorative plaques are present. Soon after you pass a fallen tree leaning on another, the trail veers left and takes you to Aman's Grave **[5]**. Here you see a large boulder with a plaque that describes Jacob Aman, another notable community member who happens to be buried beneath the rock. This spot was one of his favorite places and his choice for a final resting place.

The trail winds around through the woods and brings you to a junction with trails radiating from it (.9 mi.) **[6]**. Although a straight shot will take you back to the map board along the Orange Trail, the Yellow Trail makes a sharp right at this juncture and continues to wind you through the forest, reuniting you with the main trail **[2]**. Follow along to the left, retracing your steps out to the parking area.

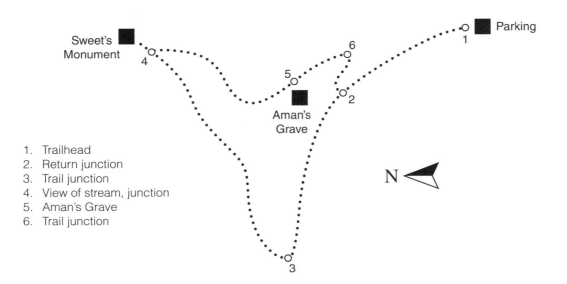

1. Trailhead
2. Return junction
3. Trail junction
4. View of stream, junction
5. Aman's Grave
6. Trail junction

Red Trail

Distance Round-Trip: 1.4 miles
Estimated Hiking Time: 30 minutes to
1 hour

Cautions: Some parts of the trail are eroding. Watch your step on the loose gravel or mud. Take insect repellent in warm months.

Trail Directions: Park in the small northern lot on the west side of the access drive, south of the trailhead. Start at the end of the access road, to the left of where it bends right [1]. Your trail is the Red Trail. The trail is wide as you head through a canopy that includes oak and hemlock. You swing to the west, following the ridgeline, and pass a junction with the Yellow Trail (.1 mi.) [2]. Continue through beech and maple, and descend gently to where the Yellow Trail again splits off to the right (.3 mi.) [3].

Stay straight leaving the ridgeline and note the large beech trees as you pick up speed in your descent. You pass wildflower interpretive stations along the way. Spot a pond on your right but watch your step along a section of the trail that is prone to erosion. The trail bottoms out at Sand Creek. Cross a concrete bridge and quickly reach the junction with the Blue Trail (.5 mi.) [4].

As you walk across the forested floodplain, you swing south and pass several old channels of the creek. Just before climbing out of the valley, you pass a large oak tree on your right and a beech on your left (.6 mi.) [5]. Now on the ridge, you leave the dense canopy of the forest and head east as the Green Trail splits off to your right (.7 mi.) [6].

If you packed a snack, a picnic table is set along this section of the trail for your use. Beyond the picnic area, the trail swings right and briefly follows along the edge of a ravine before descending into the woods. At .9 mi., turn left at the junction with the Green Trail [7]. After the trail again bottoms out, it takes you along Sand Creek toward the Grand River.

At 1.1 mi., take the footbridge across the creek near its elbow turn [8]. Get your knees ready for the climb up the bluff, which starts soon after you step off the footbridge—this is your steepest climb along the trail. At the top, turn left at the trail marker (1.2 mi.) [9] and left again so that M-45 is to your back. You now head north, with the ravine on your left and the driveway into the park on your right.

At 1.3 mi., a large oak tree marks a spot where you get a moving view of Sand Creek flowing below you in the valley [10]. Continue north to return to your vehicle or head back to the trailhead to try one of the other trails in this scenic park.

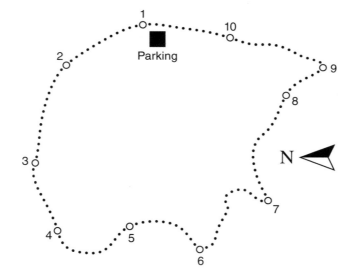

1. Trailhead
2. Yellow Trail junction
3. Yellow Trail junction
4. Blue Trail junction
5. Large oak
6. Green Trail junction
7. Green Trail junction
8. Footbridge
9. Trail marker
10. Scenic overlook

71. North Country National Scenic Trail, Birch Grove Schoolhouse

- Sleep in an old one-room schoolhouse.
- Follow the trail for a day, a week, or a season.
- Become a volunteer and help fulfill the vision of the trail.

Park Information

Designated in 1980, the North Country National Scenic Trail is a work in progress. When completed, the trail will stretch some 4,600 miles across seven northern states from Lake Champlain in New York to Lake Sakakawea in North Dakota. Michigan has the longest segment of any state, and over half of that distance is complete and certified. This accomplishment is no small feat because volunteers are doing much of the work. As the trail grows so does its footprint; the trail traverses 14 parks highlighted in this book.

The Birch Grove Schoolhouse once served as the headquarters of the North Country Trail Association. The association is the nonprofit organization working in partnership with the National Park Service to build, maintain, and promote the North Country National Scenic Trail. The schoolhouse dates to the 1880s. It was built in Park City (which no longer exists) and was moved to its present site in the 1890s. The schoolhouse is available for rental.

Directions: The North Country National Scenic Trail covers many miles in the state. Contact the National Park Service or the North Country Trail Association for more information. The Birch Grove Schoolhouse is located west of M-37, 6.8 miles north of White Cloud. Turn west onto 5 Mile Road and go 1 mile to the intersection with Felch Avenue. Turn left. The schoolhouse is on the east side of Felch Avenue.

Hours Open: Generally, the trail is open at all times and during all seasons, although seasonal or area closures may occur at the discretion of the local landowner or manager. Please check ahead for this information.

Facilities: Hiking, mountain biking in some areas, cross-country skiing, snowshoeing, camping (tent and backcountry).

Permits and Rules: Reservations and fees may be required for portions of the trail, depending on the requirements of the local managers of the trail. Please check ahead for this information

For Further Information: North Country National Scenic Trail, 700 Rayovac Drive, Suite 100, Madison Wisconsin, 53711; 608-441-5610; www.nps.gov/noco; or North Country Trail Association, 229 East Main Street, Lowell, MI 49331; 866-HikeNCT; www.north countrytrail.org. For Birch Grove Schoolhouse rental rates and facility descriptions, visit www.northcountry trail.org/wmi.

Southern
Lower
Peninsula

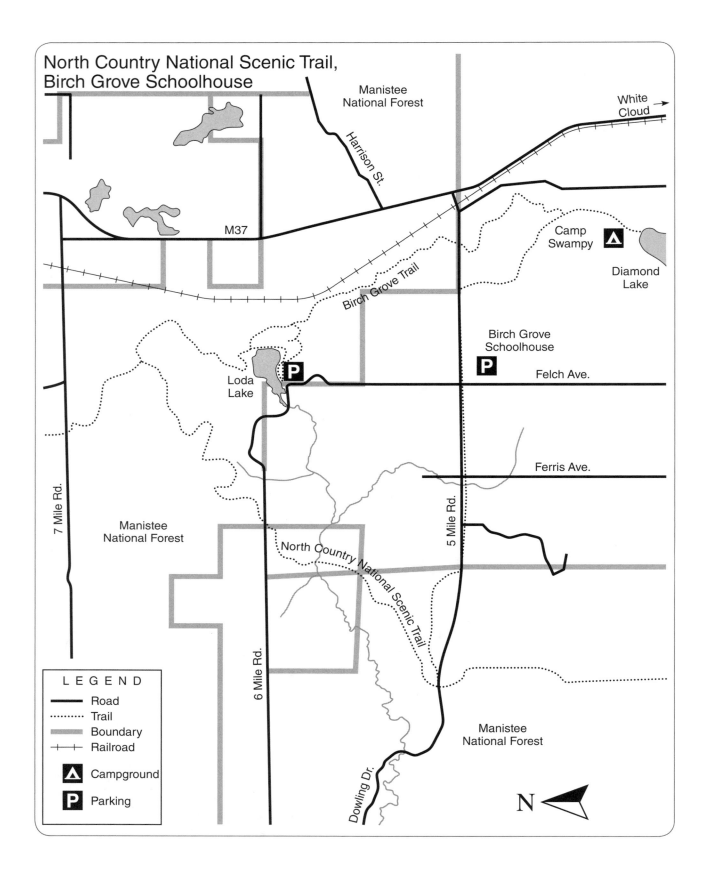

North Country National Scenic Trail,
Birch Grove Schoolhouse

Manistee National Forest

White Cloud →

Harrison St.

M37

Camp Swampy

Diamond Lake

Birch Grove Trail

Birch Grove Schoolhouse

Loda Lake

P

P

Felch Ave.

Ferris Ave.

7 Mile Rd.

Manistee National Forest

North Country National Scenic Trail

5 Mile Rd.

6 Mile Rd.

Manistee National Forest

Dowling Dr.

LEGEND
— Road
········· Trail
▬ Boundary
+–+–+ Railroad
△ Campground
P Parking

N

Birch Grove Trail

Distance Round-Trip: 9 miles
Estimated Hiking Time: 3 to 4 hours

Cautions: Wear appropriate footgear. Bring insect repellent in warmer months. Take along water and snacks.

Trail Directions: Start at the Birch Grove Schoolhouse parking lot **[1]**. Turn right on 5 Mile Road and go .5 mi. before turning south into the predominately oak woods with ferns and scattered pines. Follow the white blazes as the trail gradually descends along this stretch. After crossing an open area, the trail turns right on what looks like an old railroad grade (1.1 mi.) **[2]**. Follow the grade to the junction with the Diamond Lake Spur (1.2 mi.) **[3]**. It is .4 mi. to Diamond Lake. Turn left instead and follow as the trail bends sharply left, taking you north. Watch for deer.

After crossing 5 Mile Road (2 mi.) **[4]**, your feet are cushioned by pine needles. This level stretch has a mix of pine and oak. At times you find yourself walking on an old railroad grade. Shortly after walking through a red pine plantation you reach a junction with the Loda Lake Wildflower Sanctuary Trail (3.1 mi.) **[5]**. Stay to the right and follow along the sanctuary trail to the next junction (3.3 mi.) **[6]**. If you want a break, turn left to reach benches overlooking Loda Lake. Otherwise, turn right and shortly swing left to bend around the north end of the lake. Eventually climb away from the lake into mostly hardwoods. You skirt what looks to be a bog-filled lake with dead trees and tamaracks, pass an area dominated by aspen and birch, reenter pines, and walk along and off the old railroad grade to arrive at the junction with the North Country Trail near a large wetland (4.3 mi.) **[7]**. Turn left and follow the blue blazes.

You find yourself rolling over wooded slopes and descending to skirt wetlands. Shortly after walking through an area dominated by hemlock and large ferns, you cross an ORV trail (5.3 mi.) **[8]**. Nearby lies a green pool and the stumps of ancient giants. Cross a three-board ditch (5.6 mi.) **[9]** before climbing to reach 6 Mile Road (5.8 mi.) **[10]**. Turn right and follow the road a short distance before veering left.

Now off the road, the trail soon descends to cross an ORV trail again. Climb again before making a steep descent to cross a small footbridge over a creek (6.2 mi.) **[11]**. You soon enter an area affected by ORV use and misuse. After a very sandy crossing of an ORV trail, you climb into the woods (6.4 mi.) **[12]** and shortly pass through a fencerow of moss-covered tree stumps (6.7 mi.) **[13]**.

When the forest canopy opens up, walk on moss carpeting as oak and small white pines dominate the area. You arrive at an extension to 5 Mile Road (7.3 mi.) **[14]**. Go left and follow the sandy two-track through several red pine plantations, mixed hardwoods, and wetlands before climbing and turning left to arrive on the rural dirt road that will lead you past farm fields and back to the schoolhouse.

1. Trailhead
2. Old railroad grade
3. Diamond Lake Spur junction
4. 5 Mile Road
5. Loda Lake Wildflower Sanctuary Trail
6. Junction
7. North Country Trail junction
8. ORV trail crossing
9. Three-board ditch crossing
10. 6 Mile Road
11. Footbridge
12. ORV trail crossing
13. Dead stump fencerow
14. 5 Mile Road extension

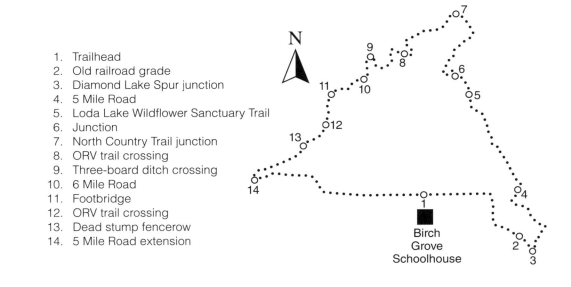

72. Manistee National Forest, Loda Lake Wildflower Sanctuary

- Seek solitude in an intimate setting.
- Enjoy the work of the Federated Garden Clubs.

Park Information

The Manistee National Forest was created in 1938 from land that was logged over, burned out, sand blown, abandoned, tax delinquent, or generally unsuitable for farming. The name comes from a Native American word meaning "the whispering through the pines." The forest contains 538,756 acres that span 40 miles east to west and 70 miles north to south across the west-central Lower Peninsula. These lands offer an abundance of recreational opportunities, including the Nordhouse Dunes Wilderness (see park #49) and some 121 miles of the North Country National Scenic Trail (see park #71).

The Loda Lake Wildflower Sanctuary is the only wildflower sanctuary in a national forest. Designated in 1949, the 72-acre sanctuary is supported by the Federated Garden Clubs. Once home to virgin pines standing 60 feet tall and measuring 54 inches in diameter, the land was farmed for a short time after the trees were harvested by the Pere Marquette Railroad. Protected species include trailing arbutus, bird's foot violet, bittersweet, flowering dogwood, trillium, club mosses, Michigan holly, American lotus, gentian, and pipsissewa.

Directions: Facilities and points of interest are spread over a large area. Contact the forest supervisor's office or the individual district offices of the Manistee National Forest for more information. The Loda Lake Wildflower Sanctuary is located west of M-37, 6.8 miles north of White Cloud. Turn west onto 5 Mile Road and go 1 mile to the intersection with Felch Avenue. Turn right on the gravel road and go north .8 mile to the parking lot entrance road.

Hours Open: Many facilities are open year-round.

Facilities: Hiking, mountain biking, cross-country skiing, snowshoeing, snowmobiling, ATV, swimming, fishing, hunting, boat launch, canoeing, camping (tent and backcountry), picnicking, interpretive trails, and visitor center.

Permits and Rules: Recreation passes are required at sites providing specific amenities ($3 daily, $5 weekly, $20 annually). Camping fees vary by site. No fee is required for backcountry camping.

For Further Information: Huron-Manistee National Forest, Supervisor's Office, 1755 S. Mitchell Street, Cadillac, MI 49601; 800-821-6263; www.fs.fed.us/r9/hmnf. Alternatively, contact the two district offices of the Manistee National Forest: Baldwin/White Cloud Ranger Station, 650 N. Michigan Avenue, P.O. Box D, Baldwin, MI 49304; 231-745-4631; Manistee Ranger Station, 412 Red Apple Road, Manistee, MI 49660; 231-723-2211.

Other Points of Interest

The **Birch Grove Schoolhouse**, the former headquarters of the North Country Trail Association, is also located on Felch Avenue just south of 5 Mile Road. The schoolhouse is available for rental. For rental rates and facility descriptions, visit www.northcountrytrail.org/wmi.

The Manistee National Forest covers a huge territory. For more information about what is available in the area, contact Mecosta County Area Convention and Visitors Bureau, 800-229-4-FUN, www.bigrapids.org; Cadillac Area Visitors Bureau, 800-22-LAKES, www.cadillacmichigan.com/index; Grayling Area Visitors Council, 800-937-8837, www.grayling-mi.com; Ludington Convention and Visitors Bureau, 877-420-6618, www.ludingtoncvb.com; Manistee Area Chamber of Commerce, 800-288-2286, www.manisteecountychamber.com.

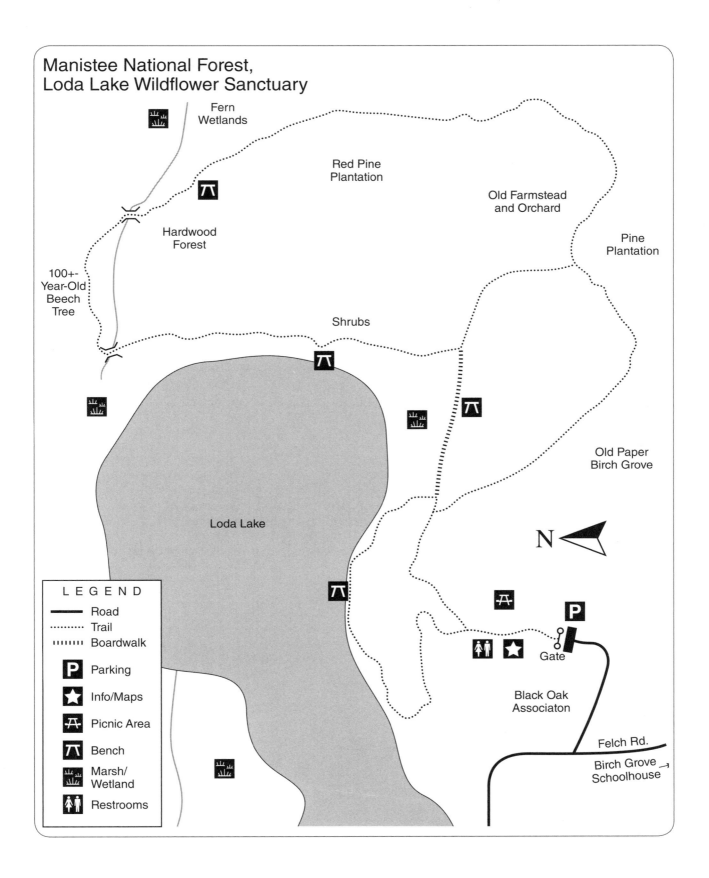

Manistee National Forest, Loda Lake Wildflower Sanctuary

Fern Wetlands

Red Pine Plantation

Old Farmstead and Orchard

Pine Plantation

Hardwood Forest

100+-Year-Old Beech Tree

Shrubs

Old Paper Birch Grove

Loda Lake

N

Black Oak Associaton

LEGEND

—— Road
········· Trail
|||||||| Boardwalk
P Parking
★ Info/Maps
Picnic Area
Bench
Marsh/ Wetland
Restrooms

Gate

Felch Rd.

Birch Grove Schoolhouse

Loda Lake Wildflower Sanctuary Trail

🐾 **Distance Round-Trip:** 1.2 miles
🐾 **Estimated Hiking Time:** 30 minutes to 1 hour

Cautions: Watch for exposed roots. Some areas may be muddy. Wear appropriate footgear. Bring insect repellent in warmer months. Don't forget your wildflower book.

Trail Directions: Start to the right of the self-service pay station at the small parking lot **[1]**. Proceed past the gate and head north to reach the information boards where you will find a picnic area with pit toilets. Pick up a trail map and continue on to the first trail junction near post #1 (.1 mi.) **[2]**. Go left and wind past a number of interpretive stops as you descend toward Loda Lake.

Turn right at post #8 to walk along the lakeshore on a carpet of moss. New vegetative growth obscures the lake at first, but views soon open up. At post #12 you find yourself at the water's edge (.2 mi.) **[3]**. Have a seat on the bench nearby to enjoy the moment and to check your brochure for the names of the plants found here. When you continue, pine needles cushion your steps. Turn left to cross a long boardwalk (.3 mi.) **[4]**. A bench has been built into the boardwalk at about the halfway point for you to sit and enjoy the wetlands. Turn left after leaving the boardwalk as pine needles again cushion your footsteps. Pass lakefront benches with views (.4 mi.) **[5]**, before crossing a small footbridge near the junction with the Birch Grove Trail (.5 mi.) **[6]**. Go right.

The trail climbs as you follow along the small stream and then dips to cross another footbridge to continue along the other side of the stream (.6 mi.) **[7]**. You skirt a wetland and pass through a red pine plantation to arrive at the remains of an old barn (.8 mi.) **[8]**. Follow the trail to the right past caged wildflowers and the old orchard before descending back into the woods.

At the next junction is a bench (.9 mi.) **[9]**. You have the option to turn right here to go to see the bird's foot violets at post #36. The best time is in early spring. When you are back at the junction with the bench, go right and continue along the old drive, descending back toward the wetland and lake. When you reach post #39 (1.1 mi.) **[10]**, turn left and climb back toward the parking area.

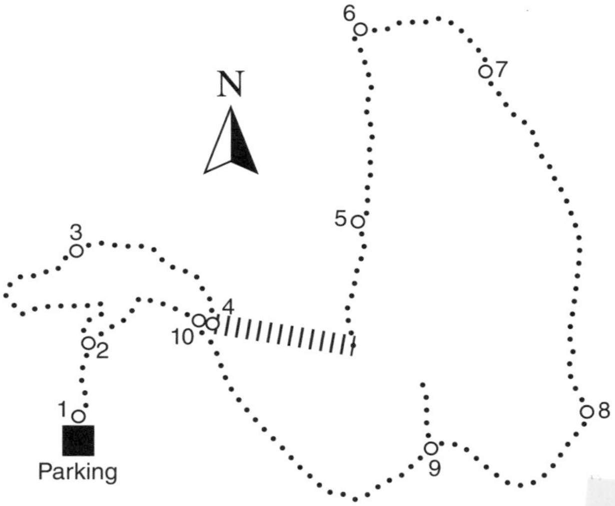

1. Trailhead
2. Trail junction
3. Water's edge
4. Boardwalk
5. Benches
6. Footbridge and trail junction
7. Footbridge
8. Old barn remains
9. Junction and bench
10. Post #39

- Escape from the crowds and enjoy, in peace, the scenic Lake Michigan shoreline.
- Stroll over wooded dunes and sandy beaches.
- Walk softly and listen carefully; you may be rewarded with the sights and sounds of nature.

Park Information

About 1,000 acres of quiet, natural beauty await you at the Saugatuck Dunes State Park. Plan on hiking, if you want to enjoy and experience it. The property was acquired in 1971 from the Augustinian Order, who used the buildings as a seminary. The structures were used as a prison and state police offices when the state took over.

Now you can adventure out over the 13 miles of color-coded trails that roll over wooded dunes, steep slopes, and sandy Lake Michigan shores. And adventure out you must, if it is the shore that you wish to enjoy. Lake Michigan awaits those who are not intimidated by the 1-mile trek over sandy dunes from the parking lot. The lake here is enticing if you like to escape beach crowds and enjoy the nearly 3 miles of Lake Michigan shoreline. The south end of this park is a designated natural area. Networks of trails lead toward the shore in this day-use park.

Directions: The park is about 1 mile north of Saugatuck. From I-96, go west on Blue Star Highway (exit 141) to 64th. Head north about a mile to 138th Avenue and then turn west. Follow the road to the park entrance.

Hours Open: The park is open daily from 8:00 a.m. to 10:00 p.m.

Facilities: Hiking, cross-country skiing, swimming, picnicking with grills, a shelter, and vault toilets.

Permits and Rules: A park fee is required for motor vehicles ($6 daily, $24 annually for residents; $8 daily, $29 annually for non-residents). This naturally managed, day-use park exhibits classic dune succession; please make a special effort to respect all flora and fauna in this fragile place and stay on the marked trails.

For Further Information: Van Buren State Park, 23960 Ruggles Road, South Haven, MI 49090; 269-673-2788.

Other Points of Interest

The city of Holland offers more than tulips and windmills. About 10 miles north of the park, the **De Graaf Nature Center Preserve**, an 18-acre nature preserve, offers several short interpretive trails as well as an interpretive center. The small area hosts a wide variety of habitats. For more information, contact De Graaf Nature Center Preserve, 600 Graafschap Road, Holland, MI 49423; 616-355-1057.

South of the park in Saugatuck, take a cruise down the Kalamazoo River and out into Lake Michigan on an old-fashioned sternwheeler, the *Star of Saugatuck.* Cruises are available from May through October. For more information, call 269-857-4261 or write to 716 Water Street, Saugatuck, MI 49453.

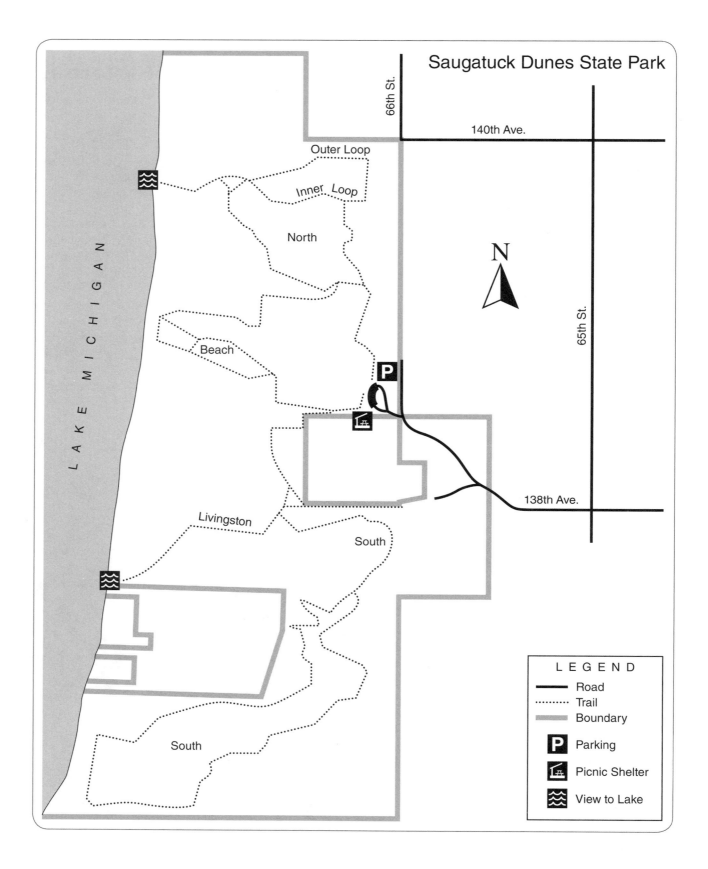

Saugatuck Dunes State Park

66th St.

140th Ave.

Outer Loop

Inner Loop

North

N

Beach

65th St.

LAKE MICHIGAN

P

138th Ave.

Livingston

South

South

LEGEND
—————— Road
· · · · · · · Trail
—————— Boundary
P   Parking
🏠   Picnic Shelter
〜   View to Lake

North Trail With Spur to Lake— Outer Loop

Distance Round-Trip: 2 miles
Estimated Hiking Time: 2 hours

Cautions: The trail (marked by white) is sandy and climbs up and down dunes. Wear sunscreen and take water. In the woods, watch your step for roots. Watch for poison ivy.

Trail Directions: Start at the north end of the parking lot **[1]**. The trail immediately enters the woods. A wide path takes you past wooded dunes. Enjoy the spring pond on your right. Walk softly, listen carefully, and enjoy the varied habitat at this edge between woods and pond. The spring bird migration can be particularly rewarding. As you continue, let your gaze follow up the tall, wooded dune to your left.

Climb away from the pond to reach post #4, where the trail forks (.2 mi.) **[2]**. The post, tipped white, has a green arrow pointing left (west). Turn left and climb through a stand of red pines and mixed hardwoods of beech, maple, and oak until you reach post #5, the junction with the Beach Trail (.3 mi.) **[3]**. Take the North Trail (white) to the right, which soon takes you down a sandy slope and onto a carpet of needles and sand. Walk slowly and enjoy the sights and smells as the trail undulates through dense pines. Take care; trails cross through here. Pay attention. You soon reach a post. Either way will get you to the main trail, but take the short jog on the left to reach the posted junction at .6 mi. **[4]**. Turn left to head to the shore. A massive wall of sand and woods rises steeply alongside you on this awesome spur to a bluff with a spectacular view of Lake Michigan (.8 mi.) **[5]**.

Retrace your steps to the post and continue straight past another until you reach another junction (1.1 mi.) **[6]**, where you find several paths. Take the path straight ahead through the open sand; climb through windswept dunes until you are at the bottom of a steep, sandy dune. Follow your gaze up the dune to the right. Now climb the steep, sandy slope where you are rewarded by a circular vista of varying dune terrain—sprawling forests, juniper, and grass-covered

dunes (1.3 mi.) **[7]**. Look back the way you came. Lake Michigan is framed between sky, tree, and dune.

From this high point, follow the sandy trail as it drops sharply and takes you to another marker (1.4 mi.) **[8]**. This vantage point offers a view of rolling, grassy, windswept dunes. The trail turns sharply to the right, travels steeply down the slope, and makes another sharp right at the next post. From here, trudge back up a slope to post #6 at the edge of the forest (1.6 mi.) **[9]**.

Turn left and enjoy the canopy of a mixed forest. The trail winds down until you reach the marsh that signals your approach to post #4 (1.8 mi.) **[2]**. Continue straight and backtrack the first part of your journey down past the wooded dunes to the parking lot.

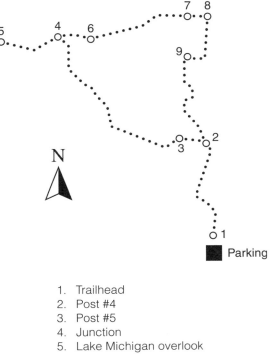

■ Parking

1. Trailhead
2. Post #4
3. Post #5
4. Junction
5. Lake Michigan overlook
6. Junction with many paths
7. Vista
8. Turn right at marker
9. Post #6

Beach Trail

Distance Round-Trip: 1.4 miles
Estimated Hiking Time: 1 to 1.5 hours

Cautions: The trail (marked by yellow) is sandy, and it climbs dunes. Take a hat, sunscreen, and water. Take care when hiking along the steep ridges. Green arrows point the way to the lake; red arrows point the way back to the parking lot. Watch for poison ivy.

Trail Directions: Start at the north end of the parking lot [1]. The first portion of the hike follows the North Trail. The path enters woods and then meanders past wooded dunes before arriving at a vernal pond (.1 mi.) [2]. During the spring migrations, this area is a birder's delight. The trail climbs away from the pond and leads you to post #4 (.2 mi.) [3]. Turn left.

The trail ascends through red pines and mixed hardwoods, and soon arrives at post #5. Take the Beach Trail to the left, which begins a climb up a ridge. At first, you will notice the steep slope below you to the left. Soon, the trail rises above its surroundings, and you walk high along the ridge as you head west toward the lake. You catch a glimpse of blue sky above Lake Michigan through the foliage just before the trail takes a sharp turn to the left and descends the sandy slope to enter the pine forest (.4 mi.) [4].

The descent continues; you wind through the woods before climbing steeply over a dune. This point has a sign. Lake Michigan is before you. You can see the continuation of the trail through the trees to your left, but it is hard to resist heading west for the lake and scrambling up the next dune to perch higher for a Lake Michigan overview (.6 mi.) [5]. Head up and enjoy a view of the lake; then come back to the trail where it continues through the woods.

Break out of trees and climb left in the sand to arrive at post #3 (.7 mi.) [6]. Head up the small dune to the right to get closer to the lake and then head east into the woods.

The trail winds and rolls through tall, wooded dunes until it reaches the posted junction at .9 mi. [7]. Veer left to stay on the inner, lower-lying loop. Wooded slopes close in on either side until you begin the steep climb out of the bowl and to post #1 (1.1 mi.) [8].

Wind to the left. Before long, notice that you are on a ridge overlooking the grounds of a refuge—first used as a seminary, later as a correctional facility (1.2 mi.) [9].

A few more steps take you to a posted junction. The trail down to the right leads to the Livingston and the South trails. Continue straight, with pines along your left. Soon the parking area comes into view. The trail veers sharply to the left, and eventually you reach the parking area just southwest of the picnic shelter.

1. Trailhead
2. Vernal pond
3. Post #4
4. Trail veers left
5. View of Lake Michigan
6. Post #3
7. Trail junction
8. Post #1
9. Overlook old grounds

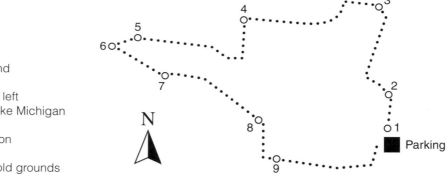

Livingston Trail

Distance Round-Trip: 2 miles
Estimated Hiking Time: 1 to 1.5 hours

Cautions: The trail (marked by red) is sandy, and it climbs dunes. Take a hat, sunscreen, and water. Watch for poison ivy.

Trail Directions: Start at the southwest end of the parking lot on the Beach Trail and wind through the woods [1]. At the junction, follow the red-tipped post left past the remnant seminary (.1 mi.) [2]. Cross a couple of paths and then reach the more well-defined post #9 junction (.4 mi.) [3].

Go right and soon stay right of post #10. The wide trail winds through tall hardwoods. At post #11, stay right and gently climb through rolling woods (.5 mi.) [4]. A ridge rises on the right. The trail descends through some good-sized beech trees.

Climb again, to the left, and roll along the flank of a ridge (.6 mi.) [5]. Look ahead at the tall, wooded slope. Your stroll rolls through heavily wooded hills. The trail skirts ridges. At .7 mi., a wooded hill rises above you and a bowl of trees lies below you—it is as if you are on a middle balcony in the forest [6].

Keep climbing. At the crest, start your descent down the back side of a dune. Pass several downed trees. At .8 mi., you are in the valley of fallen trees [7]. Shaped like an inverted rib cage, downed trees lean on slopes on both sides of the trail.

The trail levels off on a ridge, and you begin to hear waves. Descend to reach the dune grass by the Livingston Trail sign (1 mi.) [8]. A well-worn path in the sand guides you to the waters of Lake Michigan. Go ahead and enjoy the sandy beach before you turn around to head back.

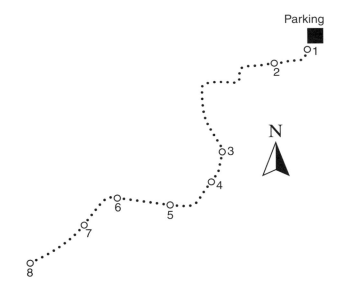

1. Trailhead
2. Junction
3. Post #9
4. Post #11
5. Climb
6. Balcony in woods
7. Valley of fallen trees
8. Lake Michigan

South Trail

Distance Round-Trip: 4.6 miles
Estimated Hiking Time: 1.5 to 2.5 hours

Cautions: The trail (marked by blue) is sandy, and it climbs dunes. Take a hat, sunscreen, and water. Watch for poison ivy.

Trail Directions: Start at the southwest end of the parking lot on the Beach Trail and wind through the woods **[1]**. At the junction, follow the red-tipped post left past the remnant seminary (.1 mi.) **[2]**. Cross a couple of paths and then reach the more well-defined post #9 junction (.4 mi.) **[3]**.

Go right and soon stay right of post #10. The wide trail winds through tall hardwoods. At post #11, veer left, following the blue-tipped posts, and soon walk along the base of a ridge (.5 mi.) **[4]**. Climb up to a post (.8 mi.) **[5]**.

Turn right and start to climb and descend through the rolling woods to reach a road and junction #12 (1 mi.) **[6]**. Stay left. Behind the sign "Saugatuck Dunes State Park Dedicated Natural Area," the trail splits. Stay right and descend.

Wow! A massive, wooded dune rises before you, and you veer left to follow along its base (1.2 mi.) **[7]**. After paralleling the ridge, you swing to climb over it (1.3 mi.) **[8]** and descend to a land bridge. Soon, another impressive wooded dune flanks the trail (1.4 mi.) **[9]**. Continue to wind and roll over, past, and through wooded dune ridges.

Climb through sand to catch your first view of Lake Michigan (2.2 mi.) **[10]**. The trail veers left at a dune, and you descend through sand. The dune to your left was cleared of tree growth—part of the dune ecosystem restoration. Then climb through dune grass to post #13 (2.4 mi.) **[11]**.

Go ahead. Climb that ribbon of sand through the grasses and treat yourself to a beautiful, secluded, sandy Lake Michigan shore. Then come back to the post and head north through the dune grass and restoration area.

At 2.5 mi., turn right along the path and walk through the restoration area to climb back into a forest of pines to twist and climb through wooded dune ridges **[12]**. The climbing intensifies. After you crest (2.9 mi.), descend past red pines on the back side of a dune and then climb through more sand and pines **[13]**. Climb to another restoration area where the trail is very sandy.

Begin a climb that swings left between the pines and open dune area. Horseshoe around a sand bowl (3.2 mi.) **[14]**. Just before reentering pines at the top, look left over the cleared bowl for your last glimpse of Lake Michigan along the ridge atop the back side of a dune.

Start descending, following the blue-tipped posts through the forest to post #14 (3.4 mi) **[15]**. Stay straight and continue descending along an old road. You soon reach another road (3.5 mi.) **[16]**. Turn right and descend to post #12 (3.6 mi.) **[6]**. Turn left and retrace your steps to the parking lot.

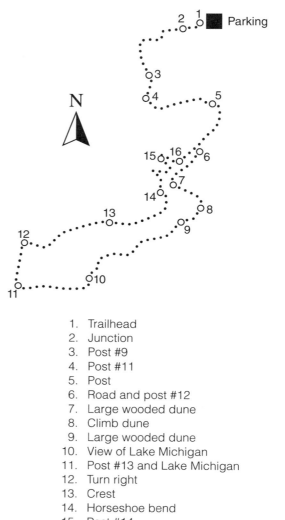

1. Trailhead
2. Junction
3. Post #9
4. Post #11
5. Post
6. Road and post #12
7. Large wooded dune
8. Climb dune
9. Large wooded dune
10. View of Lake Michigan
11. Post #13 and Lake Michigan
12. Turn right
13. Crest
14. Horseshoe bend
15. Post #14
16. Road

- Climb the challenging Dune Climb Stairway.
- Learn about sand dunes and their ecosystems at the E. Genevieve Gillette Sand Dune Visitor Center.
- Sink your toes in sand along the Lake Michigan shoreline.

Park Information

Encompassing almost 1,200 acres, the P. J. Hoffmaster State Park is a treasure trove packed with almost 3 miles of Lake Michigan shoreline, sandy beaches, and forested dunes. The 10 miles of trails that weave throughout the park give visitors a comprehensive experience of dune environments.

A vigorous hike along the Dune Climb Stairway to a platform on the top of a towering dune provides a panoramic overlook of the vast open waters of Lake Michigan. You also see the contrasting parallel lines of dunes that run along the lakeshore: the foredune, sandy and somewhat barren looking with dune grass and shrubs; and the backdune, lushly carpeted with beech and maple trees.

Although the camp and day beaches are usually crowded, the south shore, which requires a dedicated effort to access, is often quieter. In winter, you can use about 3 miles of cross-country ski trails.

The E. Genevieve Gillette Sand Dune Visitor Center, noted for its programs and exhibits on the unique dune environment, is named in honor of E. Genevieve Gillette, a tribute to her efforts in preserving unique natural areas in Michigan.

Directions: The park is located 6 miles south of Muskegon. From US 31, take Pontaluna Road west about 2 miles. From I-96, take exit 4 and follow the signs to the park.

Hours Open: Open year-round from 8:00 a.m. to 10:00 p.m.

Facilities: Hiking, swimming, camping (tent and RV), cross-country skiing, picnicking, and an interpretive center.

Permits and Rules: A park fee is required for motor vehicles ($6 daily, $24 annually for residents; $8 daily, $29 annually for nonresidents). Snowmobiles and off-road vehicles are not allowed in the park. Bicycles are allowed on paved roads only. Consuming or possessing alcoholic beverages is unlawful within the campground area from April 15 to Labor Day and in the day-use area from April 15 to June 15. Dogs must be on a 6-foot leash.

For Further Information: P.J. Hoffmaster State Park, 6585 Lake Harbor Road, Muskegon, MI 49441; 231-798-3711.

Other Points of Interest

The **E. Genevieve Gillette Sand Dune Visitor Center** provides a diverse range of programs to aid in understanding the ecosystem of the sandy, linear mounds outside its door. The visitor center is open from Memorial Day through November 1 on Tuesdays through Sundays. Call for other hours at 231-798-3573.

North of Muskegon, along the north shore of Muskegon Lake, is **Muskegon State Park** (see park #75). This park caters to anglers and boaters with its piers and channel connecting Muskegon Lake and Lake Michigan. It also offers 12 miles of hiking trails and a scenic drive along the coastline. The park is home to the Muskegon Winter Sports Complex, which features a luge run and lighted cross-country ski trails. For more information, contact Muskegon State Park, 3560 Memorial Drive, North Muskegon, MI 49445; 231-744-3480.

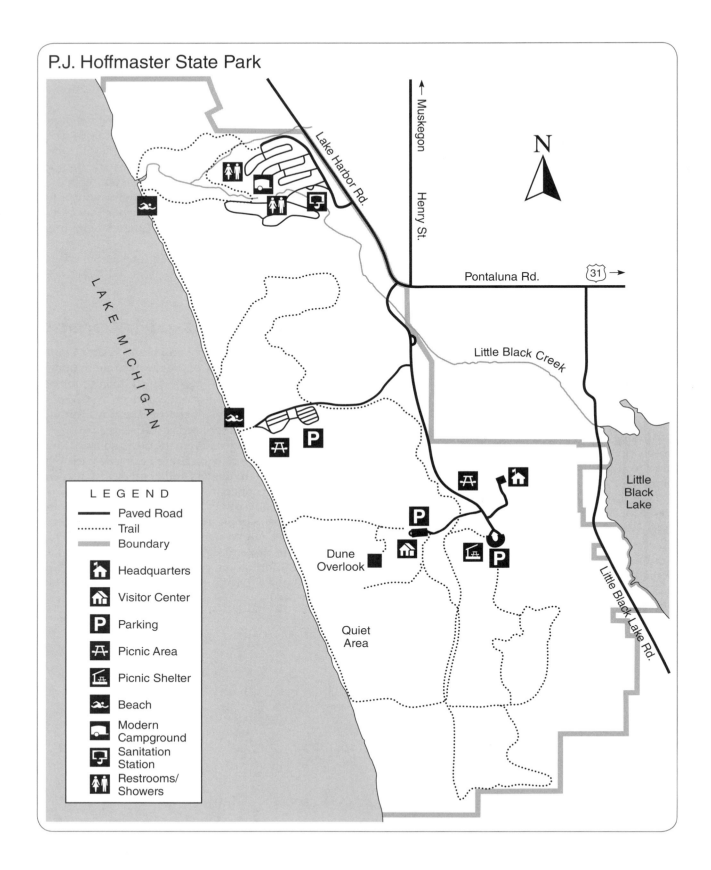

P.J. Hoffmaster State Park

LAKE MICHIGAN

Lake Harbor Rd.

← Muskegon

Henry St.

Pontaluna Rd.

31 →

Little Black Creek

Little Black Lake

Little Black Lake Rd.

Dune Overlook

Quiet Area

LEGEND

— Paved Road
···· Trail
━ Boundary

Headquarters

Visitor Center

P Parking

Picnic Area

Picnic Shelter

Beach

Modern Campground

Sanitation Station

Restrooms/ Showers

Loop of Homestead and Dune Climb Stairway

🐾 🐾 🐾   **Distance Round-Trip:** 2.4 miles
🐾 🐾 🐾   **Estimated Hiking Time:** 1.5 to 2 hours

Cautions: Roots are often exposed. Some portions of the trail go through poison ivy. Insect repellent is a must during warm months.

Trail Directions: Start the trail from the southwest end of the visitor center parking lot **[1]**. Climb a forested dune through a mix of oak, beech, maple, and pine trees to the crest, where you soon find the spur to the Quiet Area. Turn left, instead, to follow the trail through the woods, passing many beech trees. Roll through low dunes and along a ridge with bowl-shaped depressions at your side; then descend, pass a steep ravine, and arrive at post #7, a junction with ski trails (.3 mi.) **[2]**. Turn right and hike down along the ridge through oak and maple. You pass through intermittent short, open, sandy stretches as well as a number of ski trails that cross your path.

After a short descent, stay right at the junction, pass a ski trail, and stay right at the fork. Then make a sharp right at a junction to climb the back side of a wooded dune (.7 mi.) **[3]**. Descend a trough between two ridges that then becomes a land bridge that takes you to a steep, sandy dune.

At the base, the trail swings back into the woods and then onto a ridge. Quiet evolves into the lapping of waves. The trail leaves the woods, and through the shadowed tree trunks you see Lake Michigan (1 mi.) **[4]**. Soon, step down onto the sandy beach (1.1 mi.) **[5]**.

Turn right and follow the shore. Look behind you at the Grand Haven Lighthouse. Ahead of you are sand, waves, and a ridge of dunes. A wide, sandy path with a sign pointing the way to the visitor center (1.6 mi.) **[6]** is your beacon to turn inland. Head up the sandy slope. Steps assist you. Note the observation deck high above and the bowl-shaped sand blowout to your right.

Step into the shade along the boardwalk that guides you through this fragile environment around a large dune. Continue along a series of steps. At the end of the boardwalk, climb up the slope; a mountainous dune accompanies you. Cross more boardwalks. You reach the junction to the Dune Climb Stairway at 2 mi. **[7]**.

Wind your way up almost 170 steps for a sweeping view of the lake and dunes (2.1 mi.) **[8]**. A plaque at the overlook identifies as Mt. Baldy that mountainous dune that you passed while climbing up. Ahead of you, a caldera-like dune (one with a blowout) frames Lake Michigan. Catch your breath before heading down to the trail; the visitor center is only a short distance away (2.4 mi.) **[9]**.

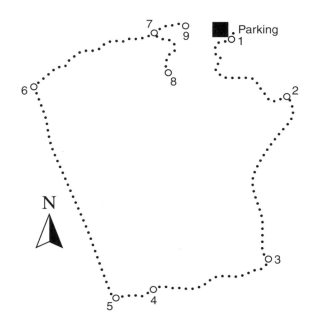

1. Trailhead
2. Post #7
3. Junction at forested dune
4. View of Lake Michigan
5. Lake Michigan
6. Sign
7. Dune Climb Stairway junction
8. View of lake and dunes
9. Visitor center

Walk-a-Mile Trail

Distance Round-Trip: 1.6 miles
Estimated Hiking Time: 45 minutes to 1 hour

Cautions: Roots are often exposed. Some portions of the trail go through poison ivy. Insect repellent is a must during warm months.

Trail Directions: Start the trail from the northeast end of the eastern parking lot for the beach area on the north side of the access drive **[1]**. Start by climbing into young sassafras trees and soon turn right at the base of a dune ridge. Follow along a narrow path as it bends around the dune and through mixed woods.

Descend along the edge of a ravine and then roll over another ridge to walk along the edge of a ravine. At .3 mi., wooden steps guide you to a land bridge **[2]**. Note how high you are. Gradually wind down off the ridge and down more wooden steps (.4 mi.) **[3]**. Notice the subtle change in vegetation as you descend, swing around a small depression, and hike onto another land bridge that remains more or less level as the sides drop and change into deep ravines.

Moss carpets your steps while you ascend past a deep ravine on your right (.6 mi.) **[4]**. Reach the top as you veer left to start descending along a land bridge. Pass through an open area and through fallen trees.

The trail turns left; a deep ravine is straight ahead (.8 mi.) **[5]**. Climb briefly before descending in the direction of the lake. Sandwiched in a narrow trough between two dune ridges, you soon climb briefly before descending again (.9 mi.) **[6]**.

After a short climb, the canopy opens and you can hear the lake (1.1 mi.) **[7]**. Climb a steep sandy slope. After enjoying the view and catching your breath, descend to the shores of Lake Michigan (1.2 mi.) **[8]**. Turn left, kick off your boots, and start your sandy stroll along the beach.

A wide path and stairs welcome you back from the beach (1.5 mi.) **[9]**. Turn left and walk to the observation deck and onto the beach area parking lot (1.6 mi.) **[10]**. You can see the east lot where you parked your vehicle. Walk about .15 mi. back to that lot.

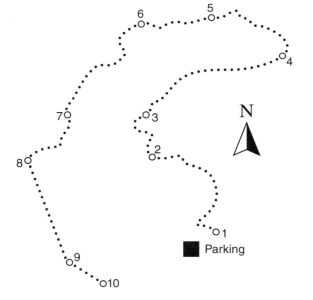

1. Trailhead
2. Steps
3. Steps
4. Moss trail
5. Turn left
6. Trough between ridges
7. Canopy opens
8. Lake Michigan
9. Stairs
10. Beach parking lot

- Cross-country ski on lighted trails.
- Learn to luge.
- Explore a rare coastal plain marsh.

Park Information

Muskegon State Park's 2 miles of sandy Lake Michigan beach rank with some of the most beautiful in the world. An additional mile of shoreline on Muskegon Lake expands the swimming, fishing, boating, and other recreational opportunities available.

Over 1,165 acres of dunes, forests, fields, lakefront, and interdunal ponds provide the naturalist, hiker, or cross-country skier with plenty of grounds to explore. And Lost Lake, not really a lake but a rare coastal plain marsh, provides the opportunity to search for the carnivorous pitcher plant. The marsh is one of only 41 left in Michigan's state park system.

Twelve miles of hiking trails and 12 miles of cross-country ski trails weave through the park. Although bicycling is not allowed on the trails because of the protected status of the dunes, a future bike route is planned that would run along the north side of Muskegon Lake, through the park, and then north along the Lake Michigan shoreline to Duck Lake State Park.

Although the camping areas and beaches are packed in the warmer months, winter is when the park shines—and not only on the 5 miles of lighted cross-country ski trails. The Muskegon Winter Sport Complex features a luge run, suitable for Olympic training. After taking luge lessons, the uninitiated can take the plunge. The complex also has a sports lodge and a lighted skating area.

Directions: The park is located about 4 miles west of North Muskegon on Lake Michigan. Take US 31 to M-120. Go west through North Muskegon and follow the signs to the park.

Hours Open: The park is open year-round. The Muskegon Winter Sports Complex is open in winter from 10:00 a.m. to 10:00 p.m. on Mondays through Fridays and from 8:00 a.m. to 10:00 p.m. on Saturdays and Sundays.

Facilities: Hiking, swimming, camping (tent and RV), group camping, picnicking and shelters, fishing, boat launch, playground, cross-country skiing, luge run, and lighted skating and cross-country skiing.

Permits and Rules: A park fee is required for motor vehicles ($6 daily, $24 annually for residents; $8 daily, $29 annually for nonresidents). Consuming or possessing alcoholic beverages is unlawful from April 15 to Labor Day; in the camping area alcohol is prohibited from April 15 to June 15. Do not pick or disturb fragile bog plants.

For Further Information: Muskegon State Park, 3560 Memorial Drive, North Muskegon, MI 49445; 231-744-3480; Muskegon Winter Sport Complex, 462 Scenic Drive, P.O. Box 3085, North Muskegon, MI 49445; 231-744-9629 or 877-TRY LUGE.

Other Points of Interest

Duck Lake State Park stretches from Lake Michigan to the northern shore of Duck Lake. Besides a beach and picnic area, a boat launch, and fishing opportunities, this park allows the hunting and snowmobiling that Muskegon State Park does not. Contact Muskegon State Park for more information.

P.J. Hoffmaster State Park (see park #74) features 3 miles of Lake Michigan shoreline, the Dune Climb Stairway, forested dunes, hiking trails, and the E. Genevieve Gillette Sand Dune Visitor Center. For more information, contact P.J. Hoffmaster State Park, 6585 Lake Harbor Road, Muskegon, MI 49441; 231-798-3711.

For more information on the Muskegon area, contact the Muskegon Area Chamber of Commerce, 900 Third Street, Suite 200, Muskegon, MI 49440; 231-722-3751; www.muskegon.org.

Park Trails

Although six hiking trails are identified, they are created by linking innumerable identified junctions from I through VII and A through H plus X and Y. Take a map and create your own trail from the many junctions.

Muskegon State Park

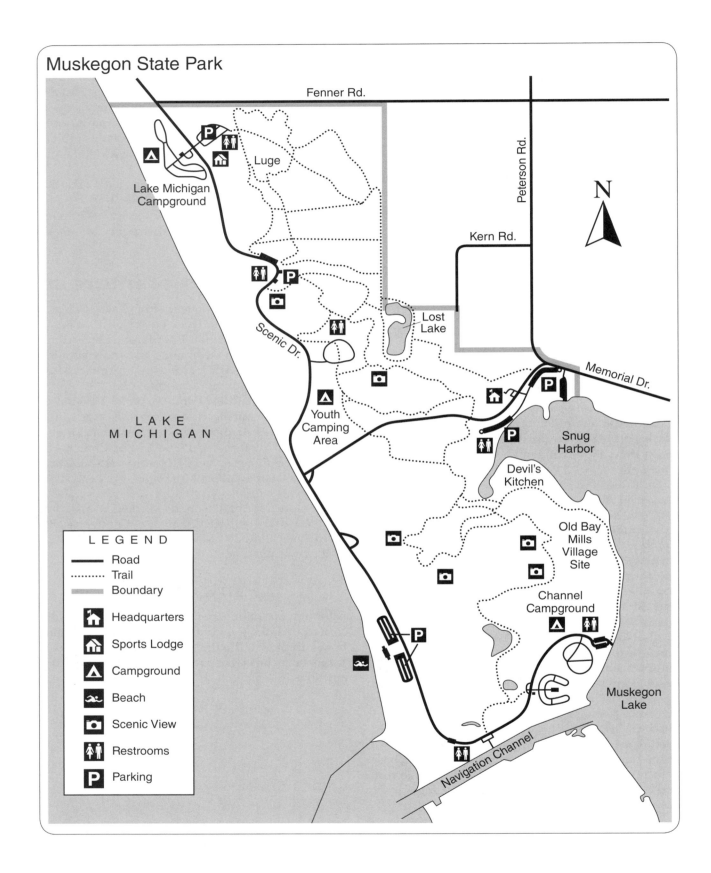

Fenner Rd.

Peterson Rd.

Kern Rd.

N

Luge

Lake Michigan
Campground

Scenic Dr.

Lost
Lake

Memorial Dr.

LAKE
MICHIGAN

Youth
Camping
Area

Snug
Harbor

Devil's
Kitchen

Old Bay
Mills
Village
Site

Channel
Campground

Muskegon
Lake

Navigation Channel

LEGEND

———	Road
·········	Trail
▬▬▬	Boundary
🏠	Headquarters
🏠	Sports Lodge
▲	Campground
〜	Beach
📷	Scenic View
🚻	Restrooms
P	Parking

Dune Ridge Trail Loop

Distance Round-Trip: 1.7 miles
Estimated Hiking Time: 45 minutes
to 1 hour

Cautions: Take insect repellent in warm months. You walk over roots and through the soft sand of a rolling dune environment; make sure that you have proper footgear.

Trail Directions: Start at the southwest end of the western Snug Harbor parking lot at post A **[1]**. Soon reach a junction. Head left to go to post B. Large ostrich ferns along the trail entertain a lush, tropical feel, yet you walk along the base of a wooded dune littered with fallen giants. Maple, beech, and hemlock predominate.

At post B, go left toward Devil's Kitchen (.2 mi.) **[2]** and on to the junction with South Camp (.3 mi.) **[3]**. Stay right and climb the steep sandy slope up the wooded dune ridge. Find post I at the top (.4 mi.) **[4]**.

Turn right to climb more, eventually to walk along a land bridge with a deep ravine on the left. The trail descends, and a depression on your right is deeper than the one on the left. Veer left at a post and abruptly climb onto a ridge for a view of sand blowouts in the foreground and Lake Michigan in the background (.5 mi.) **[5]**.

Stay left and follow along the ridge, where you are afforded views of the Muskegon Channel. Trees here are contorted sculptures twisted by wind and sand, exposing roots. Stay right at post II (.6 mi.) **[6]** and then horseshoe around a bowl.

Start down the sand through fallen or contorted trees that are trying to keep a foothold in the shifting slopes. Soon, keep your eye to the left for the next post that guides you left onto another land bridge. Moss carpets the slope, and ravines deepen around you. Catch an occasional glimpse of Muskegon.

Climb along the ridge to an overview of grass-covered dunes; lighthouses are off in the distance in the channel. Keep climbing the sandy slope and see the dune contrasts; the back is wooded, whereas the front is open sand and grass.

The trail rolls down and up onto a sandy ridge with views of Muskegon Lake and downtown Muskegon. Notice the full crown on the very short oaks—mature trees buried in sand (1 mi.) **[7]**.

Make a hairpin turn left (1.1 mi.) **[8]** and descend to another land bridge (there is no post, but an arrow is painted on a tree). Woods dominate, rather than sand.

Soon, stay right of a junction and descend past moss-covered fallen giants to post III (1.2 mi.) **[9]**. Stay straight, climbing again onto a land bridge, where you get views of Snug Harbor through the trees.

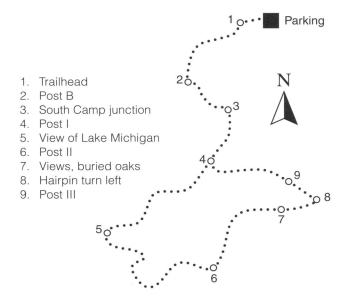

1. Trailhead
2. Post B
3. South Camp junction
4. Post I
5. View of Lake Michigan
6. Post II
7. Views, buried oaks
8. Hairpin turn left
9. Post III

Roll along the land bridge to post I (1.3 mi.) **[4]**. Turn right and descend, retracing your steps to post B **[2]**, where you turn right. Turn right again at post A to reach the parking lot.

Lost Lake Trail

Distance Round-Trip: 1.7 miles

Estimated Hiking Time: 45 minutes to 1 hour

Cautions: Take insect repellent in warm months. You walk over roots and through areas that may be wet; make sure to have proper footgear.

Trail Directions: Start at the northeast Snug Harbor parking near the boat launch and cross the paved park road (post Y on the park map) **[1]**. Enter an area of small trees and ferns in a low-lying area. Cross a couple of small footbridges on this wood-chipped path. Watercress grows in the small stream that you cross.

Hike under a utility line (which you barely notice in the lush environment of ferns and cattails) and cross a couple more footbridges (.1 mi.) **[2]**.

The trail swings right into a forest of hemlock, maple, and beech. Turn right and walk along the back side of a wooded dune (.2 mi.) **[3]**. Ferns, hemlock, and fallen trees embroider the landscape. Note the roots and fallen trees draped with moss shaped like serpents.

Break out into an open area with scrubby oak and white pine trees (.4 mi.) **[4]**. Follow through dry flatland to Lost Lake (.6 mi.) **[5]**—a coastal plain marsh. Ducks pepper the water, breaking up the enveloping trees mirrored in the water. Keep an eye out for the carnivorous pitcher plant that inhabits the area.

You see a bench to the right. Save that for later. Turn left and walk among young white pines along the edge of the lake to a post (.7 mi.) **[6]**. Turn right and walk the west side of the lake over roots. The trail swings left along marsh grasses; the trail has moss tufts tucked in the toes of exposed roots. You soon turn right to arrive at post X (.8 mi.) **[7]**.

Stay straight to post 12 (.9 mi.) **[8]**. The ski trails are numbered, and this one is the lighted trail. Turn right to follow near the north side of the lake. Soon, turn right at an unmarked trail. You see the wooded hill that you skirted earlier on the other side of the lake. Swing right, following near the east side of the lake to reach that bench that you saw earlier. Family members of past owners of the land dedicated this bench. Have a seat and watch the waterfowl before turning left at the junction **[5]** to head back.

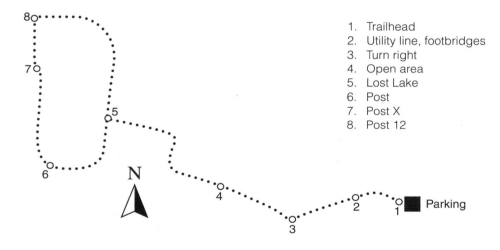

1. Trailhead
2. Utility line, footbridges
3. Turn right
4. Open area
5. Lost Lake
6. Post
7. Post X
8. Post 12

- Explore more than 5 miles of trails with a park naturalist or on your own.
- View nature from elevated platforms, towers, boardwalks, and woodchip nature trails.
- Take a specialty class on photography, canoeing, or nature awareness.

Park Information

Almost 800 acres, blanketed by upland meadows, swamp forests, marshes, and dry forest are open to exploration on an elaborate trail system. You cross boardwalks, bridges with benches, and overlook towers, walking along woodchip and natural trails. You meander on ridges high above the Paw Paw River and cut through wetlands in this variety of habitats. Come and learn more about the environment.

Sarett Nature Center offers more than trails to help you discover the natural world. Naturalists at the center educate visitors on a variety of environmental topics—bird study, wilderness appreciation, and winter ecology, to name but a few. Public programs include guided field trips and extended outings. Call for an extensive list of programs and classes. The center features exhibits, meeting rooms, a bookshop and library, and an observation room for viewing the birds attracted to the feeders outside.

Directions: The center is located about 8 miles northeast of Benton Harbor. From east of Benton Harbor, at the junction of I-94 and I-196, head north on I-196/US 31 for about a mile to the Red Arrow Highway. Head southwest on the Red Arrow Highway for about one-eighth of a mile to Benton Center Road. Turn north (right) and go about three-quarters of a mile to the entrance of the nature center, located on the west side of the road.

Hours Open: The trails are open year-round from dawn until dusk. Hours at the nature center vary. Tuesdays through Friday it is open from 9:00 a.m. to 5:00 p.m., Saturdays it is open from 10:00 a.m. to 5:00 p.m., and Sundays it is open from 1:00 p.m. to 5:00 p.m.

Facilities: Hiking and interpretive center.

Permits and Rules: No fee is required; Sarett is a private, nonprofit organization, supported by donations, contributions, and membership. Your support is vital to the continuation of the programs offered at the center. Visitors are encouraged to join. Enjoy the natural setting, but do so without pets, without picnicking, and without picking wildflowers or other plants.

For Further Information: Sarett Nature Center, 2300 Benton Center Road, Benton Harbor, MI 49022; 269-927-4832; www.sarett.com.

Other Points of Interest

Two public beaches in St. Joseph offer swimming, picnicking, boating, and pier strolling. **Tiscornia Park**, located north of the St. Joseph River Channel, provides easy access for a stroll along the North Pier, which has two lighthouses. **Silver Beach County Park** is located on Lake Michigan and has a beach boardwalk, amphitheater, and access to the 1,000-foot South Pier. For more information on these and other parks, contact St. Joseph Today at 269-985-1111; www.sjtoday.org.

Park Trails

West Marsh Trail (🥾, .2 mile). Start from the west end of the Lowland Trail. The trail weaves through a marsh and goes out to the West Marsh Tower.

Tamarack Trail (🥾, .2 mile). Loop off the River Trail through meadows to the Tamarack Tower.

River Trail (🥾🥾, 1 mile). This main trail stretches eastward through the park. It goes to the River Tower, where you view the surrounding wetlands and slow-moving waters of the Paw Paw River, and leads on to the river itself. About .3 mi. along the River Trail, a spur leads to the North Marsh Tower. This area overlooks the marsh that is flooded by the Paw Paw each spring.

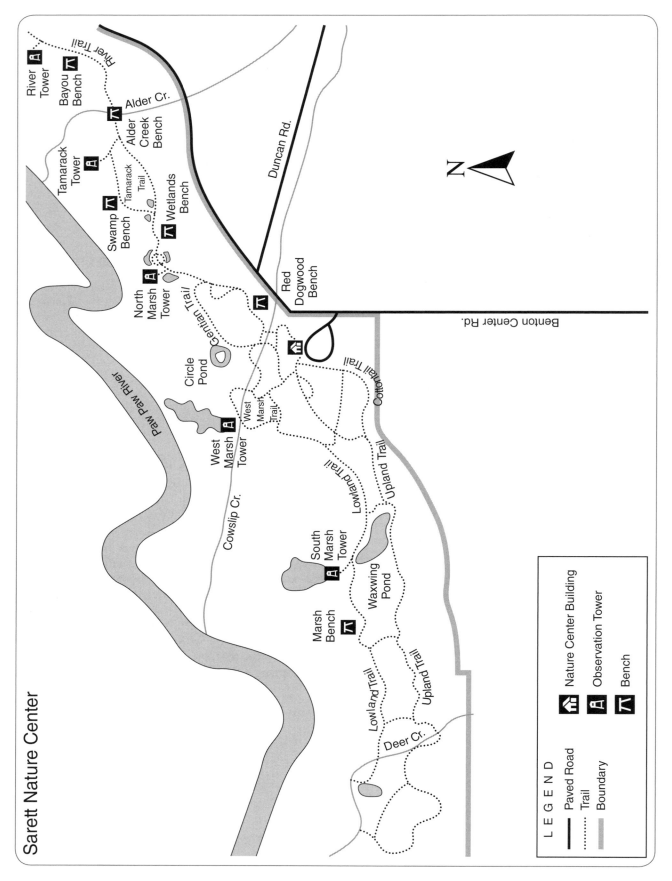

Sarett Nature Center

River Tower

Bayou Bench

River Trail

Alder Cr.

Alder Creek Bench

Tamarack Tower

Tamarack Trail

Swamp Bench

Wetlands Bench

North Marsh Tower

Gentian Trail

Circle Pond

West Marsh Tower

West Marsh Trail

Paw Paw River

Cowslip Cr.

South Marsh Tower

Marsh Bench

Waxwing Pond

Lowland Trail

Upland Trail

Lowland Trail

Upland Trail

Deer Cr.

Duncan Rd.

Red Dogwood Bench

Cottontail Trail

Benton Center Rd.

N

LEGEND

— Paved Road
····· Trail
— Boundary

🏠 Nature Center Building
Ⓐ Observation Tower
🔼 Bench

River–Gentian–
Two-Board Trails Loop

Distance Round-Trip: .5 mile
Estimated Hiking Time: 30 minutes

Cautions: Take insect repellent in warm months. Bring binoculars. Watch that you don't step off the boardwalks or into the fragile, wet environment along the trail.

Trail Directions: Begin at the west end of the nature center parking lot **[1]**. Be sure to stop at the center for advice on what might be blooming and what trail will take you in sight of it. Look out the viewing windows at the center to observe birds and small mammals at the feeders and take in the panoramic view of the Paw Paw River valley in the background.

Head west from the parking area and quickly reach a junction. Turn right at the sign board and descend from the bluff on steps. A bench waits near a large, fallen oak tree. Walk through the cut; the fallen trunk is neck high. Follow the River Trail as it splits right and passes a splash of wildflowers that precedes a footbridge over Cowslip Creek (.1 mi.) **[2]**. Turn left to cross the bridge and continue straight on the Gentian Trail (a boardwalk), as the River Trail splits right and the Treehouse Path goes left.

Pass through cedars to reach a lush, open area on the right. In August and September, look for wildflowers such as fringed gentian (a protected Michigan wildflower), the pitcher plant (a threatened species), turtlehead, and the showy, scarlet-red cardinal flower. Stop at the observation decks to view wildlife at the algae-covered Circle Pond (.2 mi.) **[3]**. Then briefly step off the boardwalk for a short walk through tall grasses. Step back on the boardwalk by the black willow tree and find yourself again under fragrant cedar trees. Take note as you pass other plants in the marsh. Look for iris, arrowhead, and skunk cabbage.

Turn right when you reach the River Trail (.3 mi.) **[4]**. Then turn right to walk the unmarked trail known as Two-Board Trail, so named because it is only two boards wide, rather than the usual three boards of other trail boardwalks. Cattails and lilies stand out here, and you get a view of the nature center up on the bluff to the south.

Turn right when you again reach the River Trail. The path may be spongy here as you walk through the thick shrubs and grasses. At .4 mi., you reach the Red Dogwood Bench **[5]**. This raised bench structure provides a good platform from which to sit quietly and watch wildlife atop the surrounding shrubs.

When you are back on the trail, you quickly cross a small footbridge and snake through small willows to arrive at a trail junction. Turn left onto an unnamed connector path and cross over the Cowslip Creek to arrive at the campfire area (.5 mi.) **[6]**. Then begin to climb back up the bluff and arrive at the east end of the nature center.

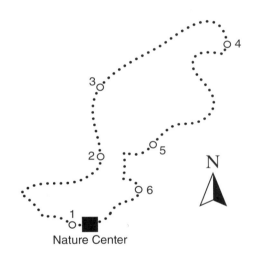

1. Trailhead
2. Cowslip Creek
3. Circle Pond
4. River Trail, halfway point
5. Red Dogwood Bench
6. Campfire area

Lowland–Upland Trails Loop

Distance Round-Trip: 2.1 miles
Estimated Hiking Time: 1 hour

Cautions: The trail crosses boardwalks that sometimes give way like worn-out car shocks and are slippery when wet. Roots are sometimes exposed. Poison ivy grows along the trail. Take insect repellent in warm months.

Trail Directions: Start at the west end of the nature center parking lot to a sign board **[1]**. Turn right to follow down and through a huge fallen oak, left at a junction, and past a soil cellar (or a contraption that looks like a cellar). Stay to the left at the West Marsh Trail junction and then duck under a canopy of trees.

Pass the second spur for the West Marsh Loop (.1 mi.) **[2]**; climb up the hill and begin to walk along the ridge over the floodplain of Cowslip Creek. The trail continues to rise, and you pass a switchback spur (.2 mi.) **[3]**. Head down steps to the lowland. Soon, moss cushions your steps. Skunk cabbage announces the beginning of a planked boardwalk (.3 mi.) **[4]**.

Walk the planks through ferns and irises. Pass Waxwing Path and the overlook for Waxwing Pond (where waxlike lily pads cover the surface). At .4 mi., you arrive at the spur for the South Marsh Tower **[5]**. You can walk the short stretch out to the overlook where the decking stands high above the swamp, home to silver maple, willow, elm, and alder trees.

Continue on the main boardwalk through the lush wetland. Benches overlook the cattails and willows of the marsh (.6 mi.) **[6]**. Soon you duck through a wall of shrubs, cross a small stream, and enter woods. At

.7 mi., pass the Marsh Marigold spur and step off the boardwalk to stay to the right along the Lowland Trail **[7]**.

A ridge rises to your left. The trail climbs and swings left just before you pass Hickory Path (.8 mi.) **[8]**. Head down and cross the watercress-clogged Deer Creek. Pass Deer Creek Path (.9 mi.) **[9]** and an algae-laden pond to reach an observation spot at Deer Creek (.9 mi.) **[10]**. Then turn back and go right on Deer Creek Path.

At 1 mi., turn right and soon reach another observation spot at Deer Creek on the right **[11]**. Climb to the left and wind around and up steps (1.1 mi.) **[12]**. Next, you walk high among youthful oaks and pass a metal truck bed with "Michigan Fruit Canners" whispering through its rust. At 1.1 mi., you reach Deer Creek Path **[13]**.

Stay straight along a ridge until it cuts down to a boardwalk and back over Deer Creek. Climb back to a ridge, passing Hickory Path before winding down a steep switchback. At 1.5 mi., you pass Marsh Marigold Path **[14]**. Step back onto a boardwalk. Ferns blanket the trail, and you again pass the green Waxwing Pond. Soon, climb high to a ridge and enjoy the view from an observation deck (1.7 mi.) **[15]**.

At 1.9 mi., you reach the Cottontail Trail junction **[16]**. Go left, cutting through a field before reentering the woods. After the junction for Woodchuck Run, you pass through a hallway of shrubs. You then reach a boardwalk and overlook (2 mi.) **[17]**.

Have a seat and soak in the view of the floodplain and the river valley below, or enjoy the view from another overlook platform a few steps farther. Look over the lowland where you hiked earlier; then head back to the center.

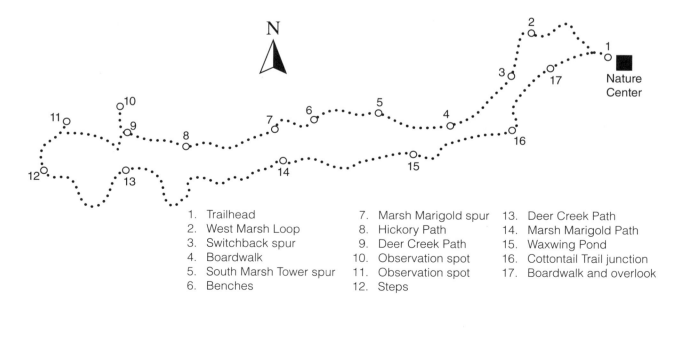

1. Trailhead	7. Marsh Marigold spur	13. Deer Creek Path
2. West Marsh Loop	8. Hickory Path	14. Marsh Marigold Path
3. Switchback spur	9. Deer Creek Path	15. Waxwing Pond
4. Boardwalk	10. Observation spot	16. Cottontail Trail junction
5. South Marsh Tower spur	11. Observation spot	17. Boardwalk and overlook
6. Benches	12. Steps	

- View what wind, water, and sand have shaped—the Great Warren Dunes.

- Walk along one of Michigan's most beautiful beaches.

- Revere one of the last-known stands of virgin beech and maple in southern Michigan.

Park Information

Although Warren Dunes State Park and Warren Woods Natural Area are two distinct units separated by 7 miles, they are united not only in name but also in origin. Both parks evolved through the foresight of Edward K. Warren, who, in the 1870s, purchased the land that is now called Warren Woods Natural Area. His effort preserved one of the few remaining virgin beech-maple forests in Michigan. He continued to purchase undeveloped land, including the land that eventually became Warren Dunes State Park. Both areas are administered by Warren Dunes State Park.

Warren Dunes State Park contains 1,952 acres that stretch along 3 miles of sandy Lake Michigan shore. Home to windblown dunes and hilly terrain blanketed with oak and hickory, the Warren Dunes offer a superb study of plant succession. Dunes rising up to 260 feet provide spectacular viewing and climbing. Almost 6 miles of trails traverse the varied terrain.

Warren Woods Natural Area is for day use only. About 1.5 miles of well-worn paths loop through the natural area, across and along the Galien River. Virgin hardwoods provide spectacular colors in the fall.

Directions: From I-94, Warren Dunes State Park is about 12 miles south of St. Joseph. Take exit 16 and follow the Red Arrow Highway south to the park entrance. Warren Woods Natural Area may be reached from exit 6 and by heading east on Elm Valley Road to the posted entrance. An alternate parking area is on Warren Woods Road, which is 1 mile north of Elm Valley Road and can be reached via Three Oaks Road.

Hours Open: Open daily.

Facilities: Warren Dunes State Park: hiking, swimming, fishing, hunting, cross-country skiing, camp-

ing (tent and RV), picnicking, and interpretive trails; Warren Woods Natural Area: hiking and picnicking.

Permits and Rules: A park fee is required for motor vehicles ($6 daily, $24 annually for residents; $8 daily, $29 annually for nonresidents). Pets must be on a 6-foot leash. Dogs are not allowed on the beach. Alcoholic beverages are prohibited from March 1 through September 30.

For Further Information: Warren Dunes State Park, 12032 Red Arrow Highway, Sawyer, MI 49125; 289-426-4013.

Other Points of Interest

Located about 4 miles north of Warren Dunes, **Grand Mere State Park**, a day-use park, has Lake Michigan beaches, access to three inland lakes, a picnic area, and a hiking trail. Day passes may be obtained from Warren Dunes State Park.

Park Trails

Yellow Birch Loop (🥾, 1 mile). Start west of the parking area on Floral Lane, off Red Arrow Highway, north of the park entrance. The trail passes through meadows, bottomland hardwoods, and wetlands.

Golden Rod Loop (🥾, .3 mile). This trail starts at the parking area on Floral Lane. It passes through meadows and bottomland and is a favorite of bird watchers.

White Tail Loop (🥾🥾, .8 mile). Start this trail off the Nature Trail, just northwest of the organization campground. The trail climbs up into the natural area.

Red Squirrel Trail (🥾🥾, .7 mile). Access this trail from the Nature Trail near the organization camp. It climbs through hardwoods and passes through the park's natural area open dunes to exit along the Blue Jay Trail.

Oak Ridge Trail (🥾🥾, .2 mile). This trail links the Red Squirrel Trail and the Blue Jay Trail, passing through woods and onto open sand.

Warren Woods Natural Area

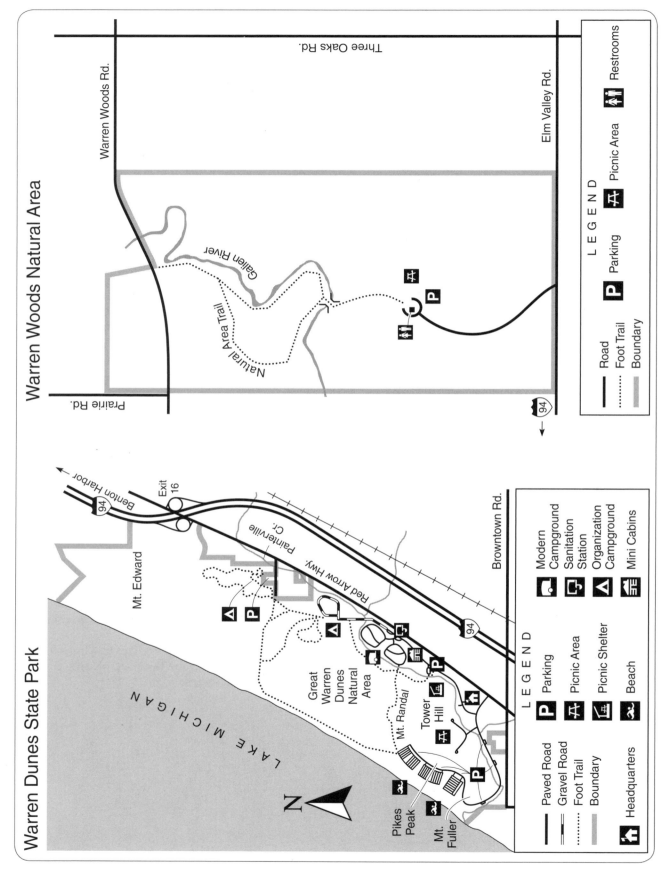

Galien River

Natural Area Trail

Warren Woods Rd.

Three Oaks Rd.

Prairie Rd.

Elm Valley Rd.

94

LEGEND

Road
Foot Trail
Boundary

P Parking

⚞ Picnic Area

🚻 Restrooms

Warren Dunes State Park

LAKE MICHIGAN

N

Benton Harbor

94

Exit 16

Mt. Edward

Painterville Cr.

Red Arrow Hwy.

Great Warren Dunes Natural Area

Mt. Randal

Tower Hill

Pikes Peak

Mt. Fuller

Browntown Rd.

94

LEGEND

Paved Road
Gravel Road
Foot Trail
Boundary

⌂ Headquarters

P Parking

⚞ Picnic Area

Picnic Shelter

Beach

Modern Campground
Sanitation Station
Organization Campground
Mini Cabins

Nature–Blue Jay–Beach–Mt. Randal Trails Loop

Distance Round-Trip: 4 miles
Estimated Hiking Time: 2 to 2.5 hours

Cautions: Portions of the trail flood, so wear proper footgear. The trail can be hard to follow in the sandy dunes. Take sunscreen, insect repellent, and water. Watch for poison ivy.

Trail Directions: Begin at the west end of the picnic shelter parking lot (which is about halfway between the park entrance and the campgrounds) **[1]**. Start along the Nature Trail, which has interpretive posts. Pick up a brochure to follow along.

Head west over Painterville Creek to the fork. Turn right into the hardwoods along the back side of a dune. Flanking the creek, the trail is prone to flooding. Transient paths that swing up the back side of the dune (called Mt. Randal) help you skirt around any water. Go past the Mt. Randal junction (.2 mi) **[2]**.

The trail passes a footbridge, bypasses the campground, and merges with an old road (.8 mi.) **[3]**. The organization camp is nearby, as are the junctions for the White Tail, Red Squirrel, and Oak Ridge trails. Continue along the back side of a dune. At 1.2 mi., you reach Floral Lane **[4]**.

Turn left here along the Blue Jay Trail and begin a gentle climb around a wooded slope and into the Warren Dunes Natural Area. The trail climbs steeper and rises above the ravine to your right. Your first real climb, however, comes at 1.3 mi. when you trudge through sand **[5]**. Pass the Oak Ridge spur and then rise to a crest to take in the Lake Michigan view (1.5

mi.) **[6]** before descending through a trough. Follow this wave of dunes toward the lake, stopping to notice the sandy blowout at 1.6 mi. **[7]**. Feel the breeze that helped shape this bowl. Continue past the Red Squirrel Trail junction

At 1.8 mi., you arrive at the last crest before the lake **[8]**. You could step down and follow along the shore, but you would miss the blowouts that you can see from the vantage point along the ridge of the Beach Trail. Turn left. As you scan the bowls of sand, look for vultures in the trees.

Follow the sandy ribbon through the dunes. At 2.1 mi., skirt some oaks that are being buried alive by dune development **[9]**. Follow an unmarked path and climb steeply up a dune (2.4 mi.) **[10]**. Pass a couple more blowouts, skirt woods, and pass an unmarked junction to arrive at the day-use area (3 mi.) **[11]**. The trail bends away from the lake. Just off the day-use parking lot is a sign that points to the campground. Follow this to the left, climb up the sand, reenter the woods, and follow the Mt. Randal Trail.

The trail adventures back across the wave of dunes, mostly through oak-hickory forest, and it occasionally teeters along ridges above steep ravines. Stairways in the forest, made either by the roots of trees or by man, at times ease the stress of climbing up and down the crests and troughs. A final series of steps winds down to a buried bench where Mt. Randal sweeps up to your right (3.6 mi.) **[12]**. The trail continues winding down, passing a bench that offers relief for your knees as well as your eyes (it overlooks a pond). Sit and enjoy the respite before heading down again and reaching the Nature Trail junction at 3.8 mi. Turn right and head back to the parking lot.

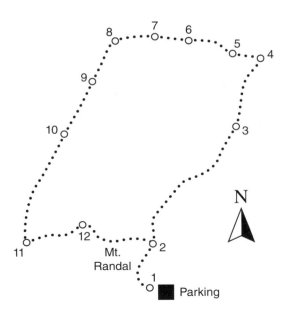

1. Trailhead
2. Mt. Randal junction
3. Old road
4. Floral Lane
5. Ascend dune
6. View of Lake Michigan
7. Blowout
8. Lake Michigan
9. Buried oaks
10. Climb up dune
11. Day-use area
12. Buried bench

Warren Woods
Natural Area Trail

Distance Round-Trip: 1.1 miles
Estimated Hiking Time: 45 minutes to
1 hour

Cautions: The trail may be hard to follow. Downfalls may obscure the route. Portions of the trail are apt to flood. Some sections along the Galien River have eroded into the water, making the path precariously narrow. Wear proper footgear. Watch for poison ivy.

Trail Directions: From Warren Dunes Park, turn south on Red Arrow Highway for 7 mi. Turn left on Union Pier, which will become Elm Valley. The park entrance is less than 4 mi. away. Watch for the park sign on the left. The trail starts on the northeast end of the parking lot **[1]**. Follow the wide trail that winds through mature woods. Thanks to Mr. Edward Warren, many trees were spared the ax. Some of the trees in the park are so large that two adults would have a hard time hugging one of them.

Wind down through the woods to steps that take you down the steep slope to cross the bridge over the Galien River (.3 mi.) **[2]**. Immediately make a hairpin turn to the right of the bridge. You will be walking along the bank of the river.

The trail is more rugged here as you follow the bank. Pass a bench among the fallen giants (.5 mi.) **[3]**. At .6 mi., the trail narrows where a tree fell over the bank, taking some of the trail with it **[4]**. Every so often you are rewarded with an opening to the river.

Pass the paw paws that envelop an ephemeral stream. On the other side of the river, look for a ridge that rises from the banks.

The trail becomes laden with roots. The river bends right, and you have a short climb before winding up to a junction (.9 mi) **[5]**.

Turn left and descend through the woods. Pass through a mass graveyard of fallen soldiers of the woods before arriving back at the bridge (.8 mi.) **[2]**. Climb up the stairs and rest on the bench at the top before heading back along the wide path to the parking lot.

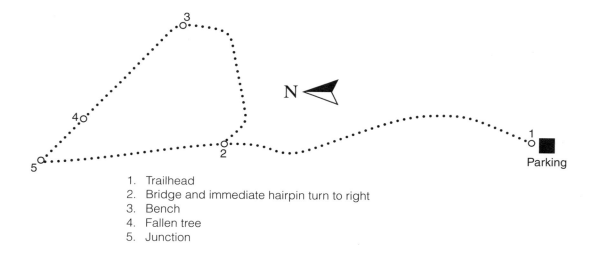

N

1. Trailhead
2. Bridge and immediate hairpin turn to right
3. Bench
4. Fallen tree
5. Junction

About the Authors

Roger Storm has been involved with trails since 1985. He currently works in the Real Estate Services Section of the Michigan Department of Natural Resources where he acquires land, or rights in land, for multi-use trails. He also served as the first state director for the Michigan chapter of the Rails-to-Trails Conservancy.

Susan Wedzel operates her own business—Wedzel and Associates—which specializes in real estate appraising and consulting. She has been a technical writer since 1986. She dabbles in outdoor photography and has had photos appear in trail-related publications.